PEDESTALS AND PODIUMS

PEDESTALS AND PODIUMS

UTAH WOMEN, RELIGIOUS AUTHORITY, AND EQUAL RIGHTS

Martha Sonntag Bradley

Signature Books • Salt Lake City • 2005
A Smith-Pettit Foundation Book

to Bob

Grow old with me and be my love

Jacket design by Ron Stucki

www.signaturebooks.com

Pedestals and Podiums: Utah Women, Religious Authority, and Equal Rights was printed on acid-free paper and was composed, printed, and bound in the United States of America.

2010 2009 2008 2007 2006 2005 6 5 4 3 2 1

Library of Congress Cataloging-in-Publication Data
Bradley, Martha Sonntag.
Pedestals and podiums : Utah women, religious authority, and equal rights / by Martha Sonntag Bradley.
p. cm.
Includes bibliographical references and index.
ISBN 1-56085-189-9
1. Mormon women—Utah—Political activity. 2. Equal rights amendments—United States—History—20th century. 3. Feminism—Religious aspects—Church of Jesus Christ of Latter-day Saints—History—20th century. I. Title.

BX8641.B73 2005
305.48'6893792—dc22

2005051718

Contents

INTRODUCTION

This is a story which has had strange and potent intersections with my life. In June 1977, I was a young mother with three children—my blonde wonder ready to begin kindergarten in the fall and two adorable daughters who were one and two years old. Purely by coincidence, I bumped into the women's movement the day I attended the Utah International Women's Year (IWY) Conference in Salt Lake City.

For me it was a stunning, shocking, stupefying day. From the beginning, I felt as if I had stumbled, then found a precarious new balance standing on a narrow bridge with dangerous drops on either side. It was a day of confusion and chaos—women crowded into hot rooms, often outnumbering the available seats. The aisles were an obstacle course of strollers in which babies fretted in the heat or slept in sweaty exhaustion. The din of speakers trying to make themselves heard, audience members responding and talking among themselves, wailing children, and the overflow noise from other rooms was mind numbing. It was one of those days when you're confronted head-on with how much you don't know.

The noise continued to wash over me as I stepped into the balloting booth. Confused, I read over the list of resolutions on the ballot I was supposed to vote for or against, but I realized I had not even begun to think about what my position as a woman in the world should be. Again I wanted—more than anything else, it seemed—to understand what it all meant.

That moment had a profound impact on my life which I vividly, even sensorially, recall, a moment that forever marked my life—a moment of "before" and "after." I became a feminist although I did not yet know what that implied. More than a decade would pass before I could begin to say I understood the women's movement and even longer before I felt it was making a difference in my own life. But for my young, naive self, that warm June day was as defining a moment as I had ever experienced.

In the twenty-five years since then, I have heard other women speak of the eleven years between 1972 and 1983 in much the same way. For many of us, it was the decade when we were students or young mothers or were undertaking our first jobs. We were still shaping our lives. Perhaps we were more alert then, or focused on what mattered—on what held out the promise of meaning—but we knew this was deeply important even when we were not exactly sure what "this" was. Women were talking about changing the world, and we believed we could have something to do with it.

At the same time, many of my friends seemed unaffected by what was going on around us. From what I could see, their lives proceeded as if nothing was in the air, as if their lives had absolutely nothing to do with those "other lives over there." In hindsight, the disconnect is remarkable to me and I have always wondered why feminism touched only some of us, why it does not seem to matter at all to many young women today.

For me, the time evoked memories of childhood. I am the only sister in a family of three brothers and I grew up headstrong and spirited, euphemisms of course for stubborn and difficult. I had all four adjectives thrown at me in various tones of voice and confess that I usually responded in kind. My mother and I squabbled endlessly over insignificant things. Still, my parents made me feel treasured and valued. The women's movement, on the most personal level, was a sturdy reminder that we women are powerful and talented, with hearts big enough to save the world. The messages of distrust and disrespect from other quarters were simply wrong.

Fifteen years after Utah's IWY conference, I delivered a paper in October 1992 on my experiences there at the LDS Church's Brigham Young University. This paper was based on a series of interviews my students and I had conducted with women who had helped plan the IWY conference, who had attended the conference themselves, or who were delegates to the national convention. The room at BYU was packed with women, many of whom I recognized. There were several women from the LDS Relief Society general board including Aileen Clyde, my personal heroine. Most of them I did not know; and I assumed, somewhat naively, that they were there because they were interested in the story. I was wrong.

After sociologist Marie Cornwall and I had delivered our separate papers and opened the session for questions, the room exploded into bedlam, it seemed to me. Accustomed to the traditional civility of academic discourse, I was surprised and dismayed. Women in the back and at both sides stood up and shouted sneering questions and criticisms that pierced the air like spit balls. I began to feel irrelevant to this exchange that seemed in some ways to be scripted. I felt as if I were disappearing into the wall behind me, and wished I could. The anger, the division, the bitterness, and the suspicions surrounding the IWY conferences and the Equal Rights Amendment (ERA) were being reenacted in front of my eyes. I found out later that many of these women had come to our session with the express purpose of disrupting it. Some had sent letters to the university president complaining about the topic and challenging the research money granted to support the research.

It would be seven years before I picked up this research again. It had proven to be a sort of hot potato each time I had touched it, and each time it had raised fresh blisters. But the story is compelling enough to draw me back again and again, demanding that I pay attention, that I find out what it had meant.

The issues seemed to be crystal clear to those in the pro and con camps. However, it is important to acknowledge the great range of responses among Mormon women. Some chose to become politically involved, join coalitions or committees, march at demonstrations, or lobby sessions of the legislatures. But far more women did nothing. The silence, which is like the apparently unruffled surface of a lake as storm winds build, is noteworthy. For thousands of Mormon women and other women throughout the country, the campaign against the ERA seemed simply irrelevant and uninteresting. They could not see its impact on their own lives which, for the most part, were contented and focused on practical tasks. The messages they heard coming from their church matched their own sense of their position in the world, particularly the Mormon world, but they failed to perceive a threat and chose to not do anything at all. Why fix what was not broken?

Others faced the fight against the ERA as a sort of short-time assignment, not all that different from an assignment to show up at the church's Welfare Center for a day of canning apples or tomatoes. They supported the battle because they were asked to do so by church leaders whom they respected and, more importantly, obeyed, if called upon to do so. The church's concern about the position of women was a great comfort to them, an assurance in a world of change that they did not necessarily choose to understand or address. This was certainly true for me.

Good, faithful, intelligent women fell into both categories. Women worthy of anyone's respect, whom I greatly respect, willingly, even eagerly, accepted the church's position, supported the anti-ERA campaign or other church programs impacting the lives of women, and found ways to weave this narrative into their own personal stories or narratives that explained their lives.

Today, in many ways, the situation regarding women is less straightforward than it had been back in the 1970s. Those of us who still care about feminism inhabit a world that is seemingly indifferent. In some quarters, feminism is treated with more derision than devil worship; many others simply could not care less. Under the illusion that enough has been accomplished, that the position of women is good enough, many women and men alike seem to go about their lives without ever giving feminism a second thought.

Others are afraid to let their feminism show. As a teacher, I have heard students undercut their own positions on gender issues by prefacing their opinion with the little apology, "Now, I'm not a feminist, but . . ." as if that means they would be crazy or off center if they were—that they would not be someone one could trust. At a recent conference, a middle-aged scholar prefaced her remarks with a similar disclaimer: "I don't want you to think I'm a feminist, but . . ." What is it about feminism that creates such avoidance?

It has been disturbing to me, at this point midway through my life, to hear students, colleagues, even friends equivocate about women's rights. Perhaps the most damaging backlash, the result of the decade-long debate over the ERA, is the enduring stigma that still brands and dismisses the strong, bright, and articulate young women just emerging into the world. Identifying oneself as a feminist, as one did in the 1970s, can be risky business.

In 1979 Utah journalist Linda Sillitoe wrote a personal reaction to the excommunication of Mormon feminist Sonia Johnson that raised another important issue.[1] Johnson, a Mormon mother with Cache Valley roots, was the founding president of Mormons for the ERA. Sillitoe decided to title her personal, privately circulated rumination "Don't Use My Name." A strong woman herself, but thinking of her own church membership, job, and family, Sillitoe reflected on what it meant to try to purge the bitterness over the injustice she had witnessed. The title was also drawn from dozens of interviewees who expressed strong feelings on the issue but masked themselves in anonymity for fear of retaliation. Might they suffer the same fate as Johnson and other women who spoke out? Might they be shunned by their local congregations? Might they be expelled from their church as Johnson was? They were not ready to take the chance. Sillitoe called this phenomenon the "invisibility factor," an idea she felt was key to understanding the psychology that ran through the 1970s and which continues to drive some women's (and men's) reactions to feminism.

Sillitoe noted the contradiction in being invisible: "The author cannot sign [her name], and to me that is the ultimate irony: that a statement of fear, love, and immobility must remain immobile—because of fear, and love." To understand how Mormon women felt about Sonia Johnson and her excommunication, Sillitoe spent hours on the telephone. "Interestingly," she wrote, "virtually every Mormon woman I have spoken with has assessed her own vulnerability, no matter how 'closet' a feminist and/or ERA supporter she might be—and none of them have been 'Sonia Johnsons.' Many softly blamed the bishop for their reticence, either because they were such good men or such unpredictable or vindictive men, whichever. Regardless, they felt endangered by the power the bishop held over them. They felt vulnerable."

The "general ignorance of the facts surrounding Sonia's excommunication" also surprised Sillitoe, who noted the "painful polarization" that pitted ERA supporters against supporters of the church, dividing families, friends, and wards and also, for some, defining their relationship to God. Despite a level of ignorance about the ERA itself, LDS church leaders relied on the collective force of obedient members who wielded tremendous political power in several key states—a power that reflected not the actual number of resident Mormons but the church's ability and will to mobilize the faithful to express the church's position through political action.

Although Mormon critiques of the ERA often read like legal arguments, church leaders from the beginning labeled the debate a moral issue—even while focusing almost exclusively on the appropriate role of the federal government, the use of law, and the meaning of the Constitution. True for the growing troops of the Christian Right that talked of "moral issues" but based its reasoning on legal arguments, the Mormon Church was joining a larger movement sweeping the country, reacting against the social change threatening the traditions America stood on.[2] The Mormon pronouncements were often prefaced by an appeal to free agency (i.e., free choice), but the implication was that a "good woman" would see only one real choice: to obey her inspired leaders and reject the ERA. The alternative was rebellion against the church or even against God and would certainly end in social and possibly ecclesiastical consequences. The result was that many ties of love and many years of conditioning tugged women in the direction these statements were intended to point them. Some feminists among the church membership were torn, feeling that theological beliefs nurtured by the church pointed them in the direction of fuller opportunities for women: the value of free agency, the ideal of eternal progression that did not accept social restrictions, woman-centered loyalty rooted in strong mother-daughter relations, and a love for the ideals of the Mormon women's Relief Society organization. But even those who moved into feminism *because of* the strength of their belief in Mormonism did so over daunting barriers of loneliness, agonized soul-searching, fear, and anger.

Interest in the ERA periodically resurfaces. The amendment died in 1982, but supporters continue to try to breathe life into the cause by lobbying the U.S. Congress and state legislatures. In the 1970s opponents of the ERA warned of dire consequences if it passed: co-ed bathrooms, women draftees, and the repeal of spousal support laws. Ironically, these social changes occurred without the ERA, including co-ed college dorms, women fighting beside men in Desert Storm, and alimony laws that are gender-neutral where need, contribution, and support issues are considered.

Mine is a generation that watched Billie Jean King trounce Bobby Riggs on the tennis court. Raised on *Donna Reed* and the *Brady Bunch,* we have taken notice of the subtleties of the *Cosby Show* as women began wearing suits to work and speaking from positions of power, expanding traditional roles to include more than tending husbands and children, to include public lives. Career opportunities, school funding, and sexual harassment became focal points of popular attention. Activists gave up on the 1970s issues of the ERA and reproductive rights—after all, *Roe v. Wade* was the law of the land, with access to first-trimester abortion—and turned instead to the hot-button issues of child support, protection against domestic violence, stalking, and better justice in rape cases. Sexual abuse, a devastating plague that fell unequally on girls under eighteen, was no longer shielded by the secrecy surrounding unspeakable crimes. Political action committees helped elect more women to office. Female representation in legislatures shifted significantly.

As a result of these societal shifts, some now view the ERA as a historical relic, obsolete and irrelevant. With women sitting on the Supreme Court, running companies, and playing professional sports, the ERA might seem unnecessary. But for others, federal legislation remains essential. Even as a symbol, the amendment holds great potency. From the first, ERA supporters have asked the question: How much value and respect does the United States show women?

In the late 1990s, two states, Iowa and Florida, passed amendments in their state constitutions that, for the first time, included women. The ERA was re-introduced into the Illinois and Virginia legislatures and debated by the general assembly in Missouri. While the original debate over the ERA was raging in the early 1970s, Ruth Bader Ginsburg, at the time a professor of law at Columbia University but soon to become the second woman to sit on the U.S. Supreme Court, asserted that without a federal amendment there would be no incentive to change laws that discriminate on the basis of gender. Writing in the 1973 issue of the *American Bar Association Journal,* she noted that despite the passage of the Pay Equity Act, Title VII of the Civil Rights Act, and Title IX of the Education Act, hundreds of laws at both the state and federal levels continued to discriminate according to gender.

Court cases such as *Reed v. Reed* (1971) and *Frontiero v. Richardson* (1973), which Ginsburg helped to argue, caused legislatures to reconsider laws that differentiated on the basis of sex. Soon the U.S. Supreme Court ruled that, under the equal protection clause of the Fourteenth Amendment, laws containing gender-based classifications must have a demonstrably rational basis. In *Craig v. Boren* the Court raised that standard so that gender discrimination would have to be shown to be substantially related to important governmental interests. Finally, as a Supreme Court judge, Ginsburg wrote the court's majority opinion in *Virginia v. U.S.* (1996), stipulating that sex-based discrimination requires an "exceedingly persuasive justification." The majority opinion struck down the barrier that had kept women from attending the formerly all-male Virginia Military Institute. Despite these advancements, gender discrimination is not as widely prohibited as discrimination based on race and ethnicity. The Fourteenth Amendment helped many but not all Americans. Without an amendment to the U.S. Constitution guaranteeing the equality of women, laws protecting women's rights could still be amended or even repealed.[3]

However, this book is not a treatise on the continuing need for an Equal Rights Amendment. Rather, it traces the high-voltage intersection of two national trends—feminism and the Christian Right, with a focus on Mormonism—during a vivid decade in American history.

Nationally-known African American feminist writer bell hooks indicates how nuanced the status of women in the United States is:

> Many women do not join organized resistance against sexism precisely because sexism has not meant an absolute lack of choices. They may know they are discriminated against on the basis of sex, but they do not equate this with oppression. Under capitalism, patriarchy is so structured that sexism restricts women's behavior in some realms even as freedom from limitations is allowed in other spheres. The absence of extreme restrictions leads many women to ignore the areas in which they are exploited or discriminated against; it may even lead them to imagine that no women are oppressed.[4]

The goal of feminism, according to hooks, has been to ensure that all people enjoy the same range of choices as those in the most privileged class. This can only be accomplished through a reordering of society to replace alienation, competition, and dehumanization with "intimacy, mutuality, and camaraderie."[5]

Besides the battle over the ERA, the formation by the United Nations of a commission to study the status of the world's women engendered the so-called International Women's Year and stimulated a worldwide discussion on the status of women. In the United States this included a series of statewide conferences and a climactic show-down in Houston, Texas, the country's first national conference on the status of women since the battle for suffrage two generations earlier. A survey conducted in advance of the Houston meeting by the National Organization of Women indicated that the ERA, reproductive rights, and other controversial feminist ideas would be endorsed overwhelmingly at the conference. And they were. But the conservatives, who sensed a liberal agenda, reported that they felt invalidated and excluded. In fact, the decade was one of profound division among women over issues that impacted their lives directly. The lingering effects are with us still.

Much of this turbulence fell during the administration of LDS President Spencer W. Kimball, a gentle and beloved leader, twelfth president of the American-based church of 3.2 million members worldwide at the time. The *Los Angeles Times* ran a feature story about him in 1974 when he attained leadership at age seventy-nine. Kimball, who was born at the end of the nineteenth century, said he felt called to counter such social ills as "the loosening of the marital bonds and juvenile delinquency." The church had always stressed the importance of the family unit in its faith structure even though the ideal family unit in the nineteenth century was polygamy. Thus, social change had affected the Mormon people in a particular way. "We try to be not of the world," President Kimball told the *Times,* "but it's impossible to be entirely unaffected by it. We have some broken homes, some divorces, some immoralities at times. We try to handle it." He emphasized that the LDS woman, within the family, was not a second-class citizen. "While we stress the importance of the woman's role in the family life, which is basic, we don't make them servants, and we don't force them to work, or to leave off all the other things. . . . They are cultured, and in many cases they've studied." Young women, he said, were allowed to become missionaries when they turned twenty-three, compared to nineteen years of age for young men, although "they are not encouraged to do so," he acknowledged.[6] He said he himself was married to a strong woman, Camilla Eyring Kimball, who despite her traditional lifestyle of family care, gardening, baking bread, and bottling vegetables was also well-known for her intellectual curiosity, insatiable reading, and steady accumulation of university courses.

Less than three years after the *Times* article, the *Salt Lake Tribune* published a piece headlined "BYU Women Oppose ERA, Survey Says, Men Prefer 'Pretty Faces.'" This disconcerting survey of women students at BYU revealed that 76 percent opposed the ERA but that 86 percent said they had been the victims of sexual discrimination. Shirleen Jones from Pingree, Idaho, worried about the negative side effects of the ERA. "It might take women out of the home," she said. Gretchen Pike of Pelham, New Hampshire, said: "Women belong in the family, supporting their husbands and raising their children, not going off being selfish and thinking of themselves." A poll of the men was especially telling. When asked about their ideal mate—the girl they wanted to marry—100 percent said physical attractiveness was vital. When asked, "What is the first thing you look for in a girl?" they responded variously, most emphasizing "a good figure and a pretty face," while three said "intelligence" and four said spirituality or a "strong testimony" were important. Dean Brown of Culver City, California, explained: "It is said that if given a choice between marrying an ugly girl with a good spirit or a cute girl with no spirit, marry the cute one because you can give a girl a good spirit, but you can't give an ugly girl good looks."[7]

Several years earlier, the LDS magazine for adolescents, in an article titled, "What Is a Girl Good For?" proposed that this was a question "the young woman of today asks":

> One hears a lot of talk about what today's girl is good for. One sees the word in print. But opinions vary greatly. Girls are counseled to marry and have families—to fulfill the measure of their creation. But if they do, they are charged with adding to the problem of the population explosion. They are taught the same subjects as boys in school and trained to compete with them in the world of commerce. On the other hand, they are reminded that their place is in the home. What is the truth? The dichotomy can be disconcerting.[8]

In this gendered discussion, author Elaine Cannon explained:

> One thing of which an LDS girl is certain is that her role in the Church and in life will always be different from that of a boy. She has not been

> given the priesthood. God's power is not used through her exactly as it is in men. But a girl does have a power. Hers is the power to bear children, yes, but also to love, and with heart and hand to comfort, teach, and train, to heal and care for both old and young, man, woman, and child alike, wherever her service may take her.

Thus, service rather than leadership was ultimately what a "girl is good for."

Perhaps this kind of language and imagery should not sadden me, but I confess that it does. Is not service part of being human? Should service not be what boys are good for? The evident difficulty in identifying what a "girl is good for" injures women and men alike. Women are good for everything, not because someone finds the words to tell them they are, but because it is already in them to be so. Most importantly, the discourse about the position of women in the Mormon world was argued with rhetoric which failed to satisfactorily explain the difference.

Women of my generation grew up in households with mothers whose sense of self was tied to 1950s obligations of perfect womanhood. To those of us following them, the messages our mothers lived by seemed contradictory and even destructive. Consider, for example, *Fascinating Womanhood,* Helen B. Andelin's advice for the perfect woman, a book that sat on the bookshelf in our family room next to Steinbeck, Faulkner, and recordings of Mario Lanza. Like the other books, I took *Fascinating Womanhood* down and read it. I watched eagerly to see if my mother asked my father for help because he was "stronger." I had seen her move a piano by herself and knew she could do anything she set her mind to. But I was suspicious of her every move for a while.

The LDS *Church News,* published weekly, celebrated Andelin's willingness to speak out against "women's liberation" in a day when other religious women seemed reticent to challenge the more experienced public debaters of feminism. Andelin was the mother of eight children, three at BYU or on LDS missions in the 1970s. "I feel strongly that the women's lib movement will fail," she told the *Church News.* "Everything they stand for is against the basic role of women. They want to do away with the woman's place in the home, yet without the structure of the home, the whole nation would be weakened." She questioned feminism's position on individual freedom, which argued that wives and mothers lose freedom by choosing to be full-time care givers and homemakers. "We need woman power in the home," she asserted. "If a woman will stay in the home and make a career out of it, she has the ability as a mother to make the world a different place."[9]

Andelin said she had come across a series of booklets written in the 1920s called "The Secrets of Fascinating Womanhood," with ideas about how to manage happier marriages. She combined these insights with her own background in Mormonism and experience as a wife and mother to begin holding seminars for women. Soon her seminars were overflowing with as many as 170 eager disciples at a time, and church members clamored for her how-to advice for a happy marriage. Her resulting book, *Fascinating Womanhood,* fit well with other conservative attempts to protect the American family in the wake of the Cold War and with the Mormon spin on what had been called the cult of true womanhood.[10] Andelin portrayed her ideal woman as one who knew how to keep her man happy by making him think he was stronger and cleverer—that she should pretend to wilt and expire in the absence of his manly protection. For many women troubled by an unfulfilled marriage or the specter of rising divorce rates, *Fascinating Womanhood* promised to create unbreakable bonds of domestic romance. For many other women, troubled by the deceit and manipulation they were asked to deploy, *Fascinating Womanhood* was asking them to compromise their integrity in the name of the family.

A student editorial appearing in December 1977 in the University of Utah's *Daily Chronicle* captured this failure to take women seriously. The anonymous writer, who described herself as a "Houston observer," blamed the media for failing to present the truth of the women's movement. "The media has made every attempt to make a sham of the women's movement either by reducing it to a ridiculous group of bra burning malcontents or militant man-hating tigers." She criticized the press for distinguishing between "pro-family" Utahns and anti-family feminists when the latter were equally family friendly. With convenient sound bites, society had effectively boxed up women into tight little packages that left no room for individuality, personal expression, or growth. Both sides did it.

What I offer in this book is my own vantage point in the continuing debate over the rights and responsibilities of Mormon women, a debate that is politicized, despite being conducted largely in a church setting, and one in which rhetoric has played a supremely important role. I hope my insights prove to be useful in clarifying of one position and a positive contribution to that debate.

This project has benefitted greatly from the tremendous resources found in various archives and historical libraries. Clearly, women knew this decade carried significant weight. Many knew they were making history and acting on a national stage. They kept their records. Many women gave their files to the Utah State Historical Society, the University of Utah, or Brigham Young University. Thus, an immense and thorough record of these events is readily available for research. Many of the relevant files planned for disposal by the LDS Church archives ended up at the University of Utah's Special Collections and are therefore also available for the use of researchers.

Beginning in 1992, several of my students and I interviewed women who have been a part of this story. These interviews are still in my possession on tape and in typescript, although not yet in a finalized form. They are destined to become part of the documentary record in the Harold B. Lee Library at BYU. In my source notations, these are designated as part of the "IWY Project." The voices captured in these interviews lend additional power to the narrative, otherwise drawn from official documents, newspaper reports, and secondary sources; and their vivid sensorial memories add an important element to these events. It was not infrequently that my students and I sat with someone who, in remembering these painful years, allowed tears to flow unchecked while she recalled what had occurred—what she had cared about or worked for and what had changed or not changed since that time. The interviews were sponsored in part by support from the BYU Women's Research Institute and the University of

Utah. They represent a balance between conservative and liberal voices, professional women and stay-at-home mothers, students and elderly women. Every attempt was made to be fair in the choice of women to interview and whose voices would contribute to this narrative. Many of the women we interviewed gave us their personal files, shared their letters and journals with us, and gave us the boxes of books, pamphlets, and papers they had saved all these years. Again, they knew these records were important, that they had helped shape history. It has been one of the rich rewards of researching this history that so many of the players are still alive, have continued to play public roles, and have reflected seriously on the significance of that decade.

The documentary record includes a huge outpouring of official publications from the LDS Church, but it has not been easy to detect the personal input of individual church leaders. Spencer Kimball, for example, made only infrequent mention of the church's campaign against the ERA in his journal.[11] There are almost no personal responses available from other significant players on the General Authority level. That part of the story is left for someone else to write.

As important as the events beginning in the late 1970s is the historical context for these developments, which is why nineteenth-century views of women and female activism, both nationally and within the LDS Church, are the subject of the first chapter in this book. Opponents and proponents of the ERA have both used Mormon history to prove their points. It is important to know the historical relationship of Mormon women to their church and their early participation in the women's movement, as well as how the church interpreted a woman's role and the issues that were important to both. The second chapter describes the efforts by national activists to pass an equal rights amendment beginning in the 1920s and continuing to the 1970s.

I found that, in key ways, the campaign against the ERA was a battle fought rhetorically with alternative imagery portraying the role of women, the nature of woman, and the potential impact of an equal rights amendment on the position of women in the world. Chapter 3 analyzes the rhetorical arguments, mediums, and discourse employed in this struggle, particularly the rhetorical stance of the Mormon Church in its anti-ERA campaign of the 1970s.

The next several chapters span the years between 1972 and 1983 and detail the campaigns, including the anti-ERA effort organized by the Special Affairs Committee of the LDS Church in Iowa, Florida, Nevada, New York, Virginia, and other key states in the ratification effort. These chapters focus as well on the mid-1970s when IWY conferences were held internationally within each participating nation and in each state of the Union. The final chapters focus on the efforts of individual Mormon women to organize in opposition to the church's official position in such organizations as Mormons for ERA (MERA); the story of MERA's most prominent leader, Sonia Johnson; and one women's group in Utah, the Alice Louise Reynolds Forum, which provided an outlet for those who were reevaluating their lives as LDS women in the wake of the decade's disturbance and the church's campaign.

Ironically, I can fully relate to both of the opposing points of view. I spent fifteen years as a "stay-at-home mother" and the next several years to the present time as a professor. My sense of a woman's life is that it is rich with choices, complex with competing pulls on her time and energy, but that it also holds out rich rewards. It is true that the LDS Church's campaign against the ERA was one of many. In important ways it mirrored the efforts of others—Protestant religious groups, conservative political action committees, and special interest organizations that first formed to fight the ERA and then transferred their attention and focus to other issues on the American political landscape. I will not anywhere in this book say that this campaign was wrong, but will instead try to understand how it worked and the impact it had on individual women's lives, the position of Utah in the context of Mormonism and Utah society, and the long-term implications of such a campaign on the women's movement more generally. In large measure, this was a war of words. But they were words that ripped apart women's lives, threatened to destroy their self-respect or dignity, and that divided women from each other in profoundly important and meaningful ways. Originally motivated by fear of change, one of many deep and weighty transformations was that women became afraid of each other. Rather than searching for common ground, this was a time when women pulled apart, believed the rhetoric of suspicion and alarm, and contributed to the dichotomies that separated feminists from more traditional women and rendered them powerless at reaching reconciliation.

It has been thirty years since the ERA was passed by the U.S. Senate and House of Representatives. I have heard countless women speak of that period as if it were their coming-out party. Regardless of where each woman positioned herself, it was a time of social upheaval and change. It forced Americans to examine the ways we relate to each other as men and women, our relationship to the law, the ways we build community, and our options in negotiating marriages and raising children. Many women had experiences similar to mine through events like the IWY that caused a sea change in their lives. Set adrift, women rewrote their scripts or took decades to begin to process and consider what it had meant for them. For others, the turbulence of the change and the violence of the backlash made them cling more tightly to traditional religion and family structures as a source of stability and meaning.

The willingness of the women to share their stories made this book possible. For many, these stories were intensely personal and painful. Other women have chosen to keep their stories private and untold. For those who shared, I value their gifts and respect both the giver and the responsibility that comes with hearing. Their stories will become part of the reader's understanding as we all find our lives inextricably linked. What we women did, separately and together, impacted all of us.

Among many to whom I am indebted are first of all the staff of the University of Utah's Special Collections archives in the Marriott Library. They were particularly helpful in passing on box after box of rich materials for my perusal. They were infinitely patient as I repeatedly exclaimed: "Can you believe this?" or "Look at this!" Much of it was really too good to believe—exactly on topic. I was deeply moved by the sense of historical significance that prompted women such as Linda Sillitoe, Sonia Johnson, Sharon Kreigher, and Kathryn MacKay to save their correspondence, the pamphlets they picked up at various demonstrations, and their personal notes. They knew the importance of this story.

Lavina Fielding Anderson's fine ethical and moral sense is evident throughout this manuscript through her editing, her friendship, and her leadership. She is an endless source of inspiration and wisdom. The Signature Books team made the final stage of the production of this book a grand ride. Ultimately, they make it happen, and they always make it excellent, rewarding, and right.

As always, my children also made this book possible. The first three were babies when this story began, and the last three are now adults, my friends and strength. It was perhaps necessary that I complete this project—despite the many disruptions and temptations to push it aside—because of these children: my two amazing sons—Jason and Patrick—my four powerful daughters—Elizabeth and her husband Mark, Rachael, Emily and Jerol, and Katelyn—and the woman my son Jason married, Sharley; the woman Patrick may some day make his life with; grandchildren Aspen, Dylan, Kristin, the beautiful new baby girl, Stella Rose; and the others who will come. For me, the women's movement was about making a rich, full life possible for every one of us. It is a journey that is still incomplete.

1. The Uses of History

> Utah is the land of marvels. She gives us, first, polygamy, which seems to be an outrage against "woman's rights," and then offers to the nation a "Female Suffrage Bill." . . . Was there ever a greater anomaly known in the history of society?
>
> —*Phrenological Journal*, 1871

When Sonia Johnson, Mormon mother of four, testified in favor of the Equal Rights Amendment before a U.S. Senate committee in 1978, she invoked the long history of Mormon participation in the woman's rights movement. When Beverly Campbell, also a Mormon mother, stood in front of the LDS Citizens Coalition in Virginia in opposition to the ERA, she too recited historical precedents to justify her position. When Mormon women opposed or supported the ERA during the campaign over ratification, they cited the history of their predecessors to support their argument. They looked to women in the past to improve the lives of women in the present.

In both the first and second waves of the women's movement— first in the nineteenth and then the twentieth century—Mormon women stood on clearly articulated and fervently defended platforms, rhetorical positions which measured feminist ideas against the Mormon worldview. In the 1970s women on both sides of the battle over the ERA believed they were fighting for a better world for all women. They believed that their female ancestors had modeled activism for them, and they very consciously followed in their footsteps. The accomplishments of nineteenth-century Mormons seemed at once justification of the fight for equal rights or proof positive of the blessings that would come from following their priesthood leaders and the "official policy" concerning opposition to the ERA.

What concerns most worried Mormon women in the nineteenth century? Would they have understood the questions asked by women in the 1970s?

The lives of women such as Eliza R. Snow, Zina Diantha Huntington Young, and Emmeline B. Wells suggest the same social forces, economic shifts, and demographic changes that altered the lives of all American women impacted nineteenth-century Mormon women. They were daughters of the Second Great Awakening, a religious revolution that empowered women with access to their own spiritual lives. Joseph Smith also profoundly shaped their thinking. They saw him as a prophet and believed he talked to God. Their devotion to his teachings formed their lives as women.[1]

The participatory nature of religion during the revivals of the early nineteenth century gave women a taste of spiritual and actual power, pulling them into religious activity in new ways. Here they seized sacred space traditionally occupied by men. Religion changed them in the process and they, in turn, shaped the Mormon world. Conversion to Mormonism separated them from their earlier lives and gave them real work to do—building what they considered to be the kingdom of God. Women played a role in this kingdom building, contributing as wives and mothers but also as faithful members of a community of saints. Like the republican motherhood of an earlier generation, women inculcated Mormon values, beliefs, and devotion in their children, expanding the base of Saints with their offspring.

One historian of American women, Anne Firor Scott, astutely noted the level of Mormon women's participation in religious activity:

> Like other Americans, Mormons believed in separate spheres for men and women, but in their case the separation was at once more stringent in ideology and less stringent in everyday life than elsewhere. In theory and in theology, men were responsible for all public life, and in private life they were expected to rule their families. At the same time, the exigencies of the Mormon situation required women to be in charge when men were away, as they so frequently were, on church business. Plural wives were often expected to earn their own keep and take full responsibility for their own children. The makings of a paradox are already evident. More was expected of Mormon women than of almost any other women in the country, but at the same time their responsibility to obey members of the priesthood was unquestioned.[2]

Also paradoxically, Mormon feminists and anti-feminists used the content of nineteenth-century women's lives to fight either for or against the ERA.

Mormonism's First Feminism

Four years after the death of Joseph Smith and one year after the Mormon pioneers entered the Salt Lake Valley to begin their settlement efforts, a group of American women met at Seneca Falls, New York, in July 1848 at the first women's rights meeting. Their grievances were voiced in a formal document, "Declaration of Sentiments," which enumerated the limited legal rights of women, their restricted opportunities for education, and the curbs on women's public involvement. After that first gathering, these same women held a series of meetings at various locations throughout the United States to clarify issues involving all women and to refine the organizational efforts of the leadership.

As was true of the 1960s, social changes impacted the reality of women's lives in the nineteenth century. Women had previously been the guardians of the hearth, given principal responsibility for socializing and nurturing the family's children and caring for the needs of their husbands.

They were, in the words of family historian Carl Degler, "responsible for the ethical and spiritual character as well as the comfort and tranquility of the home," assigned this psychological duty because they were considered "the moral superiors of men."[3]

One keen-eyed visitor to the United States, Count Alexis de Toqueville, identified the difference between the male and female spheres in the 1830s. He saw the value of this distinction, believing that it enabled true respect between husbands and wives. "Americans," he wrote in *Democracy in America,* do not believe that men and women should perform the same tasks or occupy the "same offices, but they show an equal regard for both their respective parts; and though their lot is different, they consider both of them as beings of equal value."[4] However, separate spheres guaranteed that women would lead lives confined to the domestic sphere while their husbands "represented" them in the public sphere.

This barrier was breached as the perceived moral superiority of women drew them into voluntary associations to deal with issues of public morality. American women joined charitable and humanitarian clubs in droves during the nineteenth century. In this way they created female networks, developed new skills in organization and politics, and made substantial contributions in reform and benevolence. More importantly, the boundaries of their private lives expanded to include public exposure, although within safe contexts. Female societies, providing the stepping stone into the public spotlight, were seen as logical and desirable extensions of home responsibilities. Initially as missionaries or crusaders for moral education, temperance, or abolition, but eventually demanding equal rights, women from the expanding middle class were cognizant of their increased roles and responsibilities and seized these opportunities with enthusiasm. Applying the talents they had developed in the domestic realm to the community outside their home, they became "social housekeepers," guardians of moral values in the public realm carved as a middle ground between the two.

The earliest female associations, in helping orphans, widows, and destitute mothers, engendered empathy for victimized women and, in the process, condemnation for the victimizing actions of irresponsible men and unjust laws. Women fought against the evils of alcohol with a religious sense of mission. Temperance filled them with righteous indignation and gave them a place to spend the emotional energy that came with it. Women created and managed orphanages, schools for the poor, refuges for abused or neglected wives. Regardless of the avenue they took or the method they used for distributing aid, they imbued female values into their work. This became appropriate women's work. As they ventured into public life, they traveled on safe ground, never challenging the traditional roles designated for them by their husbands or fathers, their clergy, or political leaders. This new area was an extension of the space they already knew. It was public domestic space, and they capitalized on the "gender consciousness associated with woman's sphere."[5] Formed to serve a variety of different agendas that tended to be more general than doctrinaire, the main impulse seemed to be to render aid where possible and to associate rather than to reform society in general.[6] This shift was grounded in a body of widely read public literature.

Simultaneously, as historian Barbara Welter documents, there was a powerful prescription to adhere to the "cult of true womanhood," a body of ideas perpetuated through church, tradition, and the mass media about the appropriate role of the "true"—meaning good—woman:

> Woman, in the cult of True Womanhood presented by the women's magazines, gift annuals, and religious literature of the nineteenth century, was the hostage in the home. In a society where values changed frequently, where fortunes rose and fell with frightening rapidity, where social and economic mobility provided instability as well as hope, one thing at least remained the same—a true woman was a true woman, wherever she was found. . . . It was a fearful obligation, a solemn responsibility, which the nineteenth-century American woman had—to uphold the pillars of the temple with her frail white hand.[7]

Women received this message from their parents and clergy, women's magazines, and instruction books which contained what appeared to be a recipe for perfection. Its message was simple: a woman was expected to be pious, pure, domestic, and submissive. These powerful prescriptive ideas drew boundaries around appropriate behavior and acceptable dreams that women could fulfill only if they followed the guidance of those around them who knew best.

Without these four key attributes of true womanhood, "no matter whether there was fame, achievement, or wealth, all was ashes." But in possession of them, a woman was "promised happiness and power," according to Welter.[8] Woman was portrayed as a purer vessel than man, pitted and hardened by exposure to the world, and religion was thought to be at the core of a woman's nature. Religious sensibility was a gift given women by God. Logically, religious activity was private and therefore domestic, and it kept a woman home instead of wandering into places she should not go. The opposite was also true. A woman without religion was an unnatural being too awful to contemplate. Sexual purity was part of this religious orientation, reflecting a woman's true nature. Women were taught to defend their virtue at all costs. A woman who had lost her virtue was a pariah in good society. Men were by nature more sensual, so they were fairly easily forgiven if they seduced her from the path of righteousness.

Perhaps the most quintessentially feminine of the virtues was submissiveness, and women responded to this, accepting the instruction that was offered and deferring to men. With all the information they received over the pulpit, from ladies' journals and novels, from their parents and teachers, they understood what their position in the social hierarchy was and resisted efforts to remove them from their subordinate sphere. Education, it was believed, would pull a woman away from her proper role and fill her head with ideas that were impure, irreligious, and damaging. A woman's Bible was all the reading she needed.

The concept of true womanhood was a cultural shibboleth inevitably limited to the middle-class women who could afford such luxuries. Meanwhile, outside their orderly parlors but as nearby as the immigrant women working in their kitchens and sweating over their lacy laundry, urbanization, industrialization, and other economic and social forces swept across the country. Inevitably, women fitted for true womanhood no longer fit into such a society. According to Welter, in the last quarter of the nineteenth century, the impact of the Civil War and eventually the social reform of the progressive era "all called forth responses from woman which differed from those she was trained to believe were hers by nature and divine decree. The very perfection of True Womanhood, moreover, carried within itself the seeds of its own destruction. For if woman was so very little less than the angels, she should surely take a more active part in running the world, especially since men were making such a hash of things."[9]

It is perhaps ironic that the emancipation of slaves highlighted the inequities of the legal situation of women, stimulating the women's movement in a major way. Before the Civil War, the vote was an issue that states addressed, along with women's property rights, their change in status with marriage or divorce, and their legal positions as parents. Under the "femme covert" concept, women were considered to be literally the property of their husband in marriage. They had no property rights, custody of their children, or contractual relationships. While state constitutions gradually broadened the suffrage to include white males over twenty-one, then all males, they did not in most cases extend the vote to women.

In part, true womanhood was a powerful means of social control that sought to maintain hierarchies and lines of authority. By emphasizing the domestic dimensions of a woman's influence, it kept women "pure" for their role as mothers and wives. Pure and pious women could teach their children what it meant to be an American, what duties were demanded of them in the Republic, and what the restrictions of their class meant in society. The emphasis was stimulated by the erosion of the family by urbanization as well as by the desire to preserve the status quo.

It was immediately apparent to the settlers of Utah that in the arid valley of the Great Salt Lake, the lofty concept of true womanhood needed to be adapted in order to survive. Women managed the home and their children, contributed to the family's economy, sometimes supporting the family in the absence of the father, and played a role in the community as well. It could not have been a more dramatic contrast between customs in the East and West. While a true woman in New York might be accomplished at needlework or might entertain her guests with French poetry or a piano sonata, in Utah it was far more important to be practical than decorative. Skills at a loom or a stove were more desirable than setting an elegant table.

Ironically, plural marriage strengthened many Mormon women who had to learn to be independent and resourceful and sometimes supported their families for years while their husbands attended to other families or served a series of proselytizing missions. Although there was nothing inherently dainty or delicate about either piety or purity, especially if either was under attack, the cult of true womanhood too often fostered moral and physical martyrs, as much prisoners of their fragile sensibilities as spokespersons of these values. In contrast, a plural wife was obliged to be strong, to make prudent decisions, sometimes on her own, and to find workable answers to questions raised by the day-to-day problems of raising children, earning a living, and relating to the world around her. It was a matter of survival. It is again ironic that these women were pitied by the outside world for their "powerlessness" and "oppression." Plural wives like Zina Diantha Huntington Young, Emmeline B. Wells, and Bathsheba B. Smith, all of them leaders of Mormon women, became the most vocal defenders of plural marriage.[10]

As was true of almost everything in nineteenth-century Utah, Brigham Young's attitude toward women greatly influenced their future. A legendary community builder and much-married polygamist, he believed that women had something important to contribute to building God's kingdom, and he expanded avenues for community involvement for them. Indeed, he in fact welcomed their contributions. Acknowledging the difference between male and female spheres, President Young communicated an openness to women's duties on 18 July 1869:

> We believe that women are useful, not only to sweep houses, wash dishes, make beds and raise babies, but that they should stand behind the counter, study law, or physic, or become good bookkeepers and be able to do the

> business in any counting house, and all this to enlarge their sphere of usefulness for the benefit of society at large. In following these things they but answer the design of their creation.[11]

To back up this sweeping manifesto, Brigham Young promoted women's education, insisting that his own daughters attend the finest local school, for instance. The University of Deseret in Salt Lake City admitted eighty-eight women and ninety-eight men its first year.

Fifty miles to the south, Brigham Young Academy (BYA) organized a "women's section" in the 1870s to offer home economics and teaching, with the implication that professionalism, even in these spheres, was important. Young's daughter, Susa Young Gates, was a trustee of the academy. When she spoke at the dedication of the Department of Domestic Science in the 1870s, she stated the school's goals as instruction for "both men and women[, who] shall be taught how to live in the home . . . [and] some branch of mechanics suitable to taste and capacity. Men should receive instructions in industrial areas and women in domestic work."[12] Her life was disrupted by divorce when she was a young mother, which may explain why Gates, through the *Young Woman's Journal,* encouraged girls to prepare for the unpredictable. A woman, she advised, should "perfect herself . . . in professional work . . . and toward this the course of her training must be directed. She must decide what her natural aptitudes and inclinations are, and so far as lies in her power let these determine her choice of work."[13]

Such open doors for Utah's women, it should be recognized, did not violate the "separate spheres." Brigham Young's counselor Heber C. Kimball spoke at length about the requisite submission and subordination of women as an essential element in both divine and human social orders. Young spoke often and passionately about the correlation between the church, the family, and Christianity itself, maintaining that each was hierarchical or ordered in ways that made good sense, that prevented chaos, and that led to a natural evolution of relationships. His own family was the model, his wives examples of deference, cooperation, and loving relations.[14] Young's understanding of the biblical patriarchal order placed men at the feet of Christ with responsibility for the women and children who depended on them. Wives were considered a stewardship "to improve upon in building up and establishing the kingdom of God," as were the children of a father of many. Rather than making men tyrants, according to this view, men were accountable to God "and you cannot avoid it, without suffering a loss," as Kimball warned in 1857.[15] Apostle Orson Hyde described "the order of heaven" as placing "man in the front rank; hence he is first to be addressed. Woman follows under the protection of his counsels, and the superior strength of his arm. Her desire should be unto her husband and he should rule over her."[16]

Kimball often used the ideal relationship between a husband and wife to illustrate the deferential order of church governance, asking whether a woman has a "good spirit" if she is "contending against her husband, . . . when she is commanded to be subject to her husband, even as we are to Christ? Is it not just as necessary that women should be governed, as that men should be? I want to know what good a wife is to me, unless she will let me lead and guide, and let me govern her by the word of God." More importantly, he continued, "when a wife is obedient to her husband there is union, there is heaven." For him, anything else created disorder or the "sin of confusion."[17]

It was with their husbands' approval, while the men remained at home, that Utah women ventured into the world to espouse women's rights. Despite the distance between the Great Basin and the eastern centers of the women's movement, Mormons were among the earliest and most ardent defenders of female suffrage. As political activists, they planned and staged meetings attended by thousands of women, published their own newspaper advocating carefully defined positions, and campaigned throughout the Territory of Utah. This political cause flourished through the quasi-sponsorship it received from the church's Relief Society, a charitable group reorganized in 1867 after about twenty years' dormancy. With his blessing and through his direction, Joseph Smith in 1842 founded the Female Relief Society of Nauvoo as one of the first women's organizations in the United States. In carrying out charitable work, it was in step with what other nineteenth-century American women were doing in contributing to the larger world while they carried out their own home responsibilities. The critical role of the new Relief Society work was to create an effective network of women in the territory and to teach them organizational skills.

Operating with a remarkable degree of autonomy and creativity, the effect of the Relief Society on the lives of individual Mormon women cannot be overestimated. It extended the scale of their lives from the domestic to the public and provided them with public speaking opportunities, enlisted them in direct service to the community, and engaged them in the issues of the women's movement on a local basis. It allowed them to be leaders, raising money and managing budgets, trading in real estate, and bartering in home-manufactured goods. Among their organizational efforts was a variety of economic, social, and humanitarian programs such as grain storage, production of silk, operation of local cooperative stores, professionalization of training for maternal and child health care, and more traditional service to the sick and needy.

These activities were tremendously important in both a corporate and private sense. Women learned to expect more of themselves, to understand their capabilities, and to contribute in real and meaningful ways. Their contributions were not only valued, they were essential, and it helped the community rise to a new level. In the words of historian Anne Firor Scott, these women

> played a vital part of a highly structured thoroughly male-dominated organization but who nonetheless played a vital part in its creation and maintenance. What at first glance seems an anomaly may be partly explained by the fact that Brigham Young's bold effort to establish a tightly knit community in a remote, initially inaccessible part of the West required mobilizing every bit of available energy. When capital had to be conserved, women, who established consumption patterns, had to be part of the effort. Furthermore, as long as the church practiced polygamy, the loyalty and support of the leading women was essential to survival.[18]

Unquestionably, the women exercised significant autonomy in such efforts; but simultaneously, their area of activity was encompassed by the larger male sphere of influence. Relief Society general president Eliza R. Snow strongly maintained that women could not achieve equality outside the authoritarian structure of Mormon doctrine and practice. Women should submit or at least defer to the authority of their priesthood brothers, she asserted. In her view, according to Mormon historian Carol Cornwall Madsen, "empowerment . . . came through spiritual channels, not secular, and was thus not subject to the secular indices of equality. She was herself a model of a strong, independent, and resourceful woman while fashioning her life and actions in harmony with her ecclesiastical superiors."[19]

Besides the Relief Society, Mormon women had their own independent publication, the *Woman's Exponent,* founded in 1872 and published for the next twenty-seven years entirely by women. Initially the publication disclaimed interest in such controversial issues as suffrage; but not long after its founding, Emmeline B. Wells, who became its second editor, made women's rights a central concern through editorials and by reprinting articles from other suffrage papers. For more than twenty years, the masthead slogan read: "The Rights of Women of Zion and the Rights of Women of All Nations."[20] According to political scientist Judith Rasmussen Dushku, "The history of the *Exponent* testifies both to the vigor with which Mormon women agitated for the goals of the national movement and to the widespread official support which made such agitation possible."[21] According to Susa Young Gates, Brigham Young wanted women to have their own paper because it would "contain a portion of Church history, the record of the works and experiences of women."[22] The *Exponent* kept the women abreast of meetings, reprinted speeches and essays by female leaders, and was the official voice of the Relief Society. The *Exponent* defined feminism broadly as a vehicle for the expression of women's voices about issues that impacted their lives. Themes of injustice, inequality of opportunity, and a conviction of the equality of the sexes permeated essays throughout the paper's history.

It was no coincidence that the first issue was published on Brigham

Young's birthday, reflecting his belief that a woman's publication would have a unifying effect, enthusing the women about various industries including home manufacture, and that it would be an effective vehicle for theological debate. But as a publication by and for women, the *Exponent* expressed energy and devotion to what Dushku identified as "a desire to encourage women to speak for and to women, a sense of injustice and inequality of opportunity, [and] a conviction of the absolute equality of the sexes." These three qualities appeared "not only in the vigorous editorials of Emmeline B. Wells, but in letters from correspondents in remote places."[23] When Wells reprinted articles from sister publications in the East, the paper became a vehicle to keep Utah women current on national concerns.

Wells acknowledged the profound influence of Elizabeth Cady Stanton and Susan B. Anthony as heroines and sources of inspiration, saying "the seed was planted in my soul by reading *The Revolution* [Stanton's and Anthony's radical journal]. . . . I could never have done the work I have done in this territory had it not been for the work Miss Anthony did before me."[24] For Emmeline B. Wells and her fellow polygamist wives, plurality was a women's rights issue that gave "women the highest opportunities for self-development, exercise of judgement, and [that] arouses latent faculties, making them more truly cultivated in the actual realities of life, more independent in thought and mind, noble and unselfish."[25] Independence was the veiled theme in a September 1874 essay, written as a reflection on the complicated position of women in plural marriage:

> Is there then nothing worth living for, but to be petted, humored and caressed, by a man? That is all very well as far as it goes, but that man is the only thing in existence worth living for[,] I fail to see. All honor and reverence to good men; but they and their attention are not the only sources of happiness on the earth, and need not fill up every thought of woman. And when men see that women can exist without their being constantly at hand, that they can learn to be self-reliant or depend upon each other for more or less happiness, it will perhaps take a little of the conceit out of some of them.[26]

Like feminists in the East, Utah women were concerned about health, economic, legal, and social issues.[27] In response to an invitation from woman's rights activists Susan B. Anthony and Ida Husted Harper, Wells described the paper's special mission: "From its first issue it was the champion of the suffrage cause, and by exchanging with women's papers of the United States and England it brought news of women in all parts of the world to those of Utah."[28]

Utah women lived under a fairly unusual legal situation because the Mormon-dominated territorial legislature nullified common law during the early years and gave local probate courts power to set their own legal precedents. One consequence was to liberate women from the restrictions imposed on property and exclusion from other legal rights that, in other parts of the country, belonged only to single women. The Married Persons Property Act in 1872 gave married women the right to maintain control over property and legal means to maintain their own households or to supplement the family income.

In addition, the church's Young Ladies' Mutual Improvement Association (YLMIA; organized in 1870 as the Retrenchment Society) raised $3,000 in 1900 for construction projects and to aid the needy. In 1889, Susa Young Gates began publishing the monthly *Young Woman's Journal* as the organization's voice.

Many in the national suffrage organizations opposed Anthony's friendship with Mormon women, which began in 1871 when Anthony and Stanton first visited the West. Anthony's biographer noted that she valued these new friendships and decided to regard Mormon women "as she regarded her conventionally married friends. There were no obvious signs of difference between them and these intelligent Mormon ladies."[29] Utah women actively campaigned for suffrage after that visit, sending petitions in support of the Sixteenth Amendment, which was intended to enfranchise all women. As a result, Wells was invited to the annual convention of the National Suffrage Association in Washington, D.C., in January 1879, accompanied by Zina Presendia Young Williams, daughter of Brigham Young by a plural wife, Zina Diantha Huntington. There,

Stanton and Anthony welcomed the two Mormons and invited them to address the convention. While in the nation's capital, Wells and Williams unsuccessfully lobbied Congressman George Edmunds, author of a punitive 1882 anti-polygamy bill, to moderate his zeal. When they returned to Utah, the two women plunged into the campaign for suffrage with renewed vigor.[30]

This relationship came at a high price for Anthony and Stanton. In fact, the issue of Mormon participation drove a wedge between the more conservative American Woman's Suffrage Association under Lucy Stone and Julia Ward Howe and the National Woman's Suffrage Association led by Stanton and Anthony, which welcomed any members who supported suffrage. As president of the group, Stanton refused to exclude "Mormon women, black women, and Indian women."[31] According to historian Elizabeth Clark, for some "the woman's movement implied less a battle for social power and more a struggle for broader experience and usefulness. . . . The movement was philosophically driven more by the belief in the dignity and value of the individual and the right of each to reach his or her highest potential than by ambition for social or political status."[32] Feminists like Margaret Fuller argued that women should have the same opportunities as men: "What woman needs is not as a woman to act or rule, but as a nature to grow, as an intellect to discern, as a soul to live freely, and unimpeded to unfold such powers as were given her when we left our common home."[33] Such women believed that nothing short of a revolution could effect this kind of change. In a new twist on Manifest Destiny, they advocated their right to a different future. What they shared was a vision of a world in which men and women could march together toward greater personal development. They believed that a social transformation was inevitable and that it would be of great benefit to men as well as women.

When Stanton stepped down, Susan B. Anthony became the next leader of the group. As president, she came to Utah on numerous occasions, meeting with the Relief Society and the suffrage associations. After Utah became a state in 1896, Anthony returned to celebrate the state constitution's restoration of the women's vote after six years of intense lobbying on the local level.

The division between the American and National suffragists typified the divisiveness among American women in general. Ironically, suffrage's most ardent and vocal opponents, like its defenders, were women. The philosophical and methodological differences that separated women concerned issues of legal equity, the meaning of the difference between male and female spheres, and the need for the vote. In 1878 when a group of non-Mormon women in Salt Lake City organized an anti-suffrage society, Emmeline B. Wells lamented: "We never thought that woman could rise up against woman" and predicted an adversarial situation of "diamond cut diamond."[34]

It is not surprising that the first victories for women's suffrage occurred on the fresh slate offered by the American West. Although the settlers brought with them the attitudes, values, and customs of the East or their European homelands, each individual was newly valued on the sparsely populated frontier. Day-to-day exigencies demanded that both women and men contribute fully. Women could not be pampered and sheltered when so much had to be done by both men and women in building communities. Because women's contributions had real economic and social value, their relative prestige increased. Wyoming Territory, with only a thousand white women, had only a faint administrative shape and was therefore "unencumbered by any existing legal impediments."[35] In 1870, the same year as Utah, its territorial assembly granted women the vote. Utah, with its greater population of 17,179 white female citizens, was the first to hold an election; in February they beat their Wyoming sisters to the polls.

Historians have disagreed on how Mormon women were able to obtain the vote without a strenuous campaign. Apologists have seen it as evidence of egalitarianism in pioneer Utah, while their critical counterparts have interpreted it as an extension of ecclesiastical and patriarchal influence. Carol Cornwall Madsen suggests the key influences on this initial suffrage bill: First, the national campaign, which had a marked influence on Utah's literate and well-informed women. Second, the intercontinental railroad would be completed in Utah in 1869, and among the changes predicted was an influx of non-Mormons. Brigham Young welcomed the railroad but anticipated a greater cultural war between insiders and outsiders. He therefore moved toward economic consolidation, stronger social boundaries, and sharper political affiliations; granting women the vote increased the number of voting Mormons. Finally, the easy transition to female suffrage in neighboring Wyoming, according to Madsen, gave Utah a non-threatening example.[36]

LDS historian Thomas Alexander sees suffrage as part of the evolution of Mormon attitudes toward justice.[37] He notes the cooperative economic programs in Utah that sprang from the earlier church doctrine of consecration and stewardship. Moreover, Alexander sees as important the involvement of Mormon women in philanthropy through the Relief Society and active engagement in public discourse over the shape of their communities. In this process of community betterment, the seeming contradiction between plural marriage and women's rights was reconciled by identifying them with familial ideals. In fact, Alexander argues, Mormon society in the 1890s was a "natural matrix for the radical idea of woman suffrage."[38]

By contrast, Utah historian Beverly Beeton emphasizes the tactical decision by the church to "counter the image of downtrodden Mormon women, thus stemming the tide of anti-polygamy legislation, and the desire to find lobbying power and congressional support in the move to achieve statehood." Beeton believes that Mormon leaders also saw the advantage of having support from national suffragists in the fight for statehood.[39] Historian Eleanor Flexner agrees that there was probably an "interplay of other forces" such as the threat of military intervention in an area that had behaved more like a theocracy than a democratic republic. The introduction of the Cullom Bill in Congress in 1869-70 launched an extended campaign to eradicate plural marriage. What better way to fight these measures than to recruit the help of women and to give them a voice in the political affairs of the region?[40]

Mormon women came out in droves to oppose the Cullom Bill, staging mass protest meetings in the Salt Lake City Tabernacle. They spoke passionately from the pulpit about their devotion to God and the principle of plural marriage. Empowered in part by the Relief Society, which gave them the organizational channels for such meetings, they also demonstrated the empowerment of ideas. Their commitment to the Mormon way of life and doctrine filled them with a sense of righteousness, giving new and public importance to suffrage.

The Cullom Bill passed the House of Representatives but died in the Senate. However, its restrictions were flaccid compared to those of the successive Edmunds Act (1882) and Edmunds-Tucker Act (1887) that would outlaw plural marriage, escheat church property above $50,000 total, and disfranchise Mormon women. National suffragists, as well as Utah women, protested that it piled injury upon injury, penalizing all Mormon women rather than just those in plural marriages. In this way, the act was seen as anti-suffrage as much as anti-Mormon. Nevertheless, Mormon women were not refranchised until Utah became a state in 1896. The long-sought status of statehood became stage for a final scene in the drama over both polygamy and female suffrage.

Paralleling the suffrage campaign, equity issues had long been the material of essays appearing in the *Woman's Exponent.* Emmeline B. Wells, writing under the pseudonym "Blanche Beechwood," called for better working conditions for young women in eastern sweatshops: "Give them equality in all respects and let each work with the same chance of success according to the labor performed, without the consideration of sex, and there would soon be a vast change which would be of material benefit to the existing state of society."[41]

Familiar herself with scores of talented, powerful women, Wells saw no reason to hold them back, but instead recognized the importance of providing them with ever-greater opportunities for growth and development. As she predicted: "Let [women] have the same opportunities for an education, observation, and experience in public and private for a succession of years, and then see if she is not equally endowed with man and prepared to bear her part on all general questions socially, politically, industrially, and educationally as well as spiritually."[42]

In another *Exponent* article, a writer identified as "E" (perhaps Emmeline herself) challenged the status quo on employment equity: "Custom has said . . . that women must only earn a living by a few circumscribed modes of employment; and although there is a reaction against this worse than absurd idea, the custom still obtains too largely, and the needle and midnight candle are yet considered, by too many, the proper appliances of woman's sphere."[43] Although these issues were more relevant to large urban populations than those in Utah, Wells and others were cognizant of the connections they had with women throughout the world.

The decade preceding Utah's constitutional convention was particularly significant. Just four years after passage of the Edmunds-Tucker Act in 1887, the Territorial Suffrage Association organized in Salt Lake City with 100 members. Margaret N. Caine, wife of Utah's delegate to Congress, was its first president. Before long, branches appeared in most Utah towns. Meetings were announced in the *Exponent,* much like those of the children's Primary organization, the YLMIA, or the Relief Society itself. The association kept Utah women cognizant of national issues and channeled their efforts. At one national suffrage conference in Washington D.C. in 1891, only one state or territory sent more delegates than Utah. The group maximized its impact through newspaper articles, editorial exhortations in the *Woman's Exponent,* and lectures throughout the territory by drawing on the overlapping personal and structural network of the Relief Societies.

While opponents to woman suffrage gathered 15,366 signatures on petitions to present to the state Constitutional Convention in 1895, suffrage advocates amassed 24,801.[44] In the other controversial area of polygamy, the church relinquished public support for new plural marriages with its Manifesto of 1890. This paved the way for the abandonment two years later of the church-aligned Peoples Party and integration into national politics by affiliating with national parties. Members of both national parties in Utah supported female suffrage; nevertheless, debate on this issue still raged at the convention. Some delegates feared that suffrage would alienate members of the United States Congress and derail statehood efforts. For them, suffrage was not worth the political risk. LDS authority Brigham H. Roberts, a Democrat, represented this view, while Republican Orson F. Whitney urged the merits of universal suffrage in general and the importance of doing justice to women.[45] Apostle Heber J. Grant stated that he was "decidedly in favor of equal suffrage for the sexes" and wrote to another apostle, "I am as ardent a woman's suffrage man as can be found."[46] A third apostle, Joseph F. Smith, addressing a Relief Society conference, argued on the basis of simple justice: "If a man can perform labor for which woman is physically disqualified, let him enjoy the monopoly of it; let the same be said of woman. By what process of reasoning can it be shown that a woman standing at the head of a family, with all the responsibility resting upon her to provide for them, should be deprived of the avenues and ways or means that a man in like circumstances may enjoy to provide for them?" He chastised women "who seem to glory in their enthralled condition, and who caress and fondle the very chains and manacles which fetter and enslave them! Let those who love this helpless dependent condition and prefer to remain in it enjoy it; but for conscience and for mercy's sake let them not stand in the way of those of their sisters who would be, and of right ought to be free." He responded trenchantly to the argument that women would be compelled into civic service: "There are many men in every community who never sat on a jury, never having been called to do so, nor to be a soldier, or to do any duty, nor to be sheriff, policemen, marshals, nor even governors or judges, and yet they have possessed all the qualifications to fill any of these positions. Therefore why shall the woman be compelled to do things because she has the franchise that men are not compelled to do!"[47]

Such thoughtfulness and willingness to engage in public debate are impressive. Clearly more than a political gesture to solidify the influence of the patriarchy, suffrage was a moral and ethical issue of broad and sweeping significance. The public nature of the debate measured the

Mormon community's engagement in evaluating the role women would play. It is evident that suffrage proponents believed that a good society would be marked by justice, by respect for the different natures of men and women, and by concern for maximizing the potential of individual members. For them, suffrage was a legal right and privilege by which change would be implemented. The ideal Mormon community, still evolving, saw in this a way to maximize the contribution of both men and women. It is clear that in the early years, the Latter-day Saints believed they were embarking on an important experiment, finding a better way of living. They self-consciously presented their communities and way of life to the world for its review. In the 1890s the dialogue over relations between the sexes was an integral part of that experimentation. Church leaders were not on the fringes of the discussion, but at its center, and their public reflections reveal a process of wrestling with moral questions, trying out answers on audiences who might not always respond positively, and remaining committed to a dialectic that might result in better answers. Exciting to witness, this early discussion was energetic, free, and unfettered by public relations policy or by the prescriptions of a political campaign.

Running parallel to Utah's contest with the federal government and bid for statehood was the national movement to refine state campaigns in favor of suffrage referendums. Persuasive literature on both sides flooded the nation, resulting in numerous petitions to Congress for a federal amendment to the Constitution. At the same time, the first generation of college-educated women plunged into social service. Women like Jane Addams, founder of Chicago's Hull House—prototype for the settlement house movement to provide housing and a support center for immigrants and poor women—integrated traditional womanhood into an expanded social role with a greater awareness of the particular needs of women and children.

Suffrage was a campaign that lasted for three generations, longer than any other in American history. It defined a separate sphere of political life for women and created networks of female power and influence focused on a common cause. The endless round of publications, speeches, conventions, and petitions created a community with a feminist context. "The Woman's Movement," wrote Charlotte Perkins Gilman in 1898, "rests not alone on her larger personality, with its tingling sense of revolt against injustice, but on the wide, deep sympathy of women for each other."[48] It is apparent that, in the view of such feminist leaders as Susan B. Anthony and Elizabeth Cady Stanton, the suffrage campaign was in part a crusade to better educate women about politics and identify and mobilize a constituency.

Besides suffrage, Utah women matched national efforts at social reform. One of the first states to establish a settlement house modeled on the Chicago experiment was Neighborhood House on Salt Lake City's west side. Women legislators such as the prominent art patron Alice Merrill Horne and equally prominent physician Romania B. Pratt took part in these efforts. Utah was one of the first states, in 1896, to pass protective legislation prohibiting women and children from working in mines.[49] Such laws moved women into a category of citizens in need of special legal protection; in this area, they were not considered equals with men but beings with different capabilities and needs. The legislation was fully harmonious with the national concept of *parens patria*—that government has a parental responsibility to care for those unable to care for themselves.

During the Progressive Era from the last years of the 1890s until approximately the outbreak of World War I, women assumed an ever-expanding public role. The "true woman" became the "new woman," who asked provocative questions such as whether she should attend college or what should she do with the education she received. Each of these issues generated repercussions in terms of how women would emerge into mainstream society. Women's historian Nancy Woloch analyzed the safe and conventional rhetoric often employed to couch these questions which, as Woloch found, contained a thinly veiled subversive potential:

> Women responded to such challenges by citing the values of home. A cover for self-assertion and rubric for a feminine value system, "home" was

> a code word with many meanings. It was sometimes a euphemism for Anglo-Saxon superiority; foreigners, for instance, had to be taught the values of the middle-class home. It sometimes stood for female control over male sexuality, as in the crusades against drunkenness and prostitution. And it was sometimes part of a campaign against business run rampant, since the goals of many women's groups in the progressive era were to remedy some evil of industrial capitalism—whether to end child labor, protect women workers, or get the impurities out of milk.[50]

A strong influence on women's roles was industrialization, simultaneously reducing women's economic contribution to the family and increasing her leisure time. Woloch continues: "She was the product of urbanization, which brought her into contact with other women and also into contact with the 'other half' or 'submerged tenth.' She was the product of prosperity. . . . She was [also] the product of an old ideology, which gave her first claim on rectitude, made her a guardian of culture, and legitimized the single-sex association."[51]

Both prosperity and leisure facilitated education for the "new woman." Only 1 percent of Americans attended college in 1870, 21 percent of them women; but by 1910, 40 percent of American collegians were women.[52] During this period, the number of institutions of higher education that admitted both women and men increased five-fold. Graduating women, in turn, moved into new professions, creating a further ripple effect.

Another impact of education was the application of "scientific" techniques to mothering and home management[53] A woman's moral preeminence and responsibility for curing the evils created by the industrial city remained principally her nurture of children. However, the National Congress of Mothers, organized in 1897, defined her role further as an agent for reform. These two roles had come to be seen as harmonious, even synonymous. "Scientific motherhood," announced one mother at the group's first meeting, would produce a "grander, nobler, race" while reforming drunkards and criminals. It would lead to the "abolition of asylums . . . the elimination of selfishness, the death of oppression . . . the uplifting of mankind."[54] The push for scientific motherhood generated the kindergarten movement, a woman's right to claim legal guardianship of children, a program of wholesome recreation including the construction of playgrounds, foster homes to replace orphanages, juvenile courts, and further restrictions on child labor. One university in 1915 argued on behalf of its women students: "The woman's place is in the home, but today would she serve the home, she must go beyond the home. No longer is the home encompassed by four walls. Many of its most important duties lie now involved in the bigger family of the city and the state."[55]

In Utah the Relief Society played a vigorous role in this area. Eliza R. Snow, the society's president from 1866-87, emphasized charitable and educational efforts. Her successor, Zina D. H. Young, expanded these programs during her tenure from 1888-1901. Her successor, Bathsheba Wilson Bigler Smith, supported such causes as clean milk for babies and children, an expanded nursing program, and educational courses for the general Relief Society membership.

The fifth president, Emmeline B. Wells, had edited and published the *Woman's Exponent* for thirty-five years when she became leader of the Relief Society in 1910. No woman would be more central to women's rights in Utah nor more connected to the national movement than Wells. She immersed herself in issues that seemed to matter most to nineteenth-century feminists: suffrage, equality of opportunity, education, and poverty. She abandoned earlier programs such as cooperative stores and halls managed by local women in favor of the centralized grain storage begun earlier in response to Brigham Young's suggestion, developing it into an impressive avenue for large-scale welfare and expanding it beyond the boundaries of the state. Selling wheat to the federal government during World War I symbolized Mormonism's full participation in the life of the nation and LDS women's full involvement in that participation.

Mormonism's Second Feminists: The Equal Rights Amendment

The tradition of Mormon women involved in a national political campaign—the fight for suffrage—foreshadowed another crucial era in the intersection of Mormons with the national women's movement, this time centered around the Equal Rights Amendment. In both cases, questions were raised about the differences between men and women, the need for women to be protected by the law, and the appropriate roles of women. But the 1970s generation of feminists challenged and redefined previous assumptions of appropriateness, protection, and gender differences. While the first generation assumed that women would be wives and mothers as well as activists or workers, 1970s liberationists challenged whether women ought to choose motherhood at all. An ecological awareness drove decisions about family size; and once women entered the workforce en masse, they experienced inequities that had not seemed relevant to earlier generations.[56]

Books like Betty Friedan's *The Feminine Mystique* (1963) touched a nerve nationwide in articulating inchoate dissatisfactions. After two decades of post-war prosperity, a generation of women emerged that was uneasy with maternity in the wake of the baby boom, affluence to the extreme of conspicuous materialism, and isolation in suburbs that left women feeling disconnected from each other and from sources of meaning. It was a time that asked for, and produced, a paradigm shift. In this state of *anomie,* new assumptions, rules, and ideals emerged. At times strident and passionate, Friedan argued that America's women had been persuaded to define their lives as managers of children, housekeepers aided by machines, and expert consumers. The result was a generation of well-educated but extraordinarily unchallenged women who were driven to "psychoanalysis, extra-marital affairs, alcoholism, meaningless hobbies, more and more 'adult education' that led nowhere, or equally insignificant 'do-goodism.'"[57] Friedan ignored the millions of women who found genuine satisfaction, rather than distraction, in their families and involvement in education, hobbies, and community service; but for millions of women, she offered a blueprint for a new life and her book became an immediate bestseller.

Mormon women felt these currents of change and reacted with the same diversity of voices as heard across the country. In their reaction, many consciously hearkened back to their nineteenth-century predecessors. By the 1970s, nineteenth-century Mormon women had become icons of mythic strength, expansive roles, and profound spirituality that fitted them to be partners, though not equals, with their priesthood counterparts. They seemed to model what a modern woman desired—personal and public power, private influence, equality, respect, and the genuine satisfactions of good marriages and fulfilling motherhood. Whether the reality of women's nineteenth-century lives matched the twentieth-century image they evoked mattered little. The stories about their predecessors provided common ground for Mormon women, offering them powerful and, for them, believable role models. More importantly, these role models sanctioned both domesticity and full involvement as activists in working for women's betterment. Whatever path an LDS woman chose, her pioneer foremothers had set the standard to follow.

Two examples illustrate this point. Loneta Murphy of Provo, speaking at a rally in December 1979 in Salt Lake City in support of Sonia Johnson, then undergoing excommunication in Virginia, announced proudly: "Equality of Rights under the state constitutional law are provided males and females equally—ALL CIVIL, POLITICAL AND RELIGIOUS RIGHTS AND PRIVILEGES. EQUAL LEGAL RIGHTS have been ours since Utah Statehood in 1896. I call this Utah's Best Kept Secret!"[58] Sixteen months earlier, Barbara Bradshaw Smith, then general president of the LDS Relief Society, took issue with Sonia Johnson's testimony at a Senate subcommittee hearing on the ERA, evoking the same history as Murphy but to prove Johnson in error. Smith's letter to Johnson read:

> I would like to respond to some of your comments in the spirit of the gospel of love which motivates the lives of both of us. The women you quoted and characterized as "women of great prominence," including Eliza R. Snow, Susa Young Gates, and Emmeline B. Wells, were indeed great early leaders among Mormon women. I think, however, that they would be surprised to be included in your protest paper. Unlike the "Mormons for ERA" they were never in opposition to the First Presidency and it is a sad misrepresentation of their great testimonies to suggest that they set themselves up in opposition to the Brethren when they supported the suffrage movement.[59]

Mormons for ERA affirmed their conviction that God himself had spoken to the prophet Joseph Smith in terms that could appropriately be applied to the Equal Rights Amendment. "We have been warned in modern revelation," read one handout circulated by the group, "that if we are not willing to be equal in worldly things, we cannot be equal in heavenly things, and we are urged to be 'anxiously engaged in a good cause.' Our cause is the cause of human equality, the same cause so courageously defended by our forebears. Our constant prayer is that we may live and work to see realized what they so ardently dreamed."[60] Their choice of language is interesting, both positioning their modern efforts within the context of their religious heritage and applying scriptural rhetoric to the cause. Supportive of Mormon leaders and modern-day revelation, Mormons for ERA argued that Joseph Smith's revelations mandated women's rights.

But the cause of human equality (perhaps a reference to communal living, certainly not civil rights) was a phenomenon of the last quarter of the nineteenth century, not of Joseph Smith's day. It's impetus sprang primarily from the larger national suffrage movement, not from the Doctrine and Covenants. Besides suffrage, other social elements shaped the meaning of women's rights in Utah. Though suffrage was always a complex social issue, pitting tradition, concepts of social stability, and traditions of propriety against concepts of individual freedom and democracy, giving the ballot to Utah women involved even more tortuous questions.[61]

Of broader significance, however, is how history was used or remembered by women on both sides of these issues, drawing on a shared sense of persecution from the exodus from Illinois to the Great Basin and the era of settlement, all of which bound Mormons to each other and heightened the significance of their collective activities. Searching for greater understanding of who they were as women in the 1970s, feminists and those defending a more traditional point of view looked to these common sources of inspiration.

For some, the fact that nineteenth-century women were allowed to participate in the suffrage movement seemed to be in sharp contrast to the proscriptions against supporting the ERA. For opponents, the involvement of pioneer women in professional and public areas was a surprise, no doubt brought on by the unusual circumstances of the times. For both sides, the respect of nineteenth-century Mormon women by their male counterparts was significant, but especially for those who wanted to build what they perceived to be a fairer way of life.

Either way, a curious set of dichotomies existed between tradition and innovation, obedience and free agency, loyalty and independence, feminism and homemaking. Such dichotomies seemed impossible to reconcile. They dealt with impossibly simplistic categories. Exclusionary and restrictive, they failed to capture the richness and complexity of the lives of real women living in a different time than their pioneer ancestors. Nevertheless, Mormon women anchored their views in what they saw as the respectable past of their forebears, skipping the first half of the twentieth century to focus almost entirely on the first generation of Mormon women. Both sides created an image of women upon whom they could hang their dreams in either the fight for or against the Equal Rights Amendment.

2. A Brief History of the Equal Rights Amendment

All persons born or naturalized in the United States, and subject to the jurisdiction thereof, are citizens of the United States and of the State wherein they reside. No State shall make or enforce any law which shall abridge the privileges or immunities of citizens of the United States; nor shall any State deprive any person of life, liberty, or property, without due process of law; nor deny to any person within its jurisdiction the equal protection of the laws.

—U.S. Constitution, amend. 14 (1868)

The right of citizens of the United States to vote shall not be denied or abridged by the United States or by any State on account of race, color, or previous condition of servitude.

—U.S. Constitution, amend. 15 (1870)

The right of citizens of the United States to vote shall not be denied or abridged by the United States or by any State on account of sex.

—U.S. Constitution, amend. 19 (1920)

For twentieth-century women, the Equal Rights Amendment symbolized equality in the same potent way that suffrage had to nineteenth-century feminists. The successful ratification of the Nineteenth Amendment in 1920 was the voice of the nation assuring American women of equality at the ballot box. The failure of the Equal Rights Amendment in 1982 was the voice of the nation assuring American women that they did not need Constitutional protection against infringements on their rights. Those sixty years saw the issue of women's equality rise from unconsciousness to become the nation's most bitter and divisive issue for a brief time, played out against a lengthy and complicated history.

English common law involved complicated disadvantages for women touching on every aspect of social life: legal rights, family structure, religious beliefs, access to education, and economic parity. For every woman, the question of equality existed on at least two levels: as a principle and as a set of intensely practical questions about living one's daily life. The principle was an abstraction. Everyone in the United States should be recognized in the same way by virtue of the Constitution. The Civil War and its aftermath resolved the exclusion of black men from Constitutional inclusion. Now women were insisting their equal place in the document.

What is stunning is how much confidence women activists of the late nineteenth century put in the ability of suffrage to create a new world for women. Those who threw their energy into the movement believed that when women voted, they would vote differently than men. As a result, the lives of women would be better. It seemed to be a logical conclusion and seemed to justify the emotion and fervor of the suffrage campaign. More than a legal or political technicality, suffrage was for this first generation of feminists a potent symbol. In the same way, the concept of Constitutional equality defined the women's movement between 1923, when the first equal rights amendment was proposed as a piece of legislation, and 1982 when ratification failed.

Passage of the Nineteenth Amendment

The antebellum period saw relative legal neglect of women. The good society the Founding Fathers envisioned assumed a subservient role for women even though the Constitution used basically gender-neutral language, as did the Articles of Confederation. For approximately four decades after the Civil War (1880-1920), a period loosely called the Progressive Era, the legal and social advances connected with emancipation and Reconstruction offered what seemed to be new opportunities for women. Activists attempted to benefit from the provisions of the Fourteenth Amendment—initially through the privileges and immunities clause and then through the language of due process and equal protection, both cited above.[1] These attempts were generally unsuccessful.

During these decades into the early twentieth century, the more liberal social thinkers in America, loosely affiliated as "progressives," shared a worldview that embraced immigration, industrialization, and urbanization. Based in part on environmental determinism,[2] they sought to improve work conditions for men and women, successfully restricting the number of hours worked but not achieving pay equity. "The politics of gender and the politics of class were inextricably combined," comments Joan Hoff-Wilson. "This clash of social visions was intensified in the late 1920s."[3]

Progressivism was one way women such as Jane Addams, Florence Kelley, and others first entered the public arena as "social housekeepers." These college graduates produced a small army of women ready to change the world, convinced that education both privileged them and obligated them to give back to society what they had been given. An expansion of the political agenda of suffragists, their commitment to education and especially to social work, filled them with a passion not unlike religious fervor. They filled the ranks of the women's organizations which had focused on suffrage, where they learned to organize, mobilize other women, and to exert political influence on candidates and politicians in office. According to women's historian Nancy Woloch, "By capitalizing on moral superiority and domestic ideals, with which many women identified, suffragists could simultaneously combat their opponents, prove their respectability, and attempt to gain wider support."[4]

Protective Legislation for Women

The Nineteenth Amendment was not ratified in a social vacuum, but was part of the broader Progressive era when activists tried to guarantee women the right to earn a living wage, resistance coming from those who did not want women in the workplace at all. The contest ran concurrent with the suffrage debate and was not ended by passage of the Nineteenth Amendment.

Although economic privation forced some women into the workplace, by 1890 only 20 percent of working-age women were employed outside the home. Of that total, 60 percent were domestic servants, 30 percent of them foreign born.[5] The second most likely type of employment was in manufacturing or industry. Between 1912 and 1917, according to historian Grace Abbott, 500,000 women under age thirty arrived on American soil.[6] Many of them immediately looked for jobs, most often in factories and at menial wages. Women's historian Mary P. Ryan said women "swarmed into the garment industry, food processing plants, laundries, cigar factories, and even the metal trades." Whatever the locale, the division of work was basically the same. "The first principle of the sexual division of labor," Ryan writes, "decreed that women would be relegated to unskilled tasks."[7]

Although the contest over economic equality was subtle and nuanced, in simple outline it could be seen as two competing worldviews that represented variant "ideals" for women. On the one hand was the ideal of "true womanhood"; but increasingly after the turn of the century, the "New Woman" moved onto a public stage and claimed power for herself. Nancy Woloch suggests that the "New Woman of the progressive era, vigorous, confident, and assertive, had left her mark on public life." Moreover, "by demonstrating her concern for social welfare and her ability to participate in public life, the New Woman contributed to the effectiveness of arguments for woman suffrage."[8] This view worked best for educated middle-class individuals in intact marriages, for whom kin and friendship networks provided social and emotional support and who had further support from "respectable" religious affiliations. For them, womanhood was a separate sphere with its own duties, demands, responsibilities, and fulfillments. As a wife and mother, this New Woman provided a haven-home for her children and her husband, who dealt with the outside commercial and political world on behalf of the family. Respected, appreciated, and autonomous within her sphere as long as she fulfilled her required roles, she had strong economic, social, and theological reasons for remaining within them. As long as she felt no need for power or protection through the law and was not victimized, either by family or changing life circumstances such as widowhood, she regarded with dismay the "unwomanly" behavior of those who sought to erase distinctions between the gendered spheres. But as Ryan characterizes the situation, middle-class women emerged from the home—which Ryan calls "domestic confinement"—and joined "mass organizations headed by members of their own sex. By the second decade of the twentieth century, women had formed a veritable army composed of many well-organized divisions, strategically linked, and positioned on the outer flank of the home."[9]

The second competing worldview was the egalitarian ideal of full participation in U.S. political, social, and economic life, symbolized by possession of the vote and access to paid employment with a sufficient wage to make a woman economically independent. Questions driving the debate were complex. Men's and women's physical differences made it logical that they were emotionally and intellectually different as well. Could they be equally competent at the same jobs? Men were the principal wage earners for their families; should women receive equal compensation for the same work? Should women work at all? Should women be protected in certain work environments? Women had gained more political, educational, legal, and economic benefits and opportunities than ever before, and what they lacked was legal equality. Women were still considered a special class of citizens deserving and needing special assistance and protection under the law.

Thus, an area of common ground between the two worldviews was support for legislation protecting women. Even those of the"true womanhood" mold who were satisfied with their lives responded sympathetically to the plight of women in less fortunate circumstances; the victim status of marginalized women and their children placed them in the already familiar category of objects of charity. Protective legislation masked the transition from a laissez-faire federal government to an interventionist one. Once the government had the power to help, it did not relinquish it, thus keeping the door open to continued intervention on women's behalf. From a feminist perspective, this was a positive step. However, it came with its negative assumption that women were frail, vulnerable, and generally ill-suited for the world, in particular the workplace.

One of the earliest, and certainly the most important, U.S. Supreme Court cases that set the stage for protective legislation was *Muller v. Oregon,* decided finally in 1908. A laundress had challenged an Oregon law which limited women in factories and laundries to no more than ten-hour work days. The state arrested the employer, who had forced the woman to work overtime in violation of the law. The Court upheld the Oregon law, establishing that "sex is a valid basis for classification" and thus providing judicial precedent for protective legislation. The brief in support of the opinion was written by Justice Louis Brandeis and read into the record by Justice David Brewer. It innovatively accepted testimony from the new field of social welfare to show that women were more vulnerable to occupational diseases and work hazards than men. More importantly, "the performance of maternal functions," wrote Brandeis, and "woman's physical structure justify special laws restricting or qualifying the conditions under which she should be permitted to toil." Upon such protection depended "the well-being of the race." He appealed to history: "Woman has always been dependent upon man. He established his control at the outset by superior physical strength, and this control in various forms, with diminishing intensity, has continued to the present." Government, he argued, was the surrogate, benevolent male "to protect her from the greed as well as the passion of man."[10]

The upshot of this case, while definitely setting some limitations on the physical exploitation of women in sweatshop conditions, defined women as a class of citizens who were not able to care for themselves. Legally, women had the same status as children and could not enter into contracts or make binding decisions:

> It is still true that in the struggle for subsistence she is not an equal competitor with her brother. Though limitations upon personal and contractual rights may be removed by legislation, there is that in her disposition and habits of life which will operate against a full assertion of those rights. She will still be where some legislation to protect her seems necessary to secure a real equality of right. Doubtless there are individual exceptions, and there are many respects in which she has an advantage over him; but looking at it from the viewpoint of the effort to maintain an independent position in life, she is not upon an equality. Differentiated by these matters from the other sex, she is properly placed in a class by herself.[11]

In the wake of this case, many states passed further protective legislation to keep women out of unhealthy occupations, simultaneously confirming an inherently inferior status.

Such legislation, intending to soften working conditions for women, limited the number of hours they could work, improved their work spaces, and increased their base wages. Short of unionization, these measures addressed the environmental circumstances for those who had little political or social clout to evoke change for themselves. As in the Muller case, there was special concern about potential injury to a woman's reproductive capacity. Massachusetts passed the first law that limited a woman's workday to ten hours, and other states soon followed, among them Utah, which in 1896 prohibited women from working in mines or in restaurants that served liquor.[12]

One of the proponents of this kind of protective legislation was the National Consumers League, established in 1891 by Maud Nathan and

Josephine Lowell. According to Florence Kelley, its articulate social-reformer leader, "Sex is a biological fact" upon which "social and domestic relations" are based, even though the "political rights of citizens are not properly dependent upon sex." Her view was that women carried "the burden of maternity" and that it was unfair for men, who "are not susceptible, in the same manner as women, to poisons now increasingly characteristic of certain industries, and to the universal poison of fatigue," to overlook this gender difference.[13] According to Woloch, the National Consumers' League "cut across class lines by a campaign that would benefit middle-class homemakers and women workers" by awarding a "white label" to factories and stores with sanitary conditions.[14]

Another protectionist, Alice Hamilton (1869-1970), herself a pioneer in the field of industrial health, urged that women be forbidden from working night shifts. "The father of the family, if he works at night," she reasoned, can "sleep during the day and yet have his meals served to him and his children cared for; the mother cannot."[15]

After the end of World War I, the U.S. Department of Labor created the Women's Bureau and mandated it to guard the interests of female workers. The National Woman's Party sponsored a study through this division on the impact of protective labor laws. The 1928 report confirmed what most thoughtful observers and activists already knew to be true: "In almost every kind of employment, the real forces that influence women's opportunities are far removed from legislative restrictions of their hours or conditions of work." These forces, according to the report, were natural ones—"the types of service at which the two sexes excel."[16] In other words, certain types of work were considered appropriate for women because they were natural extensions of her domestic sphere—domestic services, nursing, and teaching. It was apparent that a man's ability to support a household, as elaborated in the Brandeis brief, was a primary underlying concern—not just a woman's health or life-cycle themes. Needless to say, many employers resented being dictated to on matters of workplace safety or mandatory ceilings on work hours for their employees.

The first federally funded social welfare measure was the Sheppard-

Towner Maternity and Infancy Act of 1921, a bill informed by protectionist ideology. Sponsored by Texas Senator Morris Sheppard and Iowa Congressman Horace Towner, this act distributed federal matching grants to states for prenatal and child health clinics; published information on nutrition, hygiene, and midwife training; and organized nurses' visits to pregnant women and new mothers. The bill addressed the impact of high infant and maternity mortality rates. Women's organizations made the bill's passage a top priority the very year after women received the vote. Known as the "maternity bill," its author was Julia Lathrop, chief of the U.S. Children's Bureau. It was introduced into Congress by Jeannette Rankin, the first woman member of the House of Representatives. Passionately opposed by right-wing groups and by the American Medical Association, which considered it a threat to home and a step toward state medicine, it nevertheless sailed through Congress by a large margin.

Sheppard-Towner allotted an annual appropriation of $1,240,000 for five years. By 1925, Utah had come on board, passing laws that mandated medical inspections of schools and requiring that school children have their teeth examined.[17] Women led the Children's Bureau, aided by volunteers from women's clubs and parent-teacher organizations. But despite these fine efforts, the bill was repealed in 1929. Federal funds were restored for maternal and infant care with the 1935 Social Security Act, but public health services were not available for women and children of all social classes.[18]

Activists continued to push for protectionist measures in line with the Sheppard-Towner Act. Esther Dunshee, a member of the League of Women Voters, worried about the "biological difference between men and women" and the assumption that "conservation of our womanhood means the preservation of the race."[19] She was in agreement with the arguments made in *Muller v. Oregon* and earlier cases that women were more susceptible to disease, less suited to heavy manual labor, and more in need of limited working hours. Women's health had to be safeguarded or the human race itself would be damaged. Heavy emphasis was placed on women's "special" psychosexual nature, her different mission in life, her frailty, and the possibility of exploitation of her "weaker" status physically and economically.[20]

A National Woman's Party spokesperson, Doris Stevens, countered in 1924 that "protective legislation, no matter how benevolent in motive, unless applied to both sexes amounts to actual penalization." She found that women were hampered in their ability to protect themselves because they are not treated as equals. "Modern woman does not want the support granted to a dependent," she continued. "She wants to and should be an equal partner."[21]

In the tradition of Justice Brandeis, Felix Frankfurter, who was then a professor at the Harvard Law School, crafted an argument in 1924 which established a pattern used throughout the history of the ERA:

> The legal position of woman cannot be stated in a single simple formula. . . . The law must have regard for woman . . . as an individual, as a wage-earner, as a wife, as a mother, as a citizen. Only those who are ignorant of the nature of the law . . . or indifferent to woman's industrial life will have the naivete or the recklessness to sum up woman's whole position in a meaningless and mischievous phrase about "equal rights." . . . Law must accommodate itself to the immutable differences of nature. For some purposes . . . the law must treat them as men and women. The Woman's Party would do away with all the differences which arise from the stern fact that "male and female created He them." The Woman's Party cannot amend nature.[22]

Protectionism suffered a setback in 1923 when *Adkins v. Children's Hospital* threw out a minimum wage standard in the nation's capitol. The U.S. Congress had created a Wage Board to determine adequate minimum compensation for women and children, but the Supreme Court ruled that this infringed on Fifth Amendment guarantees of life, liberty, and property. The lower courts similarly had ruled that the idea of a minimum wage for women was incompatible with the principle of equality under the law.[23]According to the majority view, employer and employee had the Constitutional right to make contracts as they saw fit, while a Wage Board represented an unjustified interference with that right. Justices William Howard Taft, Oliver Wendell Holmes Jr., and Edward T. Sanford argued in a dissenting view that Congress had the police power to correct recognizable evils. *Adkins v. Children's Hospital* was overturned in 1937 by *West Coast Hotel Company v. Parrish* which ruled that some government intervention in contracts between employers and employees is not unconstitutional.[24]

In some circles, the assumption that women needed protective legislation was so strong that in 1921, Wisconsin, the only state with an equal rights amendment,[25] made an exemption for protective labor legislation. But Wisconsin failed to divert the debate because its judiciary was considered to be politically liberal and out of step with the rest of the country.[26]

The Proposed 1923 Equal Rights Amendment

One of the benefits of protective legislation in the 1920s was the debate over the significance of gender differences, along with related discussions about whether government intervention was necessary and whether the Fourteenth Amendment could be applied to women. Protectionists were generally opposed to an equal rights amendment, and the conflict was thus not so much women versus men as women versus women—a foreshadowing of the 1970s.

The first formal proposal for an amendment occurred in 1923, three years after ratification of the Nineteenth Amendment. Alice Paul (1885-1977), who spearheaded the movement, was born to a Quaker family in Moorestown, New Jersey, and developed a method of "Gandhi-like passive resistance," according to historian Amelia R. Fry, which in other words meant non-violent civil disobedience, combined with more traditional political posturing.[27] In 1913 she split with the protectionist National American Woman Suffrage Association (NAWSA) and, with a group of like-minded women, formed the rival National Woman's Party, which proclaimed the need for a Constitutional amendment.

As a girl, Alice Paul attended Quaker schools, then graduated from Swarthmore College and spent a year studying the conditions of the immigrant poor on New York's lower east side. In this training ground for so many of America's Progressive reformers like Jacob Riis or Edward Bellamy, Paul worked for the Women's Trade Union League and the Henry Street Settlement on a project designed to encourage labor unions to admit women to their ranks. In 1907, Paul was awarded a master's degree from the University of Pennsylvania. Next she attended the Quaker Woodbrooke Institution associated with the University of Birmingham in England. Educated and equipped with practical experience in the field, she turned her focus to women's rights. Paul returned to the United States in 1912 and joined NAWSA's campaign for a federal amendment for suffrage. It was the next year when she led a small committee called the Congressional Union out of NAWSA to become the National Woman's Party (NWP). Civil disobedience and nonviolent demonstrations —pickets, parades, and demonstrations—became her specialty for keeping women's rights in the public eye.

Much of the difference between the National Association and its offshoot, Alice Paul's party, was in tactics. After 1915, NAWSA shifted from its emphasis on educating the public to more straightforward and focused efforts to influence legislators. The NWP, by contrast, organized massive rallies, staged pickets in front of the White House, condemned the political party in control, negotiated, debated, conducted a vigorous publishing campaign, and used other tactics which were controversial for the time.[28] As a result, Paul and her more radical followers resurrected "the long-dormant campaign for a federal amendment and created a determined Congressional lobby."[29] While NAWSA lobbied more in the tradition of the Susan B. Anthony faction of first-generation activism, Paul's group revived radicalism. Alienating and, in fact, embarrassing NAWSA by their tactics, Paul and her supporters had a demonstrable impact. According to historians Ann Firor Scott and Andrew Scott, "nervousness about what the radical women might do next encouraged both Congress and the president to . . . embrace the more conservative suffragists as the lesser evil."[30] The fact that both groups had the same goal masked their deep disagreements over politics, philosophy, law, and language. These differences erupted after the passage of the Nineteenth Amendment. Paul fought to keep the NWP neutral on the issue of protective legislation while simultaneously advocating a clause that would prevent a change in any of the industrial protections already in place.

Rejecting those who argued that change must come slowly and that attitudes must evolve over time to support change, Paul was the white female equivalent of black activist W. E. B. DuBois. Defining the left spectrum of black activism in the early twentieth century, DuBois demanded equality of rights for blacks in the present rather than waiting for social evolution as advocated by Booker T. Washington and others. For the thirty-eight-year-old Paul, a Constitutional amendment would eliminate the need for protective legislation. According to one historian of the ERA, she centered her belief on the idea "that women should be treated as individuals under the law just as men were, not as a class subject to mass governmental regulation. The ERA would do away with this underlying across-the-board inequality that permeated so much of women's lives. Once it was ratified, 'then,' Paul would say, 'we shall see.'"[31] She died in July 1977 at ninety-two while the ERA still hung in the balance. Reflecting on her lifetime of service to women's causes, she once said: "I always thought once you put your hand on the plow, you don't remove it until you get to the end of the row."[32]

Ever controversial, Paul repudiated the positions of such stalwart suffragists as Carrie Chapman Catt (1859-1947), Florence Kelley (1859-1932), and Jane Addams (1860-1935), each of whom had supported both suffrage and protective legislation. They had argued for suffrage not because women were the equals of men but because women were different—with differences, they felt, that were complements to male strengths. Together, men and women provided the fuller strength that came from diversity. In fact, the influence of this logic was so strong, it seemed as though the vast majority of suffragists opposed the Equal Rights Amendment when it first surfaced in the 1920s.

Catt and Addams were close to the end of their long and active lives when the ERA was introduced. Florence Kelley, who was sixty-four years old in 1923, had been the dominant force behind passage of child-labor legislation, limitations in working hours, and wage laws for working women. Kelley saw herself as participating in a class struggle against the oppression of poor women and children.[33] As part of the first generation of college-educated women, having graduated from Cornell University in 1882, Kelley exhibited a profound sense of *noblesse oblige* as she led the community through social legislation.[34]

Kelley began by teaching evening classes for working women in Philadelphia. Then she traveled to Europe to attend the University of Zurich, where she became familiar with the work of Friedrich Engels published in 1844, *The Condition of the Working Class in England,* not published in the United States until 1887. After returning to the United States in 1886, she wrote and published the pamphlet, *Our Toiling Children,* in 1889.[35] She married, divorced in 1891, and moved into Hull House, Jane Addams's Chicago settlement house. Here she became an ardent worker and advocate of the urban poor. Her writings during this period, such as her contributions to *Hull House Maps and Papers* compiled in 1895, painted a vivid and compelling image of the horrendous working conditions of immigrants. Her work influenced an 1893 Illinois law that limited the working hours of women, regulated tenement sweatshops, and prohibited child labor.[36]

She favored gradual situation-by-situation change rather than the blanket protections offered by a Constitutional amendment. Men also needed protectionist legislation, in her view. By contrast, the ERA would invalidate the wide range of labor and health legislation women had worked hard to secure over the past thirty years; so as Kelley saw it, the amendment would actually endanger women. Her National Consumers League therefore officially opposed the ERA in 1922. Other women's groups acted similarly, including the Women's Christian Temperance Union, the National Mother and Parent Teachers' Association, the American Association of University Women, the National Council of Jewish Women, the League of Women voters, and the U.S. Women's Bureau led by Mary Anderson.

Women's Issues in the 1930s

Not surprisingly, between 1920 and 1940, more educated women entered the work force than ever before. Nevertheless, few earned the same wages or achieved the same status positions that were available to men. Career women were "social housekeepers or assistant professionals."[37] They imparted social service in education, medicine, and social work but were less visible in business, politics, or industry. As Mary Ryan suggests, their careers were closely tied to women's domestic lives and were considered appropriate extensions of that role.[38]

Much of the theory and philosophy underpinning protective legislation became moot in the economic disaster that swept the nation with the stock market crash of October 1929 and the resulting nationwide depression. Indeed, most of the legislation during this period impacted women's issues negatively. The Federal Economy Act of 1932 prohibited federal employment for spouses of other federal employees. This bill required that women whose husbands were employed be fired first in times of recession or cutback. During the 1930s, twenty-six states had laws which prohibited married women from working, and many public schools, public utilities, and department stores had rules against hiring married women.[39] Despite this opposition, the employment of married women increased by 50 percent from 1930 to 1940.[40] Still, national women's groups suffered losses. The unresolved debate between those who saw separate-sphere maintenance and those who believed in full legal equality contributed to the internal disagreement in the women's organizations. Although the movement continued to mobilize issue-by-issue support to protect women from long hours and poor wages and to affirm the importance of equal treatment, it limped along from 1929 to the 1940s.

A bright spot was the strength of Eleanor Roosevelt, who supported women's causes as the wife of U.S. President Franklin D. Roosevelt, influencing the appointment of women to key policy-making positions such as Frances Perkins in 1933 as U.S. Secretary of Labor, the first female member of a presidential cabinet.[41] Another bright spot was the Supreme Court, which overruled such previous decisions as *Adkins v. Children's Hospital* and upheld federal and state minimum wage laws for both men and women. These decisions helped pump life back into protectionist efforts and incidentally improved somewhat the position of women in industry; but by 1939, twenty-one states still did not have minimum wage laws.

Throughout the Depression and the New Deal, despite limited national interest in women's issues, Alice Paul worked to solidify her power, establishing and refining a network of women in support of the ERA. She persuaded the National Business League, Professional Women's Clubs, the National Association of Colored Women, Women's International League for Peace and Freedom, and other national groups to support the ERA and arranged similar alliances on the local level. A landmark day for Paul was May 30, 1936, when the House Judiciary Subcommittee made a positive report on the ERA. Representatives of the groups Paul had persuaded to support the ERA had testified at the hearing. The next year, subcommittees of both the House and the Senate gave the ERA their approval. In 1938, two years after the House subcommittee first considered the Equal Rights Amendment, the Senate Judiciary Committee referred it to the floor.

The Republican Party supported the ERA in 1940 but found that the opposition was significant. Even so, the National Woman's Party became identified with the Republican Party, effectively alienating such prominent Democrats as Eleanor Roosevelt. The AFL and CIO opposed the ERA until the 1970s.[42] Questions raised by later generations of female activists over credit, child care and health, child custody, and spousal abuse would not be addressed until the 1960s. An anonymous woman writing in a popular ladies' magazine argued circularly but comfortably that while "women are and of right ought to be equal with men, [they] can never be on a level with men . . . just because nature made them differently and society has so long placed them in a position different from men."[43]

Suffrage had been the focal point of the women's movement for half a century. Once it passed, feminists failed to achieve a new consensus, and activism during these years was more an expression of progressivism than of feminism. According to historian Nancy Woloch, "Large surviving groups such as the General Federation of Women's Clubs, now apolitical, and the civic-minded League of Women Voters had melted into the suburban scenery."[44] Even though the fight for an ERA continued into the 1950s, feminism retreated into the background.

Women's Issues in the 1940s and 1950s

Feminism declined again in the 1940s as women's energy was channeled into World War II. On the other hand, the war dramatically changed the employment situation. The War Manpower Commission estimated that four million new workers were required to bring to capacity the production of munitions in the war industries. Colorful posters trumpeted a call to arms for the Women's Army Corps. Advertisements in the *Ladies Home Journal* pictured women operating heavy machinery. These images of strong women confidently taking charge in traditional male roles popularized and seemed to legitimate powerful women working for the country's interest.[45] Protectionist rhetoric diminished.

Fifty percent more women entered the workforce during the war years, 1941-45, than before.[46] By 1944, 75 percent of the women in the war industries were married; 60 percent were over age thirty-five.[47] As might be expected, the issue of child care became an increasing part of the debate over their presence in the workplace. However, the government's position on child care was inconsistent, and its response to the entrance of millions of American mothers into industry was sluggish.[48] For instance, in 1943 the Children's Bureau and the Women's Bureau both opposed child care centers since they would encourage women to leave their homes.[49]

Although surveys conducted close to the war's end suggested that between 75 and 90 percent of American women wished to continue working after the war, men in positions of power in business, government, and industry decided otherwise. Soon after the war's end, aircraft companies fired 800,000 women. International Business Machines reenacted its policy against hiring married women.[50] By November 1946, two million women had lost their jobs and returned home.[51]

Described by some feminists as the "years of doldrums," the post-war era saw the cult of true womanhood reemerge in the "kitchen mystique" of the suburbs.[52] Traditional support slumped, with membership in the National Woman's Party dropping due to "an internecine fight for control of the party."[53]

Simultaneously, the contest over the Equal Rights Amendment heated up again. In 1946, Paul's version of the ERA, cast in the same language that would be used in 1972, was adopted by the Senate committee and passed by a margin of three votes on the Senate floor.[54] Voting against it was Senator Abe Murdock, a Democrat from Utah, who also opposed protectionist legislation he felt "discriminate[d] against men . . . in favor of women."[55] Opponents of the amendment organized the "Committee to Defeat the Unequal Rights Amendment," arguing that inequality was a good thing. Surprisingly, the group included some of the giants of feminism such as Carrie Chapman Catt, Eleanor Roosevelt, Frances Perkins, Mary Anderson, and Mary McLeod Bethune. Their fear was that the amendment would produce a loss of Social Security provisions and other "privileges" for wives and mothers. In 1947, Alma Lutz, spokesperson for the National Woman's Party, countered: "Human rights and fundamental freedoms are above physical structure and biological function. . . . They belong to every human being, and need no safeguards before they are offered to women."[56]

In the 1950s opponents tried a new strategy of adding riders to the ERA. In 1950, 1953, and 1960, Senator Carl Hayden of Arizona added a rider to preserve protective legislation, which would have nullified the amendment's intent. ERA defenders responded with emergency lobbying just to keep it alive in committee.

During the 1950s, Alice Paul worked with the remaining NWP loyalists to continue their lobbying efforts and to keep the amendment alive in Congressional committees. At age seventy-nine, she helped gather support among legislators for the language of what would become Title VII of the Civil Rights Act, tirelessly working to get the word "sex" written into the bill.

It was an uphill battle. Post-war anxiety over Communism and the changed world order impacted the ways families and communities interacted. The family seemed to hold the promise of future stability, with women as guardians of the home, defenders of the future. Much like the rhetoric of republican motherhood of the eighteenth century and the cult of true womanhood in the nineteenth, women were seen as responsible for socializing a future generation of American citizens, perpetuating the values and behaviors that had made America great. In an ideological struggle such as the Cold War, the perpetuation of patriotism and allegiance to democratic principles were clearly part of the body of ideas women were expected to teach their children. In such a setting, separate spheres, not equality, made the most sense in the popular mind.

The unrest of the 1960s stirred new interest in the ERA. The Civil Rights movement created an environment that was ripe for women's issues and generated much of the passion that incubated feminism. When the Civil Rights Act passed Congress in 1964, with its Title VII prohibition of discrimination in employment, women asked when it would be their turn for employment equality. Congressman Howard W. Smith, chair of the Rules Committee, recommended that the Civil Rights bill be amended to include sex equality, saying he wanted to address "the imbalance of spinsters." His proposal was accepted.[57] However, two years later when the Third National Conference on the Commission on the Status of Women met in 1966, it voiced concern over the fact that the sex discrimination provisions of Title VII were not being enforced. A group of women, including Betty Friedan, responded by founding the National Organization of Women with the purpose of more completely changing the system.

During the late 1960s, the ERA appeared before committees in both the Senate and the House of Representatives on numerous occasions and received considerable support,[58] although it failed to pass into law. During the same years, abortion reform laws passed in numerous state legislatures, and candidates for state and national elections increasingly developed platforms on women's issues. The legislative history for the real battle over ratification of the ERA began in 1970 when the Senate Subcommittee on Constitutional Amendments opened its first hearings since 1955.[59]

As the debate over woman's rights progressed through the latter part of the twentieth century, it continued as it had before, not as a trajectory of unimpeded progress but rather like the course of ocean waves, a complex movement forward and falling back, driven by forces not entirely exposed or understood. It followed decades of dramatic social, economic, and political change. Caused in part by shifts in international power stimulated by the two world wars, the position of women in American society had in fact changed; but there were serious differences over what was in a woman's best interests, even among those who were most ardently committed to women's rights. In many cases, female activists had succeeded in accomplishing what they set out to do only to discover that hoped-for legal or political advances failed to materialize in social relationships or vice versa.

To opponents of the ERA, the societal changes occurring around them seemed to threaten their basic worldview. For instance, the official statement issued by the LDS First Presidency emphasized the importance of protecting differences between men and women. Anything that might make women more like men or men more like women ran counter to the natural order and God's plan. An ungendered world would be a dangerous place. In much the same way that protectionists during the Progressive Era had wanted women to enjoy special treatment, opponents to the ERA thought that feminism threatened the cultural cohesion surrounding the definition of an "ideal" woman and her role in society in light of her special nature and class status. The ERA would change gender-defined roles of mothers, wives, and daughters beyond comprehension. Playing on this fear, the grass-roots movement proved effective in fighting feminism and in defeating ratification of the ERA.

Another characteristic of ERA opponents was their membership in the social justice wing of the Progressive movement. Their emphasis was on the inequities between the rich and poor, the educated and uneducated, and those for whom democracy provided a safe haven versus those who seemed unprotected. For an earlier generation, the temperance movement had trained abolitionist women who went on to work for women's rights. Progressivism's difficult fight for legislation protecting working men, women, and children gave its female supporters valuable experience in working for change. But important divisions among the women's rights workers at this point centered on how best to improve the status of women. Legal historian Karen Offen suggests that late nineteenth-century feminism inherited a "radical individualism" or emphasis on securing for women the individual political and civil rights held by most men.[60] Early twentieth-century feminism, based on a doctrine of "equality in difference" and stressing biological and socialized differences between women and men, focused on ways to preserve the differences rather than eradicate them or pretend they did not exist. Feminists who advocated protectionism fell into the latter category because of their social or group approach. Theirs was a variety of feminism more widespread than that based on individual rights.

The "doctrine of difference" surfaced at various times in the guise of separate-sphere arguments or as an idealized version of family and the woman's role in it and her relationship to the political world around her. Feminists who embraced elements of the Victorian view of true womanhood, including maternity, morality, feminine character, and values, found that this rhetoric struck a persuasive chord. Their belief in the meaning of difference, according to historian Mary Frances Berry, "indicates that many women were trying to preserve a female haven—rooted in social and biological feminine behavior—a haven from male culture and male institutions."[61] Carroll Smith-Rosenberg suggests that the communication of this distinctly female world had been largely lost soon after the turn of the century when women began adopting more male forms of communication. It was during the further evolution of the women's movement during the 1920s that women recognized the power of a distinctive rhetoric and revived it to particularize the discourse of women.

For Smith-Rosenberg, language can be a key to understanding the rift between the competing women's groups, which had become insurmountable by the 1920s. For her, the rift was more than just disagreement over tactics or what type of legislative or legal approach would best serve the interests of women. Rather, they spoke in "hostile languages," manifesting their variant psychological realities. For these individual groups whose key issues were matters of sexuality, entrance into professional life, and social reform in general, their basic, differing orientations prevented them from agreeing about what strategies would be appropriate to evoke requisite changes or about what those changes would mean for women's lives. In short, the rhetorical differences reflected fundamental disagreements over the proper way for women to conduct themselves, especially when agitating for change. How women spoke about these issues in turn reinforced competing worldviews, which would inform the political debate and result in profound ramifications for the lives of all American women.

3. The Poising of Nation and Church to 1972

> As the Equal Rights Amendment issue is activated in some states, we suggest that you urge members of the Church, as citizens of this great nation, to join others in efforts to defeat ERA.
>
> —Apostle Ezra Taft Benson, 1976

Barely out of the shadow of World War II, *Life* magazine issued a thirteen-page special section in 1947 on "The American Woman's Dilemma" outlining the gap between traditional ideas and the broadening public realm of women's lives.[1] According to *Life,* women's choices had expanded beyond that of finding a husband to include the world outside the home. But exactly what form would their involvement in the world take? According to historian William H. Chafe, "one of the byproducts of the era . . . was a deepening sense of bewilderment among many American women over how to define their identity."[2]

During the 1950s the cult of domesticity was reinforced by women's magazines, the new popular medium of television, and society in general. Women were portrayed as having found new meaning in the management of their households. *Ladies Home Journal*, *McCall's*, *Better Homes and Gardens*, and other clones featured happy "true women" with a ruffled apron over a pretty dress cleaning their kitchens to spotlessness, vacuuming their wall-to-wall carpets in high-heel shoes, setting breathtaking tables for dinner parties, or reading to their well-groomed, cheerful, and numerous children.[3] The true woman provided comfort and sustenance for her husband and advanced her man's career by serving as a brilliant hostess.

The 1960s Prelude

But some women were swimming upstream against the home-bound current. The national income nearly doubled in the 1950s and doubled again in the 1960s. By 1960, twice as many women worked than in 1940. In fact, 40 percent of women over sixteen had jobs. Perhaps more important for its implications for the family, the number of working mothers increased by 400 percent during these same years; 39 percent of women with children under eighteen had outside employment in 1960.[4] The majority of new postwar jobs went to women in urban offices, shops, or light industry. The tension between the demands of suburban domesticity and the realities of employment factored into the feminist movement of the 1960s.

The fifties are ironically often portrayed as a decade of simple consensus. The ideal middle-class life consisted of a blonde-brick ranch house, a nuclear family, a wood-paneled station wagon full of Little Leaguers, and domestic contentedness. But America was never as homogeneous or driven by consensus as the ideal suggested. As women moved out of the home to contribute financially, roles inevitably changed in ways that strained traditional systems of familial authority and the gendered division of household work. Women traditionally had little prestige or status as housewives; but as wage earners, their position shifted. Robert Blood suggests that "a working wife's husband listens to her more. She expresses herself and has more opinions. Instead of looking up into her husband's eyes and worshiping him, she levels with him. . . . Thus her power increases, and relatively speaking, the husband's falls."[5] While Blood's equation may exaggerate the importance of a single factor in changing social patterns, it does acknowledge the correlation between economic and social changes. Americans had more disposable income, so consumerism mushroomed. Within a decade after the end of the war, about 60 percent of American families owned their own homes.

The dialogue over women's identity failed to find answers in the 1950s, but it set a wide stage for the women's movement of the 1960s. What was soon to be called the "woman problem" was largely a question of identity. The editors of *Harper's* magazine caught the dichotomy that women experienced—yearning to expand their roles but not yet fueled by powerful ideas—in the fall of 1962. Many women were "ardently determined to extend their vocation beyond the bedroom, kitchen and nursery," but few demonstrated any interest in feminism as a movement, the magazine asserted.[6]

The decade of the 1960s challenged virtually all of America's institutions. Young people, minority groups, and activists fought ardently against "the establishment." From my perspective as a historian, the 1960s and 1970s saw more social change than the nation had tried to absorb since the 1920s. The anxiety that raged over adjustments during this period was submerged in symbolic programs—busing, school prayer, sexual liberation, peace in Vietnam, reproductive rights, and the ERA. All of these issues tested moral and religious strictures, the relationship between public and private, and the place of government in the lives of citizens. Any highly charged political issue has an emotional element that surpasses reason even though reason is often the only tool for trying to contain the emotion and sustain dialogue about it. Such tensions have a way of exploding quickly into the "ultimate" answer of violence as happened repeatedly at key points in the national debate over the civil rights movement and the anti-Vietnam protests. Such responses are eloquent testimony of the fearsomeness of the change the issues threatened.

Yet the time was ripe for change. During the 1960s the women's movement competed with the Vietnam War for headlines, as well as with student protests and the civil rights movement. Gradually, a critical mass of women saw the potential for change and responded to the call for an end to discrimination. The larger society seemed responsive as well, recognizing the need for guaranteed equality in the lives of all its citizens. It is not surprising that the various movements coincided since all were advocating profound changes in relations between human beings and groups of individuals.

French writer Simone de Beauvoir's *The Second Sex,* published in America in 1952, was an early forerunner of serious, primarily academic reflections on women's status. A decade later came the first work to become an enormously popular and hotly debated best-seller: Betty Friedan's landmark *The Feminist Mystique,* published in 1963. Friedan, herself a long-time activist, wrote about "the problem that had no name," the profound smothering uneasiness that plagued a whole generation of women. According to Friedan, this anxiety stemmed from the powerful social messages that women could only find fulfillment in their roles as wives, mothers, homemakers, and consumers. These constricted roles worked well for some women. A 1962 Gallup poll confirmed that three out of five women were "fairly satisfied" with their domestic roles as mothers and wives.[7] Still, other women were unsatisfied, depressed. Sometimes they burst through social restraints to find some new area of fulfillment, negotiating more authentic relationships with husbands and children, finding new fields for their talents, and fulfilling their own identities. Others poured the same energy into maintaining the status quo, finding financial security and self-sacrificing motherhood not only worth the effort but also the only career worthy of commitment. Some found themselves driven to escapism, secret alcoholism, damaged and damaging relationships, and unfocused dilettantism. *The Feminine Mystique* clearly set out the issues that would become basic to liberal feminism: the need to take women seriously and the urgency of immediate change. Friedan captured the ideological framework of the movement at that point in time, charging that American women had been victimized by a social construction, the "feminine mystique," that had limited the definition of happiness.[8] For anyone who felt she had little identity apart from being someone's wife or mother, there was suddenly a name for her dissatisfaction.

In the decade following 1965, divorce rates doubled and the number of children born to unmarried women increased. Birth control pills and antibiotics encouraged freer attitudes toward sexual practices and challenged the traditional taboo of premarital sex. Activists working for gay and lesbian rights emerged during this period as well.

By the mid-1960s, the women's movement was in full force.[9] The conservative wing of the movement was represented by the National Organization for Women (NOW), organized by Betty Friedan in 1966. NOW offered a political-reform approach to equality that emphasized the importance of changing public opinion, its defined purpose being "to bring women into full participation in the mainstream of American society now, exercising all the privileges and responsibilities thereof in truly equal partnership with men." This "Statement of Purpose" continued:

> NOW is dedicated to the proposition that women first and foremost are human beings, who, like all other people in our society, must have the chance to develop their fullest human potential. We believe that women can achieve such equality only by accepting to the full the challenges and responsibilities they share with all other people in our society, as part of the decision-making mainstream of American political, economic and social life.[10]

Supported primarily by well-educated professional women, NOW emphasized the necessity for progressive legislation.

At the other end of the feminist spectrum were the women's liberation groups composed of younger, more radical women who had cut their political teeth in the peace or civil rights movements, sometimes as students, and who were convinced that sexual equality was the principle objective. Radical feminist Kate Millet wrote that the problem with America was an "oppressive ideology" in which all that could be "described as distinctly human . . . [was] reserved for the male." The answer for Millet was the end of patriarchy, changes in the structure of the family, and the demolition of stereotypes about women.[11] Between these conservative and liberal wings of the women's movement lay the core agenda of American activists: equal pay, an end to job discrimination, repeal of abortion laws, and an expansion of the traditional role of women.

By the end of the decade, feminists had picketed the Miss America contest, demonstrated outside political conventions, and stormed into male clubs, restaurants, and bars across the country. In an era marked by protest, women had found their voice; but in some ways the fight had only just begun. Women's liberation was a movement of immense complexity, but its most important symbols would be abortion rights and the Equal Rights Amendment.

For many religious women, supporting feminism meant unknowable, uncontrollable, and almost certainly undesirable change.[12] They were committed to the historical centrality of home and family in a woman's life. They were nervous about the idea of competing with men, reluctant to exhibit unfeminine behavior, and conceptually unable to see themselves as systemically oppressed as long as they were treated kindly by the men they were closest to.

Simultaneously, the wide differences among feminists about precisely what needed to be done shifted dramatically according to economic class and race. Some women chose not to work, but the reality in the 1970s was that 75 percent of all white women and 81.7 percent of all minority women worked full time.[13] Many black women, according to black feminist writer bell hooks, did not consider "permission" to work an important objective. They had always worked and had always been exploited. "Sexism as a system of domination is institutionalized," she commented, "but it has never determined in an absolute way the fate of all women in this society. Being oppressed means the absence of choices. It is the primary point of contact between the oppressed and the oppressor. Many women in this society do have choices (as inadequate as they are); therefore exploitation and discrimination are words that more accurately describe the lot of women collectively in the United States."[14]

The persistent discrepancy between the work experience of men and women is evident in a comparison of median earnings for full-time workers in the mid-1970s. White men typically earned an annual income of $12,104 for full-time work. For black men, the figure was $8,524. White women earned $6,823, almost half the income of their male counterparts.

The difference between black men's and black women's earnings was less—for women, $6,258.[15] By 1975, 53 percent of all married women were working, as were 46 percent of all women with children under eighteen.[16] Equally interesting is the fact that 6.8 million families—12 percent—were headed by women in 1974, an increase of over 1 million between 1970 and 1974.[17] These statistics painted a picture of the reality of most American women's lives that was a far cry from the suburban picture windows and station wagon. Issues of equity—equal treatment under the law and in the workplace—had new relevancy for the generation of women fully employed in the 1970s.

Feminist ideology created a framework of ideas for political change. The women's movement became a revolution in the ways people were accustomed to being together in families, communities, and in the workplace. Friedan's book voiced the concerns of women who were confused by changes in society which seemed to render much of their experience in the home irrelevant. Other foundational feminist texts followed in the opening years of the 1970s: Kate Millet's *Sexual Politics*, Germaine Greer's *The Female Eunuch*, and Mary Daly's *Beyond God the Father: Toward a Philosophy of Women's Liberation*. These and books like them asked women to recognize their historic oppression, to question the ideological framework sustaining it, and to join other women in opposing it. During the 1960s and early 1970s, America handed women a wide array of laws, rules, and concepts about women's public and private realms, or about their self-image, in other words. That a woman's chief value was in providing support services for her husband's career was fundamentally challenged.

Some of the broad range of demands that became a part of feminist ideology were, in fact, contradictory. For instance, liberal feminists, beginning in the late nineteenth century, shared and still embrace some of the following beliefs:

- Women have historically been disadvantaged and discriminated against.
- Such discrimination creates an imbalance in social life that disadvantages both women and men.

- It is just and, in fact, moral to oppose this discrimination
- Girls and women are socialized in ways that limit their roles. They need access to the image and talent-building opportunities that have historically been available to men.
- Women and men are equal in virtually all respects except biologically, and should be socially, professionally, and legally equal.[18]

Another useful definitional point along the feminist spectrum has been cultural feminism. At its base was a matriarchal vision of a world guided by strong women, reflecting female concerns and values. Historically these concerns included pacifism, cooperation, and the harmonious regulation of public life. In the late nineteenth century, these values were exhibited in a utopian vision of the matriarch of a forgotten era—a former time of mother-rule which some believed had typified ancient societies. Charlotte Perkins Gilman had written a matriarchal utopia, *Herland,* in 1911, and Elizabeth Cady Stanton's *The Woman's Bible*, published in 1895, had posited a Heavenly Mother and religious authority in a female priesthood. Both liberal and cultural feminism grounded the overall movement throughout the nineteenth century and into the first two decades of the twentieth.[19]

Socialist feminism began around 1900 by marrying Marxist theory with liberal feminism's emphasis on equality.[20] Identifying the sources of women's oppression in patriarchy and capitalism, socialist feminism dealt with power issues in domestic and societal realms.[21] As an extension of this tradition, radical feminism was born in the 1960s in response to sexism, initiated by Eastern liberals identified with the "New Left." According to Maxine Hanks, "Radicalism seeks . . . liberation . . . through the creation of female systems and discourse. It seeks women's control over their own bodies and lives, as in women's healthcare and laws against sexual harassment and pornography."[22]

At least two of these philosophical positions embraced the ERA as a powerful symbol of the nation's concern for its women, although few saw the ERA as a panacea for the country's social ills. However, it was thought that ratification would send a strong message to local governments to erase the legal disadvantage of women. As had been true in the mid-nineteenth century, women joined various groups, wrapped around such issues as consciousness raising, the right to reproductive choice, and the need to remove barriers to women's full involvement in society, according to the preference of an individual woman.

Political Developments in the Women's Movement

The civil rights movement portended changes in the legal status of women. As African Americans protested their second-class status, so did women; and the 1964 Civil Rights Act, Title VII, prohibited employment discrimination based on race, color, religion, sex, or national origin. In 1978 an amendment to Title VII required employers to provide benefits for pregnancy-related disabilities.

Practically all state governors created Status of Women Commissions in the 1960s to participate with the federal Interdepartmental Committee and the Citizens Advisory Council on the Status of Women. Eleanor Roosevelt chaired the President's Commission on the Status of Women until her death in 1962. The year after her death, the commission documented inequalities in education, employment, legal status, and political standing of women.[23]

In 1966 at a national gathering of commissions on the status of women, concerns were raised about enforcement of Title VII's sex discrimination provisions. It was unclear what legal authority would take the initiative to investigate and prosecute such cases. In part, the National Organization for Women was founded to address this concern; from the first, NOW was involved in tracking progress in enforcement of workplace equality.

Largely because of pressure from women's groups, Congress enacted a series of important laws for the benefit of women—a series of Congressional acts, executive orders, and guidelines to enforce affirmative action. Leading off with the Equal Pay Act of 1963, these provisions created a more equitable situation in the work force and helped to prevent discrimination on the basis of sex.

This greater attention paid to the legal status of women provided momentum for Equal Rights Amendment supporters. By the late 1960s, the amendment had found considerable support in the House of Representatives, although it repeatedly failed to pass. In several states, abortion-reform laws were passed. Politicians more frequently included women's rights planks in their platforms and employed women on their campaign staffs. Employment reforms were popular, but abortion and child care issues caused more controversy because they seemingly threatened the family.

Opponents claimed the Fourteenth Amendment already guaranteed equality for women, which was the conclusion of President Richard Nixon's 1963 commission—that its "equal protection" clause, along with the rights guaranteed "all citizens" by the Fifteenth Amendment, necessarily included women. The federal government, for its part, set about implementing this view in a landmark case involving the American Telephone and Telegraph Company. AT&T had promised in 1973 to pay $15 million in back wages to 15,000 employees and to provide goals and timetables for the increased use of women and racial/ethnic minorities in contracted work with the federal government. The agreement was cooperatively brokered by the Equal Employment Opportunity Commission, the Labor Department, and the Justice Department.[24]

The Early 1970s

The need for an amendment that mentioned women specifically was demonstrated at the end of the nineteenth century. In 1894 the U.S. Supreme Court agreed to consider *In re Lockwood,* a case that allowed states to limit the legal definition of "person" to men. Belva A. Lockwood filed a petition to the Supreme Court of Appeals of Virginia to admit her to practice law in that court. Lockwood had for years been a member of the bar in Virginia, several other states, and the District of Columbia. When she applied for admittance before the state supreme court, however, it denied her application. The U.S. Supreme Court identified the core issue as whether, in the state law in question, "the word 'person' as therein used is confined to males, and whether women are admitted to practice law in that commonwealth."[25] Its answer was no. Without recognition as "persons" before the law, women's ability to make contracts, hold office, and practice professions was in jeopardy, not a right but a privilege that existed at the whim of a state court and according to the tides of public opinion.

From 1894 on, state courts often maintained that women were not, in fact, "persons" for professional or political purposes. Finally, seventy-seven years later in 1971, the U.S. Supreme Court reversed the legal principle of *In re Lockwood*, finding in an Idaho case, *Reed v. Reed,* that the probate code of that state gave preference to men in appointing an administrator of a decedent's estate. Sally Reed, who appealed a probate order, argued that this provision was based solely on "a discrimination prohibited by and therefore violative of the Equal Protection Clause of the Fourteenth Amendment."[26] The Fourth District Court of Idaho reviewed her appeal and, finding that the provision did violate the Equal Protection Clause, removed this sex-based disability by voiding the law. This was upheld by the Supreme Court. Even so, skeptics pointed to the court's reluctance to use a "strict scrutiny" standard in evaluating the legality of sex discrimination, as it had with race legislation under the Fourteenth Amendment.

Another landmark event was the 1972 passage through Congress of Title IX of the 1972 Educational Amendments Act. Title IX's origin was the 1965 Presidential Executive Order 11246, which prohibited federal contracts with a company that discriminated on the basis of race, color, religion, or national origin. On October 13, 1968, President Lyndon B. Johnson amended the order to include discrimination based on sex. It was a three-letter addition with sweeping implications.

Researcher Bernice Sandler identified a connection between federal contracts and discrimination on college campuses,[27] and Representative Martha Griffiths (D-Michigan) presented her views to Congress on March 9, 1970. Three months later, Representative Edith Green (D-Ohio) chaired the subcommittee that sponsored the first Congressional hearings on education and the employment of women. When first presented, Title IX proposed to amend Title VII to cover employees in higher education. At the end of the hearings, Sandler was asked to help draft a bill sponsored by Senators Birch Bayh (D-Indiana) and George McGovern (D-South Dakota).

It would be three years after Title IX was voted into law on June 23, 1970, and signed by President Richard M. Nixon that the Department of Health, Education, and Welfare drafted specific regulations, summarized as follows:[28]

- Schools would identify a Title IX coordinator to oversee compliance efforts and investigate complaints. All employees and students would be provided contact information for the coordinator.
- School systems had to conduct one-time self evaluations and modify practices to comply with Title IX.
- School systems were obligated to take affirmative action or remedial action to increase the participation of students where bias was evident.[29]

This development seemed to be in concert with the intent of the proposed Equal Rights Amendment, which by 1970 had gained support from U.S. Presidents Lyndon Johnson and Richard Nixon, the President's Task Force on the Status of Women (reversing its 1963 stand), and the Citizen's Advisory Council on the Status of Women. Trade unions and the federal Women's Bureau continued to support protective legislation.

In May 1970 the Senate Subcommittee on Constitutional Amendments began hearing testimony on the ERA after a pause of fifteen years. Forty-two witnesses—lawyers, legislators, and representatives of women's groups—testified, most of whom favored the amendment. Martha Griffiths (D-Michigan) brought the amendment out of the House Judiciary Committee over the objection of the committee's chair, Emmanuel Cellar (D-New York), a longtime opponent. On August 10, 1970, the amendment passed the House 350-15 after a full hour of debate.

In early October the Senate debated the amendment for several days. However, before taking legislative action, it adopted by a vote of 36-33 a bill that exempted women from the draft, thereby diffusing one of the objections to the ERA. Even though more than eighty senators were listed as sponsors of the ERA, the 91st Congress ended without passing it.[30]

The next year, the House Judiciary Committee specifically considered whether the ERA would "impair the validity of any law of the United States which exempts a person from compulsory military service or any other law of the United States or any State which reasonably promotes the health and safety of the people."[31] Ultimately resisting attempts to modify the language of the bill, it was forwarded to the entire House of Representatives, which passed it 354 to 23 on October 12, 1971.[32]

To this point in time, the LDS headquarters had not taken a position on the issue. Mormon Congressmen tended to vote along party lines, those supporting the amendment including Democrats Richard T. Hannah and John E. Moss of California and Morris K. Udall of Arizona. However, a Mormon Republican from California, Delwin M. Clawson, voted in favor, while Utah Democrat Gunn McKay voted against; and the other two Republicans, Utah's Sherman P. Lloyd and Idaho's Orval H. Hansen, abstained.[33]

When the bill was forwarded to the Senate on March 20, an attempt was made to add language providing that "neither the United States nor any State shall make any legal distinctions between the rights and responsibilities of male and female persons unless such distinctions are based on physiological or functional differences between them." But the subcommittee rejected this proposed amendment 15 to 1. The committee subsequently also rejected proposals to modify equality in matters of child support, protective labor legislation, sex crimes, privacy, admissions policies at institutions of higher education, the draft, and military service. Within the halls of Congress, as the votes show, there was little opposition to the original wording of the amendment, the only organized public resistance during the debate phases in either the House and Senate having come from politically conservative groups.[34]

On March 22, 1972, the Senate approved an unamended version, 84 to 8, signaling a major triumph for the decades of work by many women's organizations as well as an awareness by politicians of the tides of social change.[35] Utah's Wallace F. Bennett cast his Republican vote against, while Utah's Democratic Senator, Frank E. Moss, voted for, as did Nevada's Mormon Senator, Howard W. Cannon, also a Democrat.[36]

Supporters predicted quick ratification. In fact, twenty-two state legislatures approved the amendment before the year's end. But thereafter, as historian Mary Frances Berry described it, "the slow, trench warfare began."[37] By November 1978, six years later, only thirteen more states had ratified and four had rescinded their earlier votes—Nebraska in 1973, Tennessee in 1974, Idaho in 1977, and Kentucky in 1978.[38]

Within a year after the amendment was sent to the states for ratification, groups were formed to fight it. Phyllis Schlafly's STOP ERA became the most powerful and successful, in part because of Schlafly herself.[39] Educated at a Catholic girls school, Academy of the Sacred Heart, and Maryville College of the Sacred Heart, Schlafly had worked at a small federal arms factory during World War II, then went on to receive an M.A. in political science from Radcliffe College in 1945 and to work for various congressmen in Washington. In 1952 she ran as a Republican for the House of Representatives from Illinois's Twenty-fourth District, lost, and nonetheless became anchored in Illinois politics. She was repeatedly a delegate or alternate delegate to the Republican National Conventions.

Schlafly had become nationally prominent as a fervent anti-Communist when she campaigned for Joseph R. McCarthy during the early 1950s and, along with her husband, founded the Cardinal Mindszenty Foundation in 1958 to alert the world to Communism. All told, she was an eloquent and compelling spokesperson for a traditional point of view. She spread her influence both in person and through her many publications including her monthly *Phyllis Schlafly's Report* and eight books. She contributed to Barry Goldwater's 1964 autobiography, *A Choice, Not an Echo*.

Schlafly's first public statement concerning the ERA came in February 1972. "What's Wrong with 'Equal Rights' for Women" laid out her main arguments to a female audience. Principally, she wrote, the ERA threatened to divert control over personal matters to the government and from the states to the federal government. Countless days on the road, Schlafly delivered passionate speeches, usually beginning by thanking her husband for allowing her to participate in the campaign—a deliberate tweaking of feminist noses. In 1976 she founded the Eagle Forum, which has since become a formidable force in Utah politics. Described by one reporter as "the anathema of the women's movement," Schlafly began a campaign of national dimensions after the ERA passed Congress in 1972. She mobilized a response among many groups that perceived a threat to the future of American families. Over time, she expanded her position to include opposition to military service and financial support laws for women.

Called by some the "Gloria Steinem of the Right," Phyllis Schlafly was indeed a powerful voice for the opposition. Sally Quinn of the *Washington Post* described her as a "walking contradiction": "Her outward demeanor and dress is one of a feminine, bridge-playing, affluent housewife. She smiles a lot, giggles, worries about her appearance and makes polite conversation." Yet, "on the podium she comes on like a female George Wallace. She is tough and aggressive, totally unlike the role she espouses for most women."[40]

The Mormon Church in the 1960s

The Mormon Church unquestionably subscribed to the broad range of conservative attitudes where women were concerned. During the Great Depression of the 1930s, the more liberal years of World War II when new opportunities opened for women, and during the national retreat to domesticity of the 1950s, Mormons dealt with the same secular challenges the rest of the nation faced. Utah was no longer the isolationist refuge it had been in the nineteenth century. LDS women were fully in the world and pressed up against the same social stresses as American women everywhere. Nationally known sociologist Thomas O'Dea wrote in 1957 that Mormon youth demonstrated flexibility within the context of faith when addressing such challenges:

> The fact is that the Church of Jesus Christ of Latter-day Saints is still a vital institution. Conflict and strain have not been sufficient to prevent its orderly functioning over the last many decades. It may not be so well adapted or prepared to meet new problems as it was in times in the past, yet all transitions and all reorientations are difficult. That its values still provide a meaningful context to great numbers of its adherents cannot be denied. Its flexibility in the past and its viability under the most adverse conditions do not augur badly for its future.[41]

Even as the national mood became more liberal during the 1960s, Mormonism's conservatism did not translate initially into opposition against the ERA, even from the First Presidency.

The Mormon Church successfully negotiated a passage into modernity in the first half of the twentieth century. Instead of traditional communitarian values, Mormons became ardent proponents of capitalism.[42] They gave up their own political party and heartily espoused national politics, rejecting even Republican Apostle-Senator Reed Smoot, who had served for thirty years, to give their vote in 1932 to Franklin D. Roosevelt's Democratic Party.[43] The church exchanged its beleaguered image of polygamy for a glittering constellation of monogamous family values;[44] and after being seen as vilely un-American during the nineteenth century, its enthusiasm for sending volunteers to the Spanish-American War, World War I, and World War II, and by generously oversubscribing its war bond quotas, Mormons achieved new status as super patriots.

Furthermore, after energetically participating in the Progressive Era projects of civic betterment during the early twentieth century, the Mormon Church had actually moved briefly to the cutting edge of contemporary sociology. Under the leadership of Amy Brown Lyman, the church's Relief Society president between 1940 and 1945, Mormon women moved in step with the national reform organizations engaged in social welfare work. Trained at the University of Chicago in sociological philosophy and methods, Lyman saw the role of the Relief Society as evoking real social change. Throughout World War I, the Relief Society took part in a wide range of welfare projects including selling 200,000 bushels of wheat gathered by local Relief Society units to the federal government for war relief. In most Utah communities, each local Relief Society became a chapter of the Red Cross, amassing thousands of volunteer hours. In the early years of the Great Depression, its social workers struggled to meet the needs of those who suffered from economic displacement during the Depression. Lyman oversaw the organization of the Relief Society Social Service Department. As a woman, she symbolized how the focus of the Relief Society had shifted from suffrage and women's rights to social service and community outreach.[45]

Parallel semi-autonomous organizations had existed since the 1880s for LDS children (Primary Association) and teenage girls (Young Ladies/Young Women's Mutual Improvement Association) that, like the Relief Society for adult women, included independent budgets, publications, curriculum, and activities. Despite efforts during the 1920s and 1940s to pull the various auxiliaries under one organizational umbrella, each maintained autonomy for another two decades until the late 1960s. Though extremely supportive of the broader ecclesiastical agenda of Mormonism's male General Authorities, these auxiliaries maintained thriving and creative educational, cultural, and fund-raising programs. Their general officers, though appointed by the First Presidency and usually selected from among women attached to the male elites (Amy Brown Lyman, for instance, was married to an apostle), proved to be strong, capable leaders in their own right. Representatives from the Relief Society and from the YWMIA had been among the founding members of the National Council of Women (NCW), and they continued to provide distinguished service to those organizations through the 1960s. Belle Smith Spafford, general president of the Relief Society from 1945 to 1974, also served as president of the NCW from 1968 to 1970.[46]

This kind of national and international service grew naturally out of the participation of Mormon women in community outreach since the turn of the century. During the Progressive Era, Mormon women established milk and infant care stations at Salt Lake City's settlement house (Neighborhood House) and at other public locations on the city's west side. The Relief Society helped promote "Children's Year" in 1918-19, a campaign for children's health, and even earlier sponsored a "Baby Day" that focused on health and nutrition.[47] According to Jill Mulvay Derr, Janath Russell Cannon, and Maureen Ursenbach Beecher, authors of the most recent Relief Society history, the Progressive Movement probably influenced the Relief Society's "support for legislation for women and children, its cooperation with community agencies in charity work and in campaigns for public health and community betterment, and its . . . education program," all of which were in harmony with the national agenda.[48] In a demonstration of their enthusiasm for reform, the women at a Relief Society conference in October 1911 rose to their feet "to express their approval of the stand for a clean, moral government."[49]

Beginning in 1896 with Democrat Martha Hughes Cannon, ten women had made their influence felt in Utah's senate and 130 had held counterpart positions in the House of Representatives during the state's first eighty years.[50] As in other Western states, the Utah legislature passed protective legislation in 1911 restricting women to nine-hour days and fifty-four-hour work weeks, then to eight-hour days and forty-eight-hour weeks. In response to lobbying by the Utah Federation of Women's Clubs, the Utah legislature set a minimum wage for women and pushed for the establishment of a commission to supervise wage and working conditions.[51] These goals were achieved in 1933 with the passage of the Minimum Wage Law, giving power to a State Industrial Commission to establish minimum wages, maximum hours, and conditions of work.[52]

In 1923, the year Alice Paul presented the ERA to the U.S. Congress, the Utah Women's Legislative Committee (later the Women's Legislative Council) lobbied for better employment conditions for women, child welfare, and regulation of community vices such as racing, liquor, and gambling. Significantly, its emphasis was on protective legislation rather than equity, thereby appealing to paternalism rather than challenging the patriarchal structure of the society. In 1945 the group went on record against passage of a woman's rights amendment.[53]

In 1950 when the third version of the Equal Rights Amendment was moving through the U.S. Senate, the Relief Society general presidency, then consisting of Belle S. Spafford, Marianne Clark Sharp, and Velma N. Simonsen, assumed that First Presidency counselor J. Reuben Clark (Sharp's father) would oppose the ERA because of his strict constructionist view of the Constitution. However, on the day of the Senate vote, Clark suggested that the Relief Society presidency "keep out of it" because "there will be some of the women who think it is a good thing."[54] There is no description of the Relief Society's response to the ERA's passage, either in the *Relief Society Magazine* or in its official history. Occurring first in the wake of the Nineteenth Amendment, the ERA was becoming entwined in the politics of the various women's political organizations at the same time it was obscured by the shadow of the Nineteenth Amendment.

Mormonism's Messages to Women in the Early 1970s

In response to the turmoil of the 1960s, LDS leaders intensified their conservative messages in many areas of personal and social life. In the years immediately preceding the Congressional vote on the ERA in 1972, the church repeatedly condemned the events and issues they perceived as threatening to the family such as abortion, homosexuality, and sexual promiscuity. It was more the youth counterculture than the women's movement that seemed to be the intended target of these messages; however, the action was the same in both cases: a stern reminder that mothers should tend to their home responsibilities and teach correct values to their offspring. Thus, a strong foundation of what was expected of women was reinforced before the political implications of the ERA developed.

When the condemnation of feminism came, it was, perhaps not surprisingly, through the church's magazine, the *Ensign*. The magazine had just replaced all former periodicals published by the church's auxiliaries, including the half-century-old *Relief Society Magazine* and publications of mission organizations. In its very first issue, January 1971, ninety-four-year-old church president Joseph Fielding Smith, writing on behalf of the First Presidency, cautioned that "respected magazines proclaim 'the myth of motherhood' and champion the more radical ideas of women's liberation."[55] He countered that women who remained in the service of their families within the home were performing the gendered role for which God had fitted them with special gifts. Gender, in this context, was not about socially determined expectations but rather a position that was ordained and sanctioned by God. Mormons found this argument irrefutable. It was a potent argument with Mormon feminists, as well, who likewise maintained profound commitments to home-making and the importance of motherhood but who also found in the expansive theology of eternal progression the encouragement they sought to strive for personal betterment.

A second article in the same issue of the *Ensign* by Apostle Thomas S. Monson, "The Women's Movement: Liberation or Deception?" identified some of what he considered to be the most troubling issues: the "goals and demands that are now being made by some women: free abortion, free childcare, and equal employment." He spelled out four guidelines for women that simultaneously reassured them about their identity and strengthened their task assignments:

> 1. Every woman has been endowed by God with distinctive characteristics, gifts, and talents, in order that she may fulfill a specific mission in the eternal plan; 2. The priesthood is the central power of the Church, but "men have no greater claim than women upon the blessings that issue from the Priesthood" . . . 3. The home is the basic organization to teach an individual to walk uprightly before the Lord; 4. Compassionate service and sensitivity to the needs of others are the principal purposes for which a women's program was organized.[56]

Three months later, H. Burke Peterson of the Presiding Bishopric addressed the April 1971 general conference of the church, describing various women's roles as incompatible opposites. "One of the greatest tragedies of our day," he said, "is the confusion in the minds of some which would cause mothers to go to work in the marketplace." He implied that working women were motivated by materialism and that neglect of children was the inevitable consequence of employment:

> Our Father in Heaven would rather have you . . . read stories in the afternoon to a little girl in a faded blue hand-me-down dress than have her entertained by a color TV because you are away working to make payments. He would rather have a child come home from school to a mother ironing clothes and baking cookies, than to come home to a hired housekeeper because mother is away learning typing or shorthand to improve her job qualifications.[57]

Because the voice of mainstream Mormon women was less frequently heard than that of the authoritative males and divergent women, a powerful impression emerged that mainstream women must be united in supporting traditional family values and concentration on home duties. This view was probably well-founded. An article in the August 1973 *Ensign,* "LDS Women Unaffected by Women's Lib," presented the results of a survey of Mormon women in Utah and Colorado. The article began with an overview of the basic claims of the women's liberation movement, which according to the author were that women are "exploited and oppressed in contemporary society" and "women do not have equal opportunities for education and jobs." She quoted a national activist who reportedly asserted that "marriage and the family are instruments of women's oppression," while men are "dehumanized by foolish ideas of masculinity."[58] The author had gathered statements from 133 LDS women in Colorado and Utah, all but 15 of them married (the 15 were college students), and concluded that most Mormon women valued their motherhood, felt equal with their male counterparts, and considered abortion evil. Although she did not cite statistical data for these conclusions, she asserted that 85 percent of her sample opposed employment outside the home but that 93 percent did not think it unfeminine to do traditionally male chores. Despite the limitations imposed by such a small, non-random sample and the stereotyped version of the goals of women's liberation, this survey offered support for the perception that Mormon women subscribed to a different view than those in the national women's movement, that the rank-and-file upheld the traditional viewpoint taught by church leaders.

"No Greater Calling: The Woman's Role," an October 1973 general conference address delivered by N. Eldon Tanner of the First Presidency, centered on what he saw as a connection between women's liberation and the devil. "We hear so much about emancipation, independence, sexual liberation, birth control, abortion, and other insidious propaganda belittling the role of motherhood," he said, "all of which is Satan's way of destroying women, the home, and the family—the basic unit of society."[59] By identifying Satan as the source of such modern forces as women's liberation, changing mores, economic change, and dislocation, the church shifted the grounds of the dialogue. Rather than determining whether these social forces were good or evil based on their effects, they became evil because of their origin. It became less possible to study whether these social trends did, in fact, draw men and women away from their "eternal" roles in families. Inadvertently, perhaps, Tanner's rhetoric created an adversarial relationship between traditional Mormon women and proponents of women's rights, leaving no middle ground. One either was loyal to the church or was not; there was no room for personal interpretation or diversity of experience.

Seven years later Ezra Taft Benson, president of the Quorum of the Twelve Apostles, reinforced the dichotomy between working women and faithful women in an October 1980 general conference address. Drawing the line beyond which Mormon women were cautioned not to venture, he warned:

> Contrary to conventional wisdom, a mother's place is in the home! I recognize there are voices in our midst which would attempt to convince you that these truths are not applicable to our present-day conditions. If you listen and heed, you will be lured away from your principal obligation.
>
> Beguiling voices in the world cry out for "alternative lifestyles" for women. They maintain that some women are better suited for careers than for marriage and motherhood. These individuals spread their discontent by the propaganda that there are more exciting and self fulfilling roles for women than homemaking. Some even have been bold enough to suggest that the Church move away from the "Mormon woman stereotype" of

homemaking and rearing children. They also say it is wise to limit your family so you can have more time for personal goals and self-fulfillment.[60]

Benson acknowledged that some women worked because they were divorced, widowed, or not yet married; and rather than blaming single mothers, he concentrated instead on employed mothers in intact marriages, drawing a picture of seemingly irreconcilable dualities. "I do not wish to wound any feelings," he said, "but all of us are aware of instances of active Latter-day Saint families who are experiencing difficulties with their children because Mother is not where she should be—in the home." He blamed divorce largely on working women, then read approvingly from letters sent by women whom he described as "successful homemakers—intelligent, faithful women—who understand their callings in this life." One woman wrote: "Being a wife and mother and having a family is my first priority. . . . What job in life could possibly be more important than molding the character of another human being?" Failure in the home was directly connected to outside employment. "Now can you see," Elder Benson asked, "why Satan wants to destroy the home through having the mother leave the care of her children to others? And he is succeeding in too many homes."[61]

Relief Society lessons through the 1970s likewise emphasized traditional roles, warned against dangerous ideas, and clarified relevant church doctrines to help women stand firm against feminist infiltrators. Although traditional Mormon women for the most part remained silent, others tried to find a middle ground and respond to these tensions. According to feminist historian Maxine Hanks, Mormonism simultaneously developed its own brand of liberal feminism in the 1970s. Expressed through the appearance of independent periodicals such as *Exponent II*, *Dialogue: A Journal of Mormon Thought*, and *Sunstone*, and the new Women's Research Institute at Brigham Young University and other organizations, some of them informal, this burgeoning feminist consciousness created avenues for discussing issues relevant to the lives of Mormon women.[62]

In the summer of 1971, *Dialogue* published a special women's issue, which because of the color of its cover became known as the "pink issue."

A theme in this collection of essays was the diversity of Mormon women and the need to expand the spectrum of expectations. Historian Claudia L. Bushman edited the issue. "The standard model for Mormon womanhood," she wrote in her introduction, "is the supportive wife, the loving mother of many, the excellent cook, the imaginative homemaker and the diligent Church worker, a woman whose life is circumscribed by these roles. This model has been so clearly presented to us in sermon and story that we feel strong responsibility to cleave to that ideal and guilt when we depart. . . . We argue," she continued, "for acceptance of the diversity that already exists in the life styles of Mormon women. We have too many native differences to fit comfortably into a single mold." Bushman, as many Mormon women, carefully positioned her statement an an assertion of faith and reminder of the historical position of women. Although women "have always been valued in the Church," she wrote, they had never been "encouraged to say much. We hope that now and in the future more ladies will speak out and what is more, be heard."[63]

The contributors to this special edition were presented as women of faith who were also well educated and informed on current issues. Many were professionals and most had several children. Before writing their essays, the women met together first to "discuss their lives." Bushman explained that "the Women's Liberation movement was then in full flower, making converts and causing all women to search their souls before reaffirming their traditional commitments."[64] The range of opinions on key issues made for interesting and lively discussion, she disclosed.

> While to all outward appearances we had nothing to complain of, the first meeting was an impassioned exchange of frustrations, disappointments and confessions. . . . The effect was cathartic. We decided to meet again and have come together irregularly ever since.

One of the topics of interest was the model of the ideal Mormon woman: "Our group, largely made up of supportive wives and loving mothers who are also excellent homemakers and Church workers, has discussed the genesis of that model, how much of it is scriptural and how much traditional, and whether other models have met with acceptance in Church history."[65]

Another article that tried to mediate a middle ground appeared in the March 1976 issue of the *Ensign*, written by Lavina Fielding, the magazine's associate editor. Fielding was a well-educated single woman, thirty-one years of age, and her reflections on the issues facing women were insightful, sensitive, and based on a devoted relationship to the church. Women, according to her, dealt with a spectrum of challenges ranging from marriage to church service. Never simple, the life of a woman was pulled in endless directions that could be strengthened by the church's guidance.

> Even a marriage strengthened by the power and promise of temple covenants has no guarantee of success. . . . The Church provides strong support for a woman who wants to be a mother. . . . At the same time, some women feel . . . undue pressure . . . to have as many children as . . . [they] can, at the same time holding up high standards of performance as a mother. . . . Yet, like other couples in today's society, Mormon couples usually can choose to remain childless or to choose a predetermined number of children.

Fielding noted the strains that could be caused by church service when it did not accommodate a particular situation or the complications when a mother worked. Emphasizing the importance of caring for children, she went on to recognize the value of a variety of female contributions:

> Even though a woman's most important contribution is in the home to her family, it need not be her only contribution—if she has the active support of her husband and family in her choice and if that choice received the approbation of the Lord. I would imagine that the Lord would not give his approval with any great frequency, but there will be situations and times when he does and will approve of a woman working outside the home.

She encouraged women not to judge each other but to seek answers through the scriptures and by listening to the prophet, as well as through personal inspiration.[66]

Through the decade of the 1970s, the church leadership continued its strong emphasis on the sanctity of the family and on women's God-assigned responsibilities in the home. But in 1970 it was not yet a given that feminism would be incompatible with church membership. In fact, it seemed that feminism and homemaking were possible and even desirable given Mormonism's generally positive suffrage history and lack of official action against the four earlier versions of the ERA (1923, 1943, 1950, 1953). Women sought a middle passage that would include both traditional responsibilities and expanded opportunities. There was not yet reason for observers to foresee the massive mobilization that would hurl the time and money of thousands of Mormon women and men against the ratification effort, divide woman from woman in every congregation, and become the decade's most predictable litmus test of religious orthodoxy.

By the mid-1970s, the so-called Correlation Movement, which was the strong centralizing and streamlining of church headquarters, brought the auxiliaries under central administrative control with male priesthood functioning as its "central force."[67] Expansion into an increasingly broad international arena and greater consideration of the relationship between the church's policies and its national public image marked the decade of the seventies.

Early Ratification Successes

Congresswoman Martha Griffiths of Michigan, the ERA's chief female sponsor in the U.S. House of Representatives, had in March 1972 distributed an article to her Senate colleagues, "The Equal Rights Amendment: A Constitutional Basis for Equal Rights for Women," written by law professors and published in the *Yale Law Journal* in 1971. Birch Bayh, chair of the Senate Subcommittee on Constitutional Amendments, inserted the article into the *Congressional Record*.[68] This influential essay provided a comprehensive argument for the amendment, which supporters and opponents alike used as an outline for organizing key issues in the debate. One of its authors, Yale law professor Thomas Emerson, recommended that "the major political action—passage and ratification of the amendment—can be accomplished by a strong nationwide campaign of limited duration, and the amending process is designed to elicit national ratification for changes in basic governing values."[69] This vague reference to campaigning seemingly envisioned only national efforts. However, it was ultimately state campaigns that proved to be decisive.

Congress had not imposed a time limit for ratification for the first four versions of the ERA, but following a precedent set by Amendments Eighteen through Twenty-two beginning in 1921, seven years had become the conventional limit.[70] No one took the deadline very seriously in 1972 because it was so universally believed that ratification would be straightforward and swift. Twenty-two state legislatures approved the amendment the same year it was passed by Congress. In Hawaii, Idaho, Colorado, and California, where Mormons comprised significant percentages of the population, LDS legislators voted for the ERA. In states without LDS representation in their legislatures, rank-and-file Mormons encouraged its passage, especially in Maryland where Beltway Mormons were prominent near the nation's capital and in Massachusetts where a small Mormon community thrived in the Boston area.[71]

Idaho ratified the ERA with a landslide vote of 58 to 5 in the House and 31 to 4 in the senate in March 1972. Nearly every legislator from the Mormon counties of southeastern Idaho voted yes. "I don't believe in women's liberation," said Republican representative Elaine Kearnes of Idaho Falls, "but I will go along with the women on this issue."[72]

Five years later, the amendment seemed to hit a wall. Thirteen more states had ratified, but four, including Idaho, had rescinded ratification, and progress came to a dead stop. What had changed? Who built the wall the amendment had slammed into, and why, considering that virtually every national poll from 1974 to 1982, the year the amendment ran out of time, a majority of Americans supported the measure. A Harris Poll in April 1982 found that support was at its highest level since 1976, with 63 percent of Americans in favor.[73]

However, as Mary Frances Berry suggests in her history of the ERA, jubilant supporters failed to analyze the arguments their opponents developed or to prepare an advance strategy to assure passage in at least thirty-eight states.[74] Opponents had the easier task—they needed to control only thirteen states, not a national consensus. Berry further notes that the states that quickly ratified had a history of protective legislation: "In Alaska and Hawaii, which ratified quickly, the wounds of the earlier Prohibition, suffrage, and child labor debates had never been inflicted. These two were not even admitted to statehood until the 1950s. Most of the other states that ratified without much conflict in 1972 and 1973 had already resolved their positions in favor of women's rights by enacting equal protective labor legislation for men and women."[75] With the exception of Illinois, most of those that did not ratify in 1972-73 had not previously enacted protective legislation. A further stumbling block in Illinois was that its constitution specified a three-fifths majority vote in the legislature for ratification.

Like their counterparts nationwide, Mormons aligned themselves with values that had long been at the center of the American dream: family, motherhood, religion, a white frame house with a picket fence. The Cold War anti-Communism and experiences of veterans, who had been part of an all-male fighting force, helped frame this worldview. ERA proponents relied on more abstract values for their arguments, all basic American values—equality, justice, fairness. Both views obviously could evoke powerful emotions and convey real benefits, but the debate rapidly polarized until it was being conducted in short inflammatory exchanges—with rhetoric rather than reasoned discussion.

4. The Arguments and the Allies

> While the motives of its supporters may be praiseworthy, [the] ERA as a blanket attempt to help women could indeed bring them far more restraints and repressions. We fear it will even stifle many God-given feminine instincts. It would strike at the family, humankind's basic institution.
>
> —LDS First Presidency, 1976

When the ERA passed both the House and Senate in 1972, ratification appeared to be a *fait accompli.* The Senate vote of 84 to 8 signaled what most saw as a deep-rooted national consensus, a natural result of the social revolutions of the 1960s. The student revolt, the push for civil rights, and the subsequent cultural revolution signaled a willingness to depart from tradition. Changes of all sorts seemed not only possible but highly desirable. Past institutions no longer had an automatic advantage. Under the leadership of Betty Friedan, the women of NOW captured the spirit of progress and advocated legal and societal changes because "women can and must participate in old and new fields of society in full equality or become permanent outsiders."[1] Moreover, NOW demanded that the Constitution work for women. "WE BELIEVE that the power of American law, and the protection guaranteed by the U.S. Constitution to the civil rights of all individuals, must be effectively applied and enforced to isolate and remove patterns of sex discrimination, to ensure equality of opportunity in employment and education, and equality of civil and political rights and responsibilities on behalf of women, as well as for Negroes and other deprived groups."[2] No one was talking about counter-revolutions. However, anyone attuned to the cyclical nature of history may have noted that momentum for the ERA coincided with the end of the exhausting, expensive, and inconclusive war in Vietnam, which should have portended a conservative backlash opposed to socio-economic reforms.

Within this broad context appear the moves and countermoves of defenders and opponents of the ERA. The ERA's trajectory shows its Congressional passage and early ease in passing state scrutiny left feminists and politicians unprepared for the conservative backlash which appeared with such fury and force that proponents were stunned—knocked off balance and left fumbling for some new strategy to maintain an equal rights agenda. But for opponents, the women's movement itself had come to be seen as a threat to their most cherished institution: the nuclear family. The ERA became the symbol of what was wrong with society. Stopping it would halt disintegration, purify moral turpitude, clarify political chaos, and redeem ill-advised legal change. In short, by rejecting feminism, according to these conservative groups, one challenged the heart of the national liberal agenda that had been gathering force since the 1950s.

At first ERA boosters reacted in a scornful and dismissive way. Rather than accept the fears raised by conservatives about unisex restrooms and decriminalization of rape and engage people in mutually respectful dialogue, liberals saw these boogeymen as too ludicrous to even deserve a response. The further entanglement in anti-ERA rhetoric of topics of homosexuality and abortion indicated that for traditional women, these seemed to be part and parcel with the ERA's aim of allowing women the right to make their own choices. Whether such arguments were true or not was irrelevant. What was true was that this language and imagery employed by opponents revealed that traditional women felt vulnerable in having to move beyond conventional female roles and consider a wider spectrum of respectability.

One historian of the ERA commented on "the profoundly irrational beliefs" of the opponents, while at the same time ignoring the sometimes equally irrational beliefs that powered the ERA's proponents. She was absolutely correct in saying that these beliefs may have been "non-negotiable. Two value systems, two world views, two cultures suddenly impacted, but only one side knew it back in 1973."[3] Nowhere was this description truer than for Mormonism's women as the national debate over ratification began in 1973.

Feminists pitted against homemakers, Mormons against Mormons, conservatives against liberals, heterosexual marriage against homosexual union. These dichotomies were seemingly irreconcilable. Demonized by ideas or labels that burned like cattle brands, feminism was the catch-all for modern society's woes, the scapegoat for citizens who were apprehensive about what the next change would be. Women struggled to decide for themselves who they were in the context of a new world they did not recognize and almost certainly did not trust.

The Mormon Church was not quick to engage in the battle, but was nevertheless relentless once it committed itself; for many of its women, its direction was a lifeline. The unwavering position of the church is evident in the many public speeches, articles, and circulars distributed at the time. However, only by probing this body of discourse—what it said, what it did not say, and what meanings emerged out of familiar patterns—can one understand the true underlying message.

In undertaking a rhetorical analysis of the church's arguments, the first theme of note is the identification of the ERA as a "moral issue." Equally important was the message—one lost on most outsiders—to heed the "living prophets," which meant to obey the church's leadership—the General Authorities and especially the First Presidency. The backdrop to the anti-ERA statements was the emergence of the so-called Priesthood Correlation Program, simultaneously implemented during the

1970s, much to the detriment of the church's women's programs. Also of significance was an unexpected alliance between Mormonism and the Religious Right, a surprising development considering the usual theological disagreement and even hostility between Mormons and other conservative religions.

The Rhetorical Construction of ERA Arguments

The Greek philosopher Aristotle described rhetoric—that is, language, whether written, verbal, or visual—as a particular means of persuasion. Contemporary writers who study the uses of rhetoric suggest that it is "the art of manipulating the soul of the hearer through language, whether informative, persuasive, or poetic," and as "a means of so ordering discourse as to produce an effect on the listener or reader." Rhetoric is thus "called forth by the exigencies of a problem within a situation in which an audience can mediate change." Finally, it can be "the use of words by human agents to form attitudes or to induce actions in other human agents."[4]

Importantly, rhetoric—this particular type of carefully chosen language—is not simply communication but rather the use of language in a way to evoke a desired result. It is a premeditated act of persuasion—an attempt to mobilize one's audience in a particular direction on a particular issue. Rhetoric is contextual and therefore must adapt to changing times; and this means that by noticing shifts in rhetorical strategies, one sees, among other things, how women fit into Mormonism at various historical moments. The LDS Church's official policy statements regarding women had cultural, political, and social significance as well as profound weight in the fight against the ERA.

Suppressed gender conflicts are implicit, and ideas about government, theology, and social systems are embedded in the church's story about women—a story that has taken on mythic dimensions. The assumptions underlying church documents reveal a system of ideas about the role of women and their position in the Mormon world, the significance of their relationships with men, and the theological relation between gendered "duties" and salvation. The church's statements were written squarely within emotional norms, using familiar vocabularies, and marking boundaries between Mormon and non-Mormon thought with coded language and connotatively freighted terms. The arguments presented instructed women about how they should feel, which experiences to value, and which to shun. They portrayed the ERA as a threat to the sacral world and gave instructions on how to combat those threats. The rules and behaviors governing the everyday lives of Mormon women were situated in a cosmic battlefield of salvation and condemnation—infinitely comforting to some women seeking certainty, infinitely troubling to others who could not dismiss the questions raised by the ERA.

The central rhetorical concern on each side of the verbal battle over the ERA was its potential for change. No one doubted that the amendment would initiate seismic shifts in the cultural landscape. Supporters welcomed these promised changes for their potential to better women's lives, enhance their personal relationships, improve their ability to care for their children, and open doors to economic and professional opportunities. Opponents saw the same changes as threatening to women's worlds, destabilizing family life, and leaving women without needed economic and legal protections.

Official instructions to Mormons to eschew the women's movement in general and the Equal Rights Amendment in particular delineated the tasks and roles necessary to produce both happy and secure families and eternal salvation. Historian Vella Evans suggests that after 1970, the church "retreated deeper into the sanctity of home and motherhood while much of the rest of the nation . . . accepted expanded options for women."[5] Apostle Thomas S. Monson linked "women's liberation" with woman's "deception," pointing to such things as "free child care" and "equal employment" as the obvious "evils of the woman's movement."[6]

Peter James Caulfield, a student of the ERA, suggests that the LDS Church was able to rhetorically exploit "some latent fears and anxieties vis-á-vis several ERA-related issues, e.g., fear of freedom, fear of physical limitations, and fear of physical danger (for women) and fear of loss of power and fear of competition (for men)." At the same time, "pro-ERA forces either underestimated or chose to ignore these same potential fears and anxieties and made [other] rhetorical choices."[7] According to Caulfield, both pro- and anti-ERA rhetoric took advantage of an existing mindset to reinforce assumptions already held:

> 1. The Equal Rights Amendment represented at least a symbolic challenge to traditional sex roles, which had not only the sanction of centuries, but which crossed virtually all racial, cultural, and religious boundaries. Such a profound challenge contained, in and of itself, great potential for eliciting fear and emotional reactions in many people.
> 2. Anti-ERA forces accurately perceived and effectively exploited this fear, as well as nostalgia for a more stable, less confusing, safer past felt by many men and women in their audiences.
> 3. Pro-ERA forces . . . tended to focus their rhetoric on rational, economic arguments and to skim over, trivialize or altogether ignore the most fear-intensive issues.[8]

How did the LDS Church build its arguments against the ERA? Its response was more specifically to the larger women's movement and the image of feminism rather than to the ERA itself. The ERA was the symbolic battleground over feminism in what Caulfield calls a "process by which secular issues become 'moral' [and] 'spiritual' concerns may be manifest, showing how authoritative discourse may define and form the official Church response [while at the same time] establishing certain constraints that the leadership feels compelled to follow, and afterwards how member response may require the leadership to reevaluate a particular issue."[9]

Identifying Moral Issues

The most important positioning strategy was the church's decision to declare the ERA a "moral issue." Without access to official minutes or personal reminiscences by church leaders, it is impossible to reconstruct the thinking and discussion of the First Presidency, which consisted of Presidents Spencer W. Kimball, N. Eldon Tanner, and Marion G. Romney. However, it is evident from their statement of October 12, 1978, that for them, the amendment created uncertainty about the future and changed the position of women, thereby threatening the family.

How to distinguish between "moral" and "political" was a fuzzy concept. Members were not invited to participate with leaders in making these decisions. The institutional advantage was that it allowed leaders to determine what was moral without the need for consistency or justification. During the early 1960s, for instance, African American activists attempted to convince church leaders to take a stand in favor of civil rights, but the First Presidency declined to do so until late 1963, insisting that it was a strictly political issue. President Hugh B. Brown of the church's First Presidency walked the tricky line of supporting the policy of not ordaining black men to the priesthood but also stating his conviction that discrimination on the basis of race was immoral. At the 1963 general conference he said:

> We believe that all men are the children of the same God, and that it is a moral evil for any person or group of persons to deny any human being the right to gainful employment, to full educational opportunity, and to every privilege of citizenship, just as it is a moral evil to deny him the right to worship according to the dictates of his own conscience. . . . We call upon all men, everywhere, both within and outside the Church, to commit themselves to the establishment of full civil equality for all of God's children.[10]

Without clearly defined criteria for differentiating moral from political issues, such distinctions depended solely on the judgment of the leadership.

On numerous occasions, LDS leaders stressed that only the First Presidency and the Quorum of the Twelve Apostles—the two highest governing bodies of the church—could declare a subject to be "moral"—hence worthy of full institutional involvement. Without such a declaration, church members were counseled to use care in distinguishing between what they could do as citizens under the Constitution and what the church could do as an organization.[11]

In the nineteenth century, Mormons participated freely in local politics with the often counterproductive habit of bloc voting, allowing a dominant position in Illinois politics in the 1840s but contributing to the assassinations of Joseph and Hyrum Smith. Abstaining from political involvement seemed less an option in nineteenth-century Utah, especially after it became apparent that most federal appointees in Utah Territory entertained considerable hostility toward the Mormon system. However, the dismantling of the church's political party in 1893 as a condition for statehood and a history of bad experiences in trying to control Utah politics convinced the church that heavy handedness could be politically and socially costly. On most issues, according to political scientist and BYU professor David Magleby, the church "has remained neutral, admonishing its members to study the issues and vote according to their conscience."[12] In 1951 a member of the First Presidency said:

> The Church, while reserving the right to advocate principles of good government underlying equity, justice, and liberty, the political integrity of officials, and the active participation of its members, and the fulfillment of their obligations in civic affairs, exercises no constraint on the freedom of individuals to make their own choices and affiliations. . . . Any man who makes representation to the contrary does so without authority and justification in fact.[13]

According to Magleby, the church rarely takes an official stance on candidates or political issues even though its substantial political power, particularly in Utah, Idaho, Arizona, and Nevada, would allow it to significantly affect elections. In addition, the church wields significant influence through its business and corporate interests. Politically, the church "has been most visible . . . in discussions of moral issues," Magleby writes, and the church's policy on the ERA sparked what he characterizes as "significant local organizing by private Church members acting on their own accord against the amendment in Florida, Illinois, Maryland, Nevada, and Virginia. Not all Church members opposed the amendment. Some had spoken publicly in support of the amendment before the Church position was announced."[14]

In an instructional letter to general, regional, and local church leaders on April 1, 1974, the First Presidency of Elders Kimball, Tanner, and Romney wrote that

> the Prophet Joseph Smith [founder of the LDS church] has said: "It is our

duty to concentrate all our influence to make popular that which is sound and good, and unpopular that which is unsound." While exercising no constraint on the freedom of individuals to make their own choices as to political parties, candidates and issues, the Church urges its members as informed citizens of the respective countries to be actively involved in supporting candidates and issues which will protect liberty and strengthen the people who are governed. Freedom demands continuing responsibility.[15]

Although the presidency did not specify a particular issue in relation to this counsel, it seems likely from the context of the times that they had the Equal Rights Amendment in mind. The responsibility they reminded members of was to be informed of current issues and sensitive to relevant counsel by church leaders. Still, the final decision about how to act, as this letter reinforced, was left to an individual's personal conscience after study, reading the scriptures, and prayer. This was the church's official policy throughout most of the 1970s.

The argument about whether the ERA was moral or political underwent significant refinement through the decade, mostly in the direction of stronger official statements responding to challenges and counterproposals from those who disagreed. On October 12, 1978, the First Presidency again wrote to the church's general, regional, and local officers—although this list did not include the female auxiliary heads at any level—specifically addressing the Equal Rights Amendment and declaring it a "moral issue." The First Presidency affirmed the church's historic respect for women and conviction that they not be discriminated against, but found that "the matter is basically a moral rather than a political issue; and because of our serious concern over these moral implications, we have spoken against ratification, and without equivocation do so again" (see Appendix D).[16]

The lapse of six years between Congress's passage of the ERA and this First Presidency statement meant that Mormon authorities had not rushed precipitately into the fray. Rather, they advanced step by step, gradually increasing the authoritativeness of statements and the level from which they came. At this point, however, the only level they refrained from summoning was a joint statement of the First Presidency and Twelve Apostles or a revelatory document submitted to a general conference for canonization.

The justification for such a strong position was carefully laid out in March 1980 in the church's clearest articulation of its position on the ERA. It quoted an earlier policy statement of June 29, 1979: "Strictly political matters should be left in the field of politics where they belong. However, on moral issues, the church and its members take a positive stand. Latter-day Saints must ever be alert and united in fighting any influence which tends to break down the moral and spiritual strength of the people." The church had sometimes intervened on issues affecting church members, but "the many and varied circumstances in which our Church members live . . . make it inadvisable for the Church to involve itself institutionally in every local community issue. These challenges are best responded to by members as they meet their obligations as citizens—preferably in concert with other like-minded individuals." Even more importantly, the statement asserted: *"Only the First Presidency and the Twelve can declare a particular issue to be a moral issue worthy of full institutional involvement."*[17] This established a precedent for involvement in select issues of the church's choosing, spelled out who among the leadership had authority to make that decision, limited church involvement to matters the church deemed to be moral, and reasserted citizen action in politics.

Almost certainly for most Mormons, a First Presidency statement was authoritative on any issue, but it was also considered necessary when previous church leaders had seemed to have made contradictory pronouncements on a topic. For some Mormons, a church statement was to be weighted against ultimate principles and the individual was to decide how it squared with issues of equity and justice. But there were far fewer such Mormons. In addition, in a long history of authoritative statements from the male leadership, women were only occasionally consulted but had to live in the particular situations created by such statements.

Rhetorically, the Mormon discourse was one of cause and effect, of promise and warning, drawn from the larger national debate. Across the country, anti-ERA forces spoke with a carefully articulated point of view that warned consistently, though often vaguely, of dire negative consequences to women and the safety of their families. In the case of STOP ERA, this strategy was symbolized by the position taken by Phyllis Schlafly. The same arguments filtered down to Mormon audiences: vulnerability to a military draft (a telling issue, given the nightmare of Vietnam jungles); the destabilization of domestic relations, linked to the rising rates of divorce and illegitimate pregnancy;[18] and tension between federal and state authority. Those who advanced such arguments cast themselves rhetorically as defenders of cherished values and characterized their opponents as militant, bra-burning, radical man-haters who insisted on abortion on demand.

ERA supporters tended to be less cohesive and spoke in a variety of voices ranging from intemperate to reasoned but often stressing the probable social, economic, and educational benefits of the amendment. They cited the gradual historic emergence of women from non-personhood and oppression to the present, stressed the values to children and men of a more egalitarian society, and portrayed themselves as champions of equality for all women, including women of color and the poor.

Aristotle counseled that, in structuring persuasive public speech, one should find "common places" in which to locate arguments, making them accessible and acceptable. It is not surprising that pro- and anti-ERA forces claimed a proprietary interest in domestic relations, the proper role of government, morality, and social cohesion. Caulfield identified ten themes over which women on both sides wrestled in their public discourse:

1. The nature of men and boys.
2. The nature of women and girls.
3. The structure of the family.
4. The role of religion.
5. The role of law.
6. The nature of morality.

7. The economic situation of women in relation to men.
8. What is just or unjust with regard to women and men.
9. The nature of opponents.
10. And the past, present, and future in relation to all of the above.[19]

For most Mormons, the living prophets had answers to all of these questions. The official statements and public addresses given by church leaders between 1976 and 1980 linked the appropriate roles of men and women, girls and boys, to God's will as manifest in human creation. Anchoring traditional Mormon ideas about the differences between male and female and the meaning of those differences in biblical tradition, men were to be protectors and wage earners while women were to be nurturers and supporters, dependent on their husbands for financial support. Boys and girls were to be trained to do and expect the same. The stability of the family, the most basic institution of society, depended on it. Divorce, homosexual marriage, and nontraditional families were proof positive of the efficacy of this point and were linked to virtually every social ill—juvenile delinquency, teenage pregnancy, poverty, and religious apostasy. In fact, religion rather than social mores or currents was the only true and legitimate authority. Those who looked to secular structures were misguided and inevitably would end up with heartache. From the official Mormon position, localized legal solutions to questions about equality best served the needs of nuclear families. What advanced the good of families, most simply, in the context of the debate over the Equal Rights Amendment was the moral good. The opponent was a gaggle of feminists, representing the fears and anticipated disasters that would follow a Constitutional amendment altering the status of women in American society.[20]

Authority in Mormon Discourse

It is important to understand how Mormon women heard these LDS statements from various levels of the church organization over the next decade. In addition to basic scriptures—the Bible, Book of Mormon, Doctrine and Covenants, and Pearl of Great Price—the church's general authorities are considered to be a source of modern revelation when they speak under inspiration of the Holy Spirit during semi-annual general conferences and other forums. The conventional position of faith was that such instructions are to be taken as God's word with the binding force of ancient scripture.

Throughout the 1970s, several themes running through the body of official church literature created boundaries between Mormons and the secular world, including sharper behavioral guidelines and specific responses to political situations. In 1984 sociologist brothers Gary and Gordon Shepherd published an analysis of the themes addressed in LDS general conference addresses from 1830 to 1979. The burden of church leadership, they asserted, was to "identify and articulate the sources of people's discontent, to define courses of remedial action, and to mobilize individuals to become personally committed in pursuit of a common cause." To keep the church relevant to the member's experiences, it was imperative to continue this tradition, and rhetorical persuasion attempted to create and maintain "definitions of reality which simultaneously disparage alternative definitions."[21] Because of the belief in revelation and the nature of priesthood authority embedded in the organizational structure, such "definitions of reality" have had profound significance:

> The ultimate source of Mormonism's unity and sense of uniqueness lies in its transcendent religious beliefs: the belief in its own sacred history as God's chosen people, in its own sacred community as the Kingdom of God or one true church, and in the sacred guidance of its authoritarian leadership. The fundamental task of Mormon leadership is, in fact, to preserve these beliefs.[22]

The alternate waxing and waning of various rhetorical trends over time reflects tensions within the church, conflicts the leadership has addressed, and steps enjoined upon members to ensure greater strength and unity. For example, themes such as building of the Kingdom of God (or Zion) on Earth and a preoccupation with the utopian nature of Mormon society were routine subjects during the nineteenth century. So were descriptions of doctrines and practices that distinguished Mormons from other churches, especially the second coming of Jesus Christ and millennialism. Both themes virtually disappeared after 1920, the decade when "modern Mormonism" made an accommodation to secular authority.[23]

In contrast to these time-bound topics, the Shepherds found that "personal morality" has been a favorite subject of church speakers and has had an expansive meaning that includes sexual morality, family values, and decisions about lifestyles that impact the family. The changing conditions that seemed to threaten morality elicited repeated warnings to avoid risky situations, dangerous practices, and temptations from unworthy individuals. The Shepherds found that the family received its most intense emphasis during two specific time periods: 1890-1919 as Mormonism negotiated its passage out of polygamy and 1950-79. They concluded:

> Today the Mormon nuclear family, rather than Zion or the Kingdom of God, appears to have become the major sociological frame of reference for conference speakers. The Mormon Church is portrayed as serving the basic needs of the family, and the family in turn is defined as the basis of the Church. Traditionally family life (in which the father is head of the house, children respect and obey their parents, and parents set a proper example for their children while inculcating the basic principles of their religious faith) is legitimated as a divine institution which must be strengthened as a bulwark against what are perceived to be the disintegrating forces and immoralities of the modern secular age.[24]

With the termination of public support for new plural marriages in 1890, followed by Utah statehood six years later, Mormonism moved during the early twentieth century from the status of sect to that of a church. German sociologist Max Weber described a sect as a marginal religious movement whose members see themselves as functioning separate from, and in opposition to, secular society. A church, on the other hand, functions as an accommodating body.[25] This distinction provides insight into the relationship between religious identity and a church's response to secular society. The idea of a church as an accommodating body demonstrates how groups allot religious authority on the basis of gender. Moreover, sects typically exhibit radical departures from traditional values and mores. But as a sect changes and adapts, it becomes more of a mainstream church. So likewise "do its margins and its concepts of marginality."[26]

In an important analogous case, sociologist Laura L. Vance in her *Seventh-day Adventism in Crisis* argued that during this process of moving from sect to church, the status of Adventist women shifted, but not in the direction of greater opportunities. When the Seventh-day Adventist church was organized in 1863, women initially held leadership positions and contributed significantly to the formation of community. But over the next several decades, women lost leadership positions as Adventism became less radical and more mainstream. This retreat during the same period when the women's rights movement was gathering momentum moved Adventism to the conservative end of American society where women were concerned. In short, between 1863 and the beginning of the twentieth century, Seventh-day Adventist women lost power, influence, and position, which was part of the cost of becoming a church.[27]

Nine Major Mormon Anti-ERA Documents

Even before the Equal Rights Amendment was passed by Congress in May 1972, the LDS church viewed the women's movement with suspicion and attacked the proposed changes feminists were advocating, calling Mormon women back to their home responsibilities. The church took a highly conservative position with three cautious concessions. First, abortion was permissible in instances of rape or incest. Second, despite the primacy of a mother's influence, especially on preschool children, the church, after some hesitation, determined that single mothers should be employed and, as much as possible, self-sustaining. Third, the church intensified its long history of encouraging education for young women even though, as one feminist wryly remarked, it still subscribed to the "mattress theory"—that education was something to fall back on in times of need rather than as part of a life plan that combined marriage, children, and careers.

Except for these concessions, the church's position was firm. The duality of viewpoints that saw women as properly making individual choices for themselves when victimized, in need, or in aspiring for personal growth versus the limited ideal role for women influenced the debate over the ERA. However, as the issue became increasingly entrenched in church policies, programs, and doctrines, the polarization became agonizingly sharp, especially when the amendment was sent to the states for ratification.

One can best see the progression of thinking about these issues in the nine documents the church produced in the 1970s and early 1980s. In these documents, the church established its position and advertised it to the membership. These were, first, an address by Relief Society President Barbara B. Smith and an unsigned editorial in the *Church News*, which seemed to test the waters before the issuance of two First Presidency statements (with variations), an unsigned but lengthy pamphlet inserted in the *Ensign* magazine, an editorial by a church public relations director, an interview with Apostle Gordon B. Hinckley, and two addresses by church apostles.

Barbara B. Smith address, 1974

The opening salvo was fired by the smallest gun, at least in terms of institutional authority. On December 13, 1974, only two weeks after publication of survey data showing that most Utahns favored the Equal Rights Amendment, Barbara Bradshaw Smith spoke to a large gathering of students at the LDS Institute of Religion adjacent to the University of Utah in Salt Lake City. Chosen to make the church's first public statement against the ERA, she called it "so broad that it is inadequate, inflexible and vague; so all-encompassing that it is non-definitive"—a quotation from the church's in-house position statement of November 1974 (see chap. 5).[28] According to one observer, Smith's statement was neither definitive nor bold, but one of "cautious restraint due to the fact that the amendment was up for a legislative vote in January of 1975."[29]

Agreeing that social wrongs against women needed to be corrected, Smith cautioned that the ERA was the incorrect approach because it would "nullify all laws covering the gamut of domestic relations in such matters as financial liability of a father to support his wife and children, or the awarding of custody of children in divorce actions, which now provide favorable treatment for women." Moreover, the ERA would mandate the military draft of women and deny the right of privacy, according to her prediction. Instead of this "blanket" approach, she said, she would recommend trusting state legislatures and courts to protect women.

The rhetorical strategies in her address reflected the same approach laid out in the church's official policy the month before. It would be the pattern in church publications from that point forward. First, a mental picture of dire consequences was suggested whereby the balance of traditional family life and the good of individual women would be disrupted. The image of women in combat was an even more frightening picture at the time. Smith focused on what were said to be structural inadequacies—that the amendment was too vague or too broad, implying that it was weakly considered. As law, it may have been well intended, but was poorly designed and based on faulty premises.[30] This reasonable rather than emotional appeal lent credibility to Smith's position, suggesting that she had a privileged or superior understanding of the issues.

Although the logic of having the head of the women's auxiliary speak on a woman's issue might seem unexceptional, it was highly symbolic for Mormonism. The church was situating a woman to establish the rhetorical pattern for defending traditional values and roles for women. Throughout the 1970s, Smith would play an increasingly difficult role: acknowledging the realities of women's lives, including some of their unmet needs, while representing the official church position. The mother of seven, she had never been employed outside of the home, but her extensive executive experience in church service prepared her for this leadership role. Much of what she would do during those years centered on mobilizing women who were inexperienced in political processes, unfamiliar with political issues, and generally unaware of the significance of the rhetoric or the reality behind the debate. It was a difficult position, but she managed it by taking a position of unequivocal loyalty to the official stance.

Fifteen months later, the church's next public statement appeared in the annual "women's" issue of the *Ensign*—the March edition, based on the Relief Society's founding in March 1842. Subtitled "Special: Women and the Church," this 1976 issue included two rhetorically significant messages. The first was from church president Spencer W. Kimball, who described the "promise and potential" of the Relief Society as that of increasing service in the home and the community. The second was an interview with Barbara Smith.

To President Smith, the Relief Society was evidence that God valued the contribution of women and had included them in his plan for the earth. "In periods of eternity when the gospel flourishes," she commented, "the women were and are organized for righteous purposes. This great Relief Society movement is a part of the restoration of all things promised by the prophets of old." Calling the Relief Society a "movement" rather than an organization or an auxiliary positioned it as parallel to the women's liberation movement, which was by itself an interesting rhetorical strategy. She defined a two-fold purpose for the movement: "compassionate service" and "programs of ongoing education."

Responding to a question about her position on the ERA, she quoted the church's position statement: the amendment was "inadequate, inflexible, and vague; so all-encompassing that it is nondefinitive." The ERA, she asserted, is "a confused step backward in time, instead of a clear stride forward into the future." Stepping out of the rhetorical stance established by the First Presidency, she captured with her own language the hope of LDS women in the face of the changes threatened by feminism. Within the Mormon context, she wished the best for women in leading lives of power, influence, and participation; but she wanted such achievements to occur within an appropriate arena as proscribed and approved by the church hierarchy and sustained by doctrine:

> I will always support—as I believe the Relief Society and the Church have always done—pieces of legislation that improve and protect woman's right to development of her full potential as a contributing member of society. I want women to have social, financial, and legal rights; I want each woman to be a valued individual, creative, and with as many options as she will develop. I want to see a woman become the best woman, the best citizen, re-

> sponsible and anticipating, both in her own country and in the kingdom of God, the best homemaker, the great individual she is capable of becoming. I want her to be self-confident, trained, a great participating partner in life, but I want to be sure that the bill enacted will provide for these things to happen. The Equal Rights Amendment is not the way.[31]

Rhetorically, her arguments were well suited to persuading her audience that it made good sense to oppose the amendment. Only by opposing it would they see her dream materialize of a civically active, informed homemaker who was loyal to her church, her family, and her country. How could anyone argue?

Church News editorial, 1975

When the ERA was first presented to the Utah legislature in January 1973, it failed by eighteen votes.[32] Proponents marshaled forces to submit it in the January 1975 legislative session when its chances of success seemed stronger. Interestingly, the church-owned *Deseret News* published a poll on November 15, 1974, which asked: "Are you in favor or not in favor of the passage of the Equal Rights Amendment?" Sixty-five percent said they were in favor of passage. Among LDS respondents, 63.1 percent supported the ERA.[33] The poll seemed to galvanize the LDS general authorities into action. Before the church entered the debate, the ERA had significant support in the legislature. But on January 12, 1975, when an editorial appeared in the *Church News* in opposition to the ERA, everything changed. This was the first in a series of statements over the next five years that would officially establish the church's opinion, lay out the arguments, and justify involvement in a political campaign because of the moral questions involved.

Beginning by referencing the organization of the Relief Society in nineteenth-century Nauvoo, Illinois, and establishing the church's position "in the forefront of those who have taught the dignified and exalted place of women," it described the church's programs to enhance women's status "as daughters of God" and its support of legislation that would "safeguard the welfare of women, the home and the family." Aligning itself with the protectionist camp, the church asserted that women over time had received "special protection and the status properly due them" including "equality of opportunity in political, civil and economic spheres."

The editorial's effect was to retroactively legitimize three statements it quoted. These were the public positions of the immediate past president of the Relief Society, Belle Smith Spafford, the current president, Barbara B. Smith, and a secular source—the *Nation's Business*. Structured in a way to appeal to logic, sentiment, conviction, and loyalty, the editorial asserted that men and women are different because God made them so. "Each has his or her role. One is incomplete without the other."[34]

It was significant that the editorial quoted a national business periodical in order to anchor the church's position. The editorial agreed with the *Nation's Business* that the amendment was "unnecessary, uncertain, undesirable." Continuing, the editorial further quoted: "It seems . . . highly doubtful that the people desire any such thing as 'unisex' in their law. But if five more states ratify the pending amendment, that is what the people will get."[35] This was an argument that, over time, would be refined, coded, and finally included in pamphlet literature, public addresses, and other more informal sources to circulate throughout the church.

Irene Fisher, head of Utahns for ERA and the League of Women Voters, reported at a press conference that four independent polls in January showed thirty-four legislators in support of the amendment, thirty-two opposed, and nine undecided.[36] According to Fisher, the numbers were negatively affected by the editorial in the *Church News*. Speaking at the same press conference, Lowell Bennion, a highly respected Mormon educator and community activist, noted with uncanny prescience that the only statement that could affect public policy was one from the First Presidency.[37] His intent was to offer reassurance that the church had not officially opposed the ERA. However, the LDS church was moving slowly but surely to close that loophole.

In Logan, Utah, the *Herald Journal* saw the church's stance as a death knell for the ERA. "The Mormon Church's attack on the Equal Rights

Amendment hit the Utah Legislature like an artillery shell—scattering in all directions and killing any chance of ratification."[38] Straw polls just before the legislative session opened indicated that the ERA was only a few votes short of passage.[39] A week later, support had evaporated. Tarnished as "not only imperfect but dangerous," the amendment came before the House of Representatives only to go down, 21 to 54. Utah became the second state that week to defeat the ERA, along with Georgia.[40]

First Presidency statement, 1976

It slowly became apparent that Barbara B. Smith, though the highest-ranking woman in the church, did not have sufficient authority to maintain a united front among Mormon women. On October 22, 1976, the First Presidency issued its first direct, public statement backing up Smith's efforts to identify the ERA as a moral issue, proclaim the church's opposition, and marshal members to fight ratification. Apparently vague warnings against unknown social changes had not been effective, so the statement presented a more specific goal for preserving the family: defeating the ERA. The First Presidency instructed Latter-day Saints to "join actively with other citizens who share our concerns and who are engaged in working to reject this measure on the basis of its threat to the moral climate of the future." If the ERA were ratified, the First Presidency—Elders Kimball, Tanner, and Romney—predicted, it would undoubtedly lead to further interpretations that could "demean women rather than ennoble them, and that would threaten the stability of the family which is a creation of God." Exactly how such demeaning family destabilization would occur was not spelled out, nor did the letter claim prophetic vision regarding future disintegration.

Nevertheless, the statement allowed little room for supporters to reply. The church had preempted the claim of moral guidance for the faithful, and this was sufficient for most members. Still, others looked for a sign that this was God's word and not political meddling.[41] The statement first appeared in the *Church News*, which many Salt Lakers receive in their daily newspaper; it was then published verbatim in the December *Ensign* magazine, which reached the national LDS audience.

The four themes addressed by the First Presidency, which were destined to be repeated over and over again in the coming months, were that the ERA (1) strikes at the heart of the family, (2) renders social relationships ambiguous, (3) nullifies laws protecting women, and (4) ignores the natural differences between men and women. This seminal statement reads in full:

> From its beginnings, the Church of Jesus Christ of Latter-day Saints has affirmed the exalted role of woman in our society.
>
> In 1842, when women's organizations were little known, the Prophet Joseph Smith established the women's organization of the Church, the Relief Society, as a companion body of the priesthood. The Relief Society continues to function today as a vibrant, worldwide organization aimed at strengthening motherhood and broadening women's earning and involvement in religious, compassionate, cultural, educational, and community pursuits.
>
> In Utah, where our Church is headquartered, women received the right to vote in 1870, fifty years before the Nineteenth Amendment to the Constitution granted the right nationally.
>
> There have been injustices for women before the law and in society generally. These we deplore.
>
> There are additional rights to which women are entitled.
>
> However, we firmly believe that the Equal Rights Amendment is not the answer.
>
> While the motives of its supporters may be praiseworthy, ERA as a blanket attempt to help women could indeed bring them far more restraints and repressions. We fear it will even stifle many God-given feminine instincts.
>
> It would strike at the family, humankind's basic institution. ERA would bring ambiguity and possibly invite extensive litigation.
>
> Passage of ERA, some legal authorities contend, could nullify many accumulated benefits to women in present statutes.
>
> We recognize men and women as equally important before the Lord, but with differences biologically, emotionally, and in other ways.
>
> ERA, we believe, does not recognize these differences. There are better means for giving women, and men, the rights they deserve.[42]

The rhetorical strategy and evidence presented here would become routine during the next five years. Notice that the statement begins with credentials in women's issues in the respectable history of LDS involvement with the Relief Society, the church's female arm, which the statement says was formed to strengthen "motherhood" and extend the influence of women into the community. In citing Utah's record as one of the first states to give women the vote, the church positions itself at the center of the earlier women's movement as a champion of gender rights, claiming for itself a sort of authority to judge the appropriateness of legal issues involving social inequities. The statement establishes, as well, the church's position on the differences between men and women, asserting "God-given feminine instincts." The picture of the future if the ERA were passed is one of damaged families, cancellation of the benefits of law, and women left in precarious and vulnerable positions socially with their feminine attributes "stifled." Against this dismaying image, the unequivocal "We firmly believe the Equal Rights Amendment is not the answer" rings prophetic—words of priesthood leaders utilizing logic coupled with religious emotion and stated as an article of faith. Without question, the statement evoked a powerful response among the church's faithful.

The First Presidency's invocation of "feminine instincts" appealed not only to nature but to theology. This theme—unavoidable gender differences inviolably linked to salvation—runs through other rhetorical arguments that will be subsequently employed. Perhaps just as important in terms of the political environment was the fact that this belief marked a boundary between Mormons and outsiders. It established the church as the defender of women in the context of God's plan for them, including the right of married women to be financially supported. Feminists felt patronized, while traditionalists felt protected.

Apostle Boyd K. Packer speech, 1977

The fourth rhetorically important document appeared only a few weeks after the First Presidency statement. On January 8, 1977, Apostle Boyd K. Packer spoke to a meeting sponsored by opponents of the proposed amendment in Pocatello, Idaho.[43] The *Church News* reported the event and the *Ensign* published the address. Elder Packer, saying his intention was to present how he "thinks" and "feels" about the ERA, chose his language and imagery carefully. He said that "of course" the church engages in public issues that are "basically moral and spiritual. This is that kind of an issue," he said about the ERA, locating the topic within the field of the Mormon gospel. Still, most of his arguments drew on logic rather than emotion, acknowledging that there were inequalities between men and women, but reiterating that the ERA was not the means "to remedy them." He read the official statement of November 1976 in full, then added his interpretation.

Packer included an emotional strategy to attract his listeners' attention by telling the story of a child sick with the highly contagious but not serious disease of chicken pox. A neighbor family, wanting to get the inevitable over quickly, exposed their son to the sick child. Unfortunately, the first child had smallpox, not chicken pox, and the second child died. Packer warned: "How often it is that our solutions become problems."[44] He applied this to Title IX of the Education Amendment Act, one of fewer than forty words, he noted, that had nevertheless resulted in "regulations put together at sublevels in the bureaucracy [which] amounted to about 20,000 words!"[45] In much the same way, the ERA would be interpreted in ways no one could foresee, he argued.

The apostle then delineated key issues that would become central to the campaign against the ERA and the women's movement in general, some of which had already been defined: The ERA violated God-ordained differences between men and women, moved the power of interpreting the laws on sex discrimination from the states to the federal courts, and threatened the integrity of the family. Although he attempted to present these dispassionately, the same ideas would become a source of fear and anxiety over the next few years, mushrooming in importance and rhetorical power. Regardless of whether they made sense or were realistic, the arguments would become accepted as true and would be further embellished with more layers of rhetorical flourishes.

As the church's representative, Elder Packer's main objection nevertheless seemed to be that too much power would be granted the federal government. "The bigger the government becomes," he said, "the more lost we are as individuals. Somehow, always under the notion that our rights are being protected, webs are combined with threads, and threads are added to strings, and strings are fashioned into cords, and cords into ropes, and ropes into bonds."[46] He felt the gradual shift of sex discrimination cases from state to federal courts had already led the country down a rosy path and that the ERA would compound the problem with "anti-family and unisex values" that would "deprive lawmakers and government officials alike of the right by legal means to honor the vital differences in the roles of men and women."[47]

This last theme was already central in the church's opposition to the ERA. "When God created male and female," he asserted, "He gave each important differences in physical attributes, in emotional composition, in family responsibility. We must protect and honor the vital differences in the roles of men and women, especially in respect to the family." The problems the ERA sought to resolve, Elder Packer said, were not in the rights of women per se but "the strength and stability of the American home—in the spiritual and moral and emotional health of families."[48]

Reaffirmation by the First Presidency, 1978

The church took a different approach on May 25, 1978, when it issued a press release titled "Reaffirmation of the First Presidency's Position on ERA," which appeared in the *Church News* and *Ensign*.[49] The immediate purpose of the news release was to respond to the proposed time extension for ratification, which the church called "tampering with and an abuse of the process of amendment." It reiterated the church's position that "men and women [are] equally important before the Lord and the law," then answered three frequently asked questions. Why had the church become involved? It was because the leadership "believe ERA is a moral issue with many disturbing ramifications for women and for the family as individual members and as a whole."

What were the church's objections to the ERA? Here the news release provided an updated version of the church's 1976 statement. Resorting again to legal arguments, the church stressed that women's rights would most successfully be guaranteed "individually under appropriate specific laws." The ERA was not, according to this line of reasoning, "the proper means for achieving those rights." In fact, building on the extreme predictions that had become part of the rhetorical approach, the church foresaw a "unisex" society in which there would be "an increase in the practice of homosexual and lesbian activities, and other concepts which could alter the natural, God-given relationship of men and women."

Other themes raised against the ERA, although not particularly different from the previous church statement, included the amendment's "deceptively simple language" and how it would "strike at the family" to create "ambiguity to the family structure"—meaning the family structure wherein a man presided over wife and children. The ERA failed to recognize biological and emotional differences in men and women, the statement continued, and "could nullify many accumulated benefits to women and children" in present statutes.

The third question, apparently asked by news media, was what alternatives were desirable for women beyond being a wife and mother. In response, the church emphasized "free agency," a strategy articulated for the first time in an official statement:

> Latter-day Saint women, from the beginning of the Church and continuing today, know how deeply the Church encourages them to exercise their free agency. They also know that in the Church, or in any organization or activity for that matter, free agency must be coupled with responsibility. Individual freedom without such responsibility leads to chaos. Latter-day Saint women are strongly encouraged to develop their individual talents, to broaden their learning and to expand their contributions to activities such as religious, governmental, cultural, educational, and community pursuits.

The statement concluded with the procedural argument about tampering "with and abus[ing] the process of amending the Constitution," although it provided no explanation for this extraordinary statement. More importantly, the statement linked abuse of the amendment process with the predicted social reordering if the ERA were adopted: "We express confidence that this nation is sufficiently strong and fair to be able to resolve problems of inequality and unfairness to women, or to any other group in our society, without abusing the amending process of our most basic document, the Constitution, as outlined above, and without undermining our most basic institution, the family."

Closely related to this "Reaffirmation" was a May 24, 1979, First Presidency letter to the chair of the U.S. Senate Subcommittee on Civil and Constitutional Rights. In it, the church asserted its public position and then added some secular arguments designed to appeal to a general sense of justice. The letter offered that the ERA would "divide and polarize this nation," that "it is unfair to the interests of women," and more interestingly that it "lacks the powerful consensus of that very large majority of people in the United States." Accordingly, extension of the ratification deadline would prove to be "deeply offensive to any sense of fairness."[50] Appealing to respect for the higher public good, the church predicted that the ERA would split the country and threaten its legal foundations, privileging one faction or the other. The church drew on imagery rooted in the Federalist Papers for this argument. Fair procedures, as protected by the Constitution, should not be distorted for the benefit of a single party over the interests of the group.

Public relations editorial, 1979

Although the sixth statement holds none of the authoritative power of the earlier official statements, it indicates how persuasive the viewpoint had become. In a brief editorial appearing in the *Royalton Guard,* a newspaper published near Cardston, Alberta, on November 28, 1979, Randall V. Douglass, a local public communications director for the church, clarified what he said were misconceptions about the church's position. This was a week before the excommunication of Sonia Johnson on December 5. Douglass opened with a statement of the church's "profound veneration for the Constitution of the United States of America" and the importance of safeguarding one's Constitutional rights, as well as a "deep and everlasting commitment to the preservation and strengthening of the family, including its individual members." Quoting Relief Society President Barbara Smith, he wrote: "We don't oppose equal rights for women. We want women everywhere to have full social, financial and legal rights. We want each woman to be a valued individual, creative, and with many options as to how she will develop. We would like to eradicate laws and practices unfair to women and men, while still keeping laws that provide for their special needs." As Smith herself had insisted: "ERA is not a panacea for all that remains to be accomplished. . . . It would lock the U.S. Supreme Court into making decisions which might be harmful to women."

Douglass closed with a reference to suffrage, stating that Mormon women "were given the religious vote" from the first. Curiously, instead of referring to political suffrage or citing the successful battle of nineteenth-century Mormon women for voting rights, he cited voting privileges as a manifestation of church membership, a technique that nevertheless had a dual rhetorical effect. First, for the non-Mormon audience, this made the LDS Church seem liberal, as a church that had always included women in its governance; but second, for Mormon readers, it overlaid the political ballot with the ecclesiastical "vote," a perfunctory ritual lacking any real impact on church governance but with the possible implication that this was something church members should approve in the same way—by vote of confirmation, in which there is rarely a negative vote cast.[51]

Douglass's editorial is a good example of the power of rhetoric to present a rewritten historical consensus. In the nineteenth century, Mormon feminists like Emmeline B. Wells and Zina Diantha Huntington Young engaged in the women's movement with full confidence that they were not only fulfilling their God-given role to build a better world but that they were also contributing to the kingdom of God. Suffrage, for the nineteenth-century Mormon woman, was part of a larger design that included economic and social reforms in search of the just society. So positive and, in fact, noble was this pursuit that Eliza R. Snow called on Bathsheba Smith and others to travel throughout the church preaching the gospel of women's rights. While some Americans criticized women like Susan B. Anthony, branding them "masculine" and "crude," Mormon women admired them and fostered their friendship.

Even though Douglass could have seen the 1970s women's movement as part of this honorable religious and political heritage, he chose to appropriate the historic form by acknowledging women's ability to vote in religious congregations with men. By changing the content from personal and social betterment to defense of the home and family, this interpretation—by Douglass and by the church in its various statements—obliterated one of the chief concerns of Mormonism's foremothers: the quest for equality with men. It positioned feminism as a new development, possibly no older than the 1963 publication of Betty Friedan's *The Feminine Mystique*. This simplistic understanding tarnished feminism's goals as wholly sinister and evil. The small group of Mormon women who had some understanding of historic Mormon feminism saw the ERA as an irresistible continuation of their heritage and were caught flat-footed when traditional women saw that history as irrelevant, faced with clear marching orders from church leaders. Nor was this handful of women historians and intellectuals successful in launching effective countermeasures, either educational or along the lines of public relations.[52]

Church pamphlet, 1980

The seventh and perhaps most influential document appeared in March 1980 when each adult female member of the church received her own copy of *The Church and the Proposed Equal Rights Amendment: A Moral Issue*, a formal articulation of the ERA policy. More than a statement read from the pulpit or advice given in a Relief Society lesson, this twenty-three-page pamphlet, bound in gray card stock and printed in a traditional typeface, was designed to look serious. For some, the fact that no authors were identified roused suspicion; for others, by now accustomed to church manuals written by unidentified committees, the anonymity reinforced its authoritativeness.[53]

Despite its intended aim, the pamphlet's text was never as clear or straightforward as it represented itself to be. It expanded on the already familiar arguments by interweaving church and other statements from other contexts and applying them to this situation, along with distinct cultural nuances. A section of the pamphlet, summarizing the belief that the amendment was "unwise, unnecessary and uncertain," was primarily legalistic; it decried the attempt to shift power from the states to the federal government and asserted that existing statutes already protected women and accomplished the same things the ERA proposed to do. The uncertain future impact of the ERA was noted: the prediction of a unisex society that condoned immoral lifestyle changes. The back cover of the pamphlet contained a list of instructions titled "What Mormon Women Can Do."

1. Become well informed. We must educate ourselves about these important issues. Then act and vote intelligently.
2. Make our views known in every appropriate way.
3. Form or join responsible citizens' groups.
4. Actively support political candidates who are honest and trustworthy, and who oppose the Equal Rights Amendment.
5. Vote and act as individual concerned citizens.

Also provided were names and addresses of local, state, and federal representatives. The document concluded with a brief admonition from church leaders to study and pray about the information: "Then we want you to act accordingly." Clearly, the intended result was a united and determined front against the ERA.[54]

Interview with Gordon B. Hinckley, 1980

Three months later, after Mormon women received the March 1980 pamphlet, the June issue of *PSA Magazine* published an interview with LDS apostle and future church president Gordon B. Hinckley.[55] In it, the journalist questioned Elder Hinckley about "the Equal Rights Amendment, priesthood for the blacks,[56] . . . the church's expanding role in the America of the eighties," and the practice of excommunication. This last question sprang from Sonia Johnson's widely publicized excommunication the previous December (see chap. 11). Elder Hinckley stated that

Johnson's bishop had "made it clear that ERA was not a matter at issue in the hearings." Rather, he said, the bishop had taken action because Johnson was "ridiculing some doctrines of the church, and, at least in one speech, was considered to be hindering the missionary effort of the church." Hinckley dismissed the notion that Mormon women were unhappy with the church's ERA stance. "I don't think the women of the church are worrying about it," he said comfortably. "Those on the outside may be, but I don't think the women of the church are. The women I see in the church don't feel the slightest concern over that situation. They have major responsibilities. We don't demean them or put them off to one side. My wife said just the other evening, 'I'd like to know where all these dissatisfied women are.'"[57]

Hinckley was a member of the Special Affairs Committee set up by the church in 1974 to "monitor public policy proposals," according to historian Thomas G. Alexander. In essence a lobbying organization, the committee, although not supporting specific candidates, offered "vigorous and open support or opposition for measures they considered moral issues."[58] Later called the Public Affairs Committee, the group comprised Hinckley, himself a conservative Republican, conservative Democrat James E. Faust, and Neal A. Maxwell, among other church leaders. Because of Hinckley's key position in terms of the church's campaign against ratification of the Equal Rights Amendment, his attitudes toward women were of particular interest.

The rhetorical effect of his approach was to minimize the perceived problem, communicating amusement rather than concern about feminism. Particularly significant is the ease with which this general authority spoke for the women of the church, appropriating female discourse in sweeping generalizations about what "the women I see" thought and felt and personalizing it with the homey example of his wife's statement. No doubt what Hinckley said was truthful and sincere. The women he saw were a small group—the wives or other relatives of other male Mormon elites—and hence most likely to be satisfied by the status quo. It is also true that these women received significant responsibilities within the limited spheres allotted to Mormon women. Hinckley's own daughter, Virginia Hinckley Pearce, would serve for five years (1992-97) as first counselor in the general presidency of Young Women, an auxiliary that instructed teenage girls in church teachings, and would later be appointed to the board of directors of Deseret Book. His stepmother, May Green Hinckley, had earlier (1940-43) served as general president of the organization for Mormon children, the Primary Association.

Ezra Taft Benson address, 1981

The ninth rhetorically important document came from the president of the Quorum of the Twelve Apostles and future president of the church Ezra Taft Benson. For working women, his address in the October 1981 general conference was a source of endless guilt and confusion. Throughout his address, he expressed concern, love, and regard for the church's women, whom he called "choice women—daughters of our Heavenly Father." As president of the Quorum of the Twelve, he spoke with authority, couched in terms of kindly paternalism, laying out the definition of the "honored place of women in the eternal plan of our Heavenly Father" while the "world is increasing in wickedness. Temptations are greater than they have ever been in the memory of any of us." The direction the world was headed, he said, was according to the design of "Satan" to "thwart the plan" of God. As outlined in this speech, the appropriate role of a woman was to be a companion with the priesthood in a complementary association, as a helpmeet to her husband. This pattern was prescribed by God before the world began. A woman's principal role, he said, was as a mother and teacher of her children. She should create a home that is a "haven of security" and love. Implying that feminist messages, or what he called the "beguiling voices of the world," were "propaganda, that will attempt to convince women there are more exciting things to do than stay at home and mother her children," he asserted forcefully: "It is a misguided idea that a woman should leave the home, where there is [sic] a husband and children, to prepare educationally and financially for an unforeseen eventuality."

The female sphere, in Benson's view, was delineated by the limited roles for which women were suited. "Radiate a spirit of contentment and joy with homemaking," he urged. "You teach by example your attitude toward homemaking. . . . Homemaking is the highest, most noble, profession to which a woman might aspire. Provide your daughters with opportunities to develop their own skills, by allowing them to bake, cook, sew, and arrange their own rooms." But even more importantly, it was best for women to remember that the female sphere is subordinate to the male sphere: "Support, encourage, and strengthen your husband in his responsibility as patriarch in the home. You are partners with him. A woman's role in a man's life is to lift him, to help him uphold lofty standards, and to prepare through righteous living to be his queen for all eternity."[59]

The basic rhetorical structure of this homily involved an appeal to the existing hierarchal order, first establishing himself as the central authority as a church leader, patriarch, caring father, and one who understood the Bible. A woman could measure herself against this forcefully described standard. Was she worthy of the blessings of heaven? The apostle's connection between Satan and the current "beguiling" voices that could tease a woman away from her appropriate role suggested that activities outside the home were sinful; thus a working woman or an overeducated woman would be doomed to an unhappy life. The cult of true womanhood never had a more eloquent spokesman than in this twentieth-century prophet.

The nine documents show the LDS Church, beginning in November 1976 and moving to October 1981, as it developed and refined its message with increasing authoritativeness. The net effect was to position the coming political campaign on an ideological foundation, provide ammunition for grass-roots campaign teams, and to light the fire of righteous indignation in women so they would go forth trusting that the moral high ground was in defeating the ERA.

Priesthood Correlation

The women's movement coincided with a structural development within the Mormon Church that influenced the role of women and their status in relation to men. Investigative reporters Robert Gottlieb and Peter

Wiley in *American Saints: The Rise of Mormon Power* saw anxiety about the women's movement as part of the reason for Priesthood Correlation, a program that subordinated the women's auxiliaries to oversight by the Brethren and created mechanisms to increase church influence on individual families.[60] Sociologist Marie Cornwall saw women as "innocent bystanders," not targeted but wounded in the effort to streamline and rationalize the organization both at headquarters and in the field.[61]

Beginning seriously in the 1950s, the correlation movement was headed by Apostle Harold B. Lee, who became church president in July 1972. He had long been interested in this kind of reorganization. As chair of the Correlation Committee, formally organized in the 1960s, he had led the effort to standardize church doctrine, programs, and policies, ostensibly to bolster the family. As early as 1964 when David O. McKay was still president, Elder Lee explained at general conference: "We have endeavored to proceed . . . in an orderly and logical manner: first, by placing the priesthood quorums as the Lord has directed us in his revelations; second, by giving strength to the home; and third, by a total correlation of the curriculum and activities of all the organization, priesthood, auxiliaries, institutions, and seminaries."[62]

From that point on, regardless of where a member lived, the church organization and especially the curriculum, whether for Sunday school or other instructional settings, would be the same. Correlation promised to harmonize and unify the church worldwide. At the same time, it guaranteed greater centralization of control and less room for regional or individual variation. In 1970 the *Improvement Era,*[63] the women's *Relief Society Magazine,* the Sunday school *Instructor,* and the *Children's Friend* were shut down. Largely independent mission publications, including the respected *Millennial Star* of the British Mission, by then the oldest continuous Mormon publication, were also terminated. In their place, three age-oriented periodicals addressed the perceived needs of all church members: the *Ensign* for adults, the *New Era* for adolescents, and the *Friend* for children. Internationally, members received a slimmed-down magazine that drew selections from the English publications and reserved a four-page insert for local news. The magazines were all given the local language's equivalent of "the Liahona," the Book of Mormon word for compass. Like other correlation efforts, these publications came under the direction of male priesthood leaders, in this case through the Correlation Reading Committees which ensured that members of all ages received official policy and correct doctrine. The Young Women's Mutual Improvement Association was placed under priesthood control, as well. Independent fund-raising activities on the part of the auxiliaries were stopped. This was particularly galling to the Relief Society, where women were accustomed to raising funds for building projects and charitable efforts rather than negotiating for a piece of the operating budget.

Each of these developments was intended to strengthen traditional family structure by reinforcing the father's authority, assuring that the mother devoted full-time attention to the children, and by teaching children the same message at church and in Family Home Evenings. When Elder Lee became church president in 1972, Ruth Hardy Funk, president of the newly renamed Young Women, saw correlation as responding to Lee's fear of modern society and its impact on the members. He had, she said, "this sense of social breakdown. . . . He saw the breakdown of the nuclear family."[64]

Though President Lee served for only seventeen months before his death in December 1973, he had made the family, traditional roles and values, and gender/age-appropriate behavior for family members the central focus of all church programs. His successor, Spencer W. Kimball, energetically continued this effort. The strongest weapon the church had against the modern secular (i.e., irreligious) world was the family, characterized by patriarchal leadership, obedience, and faith. This was "the answer to the world's needs," President Kimball affirmed in April 1973. He drew a powerful image of "righteous, teaching parents; obedient, loving children; [and] faithfulness to family duties."[65]

Correlation provided more evidence of Mormonism's shift from a sect to a church. It helped seal the standardization of the message, educational materials, meeting formats, schedules, and hierarchical relationships. It positioned women in a clearly defined place and regulated their activities according to standards and policies rather than local talents or interests. In the process, the autonomy and independence that nineteenth-century women had experienced were reined in more tightly and regulated in the name of efficiency and internationalization. Women served on correlation curriculum committees and played a role in the development of programs that impacted women. Nevertheless, in the process, women lost significant power over their own organizations.

Mormons and the Religious Right

One of the ironies of the church's anti-ERA campaign was that a group of apolitical women, under the direction of male leaders who insisted that the effort was not political and working against an effort to guarantee women the right to assert themselves, became more politically active in the process. Even more ironic was how successful such women were with relatively little previous experience.

Popular literature bolstered the success of the anti-ERA effort through Helen Andelin's *Fascinating Womanhood* published in 1965 and Mirabelle Morgan's *The Total Woman* published in 1973, both of which taught the submission of women as not only a religious duty but as the path to secure, happy, and sexually fulfilled marriages. Those who made this claim acknowledged the connection between female submissiveness and religious fundamentalism,[66] taking literally God's "curse" on Eve: "In sorrow thou shalt bring forth children; and thy desire shall be to thy husband, and he shall rule over thee" (Gen. 3:16). There was nothing new about this emphasis, either in Mormonism or in the larger Judeo-Christian community, but the religious right emphasized the tenet in defense of traditional gender roles and saw it as a necessary path for personal and social salvation.

The approach was doubly familiar with its echoes of nineteenth-century true womanhood. The deferential order sustained by women continued full force with the "fascinating woman." Rather than questioning their role as their husband's supporter, women understood the hierarchy embedded in Christian theology, understood their ranking in it, and believed it necessary to create stability and security in their lives. Womanly submissiveness was necessary for a family's happiness. It kept them safe, kept them ordered, and it was a reflection of a larger pattern designed by God.

Traditional Mormon women stood squarely in the ranks of the right's opposition to social change promised by American feminism. Marching with their counterparts in other traditional American religions, they fit the profile, offered the strength evident in their numbers, and mirrored the national duality between feminists and traditional women. In March 1976 two sociologists, David Brady and Kent Tedin, published their study of women who opposed the ERA based on data gathered from among those who attended the Texas legislative hearings on whether to rescind ratification.[67] The researchers knew that the secular right and religious right tend to be middle- to upper-middle-class, middle-aged, from rural backgrounds, and that 70 percent of the women are non-working housewives. The women at the Texas hearings fit the predicted profile. Forty-five percent were over age forty-five (26 percent were between twenty-six and thirty-five), 33 percent had graduated from high school, 35 percent had some college education, and so on. The authors suggested that women's religious beliefs and values were a major source for their political beliefs, although "small town provincialism is another possible source." Interestingly, those who were not fundamentalists were perhaps "partially motivated by an 'old fashioned individualism.'"[68]

According to social scientist Ira Rohter's 1969 work, the "defining characteristic of a radical rightist . . . is his belief that there exists a vast conspiracy" of individuals who have "worked their way into positions of power and influence."[69] Therefore, those on the extreme right oppose big government (sometimes expressed as anti-statism), anti-egalitarianism, and harbor a compelling fear of a moral breakdown in society through liberal sexual lifestyles and mores, permissive child rearing, sex education, and non-mainstream lifestyles or behaviors.

Scholars have not found one representative background for members of the American right, but there is a general consensus that it manifests itself in three basic modes: religious, secular, and segregationist. For the purposes of this book, the religious right is most relevant. Religious rightists find motivation for political action when fundamental religious beliefs seem to be at risk. A literal interpretation of the Bible frequently leads to casting national and international events as a clash between cosmic good and evil forces. Changes in lifestyles or definitions of morality, particularly through increased secularization, pose a threat that must be countered in the strongest possible way, even through violence, as in the case of those who have bombed abortion clinics or assassinated doctors who perform abortions.

Perhaps the best example of a secular group, which also spoke the language of the religious right, was the John Birch Society, established in 1958. Its foundational issue was anti-Communism; but in the American political landscape, it also positioned itself as generally anti-governmental, focused on individual liberty and local rather than federal government. In December 1965, a full-page advertisement appeared in the *Salt Lake Tribune* with the heading: "What is the John Birch Society?" It described itself appealingly. Since its origins in Indianapolis in 1958, the group had operated as a nonprofit educational organization. "During these seven years we have sought to bring into the John Birch Society only men and women of good character, humane consciences, and religious ideas. For we are striving to set an example, by dedication, integrity, and purpose—in word and deed—which our children's children may follow without hesitation." Although members of the group differed in their fundamental beliefs, they shared common goals:

> (1) to combat more effectively the evil forces which now threaten our freedom, our lives, our country, and our civilization; (2) to prevail upon our fellow citizens to start pulling out of the deepening morass of collectivism, and then climb up the mountain to higher levels of individual freedom and responsibility than man has ever achieved before; (3) to restore, with brighter luster and deeper conviction, the faith-inspired morality, the spiritual sense of values, and the ennobling aspirations, on which our western civilization has been built. The long-range objective of the Society has been summarized as less government, more responsibilities, and a better world.

During the 1970s the Birch Society used its influence to fight the Equal Rights Amendment. Its dislike of big government and willingness to fight moral issues on a political stage brought its objectives in line with those of the Mormon Church.

According to a survey in the early 1970s, women affiliated with this group, not surprisingly, tended to be middle- to upper-class and were predominantly unemployed.[70] Although Robert Welch, the society's president during the 1970s, often said that his organization was religiously neutral, its rhetorical arguments against the ERA matched closely those used by other conservative religious groups.[71]

Among Birch Society educational materials was its *Review of the News,* through which it established key arguments, focused on relevant political issues, and attempted to create a consistent body of ideas as the ideological framework for the group. In the March 13, 1974, issue, Dan Smoot's article, titled "Reject or Rescind the E.R.A.," captured the essence of the society's stand:

> The idealizing of women—honoring them, especially mothers, as if on a pedestal—has always been an obvious fact of American life. It may appear to be mere ritualism in the daily routine of individual women. Yet, it is basic, not only in our romantic concept of what life ought to be like, but in our living. It has profoundly influenced our moral codes, our laws, our customs, all of our institutions, and even our taste; and it has given women a special status which they do not enjoy elsewhere. Nonetheless, politicians have long been under intermittent pressure to adopt an Equal Rights Amendment to the Constitution, to protect women by outlawing sexual discrimination. For decades Congress resisted, or ignored, the pressure. Then, on March 22, 1972, both houses of Congress, by large majorities, passed and submitted to the states for ratification a proposed Equal Rights Amendment (E.R.A.). Within two hours, Hawaii had ratified it. New Hampshire and Nebraska ratified the next day. Within two months, ten other states had ratified: Iowa, Idaho, Delaware, Kansas, Texas, Maryland, Tennessee, Alaska, Rhode Island, and New Jersey—in that order. The E.R.A. Resolution provides that, to become valid, it must be ratified by three-fourths of all State Legislatures.[72]

Smoot reminded readers that men were legally heads of families. The ERA, he argued, would victimize women, degrade them in planned ways, and, in effect, eventually victimize all people.

Thanks to the influence of LDS Apostle Ezra Taft Benson, a John Birch Society sympathizer, and his son, Reed, who was a Birch officer, a significant and influential fraction of Mormons affiliated with the society during the 1960s and 1970s. But Mormonism produced its own home-grown version of similar political leanings in the secularly oriented Freeman Institute, organized in the early 1970s and headquartered in Utah County. It borrowed its name from a Book of Mormon political party, but was later renamed the National Center for Constitutional Studies. Its founder, W. Cleon Skousen, formerly of the FBI and then police chief of Salt Lake City, and with an appointment on the BYU religion faculty, made his reputation largely through his political polemics, of which the best known was *The Naked Communist.* The Freeman Institute, like the Birch Society, saw the ERA as a major threat to the moral fiber of the United States, an assault on rights and values, and hence a natural focus for its energies. Because of cross-over membership in the LDS Church, the rhetorical arguments of both the Birch Society and the Freeman Institute are relevant to this discussion.

Although LDS Church leaders centered their ERA arguments in the moral implications based on theological issues, right-wing secular groups embraced the church's opposition to the ERA for the sake of numbers. Still, the Birch Society saw the amendment as a threat to the Constitution and a part of the "Socialist-Communist menace."[73]

The Birch Society clarified its position during the same period the Mormon Church refined its arguments. Operating in a similar cultural milieu, it is understandable that they used similar rhetorical arguments, invoking legal arguments on the one hand and the laws of God on the other. Thomas J. McIntyre and John C. Obert in *The Fear Brokers* found the tactics of the Birch Society and other groups on the religious right were grounded in a fear on the part of many Americans about what they considered to be an increasingly lax and promiscuous moral environment. "The Rightists calculated," McIntyre wrote, "that these same Americans saw abortion on demand, easier penalties on marijuana use and possession, First Amendment restraints on suppressing pornography, the Equal Rights Amendment, gay rights, school busing to achieve racial balance in the classroom, and even gun control and the new Panama Canal treaties as threats to long-held standards and values."[74] He concluded that supporters of the ERA committed a fatal strategic error in failing to grasp the fear and reaction to change in hometown America: "Without a clear, indeed empathetic understanding of the hopes, fears and aspirations of heartland America, liberals and moderates cannot mount a persuasive rebuttal to the New Right's delusive tenets or a telling counter to its tactics."[75]

In contrast, according to political scientist John Cooper, the religious right accurately represented these hopes and fears to middle America. Writing in 1970 before the ERA had become the battleground for these competing values, Cooper observed: "Rather than being a bulwark against the turn [to the] right, the church (as a whole) has been one of the prime routes of the reactionary infection in the American bloodstream."[76] Seven years later, historian Irving Louis Horowitz saw the right as ruthlessly exploiting the resources of religion for its political ends: "Far from being a humane and judicious conception of the spiritual, the new conservatism uses religion cynically, for adventurist ends. Theoretically it holds that religion is a pragmatic device for maintaining a society based on private property, order, duty. It attempts to provide a cosmic scope for imperial pretensions. A more ironic use of theology is hardly imaginable."[77] Yet for religious people frightened by the sweeping and sometimes savage social changes of the 1960s, the right promised legal and Constitutional avenues to stem the tide of moral degeneration that could propel the nation toward Armageddon.

Cheryl Arvidson, a *Las Vegas Sun* reporter, allegated in September 1977 that a coalition to fight the ERA had been formed between the Birch Society, the American Nazi Party, the Mormon Church, the Ku Klux Klan, and the Conservative Caucus. Similar charges surfaced in other states.[78] In 1978 a one-page flyer circulated in Nevada titled *The New-Right Political Apparatus: A Well Greased Machine for God, Family and True-Blue Americanism* attributed the takeover of the International Woman's Year conference in Utah (see chap. 7) to ties between major right-wing groups, particularly the Birch Society and the LDS Church, as personified by the dual allegiance of Apostle Ezra Taft Benson. The anonymous author referenced a Benson speech delivered in Las Vegas and reported in the *Valley Times* on October 2, 1975, in which the church elder had reportedly described the federal food stamp program as "moral erosion."[79] Such incursions into political territory were not without their price, as indicated by a headline in a Nevada newspaper in 1975: "Anti-Church Prejudice Grows."[80]

In addition to the John Birch Society and Freeman Institute, the LDS Church welcomed an affiliation with conservative activist Phyllis Schlafly's Eagle Forum, established in 1972. Schlafly fostered the relationship with shared literature, lectures at common events, and a series of meetings to establish friendships. In fact, she used her organization to defend Mormonism, saying it was under siege by the forces of evil embodied in proponents of the ERA. "It is clear that NOW and other radical ERAers have launched a propaganda campaign against the Church of Jesus Christ of Latter-day Saints," the forum's newsletter announced in 1980, "and they have been joined by the Justice Department, much of the media, and Phil Donahue."[81]

This article then denounced the U.S. Department of Justice's motion to disqualify a Mormon judge in Idaho from hearing the rescission decision because he held the mid-level ecclesiastical appointment of Regional Representative (see chap. 12).[82] "This was the most shocking attack on the First Amendment ever made by the US Government!" the article claimed. In response to NOW's assertion that a high-ranking Mormon official could not have the "appearance of impartiality when we know of the church's official position against the ERA and ERA extension," the article responded: "In the first place, the Judge has not had any church title since last October. Secondly, the Mormon Church does not have a professional clergy like most other denominations, but uses laymen to handle local church duties. All informed people know that Mormon bishops are not clergy but laymen. So, the entire issue raised by the Justice Dept. . . . is phony."[83] Judge Callister was not disqualified; he ruled that the Idaho legislature could in fact rescind its ratification of the ERA, which it did.

Conclusion

Those who feared ratification of the ERA acquired a rhetorical stance toward women, men, and families. According to their view, traditional domestic roles were to be protected because of the physiological, emotional, social, and even spiritual differences between men and women. Upsetting the balance could lead to social chaos and disruption. Moreover, the masculine man and the feminine woman had important family roles that needed to be preserved; religion, law, and education were to support this understanding of the foundation of a stable society. The Mormon Church's position against the ERA reflected this ideology and had the support, or at least compliance, of a great majority of its members.

Supporters of the ERA, though speaking with much more divergent voices, created a rhetoric of diversity that stressed individual differences of both men and women, even in family patterns. Persistently, they pointed to changes in economic realities and societal values that needed to be acknowledged if the general welfare of each individual American was to be promoted. What was best for the individual would ultimately prove to be best for the family. In other words, there was much that feminists and traditionalists could have agreed on in that they saw a similar problem from a different perspective. However, their concerns were expressed in such different rhetorical styles that they were unable to understand each other clearly. They drew on the ideas and symbols that were most relevant to their worldview—the ERA itself emerging as the most potent symbol of all. Both sides acknowledged pervasive injustices to women. Conservatives considered the proposed ERA to be an example of change for its own sake, threatening the destruction of everything conservatives valued most highly. For feminists, the amendment was an honorable and historically honored way of creating institutional change that would bring greater equity to a group that experienced discrimination.

Although there were certainly exceptions, it is not unfair to characterize the traditionalists as responding to and using the emotional tools—primarily anxiety about change and fear of moral decay. This was a strength since it served to mobilize women who had hitherto been content to remain uninvolved in democratic political processes, and the appeal to home and family galvanized powerful commitments that allowed coalition-building across hitherto impermeable religious barriers. Furthermore, the traditionalists did not need to produce new arguments or think their way through complex positions: They were defending the status quo. By exaggerating the issues and using scare tactics, they were able to raise the peripheral topics of immorality, homosexuality, and anti-family and anti-God positions.

On the other hand, the privileging of emotion over reason also proved to be a weakness. Although the anti-ERA battle was successful, the anti-rationalism sharply divided women. No exact figures are available, but anecdotal evidence indicates that a significant fraction of Mormon women felt the chill of social ostracism; more subtly, even if they kept their opinions to themselves and apparently continued to fit in, they no longer defined themselves as fully "belonging." Perhaps more seriously, traditionalists remained uninformed about democratic processes and unskilled in reason and compromise, while simultaneously acquiring a deeper suspicion of government, a greater willingness to accept conspiracy theories, and a level of anxiety about America's social healthiness that would develop into further irrationalism and paranoia as other issues in coming years.

For their part, ERA defenders privileged reason over emotion. This was certainly a strength, but it had an Achilles heel. They assembled impressive historical and statistical evidence on the status of American women, an approach that was unquestionably compatible with the canons of male discourse and made it relatively easy for these women to gain media exposure, but they had to resort to analogy and guesswork for their “evidence” about what would happen if the ERA were passed. This fell flat compared to the dramatically dire predictions that came from their opponents. Cool-headed arguments failed to move women in the same way or bring the issue into someone’s home and daily life. Rejecting emotional appeals as logically fallacious and unpersuasive, ERA proponents failed to understand what a powerful force emotion could be.

Social scientists Carol Mueller and Thomas Dimieri described the rhetorical stand-off when they considered the difference between proactive and reactive movements: “Reactive movements are those which seek to protect old rights; proactive movements demand new rights. . . . Reactive demands are still legitimized by the prevailing culture while proactive demands are not. . . . In this challenge phase of its life cycle, the proactive movement must define and provide symbols for legitimating new, more desirable social arrangements.”[84] Armed with rhetoric that drew on theology, social systems, and political realities, the anti-ERA movement resisted, and then attacked the rational and intellectual rhetoric of ERA supporters. In the end, it was the appeal to emotion and a rejection of reason that carried the day.

5. goals of the international women's year

> The World Conference on the International Women's Year . . . strongly urges Governments, the entire United Nations system, regional and international intergovernmental organizations and the international community as a whole to dedicate themselves to the creation of a just society where women, men and children can live in dignity, freedom, justice and prosperity.
>
> —*Report of the World Conference of the International Women's Year*

Women in the early 1970s were crowding into assertiveness training classes, wearing pantsuits to work, asking bosses for raises and greater responsibilities—subtle changes, but for some women important acts following the 1960s. As America entered the new decade, its citizens, primed by the civil rights movement, were scrutinizing issues of equity.

Like the ERA, the International Women's Year (IWY) became a watershed issue for Mormons—particularly at the Utah IWY conference. Dominating it became a symbol of commitment to righteousness pitted against the disruptive forces of social chaos sweeping the nation. The success in derailing the Salt Lake City conference provided a template for exporting the same tactics to other states in the anti-ERA fight.

In the same year Billie Jean King beat Bobby Riggs at tennis in the "Battle of the Sexes" in the Houston Astrodome, Betty Friedan met with Pope Paul VI, who told her: "We want to express our gratitude and appreciation for all you have done for the women of the world." Pope Paul gave Friedan a medallion with his likeness on it and she gave him one, called "Brassy," created by Judith Meuli, a NOW national board member from Los Angeles, as a symbol of women's equality.[1] The previous year, 1972, Helen Reddy had won a Grammy Award for her hit record, "I Am Woman," the unofficial anthem of the feminist movement.

It was also in 1972 that the United Nations, demonstrating the international awareness of the need for equity, created a commission to consider the status of the women world-wide. Virtually everywhere, it was realized, women endured repeated pregnancies and childbirth until their health broke under exhaustion and malnutrition. Many suffered abuse at the hands of husbands who, in the context of their culture, had the right, if not the obligation, to control them by sometimes harsh means. Access to education, justice, medical care, reproductive information, and means for a decent livelihood were beyond the dreams of millions of women. The United Nations proclaimed 1975 the International Women's Year (IWY) because of the growing demands for equal rights and responsibilities.

Even in America women's lives were threatened by disparities in the law, widespread spousal abuse, poverty, and a general lack of equity in social and political practice. Fifty-three percent of all women, both white and black, were either working or seeking employment, and 74 percent of those worked full-time.[2] When a woman found work, her median annual earnings were half those of a man's ($6,823 to $12,104).[3] Unemployment statistics were similar. When questioned by the U.S. Department of Labor about why they worked, 23 percent of female respondents said they worked because they had never married; another 19 percent were widowed, separated, or divorced; 29 percent had husbands whose earnings fell below the poverty level.[4] Twelve percent of all women worked in professional fields, but only 2 percent as managers or administrators; the majority worked in clerical positions (25 percent), in blue-collar jobs (20 percent), or as service workers (37 percent).

Many working women had small children. Forty-six percent with children under age sixteen worked; 63 percent had children between six and seventeen years old. Sixty-two percent were single mothers.[5] Unions counted some 5.7 million women among their members in 1975.[6] Thus, for every eight women working, only one belonged to a union.

Other numbers help create a sense of what life was like for Americans in the 1970s. In 1975 divorces exceeded 1 million for the first time in U.S. history. Only 14 percent of divorced or separated women were awarded alimony; only 46 percent of that small fraction received regular payments. At the same time, marriages declined to their lowest point since 1969, a 4 percent drop from 1974. The divorce rate per 1,000 persons reached 4.8 in 1975 compared to 3.5 in 1970 and 2.2 in 1960.[7]

In the fall of 1973, 43 percent of all college students under the age of thirty-five were women. Nearly three times as many black women enrolled in college that year—326,000—than in 1964.[8] Twenty-five percent of public college and university faculty members were women, but only 10 percent were full professors.[9]

Richard M. Nixon visited Red China in February 1972 as the first American president to do so. In November he was reelected with an impressive 60.7 percent of the vote against Democrat George McGovern. Alabama Governor George Wallace, shot when he spoke at a presidential campaign rally, escaped death but was permanently dependent on a wheelchair. By the end of the year, twenty-two states had ratified the ERA.[10] Six states made equal rights amendments to their state constitutions a ballot measure, and in each case the amendment was adopted.[11] Congress passed the Equal Employment Opportunity Act of 1972. From this point forward, the Equal Employment Opportunity Commission was empowered to enforce Title VII of the Civil Rights Act of 1964.

In 1972 Ms. *Magazine* began publication with Gloria Steinem as editor and Pat Carbine as publisher. By then, NOW had two hundred chapters and a membership of 5,800.[12] The national office published *Dick and Jane as Victims,* a 78-page booklet that analyzed stereotyped sex roles in school texts.[13] The League of Women Voters endorsed the ERA after intensive campaigning by NOW President Wilma Scott Heide and other NOW activists. The YWCA voted its support for the ERA, reversing an earlier position that the 2.4 million member organization had maintained for forty-eight years.

When Richard Nixon addressed Congress on March 1, 1973, he affirmed that his administration would "continue to support ratification of the [Equal Rights] amendment" so that "American women . . . need never again be denied equal opportunity." Despite these warm words, the White House "support" was limited to telephone calls to key leaders, telegrams, and occasional speeches by Jill Ruckelshaus or other figures from his administration.[14]

Meanwhile, opposition forces mustered as well. Phyllis Schlafly launched STOP ERA in February 1972 and attacked the amendment in her newsletter, *The Phyllis Schlafly Report.* When Supreme Court Justice Harry A. Blackmun wrote the decision in *Roe v. Wade* legalizing abortion, the Catholic Bishops Committee for Pro-Life Activities organized in opposition.

Responding to the United Nation's announcement, President Nixon in January 1974 called on Congress, the people of the United States, government officials, and interested groups to observe the IWY and consider practical and constructive measures to advance the status of women. His own presidency ended that year in squalid disgrace as the Vietnam War dragged to its own frayed conclusion. On January 9, 1975, U.S. President Gerald Ford issued Executive Order 11832 establishing a National Commission on the Observance of International Women's Year to plan "an agenda for the future." President Ford challenged the American people "to promote equality between men and women" and to correct the inequities that barred women's full participation in the nation's social, economic, and political life. Americans, he asserted, "must also support and strengthen the laws that prohibit discrimination based on sex."[15]

In April, President Ford appointed a commission of thirty-five women and men with diverse backgrounds and experience in the private sector. They were joined by two senators, appointed by the president of the Senate, and two Congresswomen, appointed by the Speaker of the House, while Ford appointed Jill Ruckelshaus as the commission's presiding officer. Its task would be to coordinate U.S. government observance of IWY, to examine the conditions of life and status of American women, and to recommend future government and non-government action. The commission's budget was $350,000, which was small compared to $2 million each for IWY activities in Australia and Canada. The commission's term was set to expire a year later, but it was ultimately extended to the end of June 1976 so it could complete its fact finding, prepare its recommendations, and deliver its final report to the president.

During that year and a half, the commission's thirteen investigatory committees conducted hearings and interviewed countless experts on women's issues and assembled relevant research and survey data. Their report, *To Form a More Perfect Union: Justice for American Women,* was a thoughtful 382-page treatise on women after two hundred years with 115 recommendations for remedial action.

At the same time that he appointed the commission, President Ford created an Interdepartmental Task Force for IWY with at least two representatives from each federal department and agency—a man and a woman—to examine how their own agency dealt with gender issues and to scrutinize programs that impacted women's lives. Forty-eight agencies submitted reports ranging in length from a single-page disclaiming responsibility to several reports between seventy and eighty pages in length, with suggestions for better addressing the needs of the country's women.

From June 19 to July 2, 1975, the United Nations' International Women's Year Conference, the world's first large-scale international meeting devoted primarily to women's concerns, met in Mexico City and recommended "Women's Year" activities worldwide. Forty-one Utah women attended as unofficial delegates.[16] "When I think of the conference," recalled Marie Scott, a community health therapist from Salt Lake City, "I think of this kaleidoscope of color and sound that . . . I had never heard before. . . . I've been places where there were thousands of people, but this was 5,000 women, and that is a whole different experience. Atmosphere, sound, the pitch that you hear is a different kind of music . . . a qualitative aesthetic difference."[17]

Although First Lady Betty Ford was not able to attend, she sent greetings to the women gathered in Mexico City. She said, "I wish you to know that the people and Government of the United States are firmly committed to the goals of the conference and to the work that must follow it if these goals are to be reached."[18] U.S. Representative to the United Nations Commission on the Status of Women Patricia Hutar wrote the official "World Plan of Action," which was adopted by the conference on July 2. It affirmed that "women want to share with men the responsibilities and the duties involved in decisions affecting peace and development as well as in decisions that affect their lives. But unless they are able to move into the top positions in their fields, their impact in national and world affairs will be negligible and the possibilities of helping other women to move ahead in their roles will be nil."[19]

Despite political disputes and confrontations between certain national delegations, the experience was, for most of those in attendance, a profound and, according to one report, "consciousness-raising experience. The discovery of common feelings and problems of discrimination among women, who are a majority of the world's population and the knowledge that the state of womanhood transcends geographic barriers inspired in many the belief that women could begin to take control of their own lives and, in the process, work for a better world with more humanist values."[20] It was a heady dream in the face of sobering realities. The commonalities of experience included discrimination, rape, spousal abuse, and the knowledge that women's issues transcended geographic barriers.

More than 8,300 women attended the conference at two separate sites: the World Conference Center and the National Medical Convention Center, both in Mexico City. The first housed more than 1,300 official U.N. delegates and staff representing 133 countries; the second hosted 7,000 unofficial, non-governmental observers, mostly women who attended at their own expense. On the agenda were four major items: (1) current trends and changes in the status and roles of women and men, (2) obstacles to equality of rights in both opportunity and responsibility, (3) the integration of women as coequals in the development process with men, and (4) the adoption of a World Plan of Action.[21] As worded in the final "Declaration of Mexico on the Equality of Women and Their Contribution to Development and Peace, 1975," the delegates affirmed their "faith in the objectives of the International Women's Year, which are equality, development and peace," and "strongly urge[d] Governments" to take measures outlined in the World Plan of Action.[22]

A separate but related conference, the so-called "tribune," which U.N. protocol attaches as part of an official conference itinerary, included general sessions, twenty panels, caucuses and workshops, film screenings, and special exhibits. The panel discussions centered on the World Plan of Action, which represented the original consensus about what might be done worldwide. The plan included topics related to education, peace, families, population control, housing, and women's health.[23] Later that year, the U.N. proclaimed the Decade of the Woman, 1975 to 1985. Each country was to stage its own events during those years, focusing on its own agenda as well as addressing the international issues of principal concern.

Many who met the Utah delegation voiced surprise at the size of the group, believing that a patriarchal culture, which they assumed Utah to be, would be unlikely to produce women who could act on feminist views. But many women in the group had spent years thinking seriously about how to reconcile their Mormonism with their feminism. Elouise Bell, an English professor at LDS-owned Brigham Young University, said: "It's difficult but we're going to grapple with it. I have faith in the ultimate good will of the people in the church to reconcile this matter." She believed the women's movement would help make the world a safer place.[24]

Margaret Wilde, former programmer and conference planner for the Women's Resource Center at the University of Utah, commented on the visual impact of the tribune when she first entered the main room: "To walk into that massive center for the first time and look at the sea of women around me, every kind of brilliant color of dress, style, complexion and hair, . . . I remember the color shock. . . . I spent a lot of time sitting looking into people's faces. . . . I was enamored with the notion that all these women from all over the world were there in one place because of an issue that was important to us all."[25]

A daily newsletter—*Xilonen*—printed in English and Spanish, stood in stacks against the walls. Banners flew, brightly emblazoned with the IWY bird—symbol of equality, development, and peace. Teri Holleran, a peer counseling specialist, was also moved by what she saw:

> The thing that struck me was how really poignant women's situation was in the world, and yet how exciting it was to get together with women from Africa, Russia and Australia, . . . walking into an auditorium and putting your earphones on and dialing your language and having that cross-cultural, cross-racial interaction. It made me confront a lot of my elitism and my classism because there was some tension there between the developed and undeveloped countries.[26]

Professor Bell was particularly impressed by the open microphone sessions where "the women of the world [could] line up and talk about anything . . . from their hearts, . . . whatever was most crucial to them as women." For Bell, Mexico City was "a turning point of my feminism. It was a realization that this was something serious. This was important. There was a lot more involved here than just a few fringe ideas, and this was serious, and it was going to have to be reckoned with. The world would not be the same again."[27]

While the U.S. Commission on the Status of Women was pursuing its task, Congress passed Public Law 94-167 on December 10, 1975, appropriating $5 million for the individual states to hold IWY conferences the following June and for a national conference to be held in November

1977 in Houston, Texas. The guidelines spelled out what each state conference should do:

> Recognize the contributions of women to the development of our country; assess the progress that has been made to date by both the private and public sectors in promoting equality between men and women in all aspects of life in the United States; assess the role of women in economic, social, cultural and political development; assess the participation of women in efforts aimed at the development of friendly relations and cooperation among nations and to the strengthening of world peace; identify the barriers that prevent women from participating fully and equally in all aspects of national life and develop recommendations for means by which such barriers can be removed; establish a timetable for the achievement of the objectives set forth in such recommendations; and establish a committee of the Conference which will take steps to provide for the convening of the second National Women's Conference . . . to evaluate the steps taken to improve the status of American women.[28]

President Jimmy Carter appointed Bella Abzug, attorney and three-term congresswoman from New York, as head of the national commission, which consisted of forty-five women from across the nation and from both political parties. A tremendous media personality, Abzug was a woman of extraordinary courage. The daughter of a Russian immigrant butcher, she studied law at Columbia University and married stockbroker Martin Abzug in 1944. They had two daughters, one of whom became a civil rights lawyer in the South and the other a peace activist in Manhattan's Greenwich Village. Standing on the opposite end of the political spectrum from Phyllis Schlafly, Abzug had defended individuals in the 1950s whom Joseph McCarthy had accused of being Communist.[29]

An ardent proponent of civil rights, Abzug wrote the first law to ban discrimination against women seeking to obtain credit, loans, or mortgages.[30] She defended a woman's right to reproductive choice by introducing bills dealing with family planning, child care, and abortion.[31] Outside Washington D.C., the American public knew her as the colorful character in outrageous hats who stood out on Capitol Hill even when not calling for an end to the Vietnam War or for the impeachment of Richard Nixon.[32] Abzug was also an adviser to the U.S. delegation to the IWY conference in Mexico City and a former member of the advisory board of the National Organization for Women. The *U.S. News and World Report* named her one of the ten most important woman leaders in 1976; her colleagues in Congress voted her third most influential member of that body.

As a body, the national commission was responsible for developing a platform and overseeing the state IWY conferences. Mary Anne Krupsak, lieutenant governor of New York, was given responsibility for the region that included Utah. A former state senator and state assemblywoman, she was well known and respected. Many of the other commissioners represented special interests. For instance, Gloria Steinem was editor and cofounder of *Ms. Magazine,* chair of the board of the Women's Action Alliance, and convener of the National Women's Political Caucus. As such, she had become an icon of American feminism—powerful and beautiful, smart, gutsy, and focused on positive change. Coretta Scott King reminded the commission of the needs of women of color. A member of the board of directors of the Southern Christian Leadership Conference, she was also a U.S. representative to the U.N. General Assembly and a well-known civil rights worker. LaDonna Harris of Albuquerque, New Mexico, was president and founder of Americans for Indian Opportunity. Others like Dorothy Haener, an international representative of the United Auto Workers union and former member of NOW's board, represented the interests of working women. Three of the commissioners were men—John Mack Carter, editor-in-chief of *Good Housekeeping;* Sey Chassler, editor-in-chief of *Redbook;* and Harry T. Edwards, a law professor at the University of Michigan, whose specialty was labor law. Betty Ford, former First Lady and advocate for women's health, and Maya Angelou, poet and author of the prize-winning autobiography, *I Know Why the Caged Bird Sings,* were also prominent, well-respected public figures.

The law required diversity on the planning committees and workshops at the state events. The committees were to include representatives of various groups that "work to advance the rights of women" and to place "special emphasis on the representation of low-income women, members of diverse racial, ethnic, and religious groups, and women of all ages."[33] The national commission established the rules for the state and national conferences, spelling out how to nominate, vote, and make recommendations. It established guidelines for recruiting attendees, running workshops, and organizing other related activities. The guidelines emphasized travel assistance, day care, and other services for women who might not otherwise be able to attend.[34] "Remember rural women," it said. "About one third of our population are non-metropolitan; they often are disproportionately poor, and are too rarely included in public meetings. Extension Home Economists, Agri-Women, migrant councils, church women's groups, Headstart Programs, local free health clinics, State departments of education, women's political caucuses, and farm organizations and unions are among those that could be helpful in rural outreach."[35] In short, IWY conferences were not to be gatherings of the socially elite and politically savvy but grass-roots convocations representing the diversity of a state's women.

Although the national commission presented each state coordinating committee a "core agenda" of fourteen national resolutions, the states were free to plan and adapt according to their own needs, including additional resolutions or even, if desired, replacing them completely. The manual of instructions advised: "It is our hope that women in every State will view the Report as only a beginning, and that the State planning meetings will actively encourage a full exploration of any issue which women in the community identify as a barrier to their full participation."[36] The national resolutions were based on extensive research and hearings held throughout the nation in 1975-76 and had been published in the commission's 1976 report, *To Form a More Perfect Union,* and dealt with arts and humanities, battered women, child care, financial credit, education, elective and appointive offices, employment, health, the equal legal status of homemakers, international interdependence, the role of mass media in employing and portraying women, female offenders in the justice system (especially young ones), older women, rape laws, and reproductive freedom.[37] The resolution on the ERA was the shortest of all, only one seven-word sentence: "The Equal Rights Amendment should be ratified."

This list of resolutions not only reflected a national consensus on the most urgent items facing women during the 1970s, it was, planners felt, broad enough to attract the interest of virtually all women. The manual for planning and executing the conferences offered suggestions for workshop discussions, listed films and guest speakers available to make presentations, and identified other resources such as bibliographies of important reading material in the belief that women nationwide would rally in support of these conferences and contribute to solutions for "ordinary" grassroots women who were not veterans of the political process.

The guidelines for Utah were the same as for other states, leaving to the State Coordinating Committee to plan and carry out the conference in terms of content and logistics. The instruction manual stated specifically that "in some decisions you will have considerable latitude and choice; in others the law, Federal policy and overall conference goals necessarily limit that choice." However, the conference's purpose was to provide an "unprecedented opportunity for high visibility and serious public attention to the unfinished business on behalf of women's rights."[38]

Looking at the International Women's Year in terms of participation, it was a great success. Most states held IWY conferences between January and July 1977, drawing more than 150,000 people together for two days. Women left their farms and offices; they came from suburban neighborhoods and inner-city ghettos; they met on college campuses, in civic auditoriums, and in outdoor arenas. However, despite careful planning by local organizers and the intent of the national commission, the state conferences proved to be contentious and conflicted. Women who wanted change and women who wanted the status quo opposed each other. Women from both sides were energized—sometimes even radicalized—by their efforts to present their case within the framework of the meetings. The ERA was a particularly volatile subject. In January 1977, as the round of state conferences began, thirty-five states had ratified the amendment and only three more were needed to constitute the required three-fourths majority for Constitutional adoption. In states that had not yet ratified the ERA, the IWY conferences exploded into emotional and impassioned confrontations. Conferences in Hawaii, Idaho, Missouri, and Utah were particularly affected.

Almost every meeting heard from groups attacking "feminists," reducing from the diverse spectrum of feminist views a single caricature. Anti-ERA groups, religious lobbies, and right-wing activists like the Eagle Forum and John Birch Society united to attack what they called the dangers of feminism and were thereby able to influence the outcome in seven states—Alabama, Florida, Indiana, Montana, Mississippi, Oklahoma, and Utah—where all the national resolutions were defeated. Twenty-nine states approved all the national resolutions. Four states took no action at all. Two defeated some IWY core recommendations and failed to act on others. Fourteen passed most of the core recommendations but took no action on others.[39]

Even though ERA ratification was a dead letter in Utah, this is where the conservative attack on feminism saw its most spectacular conservative triumph (see chaps. 6-7). Utah's convention logged by far the largest attendance with 14,000 attendees. The next closest were New York with 11,000 and California with 6,500. A majority of the people who surged into the Salt Palace in downtown Salt Lake City on June 24-25 to attend "The Voice of Womankind: Utah's First State-Wide Women's Meeting" were Mormon women, mobilized by their general and local Relief Society leaders, convinced that they were defending home, family, and righteousness. They came to oppose federal funding of child care, abortion, sex education in the schools, employment "quotas," and equal opportunity for women.[40] It was a fight with a clear victory, with many casualties.

The LDS Church and the IWY

For the LDS Church, the International Women's Year conference was a test case, a challenge to the national feminist agenda and the threats it seemed to present. The polarity, controversy, and emotion of Utah's conference stemmed directly from the church's battle against the ERA, having already effectively mobilized public support in a campaign for rescission in Idaho where Apostle Packer had rallied church members against the ERA. The IWY conference in Utah offered evidence of how efficiently women could be rallied to further the church's political objectives, the key being to call on them to defend home and family, to which they responded with fierce determination. As a result of the success in dominating the Utah meeting, the church would quickly export these same tactics to Hawaii, Iowa, New York, and other states.

What steps brought the church to the battlefield of June 1977, ready and willing to deploy forces in a no-holds-barred contest with the national feminist agenda? As we have seen, when the ERA came up for a vote in Utah in January 1973, it failed by eighteen votes.[41] Utah's legislature, made up of part-time politicians who meet for sixty-day sessions in odd-numbered years and a thirty-day budgetary session in even-numbered years, was not in session when the ERA was presented to the states for ratification in 1972. In October, rumblings on the Utah landscape made evident the variety of viewpoints that would mark the legislative debate, which began in January 1973. In October a subcommittee of the Governor's Commission on the Status of Women began studying the amendment and decided to support its passage. This commission organized a speakers' bureau to educate the public, published a brochure detailing arguments in support of the ERA, and endorsed a number of state organizations that had formed to push for ratification. During the same month, the *Deseret News* published two polls indicating that a majority of candidates running for seats in the Utah legislature favored the ERA.[42]

These moves seemed pedantic in comparison to the initially playful nature of the first opposition group originating in southern Utah. The "HOTDOGS," they called themselves—Humanitarians Opposed to the Degradation of Our Girls—took the position in December 1972 that "in proposing this amendment, the Federal Government had promised every woman in America a T-bone steak, but in effect all they were getting was a hot dog, and a spoiled one at that."[43] The HOTDOGS paid careful attention to what they supposed was the amendment's real threat to the family and what they characterized as the "Communist" nature of the women's liberation movement. Their rhetoric, according to two students of social movements John Unger Zussman and Shauna M. Adix, was as "emotional as the Governor's Commission's was calm."[44] The group sponsored a letter-writing campaign, collected signatures on petitions, produced pamphlets about the dire circumstances the ERA would bring, and ultimately made hysteria-filled speeches across the state.[45] Their work helped establish the boundaries of the ratification debate in the months before the LDS Church weighed in and the Utah legislature met in January 8, 1973.

The House Committee on Federal, State, and Military Affairs conducted a hearing on the amendment on an incredibly snowy day in January 1973. Despite the weather, it was standing room only in the auditorium of the state's capitol as a series of groups presented arguments for and against ratification. Supporters on either side interjected with spontaneous applause or muttered disapproval. It was suspected that the John Birch Society was behind the HOTDOGS. In fact, the April 1973 issue of *American Opinion*, the Birch Society's monthly magazine, confirmed that the leadership of the HOTDOGS were John Birch members and congratulated them for orchestrating the legislative defeat in Utah.[46] The themes articulated by the HOTDOGS prior to the first ratification vote in Utah portended the basic rhetoric that the LDS Church would use in its campaign against the ERA over the next decade.

It seemed certain, by the time the ERA came up for a vote on the floor of the House of Representatives on January 24, 1973, that it would be defeated despite a *Salt Lake Tribune* poll, published on January 21, indicating that 60 percent of its survey respondents favored ratification. The vote failed 51-20.

An important consequence was the organization of the Equal Rights Coalition of Utah.[47] The coalition addressed an array of issues central to the rhetoric of the women's movement such as abortion, protective legislation, family issues, and women's health, but its principal focus and *raison d'être* was ratification of the ERA. It was formed largely to counteract the negative publicity generated by the HOTDOGS and to inform about the beneficial effects of ERA. Within the year, it became clear that their fight would be an uphill battle. In 1974 two successive general presidents of the Relief Society spoke out against the ERA.[48] Even so, during the two-year period between Congressional passage and the Utah legislature's vote, the First Presidency had not taken an official position and Mormon men and women felt some liberty to take positions based on their convictions.

Irene Fisher was new to Utah in the mid-1970s, a young mother in her thirties, anxious to make new friends and contribute to the community. Charged by her optimism and enormous energy, she volunteered for the League of Women Voters. They eventually offered her a job and put her on the board of directors. Representing the league on the Equal Rights Coalition board seemed logical; but when she first started working for the ERA, she had not "realized the magnitude of what it was about." She quickly became passionate "for very fundamental reasons related to my values and beliefs about human dignity and the rights of all people."[49] She was convinced that the ERA would eliminate legal barriers which prevented women from making decisions about their own lives: "Legal barriers to full equality are especially undesirable and should be eliminated, especially as they relate to ways in which people support themselves and their families."[50]

"Some people were involved in the movement for civil rights for blacks. This was mine," Fisher later mused. "Either you were for equal rights for all people under the law or you weren't; there wasn't any halfway point." Her memories of the campaign are colored in part by the disappointment of lost battles. Initially, she remembers, "it was very optimistic and fun. We had special breakfasts for the legislators. We put bottles of Mrs. Butterworth syrup on each desk with a little apron on it with the message: 'Another woman for ERA.' We had speakers who would go around and talk about ERA." She became disillusioned when legislators quickly changed their position after the church statement was published.

But still, she said, the atmosphere was very different from the IWY. "That was very nasty."[51]

By September 1974, twenty-four of Utah's current and former women legislators had publicly endorsed the ERA. Of these, twenty-one were Mormon; eighteen were Democrats and three were Republicans.[52] After the November elections in 1975, the configuration of the state legislature shifted. Democrats established control over both houses. Eight women, the most in Utah's history, would serve in the legislature, among them Georgia B. Peterson, assistant minority whip in the Utah House. An opponent of the ERA, Peterson nevertheless was a long-time "champion of women's rights" and sponsored a number of bills intended to stamp out "prejudice."[53] Milly Oberhansley Bernard, a Democrat, first ran for the legislature in 1967 and served as majority leader in the 1975 session. Co-sponsor of the ERA in 1974, she felt the really pressing issue for her constituents was inflation. Twenty-eight-year-old newcomer Genevieve Atwood was an engineering geologist who had hoped her technical expertise would benefit the legislature in confronting environmental issues. Saying she entered politics because of Watergate, she walked her entire Salt Lake avenues district, meeting as many voters as possible. Vee Carlisle was president of the Utah Order of Women Legislators, vice president of Tracy-Collins Bank, and vice chair of the Salt Lake County Democratic Party. In the 1975 session, she intended to focus on ERA, consumerism, and the preservation of historical landmarks.[54]

Things looked rosy. On November 15, 1974, the *Deseret News* reported that 65 percent of the state's residents favored ERA ratification, Mormons at the slightly lower rate of 63.1 percent. The approval figure for non-Mormons was 73.1 percent. In Utah County, with its higher percentage of Mormons, only 50.6 percent favored the amendment. Age did not seem to make a difference, nor was there much difference between men and women. Democrats were only slightly more likely to favor passage than Republicans.[55]

Information about church decision-making for this period is not available, but it seems reasonable to suppose that the leadership looked at the survey data and realized its own members had not gotten their intended message. It also seems reasonable, in light of future events, that Apostle Gordon B. Hinckley played a key role in powering the slow acceleration through an eventually irresistible process. However, it remains unclear how tightly coordinated the Public Communications Department, reorganized in 1973 right after the ERA moved to the ratification stage, and the newly formed Special Affairs Committee were.

The new Public Communications Department was directed by veteran *Deseret News* publisher Wendell J. Ashton, but had grown out of the Radio, Publicity, and Missionary Literature Committee, organized in 1935 with twenty-five-year-old Gordon B. Hinckley as its first employee. This committee became the Church Information Service in 1957, which in turn became the External Communications Department in 1972.[56] It existed with a clear public mission of generating publicity about the church's positive achievements, handling ceremonial visits by visiting dignitaries, facilitating fact gathering for journalists, and issuing press releases when instructed to do so.

Paralleling this organization was the less public Special Affairs Committee, which may have been an outgrowth of a 1940s church committee that had conducted covert surveillance of suspected polygamists. The committee had no public presence. It was nevertheless reorganized under its new name in January 1975, a month after the *Deseret News* survey. At first said to be an information-gathering entity, the committee shifted over time to an increasing role in proposing public policy. It included three well-respected members of the Quorum of the Twelve Apostles: Elders Hinckley, James Faust, and Neal Maxwell.[57] As Hinckley's presence suggests, there was some overlap in personnel between the Public Communications Department and Special Affairs Committee.

Also in November 1974, Phyllis Schlafly came to Salt Lake City and visited Georgia Peterson and other potential recruits for STOP ERA. Peterson placed a call with Barbara Smith to see if she could bring Schlafly to see her and discuss the campaign to defeat the amendment. Smith remembered telling Schlafly, "I didn't think the Church would take a stand against the ERA, because they only took a stand against moral issues." Schlafly responded that she "felt that the ERA was one of the greatest moral issues of our day and that it would be very destructive to the family." She encouraged Smith to study the amendment, assuring her that if she did, she would surely "understand how destructive it could be."[58] Smith remembered having had "feelings" that the amendment might be important before she spoke with Schlafly and had, in fact, "discussed them with Sister Spafford," her immediate predecessor. "I did read a lot more about the ERA," she said.

After this conversation, Smith began meeting with various general authorities. Apostle Thomas S. Monson, for instance, told her "that he felt the Church would want to take some action, because they [general authorities] too felt that it would be a very destructive thing for the morals of the community and the family."[59]

When Schlafly and a relatively small group of women formed STOP ERA in 1972, it was, according to the *Phyllis Schlafly Report,* a "pro-family movement" and a "coming together of believers of all faiths who, for the first time, worked together toward a shared political goal."[60] This same group founded the Eagle Forum in 1975. "The Equal Rights Amendment was presented to the American public as something that would 'benefit women,' put women 'in the Constitution,' and lift women out of their 'second-class citizenship,'" Schlafly explained. "However, in thousands of debates, the ERA advocates were unable to show any way that ERA would benefit women or end any discrimination against them. The fact is that women already enjoy every Constitutional right that men enjoy and have enjoyed equal employment opportunity since 1964."[61]

During the winter of 1974-75, the church recruited the help of Rex E. Lee, dean of BYU's law school and future BYU president, to develop arguments against the Equal Rights Amendment. In an undated privately circulated paper, he stated that the ERA would have the counterproductive effect of limiting the rights of women. The four drawbacks he identified would appear in subsequent addresses by church leaders and in official church statements:

1. By it's [sic] nature, it will either do too little or too much.
2. The language of the proposed Amendment is so broad and so vague that it is impossible at this stage to determine whether in fact it will accomplish too little or too much.
3. Given our existing Constitutional guarantees of equality, there are serious problems with the adoption of a Constitutional amendment dealing solely with discrimination on the basis of sex that would accomplish either too little or too much.
4. In any event, the lessening of gender-based discrimination can be more effectively carried on under existing law, without the enormous drawbacks of the proposed Constitutional amendment.[62]

From this modest beginning when it seemed that a difference over how best to grant more rights to women might still be the goal, the first major step was Barbara B. Smith's address to students at the LDS Institute of Religion adjacent to the University of Utah (see chap. 4). Prior to her speech in early December 1974, Sister Smith met with Elders Hinckley and Faust of the Special Affairs Committee to discuss whether she should take a public stand. They told her "it was appropriate for me as the leader of the women of the Church to announce my stand against the Equal Rights Amendment, if I felt so inclined."[63] "I told them," she later amplified, "that I had given it careful consideration and I would like to make that kind of statement if it would be in keeping with the policy of the Church. They said they thought it would be very appropriate and that they would arrange for an audience for me to speak to."[64]

The audience the Special Affairs Committee convened was constructed somewhat artificially. School was in recess at the end of fall quarter, but about six or seven hundred students attended, as did reporters from local newspapers and television stations after being alerted by Public Communications's Wendell Ashton.[65] "I've never had such an experience," President Smith said, "with lights and cameras and microphones. I guess we had seven or eight microphones."[66] The Special Affairs Committee clearly understood how important this event was and Smith's potential as leader of the church's women to sway opinion on the amendment.

According to investigative journalists Robert Gottlieb and Peter Wiley, the three general authorities comprising the Special Affairs Committee had briefed Smith "on what to say."[67] "I worked hard," she recalled. "They told me I could work with anyone I wanted . . . [s]o I had Alice Smith work closely with me. After the talk was ready[,] I took it[,] and the Brethren approved it before I gave it."[68] "It is my considered judgment that the Equal Rights Amendment is not the way," she declared in her speech on December 13. "Once it is passed, the enforcement will demand an undeviating approach which will create endless problems for an already troubled society."[69]

Smith outlined her reasons. "It seemed to me that [women] had in America at this time unprecedented opportunities for self development and that we have economic abundance above what the women of the world have ever known. Women have the luxury of being full-time mothers as they do in some countries. Yet there is so much dissatisfaction. I tried to enumerate the reasons why."[70]

Aware of the breadth of issues facing American women that made their lives fall short in comparison to their male counterparts, she said:

> We decided that one reason would be that they didn't feel that they had equal pay for equal work. There was unequal opportunity for promotion and advancements in paid employment. Women had little voice in major public decision making. They had guilt over their failure to meet stereotyped roles. There seemed to be a traditional deference to the role of male supremacy. There were a number of restrictions as to the use of credit and credit cards. There seemed to be an inability to obtain home loans or housing. Women were being discriminated against in the administration of a child's estate. There seemed to be restrictive marital duties and parental obligations that didn't include women as they felt they should be included. There were restrictions on school entrance opportunities and also activities. There were inequalities in property rights and job benefits and inheritance. And there were other reasons.[71]

But these were not the issues Smith enumerated in her speech. On the contrary, her talk had the desired effect of paving the way for the LDS stand against the ERA, also over the next several months as Smith continued to speak on the subject, establishing herself as a committed and dedicated player in the church's efforts to defeat the amendment. She was an intelligent woman who had educated herself about the arguments and issues; in her best judgment, the ERA was not the way to resolve the problems that faced contemporary women.[72] "I just didn't feel that a blanket approach to the problem would be the answer. In fact, I stated that it would probably be a confused step backward in time, instead of a clear stride forward into the future. It would create endless litigation which might prove harmful to the solidarity of the family and the protection of the children."[73]

As Smith was interviewed on church-owned KSL radio and TV and at KBYU, she realized that the talk had caused some confusion because in the past, "people had been given the opportunity to think the way they wanted to think" on political issues, and on this topic, "no statement had come from the Church."[74]

Five years later she answered a reporter's question about the ERA and admitted to not having understood all the implications of the proposed amendment at the time. She said she relied on the ability of the prophet to see into the future: "The Prophet can so see. And if you know that, you know there is no further need for discussion."[75] It was not a position that feminists, alert to the patronizing tone of "father knows best," could respect; but for Mormon women, Barbara Smith expressed the trust and faith that was their moral compass through a troubled world.

Until this time, the general authorities had worked behind the scene, allowing Smith to be the church's chief spokesperson on the issue. On January 4, 1975, with the ratification vote in the legislature only days away, President Spencer W. Kimball declined to comment on the pending vote because it was still, for him, a "political" issue.[76]

But two days before the session opened, the LDS Church issued the unsigned editorial in the *Church News,* the tabloid-sized section of the church-owned *Deseret News,* that turned the tide. Traditionally, such editorials represented official positions, although they were usually devoted to sermon-like exhortations on religious topics. The implication in this case seemed clear to church members. The editorial described the ERA as "not only imperfect but dangerous," in fact a "confused step backward in time." The ERA was so "broad that it is inadequate, inflexible and vague; so all-encompassing that it is non-definitive." It concluded that the ERA "was not the way" because "men and women are different, made so by a divine Creator. Each has his or her role. One is incomplete without the other."[77] Faced with an uncertain vote and considerable evidence of widespread local support, the church had decided to use a rhetorical strategy that raised fear of a vague and dangerous future where the roles of men and women might be in flux, altered from a divinely created plan. Resting the argument on biblical descriptions of difference, the statement sealed the doom of the amendment in Utah. According to one historian of the period, Marilyn Warenski, the number of supporting votes dropped from thirty-four to sixteen, as indicated by an official poll.[78]

The immediate and dramatic influence of this editorial suggested the power the LDS Church could wield in the anti-ERA campaign. Tellingly, the politician who originally sponsored the ERA bill, Byron M. Fisher, a Mormon bishop, promptly reversed his position,[79] telling a *Salt Lake Tribune* reporter, "It is my Church, and as a bishop, I'm not going to vote against its wishes."[80] Fisher's position was replicated thousands of times as Mormons processed this new information. True, the *Church News* was not the First Presidency, a loophole that supporters of the ERA found comforting, but they too knew an editorial could be printed without the First Presidency's permission. For those who believed their prophet spoke to God and that instructions from the First Presidency, whether signed or unsigned, were the equivalent of divine revelation, it was a decisive moment. Elaine Cannon, general president of the Young Women's organization in 1978, captured the essence of this acceptance: "When the prophet speaks, sisters, . . . the debate is over."[81]

Utah Governor Calvin Rampton publicly supported the church's decision to oppose the amendment. On the day the legislative convened, he said at a news conference broadcast on the University of Utah's public television station, "One of the contributions any church makes to a society is to express a moral viewpoint." He predicted that the editorial would most likely have a "profound effect on the outcome of the ERA in the Utah Legislature."[82]

According to Zussman and Adix, the ratio of Mormon support, as demonstrated in various polls, fell from 63 percent in November 1974 to 31 percent in February 1975 after the ERA was defeated in Utah. Respondents in other religious groups continued to support the ERA by a 2-1 margin.[83]

At a news conference called by the Utah ERA Coalition on January 22, 1975, pro-ERA women accused the legislature of listening to the church rather than to their constituents, who according to the polls still showed high support for the amendment.[84] But on February 18 when the amendment came to the floor of the legislature, the vote in the House was 54 to 21 against.[85] By this time, public interest had been galvanized by the controversy and the gallery and overflow areas of the capitol were filled. Four hundred people gathered at a pro-ERA rally on the steps of the capitol that afternoon to sing songs, continuing into the night with a candlelight vigil. Motorcades of women from throughout the state had arrived to hear the debate in the House of Representatives.[86] Irene Fisher remembers standing on the capitol steps talking with members of a Quaker congregation who had shown up to support the vigil.[87] All but one of the women legislators spoke in favor of the amendment, while a Mormon representative stated that voting against it did not imply opposition to equal rights for women. One House member who had publicly supported ratification voted against it.[88] The amendment would not be re-introduced into the Utah legislature, but the issue was still festering two years later in June 1977 when the state IWY meeting convened.

Beginning in January 1976, women in the legislature tried to pass bills similar to the ERA that would "eradicate sex discrimination in Utah." Representatives Georgia Peterson (R-Salt Lake City) and Beth Jarman (D-Bountiful) were appointed at the beginning of the session to a committee to study sex discrimination under Utah law. According to Representative Jarman: "We started by brainstorming words, such as his, her, husband, wife, spouse, boy, girl, and feeding those words into a computer. From that we came up with 1,900 statutes in Utah laws that dealt with sex roles. From there we had a senior law student go through to find the ones that were discriminatory. We found 89 statutes and five constitutional provisions to be in that category." Compiling their own research rather than relying on data produced by special interest groups, the committee concluded in 1976 that there were four major areas in need of revision: domestic relations, legal rights of men and women, sexual abuse, and insurance and labor laws. Although the public believed women were discriminated against in employment, people were unaware of the extent of legal discrimination in other areas.[89]

A month after this research became public, offering support for those who saw the need for a sweeping amendment, the LDS First Presidency formalized its opposition with an official statement against ratification on October 22, 1976 (see chap. 4). Not only did the First Presidency take the crucial step of designating the ERA a "moral issue," meaning that opposition carried eternal significance in the on-going battle between righteousness and evil, but it voiced the fear that it "could indeed bring them [women] far more restraints and repressions. We fear it will even stifle many God-given feminine instincts." It concluded: "We recognize men and women as equally important before the Lord, but with differences biologically, emotionally, and in other ways. ERA, we believe, does not recognize these differences. There are better means for giving women, and men, the rights they deserve."[90]

The next step for the church was to organize anti-ERA activities outside Utah. The First Presidency statement was the beginning of what sociologist O. Kendall White Jr. has called an overt campaign played out publicly to convince members of the church and public policy makers that ratification would be a colossal mistake for the United States. At the same time, according to White, this statement marked the beginning of an "unofficial covert campaign, the success of which depended upon secrecy."[91] This campaign can best be understood by considering the church's *sub rosa* political activities beginning in 1978 in Virginia (see chap. 11), but the earliest organized efforts took place in the winter of 1976 and spring of 1977.

As 1976 drew to a close, thirty-four states had ratified the ERA. Only four more were needed. On December 29, 1976, Ezra Taft Benson, president of the Quorum of the Twelve, sent an official circular to all mission and stake presidents in the United States, advising: "As the Equal Rights Amendment issue is activated in some states, we suggest that you urge members of the Church, as citizens of this great nation, to join others in efforts to defeat the ERA." He attached the First Presidency's 1976 statement. In his letter, Benson used language that subtly affirmed the subordinate position of women in the Mormon world, although from the beginning, he wrote, Mormonism had "affirmed the exalted role of women within our society." The Relief Society, he said, was organized as a companion to male priesthood, and women in Utah were among the first to receive the vote; however, additional rights might nullify the accumulated benefits to "women in their present statuses." The ERA failed to "recognize inherent emotional and biological differences between males and females."[92]

A week later on January 8, 1977, Apostle Boyd K. Packer spoke to Mormons in Pocatello, Idaho, advising them to rescind the ERA. He shared the platform with Allen Larsen, Speaker of the House of Representatives in Idaho, who was also a Mormon stake president (see chap. 4). The two held a press conference afterwards. At the rally, before an estimated 2,200 people packed into the Pocatello High School auditorium, Elder Packer said: "We cannot eliminate through any pattern of legislation or regulation the differences between men and women." He read the First Presidency's statement and maintained that church leaders supported the notion of equity but not the ERA. "There are basic things that a man needs that a woman does not need," he said. "There are things that a woman needs that a man never needs, and there are things that a woman feels that a man never feels, nor should he." For him the issue of differences between men and women made the most sense. He said:

"These differences make women, in basic needs, literally opposite from men. When God created male and female, He gave each important differences in physical attributes, in emotional composition, in family responsibility." It was the responsibility of the church to protect those differences in respect to the family, he said.[93] The meeting had been called to support Idaho's rescission of its 1972 ratification of the ERA. Other church leaders spoke, including Senator Dane Watkins of Idaho Falls and Representative Rusty Barlow of Pocatello.

Elder Packer warned that the ERA might protect same-sex marriages or allow same-sex couples to adopt children. Repeating the now-familiar list of suspected abuses the amendment would cause, he predicted a military draft of women, erosion of the Constitutional division of powers, and most importantly a general "threat [to] the family." He stated emphatically what he stood for:

> I am for the equitable enforcement of existing laws. There are sufficient of them to protect the rights of women and of children and of men. Or to enact judiciously and wisely any needed legislation to correct particular circumstances.
>
> I am for protecting the rights of woman to be a woman, a feminine, female woman; a wife and a mother.
>
> I am for protecting the rights of a man to be a man, a masculine, male man; a husband and a father.
>
> I am for protecting the rights of children to be babies and children and youth, to be nurtured in a home and in a family.
>
> I am for recognizing the inherent God-given differences between men and women.
>
> I am for accommodating them so that we can have physically and emotionally and spiritually stable, happy individuals and families and communities.
>
> Without that, when the floods come, in the end what will really be worth saving?[94]

The third event in three weeks showing the church's heightened opposition occurred on January 15 when Barbara B. Smith addressed a "Rescind ERA" meeting in Coeur d'Alene, Idaho, likewise strongly urging rescission. Smith remembered the enthusiastic response and tremendous support she felt there:

> Brother Packer had been up the week before, because it had been decided by this time, more than a year later, that the Brethren would also take an official stand along with the article against ERA published as a Church editorial. They had done that in support of my stand against the Equal Rights Amendment. I was very pleased that when he was going to give his talk he invited me to visit with him, and also Public Communications, and give him any ideas that we thought would be important. Then after he had written his talk, he asked us for our suggestions.[95]

Before the month's end, the Idaho legislature, which had ratified the ERA in 1972 with a two-thirds majority, rescinded it by a simple majority.[96] The vigil held by NOW demonstrators in the capitol rotunda during the vote became a wake. On February 1, Apostle Packer repeated his Idaho address in South Carolina, adapting it slightly for this audience.[97]

That spring, the Relief Society general presidency issued an informational flyer for the church's women, *Why Mormon Women Oppose the ERA*, summarizing the position that it was "unwise, unnecessary and uncertain." Primarily a legalistic argument, this constituted new language for the Relief Society as it decried an attempt to shift power from the states to the federal government and asserted that already existing statutes protected women as much as the ERA would. Of greatest fear was the ERA's uncertain future impact, which the Relief Society felt would guarantee a unisex society that condoned "homosexual and lesbian behavior" and other lifestyle changes, all of which would threaten the family, according to the flyer.

On June 4, Barbara Smith gave an anti-ERA speech to a gathering of Mormon women in Newport Beach, California.[98] Sharing the platform with her was Phyllis Schlafly, newly prominent in her position as the head of STOP ERA. Like the American Conservative Union, Daughters of the American Revolution, and John Birch Society, Schlafly had not enjoyed national prominence before the anti-ERA campaign beyond a reputation for far-right activism. The track records of these organizations made them deceptively easy to disregard, which proved to be a strategic error for pro-ERA women. As it turned out, Smith accurately perceived Schlafly to be an important ally in the anti-ERA fight and praised her passion and dedication to family values.[99] Smith gave this California speech only twenty days before Utah's IWY conference, and the events that Smith had already set in motion would soon train the nation's attention on the Salt Palace in downtown Salt Lake City.

In early 1976, the *Ensign* had asked Smith whether one could be a good Mormon and still support ratification of the ERA. She responded that she did not want to judge anyone's standing in the church, that the responsibility for such things rested with each individual. "[But] I personally would have difficulty opposing a policy of the First Presidency," she added, although she quickly qualified her statement to say she felt women who disagreed should be allowed to speak. "I would be unhappy if we tried to limit people who express their sincere beliefs," she said.[100]

Barbara B. Smith played a challenging and uncomfortable role in this unfolding drama. With her sparkling white hair coiffed in a trademark bouffant style, her warm smile, and her soft-spoken demeanor, she seemed the ideal LDS woman. Married to Douglas Hill Smith, an insurance executive who would later serve in the church's First and Second Quorums of the Seventy, Sister Smith was the mother of seven children and grandmother of seventeen. She had served on Belle Spafford's general board before her call to head the Relief Society herself in October 1974. The appointment came only two months before she was pitchforked into national controversy with her speech at the Institute of Religion in Salt Lake City. Before her calling to the Relief Society, she had served on the Child Abuse Committee of the Utah Division of Family Services, on the board of Salt Lake City's Para-Med Foundation, on the board of the Holladay Child Care Center, and as a PTA president at two different public schools. Although she had served in church positions on both the ward and stake levels, she had no professional employment or political experience.[101] Her main qualifications were that she had strong faith in her priesthood leaders and her church, and she also soon acquired a conviction that the ERA was not the right way for American women to be protected.

As the first Relief Society president under the new Priesthood Correlation Program that severely limited the Relief Society's autonomy, publications, fund-raising capabilities, and access to its own one million members worldwide, she was in the intimidating position of being the public spokesperson on two hot-button women's issues—the ERA and abortion—during a turbulent decade until her release in April 1984. It must have been difficult for her to step forward as the woman's face of the church's opposition to the ERA, but the Special Affairs Committee had helped her define the way the policy should be articulated. A loyal standard-bearer, she set an example of supportive obedience to priesthood leaders that created stress in her life but also provided her with their immensely comforting support. She could sincerely ask Mormonism's women to make the same decisions and engage in the same activities she had.

As Relief Society president, Barbara Smith navigated her way more-or-less successfully through the IWY meetings and anti-ERA campaign. In addition to the controversial public aspects of her calling, she quietly pushed for internal changes in lesson plans, programs, and policies to better educate Mormon women about being citizens of the world. In the months before IWY, she established ad hoc committees to investigate the needs of women and to suggest possible solutions. But she unquestionably became the lightning rod for much of the firestorm generated by Utah's IWY conference.

6. planning utah's IWY conference

> The sole purpose of the Meeting is to provide an environment where women and men from all parts of the State and cultures within the State may meet to articulate their positions on a variety of social, political, and legal questions facing women today. All participants in the Meeting are not only free to but encouraged to develop their own opinions and come to their own conclusions on all issues treated by the workshops.
>
> —Utah State IWY Coordinating Committee, 1977

In February 1976, Utah's Democratic governor Calvin L. Rampton chose Jan Tyler, a thirty-seven-year-old professor of education at Brigham Young University, to chair the state's IWY Coordinating Committee. Tyler was also a member of the Governor's Commission on the Status of Women and had been involved in national-level planning for these state conferences.[1]

Tyler grew up in Los Angeles as one of eight children. After studying speech, drama, and music at BYU, she traveled to Salzburg, Austria, with the school's first Semester Abroad program. After receiving her M.A.

from Arizona State University, she began work on a Ph.D. in educational administration. At Weber State University in Ogden, Utah, she became Dean of Women, Associate Dean of Students, and Assistant Professor of Student Personnel. BYU recruited her to teach child development and family relations and to direct its Family Consultation Center. Long active in Young Republicans, she had worked on political campaigns in Arizona and Utah and had served on the boards of various nonprofit foundations. A committed Mormon, she was also a ward Relief Society president and had served on the stake boards of the Sunday School and Young Women's Mutual Improvement Association.

In 1972 Tyler was invited to meet with an ad hoc committee of the U.S. State Department to offer input on a proposal to be sent to the president. She remembered feeling impressed that, despite her youth, her opinions were valued and that this "distinguished, powerful, well-educated group of women," nearly all of whom were "several years my senior," were interested in what she had to say. She recalled, "As I left the meeting, I recall praying, 'Dear Heavenly Father, please bless these good women with the courage needed to move forth with these important plans. Please withhold the divisive forces that will surely gather to thwart their execution. And if thou canst not attend to the latter, please bless the women of this world with a sensitivity to the lights within.'"[2]

Another memorable experience for Tyler was attending a seminar in New York City with Margaret Hoopes, a colleague from BYU's College of Family Living, sponsored by the American Association of University Women and the United Nations, to preview the international meeting scheduled for later that year. "I sat listening to the symphony of various languages and dialects, the gesturing, facial animation, the colorful dress reflecting various lifestyles, customs, and religious practices," she recalled. Although everything seemed foreign, she nevertheless felt at home. "I thought I would burst with the tremendous feeling of sisterhood and wondered that I, who had been raised within a faith that so frequently uses the reference 'sister,' would discover its inclusive, not exclusive, meaning through the women's movement."[3]

Over the next several months, Jan traveled back and forth between Washington D.C. and Utah, meeting with women on the National Commission and people she had in mind for the committee she was organizing in Utah. By January 1977, she had put together a coordinating committee of bright, articulate, politically involved Utah women. She selected women she had previously worked with or who had been recommended to form a seven-person executive committee who together chose twenty-six additional committee members. Local politician Katie Dixon was the vice chair and headed up the board of coordinating councils. As an elected public official, Dixon was aware of the importance of bringing more women into public office and appointing them to federal, state, county, and city boards and commissions.[4] Years of speaking out on a variety of public issues, particularly those that impacted the lives of women, had established her as a respected, intelligent voice for women. Sharon Keigher of Salt Lake City was a second vice chair and head of the task forces board. Keigher was a member of the Equal Rights Coalition of Utah and an experienced social service administrator. Interested primarily in the problems of poverty among women, she believed that "low-income women need special attention by women's organizations to the issues of employment opportunity and day care. . . . Single heads of households," she wrote, "are suffering because of our neglect."[5] Keigher had attended the International Women's Year conference in Mexico City and had been active in several organizations addressing the issues she was passionate about—equality, improved day care, affirmative action, social service funds for programs for women and girls, and services for female offenders.[6]

Margaret "Maggie" Wilde was a consultant and technical advisor to the group, bringing experience as a former programmer and conference planner for the University of Utah's Women's Resource Center. In her thirties, she had served on the executive board of the Utah Girl Scout Council and was herself a working mother. Understandably, she was concerned about the quality of public education and the availability of good day care.[7] Fiscal officer Dorothy Littrell was a member of the Utah Society of Certified Public Accountants. Suzanne M. Grua, historian and recorder, and Marilee Latta led out on public relations and media contacts for the state IWY committee.

Tyler recognized that because of the latitude she was given to organize an executive committee of her choosing, she would become "the target for all free-floating anxiety" over potential bias:

> It didn't matter whether people were pro or anti [on women's issues], and to a certain degree, maybe one way to look at it would be to say I was successful because nobody liked me. I really worked intensely to make sure that everything was even-handed. And while I was doing that I was keenly aware of all the other forces who were right-wing pulling it their way, and others with other interests pulling it their way, and that was a difficult thing to ride through.[8]

The executive committee discussed names in late January: leaders of ecclesiastical women's organizations, women representing diverse ethnic groups, and women who had an established track record in public service. Tyler's committee was not looking for women who shared political opinions or who had a common agenda, but rather women who were an established, positive presence in the community. Some were feminists, some were not. They lacked some elements of diversity in ways that mirrored the state's own profile. Eighteen came from Salt Lake City, four from Ogden, three from Provo, two from Granger, and one each from Cedar City, Helper, Kearns, Logan, Roy, and Sunset—in short, with one exception, nobody south of Provo. All but two were Mormon. Similarly, only two were non-Anglo and most were middle class. Bringing more diverse voices were Alice Kasai, a Japanese American of the Baha'i faith, and Maria Elena Perez, who was Hispanic and Catholic. One woman was in her thirties, nine in their forties, four in their fifties, and five were sixty or older. Critics accused the committee of being liberal and pro-ERA, but Tyler defended her choices as representing the diversity of the state.[9]

Many of the women were prominent in local politics. Dolores B. Bennett, for instance, was president of the Utah Federation of Women's

Republican Clubs and third vice president of the Utah Women's Legislative Council. In her own community, she was the chair of the Logan City Zoning and Planning Commission. Norma Matheson, whose husband was elected Utah governor in 1976, was an active Democrat and community activist in her own right.

Lynne Van Dam was the a member of the Equal Rights Coalition of Utah in 1977 and a member of the board of the YWCA, the League of Women Voters, the American Civil Liberties Union, and the Utah Women's Political Caucus. She was a dance teacher and director of Ballet Folklorico of Utah as well as an actress. It was thought her broad experience would prepare her for staging a large meeting.[10] Another committee member who was prominent in the women's movement locally was Shauna Adix, executive director of the Consortium of Utah Women in Higher Education, a member of the National Association for Women's Deans, and head of the Women's Resource Center at the University of Utah. Valora Treshow was regional vice president of the American Association of University Women and a member of the Equal Rights Coalition of Utah. Her interest was in helping women assume more responsible roles in government, politics, and business. She wrote, "Women should support and assist other women to assume positions for which their talents, skills and training qualify them."[11]

Alice Kasai and Alberta Almada, previously mentioned as those who diversified the otherwise overwhelmingly white and middle-class committee, were themselves able representatives of Utah's minorities. Almada was in her forties and described herself as being interested in "the vigorous enforcement of employment laws and regulations to protect minorities and women."[12] A proud Chicana woman, she felt she had "reached the point" in her life where she was no longer afraid to "stand up and say what I feel needs to be said." She brought with her considerable organizational experience, including service as vice chair of the Governor's Policy/Advisory Council on Hispanic Affairs.

A month before the coordinating committee held its first meeting on February 8, 1977, Tyler met with LDS Relief Society President Barbara B.

Smith. In a later interview, Sister Smith recalled that Professor Tyler, whom she already knew, had publicly expressed strong opposition to Smith's "stand against the Equal Rights Amendment." According to Smith, the professor was "very much a proponent of it. I met off and on with Jan Tyler and tried to explain why the Church felt as it did and especially why I had taken the stand that I had. But she still felt that she wanted to support the Equal Rights Amendment."[13]

As they had on other occasions, on February 8, Smith and Tyler discussed how to make Utah women part of the national agenda. Tyler asked President Smith to invite Mormon women to the mass meetings scheduled for the spring and to prepare a fact sheet on the national recommendations so Mormon women would be informed.[14] Smith, no doubt in consultation with her counselors and advisors, declined to prepare a fact sheet. Possibly she saw no way to provide "objective" information since she had already committed herself to a partisan position on issues that would come under discussion; almost certainly she could not see how to generate a fact sheet reflecting the church's position that would not exacerbate political tensions in the state.

However, beginning in March she began to meet weekly with Ezra Taft Benson, president of the Quorum of the Twelve Apostles, and other male church leaders, although the men would not take part in the ongoing controversy in a visible way.[15] Smith assigned two members of her general board to study each of the fourteen national resolutions (see Appendix 1) and to present their findings to the entire board. For example, Belva Ashton was assigned to fact-find on protection for abused women. According to President Smith, this was strictly educational; the general membership was "just left free" and advised that they should "make up their own minds—that they should use the same method that we did."[16] But the educational component was not strictly confined to the board. That spring, the board conducted informal surveys of Mormon women, asking what issues they thought were most important and what they hoped the conference might accomplish.[17] The group continued to meet after the conference about once every four months for an entire morning.

Women in this post-conference group included Jean Bickmore White, Grethe Ballif Peterson, and Aileen H. Clyde, who were not members of the general board.

Long before daffodils began sprouting in Salt Lake City gardens that spring, the IWY coordinating committee was fine-tuning preparations for the upcoming conference. The full committee first met on February 8, 1977. During this meeting, the women shared with each other their dreams for the conference and the issues they felt were key for the discussion among Utah's women. They had a budget of $25,000 from the federal government and planned to write a grant application for another $14,000 from the Utah Humanities Council.

Norma Matheson later acknowledged that "everyone on that planning committee was sensitive to the fact that there were extreme viewpoints." She mirrored the committee's belief, wistful in retrospect, that "this was a great time to get a dialogue with the various interests in the state." Speaking of the group's desires, she described how all hoped for a "bringing together and examining of the issues—almost an educational effort. Having everyone know where each other was coming from and in a meaningful dialogue. The hopes were very high."[18] Matheson put a positive spin on the committee's internal dissent. More candidly, Valora Treshow, a businesswoman from Salt Lake City, described the women's diversity of opinions and styles, evident at every meeting: "Not everybody on the Coordinating Committee was focused on having an open forum. There were a lot of private agendas, I think." She saw three different working styles: "very vocal" women whose positions were immediately clear, others who were "very subtle" but who had equally strong agendas, and some who were inexperienced at "working with other women" so that "you wonder[ed] how in the world they got the appointment."[19]

The committee was not working in a vacuum. The national and local Equal Rights Amendment battle was an inseparable context for the IWY conferences. Elder Boyd K. Packer and Relief Society President Smith had both spoken against the ERA the previous month in Idaho, and the Idaho legislature had just rescinded its ratification. Despite later claims that Tyler had "stacked" the committee with liberal feminists, the coordinating committee's minutes reveal disagreement about how to organize the conference and which issues should be addressed. For example, barely ten days before the convention, Kathleen Flake reported on the program that would be presented during the conference, the minutes disclosing a sharp interchange among the committee members:

> Georgia Beth Thompson inquired as to why the AGENDA had been prepared in such a tardy manner so as to make the Coordinating Committee just a rubber stamp rather than properly fulfilling their role under Public Law 97-167; why Belle Spafford, former General Relief Society President of the LDS Church, was a speaker specifically without the consent of the Coordinating Counsel and was advised that this [invitation] had been [made] several months previously by Jan Tyler and Katie Dixon of the Executive Committee; Gaye [sic] Littleton inquired as to the separation of Church and State in planning for this meeting and the lack of prior consent being sought from the Coordinating Committee; Dorothea Livingston inquired as [to] the possibility of the prayer and the posting of the colors being offered by the Native Americans (giving a short explanation of same), and was advised by Katie Dixon that Alice Kasai had already been requested to give the prayer (Baha'i) and the Girl Scouts had already been requested to post the colors; . . . Janet Daley noted that Esther Landa was President of the National Council of Jewish Women and that no one here had protested her place on the AGENDA as Presiding Officer.[20]

Esther Landa was often mentioned as the heroine of the IWY event.[21] Tyler announced her appointment in a press release on June 13, 1977, and described her as an activist for health, welfare, and education issues in Utah and nationally. "Much of Ms. Landa's concern has been for equal rights and advancement of women," Tyler announced. "She was Director of Women's Programs in the Division of Continuing Education at the University of Utah, and Director of the first Statewide Women's Conference of that University."[22] Landa had been instrumental in creating the Women's Resource Center at the university. So, the fact that Landa also served as an officer of a national religious organization had not appeared to the committee to be her most distinguishing qualification.

It is perhaps understandable that nerves were tightly strung. The spring had passed in a hectic crescendo of logistical, organizational, and political decisions against the backdrop of national attention to the deratification movement and a stepped-up tempo of resistance headed by the Mormon Church. The minutes show that in February, the committee considered several possible sites for the conference—local high schools, the Salt Palace Convention Center, and Westminster College. Dorothy Jones and Valora Treshow formed a committee to continue their search for the most appropriate accommodations. By the end of the month, they had decided on the Salt Palace because of its large meeting spaces, ample hallways, and access to convenient transportation. The group decided to make the conference two and a half days long, beginning with registration on Thursday afternoon and a speaker at an evening plenary session, concluding with final workshops on Saturday afternoon.

At the committee meeting on February 14, women pledged to start making lists of acquaintances to recruit for various task forces. They discussed the budget, how to house delegates, office space and supplies, and airfare to the national conference in Houston. They made specific assignments. For instance, Katie Dixon was to provide various women's organizations with up-to-date information. Also, because of her experience in local government, she was asked to serve as the conference's parliamentarian. Sharon Keigher was to schedule workshops on topics determined by the task forces to be of interest to Utah women. Maggie Wilde was to arrange for mechanical equipment and to be the contact person for set-up, technical problems, and emergencies. Marilee Latta would handle public relations and media concerns. Valora Treshow was to work with three other women to finalize site arrangements. Marilee Latta would also select films to be shown at the conference and organize a speakers bureau. Other assignments included fund raising by Lynne Van Dam, Lola Redford, and Kathleen Flake; a "Men's Council" to be organized by Ted Wilson and Norma Matheson; and Etta Diamenti to act as an organizational liaison.[23]

In addition, the task force chairs were asked to begin surveying local concerns on topics agreed upon by the coordinating committee. These corresponded roughly to the areas of focus in the national resolutions (see Appendix 2): minority concerns, international issues, state history, basic needs, the environment, work and income, relationships among differing groups, civil rights, education, outreach to both adults and youth, and the Utah State Plan of Action.[24]

The committee issued a press release on March 24 articulating its goals, history, and plans. It is unclear who drafted the memo, but it promised a convention that would "echo" the first women's rights meeting in America, the famed Seneca Falls conference in New York in 1848. The conference was said to meet U.S. President Gerald Ford's challenge to confront "those inequities that still linger as barriers to the full participation of women in our Nation's life."[25] The press release outlined the following agenda:

> We will respond for or against the proposed national resolutions regarding solutions to the barriers which women still face; we will create and respond for or against proposed state resolutions; we will produce a State Plan of Action to be presented to the Governor; we will produce a State Report to be sent to the National Commission; and we will elect 14 delegates to represent us at the Second World Conference on Women to be held in 1980.[26]

The committee expressed its belief that it represented the "diversity of women in the state" and that it was "determined to be an example . . . that diversity doesn't have to divide people, but that we can work together for a common goal."

> It is our hope that the State Meeting will serve as a catalyst for healing the wounds of polarization and isolation among some Utah women. We are interested in drawing out women from 16 years old to 100 years old and over. We especially want to involve rural women, students, ethnic women, homemakers, professional women—all women. Our aim is to also reach out to women who have no organizational affiliation and those who have never attended a women's conference.

The committee went out of its way to invite men because "the interests of women and men are indivisible and we cannot talk about the concerns of women without including concerned men." The hope was that "all" would come and "join with us in this massive problem solving effort. Our invitation is COME JOIN IN THIS UNITY OF PURPOSE. LET US WORK AND REASON THROUGH THESE ISSUES TOGETHER."[27]

On the same day this news release was issued, the coordinating committee met in the governor's boardroom of the state capitol, using the first half hour as a press conference. Jan Tyler set the stage with a description of the Seneca Falls conference and the document it produced, "The Declaration of Independence for Women." She mentioned the IWY conference held in Mexico City and the upcoming conference in Houston. She then fielded questions.[28]

On April 18 the coordinating committee considered feedback from its task forces and some additional topics, as yet unaddressed, that had been identified as particularly significant to Utah women. The committee assigned additional task forces to research these new areas for a total of twenty-two themes, around which the conference program would be organized: (1) aging; (2) arts and humanities; (3) basic needs—standard of living issues including poverty and single parenthood (no parallel category in the national resolutions); (4) child development (as opposed to the national resolution on "child care"); (5) education; (6) employment; (7) enforcement of laws (nationally included as part of reproductive freedom, rape, and credit, but not as a separate resolution); (8) the Equal Rights Amendment; (9) family violence (no national equivalent); (10) health; (11) international interdependence; (12) the legal status of homemakers; (13) lifestyles (no national equivalent); (14) media; (15) men (no national equivalent); (16) minority women; (17) polarization—the divisions between feminists and more traditional women; (18) power—especially in the workplace (no national equivalent); (19) rape; (20) female offenders; (21) women in Utah history (no national equivalent); and (22) young women.[29]

Tyler told the chairs that the task forces were "our major program tool . . . the first cut at formulating these issues, so that the entire conference can take hold of them and express its opinion about them."[30] The chairs and task force committees were given four assignments: to obtain data from multiple resources and assign members to research specific areas, brainstorm, and train coordinators to provide information to relevant groups before the conference. The two-hour workshops at the conference would be overseen by a facilitator for each topic, resource people, a recorder, and a reporter. Each workshop was intended to be information-oriented and to particularly consider the national commission's resolutions.

Throughout the early part of the year, the coordinating committee met weekly, mostly to dispense with "housekeeping" chores such as finding office space and making plans for working with the media. On March 8, Tyler reported on her meeting the previous week with members of the national commission in Washington D.C. They determined that regional mass meetings should be held throughout the state beginning May 16-20.[31] The committee also continued to devote considerable care to assisting the task force chairs, its "major program tool."[32]

On April 21 the committee held a public meeting at the state capitol to provide information about the conference and clarify the terms and policies set forth by the national commission. The Resolutions Subcommittee presented a list of preliminary resolutions they felt represented a consensus of women's views throughout the state, some of them mirroring, but others starkly contradicting, the national commission's recommendations, including the following Utah variants:

WHEREAS: Five million dollars of our tax money has been spent on IWY Conferences, we ask that federal, state, and local government deny further funds to the IWY Commission or any other group which promotes ratification of the Equal Rights Amendment.

WHEREAS: We reject any movement to eliminate from children's textbooks, gender. This includes Mother, Father, Miss, Mrs[.], Man, Woman, in that they are separate and autonomous, each in his own right.

WHEREAS: We reject Title IX with it's 20,000 words. We believe in equal opportunities and facilities but we also believe one sex should not be given preferential treatment over another. We request HEW to withdraw Title IX Regulations from all education including undergraduates and especially private schools.

WHEREAS: We wish to go forward to Basic Education Concepts with Math, American History, World History, Free Enterprise Economics, English, Grammar, Spelling, Writing and Music back in the schools. [sic] We deplore the progressive education that is now present in our schools.

WHEREAS: We deplore showing pornographic films in classes on sex education. We desire to have the schools free from any sex and family life education. We reserve that right to ourselves as parents of those children.

WHEREAS: We recommend that the religion of Humanism be eliminated from school curriculum and that Evolution be taught as theory and not fact.

WHEREAS: We deny there should be civil rights for homosexuals; these become special privileges. We affirm our approval of Anita Bryant's philosophy that our children should not be taught [in the public schools] by homosexuals.

WHEREAS: We reserve the right to bring about Liberty and Justice for all. We declare that equality is a false concept and a fraud because no one is equal, no thing is equal.

WHEREAS: We believe that sexual assault should remain a crime against the victim and that it not be lessened to any extent under the common law.

WHEREAS: We affirm that marriage must be based on mutual respect and communication. Any act of sterilization is not a private matter. It is for both spouses to decide.

WHEREAS: We believe in equal pay for equal work but we reject preferential treatment for women over men—or quotas.[33]

The attendance at this meeting was disappointingly small, but these resolutions, in their determinedly conservative spirit, were a startlingly accurate reflection of the majority views that would be articulated two months later at the state conference.

The most conspicuous and controversial part of the coordinating committee's two-pronged task was finalizing the format for open-forum discussions. They brainstormed about various strategies, not wanting the artificiality and built-in adversarialism of staged debates but apprehensive about open meetings deteriorating into shouting matches. Their goal was to allow women to disagree with each other and resolve their differences civilly.[34] This format would require skilled facilitators who could present high-quality information and keep the group focused and on task.

Sharon Keigher proposed that "at least 100 staff members" from the Utah State Department of Social Services be invited to facilitate the conference workshops.[35] This idea was accepted, and the Social Services staff provided expert discussion leaders, useful data, and consultation on issues that seemed particularly relevant to the state's women. Tony Mitchell, executive director of Social Services, also assisted in planning for child care. Keigher estimated they would receive up to 1,000 children aged 3-9 and thought the elementary schools might be "staffed with volunteers supervised by qualified providers."[36] Again, this proposal was accepted. In addition to local schools, rooms at the Salt Palace itself were reserved for this purpose.

Publicity for IWY activities began in Washington D.C. on January 13 with a "Women's State of the Union Address" by Karen DeCrow, president the National Organization for Women (NOW). Intense lobbying by prominent NOW leaders such as Eleanor Smeal, who would soon be elected national NOW president, assured Indiana of becoming the thirty-fifth state to ratify the ERA on January 27 despite a major push by Phyllis Schlafly and her supporters to kill the amendment. Elsewhere the news was not so good for ERA boosters. On the same day, January 27, the forty-member Virginia Senate came within one vote of a majority needed to ratify the ERA, while in Idaho, LDS leaders Boyd Packer and Barbara

Smith delivered their speeches urging rescission of the state's ERA ratification. The legislature accommodated the request.

On February 1, Senator Jake Garn inserted Elder Packer's anti-ERA speech into the Congressional Record. The Nevada senate ratified the ERA on February 9, with Lieutenant Governor Bob Rose casting the tie-breaking vote. Pro-ERA forces celebrated, but two days later the Nevada assembly rejected it 24-15. Eleven of the negative votes were from Democrats who had run as pro-ERA candidates, using pro-ERA campaign workers and accepting contributions from pro-ERA organizations and donors. Some had voted for the ERA in the 1975 session. But according to the *Feminist Chronicles,* because of "unprecedented pressure from the Nevada Legislature's Mormon Bishops who held key positions in the state's power structure," they switched their positions.[37]

Vermont was the first to hold its state women's conference. On February 26 more than a thousand women and men braved a large snow storm to assemble and pass resolutions supporting the ERA, affirmative action, scholarships for female students, and improvements in day care. Exit polls indicated that 45 percent of the women in attendance had never attended a women's conference before.[38]

After Tennessee and Nebraska followed Idaho's lead in rescinding their support of the ERA, the U.S. Justice Department informed President Carter's counsel that, in their opinion, rescission was illegal and unconstitutional.[39] In March, California NOW announced a boycott of Nevada because of its continued refusal to ratify the ERA, and the California Women Lawyers Association encouraged its members to avoid vacationing or scheduling professional meetings there.[40] Clifford Cummings, president of the LDS Oakton Virginia Stake, following the counsel of Apostle Benson's letter to stake presidents, spoke against the ERA at a Sterling Park Ward gathering in March.[41] Florida Mormons, who were funded in part by contributions from California, lobbied strenuously against the ERA in Tallahassee. They felt jubilant when the senate refused to ratify, 21-19. An angry Eleanor Smeal noted that "two long-time supporters . . .

made a last-minute switch to the opposition that blocked ratification, following the Nevada pattern."[42]

Meanwhile, Jan Tyler and her IWY Utah committee "kept talking about outreach, trying to get as many women involved as possible," recalled Esther Landa.[43] Between January and June, committee members met with women's organizations: the Council of Church Women, the Utah Federation of Women's Clubs, the LDS Relief Society general presidency, and other groups.

Barbara Smith appreciated the potential for a statewide gathering that expressed opposition to the ERA. She knew that many of the faithful already resented national resolutions on issues of human life, family, and morality. She and other church leaders did not oppose the IWY, but they took a stance against abortion and reproductive freedom. For Smith, not to do so would have been to deny her calling as a spiritual leader of women. Furthermore, as Smith explained in her published memoirs, her two counselors, Janath R. Cannon and Marion R. Boyer, agreed that it would be "folly for the state of Utah to be represented only by nonmembers or by inactive members of the Church, and that the issues to be discussed needed to be addressed by all Mormon women."[44]

Still, the long-standing tradition of avoiding political involvement was a line the church had learned not to cross casually. Smith was determined to not politicize the Relief Society by siding with one political platform and opted instead for an indirect method. With the approval of her priesthood leaders, she asked the church's *Deseret News* to publish a series of articles explaining key issues that would be discussed at the state IWY meetings. One of these articles quoted her saying attendance at the conference was "vital for women, especially LDS women," and more emphatically that "Mormon women everywhere" should "become part of the decision making process by registering as delegates and by making themselves eligible to become delegates to the national conference."[45] "When we sent the letter out inviting wards to have women from each stake come," she later explained, "we also asked them to read the information that would be in the paper so that they would be apprised of the issues because we felt they should come knowledgeably participating in the conference."[46]

In speaking to the *Deseret News*, Smith added that the "light of the gospel" was crucial in the "deliberations of nations." "Mormon women," she continued, were "intelligent, capable representatives who can study issues with eternal perspectives in mind." She cited a "long history of conviction that each individual has responsibility for his or her actions as a citizen" and that "to let decisions of a vital nature be made without participation is unthinkable."[47] Despite her emphasis on education and independent thinking, as well as a determination to remain clear on principle and uncommitted about practice, her careful wording and partial reticence backfired. A year later she told an interviewer that regretfully her message gave "sanction" to various outside groups to "gain a foothold" so "it looked like the Relief Society [was] sponsoring certain things and we were not." There was lobbying by "extremist groups and anybody who took the opportunity to use any method they wanted to get to the women."[48]

President Smith seems to have been genuinely surprised by this turn of events as Relief Society women were increasingly subjected to the influence of conservative interest groups. She was not alone. Women on both sides of the issues were startled by the passionate responses, by the overflowing attendance at the conferences, and by the heat of the emotions. The intensity of virtually all aspects of the Utah conference shocked almost everyone involved. Across the board, women were unprepared for what happened.

As late as May, no one would have predicted the explosion. The coordinating committee minutes suggest that the decision to hold mass meetings in outlying areas, an innovation that no other state was utilizing, was made in February. One reason was that women in rural areas might not be able to attend the Salt Lake conference in June and that at mass meetings, their voices could be heard, their opinions recorded, and the results provided to the chairs of the task forces organizing the conference sessions.[49] Jan Tyler appointed Kathleen Flake to coordinate the outreach gatherings and choose the issues to be discussed there.

During March and April, Flake asked school district superintendents throughout the state to make a school available for a meeting as close to May 16 as possible. She organized committees of local volunteers to oversee the planning, scheduling, publicity, and recruitment—the first-contact volunteers being women the coordinating committee knew or were aware of from Status of Women commission files and leadership of women's and girls' groups. Flake worked with other members of the coordinating committee, who performed some of the more specialized tasks. Marilee Latta and her committee handled publicity.[50] The coordinating committee sent out recruiting letters to women's organizations, school PTAs, or other groups and individuals.[51] Georgia Beth Thompson's letter, "Participate in GRASS ROOTS DEMOCRACY!" went to women in Iron County. It emphasized that IWY "IS NOT A LOBBY GROUP. Our purpose is to listen and collect the concerns of all women in Utah. WE DO NOT REPRESENT ANY ONE POINT OF VIEW. We are merely providing a forum for ALL VOICES to be heard and so that ALL may participate in the 'grass roots' process.'" It concluded, "WE ARE INTERESTED IN DIALOGUE, not agreement."[52]

The preliminary agenda for the mass meetings showed two hours carefully scheduled for members of the committee or local political leaders to explain the IWY and the history of the event and how Utah's conference fit into the national plan. The women would receive and discuss *To Form a More Perfect Union,* which contained the national resolutions. They would also receive fact sheets that reflected the research conducted by the Utah task forces, along with questionnaires. After the chairs explained these documents, the women would divide into small discussion groups. Each group would prioritize the issues and create a separate report to the full group, which would assemble these reports and send them to the coordinating committee. During the final thirty minutes, the chair would explain the state meeting and give directions on time, how to find the Salt Palace, and how to participate in the voting, along with other information about car pools, babysitting, and literature.[53] Feedback was a critical issue. "Their voice is important," the sample agenda reminded organizers.[54]

The agenda was eventually revised to allow for an even more informal approach. The introductory lectures were dropped. The chair would group the women by sixes and ask them to brainstorm on issues that concerned them most, then prioritize the items.

Except for a sprinkling of early birds or stragglers, the mass meetings were held between May 16 and 21, usually in high schools, where the groups of six women each brainstormed in school libraries and cafeterias and produced 712 lists of issues. Exit interviews showed that the most critical topics for these women were the ERA, abortion, "preserving the family," education, and interestingly, "sexism in textbooks, scholarships, financial aid and hiring practices." Women were concerned about equal pay for equal work, sex roles, job discrimination, media violence and portrayal of women in the media, child care, pornography, Title IX, family planning, career development, rape, women in politics, credit, criminal justice, care and rights of the elderly, the status of homemakers, and federal interference in private lives.[55]

"We didn't ask women to vote 'yes' or 'no' on any issue," explained Valora Treshow of the coordinating committee. Georgia Beth Thompson confirmed this: "We simply asked them what things worried them the most, . . . what their primary concerns were. We wanted to be sure to focus on these things in our conference."[56] Attendance was typically between fifty and a hundred. Although feelings sometimes ran high and the debate was occasionally energetic, according to Kathleen Flake, "the anger usually generated by such issues was never a factor in the discussion. This, perhaps, was the most rewarding aspect of the mass meeting experience." It seemed that for the first time women with different viewpoints and backgrounds met in what she saw as a "truly open discussion on those issues with which they strongly identify." In fact, "never have so many disagreed so strongly about so much with so little rancor."[57] In retrospect, the IWY-coordinated mass meetings were the honeymoon before an acrimonious divorce.

One of the earliest meetings was sponsored by the Women's Council of Provo on April 30. According to the minutes, the chair welcomed those in attendance and the task force chairs gave three-minute presentations on issues. The group then divided into smaller groups and brainstormed priorities. Reba Keele, an organizational behaviorist at BYU, delivered a presentation on dealing with group dynamics. The meeting concluded with a question-and-answer session.[58]

Significantly, Barbara Smith received a letter written on May 23 from Norma Cheney and Barbara Reynolds, reporting on the Idaho IWY held May 21-22. They estimated that of the 1,000 women at the conference, only 10 percent were Mormon. Four of them, including Cheney, had run unsuccessfully as delegates to the Houston convention. The NOW women, according to Reynolds and Cheney, were "very radical and liberal" and "knew what they wanted, and they knew who to vote for and how to vote."[59]

The Mormon women sensed a conspiracy to keep them from full participation in the Idaho meetings. They were "told that it was to be an opinion conference and not a voting conference" and were segregated from the rest of the crowd and given incorrect information, according to the informants. "In the evening," they reported, "the LDS women were told it was time for dinner. While [we] went out to dinner, much voting was done among the rest of the women. Amendments were brought forth from the NOW organization. An amendment was passed allowing women to receive money [for] . . . counseling in lesbianism."

In an accompanying letter, Cheney noted that between 200 and 300 NOW supporters were in attendance. "It was obvious," Cheney wrote, "that they were here to push through every resolution they could to further their cause." She thought "their manner of conduct was anything but lady-like. They booed and hissed anyone who offered a dissenting argument." By contrast, they passed "such things as federally financed abortions, sex education in the schools without parental consent, end to discrimination of people because of their sex preference, and on and on. . . . These were very upsetting to us who did not wish to have this reflect the thinking of the LDS woman," she wrote.

Angered at what they saw as a takeover, Reynolds and Cheney talked early the morning of the second day and tried to strategize about ways to turn the meeting around. "We met with several other women," she wrote. "We decided that it might help us gain some direction if we could have some advice from the Priesthood." After a meeting at the local LDS Institute of Religion building with some of the "brethren we knew in the area," they drew up a dissenting opinion to present on the floor in the afternoon session to be included in the final report. The reason she was writing to Smith, Cheney explained, was because she hoped "we might be better prepared to express an effective voice in some of the resolutions that go to the national conference and eventually to the president of the United States from other states."[60]

The Idaho conference profoundly influenced the planning of Utah's meetings. Belva Ashton, a member of Barbara Smith's general board, recalled the alarm when "we started getting reports from Church women, like in Idaho, Colorado and in other places." These reports painted a picture of outrage, Mormon attendees complaining that "hey, it was railroaded. We went there, and they would not allow us to participate. They would not allow us to nominate people from the floor."[61] Colorado's meeting followed Idaho's on June 3-5 with similarly disappointing results for conservatives. To Smith and Ashton, it seemed more important than ever that Relief Society women in Utah come en masse to the Salt Palace to fight the feminist agenda, the ERA, and the liberal platform of the national commission.

Smith took her concerns to the male leadership of the church. In response, Apostle Benson called the church's regional representatives for Utah and asked them to have each ward in Utah send ten women to the IWY conference. Two days later, on June 3, Elder Benson sent a follow-up letter with specific instructions:

> Stake Relief Society presidents in Utah will be asked to: 1. encourage LDS

> women in their stake to read the *Deseret News* articles in order to become informed regarding the rules of the IWY meeting: voting times, procedures, recommendations, and how delegates are selected, including how nominations from the floor should be made; 2. select one capable and experienced LDS woman who could speak from the floor at the convention, as a concerned citizen; 3. encourage at least ten women and hopefully many more from each ward to attend the convention workshops as "registered participants" ($2 fee). This will enable them to vote and be in a position to support good recommendations, and to file a minority dissenting report if necessary. 4. encourage LDS women to call friends, neighbors or women affiliated with other churches who share mutual concerns, and ask them to attend the convention also.[62]

On June 7, Barbara Smith and her counselors sent the same regional representatives a letter to be read in ward Relief Societies urging women to "become part of the decision making process by registering as delegates and by making themselves eligible to become delegates to the national conference."[63] Smith and her counselors included copies of Elder Benson's letter for each bishop, stake president, and Relief Society president in given jurisdictions.

When Jan Tyler first heard about the letter, she "really felt like she was put in a bind because she personally was very involved with women's concerns, and she did not—had never up to that point—felt like she had to make choices between the Church and what she was doing." She talked with Kathleen Flake and other committee members. They did rough calculations of how many women might come to the conference and they guessed there might be a flood of maybe seven or eight thousand. "This is disastrous," Flake remembered saying.[64]

As chair of the fund-raising committee, Flake wrote to the First Presidency on June 13 requesting funds to accommodate the "estimated additional three to four thousand women who will respond to President Barbara Smith's and President Ezra Taft Benson's recent request that 'at least ten women and hopefully many more' from each ward in the State attend the Utah State Women's Meeting."[65] Flake's professional work was in the church's Development Office, so she made the request of her employers reluctantly. She knew the church "is a charitable society which has its own need for philanthropic support. However, because of the short time given to the Coordinating Committee to accommodate the more than 200 percent increase in attendance," the committee was suddenly in dire need of more financial support.[66] She explained that the IWY's budget would be about $10,000 short. If the coordinating committee could not raise more money, it would have to close registration—which would shut out the women who were obediently flocking to register. However, the church chose not to provide any funding. The conference budget was patched together with $25,000 from the federal government, $14,000 from the Utah Endowment for the Humanities, and $6,000 from private donors.

The state did not provide direct appropriation, but it did make in-kind contributions and significant gestures of moral support. Both Ted Wilson, mayor of Salt Lake City, and Governor Scott Matheson issued special proclamations in support of the conference. Governor Matheson designated June as Utah Women's Month and the mayor proclaimed Thursday, June 23, Women's Day. Matheson's declaration mentioned the IWY's goal of identifying "barriers that prevent women from participating fully and equally in all aspects of national life, and to develop recommendations for means to remove such barriers." Wilson's proclamation anticipated the "improved communication, increased awareness and the formulation of common goals" at Utah's first state-wide women's meeting.

According to Georgia Peterson, the task of coordinating the Relief Society and Special Affairs Committee in anti-IWY activity fell to Belva and Wendell Ashton, who were respectively in the leadership of the two organizations.[67] The Young Women's general president, Ruth Hardy Funk, who was on the IWY coordinating committee, met several times with Barbara Smith and other women leaders. On June 6, Robert B. Hales, then a member of the First Quorum of the Seventy and later an apostle, asked Funk for a copy of the address that former Relief Society President Belle S. Spafford would be delivering at the opening plenary session on June 24.[68]

Beginning on June 16, with the state conference only a week away, Barbara Smith met daily with Georgia Peterson, Moana Bennett of the Relief Society general board, Oscar W. McConkie, and Wendell Ashton to talk about delegates to the national convention and to develop strategies for the state conference.[69] Georgia Peterson had never met Moana Bennett before but learned that she wrote many of Barbara Smith's speeches and was a key member of the leadership team. Before the week's end, President Smith stopped coming to the meetings.[70] McConkie and Peterson intensively reviewed the rules for the conference. According to Peterson's recollection, the decision was made that the Relief Society would get involved but not advise women on how to vote.[71]

Florence Smith Jacobsen, former Young Women's general president and director of the Museum of Art and Church History, was adamant that the church did not involve itself in the conference. She told an interviewer: "The church itself was not involved. . . . We were women with our own opinions. We [were], of course, members of the church and [that] . . . couldn't help but influence us in our voting."[72]

But suspicion, anger, dread, and loyalty decided the battle lines that were forming, forcing women like Tyler to make difficult choices. Tyler's role as chair of the coordinating committee was complicated. On June 8, not yet informed of the Relief Society letters, she sent a memo to her committee members reminding them of the importance of what they were doing. "The closer we come to our LIFE LINES (rather than deadlines)," she wrote, "perhaps the greater our anxiety will be." She encouraged everyone to simplify their efforts and continue to give feedback. She cautioned: "We've already had fair warning that what we do will be scrutinized very carefully. Let's in sisterhood be sensitive and critical about those things which need special attention so that we can stand up—together—with confidence under that scrutiny." Appreciative of the hundreds of hours each had put into their assignments, she believed that in the future they would be proud of what they had done together. "Each of us, working together, has had a hand in creating a portion of history."[73]

This view helped Tyler maintain her emotional equilibrium during a series of unpleasant encounters with Utah's Republican senator Orrin Hatch, a strong and vocal opponent of the ERA. According to Tyler, he telephoned her several times in an attempt to "take complete control of the conference" or bully her into agreeing to mute discussions on the national recommendations.[74] Tyler did not keep her notes, but she remembered Hatch's effort to influence the final plans.[75] When someone from Hatch's staff called the IWY office, no one wanted to talk to him. Tyler said the male staff member who called "was screaming at me, telling us how we were supposed to do things and everything else."[76]

As the first day of the conference approached, suspicion, intrigue, and rumors increased and swirled around the state. Tyler attempted, in statements to the press, to disarm the growing mistrust. "There have been numerous attempts to divide women as we anticipate coming together to find solutions," she told the *Salt Lake Tribune* four days in advance. She re-emphasized their intent to seek solutions, not to "destroy personalities or to participate in divisiveness." For those "who would attend to disrupt and divide, . . . we have a compassion. To those who come with a deep desire to treat each with dignity, we join hands."[77]

Despite Barbara Smith's steadfast claim that the general authorities were not involved except in offering her counsel when requested, feminists were ready to believe that at least some church leaders had contacted groups like the John Birch Society.[78] On June 22, the Tuesday night before the conference began, a coordinating committee member was at a Bountiful High School meeting where a slate of twenty-one church-approved candidates for the national convention was passed out to conference registrants. Georgia Peterson, who had prepared the list for her organization, Let's Govern Ourselves (LGO), denied that it was an "official LDS list." "I wish I had that kind of authority. I don't," she said.[79] But for Mormon women, there was confusion about whether the list originated with LGO, the Conservative Caucus, or church headquarters. LGO provided a list of crucial sessions for women to attend with instructions about what to do at them. Another of its handouts read:

8:30. Rules Meeting—be there to vote a loud "AYE" when it's proposed that "All delegates that sent in applications to IWY be considered as nominees." This is to be proposed by one of our group in opposition to Resolution #13 (may be another [number] by then, however) which gives the Executive Committee the right to disqualify any nominee to the National Convention.

9:15. Nominations from the floor—If our "AYE" vote doesn't carry, we will move to extend nominating time to 60 minutes (prev. 30). Then we will attempt to nominate as many people from the list above as possible.

1:00-3:00 and 3:30-5:30. Variety of Workshops—attend those which interest you most and express your views and (especially) give positive alternatives and recommendations.[80]

Peterson said the LGO emerged out of meetings between the Relief Society leaders and general authorities the second week in June, that she met five times with Oscar McConkie, senior partner in the church's law firm, Kirton & McConkie, and Wendell Ashton, head of Public Communications and member of the Special Affairs Committee, and then spent two hectic weeks crisscrossing the state to promote Let's Govern Ourselves.[81] The group's main effort was to revise the convention rules, which she believed had been set up to favor the delegates nominated by the coordinating committee.

In party politics, it is not unusual to offer a list of preferred candidates or to quibble over procedural rules. So far, this was business as usual in the give and take of contrasting political views. But a runaway train was roaring down on the IWY scene. Relief Society officers, with no more information than the letters they had received, selected women in their wards to participate in the conference. Hundreds of these obedient women scrambled for information. Defensive and frightened because of the warnings about threats to their families, anxious to take the "right" action to protect them, and trusting in their leaders, these traditional women were also confused because although the principles were clear, the desired implementation was fuzzy. What were they supposed to do to protect their families? Given the level of tension, coupled with a strong anti-ERA stand and, simultaneously, the odd reserve of Relief Society leaders and general authorities to present a clear plan of action, these anxious mothers and homemakers were ripe for mobilization.

For secular right-wing organizations whose agendas already included deep mistrust of "liberal" causes like the ERA, providing specific leadership was not only easy but logical. Phyllis Schlafly's Eagle Forum was such an organization. A second group that seized the opportunity was the 120-member Conservative Caucus, led by Dennis Ker, bishop of the Kearns 22nd Ward and director of Utah's 2nd Congressional District. Ker described the caucus as a "nationwide organization for lobbying. It's non-partisan," he said, "and its purpose is to give grassroots input into the government which we feel they [government officials] don't really get from the majority of the people."[82] The John Birch Society's monthly *Utah Independent* published Ker's denial just before the IWY conference of being a Birch member but confirmed that some of his group were. Ker told the *Independent* he was organizing Mormon women to participate in Utah's IWY because of "horror stories" that had filtered in from other state IWY conferences.

When Jan Tyler became aware that Ker was planning pre-conference meetings, she telephoned and said: "It's come to my attention that you seem to have some concerns about what you think this whole conference is going to be about. I'd really like to respond to any questions you have, share any information. I want you to be informed."[83] Tyler went to his house with three other committee members; but as a measure of the polarization that existed, only Tyler entered the house after their initial reception. Tyler remembered Ker as a fairly young man in his early thirties with light brown hair, of average size and build. She later remembered, "I gave him some information and I was a little confrontational with him, not in an argumentative way, but in that 'Look, quit trying to twist things' [way]. . . . He seemed to receive what I had to say. We did dialogue and talk."[84] She left feeling that he had at least listened to her viewpoint, although he made no promises, nor would he agree to cancel upcoming meetings to warn women about the IWY's alleged hidden agenda.

The Conservative Caucus had two objectives: to stop the ERA and to disrupt the IWY's feminist goals.[85] The group never disclosed the source of its funding, but it had enough to sponsor at least fourteen meetings at locations similar to those used for the mass meetings (usually schools), publish handouts, and publicize its activities in the *Utah Independent*.[86] According to Ker, the group formulated its plans at monthly meetings at which they heard reports about the IWY conventions and discussed possible strategies and a plan to mobilize the state's women.[87] Ker insisted that the caucus did not call Relief Society women directly but simply piggy backed on the efforts of the ward Relief Society presidents and bishops. He said at least four women organized their own local meetings and invited him to speak.[88]

According to the *Salt Lake Tribune*, Ker met with Barbara Smith to offer to conduct educational meetings for the Relief Society. Smith declined, saying it would not be possible to work through church channels. Ker said he "talked with her to see what she knew about the IWY convention and told her we planned to inform our women. The next day I called her to check on some delegates who were on the slate the IWY committee was drawing up."[89] He wanted to know the proposed delegates' stands on the ERA, abortion, and Title IX. His next step was to announce a meeting at Highland High School, saying "the Mormon Church officials knew about his plans before he started his campaign."[90] He estimated that as many as 6,000 people attended his workshops during a single week. When asked if the women believed they were attending a church-organized meeting, he replied, "I don't think there is any question."[91]

Dennis Ker identified himself as a "concerned father of five children" whose only intent was to provide education. Yet, he clearly played on women's fears, warning them that the IWY proposals were deceitfully written and baited with hidden hooks. He distributed an article by Phyllis Schlafly, "Federal Financing of a Foolish Festival for Frustrated Feminists," reporting on the state women's meetings that had already been held. In addition, he provided a list of endorsements for national delegates. One of the more bizarre instructions he gave the women was to not attend the movies scheduled for the conference because they might depict pornography and aberrant sexuality.[92]

Ker was careful to maintain that he had not called Mormon women to attend his meetings, but that word had gotten out informally.[93] He planned three of the meetings himself and attended numerous others, he said. Not that he was shy about claiming partial credit for the high attendance at the IWY conference in June: "I think that before [attending my seminar,] many of the women were totally uninformed about the issues and now they are informed and [I believe] that these women will never be the same. They came with these proposals for the workshops, too. We didn't draft the proposals for them. We didn't want to tell the women what to do except we did give them information about a slate of delegates and the national proposals."[94]

Georgia Peterson belatedly became aware that Ker was using her group's name and that, to promote his meeting at Highland High School, he "was purporting that [it would] be representative of the 'Let's Govern Ourselves' crowd." She went and sat in the balcony where an estimated thousand women filled the auditorium.

Ker was seated on stage alongside Erma Christensen, an officer in the conservative American Party and writer for the *Utah Independent,* and Doris Wilson of the Conservative Caucus. When Ker began speaking, he referred to "Let's Govern Ourselves" as if he represented the group. Incensed, Peterson stood up, walked down to the stage and interrupted him at the microphone. She introduced herself and said she had never been consulted about the meeting and had not been invited. She said that even though many in the audience might be sympathetic with various right-wing groups that had planned the presentation, Peterson felt uncomfortable with the content of the meeting: "He had been saying things about the various study groups that were organized. You want to go in there and you want to march, you want to vote 'NO' on these things. And he had a list of things that he was very much opposed to. And I can't remember exactly, but what he was saying offended me to the point that I had the nerve to get up and walk up, uninvited, and take over the microphone." She added with a note self-deprecating humor, "I mean, this," referring to herself, "is a woman who has no sense."[95]

Peterson also remembered that she was so angry, there was "fire" in her eyes when she snatched the microphone and reassured the audience: "Look, you don't need to go in there and be frightened. I mean, this is a meeting of women. You can go in, you can voice your opinion, you can [take a] stand, . . . and this can be fun. This is the legislative process." Recalling the moment years later, emotion swept over her and she said in a choked voice, "I truly thought [what I said was true]." After marching off the high school stage, several women followed her and held a "mini caucus" in the parking lot.

The anecdote may seem to illustrate a fleeting moment of excessive zeal on Ker's part, but it represented a pattern of conservative hijacking of the type traditionalists suspected the liberals of. Representatives of various conservative groups asked the Relief Society general presidency for permission to hold instructional meetings for the church's women. According to Smith, the presidency consistently refused to endorse these independent pre-conference meetings. "We would only give them [the women] information through the newspapers. We said that we would not even tell them what they could or could not do," Smith recalled. "But there were those who contacted friends and held meetings to tell the women of the dangers that they would face and how they might be railroaded into accepting proposals that would not really represent their beliefs."[96]

The church's public communications spokesman, Don LeFevre, was interviewed by the *New York Times* a month after the state conference and denied that the church had instructed Relief Society members how to vote. He did acknowledge that the church had publicized its positions on the ERA, abortion, and other key issues "in case they [the women] had any questions" about these. Moreover, he said, it is standard political procedure for institutions to make public their positions and to encourage their members or constituencies to support those positions and voice their opinions by voting.[97]

As early as the first week in May, "different people" approached Norma Udall, a Special Education teacher who had chaired the mass meeting in Orem, and "asked me to run" as a delegate to the Houston conference. "Several people just sort of got behind me and pushed it, I mean, more than I was prepared for, really."[98] As a widow, she was sensitive to the way society treated older women and single women.

Belva Ashton decided to run on her own initiative. She saw an "announcement . . . in the paper," she recalled. "No one . . . suggested to me, 'Why don't you go and submit your name to be a delegate to Houston?' But I decided I would. . . . And I didn't talk with anyone—Wendell or anyone else. I just thought, 'This is something I'd like to do [and] I ought to do, I feel [so] strongly about some of the issues.'"[99] Her commitment captured the seriousness of those who similarly felt compelled to participate because the issues had deep personal and social significance to them. They felt obligated to become informed, to attend the Utah conference, and to defend traditional family and religious values at the national meeting. They knew they were challenging national trends and would be unpopular, but they felt strongly that they had been called, as a religious duty, to take a stand.

Zelda B. McAllister put her name on the ballot because she believed the feminist portrayal of the ERA was dangerous. She wrote, "The Era [sic] is made to look like an aid to women when the truth is it will take away so many of our rights and keep us from being happy homemakers, wifes [sic], and mothers."[100]

In the countdown weeks prior to the conference, religion and politics became inextricably fused in the minds of many LDS women. Numerous women received telephone calls from the same church leaders (bishops and Relief Society officers) to attend the Conservative Caucus's meetings who had asked them to attend the conference itself.[101] Still, both the Conservative Caucus and Let's Govern Ourselves denied any direct connection between these meetings and any involvement by the church.[102]

The Conservative Caucus gave women one simple task, to vote "no" on all recommendations from the national commission, and one simple reason for it, to protect their families. This single-item action list was one of the most explosive and polarizing aspects of the June conference. The Conservative Caucus, the Eagle Forum, and LGO repeatedly characterized the national proposals as an embodiment of the liberal feminist agenda, anti-family, and anti-religion. The blanket order to vote "no," which was based in fear, did not come from the Relief Society, the *Deseret News,* or any general authorities or LDS group. Still, the combination of official silence on some points and knowledge that church officials were holding strategy sessions about the conference provided an atmosphere in which rumors went a long way, hints took the place of hard information, and suggestions assumed the force of official instructions. Stereotypes reigned in place of logic. At the conservative caucuses, in the literature circulated by the Relief Society, and in the LGO meetings, a simple dichotomy pitted feminists against homemakers, the latter portrayed as guardians of home and family values. This polarization poisoned the debate on virtually every issue. The use of ecclesiastical settings, ecclesiastical language, quotations from scriptures and leaders, and the judicious mention of ecclesiastical office such as Ker's position as a bishop allowed an intense combination of anxiety and resolution to develop.

Dennis Ker was proud of the turnout and voting behavior of Utah's women. He said: "I felt after the first day that some people had had hurt feelings. The IWY committee had done a lot of work and their proposals weren't accepted, but I feel that that's because they didn't reflect the majority of the women in Utah, and we think that majority is conservative. I was proud of the way the majority of women acted. I think the views of the majority were represented."[103]

Barbara Smith realized only too late how skillfully these outside groups had used the Mormon network. In a post-conference interview, she admitted that when she first met Ker: "I was a little afraid . . . of his political stand, and so I did not give him approval even though I did listen to what he had to say and did tell him . . . that he could do whatever he wanted. But I didn't even think about him doing some of the things he did."[104] When Smith learned in early June that Ker was using her name and the church's name, she immediately notified him that this was not appropriate and that he was misrepresenting the church.[105] She did not state exactly when she took this action, but as matters turned out, it was too late. For many traditional women—as well as for Mormon feminists who saw what was happening—the church's agenda was one and the same as that of the conservative right. The reason, Ker said, that women attending his caucus meetings thought they were "being held under the auspices of the Relief Society"[106] was because women were "informed by their Relief Society presidents about [the conservative] sessions and that may have added to their confusion."[107]

Smith blamed much of the subsequent conference hysteria on those who had political agendas and preyed on the fears of the uninformed, faithful LDS women who were anxious to protect their families. In hindsight, she held herself partly responsible for what happened because "I didn't say 'Don't use the Relief Society.'" She should have been more forceful in that regard. Instead, she allowed herself to be used "by the far right."[108] "By the time these groups had contacted those who would represent the Mormon women, fears and anxieties arose and walls of defense were built. A vacuum was created because the Church and the Relief Society wanted to remain impartial."[109] It was an astute observation that she herself had been among the victims of this mobilization. The careful boundaries she had tried to observe in expressing disapproval for the ERA while simultaneously not dictating political action to the church's women were erased by the rising tide of extreme feelings and end-justifies-the-means tactics that carried on beyond the IWY conference to the ultimate defeat of the Equal Rights Amendment. By 1982 when the period for ratification expired, the church was standing firmly on the traditional side of the gulf dividing American women. For at least some Mormon women who sincerely believed in equality, there was no way to bridge the gap and remain Mormon.

7. Turmoil, June 1977

> The women themselves came ready to block anything that was said, for they did not want to be falsely persuaded to accept attitudes or actions that could be damaging to them or to the Church.
>
> —Barbara B. Smith, General President of the LDS Relief Society, 1977

Calling Out the Women

As Utah's bishops and Relief Society presidents called women in their wards to invite them to attend the upcoming IWY conference, the most important detail communicated, whatever the exact phrasing, was that the call had originated with "the Brethren" at church headquarters. This call to arms, issued through priesthood channels, could only have produced the kind of dramatic scene that would play out later that month.

Ironically, some of the women were contacted because they had shown an interest in "women's issues." But for most, an interest in "women's lib" disqualified them from consideration. Some women heard about the conference through other means and attended based on other reasons, whether or not they had received a church calling. Some went simply because they were interested in the subjects. In Provo, when Charlotte England's Relief Society president telephoned her and encouraged her to go, it stirred her curiosity. "This would be an interesting conference for my daughters and myself to attend," she said.[1] Daphne Dalley, a resource manager from Cedar City and already an ERA supporter and active Democrat, saw the IWY as a way to become better informed and to "converse with other women about women's issues." She learned about the conference from the League of Women Voters. With three or four friends from the league, she "got up at about four o'clock in the morning and drove to Salt Lake."[2]

Others were more hesitant. One of Belva Ashton's young neighbors received the summoning call and obeyed but confessed to Ashton after the conference: "I was told to go, or asked to go, but I felt totally out of my element. I didn't know the issues. I went totally ill-prepared." She obeyed because she "thought she was defending hearth and home" and understood that she was "to vote no on practically everything." Overall, it was not a pleasant experience for this woman, whom Ashton believed was victimized and, with other women like her, frightened but resolute, believing she was "fighting some big, evil monster from the outside."[3]

Mary Blundell went to the conference to show her support for the ERA. As a member of the Equal Rights Coalition, she wanted all laws removed that discriminated against women, particularly against women of color.[4] In her fifties and a former member of the Utah Federation of Business and Professional Women, Blundell had worked most of her adult life in Texas and was acutely aware of racial discrimination.

Final Preparations

The night beforehand, the coordinating committee held its final preparation meeting for the state conference. Jan Tyler ran down a list of last minute details. Alice Kasai would give an opening prayer. There would be six microphones on the floor. The voting machines needed to be returned on Monday. Mary Anne Krupsak, the first woman to be elected as New York's lieutenant governor, was present. Politically experienced after two terms in the state assembly and as a national IWY commissioner responsible for Utah, she congratulated the committee on their efforts, perhaps reassuring them in the face of predicted crowds and unpredictable problems. "I have never seen a state that has done such a marvelous job of preparation," she said, "from the Mass Meetings arranged by your Outreach Committee [to] the extra planning on workshops and their excellent preparation so that all people attending could get the very best information afforded by expert planning, speakers, and quality of work done by the various committees. You have done so much."[5] She volunteered to make an introductory statement at the opening session. Marilee Latta announced that because of the anticipated crowd, "we of the Coordinating Committee must present a united front at all times," as Suzanna Mae Grua recorded in the minutes. All knew that they faced an uncertain outcome and that the immense logistical pressure would be overcome only if they put their differences behind them.

The Program

Participants were invited to choose among twenty-one workshops held concurrently during four time slots. In other words, each participant could attend four sessions if she so chose. As previously mentioned, the committee invested careful thought in planning in order to avoid confrontation or disorder. As will be seen, the plans came to naught as workshops quickly deteriorated into divisive, chaotic affairs, stirring up more emotion than anything seen in the state since the Great Indignation of the 1880s—the mass meeting where women protested the federal crackdown on polygamy.

Many of the workshops were the same as originally conceived by the coordinating committee's task forces. Unchanged were the topics of aging, arts and humanities, basic needs, child development, employment, enforcement of laws, the ERA, the legal status of homemakers, lifestyles, media, men, minority women, polarity (originally termed "polarization"), power (elective, appointive, personal), women offenders, and women in Utah history.

Six preliminary topics would not make it to the convention floor: education, family violence, health (perhaps more accurately narrowed down to "reproductive health"), international interdependence, rape, and young women. Five additional topics were added: child abuse, mental health, women as students, child development, and teenage pregnancy.

Registration Thursday evening was light, but Friday morning at 8:00 o'clock, Esther Landa saw crowds of women in front of doors long before they opened, all anxious to get in and register.[6] Long lines would continue to be the norm on Friday and Saturday, complicated by the number of children, shortage of registration materials, and hot stuffy air in the Salt Palace Convention Center.

Plenary sessions in the assembly hall, the largest space in the building, were presided over by Landa. Unquestionably a woman of stature, she was national president of the National Council of Jewish Women and former president of the League of Women Voters.[7] The coordinating committee had sent her literature from the national commission and state committee so she could familiarize herself with the key issues.

At the first session, Alice Kasai pronounced the invocation and the Girl Scouts, led by committee member Dorothea Livingston, presented the colors. The congregation then sang "America the Beautiful," accompanied by Kathryn F. Kirk.

In keeping with the guidelines of the national commission, parliamentarian Adelyn Logan explained the ground rules for the two-day event. She introduced the workshop leaders, coordinating council chairs, professional staff, and coordinating committee members; these were accepted by motion, as were the state meeting rules. Logan explained Public Law 94-167 and called for nominations for the Houston delegates. Utah would be allowed fourteen, she explained, as determined by population. Guided by Roberts's Rules of Order, two hundred delegates were nominated within the next twenty-four hours. Logan invited women to talk with nominees in the assembly hall's southeast corner between 11:45 a.m. and noon. The election was scheduled for the next day.

Then Mary Anne Krupsak of New York delivered a rousing call for Utah's women to unite in the effort to improve the status of all women.

Committed to the idea of representative government, she portrayed the conference as an essential piece in the democratic process. This was a way the voices of women could be heard, she said.

Jan Tyler presided over the general session which began at 10:15. Belle S. Spafford, the immediate predecessor of LDS Relief Society President Barbara Smith, read her speech, "Today, the Prelude for Tomorrow."[8] Involved in women's issues even before she became Relief Society president, Spafford had attended every conference of the International Council of Women since 1937 and had been president of the National Council of Women from 1968-70. She warned listeners to beware of excess in their efforts to change the world because, she said, these attempts sometimes backfire and can "lead the overzealous to faulty attitudes and extreme attitudes. In trying to solve problems, one needs to be alert not to create new problems that may be as detrimental as those one would eradicate." Liberation carried "to the extreme can surrender to license," she warned, "and license, in turn, can embrace behavior that is antisocial."

Well loved by Mormon women, Spafford was the emotional favorite of the mainstream audience, which received her with resounding applause as she said she "support[ed] equal pay for equal work and equal credit regulations" but deplored "anything that would adversely affect the femininity of women or impair the quality of her home and family life." Taking full advantage of her platform and moving from generalities to specifics, she strongly asserted that she was "philosophically and morally" opposed to the ERA, which would "introduce a feminist philosophy into the U.S. that is against the nation's viewpoint that the male is the head of the household." She added, "We believe in taking care of our husbands, families, for love. We don't want to do it for money."[9]

In some ways, her remarks were reminiscent of nineteenth-century orators such as Booker T. Washington, who repeatedly told fellow blacks that society would change slowly and that there was peril in moving too quickly or leaping into the unknown. Spafford acknowledged the need for greater equity for women but advocated moderate change, though without condemning feminism per se. Still, the implication was clear. For a traditional woman seeking balance in her own life—a desire for greater recognition, but primarily as a woman, and respect for her responsibilities to her family—Spafford's speech was a polite voice celebrating women and carefully remaining aloof from feminism.

In the afternoon between 1:30 and 3:15 p.m., ten workshops were held in rooms spread throughout the building. The topics included aging, child abuse, education, employment, enforcement of laws, lifestyles, mental health, power (elective, appointive, personal), and women offenders. At 3:30 p.m. another round of ten sessions began, this time on the arts and humanities, basic needs, child development, the ERA, media, men, minority women, rape, reproductive health, and women in Utah history.

Jan Tyler had asked workshop chairs to study the particular issues carefully and identify resource people locally who might be able to add their expertise to the discussion. She asked the chairs to gather and condense information and produce handouts to explain pros and cons. Balance in presenting differing views was emphasized. In the plenary session, each chair was to present the recommendation of the workshop, assuming the attendees had expressed a consensus, along with the national and state recommendations as listed on the "Voice of Womankind" program. Each chair was to leave ten minutes to field questions from the floor.

A film festival ran for two hours Friday evening, mostly documentaries on a wide range of topics: *The Black Woman; Day Care Today; Does Anybody Need Me Anymore; Children as People; Chris and Bennie; ERA and the American Way; I Is for Important; Images of Country Women; Joyce at Thirty-four; Men's Lives; Mothers after Divorce; Time Has No Sympathy; What I Want; When Women Get to Hurting; Woman to Woman*; and *Womanhouse.* Most were chosen for topics being discussed in the workshops. As can be seen from the titles, they ranged from issues about women of color to abused women, from the needs of young girls to those of aged women. Although some touched on issues of sexuality—a source of alarm for some attendees—the majority did not.

Self-proclaimed anti-feminist Margaret Mahoney, a Winchester, Massachusetts, attorney, was the plenary speaker Friday afternoon. She ran away with the session when she cried: "Has the pedestal become a cage? To the feminist, yes. To the anti-feminist, the pedestal has never been a cage. It never has been and it never will be." She maintained that she was "philosophically and morally" opposed to the ERA and warned that it would "introduce a feminist philosophy into the United States that is against the nation's viewpoint that the male is the head of the household." The crowd burst into cheers, especially when she echoed Belle Spafford: "We believe in taking care of our husbands, families, for love. We don't want to do it for money."[10]

Beginning at 7:00 p.m., an open-mike session encouraged women to express their views. All afternoon and evening, the Salt Lake Festival of the Arts presented local art by women in rooms adjacent to the workshop meeting spaces.

Saturday registration opened at 8:00 a.m. and closed at 2:00 p.m. The *Salt Lake Tribune* noted a continuation of the "anti-ERA, pro-family chorus, . . . a convention split by openly hostile factions."[11] At 8:30 a.m., Janet Darley, chair of the voting committee, explained the location of the voting booths and procedures designed to streamline the voting. The women would use computerized punch cards in private booths. The punch cards were consecutively numbered and voters' names would be recorded (unregistered women would not be permitted to vote). Each voter would be allowed six minutes in a booth. Balloting would start at 9:00 a.m. and close at 3:00 p.m. The results would be tabulated within forty-five minutes after the polls closed.[12] Darley reminded the women that the candidates' names were posted on the east wall, along with biographies, but that nominees were not allowed to campaign.[13] Women were to vote on the national platform as well as national delegates. She ended with a short credentials report on the committee's authority to fulfill public law in connection with the national IWY celebration.

Lola Redford spoke at 9:15 a.m. As the director of Consumer Action Now and Mormon wife of film star Robert Redford, she had distinguished herself in promoting the interests of women and children and had served on the National Women's Political Caucus advisory board. Speaking movingly about the plight of women in poverty throughout the world, she linked Utah's efforts with those on the international stage. Community activism, she reminded the audience, begins with simple, grassroots efforts. She said her own consumer group began with twenty volunteers. "We are trying to do something about the things we believe in," she said.[14]

A member of the coordinating committee, Dolores Bennett, presided over the 1:00 general session where Helvi Sipila of Finland, general secretary of the International Women's Year and assistant secretary general of the United Nations for social development and humanitarian affairs, spoke. Sipila was also involved as president of the International Federation of Women Lawyers, president of Zonat International, vice president of the International Council of Women, and committee member of the World Association of Girl Guides and Girl Scouts. She recounted the history of IWY, the International Conference in Mexico City, and other events staged by women's groups across the world. She reminded her audience that internationally, women had identified common ground—reflected in the resolutions before them. "U.S. women, as members of the world community, need to speak out against malnutrition, illiteracy, disease, economic disadvantage and other human suffering," she pled. "Indeed, we may ask what was the human right-to-life of those 10 to 20 million children, mostly in developing countries, among the 125 million children born during the International Women's Year, who had to die before they were even a year old?"[15] Sipila had been warned that she might be booed during the Utah conference—certain speakers at earlier IWY events had been—but to the contrary, she received a rousing standing ovation.

During the general session on Saturday afternoon, a woman who seemed typical of the crowd made a motion. Probably speaking before the largest audience of her life and reading from a notepad in her hand, she spoke into a hand-held microphone: "We, the participants of the largest IWY meeting in our nation, appreciate this opportunity to make our views known. However, we feel that our tax dollars are being spent to promote a pro-ERA stand to which we are diametrically opposed. Our tax dollars are also being used to promote other views on issues pertinent to women, to which we object."[16] The key phrase here was "diametrically opposed." The time had come for Mormon women to take a stand, and they let it be known that they would not tolerate compromise.

The Battleground

The coordinating committee had planned a rich, lively, thoughtful program that turned into a battleground. Even without the roiling emotions of fear, suspicion, bewilderment, and anger, it might have been catastrophic simply because of the numbers. The committee had anticipated up to 4,000 women. By the sticky, sweaty end of the conference on Saturday afternoon, 13,800 had registered, and many others who did not register came to watch and lobby in the workshops.[17] Utah's conference was twice as large as California's. Marilyn Arnold, a BYU English professor and assistant to the school's president, believed that women went so their voices could be heard. "They didn't want resolutions to be passed that wouldn't reflect the larger population of Utah. So LDS women were there in great numbers. . . . I've never seen so many polyester pantsuits in my life!"[18] Women were sitting on boxes and table tops, sharing folding chairs, leaning against walls, or sitting cross-legged in the aisles. "They came—the husbands and the wives and the kids. They'd change the babies, laying them on the floor down there, changing their diapers. It was like a zoo."

Many brought sack lunches. Others planned to walk across the street to eat at Salt Lake City restaurants, which were soon full. Nearly all day long, restrooms were crowded with lines of women waiting impatiently. Before long, paper towels overflowed from trash cans. Water splashed the mirrors and floor. There was a shortage of written materials. The rooms were hot and crowded. An inadequate number of voting booths generated tension and confusion.

With rooms overflowing, people sitting on the floor and outside in the hall, Betty Kingsford found herself overwhelmed. Not having known what to expect, she was nevertheless amazed to see "people shouting and booing [at speakers] and shouting them down. The anger that was displayed" was incomprehensible. "I think that I was astounded to see how rudely treated some of the women [were] who were just merely trying to communicate a point of view, merely to express themselves. They were unable to finish sentences. . . . It was just staggering to me to observe that and think, 'What is going on?'" In the plenary session, she was so "stunned at the waves of emotion" that she found it difficult to listen.[19]

Cheryl Lynn May sensed the fear that was overwhelming the participants, as she later, compassionately, told an interviewer:

> I remember how mobbed the place was. And that these dear sisters . . . seemed to feel that they were sort of in a dangerous foray into enemy territory. And that they had been commissioned to squash some kind of dangerous conspiracy and they were sort of whispering to one another, [with] very concerned looks on their faces.
>
> My impression was that the great majority of them were lovely Relief Society sisters who knew very little about politics and did not care much about politics. But, by golly, they received orders from headquarters and they were going to be where they were supposed to be. Their confusion was only exceeded by the consternation of the conference organizers. . . . [The Relief Society] sisters had a sense of serious threat. They were [not] quite sure what it was but it was heavy stuff.[20]

Christine Meaders Durham, a Salt Lake attorney and active Mormon who later became Utah's first woman supreme court justice, said she was shocked and distressed to see the willingness to cast negative votes without first even considering the issues:

> It seemed to me that in every session that I attended or heard about they automatically voted down any proposal put forth by any proponent. There didn't seem to me to be any give and take. There didn't seem to be any depth of consideration or thinking. It was basically [that] these issues—these issues affecting women . . . threaten our conventions and our traditions, and we are going to roll them down without looking at their merits independently. And I found that very depressing.[21]

Ramona Adams from Salt Lake City called it "ignorance in action."

"People were angry. A lot of the women were upset. They came as if they had the answers to things, and they didn't even know what the questions were. They were in several places that I went, and—I can't remember specific ones—they were really heckling. They heckled the people. It was rude."[22]

Durham gave a speech at the ERA workshop, whose double sessions topped attendance records for the conference with more than 4,000 women crowding into the rooms. Durham's presentation was even-handed. Aileen Clyde described her as an "absolutely splendid debater and thinker who kept everything very rational and very logical and historical."[23] Durham saw the ERA as a "standard, a guide" for the states, something that would not "impact a woman's ability to make personal choices."[24] It was necessary for the country "to change our view for equal treatment of men and women under the law. We can't expect our legislators to do it for us."[25] Although Durham remembered "clapping and booing," she recalled that these outbursts came during the question-answer period— that no one interrupted her prepared comments. In her mind, her debate with Rex Lee went well.[26]

Durham was lucky. Shauna Adix chaired the alternative lifestyles workshop, which exploded with emotion:

> Long before the scheduled meeting time, people were lined up in front of the door. The assigned room had a stated capacity of 72. We allowed as many extra persons in as we dared and just barely had open aisles to the doors, front and back in the room. There was much concern from the people on the outside about wanting to come in and we were late in starting from trying to explain that we simply had no more room in the inn. The outside noise was so great that we could not hear, but each time we opened the door to ask for quiet, the annoyance and anger seemed only to heighten. At one point, someone banged so vociferously on the door that one of the task force members opened it to ask for quiet—and was immediately flung against the wall as two women forced their way into the room. . . . I explained that we were going to make no recommendations, which was met by many with complaints and challenges as to the legality of such a stand, but it did cause some people to leave. As they left, others pushed

> their way in until we had close to a hundred women in the room. One of the members of the task force went to find other space and returned with the report of a larger available room. The women in the room refused to leave (fearing, I suspect, that they would lose their front row seats) and finally, in an attempt to compromise, two task force members offered to go with the overflow group to the new room while the original group stayed.

The workshop fell apart when one woman, speaking from the floor, called lesbians "degenerates." Another woman challenged this label, identifying herself as a lesbian. At this point, some women walked out, others refused to leave, and pandemonium broke out.[27]

Daphne Dalley, who attended this workshop, remembered that the woman who identified herself as a lesbian was harassed with shouts, hisses, and verbal abuse:

> I guess I was just shocked. I had perceived myself to be a very traditional Mormon woman up to that point. . . . If this was traditional Mormon womanhood in this conference, in this room, I was not a traditional Mormon woman, and I had no desire to be one. I just thought, "This woman deserves to be listened to. She has value as a human being. There's no reason to make her feel less because of her choices." I'm sure it took a lot of courage to stand up there and say what she did.[28]

Even a topic as uncontroversial as education exploded out of control. Reba Keele, then director of the BYU Honors Program, and Lisa Bolin Hawkins had spent long hours organizing the workshop, carefully drafting the language of the recommendations and preparing the supporting materials. Lisa was a law student in 1977 who had come to the conference because she was concerned that the "special needs and rights of women and children needed to be more carefully considered by legislators [and] justice and law enforcement agencies in Utah and the United States."[29]

The most painful moment for them came after the workshop when they presented their group's recommendations before the large session. They were both stunned when a woman who had been in their session "stood up at the microphone and said, 'I thought that we had learned some good stuff in education, but I have just been told that to vote in favor of any of these educational proposals will be a vote in favor of the ERA.' And that was it. That's all she said." Hawkins jumped to her feet and seized the mike. "That's not true," she exclaimed passionately. "That's not true. It has only to do with education." Too shaken to continue, she sat down. Then, as Keele remembers:

> A woman in front of us with a garment line under her blouse[30] turned around and, with the most hatred I have ever seen in a person's eyes and voice, looked at Lisa and me and said, "We don't need women like you in this state. Why don't you leave?" And we just sat there stunned. All those months of work, all the attempts to be empathetic toward the conservative positions. All those attempts to make sure that this was carefully discussed and that we didn't do any railroading.[31]

Hawkins was frightened by what she described as the "mob psychology" as women caught up in the fight acted in ways she had never seen before. "They were being rude to other people," she said, "shouting other people down, interrupting, not following the rules that had been made up for large gatherings of this kind so that different people can state their case."[32]

One of the task force members, Cynthia Boshard, who was also a journalist, sensed early that the conference was spiraling out of control: "We started to see that people were beginning to crowd their way into workshops that were already overcrowded. We had people at the door holding the crowds because of fire codes. People just got nasty and they were mean and vicious. They were critical of our attempts to make compromises."[33]

Patricia Brim, a Mormon from the affluent Federal Heights neighborhood in Salt Lake City, called the conference "an appalling and utterly frightening take-over by a consolidated, professionally organized and controlled majority." She recognized that the conference had generated suspicions and accusations from the beginning, but "hostility mounted as the conference progressed and as committee members and workshop coordinators saw months of work in research and preparation wiped out in one day."[34]

For many, participation in the conference was an overwhelming experience. The Salt Palace was bursting with women, all of whom were going in different directions with something specific to accomplish. It was easy to feel dazed as if one were spinning in circles. Too many bodies pressed into too small a space. The air was heavy and muggy. The noise was deafening, disorienting. Child care was available, but bringing children into this chaos was a risky proposition. Like everything else, the child care facilities, planned to accommodate a few hundred children, were completely overwhelmed. Children struggled and wailed in their mothers' arms or dozed uneasily in back packs if they were not lying listlessly in strollers, their cheeks pink with the prickly heat, or wandering confused and crying behind their mothers in the halls.

The "Women in History" workshop featured four Mormon historians: Maureen Ursenbach Beecher, Kathryn MacKay, Cheryll Lynn May, and Jill Mulvay. May, a political science instructor at the University of Utah, enthralled the audience with her deep voice and clear, articulate way of expressing herself, which never failed to inspire others to become better informed. Unfortunately, the positive response to this workshop was uncharacteristic for the conference.

Elsewhere the predominant tone was one of mutual suspicion and polarization, which effectively destroyed any opportunity for dialogue. For Cynthia Boshard, the strongest memories that still lingered fourteen years later were of disgust and betrayal. She remembered how committed the organizers were to doing everything by the book, according to the guidelines, and how she looked around at the hordes of angry women and thought:

> "You people are trying to change that. You're taking the information out of context, twisting it around to meet your own sick need that comes out of paranoia, fear, or whatever. . . . You are being directed by men, and you don't even know about the issues that we are talking about." And as I got with other members of the organizing committee and other people who had been in some of the sessions, it was just like we'd been run over, like we'd been hit; the life had been knocked out of us, and what's going on?[35]

Boshard was not exaggerating about the male presence at the conference. Although it was for and about women, Keele found the active role of a large number of men unnerving: "They were there to help coordinate and make sure that the right people got elected. Now, I didn't see any of these men at our small group session"—her workshop on education—"but in the large group, they were ubiquitous. They were everywhere. Always around the margins. Always with these walkie-talkies, always having certain women going to talk to them and then they'd bark into the walkie-talkies."[36]

Sharon Keigher was particularly disappointed over the lack of moderation. Many of the task force chairs came to her in tears of frustration because participants had been so unwilling to hear other points of view or consider recommendations. She said, "The task forces have been working on their proposals for months. The meetings were always open, and anyone could have come."[37]

Georgia Peterson of the conservative Let's Govern Ourselves (LGO) caucus was a major player in mobilizing attendance and trying to influence voting, but she too was dismayed by how people functioned in this emotional environment:

> Women were coming up to me, saying "Tell us how to vote, tell us how to vote!" And I said, "Come to the caucus" (the medium-size Salt Palace room allocated to LGO), and the room was packed, women sitting on the floor, all around the outside of the room. . . . I was really saddened that women were so totally uninformed about what was going on. And I remember giving a speech at that particular time where I said, "Think! Think! You decide what you want! And think! You have a God-given mind. Use it!" And I know that women thought I was very harsh; there were many women whose feelings were hurt when I said that. I was totally dismayed that women did not know . . . what effect they can have on politics and government.[38]

Friday night, as the first day's events dragged to their sweltering, bewildering close, the crowd of Mormons was reluctant to leave because of rumors that had circulated about the Idaho conference, which was said to have been adjourned and then reconvened in order to pass "what they wanted to," as Esther Landa had described it. "The women in Utah were afraid that the same thing was going to happen, so it was about midnight when we finally got them to adjourn." The resourceful Landa appealed to Barbara Smith to come to the stand and tell the women to go home, explaining to her: "You know, I think you've got to get up there and say something to calm this group down and indicate to them if we adjourn, we'll be back the next day."[39] This tactic succeeded.

Gloria Firmage from Salt Lake City recalled the surreal ending to the day's events: "Everybody was frustrated with this tension that was so thick you could cut it. Nobody wanted to go home because they were fearful that something would happen while they were gone, until Sister Smith stood up and said, 'Ladies it's time to go to bed. It's time to sleep. You know, this is ridiculous. We're human beings. We live in the same community. We need to be talking, not fighting. Not boxing in a ring, do you understand?'" To Firmage's thinking, boxing was the perfect metaphor. "It became a shadow box. It was like both sides fighting a shadow that wasn't even there. When you shadow box, you know, you are fighting an image that doesn't have any reality."[40]

Dazed and overwhelmed, the organizers gathered that sultry midnight to figure out what to do. Broshard remembers: "We all got together to sort of talk about the process, about what had just happened." She said they were "dumbfounded." The question on everyone's mind was, "When we all vote in the big session tomorrow, what is going to happen?"[41]

Saturday morning began with an intensity that was already at fever pitch. Women streamed into the Salt Palace past a small group of picketers, about seventy women strong, who carried signs and chanted: "Not the Church. Not the State. Women Will Decide Our Fate." The protestors objected to the "unrepresentative" composition of the meetings. Irene Fisher, president of the Salt Lake League of Women Voters, said that sixteen statewide organizations were represented in the picket line, a demonstration planned that morning during an early caucus. The placards read: "IWY Asked for Women: You Send Sheep," "Remember the

Day You Were Persecuted," "Ten from Every Ward Has Brought a Plague of Pickets," and "Twelve Thousand Vote Ms. Smith's Mind."[42] Fisher explained :

> Their negative strategies have blocked all attempts at rational consideration of differing viewpoints. The refusal of this element of the delegate body to indulge divergent opinions, the rude and often irrational behavior exhibited by these delegates, and their complete unwillingness to consider IWY proposals, not to mention the outright thefts and destruction of printed materials belonging to some of the (protesting) organizations was inexcusable and undemocratic. Months of planning, research, financial support, and hard work were blatantly destroyed in one day, indicating the ignorance that is inherent in calculated bigotry. We are confident that the tactics exhibited in Friday's session are not characteristic of responsible members of the LDS Church and other Utah citizens, but their voices were clearly unheard.[43]

Another spokesman for the protesters, Nan Carter, said the church's influence was evident and that in her mind it "violate[s] the doctrine of a separation of church and state."[44]

The Voting

Thousands of yellow voting cards flashed in the air during the negative vote for the ERA, and women cheered as it went down in defeat.[45] Coupled with a resolution opposing the appropriation of any more tax dollars for the IWY, Utah's women, by an overwhelming majority, took a position squarely against the women's movement.

Daphne Dalley and her friend, Barbara Starr, felt astonished and defiant during the voting. The wave of yellow cards rose "as people would vote against everything and then we would raise our little cards and vote the way we felt. It just became more and more evident to me how much out of the main stream I was in terms of my personal opinions, what I thought my level of awareness was of women's issues, . . . almost 180 degrees opposite."[46]

Three separate votes were conducted at the conference. The first, to consider twenty-five national resolutions, took place Friday in the voting booths set up throughout the Salt Palace where long lines of registered women waited with ballots they were issued when they registered. The women were also asked to elect fourteen delegates to the national IWY in Houston. Second, during each workshop, the chair presented the state resolution, accompanied by the task force's recommendation which was usually in the affirmative. Fourth, resolutions that made it successfully through the workshops were presented at the Saturday plenary session when attendees were asked to vote by raising their hands. Some women, holding yellow cards, voted down every single resolution that came from the national IWY commission. In addition, all fourteen of the women elected to the national convention were anti-ERA delegates from the Let's Govern Ourselves list.[47] It was a stunning victory for Georgia Peterson.

By law, any bona fide female resident over age sixteen could vote. Large numbers of women came convinced the voting would be rigged and the majority view would be disfranchised, yet these women and their allies, voting en bloc, emerged as the overwhelming victors in the balloting, electing a monochromatic slate of national delegates and defeating every national resolution. Esther Landa felt disgusted by the crowds of women who voted no on everything without having studied the issues. "They just got the call to come and then they got this brainwashing by the men and they just automatically voted no. We probably could have had a resolution that the earth is . . . [not] flat," she later said, "and they would have voted no. But I did have the feeling that toward the end they maybe were listening a little bit better."[48]

Reba Keele waited in the voting line and noticed women holding their LGO lists and overheard one "say to the woman in the next booth, 'I can't find so-and-so on the ballot,'" while another announced her progress through the list: "Well there are ten down . . ." Numbly, Keele realized that they were marking the LGO recommendations.[49] Charlotte England questioned the women she was with about why they were voting that way. They said, "Well, this is what they wanted us to do; we want to vote against these things, because they're very dangerous." But England thought some of the issues seemed good for women and commented that this was her "first realization" that "we were being kind of pushed into something to vote a certain way without really thinking or asking if that was really a good thing to vote on. And it bothered me."[50] The car pool of women she was with talked about the vote and the conference on their way home to Utah County that night, and Charlotte realized she was the only one in the car who felt the way she did.

By contrast, some women cast reasoned and reasonably negative votes. Dorothy Littrell, the committee's fiscal officer, voted "no" on the employment proposal because she objected to federal interference in one's private life. "I object to women being classified as a minority in order to receive special benefits," she explained. "I object to a quota system for jobs for women without regard to qualification. I also object to being part of a world plan of action which my government and my tax dollars are subsidizing."[51]

The results of the balloting reveal how effectively the pre-conference caucus meetings had been (see Appendix 4). The women of Utah voted overwhelmingly against the national platform, including such apparently helpful provisions as:

1. The President should take steps to require that women (1) have equal opportunities for appointment to managerial and upper level posts in Federally-funded cultural institutions, such as libraries, museums, universities and public radio and TV; (2) are more equitably represented in the staffing of grant-awarding agencies; (3) benefit more fairly from government grants, whether as individual grant applicants or as members of cultural institutions receiving Federal or State funding.

    - Agree: 1,486 (15.5%)
    - Disagree: 8,041 (83.8%)
    - Don't know: 73

2. The Federal government should assume a major role in providing

universal voluntary child development programs with ability-to-pay fee schedules and with direct parental involvement in operation.

- Agree: 693 (7.2%)
- Disagree: 8,858 (92.1%)
- Don't know: 67

3. Bilingual vocational training and education programs should be extended and significantly expanded.

- Agree: 1,148 (11.9%)
- Disagree: 8,326 (86.3%)
- Don't know: 177

4. Homemakers should be covered by Social Security.

- Agree: 1,405 (14.5%)
- Disagree: 8,039 (82.9%)
- Don't know: 247

5. Equal Rights Amendment

- Agree: 666
- Disagree: 8,956
- Don't know: 84[52]

Why would women react with such sweeping negativism to such resolutions? As was evident from the comments and priorities that came out of the mass meetings, the vote reflected what Utah's women perceived to be the feminist agenda. Abortion, ERA, and even discussions about child care seemed to threaten the lives they knew and represent an uncertain future. Not surprisingly, a Republican distrust of big government was a prominent factor, which meant that the proposals were tainted not just because they were feminist but because they allowed the federal government to assume responsibility for new areas of women's lives. Expanded social services programs fell into this category. Beyond that, a general satisfaction with life on the part of the majority of women in attendance prevented them from empathizing with those who were different or whose situations were more challenging.

Post-Conference Responses

When the delegates streamed out of the Salt Palace after the final vote on Saturday, the hot summer night was filled with mixed comments and feelings. Those who had come as foot soldiers in a battle to defend their families, as well as cherished religious values, felt vindicated, triumphant, and determined to do the same in Houston. Ironically, they had been politicized without having learned much about the political process. Those who came because they were interested in women's issues and encouraged that the IWY symbolized more serious attention to women's needs were stunned, angry, discouraged, and alienated from their traditional sisters on the other side of the wide gulf that had opened up. And almost without exception, women on each side felt bitterly mistrustful of women on the other side. Perhaps the greatest casualty of the IWY conference was the feeling of sisterhood with other women. For many Mormon women, "sisterhood" had become a shrinking circle wherein admittance was controlled by politically proper shibboleths.

Barbara Smith had attended the conference but had not spoken from the floor or put her name forward as a candidate. She scrupulously made no comment about the outcome of the vote, offering neither public congratulations to the winners nor condolences to the losers. Nor did she make public her feelings about the monolithic defeat of the proposed resolutions or the election of the all-conservative delegates. Instead, in an interview the next month, she focused on the process by which these ends had been accomplished, expressing cautious disappointment and disapproval:

> The women themselves came ready to block anything that was said, for they did not want to be falsely persuaded to accept attitudes or actions that could be damaging to them or to the Church. Some had been told that they would be safe if they voted no on everything. The Latter-day

Saint women came by the thousands. They attended the workshops and defensively participated. I was told that sometimes they would not even listen to those who were presenters.

Admitting that the Relief Society shared some blame for not better educating women about politics and current issues, President Smith added: "I feel that a combination of factors contributed to that state of mind. Primarily, Mormon women are generally uninformed about the women's movement because they don't see a need to be informed. People were able to play on their fears and feelings and we saw what comes of it. If people are uninformed, they are easily panicked."[53] Smith met with stake Relief Society presidents to gather reactions and summarized the input she received in the neutrality of carefully phrased passive verbs:

> It was strongly expressed that Mormon women wanted more information, help with skills in parliamentary procedures, and a clear understanding of the expectations so that they might participate more effectively in future community and state meetings. We decided to provide instruction in the curriculum and to encourage Relief Society members and leaders to constantly strive to be more knowledgeable about, and responsive to, the issues involved in each community, not just those pertaining to the IWY. Women were encouraged to learn how to conduct themselves in public forums, how to have influence as individual citizens, and how to use parliamentary procedures in public meetings.[54]

The Relief Society had learned a potent lesson. There was a down side to mass gatherings of anxiously obedient and frightened women: a potential for chaos, stereotyping, and emotional violence. But the Relief Society had also learned the brute fact of the advantage of superior numbers in a political contest.

In retrospect, the dream of dialogue among Utah's women had been doomed from the start for two reasons: (1) the majority of participants were politically uninformed women who depended on other people for direction, and (2) paranoia over the ERA irrevocably poisoned the atmosphere. Thousands of women, mobilized through a structure they trusted, hearing language that was familiar, honestly believed they were defending the truth against a destruction-bent conspiracy from the left. The agenda of the Conservative Caucus, Let's Govern Ourselves, and the Eagle Forum triumphed magnificently because they mirrored the objectives of the LDS Church. To many women, the instruction to vote no on every issue felt right.

Yet Jan Tyler and a number of the coordinating committee were themselves active Mormon women who were educated and politically savvy. Why did they fail to foresee and channel this explosive energy into less catastrophic channels?

At least one "concerned participant" saw the conference debacle as a failure of the committee's leadership and raised some thoughtful questions on this issue. Dorothy L. Behling thought that it was a mistake not to spend time during the opening sessions on parliamentary procedure,[55] the history of the IWY, or basic orientation: "It could have been anticipated that when all those numbers showed up on Friday that their basic frame of reference was anti-ERA, anti-abortion. Was it not the responsibility of the governing committee to assess that and provide on-the-spot information which separated those issues from the other issues to be discussed in the workshops?" For Behling, the conference catastrophe seemed to reflect failures in communication and perception. Too many women came unprepared, expecting the worst and failing to exercise the power to discern the difference: "Many of the issues, beautifully worded and thoughtfully prepared, were given little or no ear. Was this only the bigotry of the women or should the leaders take some of the responsibility for the lack of adequate preparation? Perhaps the committee and a large percentage of women were both defensive and ceased to draw on all their resources at a critical encounter."[56]

For Barbara Hales, the chaos was due largely to the lack of civic experience for the majority of participants. "They had no regard or respect for parliamentary procedure. . . . They had been assigned certain roles to play, and they reminded me of Stepford wives. . . . A group of people who had no information, who did not want any information other than having been given marching orders, . . . came in intent on saving us all from this wicked IWY group that was going to give women some access to the American dream."[57] Patricia Hill wrote a "Minority Report" in the aftermath and criticized the bad behavior of those who attended the conference unprepared. She wrote: "The ignorance or unwillingness of the majority of women to understand the problems of working women, divorced women, uneducated women, poor women, and minority women was absolutely devastating. Some progress in educating women in these areas was made in the workshops, but as soon as any of the proposals (as compromised as they were) were made to the floor of the entire body, most proposals were defeated."[58]

Many of the traditional women felt misunderstood and unfairly stereotyped. Dalley told of a friend who returned home to Cedar City with some other women from her ward, upset by the emotion and the confusion of the conference. The women talked about the news coverage in the morning paper. The media had called Mormon women sheep, saying "they don't have opinions of their own, they're all coached by men [in] all of these things." The women "were very angry," Dalley recalled. They said, "How they could say that about us? How can they say we're sheep? How can they say we don't have an opinion?" The irony, in Dalley's mind, was that these women had attended because they were asked to and voted no on all national resolutions.[59]

Only a month after Utah's IWY, Esther Landa spoke at a regional luncheon of the Delta Kappa Gamma Society at the Hotel Utah. She mentioned how the controversy over the ERA and abortion had became "so intense, so bitter, so divisive that civilized dialogue . . . seemed almost impossible." Like other women's advocates, she had hoped the meeting would stimulate dialogue among diverse women. Instead, "what started out to be an idealistic, open, democratic discussion, an educational and informative experience," became politicized. As a result, "the whole future of the women's movement" hung in the balance. In her opinion, gender stereotyping deprived both men and women of their potential; it was "human liberation" that was at issue.[60]

Another minority report was written by Linda Schrenk, suggesting that the conference turned out to be contrary to Constitutional principles in that it had failed to represent a diversity of views. It was democracy unchecked by constraint of law—specifically the barrier between church and state, for instance.[61]

The task of understanding Utah's IWY conference is far from complete. One woman said she waited seven years before she talked publicly about it. The conference had stirred up so much anger and confusion, she did not know how to handle it. For Marilee Latta, it was "sort of like going to Vietnam. It was like being in combat for one day, . . . it was so overpowering. And it made such a difference in all of our lives that it was the type of thing I couldn't discuss. I couldn't talk about it. I didn't want to talk about it for years. It was that impactful."[62]

Cynthia Boshard commented on her emotional damage control:

> It's hard to find the words for it, and in 1977 there were a lot of words, a lot of feelings for it. But so many of us, and me, speaking for myself, have suppressed that, or worked beyond that. I put those feelings away a long time ago and try not to go back to it because they are so painful and so hurtful. It was such a bad experience for me about this state and the leadership of the Mormon Church who I think—or thought then—were well-intentioned. . . . When it was all over [I felt] . . . it was cruel, and it was dirty handed, and there was not one ounce of Christianity in any of what they were doing because they were acting so much out of fear. I started to understand how Christian wars get started.[63]

For Jan Tyler, the IWY was "not the beginning or the end of anything. It is part of a process we have to go through until people are ready to focus on issues and solve problems."[64] Speaking with objectivity fourteen years after the conference, she defined the event as a "vision" of future options:

> It was an opportunity that wasn't [realized], in my honest opinion, but the vision of . . . maybe the first opportunity, at least in modern times in this state for women to come together around something that was theirs [even though] it had been highly politicized. . . .

> It was like I was watching fourteen births at once. Even [for] those of us who had our own earlier awakenings it was a . . . jolting consciousness of a different kind. Without exception every woman who was there was radicalized, either very conservatively or, if you already had some kind of awareness, you were radicalized—more radicalized. . . . and it was painful to watch those births that were mishandled. There was not a natural process of discovery and joy and information and learning and being able to process this yourself.[65]

Christine Durham agreed that even the negative aspects of the conference had a positive side:

> The IWY had the effect, partly because it was so awful and so negative, of getting that message out to a lot of people in a big hurry. And the net result, within five years, was that there were far more well-informed, involved activist women around the community who were saying, "There have got to be changes. Things have got to be done."
>
> There were hundreds, perhaps thousands, of women who were sensitized as a result of the IWY conference who started looking around them—looking around in their schools and their neighborhoods and their communities and their offices and their professions and saying, "Gee, I never quite saw the world before. It doesn't look quite right to me. What needs to be done about it?" And they got active and started doing things about it. I think there's a direct correlation. I'm hopeful that would have happened without IWY, but as I said, I think IWY enhanced the process in our state.[66]

Utah's politicians took a keen interest in the outcome of the conference. Utah Congressman Dan Marriott congratulated the delegates on July 6, saying he cared deeply about women's issues and felt they could "make no greater contribution or experience greater reward than in the home." He was pleased that Utah was "instrumental in putting aside once and for all the interests of the few extreme elements [in order to] present the will of the majority. Only then can the rights and freedoms of women and men truly be protected."[67]

In mid-July, Utah's Democratic governor Scott Matheson, whose wife had served on the coordinating committee, called an informal meeting of the Governor's Commission on the Status of Women and instructed them to thereafter direct their energies toward improving the legal status of homemakers, a goal clearly endorsed by the women attending the IWY meeting.[68] Eleanor Lewis, chair of the commission, stated that another goal springing from the IWY conference was to establish women's rights commissions throughout the state. "More moneyed women than not are privy to activities of the commission because poor women cannot afford to travel to the capital for meetings and events," she said. "We need this local input, at the grass roots."[69]

Much of the emotional work of processing what had occurred was painfully private, but some women expressed themselves through letters to their local newspapers. One woman wrote to the *Salt Lake Tribune* to challenge Barbara Smith's insistence that the church had not been involved in influencing votes:

> Having attended an LDS Sacrament meeting as well as a Relief Society meeting just prior to the conference, I am in disbelief as to how Mrs. Smith and the group she represents could deny such accusations. At both meetings, all women were urged to be in attendance at the meetings and to vote according to the teachings of their church. Statements were voiced such as "We want the vote to go our way" and "we can rule by our numbers alone, so please attend." This was followed up by the Relief Society visiting teachers carrying the same message to those on whom they call.[70]

Neither Smith nor any other spokesperson responded. In an interview with the *New York Times* a month later, Public Communications spokesman Don LeFevre admitted the church had been involved: "The Church has always been concerned with threats to the stability of the family and the home. We don't make any excuses for our women's participation. We're proud of them. Other women's groups could probably take a note from their book."[71]

Indeed, the John Birch Society's publication, the *Utah Independent,* gloated at the sweeping defeat of national resolutions and the overwhelming election of conservative delegates. It mocked the disappointment of the coordinating committee over the chaos that had ensued: "The highly-publicized 'Voice of Womankind' rang out from the State Women's Meeting at the Salt Palace last weekend . . . but organizers didn't like the way it sounded! They apparently expected Utah housewives to mindlessly echo their deceptive pro-abortion, pro-ERA recommendations and to endorse their feminist slate of nominees."[72] Perpetuating a conspiratorial approach, the *Independent* added: "They threatened to close down the Right to Life booth because its representatives had been distributing a pro-life, anti-ERA slate. Yet they openly campaigned, from the podium, for members of their own carefully-selected list." The *Independent* insisted that organizers "conveniently lost" recommendations from the Reproductive Health Workshop and "suppressed the views and the candidates which were not their own, shutting off the microphones of those they had promised could speak or those who had proof of IWY inaccuracies."[73] Typical of the exaggerated claims made before the conference, whatever incidental mistakes occurred amid the conference confusion were interpreted as intentional injustices, while the crowds of women shouting down speakers and preventing all views from being fairly heard were simultaneously celebrated as a great success. I have not found any evidence of committee members intentionally subverting the efforts of special interest groups to distribute literature, voice opinions, or get their candidates elected.

Aileen H. Clyde of Springville, Utah, attended the conference. She would later became a counselor in the general presidency of the LDS Relief Society. Clyde sent a carefully worded letter to the editor of the *Provo Herald:* "The meaning and importance of the Women's Conference held in Salt Lake City this past weekend invites continuing study. . . . I hope that both the women participants and the women they are credited with having represented will examine carefully their own understanding of the twenty-five issues presented there so that they can have a constructive influence as our society continues to focus on the rights of women as persons." She expressed dismay at the lack of participation in the earlier mass meetings held around the state and at what she perceived to have been the manipulation of voters by the Conservative Caucus and its leader, Dennis Ker:

> May I suggest some inferences I could make from this. (1) Mr. Ker found these women easy to mislead. (2) Mr. Ker found the women had misled themselves. (3) These women were so full of pre-conceived notions that such group participation clouded their judgment about the difference between church and political sponsorship. (4) These women forgot temporarily the counsel of their Church that they should never use their Church callings for political purposes. . . . That Utah had the largest Women's Conference participation in the United States is noteworthy to the extent that it was Utah women representing themselves. To the extent that the large attendance resulted from political manipulation of Utah women's Church loyalty, it might not be so exemplary.[74]

Another letter to the *Salt Lake Tribune* commented on other ironic dichotomies:

> Anti-ERA women call themselves "pro-family"—as if they consider the rest of us to be anti-family. How can widowed and divorced women, who are fighting to gain the benefits and wages that only men have enjoyed in the past, be labeled "anti-family," when many of them are the sole support of their families? These women (my daughter is one of them) work long, hard hours at a daytime job, then go home to clean, cook, sew, etc., for several hours more. After they pay babysitting or nursery fees for the care of their children, most of them find it difficult—if not impossible—to make ends meet. Certainly, they have to forego all of the luxuries their more fortunate sisters take for granted. After reading the list of names and backgrounds of Utah's elected delegates to the IWY conference, I realized the majority of these women, as wives of prominent and/or well-to-do men, have never had to depend upon their own earnings for their families' livelihood; they've had the time and the money to pursue the careers they wanted, instead of wasting their talents in a stenographers' pool, a department store sales force, or a restaurant's waitress crew, at a salary most men would scorn. . . . The Utah elected delegation's indignant reaction to the appointment of at-large delegates to the national IWY conference was

amusing, since their arguments that it was a biased, unrepresentative group could also have been applied to them.[75]

Alan Rasmussen from Salt Lake City regretted what he assumed was gridlock created by irreconcilable and inflexible viewpoints on both sides. "As an active Mormon," he wrote, "I must apologize for the shabby way some of my co-religionists treated so many of the non-Mormons at the recent IWY conference."[76]

Few letters were able to achieve such emotional equilibrium. The columns of both the *Salt Lake Tribune* and the *Deseret News* spilled over with angry, heartfelt expressions such as this:

> The booing and the hissing of the minority by some conservative fanatics and the mindless sheep that followed them, and their refusal in some instances to even let the minority speakers finish their presentations, were just too much for (my wife and me) and were, in my opinion, the height of intolerance and bigotry.[77]

Another letter the same day read:

> So congratulations to you, my fellow Mormons. You won the battle, but you lost the war. You won your points against the ERA and the other positions presented at the conference, even to the extent of voting down teaching little girls in public schools how to recognize potential rapists. But you set both Mormon/non-Mormon relations and the entire missionary effort of the church in this valley back 50 years. How can I face my non-Mormon friends after what you have done? How can you face yours? Do you even have any non-Mormon friends? . . . To maintain consistency with its teachings, the First Presidency of the LDS Church should come out publicly and roundly condemn the shameful tactics displayed at this conference. Let the majority rule—but let it rule in dignity, fairness, and courtesy."[78]

Kathleen Christison's letter to the editor the next day described her pride at seeing democracy in action, tainted by her horror as she watched thousands of "people who either could not or did not choose to think for themselves." She acknowledged that her local Relief Society president had asked her to attend the conference and that she had gone willingly, invigorated by the prospect of becoming informed and involved. Nevertheless, during the general assembly, as she heard resolutions voted down one by one almost mechanically, she "didn't know whether to laugh or cry. Not because the women who were elected as delegates are not intelligent forthright individuals who, for the most part, will represent my views, but because we do not have among them a fair representation of the culture of the women of this state." She concluded:

> Utah women have spoken out in unmistakable terms. The debates and votes . . . left no doubt that the women of this state hope to cling to traditional values and lifestyles against the winds of change blowing across the country. They left no doubt that they distrust and resent the intrusion of federal government into so many aspects of our lives. They stated clearly and unequivocably [sic] their belief in the home as the basic unit of our society. Picketers and some others charged that the conference was not really representative of Utah women. It is certainly true that liberal voices were often drowned out at the conference, and it is unfortunate that, with feelings running high in a conference of such unprecedented size, other points of view were sometimes not listened to.[79]

Fiscal officer Dorothy Littrell felt bitter about the subversion of the process and of the committee's careful preparations. Three week after the conference, she and others signed a brusk letter to the editor: "As active Mormons and Social Relations and Gospel Doctrine teachers in the church, we must express our disappointment at the anti-Christian behavior displayed by so many of the LDS women at the International Women's Year Conference."[80]

A letter from two other dismayed and embarrassed Mormon women questioned the negativity that prevailed, fueled by the doctrine that feminism opposes the family. Sisters-in-law Kathryn Wadsworth Davis and Mirian Bailey Wadsworth wrote:

> We are supposed to be first and foremost a Christian church grounded in the teachings and lifestyle of Jesus Christ. Obviously many either forgot

this or never knew it. . . . It will be difficult to heal the wounds and mend the bad feelings that were generated. If anything good can come out of this unfortunate affair, it might be that many eyes will be opened to see that all is not well in Zion.[81]

Of all the writers, Christison captured the paradox neatly. One's feelings about the success of the conference depended not on the conference itself but on one's political leanings. From a conservative perspective, it had been a success in that it was representative of Utah's women and gave a clarion expression of Utah's values. From a liberal perspective, it was a terrifying reversal of women's minuscule progress toward equality, a cynical power play to deny fair treatment of half the state's citizens, and worse still, an embarrassing display of ignorance as women worked against their own best interests—in other words, a representation of everything that was wrong with Utah.

Tyler tried to find comfort where she could, knowing that at least in some respects the future lay in the hands of the Houston convention. She was encouraged that women telephoned her after the state meeting saying they had been "thinking about things they've never thought about before. A lot of them are beginning to transcend their own conditions, and say that 'there are other women in the world who find themselves in circumstances very different from mine.'" Tyler held the hope, despite the position taken by the church on women's issues, that traditionalists and feminists might still find common ground. "That doesn't mean that there isn't some pain and introspection that goes on, dealing with issues you might otherwise have ignored. That isn't to say it's an easy thing," she continued. Many people think that if "they don't buy the whole package of women's rights issues, they're somehow shut out of the movement altogether. If the women's movement is going to define itself as just another part of society that's exclusive, then it's really in trouble."[82]

It was some comfort that a *Deseret News* editorial recognized the efforts of the coordinating committee to address diverse viewpoints, bring a variety of voices into the arena, and adapt to the problems that sprang up along the way: "Special commendation is due to the women who worked so hard to organize and bring the conference off. The throng of some 13,000 women—more than twice the size of the next largest state conference—created severe stresses. They were met, in the main, with good humor and tolerance not only by the workers but by the thousands of women who were inconvenienced by shortages of seating, materials, and time." The paper particularly commended Esther Landa and the coordinating committee for "the balance, dignity, composure, and sense of fairness they displayed under extremely trying conditions."[83]

Tyler wrote to Kathryn MacKay, another disillusioned committee woman, after two years had passed:

> I, like thousands, learned a great deal after IWY. Continually, since that event, other lessons come into focus, as I am prepared to learn them. One of the things I determined early was that I no longer wanted to work with groups of only women. So these past two years have been unattached to any one-gender organizations, although I've continued to be supportive and make contributions—I just ceased to "belong." I also determined that this whole "women's issue" was far larger and had implications for a far wider range of people than I was seeing and associating [with], . . . which I'm sure has been very confusing to some people. . . . I was [impressed] . . . at the Houston meeting as I watched Gloria Steinem working on the convention floor with the minority women. Her role as a facilitator, a "coach," a supporter of their search, as one who could lend her experiences and vision in encouraging others to reach for and be all they could, fascinated me and I knew that I could in some similar way do that also.[84]

In a more discouraged moment, Tyler admitted that despite her best efforts, the "unfortunate things" at Utah's conference "gave me personal pain,"and she could not understand how women who "profess[ed] a tremendous concern for life" could be so "abusive in their actions toward others."[85]

Traditional women came away from the conference generally satisfied by their efforts. Claudia Aldredge of St. George wrote on July 4: "I believe that the outcome of this conference [reflected] the views of interested Utah women, as this is how the majority voted. We, the majority of women present, are merely concerned about doing what we can to preserve the family unit. We merely turned out to vote and I, for one, was surprised to see so many anti-ERA persons in attendance."[86]

An incongruous symbol for Mormon women was a nearby art exhibition, "The Women: A Perspective from the Past," which opened at the Relief Society Resource Center in conjunction with the IWY. The display offered brief glimpses of women from pioneer times to the present. The curator, Ann Madsen, wife of a BYU philosophy professor, said it was intended to let women show how they tried to "surround themselves and their environment with beauty, making their homes pleasant places for themselves and their families."[87] This message of sweet gentility was already hopelessly out of date. Emboldened by the belief that they were defending everything they cared most about, Mormon women had just embarked on a political cause that would become more hard-edged as they demonstrated a willingness to do virtually anything, however mean-spirited, to achieve their goal.

The IWY conference was the proving ground for the upcoming national fight against the so-called feminist threat of the ERA, and the strategies used here would be multiplied elsewhere, including the use of telephone trees provided by the church organization, repetitive instruction to toe the party line, mass literature and information drives, heavy lobbying, and bloc voting. Church leaders had learned how to mobilize an inexperienced but devoted mass of foot soldiers in a holy war against feminism.

8. The National Convention

> For the 20,000 women, men, and children who were there, for the millions of Americans who read about it, listened on the radio, or watched on television, the National Women's Conference, held in Houston . . . was a unique experience. It was a first in so many ways.
>
> —*The Spirit of Houston*

The many ways the IWY conference in Houston was "a first" included the first time in the United States for a national meeting with government sponsorship to act on issues impacting women's lives. It was the first time women would elect their own representatives for a government conference. And it was the first time such a diverse group of women representing all ethnic, racial, and religious groups, and from every economic class, would meet. Held the same weekend that Egyptian President Anwar Sadat made his memorable first visit to Israel, this conference was also making history.

According to the National Commission on the Observance of International Women's Year,

> Mothers, daughters, and grandmothers. Single, married, divorced, or

widowed women. Homemakers. Working women. Students. The President's wife and two former First Ladies. Members of Congress. Public officials. Leaders of the Democratic and Republican national committees. Representatives from every major women's organization in the country. Disabled women. White, black, Hispanic, American Indian, Eskimo, and Asian American women. Women of fame and women who lead ordinary lives. They were all there, together.[1]

The U.S. Commitment

Groundwork for the conference began when the United Nations issued its proclamation in 1975 establishing International Women's Year. Fueled by rising demands for economic and social equity, IWY was intended to focus world attention on improving women's lives. On January 30, 1974, President Richard M. Nixon called for Americans to support the year-long observance.

His successor, Gerald Ford, issued Executive Order No. 11832 on January 9, 1975, creating the national commission "to promote equality between men and women." At the head of the thirty-five women and men comprising the commission, President Ford appointed Jill Ruckelshaus as its presiding officer. Ruckelshaus was an attorney, mother, and government official for whom the women's movement had been nothing short of a movement for freedom, both "for those who work outside the home and those who dedicate themselves with more altruism than any profession I know to being wives and mothers, cooks and chauffeurs, and child psychologists and loving human beings."[2]

The commission was to address "those inequities that still linger as barriers to the full participation of women in our Nation's life." President Ford underscored that Americans should "support and strengthen the laws that prohibit discrimination based on sex."[3] In response, the commission created thirteen committees to investigate discrimination and prepare specific recommendations for the president. In June 1976 the commission issued its 382-page report, *To Form a More Perfect Union,* with 115 specific recommendations.

The report was surprisingly thorough in considering homemakers, women in the workplace, the image of women presented by the media, the Equal Rights Amendment, women in the arts and humanities, women of color, and legal issues impacting women. A poll of 1,522 women by Market Opinion Research asked, on behalf of the commission, how satisfied they were with their lives, what they perceived their status to be, what they would like to be doing, and whether they welcomed or resisted changes in their roles.[4]

The United Nations sponsored its international IWY conference in Mexico City in June 1975 (see chap. 5). Understandably, the meeting did not take place without some problems where many delegations were led by men who voiced the official viewpoints of their governments. Logistical problems in providing lodging, meeting spaces, and translation services for 1,300 attendees from across the world frazzled nerves. Besides the official delegates who came from 130 countries, 7,000 other individuals, mostly women, came at their own expense.

Senator Charles H. Percy of Illinois, a Congressional advisor to the U.S. delegation, observed: "The Conference was an opportunity for women to meet, find reassurance in each other's experiences and gain new challenges in each other's ideas. The Conference toughened and matured the international women's movement. Women . . . began . . . building the informal associations and networks so important in the exercise of influence and power."[5] But for many, the coming together of women from around the world, sharing common concerns regardless of their homelands, was itself a profoundly moving experience. The realization that the "state of womanhood transcends geographic barriers inspired in many the belief that women could begin to take control of their own lives and, in the process, work for a better world with more humanist values."[6]

Listening to Women

Early in 1975, Representative Bella Abzug (D-New York), who had been in Mexico City, introduced a proposal for a national women's conference to be held as part of the U.S. bicentennial celebration. The House of Representatives passed Public Law 94-167 on December 10 and the Senate followed thirteen days later. President Ford signed the bill into law the day before Christmas. It provided for state or regional meetings leading to a national conference, which it said should "assess the progress that has been made to date by both the private and public sectors in promoting equality between men and women in all aspects of life in the United States." It also called for a second National Women's Conference at some future date "to evaluate the steps taken to improve the status of American women" in the wake of the first conference.[7]

Congress appropriated $5 million for the activities and encouraged "special emphasis on the representation of low-income women, members of diverse racial, ethnic, and religious groups, and women of all ages." More than half the funding was divided among the states for their conferences. Money also went to scholarships and grants for women who might not otherwise be able to attend.

The national commission appointed a conference chair for each state in concert with the state's governor. The state committees were to represent a cross-section of the female population. As mandated by the commission, all meetings were to be open to the public and conform to Roberts's Rules of Order. Women over sixteen could register, speak, and vote. As in Utah, state or territorial coordinating committees set local agendas, researched resolutions, and prepared for workshops, mass meetings, and other events. Although the national commission identified a core agenda of sixteen issues and drafted workshop guidelines for these topics, each state committee had the right to shape its own agenda and choose speakers, films, and other events according to its perception of local needs and interest.

As a result, each state's committee exercised significant control in shaping the conferences and selecting a slate of resolutions for discussion. Each conference had provisions for receiving proposals from the floor. Although Utah was the only state to hold local mass meetings, Indiana, North Carolina, and Puerto Rico held regional gatherings and Arkansas formed outreach committees to conduct research on rural education and equity in the workplace. The District of Columbia held a two-day hearing at which women were invited to testify.[8]

More than 150,000 women (and some men) attended the state and territorial conferences. Women from isolated farms in the Midwest came, as did professional women wearing power suits and carrying attaché cases. Homemakers and educators, waitresses and physicists all met together on college campuses and state fairgrounds, in civic centers or in outdoor arenas. The conventions were intended to identify issues peculiar to the different states, but they in fact became single-issue "battlegrounds for the Equal Rights Amendment and legalized abortions" according to one reporter.[9]

The first of the conferences, held in February 1977 in Montpelier, Vermont, was billed as a one-day "Women's Town Meeting" and drew more than a thousand women, many of them taking advantage of free bus service and child care. Others came because they were simply curious. After a keynote speaker and workshops, participants voted on resolutions and elected delegates during a plenary session. In a post-conference poll, 45 percent said they had never before participated in a women's meeting and had attended largely due to their own personal interest.[10]

The most popular session was "Women's Health Resources in Vermont," which included a discussion about family planning, abortion, and other health issues. Other sessions included the unique problems of French-speaking women in the northeastern part of the state and the problems of urban women whose children had moved into the country. A workshop moderated by a male reporter from the *Boston Globe* explored problems faced by homemakers.

The chair, Lenore W. McNeer, was director of human services at Vermont College. In her concluding remarks, she voiced the hope that legislators had heard what the women at the conference had said and would make necessary changes in the law. In fact, two weeks later, the Vermont legislature revised a rape law that feminists had long lobbied for.[11]

The next month, on May 6, more than 780 women crowded into the auditorium of the University of Alaska, the largest meeting room in Anchorage.[12] Simultaneously, more than 1,200 women and men from Georgia met in the elegant Sheraton-Biltmore Hotel in Atlanta to hear Bella

Abzug, presiding officer of the national commission, talk about why American women needed the Equal Rights Amendment. Georgia had voted against ratification, and the coordinating committee mirrored the state's division over the issue.[13]

Valeria Harper, star of the popular television sitcom *Rhoda,* opened the state meeting in Boise, Idaho, on May 21-22, urging equal rights for homemakers. Even though Idaho had rescinded its ratification of the ERA in January, participants nevertheless adopted all of the national resolutions—an action that dismayed Mormon attendees.

Eight states held their conferences in early June. Seven voted to support all the core resolutions and elected national delegates who were seasoned defenders of female equality. Resolutions that reflected local concerns included Washington D.C.'s request for independence.[14] In Arizona, where migrant workers comprise a significant proportion of the labor force, women "refused to eat lettuce cultivated by non-union labor."[15]

Most of these meetings avoided heated controversy even while generating lively debate. An exception was Missouri, where the ERA had not been ratified. At Washington University in St. Louis on June 10-12, there was a tense mood among the 2,500 attendees. Distinguished alumna Phyllis Schlafly, president of STOP ERA, boycotted the state conference. She also refused to attend any other state meeting and specifically declined an invitation to serve on the Missouri coordinating committee. Her decision complicated efforts to achieve balance because anti-ERA forces felt they should follow her lead. Approximately 400 people registered the first day, fewer on Saturday, and fewer still on Sunday. Puzzlingly, however, an improbable total of 861 voted on the resolutions and for delegates. According to the official report sent to the National Commission, a coalition of anti-abortion and anti-ERA groups bused five hundred men and women to the conference site with "a handbill and a list of their own 'New Suffragist' candidates printed on yellow paper."[16] The thirty women elected to attend the national convention were all from the New Suffragist slate—and all, despite the name, opposed equality for women. Although few people registered to attend the conference, 1,164 participated. In the confusion, the meetings ended without passing any resolutions.[17]

Fireworks also punctuated the California conference, which attracted 6,500 to the University of Southern California campus. Despite efforts by the coordinating committee to create balance in the workshops and to represent different ethnic, occupational, and other special interests, conservatives and liberals squared off at each other, contesting every issue, including the site choice, workshop topics, and how the votes would be counted. One workshop questioned whether the women's movement was the principal obstacle facing contemporary women. After several nights of caucusing, speeches, and deal-making, the Californians elected ninety-six delegates. Among them were forty-five Caucasians, fourteen African Americans, twenty-one Hispanics, and ten Asian Americans. Thirteen identified themselves as lesbians and thirty came from low-income families. The final report marveled that anyone could have expected consensus from a body as "diverse as that meeting in California simply because women are still stereotyped as a class. What would happen," the reporter of the California meeting, Suzanne Paizis, inquired, "if you brought men together from all walks of life to discuss 'Credit Factors Influencing Your Life'? Who would expect bank presidents and hard core unemployed to attend or interact in those circumstances? Visualize thousands of neurosurgeons, truck drivers, school administrators, interior decorators, custodians, management consultants, tennis players, and salesmen spending three days in a parliamentary session to come up with recommendations on fifty different subjects."[18]

Minnesota's conference, attended by 4,500 individuals, concluded on June 5 in a spirit of cordial optimism:

> Recognizing that we will never all agree on every issue, we pledge to bind ourselves together in love, to continue to work on the concerns of universal importance—the need for our personal dignity, the relief of our suffering, the achievement of our aspirations—so that we can go on to that great

victory: equality for all women, not only in Minnesota, but around the world.[19]

Despite this pledge, a sour note occurred in a confrontation between anti-abortion and pro-choice groups.[20]

In marked contrast were a few even pricklier conferences. Utah was not the only state to express overwhelming mistrust of what it saw as a liberal agenda. In Ohio, which held its conference on June 11-12 in Columbus, a split among feminists allowed the "right to life" coalition to pick up 80 percent of the delegates. Since only 10 percent of anti-abortion delegates favored the ERA, this turn of events was doubly political. Abortion was as hotly contested an issue as the ERA in most states. At the Oklahoma meetings on June 16-18, attended by 1,400, a coalition of local Christians elected a full slate of anti-ERA delegates, passed a resolution that "homemaking is the most vital and rewarding career for women," and in a single bloc vote defeated the national core agenda and ended the meeting.[21]

The Washington D.C. convention elected twelve women headed by Ann B. Turpeau, chair of the D.C. Commission on the Status of Women. The other delegates represented a cross-section of the city.[22] Organizers had attempted to prevent "extremist groups" such as "Right to Lifers and radical feminists" from participating, and the conference was, in fact, the scene of some heated debates on abortion and lesbianism. Ultimately, the conference endorsed abortion on request "regardless of the ability to pay," repeal of laws prohibiting consensual sexual acts among adults, and a study of the impact of welfare reform on women. The Reverend Imagene Stewart of the Church of What's Happening Now ended the ceremony with a rendition of "I Am Woman." Wearing a gold-encrusted silk outfit, trouser legs tucked into black boots and a three-color hat that said "Free D.C.," she roused the audience and left them feeling they would have an impact on Houston. "This delegation is going to keep it together," said Bennetta Washington, wife of Mayor Walter Washington, a delegate-at-large for the Houston conference.[23]

In some states, men with walkie-talkies monitored the events at the conferences. This happened in Alabama, Hawaii, Illinois, Indiana, Mississippi, and Ohio, and in all six states where men directed the women how to vote, the anti-feminists voted down all of the national resolutions including aid to the handicapped. Similarly, in Montgomery, Alabama, on the weekend of July 9, attended by 2,000 people, the conservative forces prevailed in electing twenty of the twenty-four delegates to Houston. Like Utah, they repudiated every single national resolution.

Mormon Influence outside Utah

The state conferences that included a contest between traditional and liberal women were, in part, the result of the LDS Church capitalizing on the lessons learned in Utah and mobilizing women under priesthood direction in at least five states, a development not fully appreciated at the time. Utah's conference concluded on June 25. Although Mormons represented less than 2 percent of Washington State's total population, they represented half of the 4,000 women registered for the state meeting in Ellensburg, July 8-10, according to the *Seattle Post-Intelligencer.* They joined other conservative women who believed the fight against the ERA was a moral issue; but for many, the resolution jointly supporting minority rights and the ERA presented an ethical dilemma: "Many opposition women were so torn that they abstained, but a few rose slowly and tearfully to vote 'yes' for the minorities. ERA and all. Black women rushed over to embrace them. After a stormy session and a recount of ballots that took days, a majority of delegates favoring ERA was elected."[24] About half of the delegates, according to the *New York Times,* were Mormon, and they rejected the ERA resolution with very little "dialogue."[25]

Attended by about 1,787 women, Montana's conference, held July 8-10, the same weekend as Washington's, quickly deteriorated because single-issue groups dug in their heels over abortion, the ERA, and compulsory military service for women. According to Jean Dimich, chair of the Montana nominating committee, many of the women opposed to the ERA and abortion wore beehive pins, apparently signals of their LDS membership.[26] About two hundred women walked out the first night, saying that the meeting had been taken over by the "ultraconservatives."

Some returned for workshops on Saturday, but each competing group had put together its own lists of proposals for the state's fourteen allotted delegates.[27] About half of the elected delegates were reportedly Mormon, and they were definitely anti-abortion and anti-ERA. Judy Smith of Missoula told the *Salt Lake Tribune* she saw men with walkie-talkies ushering groups of conservative women into rooms where policies and procedures were discussed. The men coached the women on what to say and how to operate the microphones as if they were children, according to Smith.[28] One walkie-talkie carrier, Jack Piippo of Bozeman, said as many as half the women at the conference were LDS Church members. He told the *Deseret News* his ward leaders recruited him; the women were told by their ward Relief Society presidencies to attend. According to Mary Munger, head of the coordinating committee, all fourteen delegates to Houston were on record during the state conference as having opposed abortion and the ERA.[29]

The New York conference drew 10,000 participants to Albany to elect eighty-eight delegates. After thrashing out a plan of action, they decided on "the ERA, abortion, equal pay for equal work, women's history courses, support for mothers who stay at home, protection for widows and elderly women, universal child care—all were endorsed by an overflow meeting."[30] Chair Mary Burke Nicholas was director of the Women's Division of the Executive Chamber, a cabinet-level job within the New York governor's office. The founder of the Coalition of 100 Black Women, she and other organizers had anticipated about 3,000 women from across the state, and when almost triple that number showed up, it created a chaotic and confused atmosphere that Nicholas described as "nightmarish."[31] This unexpected turnout was in part due to a huge response of Mormon women who were quickly mobilized by their ward leaders. The ballot sheet was three and a half feet long with 320 nominations.

Among the Mormons who attended, a busload from New York City was mobilized by two church officials. They and other church members arrived in Albany from branches and wards throughout the state. Reporter Elaine Bissell described the "churning mob of a reported 8,000 women milling through the mammoth concourse level of the Empire State Plaza" in the opening hours of the conference. Women were "arriving with knapsacks and sleeping bags, in Charles Jourdan shoes and with Fendi purses, in sneakers and shorts, in Cardin T-shirts and pre-bleached Levis, with infant strollers and in wheelchairs and by stretch Mercedes, pick-up truck and Greyhound bus."[32] The Mormon women had all received a letter from the stake Relief Society presidency giving them conference information and alerting them that "matters of vital interest to us as women in the Church will be discussed and voted upon. Equal rights for women, abortion, and other topics including sex-education in the schools, pornography, homosexual rights, crime and T.V. violence have surfaced in the meetings held in other states. Delegates will be selected to represent the proposals that are voted in."[33]

According to this letter, the LDS First Presidency had authorized the creation of committees and individuals ("visiting teachers") to get women out for the event and assist them in finding child care, transportation, and housing. In addition, local members created the "Citizens Review Committee" to solicit women willing to be nominated as delegates to the national convention. Finally, the letter gave some specific instructions, or rather requests, from the Relief Society general presidency in Salt Lake City. The presidency recommended:

1) Each sister should dress modestly and in a well-groomed manner that reflects the highest ideals of LDS womanhood.
2) Each should become well-informed on topics likely for discussion so she cannot be maneuvered into an embarrassing position by well-informed persons with opposing views. We must speak intelligently.
3) We should actively participate and make our views known and heard. Overly-emotional, radical and sarcastic behavior should be avoided; We should maintain an image of maturity and responsibility.[34]

Two fact sheets accompanying the letter included details on hotel choices, special sessions of interest, and most importantly the voting times and locations. The "Supplemental Data Sheet" noted the "PRIME

IMPORTANCE" of voting down certain resolutions and voting for Mormon delegates. It said: "Elements capable of destroying family unity may be introduced in the resolutions and must be opposed. We should act as individuals—as citizens and residents of New York State—and not as any church or organization."[35]

Mark Koltko, converted to Mormonism only two years earlier, was asked by his ward leaders to take a walkie-talkie along to help organize the women from the sidelines. Church leaders assigned other men with walkie-talkies to each workshop and plenary session, keeping tabs on voting and attendance.[36] Koltko remembered that, when votes were about to begin, each observer contacted the others, and as many women as possible would rush to the site of the vote to participate. In many cases, this tactic effectively dominated the vote. Walkie-talkies were used in several other state conventions,[37] but the "flying squad" technique proved only partially effective in Albany, according to Koltko, because the capitol police were called out to help disperse the crowds.

Despite the efforts of local Mormons, New York State sent a strongly feminist delegation to Houston. Zelle Andrews, New York's National Organization of Women president, said at a press conference on July 24: "The entire slate of eighty-eight delegates and five alternates is committed to three fundamental issues—passage of the equal rights amendment; safe, legal abortion regardless of income; and civil rights for lesbians and gay men." Andrews asserted that the delegation was the largest from any state committed to those three "feminist positions."[38]

In Hawaii local LDS bishops asked the women in their wards to attend the three-day Honolulu conference beginning July 8. They were told to report to the "Traditional Values Van" where they would sign in together and be united in their opposition to the national resolutions. The bishops stressed that they needed especially to attend the first plenary session so they could vote on the rules for the conference and thereby block the influence of the feminist organizers. Ward members car pooled from church parking lots to the conference site. At Laie, women met in the parking lot of the BYU-Hawaii campus.

A pre-conference workshop for LDS women included "Feminists—Consciousness Raising (Homosexuality)" to warn them that lesbians would try to show X-rated movies, pass out pornographic literature, and promote licentious lifestyles—specifically calling the IWY organizers lesbians and degenerates. The *Honolulu Star-Bulletin* reported that "a militant bloc of conservatives led by women of the Church of Jesus Christ of Latter-day Saints (Mormon) outnumbered the more liberal faction about 2 to 1 at the Hawaii women's conference." Organizers estimated that the more than 1,500 Mormons in attendance created a heavy "conservative flavor of the Hawaii state meeting."[39] Despite this advantage, Terry Bosgra and Lissa Atkinson protested what they called the "feminist takeover" even though Bosgra and Atkinson were both elected as delegates. In a letter to the national IWY commission, the women complained:

> The parliamentarian, Clara Kakalia, was also observed to be wearing a pro-ERA wristband and she took visible satisfaction in rulings that went against the Women for Traditional Values group. . . . There were complaints that she snatched lists of candidates [from conservatives] . . . and ejected at least one Traditional Values woman from the polling place. . . . Through parliamentary maneuvering and obstruction, a small minority of pro-ERA advocates was able to totally control Saturday and Sunday sessions to the almost complete exclusion of participation by anyone else.[40]

Helen Triester, another Mormon elected to the national convention, was similarly outraged by what occurred in Honolulu, and she thought the national commission should rebuke the planning committee. She wrote:

> I lined up outside the auditorium, along with 1,000 other people, to attend another "meeting" which was billed on my program as "Coming together," and since it was given in the auditorium, I selected a seat as far down front as I could and expected it to be another session meeting, with possibly a panel of women, maybe some sincere discussion about how women might achieve associations to this end. What was presented was two Lesbians, dressed in Leotards, showing the audience how they make

> love in a pay toilet! . . . One lady in front of me vomited. Another lady was nauseated right in the lobby! And it made me sick too, to see and hear such filth.[41]

Perhaps intended to demonstrate the reality of a lifestyle forced to move in a subterranean world, this interpretive dance performance elicited disgust rather than compassion from the conservative women.[42]

According to reporter Ray Yuen, the Hawaii meeting ended the way it began—"as a confrontation between conservatives, mainly churchgoers, and the outnumbered liberals and individuals."[43] Only ten of the more than 100 resolutions from the dozen task forces made it to the floor for some 4,000 women to vote on. Only four passed, endorsing more women in elected office, improved health care for elderly women, and various educational opportunities for women.

Carlanne McCrystal, a self-avowed feminist, mourned the male presence: "There are a lot of men here who I believe are leading the women. This is the International Women's Year, and I would like to see the women leading themselves."[44] The planners felt blindsided by the unexpected turnout. "It's too bad we were unaware until too late," chair Winona Rubin said, acknowledging the resulting confusion. "I had hoped we could act on many more issues that are important to women." As for the Mormon women in attendance, they denied voting as a bloc during the conference "and repeated earlier statements that they had been 'educated' on the issues and were voting and attending as individuals." When the conference crowd filtered out of the auditorium after the last meeting, two women quietly stood at the side of the entrance holding a sign that sometimes brought cheers from the more liberal delegates as they exited. It read: "God forgive them for they know not what they do."[45]

For Mormons, the highlight of the conference came a day later in a congratulatory visit from Barbara Smith, who spoke at the Honolulu Tabernacle on July 11. As president of the general Relief Society and respected leader of Mormon women, she encouraged the audience to "continue strong," telling the women success stories that had come out of other state IWY conferences.[46]

These events racheted up the tension in anticipation of the national conference in Houston. Eleven states—Alabama, Hawaii, Indiana, Kansas, Mississippi, Missouri, Montana, Nebraska, Ohio, Oklahoma, and Utah—had elected delegates who largely opposed the national resolutions. California and New York had elected unabashedly liberal delegations who overwhelmingly supported the national agenda. Several other states sent split delegations.

Conference organizers expressed a "deep concern" over the Mormon Church's involvement and how it would play out in Houston. Several conservative religious and political groups around the country had fought against the IWY's push for greater equality for women, but the Mormon Church's campaign had been the most formidable, turning several IWY state conferences into chaos.

The highly organized opposition to the ERA in the state gatherings should have been a red flag for feminists. But instead of changing their approach to a broader appeal to women of all stripes and a message that might connect with people emotionally, they continued to emphasize education and subtle persuasion, resulting in the two sides growing farther apart over the next five years until what could be said had begun as a battle had deteriorated to something more like trench warfare. Still, on the eve of the convention in Houston, a pre-conference telephone survey indicated that only 20 percent of the delegates opposed the ERA.[47] During the conference itself, a Roper poll discussed on the *McNeill-Lehrer Report* turned up corroboration in 19 percent of the delegates who agreed with Schlafly's anti-ERA position.[48] Even so, supporters concerned about the hostility expressed at some state conferences worried that disruptive tactics might be utilized in Houston.

Houston

It was one of the most diverse gatherings in U.S. history as participants arrived in Houston from all regions of the country and all walks of life: American Indians, Samoans, Hawaiians, Asian Americans, Eskimos, Hispanics, and African Americans; secretaries, teachers, industrial workers, policewomen; politicians and philosophers. They were single, married, widowed, divorced. They were mothers, sisters, daughters, and wives. Some nursed babies during sessions. Others traveled great distances, leaving their children at home.

The conference opened on November 19, 1977, at the Sam Houston Coliseum. Meetings and displays would be held in the nearby Albert Thomas Convention Center, while plenary sessions were scheduled for the coliseum. Of the 2,005 delegates, 1,403 had been elected in state meetings, 186 were alternates, forty-seven were state IWY commissioners, and 370 were delegates-at-large appointed by the national commission.[49] The role of the at-large delegates was not precisely defined, but this group was more diverse than the slate of elected delegates. Most had been selected by state governors to create balance and reflect the demographic composition of a state, although it was also true that some of the appointed representatives were from organizations working "to advance the rights of women."[50] The national commission viewed these appointments as a safeguard against homogeneity, which meant, of course, that the traditionalists viewed them with suspicion.

An editorial in the *Washington Post* reflected this tone of mistrust:

> The National Women's Conference, which opens in Houston today, was a poor idea from the start. Such federally financed conferences . . . push ideas that don't need it and generate so much controversy over other issues that they create a public impression of even more discord than actually exists. Beyond these general liabilities, the women's conference has had special problems. . . . The conference organizers, headed by former Rep. Bella Abzug, have advanced a "plan for action" that touches every inflammatory base. . . . This platform is, we believe, overloaded and doctrinaire.[51]

But the gulf between the organizers and the elected delegates was not as great as it could have been. For instance, 64.5 percent of the state delegates were white—considerably less than the 84.4 percent of the general U.S. population.[52] Overall, the delegates tilted toward the economically disadvantaged with only 14.1 percent in an income bracket above $20,000, compared to the national figure of 25.7 percent. Middle-class women were under-represented, although Utah's delegation provided an exception to the rule.[53] There were other skewed demographic representations such as Mississippi's all-white delegation from a state whose population was 36.8 percent black. Mississippi also sent five men. Only two of Alabama's twenty-four delegates were black, from a population that was 26.2 percent African American.[54] In such instances, the national commission strove for balance by selecting black women at-large.[55] Of the 1,442 elected delegates, 97 were under age twenty-five, 192 were fifty-six or older, and the rest were middle-aged. Minnesota sent the largest number of young women: nine out of twenty-six were between sixteen and twenty-five. By contrast, almost half of Michigan's forty-eight-member delegation was over the age of fifty-six.[56] Politically, the national commission reported an "onslaught" of activity from "radical right-wing" groups aimed at "disruptions" and that these groups "hampered about one-fifth of the State/Territorial meetings. Overall, however, analysis shows that the radical right-wing influence is limited to a small number of delegates from a few states."[57]

Along with the limited number of male delegates, there were uncounted thousands of men and women who attended as guests, reporters, or advisors for workshops and special events. There were also more than 3,000 volunteers. The federal government employed more than 800 women just to help register delegates and collect money for registration fees.

Most of the Utah delegation stayed at the Ramada Inn near the Astrodome complex across town. When they arrived, the weather was hot and muggy. Everywhere they went, they seemed to be a curiosity. The official press briefing book included news articles about how the LDS Church had called ten women from each congregation to the state IWY conferences[58] and identified the church among the "radical right wing groups."[59]

All of the city's hotels were full, some were overbooked. The Hyatt Regency turned away more than 200 women when some businessmen stayed longer than they had planned. Women camped out in hotel lobbies for as long as five hours while they waited for their rooms.[60] Lines formed everywhere at restaurants, outside bathrooms, and at the elevators. "In fact there was a line for just about every human activity. While most remained remarkably cheerful," one reporter wrote, it was "grumbled that a men's conference would never be treated like this."[61]

Security alone cost about $40,000, according to Bella Abzug.[62] NBC television sent eight reporters, engineers, editors, and cameramen. ABC's *Good Morning America* fielded a crew of twelve and broadcast the entire two-hour morning show from the convention center each day. Every major newspaper had reporters in Houston, along with correspondents from a Norwegian magazine and a Canadian broadcasting company.[63]

The women of the national commission must have been exhilarated, anticipating the revolution they felt they were initiating with the convention—the first such government-endorsed gathering of women—and a plan of action that was the result of their best thinking and research, two years of work, and the attention of the world. What a heady feeling of power, anticipation, and unity they must have felt!

In reality, it was a carnival—a power struggle—and something like mud wrestling. Even so, it was a historic event no one wanted to miss. Reporter Megan Rosenfeld, assigned to the conference by her editor at the *Washington Post,* had an eye-opening experience. "The presence of so many women, not just as conference-goers but as conference-runners, was both awesome and startling. For the first time, I was one of the majority. For the first time, my colleague Bill Curry was in a minority. I felt quite comfortable: he, to my secret thought, felt uneasy the entire four days and he wasn't the only one." Rosenfeld reflected that she found herself

> less preoccupied with my appearance than I usually am and totally without the fear that I usually have in a strange city of being vulnerable to physical attack. I felt neither ashamed of being at a conference of women nor embarrassed about aspects of their behavior that were different from a convention dominated by men—babies cared for in the midst of debate, occasional tears, spontaneous singing. That these women were not experienced travelers was obvious: in some cases staying at a hotel was a rare, if not en-

tirely new, experience, and there were many who did not have credit cards.

"Ironically," she continued, "the only hookers at the convention were the ones lobbying for the decriminalization of prostitution." Most importantly to Rosenfeld, "the woman's movement, as this conference made clear, is no longer a small group of intellectuals meeting in someone's living room in New York. It has developed into a force [that is] socially acceptable [to both] presidents' wives and housewives from South Dakota."[64]

The Conference Begins

On Thursday, November 18, as women were checking into hotels and getting oriented, celebrities Rosalynn Carter, Betty Ford, Lady Bird Johnson, Billie Jean King, and Margaret Mead were among the notable women moving through the crowds.[65] Americans knew Betty Ford was a former dancer who had toured with the Martha Graham Concert Group in her youth and that, as First Lady, her public battle with breast cancer had transformed her into an activist. Pushing for a greater national awareness of health problems for women, her struggle with substance abuse had inspired her to found the Betty Ford Center in southern California. She would detail the tumultuous story in two autobiographies: *The Times of My Life* (1979) and *A Glad Awakening* (1987). The theme of the convention, "You've come a long way, baby," could have described the First Lady's own dramatic rise to national prominence. Known as a woman of courage and elegance, she epitomized the new woman of the 1970s. After publicly defending a woman's right to abortion when a pregnancy jeopardized her health or in cases of rape, she had alienated some voters. When she first confronted reporters in her first official news conference in the White House, she reiterated her stance. Not one to back down from a controversial issue, she pledged to campaign for the ERA.[66]

Rosalynn Carter, married to President Jimmy Carter, was active in campaigning for human rights issues. Described by her husband as "an almost equal extension of myself," she was acknowledged as one of his most influential advisors and diligently campaigned for the Equal Rights Amendment.[67]

Other key women in government were there as well: Provo-born Esther Peterson, consumer affairs advisor to the U.S. president; Eleanor Holmes Norton, new chair of the Equal Employment Opportunity Commission; and Mary Anne Krupsak, lieutenant governor of New York. Flamboyant Bella Abzug was the presiding officer,[68] flanked by other commissioners: Maya Angelou; Coretta Scott King; Cecilia Preciado-Burciaga, assistant provost of Stanford University; Gloria Scott, national president of the Girl Scouts of America; and Addie Wyatt, vice president of the Amalgamated Meat Cutters and Butcher Workmen of North America.

Gloria Steinem spoke Thursday night at the Jewish Community Center. A striking, articulate, and passionate proponent of women's rights and the ERA, she described the delegates assembling in Houston as "so exposed, so vulnerable—out there on the edge of history, to make a new world." She described the women's movement as a "transforming movement" rather than a revolution. "What we are trying to do," she said, "is to bring together the full scope of humanity." She accused the media of enhancing the controversy over the ERA. "We need the talents of everyone," she asserted. "If we do not establish civil rights for women whose lifestyle is different from our own, we will never be able to act morally again."[69]

Friday, November 18

Friday morning was devoted to a series of press conferences, caucuses, and coalition meetings, beginning the media circus that would continue for the next several days. Registration proved to be more chaotic than anticipated. By noon, however, things had calmed down somewhat, and a thousand women gathered in front of the coliseum to watch runners bring an Olympic-style torch that had come 2,610 miles in a relay race from Seneca Falls, site of the symbolic birth of the American women's movement. Judy Carter, Jimmy's and Rosalynn's daughter-in-law, was one of the final fifty runners.[70] Three young women athletes brought the torch down the final stretch and the crowd chanted, "E-R-A! E-R-A! E-R-A!" and "Hey, Hey, What do you say? Ratify the ERA! ERAERA-ERAERAERAERA!" Poet and novelist Maya Angelou read the "Declaration of Sentiments" she had drafted to mirror Susan B. Anthony's declaration at Seneca Falls. Abzug enthused that "some of us run with a torch, some of us run for equality—but none of us runs for cover."[71] For many, it was an emotional, unifying moment. During the last mile, a series of women like Billie Jean King passed the torch one to the other. "This whole stream of women, this whole parade of women with banners and the torch, and it was a pretty exciting moment," BYU's Marilyn Arnold later remembered. "It was a very inspiring kind of thing. Although there were some very radical kinds of views expressed, so many of them were the more solid sorts of things, and also just a celebration of womanhood. It was very exciting."[72]

Megan Rosenfeld at the *Washington Post* painted a vivid picture of the emotion, action, and drama of the opening session, "devoted largely to enthusiastic demonstrations of a unified belief in the need to demand equality for women. Cheers boomed out as the symbolic torch" arrived, "preceded by a marching band of young women in red-plumed helmets and a Girl Scout color guard." The torch was "carried up the stage" to First Lady Rosalynn Carter, who stood with the former First Ladies and other dignitaries "in a show of support."[73]

Rosalynn Carter brought a message from her husband of "concern about the outcome of your agenda," which he acknowledged was "deep." She added that she was "proud to be a part of the National Women's Conference. Never before in our history has there been such a women's meeting—in numbers, in preparation, in diversity, in long-range effect. The breadth of opinion, ethnic groups, income and occupation represented here is remarkably reflective in our whole country."[74]

Liz Carpenter, an IWY commissioner and former press secretary to Lady Bird Johnson, introduced twelve delegates and asked them to come to the stage, making a point about the diversity of the women in the room, saying: "Here is eighty-five-year-old Clara M. Beyer of Washington, D.C., retired government worker of sixty years, protégé of Justice [Felix] Frankfurter . . . mother of three sons and twelve grandchildren; the delegate from Illinois, Marge Jinrich—fourteen years with the United Auto Workers—she helps support her semi-invalid husband and five children on a paycheck of $8,500; from Minnesota . . . Mary Ann Brueschoff, who runs her own poultry farm—she was butchering geese when I called [her]. . . ."[75] The point was clear. The women stood at the edge of the stage, proud that they were there and incredulous at the size of the gathering.

Using demographics to personalize a profile of the commissioners, Bella Abzug added, "We range from the young to the not so young. Thirty-four of us are married. Four are widows. Seven are single, and one is engaged." As a group, they had seventy-four children and seventeen grandchildren. "And one is the mother of eight children." She concluded about the delegates in general: "We are a multitude. We are alive and kicking, and we shall get even livelier. The women's movement has become an indestructible part of American life."[76]

For some, the opening ceremonies were ominous—more the appearance of the anti-Christ than the harbinger of good things to come. Across town in the Astro Arena, adjacent to the Astrodome, Phyllis Schlafly held a counter-rally attended by 15,000 and predicted that "Houston will finish off the women's movement. It will show them off for the radical, anti-family, pro-lesbian people they are." She maintained that a silent majority opposed the ERA and most of the resolutions of the national commission.[77]

Schlafly was followed by others alleging the IWY commission was corrupt and promoted slanted, biased goals. The ERA itself was "sick," "immoral," "unGodly," "unpatriotic," and "antifamily," they said.[78] They voted approval for their own resolutions against abortion, the Equal Rights Amendment, and lesbian rights. Schlafly predicted, correctly as it turned out, the defeat of the amendment, but incorrectly that it would be the "death knell" of the women's liberation movement.[79] The throng of conservative women cheered, waved flags, and shook Bibles in the air, many holding children on their hips. The crowd made clear "their preference for historic sex roles."[80]

Schlafly emphasized that they "reject the antifamily goal of the Equal Rights Amendment and the International Women's Year. The American women do not want ERA, abortion, lesbian rights, and they do not want child care in the hands of government."[81] According to one observer, the audience was almost exclusively white, many of them young. "I want to keep my child at home and I don't want to be drafted," said Gale Hartschuh, a twenty-one-year-old housewife from Houston who pushed her two-month-old daughter in a stroller. "I'm afraid of what ERA will do to homelife."[82]

Schlafly's strategy of boycotting the convention and holding an alterative meeting had a powerful effect, as did the lack of balance in many of the state delegations. What better argument for the opposition than that the conference was staged, attended, and manipulated by feminists? Schlafly wanted to negate the impact of any resolutions the conference endorsed on grounds that the gathering was undemocratic. The counter-rally was fueled by the agitation against ERA ratification that was just beginning to pick up steam nationally.

The Ku Klux Klan had announced as early as September that it would try to disrupt the conference because it considered feminists to be the "misfits of society." Robert Shelton, the imperial wizard of the clan, said the KKK had infiltrated the women's movement and that some Klanswomen had been elected delegates, although he did not mention names. He promised that these women would "oppose what's going on," adding that "our men also will be there to protect our women from all the militant lesbians." Shelton concluded that "it's not safe for a decent woman to be there."[83]

Anita Bryant, another right-wing activist and television personality, also boycotted the Houston convention, saying she "doesn't believe in the Equal Rights Amendment or the National Women's Conference," which she called "pro-lesbian, pro-abortion and pro many other things that aren't representative of the thinking of most American women."[84]

For the most part, the Utah delegation felt at odds with the majority in attendance at the conference. Still, many remembered the moments when their differences seemed to dissolve. For instance, after a discussion about issues impacting the lives of women of color and various ethnic groups, the Utah delegation was the first to stand in support of the resolution. Ruth Funk thought, "I can't believe I'm hearing this because I can vote for this. . . . I didn't even look at my delegation. I just remember standing up and smiling and then looking over and seeing them all standing up. Then the whole audience looked at us and they clapped and they said, 'So you really do believe there are some things that we can [agree on].'" The black women in front of the Utah delegation turned around and hugged and kissed them. "It was a very, very moving experience, the highlight of the conference."[85]

At the same session, Utah's Georgia Peterson, founder of Let's Govern Ourselves, tried to introduce a Utah resolution and was "drowned by boos, hisses and jeers." It took the convention chair Anne Saunier twenty minutes to read Peterson's lengthy proposal that was mostly concerned with the encroachment of the federal government on women's private lives. When delegates understood the intent of Peterson's proposal, they were mollified[86] and, in fact, reacted with "resounding, deafening approval."[87] The Utah delegation considered this session the only truly positive moment of the conference.

Saturday, November 19

The plenary session on Saturday began at 9:00 a.m. in the coliseum. Waiting for the program to begin, some women sang songs and hoisted signs and banners proclaiming their ideological positions: "ERA, Yes" and "Liberated Men are More Fun" or "Women's Lib: Follow Jesus Christ and Your Husband and Your Pastor . . . REPENT!" Three wives of U.S. presidents sat together on the stage and each spoke of her experience working for women's rights and supporting her husband in improving the lives of women.

Bella Abzug explained the main task of the conference in her first address: "The mandate under which we meet does not tell us to consider whether women should seek to end discrimination or should seek full equality, full citizenship, and full participation in society. Instead, it takes a stand for equality, a position that I believe has the support of a majority of Americans. Our purpose," she continued, "is not to tell women how to live or what to do. It is simply to say that women must be free to choose what they do. Whatever women choose to do with equality, it must be ours as a matter of simple justice."[88]

During the second plenary session that day, Jill Ruckelshaus, former member of the Republican National Committee and past head of the IWY Commission, asked the group to find a way to achieve unity in support of the National Plan of Action. She reminded them that "by a recent Gallup Poll, 63 percent of all the people in this country, male and female, young and old, support the goals of the women's movement. Yet the press and many politicians claim that women cannot agree on what they want. Why is total unanimity suddenly demanded on women's issues?"[89] She maintained that the ERA "is designed to establish . . . the clear moral value judgment that all Americans, women and men, stand equal under the law."[90]

The format at the plenary session, as it had been at the state meetings, was for delegates to form lines, in this case behind eight microphones, to make motions and raise procedural questions. It was a process that clogged the session, although within a few hours the national planks began to be introduced.

The National Plan of Action

The most important work of the convention was adopting a twenty-six-issue program that had emerged from the past year's state conventions, research, and organizational efforts. The states had considered the core agenda produced by the national commission and had endorsed a handful of the 115 recommendations published in *To Form a More Perfect Union.* The states had also passed more than 4,000 resolutions reflecting local concerns, as well as fears about feminist goals harming the family. If a recommendation had the support of twelve or more states, it was included in the proposed national plan. The national commission also exercised its option and added additional recommendations.[91] Collectively, resolutions touched virtually every aspect of a woman's life.

Utah's delegation sent its version of the resolutions to the national commission on August 1.[92] A sixteen-page report, it summarized the expressed will of the majority in attendance at the June conference. Prominent themes included opposition to the ERA and abortion, a "call to strengthen" the family, "placement of the responsibility for sex education with parents, not the public schools," and "an aversion to increased governmental intervention to solve problems." Utah's plan included no recommendations concerning women as educators or an increased ability for women to determine their own futures. It did recommend a family court system, better reporting of "women's activities, [which should] be reported in the media on their merits, and not sensationalized because they are women's activities," improved programs for female offenders, and more stringent enforcement of anti-pornography legislation. Taken altogether, it was a conservative manifesto that challenged the national resolutions. The more mainstream proposals, as reflected by the national list, ran in the direction of extending social security benefits to homemakers, providing counseling services for displaced women, requiring pregnancy disability benefits for employed women, establishing comprehensive child care facilities, funding educational and job programs for poor women, and ending discrimination against women in the workplace.

The national plan was titled the "Declaration of American Women 1977." It began: "We are here to move history forward. We are women from every State and Territory in the Nation. . . . We speak in varied accents and languages but we share the common language and experience of American women who throughout our Nation's life have been denied the opportunities, rights, privileges and responsibilities accorded to men."[93] It was a bold and comprehensive plan.

Plank 21 was titled "Reproductive Freedom," but no one had any doubt that this term camouflaged a reference to abortion, which feminists phrased as a woman's right to choose for herself. In a sense, it was a defense of the status-quo:

> We support the U.S. Supreme Court decisions which guarantee reproductive freedom to women. We urge all branches of Federal, State, and local governments to give the highest priority to complying with these Supreme Court decisions and to making available all methods of family planning to women unable to take advantage of private facilities. We oppose the exclusion of abortion or childbirth and pregnancy-related care from Federal, State, or local funding of medical services or from privately financed medical services.[94]

The vote on this controversial plank came after twenty minutes of debate that confirmed how polarized the convention was on this issue.[95] Speakers on both sides stepped to the microphones located around the auditorium. Anne O'Donnell, a nurse from Michigan, spoke with a tremor in her voice: "The promise of a women's movement will be destroyed if you go on record as approving this destructive resolution."[96] During the vote, pro-abortion delegates sprang to their feet, signaling their approval and enthusiasm, while anti-abortion delegates waved protest signs. Proponents began singing "America the Beautiful" and intermittently chanting, "Choice, Choice!" and waving clenched fists. Plank 21 passed.

Of all the recommendations to the state IWY committees, Plank 11 was the only proposal that remained unmodified, having passed intact through forty-one state conferences. It read simply: "The Equal Rights Amendment should be ratified." At this gathering, not even abortion or lesbian rights would generate the same explosiveness. The ERA had been ratified by thirty-five states, three of which had subsequently rescinded their ratification. Three more were needed before March 22, 1979.

The text of the amendment itself asserted that "women will not have equality in the United States unless it is guaranteed by the Constitution."[97] What this failed to acknowledge was the debate over whether such an amendment was even necessary. The IWY filled in the gap, first of all attributing setbacks to ratification to "a well-organized, well-financed minority" that had blocked progress based on "many of the same false arguments that were used to prevent women from getting the vote, namely, that ERA would destroy the family and morality. In some States, ratification has been held up by the negative votes of as few as two or three male legislators."[98]

The official report of the convention noted the failure of the courts to consistently recognize women as persons under the Fourteenth Amendment, thereby disarming the frequent criticism that the ERA was unnecessary. While the 1872 U.S. Supreme Court had found Susan B. Anthony protected in her right to vote,[99] the Court later that same year had upheld an Illinois law prohibiting women from practicing law.[100]

Prior to 1977 the Supreme Court had struck down some gender discrimination laws, the report continued, and allowed others to stand.[101] If it had used the same rigor in interpreting sex classifications as it had in interpreting race classifications under the Fourteenth Amendment, the need for a Constitutional amendment would not be so compelling. But the Court had not, and the Fourteenth Amendment was insufficient. In contrast, the ERA would be "a more immediate and effective remedy to sex discrimination in Federal and State laws than a case-by-case interpretation . . . could ever be. The critical distinction is that[,] under the ERA, sex is a prohibited classification, not a classification that is subject to some level of judicial review and that, therefore, may or may not be sustained."[102]

Far from the deterioration of the family structure predicted by the ERA's opponents, the report predicted positive outcomes:

ERA will be	the basis for recognition of the principle (ignored in most family law) that the homemaker's role in marriage has economic value and that marriage is a full partnership . . .
ERA will insure	that the families of women workers receive the same benefits as families of men workers under the social security law . . .

ERA will insure	that married women can engage in business freely and dispose of separate or community property on the same basis as married men.

The report also counterattacked, asserting what the ERA would not do:

ERA will NOT	change or weaken family structure. Courts do not interfere in the private relationship of an ongoing marriage, and ERA will strengthen families by implicitly giving value to each spouse's contribution to and support of the other.
ERA will NOT	require the States to permit homosexual marriage. The amendment is concerned with discrimination based on gender and has nothing to do with sexual behavior or with relationships between people of the same sex.
ERA will NOT	have any impact on abortion laws. The U.S. Supreme Court decisions on abortion were made under present Constitutional provisions addressed to privacy issues . . .
ERA will NOT	require co-ed bathrooms. . . .
ERA will NOT	require that there be as many women as men in combat roles in the military service, but it will give women equal access to the skills, training, education and other benefits that military services provide.[103]

In assessing the ERA's status, the document reported that Congress had passed the proposed Twenty-seventh Amendment in 1972. It had been ratified by thirty-five states and three of them—Idaho, Nebraska, and Tennessee—had rescinded ratification. This, the report stated, was of questionable legality according to the opinion of Assistant Attorney General John Harmon, based on precedent for the Fourteenth and Fifteenth Amendments. It should be noted that in mentioning Harmon's opinion, the national commission portrayed the ERA in a light slanted toward a desired outcome because at that point in time, debate over rescission was far from over. In addition, the report mentioned that "fifteen states have not ratified," giving the impression that the remaining states might get around to it when, in fact, many of them had already repeatedly rejected the amendment.

Adding to the positive spin on the ERA, the report rolled out the bandwagon, citing the many prominent individuals and organizations that had endorsed the amendment including six U.S. presidents and 200 organizations, among them the American Bar Association, the Lutheran Church and several other major religious denominations, the NAACP and other minority groups, women's organizations ranging from the American Association of University Women to the Girl Scouts, and the AFL-CIO and other labor unions.[104]

On the conference floor, when the Equal Rights Amendment was presented, it produced the most emotional and passionate moment of the convention. Commissioner Claire Randall, General Secretary of the National Council of Churches, read the seven words, "The Equal Rights Amendment should be ratified," and pandemonium erupted, bringing the proceedings to a halt.[105] Chants, signs bobbing in the air, and a rush of energy gave a sensory richness to the room. Ann Richards, later elected governor of Texas, urged the assembly to remember that "those few of us who are fortunate enough to be in the positions we are" speak "for those who are speechless and voiceless, the divorced who may not get credit, the widows who are incapable of making a living, my own daughter, who cannot find women in the history texts of this country in the elementary schools."[106] The grandniece of Susan B. Anthony stood up during this debate and said into the microphone, in what Reba Keele remembered as a "deep deep voice, 'My name is Susan B. Anthony' and the room fell apart. The cheering, the stamping, the whole bit. It was one of those magic moments I'd never known anything like before. It was the exact contrast of the Utah hate. It was all these people who were different . . . but the contrast was that there was a rational way to talk, even if you disagreed, that was in such contrast to Utah, which had such fear that the arguments would be heard."[107] In an emotional address, Anthony called the ERA "the fulfillment of [the first Susan B. Anthony's] lifetime work, her fifty-one years spent living and dying for women. Failure is impossible," she said.[108]

Opposition to the ERA centered on a range of issues. Evelyn Pitschke of Indiana and chair of the National Association of Lawyers Who Oppose the Equal Rights Amendment thought "section 2 of the amendment gives great power to the Federal Government."[109] Jean Westwood, a Democrat from Utah and former chair of the Democratic National Committee, offered insight from a Mormon who favored the ERA: "I grew up in Utah, where women had the vote when it was a territory. They had the vote as a State, and in 1896, with the help of the Mormon Church, Utah passed in their Constitution an amendment which said, 'Women shall have equal civil, political, and religious rights with men.' I have devoted my life in politics to seeing that this privilege is extended to all women."[110]

The testimonials completed, the motion to accept the plank carried 927 to 341. This triggered the most emotional outburst of Saturday's meetings. Women chanted "Three More States, Three More States." Bella Abzug announced adjournment after a long and productive day with the words, "Good night, my loves."[111]

Sunday-Monday, November 20-21

On the third day of the convention, the same type of packed schedule faced the delegates. Beginning at noon, fourteen more planks were introduced, discussed, and voted on. To no one's surprise, the national commission's agenda prevailed. Monday would be the last day in Houston, but by then many delegates had already left, some of them in disgust.

The final plenary session, after three days of intense debate and discussion, ended with little fanfare. At 11:00 a.m. on Sunday, the delegates voted down the twenty-sixth plank of the proposed National Plan of Action which would have recommended a cabinet-level Women's Department to oversee social programs such as family planning.[112] At first glance, this seemed like an odd plank to reject; but perhaps as much as any action of the conference, it suggested that the group's diversity was real and impactful. According to one writer, it would be wrong to think

> that the conferees represented a majority of all American women; that

> claim is as hard to prove or disprove as the opponents' cries that the delegates spoke for no one beyond themselves. What was surely demonstrated, for anyone who still doubted it, was that women from all those regions, backgrounds, and circumstances not only had common concerns but an impressive amount of energy and organizing skill. The conference should finally put to rest the notion that the women's movement appeals only to Easterners or liberal Democrats or affluent suburbanites or any other narrow slice of society.[113]

To underscore that the voting had not been unanimous, dissidents staged a walkout just before the convention's end and held an impromptu press conference on the street where they sang "God Bless America."

Those who remained behind, by far the majority of the delegates, responded to a request from the presiding officer, Addie Wyatt, to figuratively join hands and voices to demonstrate a final show of unity and support. "One more time," she said, "for the Equal Rights Amendment."[114]

Conclusion

Media summaries of the meaning of the Houston convention varied, but reporters recognized it would contribute in some way to altering the course of history. Many women realized the dimensions of their common ground. Regardless of whether or not they were employed outside of the home or were Caucasian, African American, or Japanese American, they shared common experiences as women in the United States. For many, this realization reduced the isolation and social inequality they felt. An editorial in the *Washington Post* concluded that the conference contradicted the claims of the anti-feminist right:

> Watched carefully, the proceedings . . . gave the lie to the charge by Mrs. Schlafly and others that the movement is socially radical or "anti-family." The views that those critics harp on—support for publicly funded abortions and for the civil rights of homosexuals—were also those that caused the most uneasiness among the delegates. The broadest accord, on the other hand, involved the most family-oriented concerns, such as assistance for battered wives and children, and the legal and economic problems of homemakers, widows and divorcees.[115]

Speaking of a coalition formed by women of racial and ethnic minority groups, Sylvia Law of Morgan State University said, "We are learning to use power," that the coalition was the best memory she would take home with her.[116] Betty Friedan, whose *Feminine Mystique* had helped fuel the women's movement, reflected on the larger significance of the event in the context of history: "The women's movement has absolutely changed the mainstream of American life. The diversity of women— here they are young, and old, in blue jeans and suburban sweaters, square and fashionable and chic—and they are together in an incredible way."[117]

The woman who pushed the ERA through Congress in 1972, Representative Martha Griffiths, met on Saturday with women from several influential organizations—the American Association of University Women, League of Women Voters, National Education Association, National Organization for Women, and National Women's Political Caucus—and afterwards told the *Daily Breakthrough* that if the convention had been a showdown over the ERA, she was returning to Washington D.C. feeling it had won.[118] The National IWY Commission agreed. According to its final report sent to the U.S. president after the convention, "with only 20 percent of the delegates opposing some or most of the planks, there emerged from Houston a consensus on what American women need and want to achieve equal rights, equal status, and equal responsibilities with men."[119] The report emphasized consensus on the crucial eleventh plank: "Final ratification of the Equal Rights Amendment is needed, as one speaker said, 'to put women in the Constitution' and to establish a framework of justice for their efforts to remove remaining barriers to equality."[120]

Others were less certain. Regarding the enthusiasm of the floor demonstrations for the ERA, it was easy "to believe that their fervor alone," wrote reporter David S. Broder for the *Washington Post,* "would sway the relative handful of state legislators blocking its passage." But he astutely noted the political imbalance among the delegates sent to Houston, which "skewed the tone of the whole convention. . . . Because there was no significant conservative bloc to be dealt with, the main effort of the 'pro-plan' caucus representing the majority of the delegates" was to satisfy, or at least "avoid fights with," the far left. Even though the convention would "bury the idea that so-called 'women's issues' are a sideshow to the center-ring concerns of American politics," its endorsement of the ERA "would be discounted by the public's and politicians' perception that it was controlled by 'radical feminists.'"[121]

For Donna Wayment of the Utah delegation, the conference was a "federally funded propaganda tool to further the cause of the feminist movement. I fear for the future generations of this country if this becomes legislation."[122] For Wayment and her sister Utah delegates, the threats posed to the American family and the dangers of the ERA were one and the same. Both portended future confusion over the appropriate roles of men and women. The Utah group left Houston with mixed feelings and a much different story to tell.

9. Utah's Delegation

> True equity is not a product of law alone, but of law and mercy in proper balance. Legal remedies for all problems compound in our society bringing pharisaical death to the spirit of our nation. Let us turn our eyes in a new direction.
>
> —Utah's elected delegates to the National IWY Commission, 1977

The elected delegates from Utah received a letter from the chair of the state coordinating committee a week after the Salt Palace conference. It read: "We ask that you honestly evaluate your willingness and ability to assertively represent the State of Utah in the conference of this size and scope. In addition, all delegates and alternates will be expected to familiarize themselves with all national and state recommendations before the November conference."[1] Jan Tyler encouraged the delegates to be "as informed as possible" and to study the national resolutions carefully. The fourteen elected delegates, four alternates, and eight at-large delegates indicated that they were ready and willing to accept this charge.

The delegation represented the majority opinion in Utah, but in Houston they were ideologically and demographically in a minority. Of the nineteen elected and alternate delegates, seventeen were Republican, only two Democrat; one Catholic among the otherwise uniformly LDS group; eighteen Euro-American, with one Hispanic. All of them placed themselves socioeconomically in the middle class, and all stated that their principal reason for serving as a delegate was their opposition to the ERA. Belle Spafford, Belva Ashton, Elaine Cannon, Jennie Duran, and Gloria Firmage were Relief Society leaders. As a group, they were bright and capable, and they were united in their commitment to traditional religion as the source of their political beliefs.

Some of the coordinating committee found the delegates to be disturbingly homogenous. Lynne Van Dam "moved that this body file an official complaint on this delegation because we feel it is not representative of the people of Utah" with only six from outside the Salt Lake City area, four of whom were from Provo. Van Dam suggested that the committee inquire about credentialing.[2] The committee asked the national commission whether the delegation "meet[s] the standard for a balanced, State representation mandated by PL 94-167." The letter drafted by Valora Treshow explained:

> The 13,800 delegates to the Utah State Meeting chose to elect an overwhelming majority of white, middle income, Mormon, urban, 40-year plus, married representatives to the National Women's Conference. . . . While the Utah State Coordinating Committee recognizes the right of the majority to prevail, it also believes that it is the right of the minority to be heard. Because the majority ruled so absolutely at the Utah State Meeting and elected such a uniform delegation, the minority may be as thoroughly silenced in Houston as it was in Salt Lake unless the National Commission chooses to intervene in their behalf.[3]

The report expressed concern that, out of forty-two names the nominating committee had recommended, only four were elected and the others all came from Georgia Peterson's list. "This was, in part, due to illegal campaigning by the Utah Conservative Caucus, Let's Govern Ourselves (a local political group headed by delegate Georgia Peterson), and the Utah Right to Life. There is some indication that the John Birch Society was heavily involved." The report documented that "despite rules to contrary which had been accepted by delegates to the State Meeting, these groups campaigned throughout the two-day conference." The Right to Life group alone brought in more than 4,000 flyers to promote a slate of eleven of the fourteen delegates on the Let's Govern Ourselves list.[4]

Another group challenged the election on suspicion that the meeting rules had been violated. Beth Gurrister of Brigham City, representing Church Women United of Utah, felt the fact of a nearly all-Mormon delegation was evidence enough to believe that the process, which was intended to produce a "balanced representation," had been ignored.[5] However, both challenges, along with 130 other challenges nationwide, were rejected by the national commission, deciding that where there was no evidence of fraud, the delegations would stand.[6]

The Utah delegates constituted a virtual who's who of the Mormon elite from Utah. Georgia Peterson was an easy choice for chair. She had worked briefly for the FBI (1945-47), was a former Utah tax commissioner, and had served as a state representative (1969-77). As treasurer of the National Republican Legislators, she had connections outside the state equal to her current prominence on the board of the Children's Center and other activities.

Peterson had worked against the ERA since 1970. "I have support for equality in law, but not for the amendment," she explained. "I am a politician and I have sponsored and been responsible for laws on equality. State laws, that's where I'm coming from. I am possessive of states' rights to make domestic law. I don't trust the New York congressional delegation to make my laws. Personal law is what equal rights is all about." For her, the ERA was a moral issue that would impact her family. "I have felt that we didn't need ERA. Every time the Constitution is amended you lose a right guaranteed to you. States rights are eroded each time the Constitution is changed."[7] She spoke eloquently and often to women's groups. Going beyond the traditional LDS party line, she confidently addressed the legal issues of governance.

Vice-chair Dixie L. Nelson was vice president of the Murray City

Chamber of Commerce, vice president of the Utah Opera Company, and immediate past president of the Utah PTA (1973-75) and had held national PTA positions. This same high standard of public life and accomplishment characterized the delegation as a whole. Not ordinary housewives, although they had not, for the most part, worked professionally, they did have extensive records of public service in their communities and church.

The secretary of the delegation was Jayne Ann Morgan Payne, mother of twelve children and author of *To Fulfill Her Promise* and a contributor to *The Joy of Being a Woman.* Among other delegates, Jennie M. Duran was the mother of three and an elementary school teacher who had served on the Utah Law Enforcement and Planning Council as treasurer and was on the executive board of Utah Ballet Folklorico and a member of the Cottonwood Community Crime Council.

All Mormons knew Belle Spafford, and many also knew of Belva Barlow Ashton, a member of the LDS Relief Society general board. Ashton was a Deseret Gymnasium board member, as well. She and husband, Wendell, were the parents of seven children. An alternate delegate, Amy Y. Valentine, was a Spanish teacher and another member of the Relief Society general board.

Another high-profile Mormon, one who had been on the state coordinating committee, was Ruth Hardy Funk, general president of the church's Young Women program. She was the mother of four and had been a school teacher for years and had served on the boards of the Bonneville International Corporation, the Lion House Social Center, Promised Valley Playhouse, and the Deseret Gymnasium (all church-owned) and had chaired fund drives for the Red Cross and Utah Symphony. Elaine Cannon, mother of six, was a popular speaker and organizer. As the author of numerous books, including *How to Put Life in Your Life Story,* she epitomized the smart, talented, and grounded Mormon woman. She had co-edited the church's *Era of Youth,* a monthly insert for adolescents that became a separate magazine under the church's Correlation Program. In July 1978, she would replace Funk as general president of Young Women. She was selected to be the delegation's corresponding secretary.

Florence Smith Jacobsen, an alternate delegate, was Funk's immediate predecessor as president of the Young Women's Mutual Improvement Association. (The name of the organization had since changed as part of other Correlation-driven modifications.) Her aunt, Lucy Grant Cannon, had held the same position from 1937 to 1948. Jacobsen was known to be a cultured woman, committed to the arts, and was the founding director of the LDS Museum of Church History and Art and a member of the Governor's Cultural and Historic Sites Review Committee. She oversaw restoration of the Brigham Young Forest Farm House in Salt Lake City, the Joseph Smith Home in Palmyra, New York, and the Brigham Young, Wilford Woodruff, and Sarah M. Granger Kimball homes in Nauvoo, Illinois. The National Council of Women had awarded her the Woman of Conscience Award in 1968.

Naomi Udall was past president of the American Association of University Women. Lois T. Pickett was the newly elected president of Utah Federation of Republican Women and vice president of the Bountiful City Chamber of Commerce, as well as the local president of the American Legion. She received a Woman of the Year award from the Federation of Business and Professional Women.

A member of the Eagle Forum, Carol Garbett of Kearns joined Dolores B. Bennett and Donna Wayment, mothers all, in involvement in Republican Party politics and the PTA. Bennett was the delegation's parliamentarian. Margaret Mary Cassun, a self-identified "home engineer" (i.e., housewife) and chair of the Davis County Right to Life committee, was the sole Catholic delegate. She and her husband, William, were parents of three sons and one daughter.

Convention members chose four alternates. In addition to Jacobsen and Valentine, already mentioned, Gloria Paramore Firmage, wife of a well-known University of Utah law professor, Edwin B. Firmage, and mother of eight children, was Utah's Young Mother of the Year in 1977. From the southern part of the state, Anne Okerlund Leavitt was the mother of future governor Michael Leavitt and an active, politically involved personality.

Despite the high-caliber profile of the delegates and alternates, critics were quick to point to their obvious lack of diversity, as mentioned above. To broaden the spectrum of those who would go to Houston, the national IWY commission, in consultation with Utah's governor, appointed eight additional women, all known for their feminist views, as at-large delegates. Of course, their appointment rankled the regularly elected delegates.

The at-large delegates included Lynne Van Dam, who was a constituent advocate for the Utah Department of Social Services, a former juvenile court probation officer, a board member of the Phoenix Institute, and a board member of the Utah Environment Center. Married with two children, Van Dam had been a vocal spokesperson for feminist issues, a fervent advocate of the ERA, and often the collective conscience at meetings of Utah's coordinating committee. Joining Van Dam was Sandra Elaine Haggerty, a professor of communications at the University of Utah and a nationally syndicated columnist. She was the mother of three. Alberta Archuleta Almada, a member of the coordinating committee, was on the Governor's Council on Hispanic Affairs and the first president of the Community Organization Operation Program. She had five children.

The hands-down favorite heroine of the state convention, Esther R. Landa, was president of the National Council of Jewish Women and past president of the League of Women Voters of Salt Lake City. She attended Congregation B'Nai Israel in Salt Lake. She was the mother of three children. Committed to diversity, to the untapped potential that existed in the hearts of Utah's women, and universally respected, Landa was the epitome of political savvy and social grace.

University of Utah law student and LDS Church employee Kathleen Flake had overseen the state's mass meetings and nominations for national delegates. Eloise McQuown was a University of Utah professor of library science whose research on women in management and human relations made her a knowledgeable at-large delegate. She was a committee member of the National Women's Political Caucus and founder of the Equal Rights Coalition of Utah. Likewise, Reba Keele's work in organizational behavior and experience as a professor and director of the Honors Program at Brigham Young University added much to the group's breadth of expertise. Joan Draper, a senior at the University of Utah law school, had been a task force chair during the June meetings.

In a sense, any distinctions between pro- and anti-family homemakers and working women, traditional women or feminists, were meaningless given this line-up of delegates. Women in both camps were mothers and wives, community activists, and religiously involved people. Their lives were rich, active, and diverse.

Even so, Utah's Republican senator Orrin Hatch accused the national commission of "load[ing] the Utah delegation" with "left-wing radicals." In his mind, the mere fact of choosing at-large delegates showed the commission was interfering to skew Utah's representation. To Catherine Clarenbach, IWY executive director, Senator Hatch wrote that he was "increasingly anxious about the honesty of the process used by the national commission" to "break up a delegation falsely characterized by IWY as radical right wing." He had been informed that at-large delegates were appointed because of an insufficient minority representation in terms of race, education, and age, which he found to be "reprehensible" and a "blatant falsehood."[8]

The at-large delegates themselves held a press conference in Utah to clarify that they "weren't appointed to counter" the elected delegation, but to provide "balance at the national level," as explained by Eloise McQuown. They were going to Houston as individuals to express their personal viewpoints as well as the concerns of the state's women. "We see ourselves as individual women, individual women at-large. We don't see ourselves as an organized delegation," said McQuown.[9]

Lynne Van Dam reflected on the contradictions built into the objection of Mormons against social change in general and the ERA in particular: "Among the Mormon women, there is this incredible push for the family and against ERA. There is this reverence for men. Yet, the family in

Utah is in dire trouble. Here in Utah, we have a high rate of child and wife abuse, suicide, a high illegitimacy rate, a high divorce rate—all the ills of the big cities."[10] Morgan and Van Dam identified the emotional, moral, social, and intellectual spheres that had collided so turbulently at Salt Lake City's Salt Palace and correctly predicted that they would collide again in Houston. Esther Landa spoke to a luncheon of the Southwest Regional Conference of the Delta Kappa Gamma Society at Hotel Utah and said the ERA and abortion had become "overriding issues for IWY conferences" wherever they were held. Although the state conferences were intended to "recognize the contributions of women and assess the progress made in both the private and public sectors in promoting equality between men and women in all aspects of life, they had "turned into battlegrounds between those who believe in women's rights and those who either wish to perpetuate the status quo or return to earlier times."[11]

The Delegates' Preparation

Barely pausing after the strenuous conference at the Salt Palace, Utah's elected delegates began meeting weekly to plan for Houston, develop a pamphlet to describe their platform, and organize a series of public workshops. According to the group's minutes, they immediately began strategizing how to explain why they were taking the stand they were. On July 5 at one of their first official meetings, they began a list of prominent Americans who were opposed to the ERA and abortion. On it were U.S. Senator Sam Ervin, Anita Bryant, sociologist Margaret Mead, and scientist Alex Oblan. They felt this list would help legitimize the group's position and provide ammunition against the two measures they knew more liberal women would push for as necessary for women's advancement.[12] Each delegate received the assignment to make a list of reasons "why the ERA is undesirable" and research whether the IWY commission had committed crimes under federal laws by misusing funds to "further a political goal without fair representation." Also, what could they learn about the IWY leaders? Enthusiastically, the group of eighteen planned a retreat, elected officers, and made some special assignments.

On the same day as this meeting, Jan Tyler sent each delegate a copy of *To Form a More Perfect Union* and expressed the coordinating committee's desire to help them in whatever way they could. The Utah delegation responded by writing a critique of *To Form a More Perfect Union,* which they considered to be propaganda produced by a "pressure group whose purpose is to secure passage of the Equal Rights Amendment and Reproductive Freedom (abortion) recommendations."[13] They prepared an "open letter" to explain their position. Taken as a summation of the values, beliefs, and political insights of conservative women confronting the assumed feminist agenda of the national commission is instructive on the nature of the chasm separating the two. Both wide and deep, the ideological differences between conservative, tradition-focused women and those more closely aligned with the feminist movement seemed impossible to bridge.

Tyler promised to send the minutes of the Utah conference prepared by secretary Kathryn Putnam, plus a compilation of the recommendations presented from the floor and a list of the other delegates' and alternates' telephone numbers and addresses.[14] On Wednesday, July 6, the elected delegates met again to continue preparations for the November convention.

The publication

Working hard and fast, the delegates published an eleven-point platform, *Utah Women Speak,* at the end of July. The brightly colored red-and-white brochure included a beehive and snowcapped mountains on the front. It focused on such important issues as abortion, the ERA, child care, child and spousal abuse, pornography, and education from a pro-family stance. Peterson described how the delegates saw themselves as rising to a historic occasion to call others to meet the challenge: "Ultimately each age must face challenges that come, and accept accountability for its response to those challenges. It thus becomes important that, individually and collectively, we give ourselves to causes we perceive as having the greatest impact on an improved quality of life. Quality of life for all is built on the foundation of a good home and family life."[15] Speaking to a reporter, Payne stressed "the crucial issue of women," which was to be "the light and life of the home and family. Any nation is only as strong and noble as are its women who teach and inspire their husbands and children to work for the betterment of mankind both spiritually and temporally."[16]

Many were surprised to find that the delegation's anti-abortion plank was more moderate than what had been voted on during the IWY conference. The conference had adopted the position of Senator Jake Garn's proposed Right-to-Life Amendment—that life begins at conception and incest and rape are insufficient cause for an abortion. The implication was that euthanasia was similarly disallowed.[17] Margaret Mary Cassun and Carol Garbett went on record in the minutes of the Utah delegation's meeting as being opposed to Senator Garn's position because it was too moderate. Nevertheless, the delegation endorsed the LDS position that incest and rape are sufficient reasons for an abortion. From this time on, the women who made up the official delegation would meet every other week from mid-July until the national convention.

Public workshops

The delegation planned three public workshops for September 23, September 30, and early October, the latter in conjunction with LDS general conference. Their purpose was to help the delegates become "informed" and "hear both sides of each issue" in order to better anticipate the arguments they could expect to hear in Houston, as well as to better frame the arguments for presentation to the national convention.[18]

Jayne Ann Payne oversaw the planning, arranging for a meeting room, publicizing the workshops, and inviting speakers to address specific topics. She instructed workshop leaders to consult resource people, personally read about their topic, and then condense their ideas, including pros and cons, and prepare a bibliography and a handout for people attending their workshop.[19]

The committee held their meetings at the Utah State Capitol Building and announced them in newspapers and radio spots, although without making the same effort as the coordinating committee to ensure a diverse audience. In part because of the extremely tight schedule before the

November meetings, but also because of limited resources, the audiences ranged from thirty to 100 and were homogenous in terms of race, economic class, and educational level. They mirrored the delegates' profiles as white, well-educated, middle-class men and women. The participants were joined by media representatives such as Elizabeth Schoenfield and Angelyn Nelson and their cameramen and photographers, all of whom crowded into the small room reserved for the meetings.

Still, the workshops proved to be beneficial and informative. Gathering input from individuals and organizations, the events afforded the delegates a platform within the public eye. For example, Georgia Peterson was able to characterize the IWY as an attempt to destroy the American family, which she promised to defend as the cornerstone of society. From personal involvement, she said, the IWY was "undemocratic and unfair."[20]

At the first workshop, September 23, Elaine Cannon gave a thirty-minute presentation on the arts and humanities. Governor Scott Matheson arrived and was personally introduced to each delegate. Then followed half-hour presentations by Amy Valentine on credit issues, Carol Garbett on the mass media, and Lois Pickett on employment. Pickett told the group that 50.6 percent of the Utah work force were female.[21]

Paul Washeba of the *Los Angeles NOW Times,* a feminist newspaper, attended the September 30 workshop, as did Shelley Osterloh from KSL-TV. The day's topics were to be rape, reproductive health, aging, and minority women. When the media representatives introduced themselves, Washeba said simply that he was from "NOW." Assuming he was an officer or lobbyist with the National Organization of Women rather than a reporter for its Los Angeles newspaper, Georgia Peterson announced that representatives of other organizations would not be welcome and asked him to leave. According to the minutes, Peterson explained, "These workshops were designed primarily to educate and inform the delegation on the issues both pro and con" and that if Mr. Washeba attempted to return, "the workshop would be adjourned."[22]

Washeba left but, according to Peterson's prediction, soon returned and the workshop was adjourned to Florence Jacobsen's nearby house in the upper Avenues. Two weeks later on October 15 after the Mormon semi-annual general conference, the workshop reconvened in the state capitol. Washeba was once again present, but the confusion had been clarified and he was allowed to remain. Gloria Firmage served the crowd homemade bread and jam. Then, with Jayne Ann Payne, she presented a one-hour session on the legal status of homemakers. Other presentations were made by Florence Jacobsen and Belle Spafford on international interdependence, Ruth Funk on young women, Dolores Bennett on women in positions of power, and Anne Leavitt about female offenders.[23] Each reiterated the conclusions of the IWY conference in June.

Christine Meaders Durham and Eleanor Lewis gave a special presentation on the ERA and women under the law, to which IWY delegates Peterson and Payne responded. According to Durham, "Equal rights means equal responsibility."[24] In her opinion, the Constitutional amendment would put gender on notice in the workplace and public sphere but would not affect families in the private sector. Peterson and Payne countered that the ERA was not necessary because of the numerous laws already in place preventing discrimination. They argued that the broadly worded amendment would have unforeseen consequences. Payne had written a one-page handout titled, "The Equal Rights Amendment or the Equivocal Rights Amendment?" articulating the views of both sides of the campaign.[25]

After lunch, Sally Ehlinger of the League of Women Voters read a statement objecting to the workshops. She felt the delegation, instead of representing the consensus of the IWY conference, had made decisions and based policies on its own opinions. For Ehlinger, the democratic process itself was at risk. "It is understandable that [they] may be reluctant to say that the women of Utah want absolutely no national changes that affect women," she explained, acknowledging that the "decisions of the Utah IWY conference are distressing to many and unbelievable to others." But having solicited a vote, Utah needed to stand by it.[26]

In response, Michelle Van Sickle of the Eagle Forum pledged her organization's support for the positions expressed by the delegates. An unidentified woman who taught in the Head Start program and was a member of Citizens for True Freedom expressed her group's concerns about child care and education for preschoolers while simultaneously criticizing the government's intrusion into women's private lives.

So ended the delegation's educational outreach prior to leaving for Houston. Later in October, the delegation sent President Jimmy Carter a telegram protesting the agenda of the national convention. On October 27 the group met to hear reports from the other IWY conferences and to make travel arrangements. Bella Abzug had sent the delegates a reminder to make reservations as soon as possible.[27] Peterson reported that Paul Washeba and NOW had decided to sue the Utah delegation for $10,000 in damages for having violated his civil rights. The suit named Governor Matheson and Attorney General Robert Hansen as "co-conspirators."[28]

Financial conflicts

In early November the delegation further distanced itself from the National IWY Commission, calling for an audit of funds and requesting that the national Plan of Action be ruled invalid. Moreover, they asked for an official review of all state and national ballot results, a compilation of all minority reports, and a list of members of national and state IWY commissions with their stands on the ERA, abortion, and homosexual rights.[29]

National finances were not the only prickly point for the Utah delegates, who received airfare and a per diem from the state coordinating committee but paid the bulk of the costs to attend the national convention themselves. In late October, the Equal Rights Coalition of Utah alleged that the delegates had secretly formed a nonprofit organization to raise money for their political agenda. It asserted that this nonprofit, the "Utah Women's Association," had received contributions from the Ku Klux Klan, the John Birch Society, the Conservative Caucus, and the Eagle Forum.[30]

The delegates opened the contribution list to public scrutiny, but the Equal Rights Coalition immediately challenged it. Gloria Firmage pled for an end to what she saw as a smear campaign and asked the delegates' accusers to open their own financial records. "This innuendo must simply stop," she said. "People have a real misconception of what has happened. . . . We have given all the evidence that we have. We are not motivated by extremists and we're not being deceitful. Now we ask for fairness from the other side."[31] Two days later, the delegates left for Houston.

On their return, the delegates explained that they had held a fund raiser earlier that fall to underwrite those who could not afford to pay their own way. Mountain Fuel Supply Company President Bernard Z. Kastler and ZCMI's President Oakley Evans contributed the largest amounts. Federally Employed Women and the Utah Woman's Political Caucus made donations of $100 each and the YWCA donated $85. The two largest contributions from women of $100 and $500 were from individuals who had recently been awarded damages in sex discrimination suits. Most of the money, about $3,000, came from area women who sent in checks ranging from $1 to $20.[32]

In Houston

The Utah delegation arrived in Houston on Thursday, November 17, feeling beleaguered, with a pre-prepared news release in hand, "Utah Delegation Falsely Accused." They handed it out to any and all reporters they encountered. "We wonder why the IWY commission is going to such great lengths to discredit us," the press release read. "Our delegation is made up of superior women who've long been involved in professional and community activities. . . . Since when does a commission of the State Department in a free society begin to label groups as radical?" Peterson wrote.[33]

Ironically, given the impression people had of the Utah delegation, which was only reinforced by its defensive press release, the first Utahn to step into the spotlight at Houston did so carrying a sign that read "Another Mormon for the ERA." June Fulmer, who had come to Houston as an observer, was a counselor from Odyssey House, a drug rehabilitation program in Salt Lake City. She shared the final lap of the Seneca Falls torch relay from Overlook Park to the Houston Coliseum with dozens of other women.[34] A crowd of about a thousand women and men waited in a light rain for the runners as a band struck up "Yellow Rose of Texas" and the boisterous onlookers raised banners and placards into the air. The constant applause surged to a climax as the runners came in sight. When Fulmer came to a stop, a sea of reporters engulfed her with cameras and microphones, begging for a comment. Runners simultaneously surrounded presiding officer Bella Abzug, who was so recognizable in her trademark wide-brimmed hat.[35]

Mormons already had name recognition because of their take-over of the Utah conference and for setting a national record for attendance at an IWY conference. Georgia Peterson appeared on ABC television's *Good Morning, America* on Friday to spar with IWY national commissioner Elizabeth Holtzman, a Democrat from New York. On Friday night, Utah's fourteen elected delegates attended a pro-family dinner attended by approximately 300 conservative delegates. After the dinner, they caucused to plan strategies for demonstrating during the ERA and abortion votes on Saturday.

During the opening ceremonies on Friday, some 150 Utahns joined about 15,000 other people jammed into Phyllis Schlafly's counter-convention in the Astro Arena to protest the IWY, its resolutions, and its $5 million in federal funds.[36] Utah's delegation had carried petitions to Texas signed by thousands of Utahns and added them to the more than 300,000 petitions stacked under an American flag on the stage. The petitions opposed the ERA, abortion on demand, federal day care, and homosexuality. One woman told a reporter the gathering was meant to send a message to U.S. President Jimmy Carter that most American women did not approve of the national resolutions. At the rally, speakers promoted a "pro-family" platform in opposition to the official conference's "pro-plan" platform. Many in attendance said they had heard about the rally at their churches, although there had been no organized effort to recruit participants in the nearby LDS wards. For many, the meeting felt as much like a religious revival as a political demonstration.

Each day of the conference, the delegates could attend meetings or opt to attend special lectures or clinics in rooms at the Albert Thomas Convention Center. Thirty sessions billed as "Briefings from the Top" provided experts to answer questions about key issues. These included a Utah woman, Esther Peterson, former Special Assistant to President Lyndon B. Johnson, joined by Barbara Blum of the Environmental Protection Agency and Midge Costanza, Assistant to President Jimmy Carter.[37]

In dubious company with the Ku Klux Klan and other extremist groups, Mormons were featured in the official Women's Conference Network press kit that provided reporters with basic information about the conference and a seven-page document titled "Summary Sheet of Press Reports on the Tactics of Radical Right Wing Groups."[38] The Mormon Church was listed with eight other groups that had tried to subvert the purpose of Public Law 94-167. The groups were the Citizen's Forum, Conservative Caucus, Eagle Forum, John Birch Society, KKK, LDS Church, Right to Life, STOP ERA, and a more vaguely defined coalition of fundamentalist Christian churches.[39]

Utah's senators and Senator Frank Church of Idaho joined the Mormon Church in demanding an apology from the U.S. State Department for allowing press reports accusing the church of "subverting the law."[40] In an undated press release, Georgia Peterson, speaking for the Utah delegation, protested the "radical" label given them by the national commission,[41] then went on to describe the Houston conference as "no more than a government funded lobby carefully designed to quash the views of women opposing the Equal Rights Amendment and reproductive freedom recommendations." She maintained that "not only has free input of ideas and proposals been carefully muzzled, but those in charge have sought to destroy our credibility by name-calling and trying to link us with extremist groups like the Ku Klux Klan." Peterson believed that the delegation deserved better than this. She said, "In a democratic society where a diversity of views is to be both tolerated and invited, we are disappointed that a government-sponsored conference would be conducted with such strong-arm tactics."[42] Congressman Gunn McKay, a Democrat from Utah, denounced the national commission for saying the Mormon Church had instructed the delegates how to vote on the ERA.[43]

Each day of the convention, the national commission published a newspaper, the *Daily Breakthrough: Where Women Are News,* and the edition of November 19, the first day of the convention, included an article about Mormon involvement in the campaign against the ERA. "The women's movement," it read, "has discovered a new enemy—the Mormon Church—because the church has found a new evil—the Equal Rights Amendment." Officially, the Mormon Church opposed the ERA because it threatened the family, reporter Kay Mills wrote. "But Ezra Taft Benson, probably the best-known Mormon nationally and next in line to head the church, acknowledged he felt the amendment would 'weaken men.' Men are dominant, he said, because 'someone must be in charge and take leadership.'"

Mills noted that the Mormon influence was most significantly felt over the summer when thousands of Mormons descended upon the state IWYs, influencing the selection of delegates and the shape of the state resolutions. Mills quoted someone from Mormons for the Equal Rights Amendment who said the opposition was "rooted in resistance to change, and we profoundly believe many societal attitudes about men and women are unhealthy, unrealistic and need changing." Elizabeth Chittick, head of the National Women's Party and a backer of the ERA, saw the Mormons as "frightened of any challenge to the man as head of the household." Liz Carpenter, co-chair of ERAmerica, the coalition pushing for ratification, boldly criticized the efforts of religious groups to interfere with the amendment process. "I do not think we should allow [interference from] Salt Lake City, where church leaders historically over-married, or Rome, where the head of the church never marries."[44]

Mormon reporter Jack Anderson joined the outrage on learning the convention had linked Mormons with the Klan and had called Mormons "radical." Bella Abzug, he wrote, "has an unfortunate tendency to brand women of less advanced views as hate mongers of the far right. She gave her personal imprimatur, for example, to a handout lumping Mormons with the John Birch Society and the Ku Klux Klan."

Kay Clarenbach, executive director of the Women's Year Commission, acknowledged that Abzug was responsible for the "Summary Sheet of Press Reports" and agreed that it had been "improper." Clarenbach said the handout was "put together at the order of Bella—with at least the concurrence of some of the executive committee." When Anderson questioned Abzug about the handout, she denied a first-hand role in its production. However, as a result of the controversy surrounding the handout and its circulation, the State Department canceled the franking privilege it had given the commission allowing it to send out free mailings.[45]

Letters to the editor in Utah commended Senator Church for correcting what one male writer portrayed as "the unprincipled smear of the Mormon Church by the National IWY Commission," the same writer adding that "the senator merits scolding when he insists on linking the patriotic John Birch Society with the subversive Ku Klux Klan."[46] Georgia Peterson wrote a letter to *Exponent II,* a Mormon women's quarterly in Boston, suggesting that the "irony of the IWY Commission is that to achieve their goals, they attempted to discredit Mormon women by encouraging the discrimination they say they wish to end. The fact that they did not succeed brings more hope for equality than all the resolutions they adopted."[47]

From the perspective of the Utah delegation, Houston was not an "open forum for the discussion of women's problems and concerns." Rather, it had been masterminded to create a massive demonstration of support for the ERA. If true, using the IWY in this way was a premature and clumsy celebration that quickly backfired.

Utah's critique centered, in part, on the procedural and substantive inequities it perceived in the selection of at-large delegates and misguided lobbying efforts by the national commission. Nine of the at-large delegates from Utah shared the majority viewpoint of the commission. Eight were from Salt Lake County and seven worked for the government or were affiliated with government institutions. To the elected delegation, this latter fact was itself evidence the commission was stacking the deck.

The Utah delegation also objected to the way the national resolutions moved through state conventions and were voted on in Houston as if no other resolutions had emerged from the state meetings. The national resolutions, as written, were defeated in Utah, but there was no evidence of this in Houston. In Peterson's letter to *Exponent II,* she complained that "if the IWY National Commission has known from the beginning that we would not be given opportunity to deal with state resolutions in the Houston Conference, the women of the states and country have been cynically manipulated as state props toward the commission's ends."[48] Thus, it seemed that the "direction, formula, and outcome" of the national conference had been determined before the convention even convened.

An equally serious criticism centered on the lack of balance in the materials presented in the briefing book on the resolutions. The Utah delegation accused the commission of presenting one side of each issue, with a bias in favor of feminist goals. Peterson concluded: "True equity is not a product of law alone, but of law and mercy in proper balance. Legal remedies for all problems compound in our society bringing pharisaical death to the spirit of our nation. Let us turn our eyes in a new direction."[49]

In short, the Utah delegation resented much about their Houston experience and left feeling misunderstood and undervalued. Florence Jacobsen, unquestionably one of Utah's great ladies, sailed through with unflappable poise. "We knew that we would run up against a great deal of negative unacceptance," she later recalled. "They just would not accept us as being legitimate people with any authority or any ideas." Her fears were borne out. Women were dismissive of Utahns everywhere they went. "We were not received well. Even on the elevators they would make mocking remarks. If I happened to be on an elevator and I had my badge on me—we all wore our badges—'Well, there's the Utah group, we know how you're going to vote.' It was one of the experiences where you held up your head and smiled and were gracious regardless of what people said or how they acted."[50]

According to Naomi Udall, "Strangers would say, 'Did the men let you out long enough to come down here?' That sort of thing. 'Did you have to have written permission?' Everyone figured that Utah women were pawns of their husbands and the Church leaders."[51] Ideally, the national convention was held to celebrate American women and to push for the improvement of the lives of women in general, but this group, at least, felt let down by the process.

The Utahns published an open letter expressing outrage at their treatment in Houston. When they had tried to voice their views, they said, they had been shouted down, openly criticized in the press and in plenary sessions, and generally treated disrespectfully. Ruth Hardy Funk drafted the letter of complaint to the national IWY commission, not missing the opportunity to get in another dig at the commission in the process:

> It is our opinion that the IWY National Commission is a pressure group whose purpose is to secure passage of the Equal Rights Amendment and Reproductive Freedom recommendations. It is not an open forum for the discussion of women's problems and concerns. The purpose of the Houston Conference, as designed by the National IWY Commission, is not to allow the free input of ideas and proposals of women across the nation, but rather it is a massive demonstration of political sentiment in favor of the Equal Rights Amendment, designed to intimidate state and national legislatures in support of the amendment. We believe the IWY National Commission, as the recipient of public funding, should provide a forum for the free discussion of a wide range of issues facing American women, rather than perform the function of a federally funded lobbyist group for a predetermined and unpopular end.[52]

The Utah delegation was "very much in the minority," remembered Esther Landa. "There were a couple of other—two or three—states that had non-feminist delegations. So they got a feeling for what it was like to be in the minority."[53] As a Jewish woman, Landa was most concerned that anti-Israel resolutions, which had come out of various state political conferences, would be introduced.

Georgia Peterson was convinced even before Houston that "it would be no more than a farce for the passage of feminist goals such as ERA, abortion, and lesbian rights." In her November 21 press release, she expressed resentment at the commission's efforts to "try to discredit" the Utah delegation by "implying that we were against advancement for women." She summarized: "ERA, abortion, and lesbian rights are now a package deal for the feminists." She quoted Naomi Udall: "The demonstration of elation with the passage of the abortion and sexual preference resolutions will haunt me for years. American women of the majority view must be alerted to take up the crusade for support of the home and family. Battle lines have been drawn, and all that we hold dear is at stake."[54]

Post-Houston Opinions

A poll of 1,064 Americans following the Houston conference, conducted by Associated Press and NBC News, showed 53 percent agreement with the conference's approval of the ERA; 37 percent were opposed and 10 percent undecided. Fifty-three percent agreed with the statement: "Every woman who wants an abortion should be able to have one"; 43 percent were opposed and the rest unsure. Only 6 percent opposed equal pay; 92 percent favored equal treatment. Opposition to IWY decisions tended to come from older men and women, Catholics, and more conservative Americans. Despite the widespread support for the ERA and even abortion, polls demonstrated that Americans were nevertheless apprehensive about any drastic change to society's mores.[55]

When the Utah delegates returned from Houston, they were feted at a rally attended by a few hundred people and three Utah politicians at the capitol rotunda. The crowd was less than the thousands anticipated, but it was lively and enthusiastic. Women paraded around the edges carrying signs reading "My family is alive and growing in our America" and "Preserve the family unit—vote no! ERA!"

Speakers included Senator Orrin Hatch, who said the women had exhibited "dignity, foresight, and fortitude. . . . They're tremendous." His opinion of the at-large delegates was that they were unwelcome interlopers. "After they were rejected by the Utah majority," he said, it was "a farce to reappoint them under the guise of at-large delegates." Attorney General Robert Hansen and Lieutenant Governor David Monson set aside partisan differences to join in celebrating family life, the rights of the unborn, and women's rights without the ERA. "As I see forces fomenting for ERA," Hansen said, "it tends to bring womanhood down to the level of manhood. . . . Superiority has always been with the woman."[56]

The IWY national commission wrote to all delegates after the conference thanking them for making the event a success: "Your serious and thoughtful participation, your disciplined behavior and your enthusiasm and spirit all contributed to the success of an event that has captured the imagination of our nation."[57] The letter included a set of amended resolutions for the delegates' review and suggestions for further involvement to make the national plan a reality.

In March 1978 the commission announced that four Utah women would sit on the International Women's Year Continuing Committee: Georgia B. Peterson as an elected delegate and three of Utah's at-large delegates: Joan Draper, Sandra Haggerty, and Alberta Almada. The group met with U.S. President Carter to present the resolutions from the national convention, then donated artifacts from the Salt Lake meeting to the Smithsonian Institution.[58] The report they gave Carter included the minority views of Houston's dissenters. That month, Carter announced a new group to study and eliminate discrimination against women in government jobs and programs. To the official delegation of 200 women who visited the White House, he promised "an interdepartmental agency group to work with cabinet officers, agency staffs and me personally to make sure the work you did in Houston will be completed."[59] He told the Continuing Committee his domestic staff and cabinet members were already implementing the twenty-six-item Plan of Action approved in Houston.

In a cover story on December 5, *Time* magazine commented:

What happened, particularly for the 14,000 who attended the Houston

> meeting, was an end to the psychological isolation that had constrained their activities and ambitions. They learned that many other middle-of-the-road, American-as-Mom's-apple-pie women shared with them a sense of second class citizenship and a craving for greater social and economic equality. . . .
>
> Certainly, Washington and the whole nation are watching the leaders of this increasingly vocal majority. As was echoed many times in Houston, it is a particularly exciting time to be a woman.[60]

In some ways, Houston was an emotional anticlimax despite the clear winners and losers. The wives of three presidents—one Republican and two Democrat—supported the ERA, equity in the workplace, and guaranties for social programs benefitting the lives of women and children. The two thousand delegates overwhelmingly approved a package of proposals despite the hot spots that alienated conservative voters and despite alternate meetings across town to affirm anti-ERA views. Puzzlingly, no one appeared especially jubilant. In fact, the rest of the country was left with the feeling there had been a stalemate. ERA opponents and proponents alike had been damaged by insisting that the ERA meant more than the equal rights it was intended to guarantee. Each group made significant mistakes in both judgment and strategy.

Feminists had allowed a few particular issues to overshadow the larger picture. As a result, the ERA was lost in the mix of controversial social issues. According to one critic, feminists damaged themselves "by over-confidence in the guerrilla theater politicking" in the tradition of their suffragist ancestors and "over-estimated prospects of success through flirtations with the media."[61] Feminists seemed to have been fighting more for symbolic vindication than for any real power or the privilege to effect change.

For their part, by linking themselves with extremist groups, Mormon delegates formed alliances that landed them in unsavory company, which they rationalized with an end-justifies-the-means approach. They vibrated with a crusader's zeal and martyr's certitude. Being outnumbered and scorned was something that was bred into their bones from nineteenth-century foremothers who had first accepted the despised Mormon gospel and then defended the abhorred system of plural marriage. This modern generation of LDS women was ready to strike not against the intolerance of the status quo but against those who would challenge it.

10. Anti-ERA Activism in Key States

> The church has been acting like a political party. Those aren't prayer meetings they hold on Sundays. Those are precinct meetings.
>
> —Joe Neal, Nevada state legislator, 1978

On October 30, 1976, less than a week before the national election, LDS Church President Spencer W. Kimball issued a statement that made opposition to the ERA the official policy of the church. Earlier that month, Phyllis Schlafly, head of Stop ERA, met with Barbara Smith, Georgia Peterson, and possibly President Kimball—this despite the fact that little interest had been expressed in Utah about the ERA.[1] But from that point on, the campaign against ratification coalesced. Top Mormon leaders traveled to key locations to take to the platform in rare public appearances. Apostle Boyd K. Packer, for one, appeared in Pocatello, Idaho, at a rally during the successful drive to rescind Idaho's ratification. Apostle Neal A. Maxwell appeared at a public event in Florida along with Schlafly.

Four years earlier, the same Equal Rights Amendment had passed through the United States Congress and quick ratification in twenty-two states. The next year, eight more states had ratified for a total of thirty states, followed by three states in 1974 and one more in 1975.

In the November 1976 presidential election, Jimmy Carter defeated incumbent Gerald Ford with 50.8 percent of the vote. As a vocal supporter of the ERA, Carter and his wife Rosalynn proved to be valuable to the pro-ERA forces. That same year, South Dakota successfully staved off a rescission effort by 37-33, the victory coming in large part from the intensive campaigning done by the National Organization of Women (NOW) in coalition with the League of Women Voters and the American Association of University Women.[2] Recognizing the importance of the remaining states, NOW announced at its national strategy meeting held in St. Louis in January 1976 that it would renew its efforts in Florida, Illinois, Indiana, Missouri, Nevada, and South Carolina.[3] In Virginia, NOW organizers staged a hundred-mile walk for ERA.[4] The ERA had acquired the dubious honor of taking the longest time to be ratified of any Constitutional amendment. The Nineteenth Amendment, which gave women the vote, had taken fifteen months. The fourth year into the ERA's struggle proved to be the apex as no additional states lent support and five states attempted, unsuccessfully, to rescind their endorsement. Also significant in 1976, Orrin Hatch, the golden boy of the New Right, was elected to the United States Senate despite the fact that he had no record of public service. He defeated three-term incumbent Frank Moss.

In 1977, as opposition picked up significantly in the states which had not yet ratified the ERA, the LDS Church began its campaign to varying degrees in Arizona, Florida, Illinois, Missouri, Nevada, North Carolina, and Virginia. The church followed its ecclesiastical channels, contacting priesthood leaders at the state level to identify and endorse anti-ERA candidates for state legislatures. Mormon groups were soon endorsing candidates, circulating campaign materials, organizing "get out the vote" efforts, and activating calling trees. The Special Affairs Committee, which implemented the program at church headquarters, targeted states that were vulnerable in the ratification campaign. In each state, there were one or two LDS Regional Representatives who communicated with stake leaders—stakes being composed of six to eight local congregations. The latter, "wards," were headed by a bishop and two counselors. Bishops were key to the anti-ERA campaign because they implemented the grass-roots action.

Indiana became the thirty-fifth state to ratify the ERA in 1977 despite the effective, last-minute efforts by Phyllis Schlafly and her supporters to kill the amendment. The intense campaigning on the other side was directed by NOW chair Eleanor Smeal and the state NOW coordinator in Indiana, Sue Errington. It culminated in a huge ERA rally that continued undaunted during a raging blizzard on January 8. As further demonstration of the extent of their commitment, NOW members stood vigil at the capitol rotunda through the entire vote.[5]

Ratification efforts elsewhere were less successful. The Virginia senate came within one vote of ratifying the ERA on January 27, 1977, with a vote of 20-18. A majority vote of all forty members of the senate was required, rather than a majority of those who were present. The Nevada senate ratified the ERA although the vote itself was tied 10-10 and Lt. Governor Bob Rose had to cast the deciding vote. The Nevada assembly rejected it 24-15. ERA proponents were outraged to find that eleven assemblymen who had previously supported the amendment switched sides and that eight of the eleven had received pro-ERA campaign funds. Three states had rescinded their ratification by 1977, but in March the Justice Department gave as its opinion that rescission was illegal and unconstitutional.[6] There was more good news for NOW members in the wake of the 1976 election as legislative seats in key states were won away from anti-ERA legislators. However, there were also switches in Florida and North Carolina similar to what happened in Nevada.

Upon failure of the amendment in Georgia in 1978, a state senator described the vote as "history in the unmaking."[7] Eleanor Smeal and members of Virginia NOW, four thousand strong, marched on the state capitol in Richmond to call for passage of the ERA. Organized as well by a coalition of Virginia labor groups, this was the largest ERA demonstration to date but had little impact on the legislature which continued to stall. In South Carolina, the senate decided to table the vote after three legislators switched from "aye" to "nay" in a non-binding roll call to see how the measure would fair if brought to a vote.[8] In Virginia, public polls showed that 59 percent of the electorate supported the ERA. Nevertheless, the House Privileges and Elections Committee decided not to bring it out of committee. NOW activists Marianne Fowler and Jean Marshall Clark were arrested on the capitol steps and charged with civil disturbance.[9]

That same year in Kentucky, Lt. Governor Thelma Stoval, filling in for Governor Julian Carroll while he was out of state on vacation, vetoed a rescission vote. She defended her action by noting that "sixty-four percent of the people of Kentucky are for ERA."[10] The Illinois House of Representatives failed to ratify because five pro-ERA representatives from Chicago, protesting another issue, failed to casts their votes. This was a severe setback to ERA supporters, who had anticipated a victory from one of the fence sitters. Seeing that success would not be imminent but that there were still states that had not rejected the amendment outright, members of the U.S. Senate and House of Representatives proposed extensions to the ratification deadline although disagreeing over whether the extension should be seven years or half that amount of time.

In the middle of the long hot summer of 1978, NOW sponsored a march of 100,000 of all ages and races down Constitution Avenue to the steps of the nation's Capitol to deliver the message that the people of America wanted the ERA and wanted an extension of ratification. An overlay of the historic suffrage colors of purple, gold, and white was visible among the mass of people marching in 95-degree heat. President Smeal and others delivered words of encouragement and support and articulated the vision for the immediate future.[11] One month later, on August 15, the House voted to extend the deadline, although only to the end of June 1982, and in October the Senate agreed to this extension—a small victory for the amendment's proponents and a new stimulus for the opposition to step up their campaign to kill the amendment.[12]

Headquarters Strategy

While describing the LDS Church's crusade as subterranean may not entirely capture its essence, it was nevertheless a campaign functioning just beneath the horizon of visibility and was primarily a grass-roots effort by church members. Conducted in seven key states where ratification was pending or where rescission was a possibility, as well as other states (see chap. 11), the church's involvement went beyond a generalized concern over a moral issue to include active, if not always overt, participation in partisan politics.

After identifying and endorsing anti-ERA candidates for state legislatures, the church mobilized people to raise funds for those candidates and encouraged massive efforts to sway public opinion. In several states, local leaders themselves directly contacted individual members, circulated lists of endorsed candidates, and solicited contributions for candidates or for political action committees. The campaign was effective, tightly organized, and driven by a strong sense of focus, vision, and determination.

The format of the campaign mirrored the way theological and organizational directives are disseminated from Salt Lake City to LDS church members. The policy statement originated with the First Presidency, the first tier of institutional authority and power, and the instruction to form political action committees came from Apostles Faust, Hinckley, and Maxwell of the Special Affairs Committee. These men engaged the general presidency of the Relief Society, which repeatedly reminded LDS women of the significance of this political activity. President Barbara Smith issued instructions on the distribution of literature, methods for contacting legislative leaders, and use of Relief Society members to recruit campaign workers, all the while reiterating the importance of the moral rather than political aspect of the issues in justification of the use of church resources.

The initiative then passed to the church's second institutional tier: the regional representatives. Notwithstanding statements by public communications people protesting a connection to church headquarters, the

East Coast representative publicly admitted that the coalition he was connected with originated with Apostle Gordon B. Hinckley.[13] Other documents that were circulated within Virginia congregations linked the coalition not only to Elder Hinckley but also to President Kimball (see chap. 11).[14] Stake presidents, the next tier below regional representatives, staged meetings in chapels and private residences to choose Relief Society women (usually Relief Society presidents) to form executive committees for political action, and these in turn chose women from their wards to serve on the committee and mobilize friends and neighbors. The structure of the coalition activities in states such as Missouri, Nevada, Virginia, and others shadowed the organization of the church itself. Direction, authority, and power flowed from the top down in mobilizing this huge army of local members. Empowered by church leaders, Mormons struck first at the ERA, then branched out to mobilize against abortion, sex education, pornography, drugs, homosexuality, and a vast landscape of social issues they felt were ripe for reversal.

Uncertainty about the line dividing religion from politics was ultimately irrelevant to most faithful church members. Because religious leaders convened meetings and issued calls in religious terms, the obedient responded as if they had been asked to teach a Sunday School class or visit an ailing ward member. They understood the organizational structure of the church and their place in it; perhaps more importantly, they knew what was expected when their leaders spoke. Local groups assumed that if the instruction came from any of the twelve apostles, then they had the tacit approval of the church president and prophet himself.

At a key meeting in Salt Lake City on October 5, 1979, at which selected stake presidents and statewide ERA coordinators were gathered, Elder Hinckley, who would become a third counselor to the ailing President Kimball in July 1981, outlined a new method for dealing with political issues. He told the group that:

1. people should not be set apart for this work;
2. should not use LDS in [the] title of organizations; [but that]
3. church building[s] may be used for ERA education; [and]

4. any and all Church meetings are appropriate forums for discussing ERA;
5. [they] should not use Church funds; [but]
6. educating members on ERA issues [is appropriate];
7. [they should] not endorse political candidates—but [should] publish [an] incumbent[']s voting record."[15]

His instructions deviated from long-standing church policy, emphasized three years earlier in a letter from ranking apostle Ezra Taft Benson to all stake and mission presidents: "Please keep in mind that Church buildings and organizations are not to be used for this or any other political or legislative purposes."[16] A similar statement appeared in the *Deseret News* in August 1962. As historian D. Michael Quinn has noted, Elder Hinckley's "contrary instructions" to stake presidents and ERA coordinators, held in conjunction with the church's semi-annual general conference, carried weight, and one assumes that these directives were also given to regional representatives and other church officials.[17]

After the deadline for ratification was extended, the First Presidency reiterated its opposition to the ERA on August 26, 1978, in the *Church News*. The statement began: "We believe ERA is a moral issue with many disturbing ramifications for women and for the family." Painting again a picture of an uncertain future, it continued to warn against a "possible train of unnatural consequences which could result because of its very vagueness—encouragement of those who seek a unisex society, an increase in the practice of homosexual and lesbian activities, and other concepts which could alter the natural, God-given relationship of men and women."[18] This was followed by a First Presidency letter to church leaders asking them to encourage members to "join actively with other citizens who share our concerns and who are engaged in working to reject this measure." Stimulated in part by the extension in time required for ratification, the letter developed an argument that echoed earlier rhetoric.

> While the enactment or reject[ion] of the Equal Rights Amendment must be accomplished by recognized political processes, we are convinced that because of its predictable results the matter is basically a moral rather than

> a political issue; and because of our serious concern over these moral implications, we have spoken against ratification, and without equivocation do so again. We are convinced, after careful study, after consultation with various Constitutional authorities, and after much prayerful consideration, that if the proposed amendment were to be ratified, there would follow over the years a train of interpretations and implementations that would demean women rather than ennoble them, and that also would threaten the stability of the family which is a creation of God.[19]

The church thus pumped life back into the anti-ERA movement while also adding a new sense of urgency. This was evident in Virginia when a coalition was formed and tactics implemented that had proven effective during the state IWY conferences.[20]

The church's *Ensign* magazine published articles to clarify the church's position, along with speeches by regional church leaders about ratification and official policy statements that left no room for interpretation. Bishops, stake presidents, teachers, and women read them aloud and interpreted them in private. Official press packets were distributed through church channels to local newspapers, television personalities, and other individuals in the media. Early on, it was understood that this battle would be fought and won largely in the press. In March 1980 the church spared no expense in widely distributing *The Church and the Proposed Equal Rights Amendment: A Moral Issue.*

Public statements were not always interpreted consistently by church members, in part because of the inconsistency of the messages from Salt Lake City. Some ward bishoprics instructed members to not use church facilities for political purposes,[21] yet during the fall of 1978 ward newsletters repeatedly called for political action in defeating the ERA.[22] The same newsletters told members that if they wanted "to support the Prophet in his opposition to the ERA," they could call or write their Congressmen, who were identified by name. Anti-ERA candidates for political office spoke in at least one ward house, and the names of pro-ERA legislators were posted in chapel hallways, together with sample letters one might send to legislators. Petitions opposing ratification were circulated in Relief Society and Sunday school classes. One petition read in part:

"We consider the Equal Rights Amendment a nonpartisan issue and will, in the 1979 elections, vote only for those candidates who oppose ratification of the Equal Rights Amendment."[23]

Joining with other anti-ERA groups was a logical next move. Fortified by an association of shared literature, enthusiasm, and focus, such a union made it easier for Mormons to blend with secular groups in lobbying efforts. While distributing literature at the state capitol or engaging in letter writing campaigns, Mormons were careful to present themselves as private citizens acting as such rather than as Latter-day Saints mobilized by their prophet. As a result, it appeared as if there were a spontaneous, massive groundswell of antipathy for the ERA.

According to one historian: "It was precisely in states with small Mormon populations, where legislators were unaware of Mormon influence, that this strategy was the most effective because it was more likely to be interpreted as authentic, popular opposition. Thus, small Mormon minorities exerted disproportionate influence over the fate of ERA in Virginia, Missouri, Florida, Illinois, and North Carolina."[24] The success of the campaign depended on the anonymity of the group. As individuals, their point of view was more compelling since politicians responded to the desires of their constituencies. In South Dakota, Mormons comprised only 1 percent of the total population,[25] but researchers have estimated that as many as 90 percent of eligible Mormon voters registered their opposition.[26]

Money spent on the campaigns in Florida and Virginia demonstrated the advantage of having the official sanction of the LDS Church. Approximately $26,000 of $31,000 raised in one month by Families Are Concerned Today (FACT) and spent in Florida and Virginia came from Mormon donors—94 percent of it from California Mormons.[27] Clearly, the efforts by church members in various states were integrated, coordinated in Salt Lake City and designed to fight ratification wherever necessary. Opposition forces prevailed in Florida by two votes. Whether the victory was linked to FACT funds or not, one Regional Representative explained that FACT circulated funds in a way that avoided the impression of church activity. "It is not [being done by the church]," he said. "It is church people."[28]

According to sociologist O. Kendall White, such language underestimated the benefit of having the church's support: "This covert campaign depended upon the infrastructure of Mormonism—the social bonds, the Relief Society, the coordination and tacit support of top officials, the local facilities, and the local and general church media." Furthermore, funds raised so successfully were "products of this social structure, and this social structure, not simply the political beliefs and activities of citizens who also happened to be 'church people,' was responsible for the effective mobilization."[29]

One analysis of the union of Catholics and Mormons in Nevada showed that the combined organizational networks allowed them to marshal impressive numbers of workers, produce and distribute literature, and exert influence through ideological tests for legislative candidates.[30] Mormon involvement was so widespread, there was no attempt to conceal the source of the activism and seemingly no reluctance to use church facilities and infrastructure. Chapels were used for political meetings and home visitors ("home teachers" and "visiting teachers" in Mormon parlance) took literature to ward members; Relief Society telephone trees proved especially helpful.[31]

Sociologists of religion, writing after the ERA's defeat, placed the LDS Church squarely in the middle of the new Religious Right.[32] Following the release of Elder Hugh B. Brown, a liberal Democratic voice, from the LDS First Presidency at the death of President David O. McKay in 1970, and coincident with the elections of conservative Utah senators Jake Garn in 1975 and Orrin Hatch in 1977, Mormons became increasingly aligned with conservative Republican politics.

With only three more states needed to pass the ERA in early 1977, Mormons and anti-ERA activists alike focused on a handful of states.[33] The campaigns in Idaho, Kentucky, Nebraska, South Dakota, and Tennessee were directed toward rescission. In all cases, the uniformity of tactics used by the amendment's opponents speaks to the centralized direction of the battle. For the Mormons, the Special Affairs Committee functioned as a sort of clearinghouse, noting successful anti-ERA tactics in one state and duplicating them in another. All of this was coordinated by Elder Hinckley as chair of the Special Affairs Committee.

Another church member moved to the center of public controversy in April 1978 when Dallin H. Oaks, president of Brigham Young University and future LDS apostle, issued a condemnation of "repressive tactics" used by organizations threatening to boycott Utah for not ratifying the ERA. He explained to his faculty and staff: "A boycott is an ugly instrument by which to impose one's will upon others, since its efforts to penalize the adversary necessarily inflict injury on the innocent." He found the "morality" of such a tactic to be "contemptible."[34] The organizations implicated in the boycott were the American Association of University Women, American Home Economic Association, American Political Science Association, American Psychological Association, American Theater Association, Organization of American Historians, and the Speech Communication Association. The BYU president threatened to prevent any faculty from joining these groups.

Several days later, BYU's student newspaper, the *Daily Universe*, published the full text of Oaks's letter, accompanied by faculty reactions. The student editor subsequently opined: "Apparently [President Oaks] does not realize that boycotts are an accepted part of society. . . . One need wonder why Pres. Oaks chose to protest this particular boycott." Oaks wrote a stinging private letter to the student that her editorial did "not meet the standard I have come to expect."[35] A local member of the Utah League of Women Voters and wife of a BYU professor challenged Oaks. Her letter, along with one by a husband and wife, appeared in the *Daily Universe* the next day.[36] This second letter observed that two days after Oaks's statement, the LDS First Presidency had called for a churchwide boycott of television to protest unacceptable network programming, repeating Oaks's opinion that such tactics were "repressive," "contemptible," and "an ugly instrument by which to impose one's will upon others."

As political action surrounding the ERA continued, BYU invited Phyllis Schlafly to speak on campus. Curiously, the school denied a platform to Beverly Campbell, the church's official spokesperson in Virginia. For the most part, campus discussion of the ERA, at least to general audiences, was incorporated into sermons delivered by LDS church leaders at weekly devotionals.[37]

On December 9, 1979, CBS's *Sixty Minutes* aired a program about the church's policy on the ERA. The church's involvement was big news, disclosing how contingents of Mormons in Florida, Nevada, and Virginia had impacted the state ratification votes. Sonia Johnson's public excommunication had just run its course in Virginia. The Public Affairs Office reacted by preparing a packet called the "ERA Information Envelope" for stake Public Communications directors. It contained four documents: "The Equal Rights Amendment Dilemma," "An Appeal to Reject ERA," "The Risks v. the Benefits," and "Why Mormon Women Oppose the ERA." The rhetoric of each was slightly different. In the first, Mormon attorney Rex Lee laid out what he saw as the legal reasons the ERA spelled danger. The second two items attempted to show why the church was reasonable and defensible in opposing the ERA based on seemingly overwhelming benefits versus the risks of creating an uncertain future. Opposition, from this point of view, was a moral position because of the potentially negative impact on the American family. The fourth document, "Why Mormon Women Oppose the ERA," voiced the Relief Society line of opposition to military service, unisex bathrooms, and changes in divorce laws, among other issues. In addition, the packet included a newspaper clipping titled "Sonia's Bishop Was the Real Hero" and a news release "On Rebuttal to '60 Minutes' Program."

In a cover letter, Heber G. Wolsey, managing director of the church's Public Communications Department, instructed local leaders that if approached by radio or television talk shows, they should find out as much as possible about the interviewer in advance to know what approach the interviewer might take, as well as who might be in the audience. He advised them against being interviewed until they had discussed it with "someone else," a coded reference to the Public Affairs office, and given full consideration.[38]

The church's massive, often sub rosa campaign proceeded in three waves—in Idaho, which had ratified the amendment and now sought to rescind that ratification; in three states with a large enough Mormon population and political influence to offer the potential for a successful fight: California, Florida, and Nevada; and states which had not ratified and campaigns were conducted primarily after the extension of the ratification deadline: Illinois, Missouri, and on a smaller scale in North Carolina.

Step One
Promoting Rescission in Idaho

The example of Idaho is useful in understanding the LDS Church's strategy. Idaho's legislature ratified the ERA in 1972, one of twenty-two states to do so that first year; but almost immediately a movement formed to rescind it.[39] To address opposition to the ratification vote, the state house of representatives' Judiciary Committee scheduled a public hearing in Boise on February 5, 1973. Mormon bishops throughout the surrounding area encouraged members to attend and distributed a circular in their wards offering free housing, transportation, and other assistance. Members who could not attend were to contact their state representatives to voice their opinion. The language in the circular was alarmist:

> The Equal Rights Amendment has been ratified in Idaho. If we keep this, it could mean that our girls would be subject to the draft, we could be forced into common public restrooms for men and women, wives could be expected to be responsible for the financial support of their children along with the fathers, and so the children would be put in day care centers at the age of two and mothers would have to work. These are but a few of the changes it could bring into our lives.[40]

The success of this call to action, as LDS members dutifully showed up in overwhelming numbers, must have left an impression on Elder Hinckley and others of the Special Affairs Committee, which later drew on its collective memory to put the same action in motion for repeat performances elsewhere, especially after realizing the opportunity it had missed to influence the outcome of the Idaho IWY conference in 1977.

The month before the Judiciary Committee hearing, the Idaho legislature had voted to rescind ratification. It was three days before the vote that the church brought considerable public influence to bear on the legislature by staging the rally in Pocatello where Apostle Packer spoke. On the fifteenth of January, Barbara Smith spoke in Coeur d'Alene to encourage people to maintain their support for the rescission.[41] As previously mentioned, the U.S. Justice Department advised President Jimmy Carter in 1979 that the rescission was illegal.

This opinion, and the reaction from Idaho, would bring the state back into the national spotlight on May 9, 1979, when the state, along with Arizona, filed suit in federal court in Boise to validate its rescission and challenge the Constitutionality of the ratification extension. The case, *Idaho v. Freeman,* was heard by Judge Marion J. Callister, an LDS regional representative. On October 4, Judge Callister denied a Justice Department motion to recuse himself, thereby drawing the church's role in the ERA controversy more unwelcome public attention (see chap. 11).

Step Two
Mobilizing Armies of Volunteers
Nevada, California, and Florida

Political groups calling themselves "private citizens" but comprised almost exclusively of Mormon Church members began appearing in key states. In Arizona it was the Home and Family Rally Committee, in Iowa the Citizens for Family Life, the Hana Pono Political Action Caucus in Hawaii, Families Are Concerned Today in Florida, Coalition Citizens Quest for Quality Government in Nevada, Pro-Family Unity in South Carolina, and Save Our Families in Tennessee. Mormons founded the Illinois Citizens for Family Life, Missouri Citizens Council, and Virginia Citizens Coalition. In California LDS people founded two political groups, the Pro-Family Coalition and the Standard of Liberty Political Action Group. All of these organizations worked in concert, corresponding, sharing notes, and following directives from Salt Lake City. It may be instructive to consider their common agenda and tactics, which left a recognizable footprint as their activities were authorized from Salt Lake:

- The "citizen" groups organized car pools and bus caravans to bring hundreds, even thousands, to anti-ERA demonstrations at state capitols. These well-publicized public rallies were important in creating common ground between Mormon organizations and other groups.[42]

- Because of the grassroots, informal nature of their organizations, the groups did not feel it necessary to register as lobbyists or file complete reports of donations. Some did, but this was not the case in Florida or Virginia where the media investigated and found them to be illegal PACs which had neither registered nor reported significant financial activity.[43] In Arizona and Missouri where they were unregistered, the Mormon groups managed to operate under the radar and not draw attention to their guerilla status. Wherever the reporting requirements were more lenient and the groups were small enough to escape detection, they operated with more latitude.

- Church leaders initiated letter-writing campaigns with instructions to church members to identify themselves as private citizens.

- Local leaders produced and distributed anti-ERA instructional literature. It often included documents from Phyllis Schlafly's Eagle Forum and STOP-ERA. These were distributed during LDS church meetings or made available for pick-up in church buildings.

- Alliances were forged with other anti-ERA groups. This last step was particularly significant, given the church's history of insular politics and aloofness from other religious groups. Virginia Regional Representative Julian Lowe told a reporter in February 1979 that anti-ERA Mormons "have allied with other groups, . . .

whoever sees things the way we do—Catholic, Baptist."[44] Bridging barriers of mutual suspicion, the Religious Right coalesced in new ways.

During the spring of 1978, the *New York Times* ran a series of articles about the ERA and found that right-wing organizations had been surprisingly influential in frustrating ratification. Opponents, according to the *Times*, clouded the issue with fear-laden threats about homosexuality, military service for women, liberal divorce laws, and Marxism. The National Conference of Catholic Bishops, ever more entrenched in its opposition, asserted that the amendment would lead to increased abortions and threaten the family in unpredictable ways.[45]

Nevada was the first state to vote on ratification after the October 1978 Congressional extension. Nevada submitted an advisory referendum to the general public, making the state a significant test case of public opinion.[46] The legislature had already voted against ratification in 1975, 1976, 1977, and 1978. In 1975 the amendment had passed the assembly 27-13 but was defeated in the senate. The next year, ERA proponents worked hard to generate more support in the senate.

According to *Ms. Magazine*, Relief Society women were the first to organize against the ERA in Nevada in 1975. "We were given leaflets suggesting that we write letters against the ERA," said an LDS woman who chose to remain anonymous. "They told us there was no need to stamp them. The Relief Society teachers would come pick them up. The letters were saved and sent to legislators in the 1975 vote."[47] In addition, LDS bishops condemned the ERA in sacrament meetings, the principal worship services, and priesthood meetings for the church's men.[48]

When the 1975 editorial appeared in the *Church News*, the church became a frequent topic of discussion during the Nevada legislative session. The *Church News* editorial maintained that differences between men and women were determined by God and that the ERA was a "confused" step backward in time "instead of a clear stride into the future." "The timing of the editorial, coming just before the Nevada and Utah legislatures considered ratification of the ERA brought fire from ERA proponents," wrote a reporter for the *Las Vegas Review Journal.*"[49] Long-time ERA supporter Jean Ford was running for the Nevada senate from District 3. She had been told she could "write off a certain block of votes from a certain religious group in this town. I was told that by members of the Mormon Church. A lot of my supporters told me to cool it on ERA, that if I actively campaigned on that issue, it would hurt me." Politician John Shipp, a Republican in the District 3 primary, believed the influence of the church was real and something to be anticipated carefully. State Senator Helen Herr, the STOP ERA state leader and a candidate for re-election in District 3, said that "two hundred churches in Clark County —representing all denominations, not just Mormons—have been very active in ERA opposition."

State senator and LDS Regional Representative James Gibson acknowledged the church's opposition, saying: "If you're pro-ERA and that also means you're for abortion and for decriminalization of marijuana and other things that seem to go with that, then it could hurt [the] Church membership[, which] is a substantial factor in the population. I'm not sure of the impact on the election overall, but I think in a close election, it could be significant."[50] Wendell Waite, an LDS bishop and Las Vegas councilman seemed to be unaware of the citizens' organization. The church, he insisted, had "never told them how to vote. There is no organized effort of the church to work against the ERA or pro-ERA candidates that I'm aware of. Mormons are certainly involved in working for some candidates, but that's certainly their right."[51]

The Nevada Democratic Party investigated the Mormon involvement in the ERA ratification in hearings on unfair campaign practices in 1976.[52] United Press reporter Myram Borders reported that, according to testimony offered at the hearings, the Mormon political group was created "to act as a vehicle to defeat candidates favoring the Equal Rights Amendment."[53]

According to Renee Rampton, a Mormon mother of four children, her Nevada bishop, S. Mahlon Edwards, invited her in the fall of 1976 to serve on the so-called Quest Committee, explaining that he was acting on instructions from the president of the Las Vegas South Stake, who wanted volunteers for this political action committee. She declined, telling him she "could see a conflict," as she also explained to the chair of the Fair Campaign Practices Committee of the Democratic Party.[54] Rampton knew of Quest's attempt to influence the recent election. Two days before the primary, Quest anonymously mass-distributed a listing of each candidate's position on five issues: the Equal Rights Amendment, capital punishment, pornography, abortion, and marijuana. The summary of the candidates' positions claimed to be based on survey questions, but candidates, including some incumbents, complained that their positions had been misrepresented or ignored.[55]

When Quest insisted that it did not endorse candidates, it walked a narrow semantic line. In fact, the committee prepared a list of preferred candidates in two elections in 1976 and 1978, according to Rampton, who said the lists circulated in Mormon ward chapels and Catholic parish halls and that Relief Society "calling trees" were activated to campaign for anti-ERA candidates. Rampton felt that this was "dangerously close to violating the principle of separation of church and state."[56]

Ms. Magazine found that leaflets prepared by the Quest Committee were distributed by volunteers in various neighborhoods, in church parking lots, and at Relief Society meetings.[57] Rampton said that, after her talk with her bishop, she received calls from two other church members about the ERA, adding that "they had preconceived ideas."[58] Her understanding was that southern Nevada stake presidents organized Quest in early 1976. One church member showed up at her house on the afternoon of Father's Day 1976 and asked her to attend a meeting about the ERA that was to begin less than two hours later. "I declined," she said, "stating that it was Fathers Day and the Sabbath, and such a meeting was highly inconvenient and inappropriate at that time. He then asked if a representative of the committee could bring some materials to me." She agreed.[59]

Rampton asked another church member, Norene Ray, how the committee was organized. Ray told her "that the Regional Representative for the LDS Church in the Las Vegas region had met with the five Stake Presidents and formulated the plan whereby each Bishop would call two people from every ward in the Las Vegas region to act as representatives on the 'Quest' committee. She also said there were other members who were not LDS."[60] Rampton reflected on this:

> Even though the motives of those who used the LDS church for political reasons may be understandable, and certainly the concern of church leaders for good government is appreciated, I stated at the hearings that such an approach to politics as exemplified by the "Quest" committee was and is repugnant to me as a member of the LDS church and as a citizen of the United States of America.[61]

Rampton wrote to President Kimball objecting to what she considered to be an unconstitutional mix of church and state. Secretary Francis Gibbons acknowledged receipt of the letter, but Rampton never received a response.[62]

Rampton's friend and fellow ward member, Verlene Chiodini, a thirty-seven-year-old mother of two children said she declined the invitation to attend a Quest meeting because she too felt it had a predetermined agenda, that it had "decided in advance what issues it considered moral issues. I felt the implication was that if a candidate's answers didn't agree with committee's moral judgment, then the candidate wasn't a moral person."[63] The Fair Campaign Practices hearing took testimony from Cynthia Cunningham, an assembly candidate in District 8, who said the summary poll was delivered to her home two days before the primary election by a person who refused to identify himself or the organization he represented. She concluded that the "questionnaire could only have been compiled by Quest for although the responses were distorted and misleading on three of the five issues, no one else had asked me about the same combination of issues."[64] "Whoever Quest really represents and whatever their motive," she said, "their tactics are typical of dirty politics at its worst. The sheet delivered to my home wasn't identified to source and seriously misrepresented my response to questions to make me look as bad as possible based on moral values."[65] Robert Robinson, a member of the Mormon Church, defeated Cunningham in District 8 in 1976. Robinson had voted for the ERA in 1975, yet the Quest summary listed him as a "no" vote. Thomas Semmens, an assembly candidate in District 5, was interviewed by Quest. They told him the group represented 50,000 people. "Quest didn't seem concerned about my qualifications or experience," he said. "Instead they kept telling me their beliefs on certain issues, such as abortion. I gave detailed answers to all their questions but they reported only 'yes' or 'no' answers and singled out specific questions rather than all of those asked." Jan MacEacher of the Las Vegas League of Women Voters agreed that the poll had deliberately deceived voters.[66]

After the hearings on campaign practices, the committee chair, Charles Waterman, asked Rampton to submit a formal written document for the permanent record.[67] He also solicited information from the stake president, James K. Seastrand. The latter said he had first heard about Quest from Joe Bowler, who told him he represented an organization of citizens interested in "quality government."[68] Seastrand said he raised the issue at a subsequent meeting of local stake presidents. As a group, the presidents "unanimously felt they could recommend to the members of their various stakes that their members become involved as citizens in that organization." Since that time, Seastrand wrote, they had "urged members of their stake[s] to become involved in this organization and any other such organization so long as its principles and goals conform generally to the way we believe."[69] Seastrand carefully emphasized that he gave "this history so that you may clearly understand that the LDS Church did not organize 'Quest,' nor 'Nevadans Against Pornography,' nor any other citizens' organizations." As far as he knew, Joe Bowler, Charlotte McCourt, and Arda Harman were the original founders of the organization.[70]

The man who contacted Renee Rampton on Father's Day, Dean Schank, wrote to Charles Waterman on March 9, 1977, in response to Waterman's request for him to testify. Schank said he would not testify but would provide a written summary of what he knew. According to his account, Quest invited him to the Clark County Library Auditorium, where he sat behind Commissioner Jack Petitti, who had also been invited to attend. Although he "didn't know what to expect, . . . thoughts of another political pressure group or 'railroad job' by some political activists had entered my mind," he wrote. However, the meeting was different from what he had expected. "It was refreshing to see a Westside Minister open the meeting with prayer, seeking the Lord's blessing that worthy candidates would be put into office and that the citizens would become involved in the elective process. Although prayer was one of the steps used by our founding fathers it is too often forgotten today. There was no question in my mind that the persons in 'Quest' were earnest about their views. There was a patriotic and undeniable spirit to accomplish their goals. It was like watching a 'silent majority' decide to come alive."

Schank said he supported the idea of interviewing candidates to produce comparative summaries of their views. When he received the flyer just before the primary election, he "found the information to be concise, very open and quite remarkably unbiased. Which is quite difficult in political circles today." He concluded that "the real genius was the friend to friend, neighbor to neighbor grassroots approach."[71]

When asked about evidence of church involvement in the organizations fighting the ERA, Jerry Cahill, director of press relations for the LDS Church, said that "an anti-ERA meeting should not be convened in church facilities," but considering that the "Official Statement from the First Presidency against ERA" had been read from the pulpit throughout the church, this may have caused other members to speak about it in church as well.[72]

The NOW leadership believed that James Gibson, an LDS regional representative and legislative majority leader, was partly responsible for the organization of Quest. According to a document summarizing the church's activities in various state campaigns, later included in the ERA missionary packets prepared by NOW in 1981, Gibson met with stake presidents and encouraged them to direct each bishop in their jurisdiction to choose two women from each ward to serve on the Quest committee. One purpose of the committee, and the principal task of the volunteers, was preparation and distribution of the candidate endorsement sheets.[73]

Ms. *Magazine* described Gibson as the "single most powerful legislator in Nevada."[74] In his early sixties, he was a convert to Mormonism; he was also, by that time, the most influential Mormon in the region. ERA supporters believed his influence was behind the eleven legislators changing their votes between 1975 and 1977 to seal the amendment's defeat.

During this period, conservative Mormon Apostle Ezra Taft Benson spoke frequently to the John Birch Society, and his church assignments occasionally took him to Las Vegas, such as in the spring of 1976. He represented a bridge to the right-wing groups in Nevada and elsewhere when they were coalescing around defeat of the ERA. According to one analyst, the ERA suffered in this struggle of ideologies in that "some of [the ERA's] most outspoken and quotable leaders . . . espouse[d] other liberal philosophies such as abortion upon demand, lesbianism, and decriminalization of marijuana." The right wing was happy to paint the ERA with a broad brush to portray it as counter-cultural.[75]

The ERA passed the Nevada senate in 1977 with an initial vote of 10-10, with Lt. Governor Bob Rose's vote breaking the tie, then failed in the assembly by a vote of 24-15. Kate Butler, coordinator of Nevadans for ERA, criticized the "turn coats" who made this defeat possible. "These were people we supported in 1976 with volunteers and campaign donations," she said bitterly. "They indicated their support for the ERA to us then, but clearly they were talking out of both sides of their mouths."[76] Those who had switched their positions said it was because constituent polls had not shown a strong consensus for the ERA. Speaker Pro Tem Harley L. Harmon said he conducted an informal poll of registered voters in his district that showed a negative opinion of the ERA.[77]

By 1978, state legislators saw a way out of the impasse by putting the matter to a statewide referendum, and some of them pledged to abide by the results rather than take a strong personal stand. Harriet Trudell, aide to Governor Mike O'Callaghan, said she was discouraged by the changed votes: "Jimmy Carter called, and we had the Governor, Judy Carter and Maureen Reagan. Some of the top people in the gaming industry, leading businessmen, the people these guys go to for political donations, lobbied for us. But we couldn't move a vote. They were nailed."[78] Mormons held three of the most powerful senate committees: Floyd Lamb was chair of finance, James Gibson chaired government affairs, and Mel Close oversaw the judiciary.[79]

Nevada voters went to the polls on November 7 where they confronted a long and complicated ballot. Other issues had become poisoned by association with the ERA. Ironically, the ballot included a long-ignored constitutional provision that persons or women who had engaged in a duel could not hold public office.[80] One U.S. Congressional seat was up for grabs. Seven statewide offices ranging from the governorship to state treasurer were on the ballot. In total, forty state assembly seats and half of the twenty-member senate could shift in this election. A tax-cutting proposition, which passed with a 70 percent majority, shared the same page on the ballot as the ERA.

Support for the referendum came from an eclectic collection of women's organizations and from all social classes, although the greatest support seemed to come from the middle class. A small but significant minority voice among Mormons was expressed by Dorothy Frehner, whose car heralded a bumper sticker "Another Mormon for ERA." A former Relief Society president, she said she could not "believe the Lord didn't want women to have equal rights."[81] Frehner later asked that her name be removed from church rolls, saying "I feel that by staying within the formal structure of the established Church I am legitimatizing racism, sexism, and most especially elitism. I would rather live according to the principles of the Gospel as taught by Jesus Christ than that of John Birch."[82] A Mormon attorney, Lee Walker, also supported the ERA. Walker was a former state senator from North Las Vegas who said: "I voted against it because I thought that was what the majority of my constituents wanted, but they voted me out." He lost in 1976 to Wilbur Faiss, an ERA supporter. Ever an active Mormon, Walker nevertheless felt that "the amendment just says that everybody ought to be treated the same. Anything which denies that position is bad."[83]

"Equality Now," one of the groups pushing for the initiative, emphasized Nevada's traditional support for the rights of working women. In Reno, Sue Wagner, a Republican assemblywoman and the only woman in the legislature, provided leadership for ERA supporters. Friends described her as an "All American woman" with two children, a dog, a hamster, five fish, and a station wagon. She was also an active Episcopalian, and her husband, a university professor, was in support of the ERA because he thought it was "unreasonable not to be."[84] Wagner worked tirelessly for the ERA, personally canvassing 800 homes in her district in the northern part of the state, which weighed in with solid support both for her as a candidate and for the ERA.

"Catholics Act for ERA" was another well-publicized group founded by nuns who traveled to Nevada in 1978 and 1979 to hold press conferences, organize demonstrations, and pass out informational brochures. "People of Faith for ERA" was the equivalent Protestant organization that distributed materials about various candidates and arranged speaking engagements for ERA supporters.

Anti-ERA forces accused NOW of favoring "alternative lifestyles," by which they meant homosexuality, sexual permissiveness, and abortion on demand. Nevada state senator Eugene V. Echols came to believe this and said he "saw the hand of God" in the fight against the ERA.[85] Others did too. James Gibson, the senate majority leader and LDS regional representative, read into the 1977 legislative record a letter from the Catholic bishop of Nevada, the Right Rev. Norman F. McFarland, predicting trouble for the traditional family if the ERA were passed.[86] Although the statement was not binding on Catholics, Bishop McFarland emphasized that it was in harmony with the church's teachings on morality and family issues.[87] It was through such small steps, gradually over the decade of the 1970s, that an uneasy alliance formed between Mormons, Catholics, and a loose coalition of conservative Protestants.

One-fifth of the state's voters were Mormons, most prominently in and around Las Vegas and east of Reno in Sparks. When the media became aware of the Mormon political group Quest, it understood the potential for bloc voting in these high-density Mormon areas. George Franklin, a popular editorialist for the *Las Vegas Sun,* devoted a column to Mormon influence in government in Nevada in April 1978 and concluded with the comment, "Keep the pulpit out of politics, and politics out of the pulpit."[88] A columnist for the *Valley Times* was alarmed when Mormons and Catholics tried to dominate the November 1978 Clark County (Las Vegas area) Democratic convention.

Gibson spoke at an LDS conference in February 1977, telling the congregation that Mormons should "follow the [church] authorities without reservation." The next year, it was Gibson who launched the anti-ERA campaign in Nevada with what he called "Project Inform." The posters and handouts listed him as the director of the project; he also presided at some of the presentations held in lieu of weekly Relief Society meetings or at other times during the week in LDS chapels. Typically, the programs included anti-ERA speeches by LDS women and encouragement to join and participate in Quest. The literature distributed at these meetings was produced by STOP ERA, along with Karen Hayes's speech, in which she portrayed the national IWY convention as a "gathering of sexual perverts."[89]

As the advisory referendum on the ERA approached in late 1978, Gibson hired a professional political organizer to campaign against the referendum. This was, according to the hired consultant, a "political consultant's dream" because of the ready pool of volunteers who were anxious to go door-to-door, write letters, and attend demonstrations—and who would vote in great numbers themselves. It was estimated that 90 percent of the Mormons in the area went to the polls and voted.[90] Even though they represented only 10 percent of the population, they made up 30 percent of all of those who voted.[91] Just before the vote, speeches and prayers in Mormon wards voiced the worst fears of those who believed the ERA would irrevocably change the world as they knew it. Gibson spoke at a gathering of his entire stake, telling the members to "follow the [church] authorities."[92]

Proving the power of this volunteer base, hundreds of Mormons participated in a massive, overwhelming telephone and door-to-door campaign during the two weeks prior to the election. They poked leaflets into window wipers wherever they went. According to Renee Rampton, bishops collected funds from ward members to pay for the anti-ERA leaflets and candidate-endorsement flyers,[93] although the members were told they were doing so in the capacity of "private citizens" in order to observe a technical distinction between the church and its members.[94] As some legislators became impatient with the flood of letters and overloaded capitol switchboard, Mormon legislator Joe Neal exclaimed: "The church has been acting like a political party. Those aren't prayer meetings they hold on Sundays. Those are precinct meetings."[95]

In the Quest hierarchy, LDS bishops, or sometimes bishoprics, served as the group leaders and received assignments to fill quotas for neighborhood canvassing. Non-Mormons saw the "just concerned citizens" line as a semantic ruse, but LDS leaders considered it an important principle to which they adhered, if only by way of lip service. When Noreen Ray lectured women in her ward Relief Society about Quest in a meeting held for that purpose on February 15, 1978, she prefaced her comments by encouraging the sisters to become politically involved and savvy, to know what the issues and who the candidates were, and to know where and when to vote. She described Quest as a "nonpartisan, nonpolitical, nonsectarian vehicle" to help women become better informed and more politically active. "We only are interested in moral issues," she asserted. "Only moral issues. We do not endorse candidates. We do not take stands on parties. The only thing we provide—the service we provide the community—is [to] let the voter know where the candidate stands on moral issues and then the voter votes the way he sees fit."[96] Ray positioned the women's movement in terms of a secular humanist challenge to Christian faith. "Now Sisters," she said, "I want to read you something about humanism. . . . This is a quote from Betty Friedan, the founder of the organization of National Organization for Women; she's called the mother of the women's liberation movement. Listen to this. About God and Religion. 'We find insufficient evidence for the belief in the existence of the supernatural. As non-theists, we begin with humans, not God, nature, not Deity; but we can discover no divine purpose or providence for the human species, no Deity will save us, we must save ourselves.'"[97]

The phone trees that were activated in November 1978 consisted of fourteen callers per ward from forty-four wards in the Las Vegas area alone. To reemphasize the church's position, the First Presidency sent a letter to all local church leaders reaffirming its anti-ERA position and authorizing leaders to use church facilities and resources, including members, in the campaign to defeat the ERA. A circular was sent nationwide and was read in sacrament meeting quoting the recent statement of October 12: "We take this opportunity again to bring to your attention our position on this important question." It reminded members that this was a "moral rather than a political issue" and that "because of their unique capacities and responsibilities as wives and mothers, women should be the beneficiaries of such special laws as will safeguard . . . the interests of children and families."[98]

Those who missed church on November 6 had the message hand-delivered to their homes the day before the election. Those who did attend found, in many instances, that the services were partly dedicated to a discussion of the amendment.[99] Mrs. Rampton reported that in her ward sacrament meeting, the invocation included a prayer for the referendum's defeat. The member of the bishopric who conducted the service asked for volunteers for a telephone tree. It was fast Sunday. During the testimony (witnessing) portion of the service, member after member stepped up to the microphone "trembling with fear of the horrors which had been painted in their minds by all this [anti-ERA activity]." It was a stunning experience for Rampton. "I sat dumbfounded through the meeting," she recalled, "incredulous at the entire experience. Finally it ended the same way it had begun, with a member praying to close the meeting and imploring the help of the Lord in defeating the ERA." She confronted the individual who had offered the benediction, and he said, "Renee, it's from the prophet."[100]

The Relief Society entered the fray with enthusiasm by sending each female member in the state a small pamphlet titled *Why Mormon Women Oppose the ERA*. The brochure was produced by the General Relief Society during the winter of 1976-77 and sent throughout the church for distribution to the women.

In addition, Quest again distributed its candidate evaluations based on key issues, favoring those who were opposed to legalizing marijuana and in favor of the death penalty, as two examples, and identifying the candidates as conservative or liberal based on their positions on such issues. The sheets were mimeographed and distributed in LDS parking lots, throughout neighborhoods, and in other public places. Rampton said they were also passed out during Relief Society meetings. The Fair Campaign Practices Committee noted that these voter sheets were "seen in Mormon churches."[101]

Noreen Ray said that this army for God helped develop candidates for office. She mentioned the powerful emotional lure to women when "we were promised that if we would devote ourselves to informing the women of the dangers that our families are in that the Lord would be with us."[102] She did not identify who had made the promise, but the rhetorical appeal was strong and showed how successful the strategy was in creating networks based on the church organization and in drawing on a theological heritage.

It was not just the women in Nevada who were involved on a broad scale. Mormon men also distributed anti-ERA literature, especially on their monthly visits to each church member's home. The anti-ERA flyers were left on tables in chapel lobbies and appeared as inserts in the local *Beehive* newspaper, an advertising medium for the southern Nevada Mormon community. Although not an official church publication, the *Beehive* was nevertheless frequently passed out in Mormon meetinghouses and distributed in church parking lots. The September 3, 1978, edition included various types of political endorsements. For instance, it carried paid political ads such as "Re-elect Senator JAMES I. GIBSON, SENATE DISTRICT 1." This was surrounded by a black border without any statement identifying it as a paid advertisement, giving the impression that the *Beehive* itself might be endorsing Gibson. The inserts in this particular edition included a campaign leaflet for John Foley, the Democratic candidate for governor; an endorsement sheet which advertised Quest; and a Conservative Caucus newsletter with a message from the state director, Homer Hansen. Of all these, only the ad for John Foley was clearly paid for by his campaign. Another type of endorsement in the newspaper appeared as a news story profiling a certain candidate, typically including an interview, quotes from campaign literature, and details about the candidate's home life and church activity.[103]

Verlene Chiodini told the *Salt Lake Tribune* she picked up a copy of the *Beehive* and found, tucked inside, a list of candidates endorsed by *Citizens for Responsible Government,* the newsletter of the Conservative Caucus of Nevada. There was also a letter from the caucus urging LDS people to oppose liberal government programs, which it described in terms of "moral decay, fiscal bankruptcy and national weakness."[104] It is impossible to determine in every instance where the church was used for political purposes whether such activity was at the discretion of an individual member or in response to specific directions, but there was a shared interpretation of the appropriate role of the church in the anti-ERA campaign because the First Presidency had encouraged members to "join actively" in using church facilities and whatever other resources might be useful to defeat the amendment.[105]

Kent White was a church custodian in Arville, Nevada, in 1978 and reported: "While cleaning the 25th Ward Clerk's office of the chapel sometime between late September and early October, I saw at least two bundles of copies of the STOP ERA newsletter titled, 'Equal Rights—Yes! ERA—No! On the back page of the newsletter is a table of candidates who voted for the ERA and against the ERA in the previous session of the legislature. The reader is urged to vote only for those candidates who vote against the ERA."[106]

Although the call for political action went out to LDS members generally, the response was most vigorous where the LDS Special Affairs Committee assigned local leaders to create political action groups.[107] Lori Stromberg estimated that as many as 86 percent of the letters opposing the ERA in Virginia were written by Mormons, who comprised only 1 percent of the state's total population, as one example.[108]

Sheldon Rampton mentioned that literature from Phyllis Schlafly's Eagle Forum and STOP-ERA was available not only in LDS chapels but also at the Nevada LDS Distribution Center next to a stack of temple garments.[109] One of the fact sheets available at the distribution center listed short, pithy slogans that, however easy to remember, promoted only a surface awareness of the issues and their significance; a series of one liners, punchy as sound bites, filled the page:[110]

> Equal Rights—Yes! ERA—No!
> Will you lose your job under ERA?
> Will Fed. Gov't Control your church?
> The new ERA Society encourages homosexuality as an American lifestyle.
> The ERA Society will decide who has the right to live.
> The ERA will force women into combat.
> The welfare of women is not the primary goal of the leading advocates of the ERA. Their goal is nothing less than the complete restructuring of American Society.
> The New ERA Society denies God.
> The new ERA Society will destroy marriage and family.
> The new ERA Society will take away your right to own property.[111]

For a traditional audience of family-based women, the bleak scenario of the future painted by these slogans was daunting. Mormon women were taught from the pulpit that their principal role was that of wife and mother, that the threat of combat duty, homosexuality and lax morality, and the hint of federal encroachment into the right to choose one's lifestyle for oneself were horrifying predictions. It created an emotional knee jerk that definitely fueled the army of men and women fighting the ERA.

Indeed, many of those who became involved in Nevada had previously never been involved in politics.

When the votes were counted after polls closed on the night of November 7, 1978, the referendum had failed by a two-to-one margin. In addition, a slate of conservative candidates was ushered into Nevada politics. Despite the rather high-profile involvement of Mormons in the campaign and their elation at the outcome, the church's Public Communications office denied any involvement in the election.[112]

California

California ratified the Equal Rights Amendment in 1973. Nevertheless, Mormon influence in the state was significant due to many wealthy and politically well positioned Mormons who contributed to the campaigns in other states. In the fall of 1978, California Mormons rallied to help finance the anti-ERA campaign in Florida. As a result, of the total $30,000 collected for Florida's Families Are Concerned Today (FACT), 53 percent came from California. Of that amount, no funds came from non-Mormon sources.[113]

In Sacramento, eighty-seven Mormons contributed $2,355 within days of being told about FACT's need for funds. Florida held a referendum on the ERA in 1978 similar to Nevada's plebiscite and anti-ERA forces mobilized; the result was a two-to-one rejection of the amendment. The next spring the senate, after the house passed the amendment, voted against it 21-19. FACT had accomplished its mission.

Mormon activity in California began in 1976 when the church issued its official statement, but its presence wasn't noticed until 1978. It lasted until after the successes in Florida and the end of the ratification period. Diane Divoky of the *Sacramento Bee* commented in 1980: "Until recently, the role of the Church of Jesus Christ of Latter-day Saints in fighting the ERA and some related women's issues received little notice, because in their political activity Mormons simply identify themselves as concerned citizens, even when the call to action has come from Church officials."[114] In the wake of Sonia Johnson's well publicized excommunication for supporting the ERA in Virginia, NOW made Johnson a cause celebre, and the negative publicity impacted the way Mormons in California dealt with the ERA.

In the golden state, Mormons created several organizations to oppose the ERA including the Standard of Liberty Political Action Committee, better known by its acronym SOLPAC; Pro-Family Unity, eventually called United Families of America; American Association of Women, Pro-Family Coalition, and California Family Women. The first group, SOLPAC, was spearheaded by John Harmer, a conservative Mormon and former California lieutenant governor. The committee's principal activity was to raise funds for campaigns in other states, particularly in Alabama, South Carolina, Texas, and other various Western states.[115] Organized in 1977, it participated early on in a national anti-ERA strategy meeting in St. Louis. Although the group was fully functioning in 1977 and 1978, it would not register as a lobbying group until 1979. Harmer dismissed the significance of this to the *Sacramento Bee*, saying SOLPAC had put "modest amounts of money into 'half a dozen' political campaigns." In part, the funds were raised by letter from Utah's Orrin Hatch, in which the Republican Senator strategically quoted LDS President Spencer W. Kimball's statement about the importance of members becoming politically active. The board of directors of SOLPAC were all Mormons and at least three of the executive committee were LDS regional representatives. These included John Carmack of Los Angeles, Harvey Greer of Sacramento, and Jay N. Lybbert of Tallahassee, Florida. Two women sat on the executive committee, including Vivian Adams of the church's Public Communications office in Chicago.[116]

Pro-Family Unity, another Mormon-initiated group, operated out of Sacramento beginning in 1978. It incorporated in South Carolina when it opened a second office there, although its national executive director, James Dills, was an LDS bishop in Sacramento. According to the anti-ERA activist Jan Clark, a resident of South Carolina, Pro-Family Unity killed the ERA in her state. Clark and her husband moved to Illinois in 1979, and LDS leader Paul H. Dunn said they were "heaven sent here to fight the ERA."[117] By 1980, Pro-Family Unity expanded to become a nationwide group called United Families of America (UFA), and Jan Clark sat on the board of the expanded group, based in Salt Lake City. UFA had plans for research activities in "conjunction with Brigham Young University," Jan Clark said, and worked "closely with Sister Smith, and always discuss issues back and forth with her." Although UFA had a research component, it was primarily a lobbyist organization.[118]

The UFA newsletter, called the *National Family Reporter,* achieved a distribution of 15,000. The editor, Gordon Jones, a Mormon, said that "although he believes the ERA is dead politically [1980], the issues it symbolizes will not go away. . . . Safeguards must be written into legislation for women so we do not become a 'sex-neutral' society." Clifford Cummings, former stake president of the Oakton Virginia Stake, was also a board member but simultaneously responsible for organizing the Virginia Citizens Coalition.

The American Association of Women was formed in April 1980 by Georgia Peterson, a former Utah state legislator and in 1980 a state tax commissioner. Overwhelmingly Mormon, the group nevertheless included a Baptist state legislator and Karen Hayes of Nevada.[119] The final two groups were the Pro-Family Coalition led by Doris Enderle, a Mormon woman from Huntington Beach, and California Family Women, a group primarily located in Santa Clara County. These, like the others, focused on raising money for out-of-state campaigns.

Although it would be difficult to quantify, it was perhaps the affluence of California's Mormons that accounted for their heavy contributions to fighting the ERA's ratification. According to Nadine R. Hansen, an attorney and ERA supporter, her fellow Mormons in California channeled funds to three state senators running in Florida in the fall of 1979.[120] Three of the four were elected and the ERA was defeated 19 to 21. The first mention of cross-state contributions appeared on May 4, 1980, in the *Sacramento Bee* in the same article that found LDS involvement had gone unnoticed because of attempts to conceal their common religious affiliation.[121]

Jerry Cahill, director of press relations for the church, said that when "a call for Florida campaign contributions was received by church authorities in Salt Lake," they forwarded the request to church leaders in northern California. This surprising disclosure was the first time the church had admitted the breadth of its involvement. As Diane Divoky wrote, the church had previously "denied its involvement in ERA politics, saying that its stand against the amendment [was] a moral one."[122] Cahill explained that authorization for "such collections of anti-ERA funds from Mormons had been given in a letter from the head of the church, Spencer W. Kimball, and his two counselors." He said the "letter of authorization was sent to all 9,000 church officers in the United States on October 12, 1978," a month before the Florida elections.[123]

Jerry L. Gardner, the Public Communications director for the church in Sacramento, insisted that no funds had come from the church itself, although the contributors in the Sacramento area were all Mormons, many of them "high ranking officials in the church."

Victor L. McDaniel of Orangevale, a major in the U.S. Air Force, said the request for funds was an agenda item during a stake high council meeting. "They let the whole (North Sacramento) stake know," he said. "But I don't know how much further the request went."[124] Gigi Doty of Menlo Park received the pitch in Sunday school when Dale Brunken, a stake high counselor, said he had been assigned to raise a certain amount of money that had to be transferred to Florida by eleven o'clock of "a particular evening." He predicted that the goal would easily be met. When the *Sacramento Bee* contacted him, Brunken denied "knowing anything about the announcement" or of knowing who Doty was.[125]

Brunken's denial lacked plausibility in light of the facts. According to the *Miami Herald,* California Mormons raised $17,000 in less than a week. On a single day, October 30, 1978, 308 individual Mormons in the Bay Area donated $6,859. Reporter Linda Cicero compared ward membership lists to contribution lists, ascertaining that nearly all of the donors were Mormons. The only prominent exception was a $3,000 donation from Phyllis Schlafly's STOP-ERA, headquartered in Alton, Illinois.[126] "Donations, sometimes in the thousands of dollars, left the coffers of the

LDS citizens' groups and ended up with non-Mormons organizations such as Phyllis Schlafly's STOP-ERA and Eagle Forum in Illinois.[127] According to the *Miami Herald,* John Carmack, an attorney and LDS regional representative, contributed $3,000 in 1978, as did his wife, Shirley.[128] An article in the April 1982 issue of the *Florida Historical Quarterly* noted: "Because funds went to candidates or to the organization, 'Families Are Concerned Today,' as contributions from individual donors, they were not identified initially as part of an organized campaign."[129]

In February 1979 when the extension campaigns were running full force in several states, Paul McCloskey, a Republican Congressman from California, voiced opposition to religious influence. His newsletter specifically named the Mormon Church: "I have always thought that one of the most treasured concepts established by our Constitution has been that of freedom of religion." He further reflected:

> In the past, this meant a separation of church and state, with each religion free to practice its own moral values, but not to impose them on others. . . . Presently, however, several churches . . . notably the Catholic and Mormon, have argued that their moral values should be written into the law in matters such as the Equal Rights Amendment and abortion. There is a danger here as I see it, since religious beliefs are based on faith and thereby not subject to compromise. Our democratic government requires compromise and accommodation of differing views and it could be harmful if politics and religion become inextricably intertwined.[130]

At least in the funding of this anti-ERA campaign, the two were hopelessly intertwined.

Florida

The ERA had come up for ratification in each legislative session in Florida since 1972. On April 13, 1977, it failed again when at least three legislators who had previously pledged support switched sides when it came to a vote. This was all the more startling because a poll commissioned by the Democratic National Committee showed the amendment's supporters had nothing short of a gigantic majority in Florida—62 percent against 16 percent.[131] National polls demonstrated the same level of support.

According to Ken Driggs, assistant to Florida's speaker of the house, Donald L. Tucker (both Tucker and Driggs were Mormons), a campaign to defeat the ERA had been afoot in Mormon wards in Florida, and masses of Mormon men and women had attended demonstrations at the state capitol staged by Schlafly's STOP-ERA. Driggs wrote that other church members lobbied Tucker so intensely on Sundays that

> the Bishop made a plea in Sacrament Meeting to leave the man alone on his day of rest, suggesting that they get an appointment with him during office hours. During the next two weeks the lobbying by the various other factions on the Senate side became so intense that it stifled almost all other legislative matters, and the bitterness spilled over into the House. Chartered buses brought hundreds of "Stoppies" to the Capitol where they filled the halls. They dressed in red, many wearing aprons in the shape of a stop sign, and the pro-ERA lobbyists, fewer in number, adopted green as their identifying color. A great many young girls and baby strollers added to the props employed by both sides.[132]

The president of NOW, Eleanor Smeal, criticized what she called Florida's "straight political horse trading" among legislators who, she said, were "not emotionally committed."[133] In her first year as president of NOW, she had spent most of her time rallying support for ERA. As time wore on, she promoted a campaign "of increasing outrage" and urged the membership: "We need to recruit people to go to all the states, create caravans to go into every small town and hamlet and build a grassroots organization like we did in Indiana. . . . We need national boycotts, economic sanctions. . . . We have to make this too hot an issue to trade on."[134] Clearly, the feminists had been outmaneuvered; but in the future, they would refine and enlarge their organizational efforts and ability to apply political pressure. As Smeal grimly promised, "In the long run, they will regret having made us fight so hard."[135]

As was true in other states like Nevada or Arizona, Mormon activity in Florida began after the October 1977 official statement of the First

Presidency and tapered off after the 1979 referendum. In 1978, LDS regional representatives called bishops and asked them to visit ward members and ask for donations to FACT for campaigning for anti-ERA candidates.[136] When Karen Torgeson, a Tallahassee Mormon, heard about this, she telephoned the Internal Revenue Service and asked whether this would violate the regulations governing tax-exempt organizations. She subsequently called the Special Affairs Committee in Salt Lake City and expressed her disagreement with their approach, then wrote to Sonia Johnson to tell her what had happened in Florida.[137] Sonia was keeping record of this type of activities for Mormons for ERA.

Don Ladd, a regional representative in Virginia, owned land in Florida. Julian Lowe, Virginia's other regional representative, told Mormons for ERA that Ladd had appropriately participated in the church's pre-election campaign in Florida.[138] But crossing state lines to campaign against pro-ERA candidates, sending funds to support anti-ERA candidates, and sending research or information to help in campaigns became a complicated web of relationships. The same names—Don Ladd, Clifford Cummings, and others—kept showing up in other states. They were connected not only through personal business and real estate interests but also by ecclesiastical lines of authority, and they together managed a campaign of significant dimensions and national impact.

The fuzzy line separating outside religious interests from local politics was particularly troublesome to the candidates who ran against the interests of FACT. Senator Pat Frank, a Democrat from Tampa whose opponent received Mormon funds,[139] said to the *Miami Herald*: "I believe in freedom of speech and I wouldn't want to inhibit anyone from supporting the candidate of their choice. But I have a problem in terms of a tax-exempt organization using that organization to become involved in political campaigns. That's violating the intent of the tax exemption." Deputy Secretary of State Dorothy Glisson explained that groups spending more than a hundred dollars had to register to "let the citizens know where the money is coming from, to let the citizens know who the people are who are supporting" political activities.[140] According to official campaign records created and maintained by FACT, the state was divided up along LDS stake boundaries rather than political districts in determining which congregations would help which candidates. For example, in October 1978, eighty-five Mormons in Melbourne and Cocoa Beach contributed $2,031 to the campaign of B. E. "Billie" Brooks, two senate districts and over 100 miles away in the Palm Beach area.[141] As the *Miami Herald* found, such funds were matched by money coming in from California.[142]

According to the *Salt Lake Tribune,* church members contributed $15,000 to four anti-ERA candidates: state senators Van Poole, Democrat from Fort Lauderdale; John Ware, Republican from Tampa; and unsuccessful candidates "Billie" Brooks, a Republican from Riviera Beach, and David Ray, a Republican from Tampa. Each of these candidates claimed they were not aware the money was coming from Mormon sources.[143]

Responding to questions about illegal campaign tactics, Florida's secretary of state, George Firestone, began an investigation in mid-April 1980 to determine if FACT fund raising had violated state election laws which explicitly require political groups to report how much money they raise, the source of their contributions, and how the money is spent; nor could any individual or group give more than $3,000.[144] In this case, FACT had received over $20,000 from individual donors, each giving the maximum of $3,000, within the first week of the fund-raising drive.[145] According to the *Miami Herald,* candidates for Florida's legislature who opposed the ERA received thousands of dollars in last-minute contributions from Mormon church leaders. Reportedly, again according to the *Herald*'s investigation, the church had hoped to raise at least $10,000 for each candidate during the last seventeen days prior to the election. The LDS public relations office in Salt Lake City reported that $60,000 was collected during the seventeen-day period before the November 7 election.[146]

Justifying the flow of funds from California to Florida, Jay N. Lybbert, a political scientist at Tallahassee Junior College and the LDS regional representative for that area, told the *Miami Herald,* "I just talked to a few of my friends."[147] What Lybbert failed to tell the *Herald* was that he was on the executive committee of SOLPAC, although the Miami papers filled in this detail.[148] Nor did Lybbert acknowledge that FACT's financial records showed him making $414 worth of long-distance telephone calls, presumably in the fund raising effort. The president of one stake told a reporter that Lybbert called him that fall and asked him to mobilize the bishops to collect contributions from the members.[149] The *Miami Herald* reported that Richard Chapple, president of the LDS Tallahassee stake, confirmed that the request had come from a church leader. However, Chapple was quick to say that it was not a religious calling. "I realize there are people who can't make that distinction," he said. "You can take off your tie. You can put on a sports shirt. You can work in the garden and even get your hands dirty but [you] cannot divest [yourself] from [being seen] as [their] spiritual leader."[150]

Bill Evans of the Special Affairs Committee told Linda Sillitoe, writing about the story for *Utah Holiday* magazine, that he was uncertain about the financial contributions to FACT, saying he "doesn't know if money's being raised in other states to send to unratified states."[151] Speaking to the *Miami Herald* in April 1980, church spokesman Jerry Cahill admitted: "Things undoubtedly were done that on review shouldn't have been done," reflecting the fact that often local efforts were not coordinated with churchwide efforts.[152]

One of those "things" may have been shifting LDS missionaries from the proselytizing duties to canvas against the ERA. Maxine Hanks said she and other missionaries were asked to distribute anti-ERA literature in the Tampa suburbs just before the election. It is unknown if the directive came from the mission president himself or stake and ward leaders who gave the instructions to the full-time missionaries.[153]

Other churches in Florida took public stands on the ERA. Praise the Lord, a coalition of fundamentalist religious groups based in Charlotte, North Carolina, was the most active and visible in the campaign and crossed state lines to extend the fight into Florida. However, on the other side were other religious groups, the ERA receiving support from Baptist, Methodist, Jewish, and Lutheran churches, among others.

On May 17, 1979, the Florida house voted in favor of the ERA with a vote of 65-53. The senate rejected it the next week, 21-19. Senator Guy Spicola had voted for the ERA in 1973, 1975, and 1977, and Pete Skinner had voted against it in 1975 but for it in 1977. This time, both voted against. The most surprising turnaround was on the part of Senator Vernon Holloway, who earlier had promised to conform to his constituency's wishes. They expressed support by a two-to-one margin, but Holloway voted against ratification. The next year, when the ERA came up before the legislature, the senate passed it and the house did not.

Arizona

Arizona rejected the ERA in successive state legislatures starting in 1973. When the deadline was extended and the church sought to prevent ratification in states where Mormon influence was the strongest, this included Arizona with a 6 percent LDS population. The anti-ERA coordinator for the church in Arizona presented the U.S. Congress with a petition "signed by 70,000 Arizonans" expressing their opposition to the amendment.[154]

Apparently the anti-ERA activity began during the fall of 1977 and ended when the extension period expired. Documents in the Sonia Johnson Collection show that the bishopric of the Tempe Eighth Ward sent a sheaf of papers to each of the approximately 200 families in their ward. The teachers quorum, consisting of fourteen- and fifteen-year-old boys, stuffed the envelopes as a "service project," although some objected. According to church member Lou Ann Stoker Dickson, her bishopric received pressure from the "hierarchy"—meaning the stake president and his superiors—to get the message across to members, although they were also advised to do so as "private citizens." The bishopric was to tell the members "how to vote on these issues," according to her conversation with a member of the bishopric.[155]

This informational packet began with a cover letter mentioning that it was from "your bishopric" and ended with AMEN rather than signatures. This letter encouraged those who read the material "to study and pray about this information. Then we want you to act accordingly."[156] The implication was that if one prayed, one would receive the correct answer—the one already provided by the First Presidency. The packet included the names and addresses of Tempe's government representatives. The letter asserted that, "as your Bishopric, we feel obligated to communicate the counsel of living prophets to our ward members. This communication is not intended to create debate or cause division, but to inform and bare witness of the counsel all of us have received from the Lord through His prophets."[157]

The packet contained the usual statements from President Kimball, Apostle Benson, Apostle Packer, and President Barbara Smith. They were arranged in chronological order and followed a summary sheet which laid out key quotes from each document:

October 22, 1976	We recognize men and women as equally important before the Lord, but with differences biologically, emotionally, and in other ways. . . . ERA, we believe, does not recognize these differences.
August 26, 1978	We believe ERA is a moral issue . . . [We need to be] strong and fair to be able to resolve problems of inequality . . . without undermining our most basic institution, the family.
October 12, 1978	We take this opportunity again to bring to your attention our position on this important question. . . . Because of their unique capacities and responsibilities as wives and mothers, women should be the beneficiaries of such special laws as will safeguard . . . the interests of children and families. . . . We are convinced that . . . the matter is basically a moral rather than a political issue. . . . Because of our serious concern, we urge our people to join actively . . . in working to reject this measure.
July 1, 1979	We encourage all members as citizens of the nation to be actively involved in the political process. . . . The First Presidency and Twelve can declare a particular issue to be a moral issue worthy of full institutional involvement.

February 1980	The ERA is a serious moral issue. . . . For those . . . who choose to remain in the home . . . passage of the ERA may make their choice more difficult. . . . Great pressures could be brought to bear on a woman not to marry or have children. . . . The First Presidency has spoken out against the amendment. . . . In addition, many local Church leaders on stake and ward levels have encouraged their membership to keep informed and perform their civic duties. . . . Because of this counsel, many Church members have joined with other similarly minded citizens in their efforts to defeat the ERA. (See Appendix 1.)

There was also an unsigned single sheet entitled "Facts on what the ERA would do and would not do." With slight variations on familiar themes, the list focused primarily on the dire legal predictions about elimination of family support and credit laws. The ERA would not, according to this sheet, improve on existing state laws requiring equal pay for equal work or federal statutes prohibiting sex discrimination in housing and mortgages, but it would eliminate all single-sex schools.

The first sheet in the packet, the bishopric's introduction, was simultaneously respectful and didactic. All men and women were obliged to stay informed about issues of moral significance: "When you are informed, then you can intelligently speak your opinion. There is a definite responsibility that is yours: read, study and then act. They all go together with prayer." The material in the packet would help the families become informed and make wise decisions. It also gave members the opportunity to "witness the counsel all of us have received from the Lord through His prophets."[158]

As was true in similar admonitions to local members, free agency was a prominent theme at the outset, leading to a conclusion that emphasized faithfulness and obedience to the "living prophets" and eliminating personal sin "so that no excuse may exist in your life for not knowing" the right course in such matters.[159] The message was always clear: If you were faithful and obedient, you would oppose the ERA.

There was another more emotional aspect to the bishopric's interpretation of the ERA. The amendment, according to the letter, "destroys a tax exemption status of churches unless the church['s policy] coincides with Federal rules." In other words, the financial stability of the church was at risk. And there was more in that the amendment would "require 18-year-old girls to register for the draft [and] invalidates all [the] state's protective labor laws for women." While these predictions reflected the church's already well established rhetorical response to the ERA, they added on further emotional dimensions: the ERA would put teenage girls in harm's way, destroy the corporate standing of the church, muddy the legal environment, and endanger widows and others who, for one reason or another, had to work outside the home.[160]

Perhaps attempting to head off uneasiness at this deviation from the church's tradition of political non-involvement, the packet included two quotations, the first from a 1969 First Presidency message: "We recognize the urgent need of encouraging legislators and civic groups to use their good offices to combat the evils. . . . On moral issues the Church and its members should take a positive stand. We urge all members of the Church to wield their influence. . . . Latter-day Saints must always be alert and united in contending against any influence which tends to break down the moral and spiritual strength of the people." The second quotation was from another First Presidency statement, this one from 1974: "While exercising no constraint on the freedom of individuals to make their own choices as to political parties, candidates and issues, the Church urges its members as informed citizens of the respective countries to be actively involved in supporting candidates and issues which will protect liberty and strengthen the people who are governed. Freedom demands continuing responsibility."[161]

Perhaps the most notable difference between Arizona and other states was the high percentage of LDS residents, which made it relatively easy to produce a mass response through a simple call for support, even if the outreach to the membership had little in the way of logic or a presentation that one could call impressive.[162]

The Third Step:
State Campaigns after the Deadline Extension
Missouri, Illinois, and North Carolina

Initiating the third wave of state campaigns in the wake of the deadline extension, Elder Gordon B. Hinckley, as noted elsewhere, summoned "all of Missouri and Illinois stake presidents and state [anti-ERA] coordinators" to a meeting on October 5, 1979, in Salt Lake City. There, as chair of the Special Affairs Committee, he authorized them to use "church buildings" and "church meetings" to campaign against the ERA and promote candidates who would oppose it.[163] This was a reversal of the policy emphasized in Apostle Ezra Taft Benson's 1976 letter: "Please keep in mind that Church buildings and organizations are not to be used for . . . political or legislative purposes."[164]

The structure of the Missouri Citizens Council was similar to that of the Virginia Citizens Coalition. Stake and ward Relief Society presidents were chosen to be coordinators, charged with rounding up ten or more women and men in each ward to work as anti-ERA teams. Their principal responsibilities were to write letters to legislators, canvass, and lobby against the ERA. Funds were solicited from church members; some ward leaders were called into the stake president's office and told that the quota to be raised by each ward was $2,000. One local leader said he was "shocked" to be told this in the stake president's office.[165]

North Carolina

Already in North Carolina, Missouri, and Illinois, Mormon women had been working against the ERA since the church's official statement of 1976 and Barbara Smith's encouragement to be involved in the 1977 IWY meetings. Other letters and circulars originating in Salt Lake City had reached local church officials, but after the extension, the pressure mounted to organize a corps of dedicated volunteers to guarantee that the amendment would not be approved in the key states. In each effort, it was principally the women who worked to kill the ERA, their opposition rooted in the fact that "it jeopardized a way of life they had entered in good faith," as Andrew Hacker of *Harper's* magazine phrased it in 1980.[166]

The women responded enthusiastically to the direction of their male leaders.

NOW upped the ante with its own more aggressive techniques including a boycott of any state that voted against the amendment. On December 13, 1979, NOW members demonstrated outside the White House when President Carter declined to intervene against Marion J. Callister, the Mormon judge in Idaho. Carter was meeting with eighteen leaders of other women's groups during the protest.

The tactics that had been fully refined in Nevada, Florida, and Virginia before 1978 were implemented in North Carolina. There were demonstrations at the state capitol, letter writing campaigns, and ecumenical alliances. Charles R. Davis, the bishop of one North Carolina ward, gave the Relief Society president funds to use as she saw fit for the women of their ward in the way of lodging and transportation to anti-ERA rallies at the capitol.[167]

Mormons joined with members of the John Birch Society—a comfortable relationship—and of fundamentalist Protestant groups—rarely before an ally—to form North Carolinians Against ERA. The editor of the *Baptist Biblical Recorder*, published in Charlotte, confirmed that "there was a Mormon network at the core of the organization." As one indication, the chair of the Charlotte chapter was the stake Young Men's president.[168]

A study of North Carolina politics from this period cited a woman who brought five thousand letters, gathered from Mormon sources, into the general assembly chamber as proof of grassroots anti-ERA sentiment.[169] She was said to be part of the "Mormon network," a highly organized, hierarchically controlled body of workers who formed the backbone of ERA resistance in the state. This "massive" support, however, was primarily from a religious group that constituted less than 1 percent of the total population.[170]

Missouri

In Missouri another highly disciplined organization was formed in response to Elder Hinckley. Missouri activism included the production and distribution of anti-ERA materials, fund raising, and educational meetings for church members. On October 3, 1979, about 125 Mormons in Kansas City under the name "Missouri Citizens Council" attended a city council meeting to discourage endorsement of the ERA to the state legislature. Without mentioning their religious affiliation, they claimed to represent 9,000 Missouri citizens.[171] One of their publications described "an organization of public minded Citizens who are concerned for the retention of the high quality of family life. It invites all citizens regardless of race, creed or political affiliation to join the persuasion to keep the traditional, moral standards which safeguard the family. The Missouri Citizen's Council is for Equality for women."[172]

An informational packet circulated in advance of the November 1980 election included a list of candidates' positions on the ERA. It had "Points to Ponder Concerning ERA," the results of a survey of public opinion about the ERA, and names and phone numbers of candidates.[173]

The church's involvement in the election was troubling to some Mormons, including Robert Mecham, a professor of medicine at Washington University in St. Louis. He wrote to Apostle Neal A. Maxwell on December 5, 1979, objecting to the church's involvement in politics and the Missouri Citizens Council in particular. Because Maxwell was a member of the Special Affairs Committee, Mecham assumed the apostle understood what was happening and could stop it.

Of everything Mecham had observed, it was the "surreptitious" nature of the church's involvement that most bothered him.[174] The Missouri Citizens Council had denied church affiliation, creating the illusion that there had been a spontaneous groundswell of opposition to the ERA in Missouri. Mecham reported that he knew from personal knowledge that this denial was inaccurate, that bishops in his stake had "set apart or given blessings" to women to serve as their ward representatives. Eventually the group's name changed to the Missouri LDS Citizens Council and bishops were told to "invite" but not set apart members on the council—the directions emanating from the meeting with Elder Hinckley in Salt Lake City.

The council's structure was an additional problem for Mecham in that its interests were coordinated by stake Relief Society presidents under the direction of a state coordinator, a man, appointed by a regional representative. When Mecham questioned the council's state director about the relationship between this group and the church itself, the director said, "We are not an organization of the Church. . . . We work under the direction of the Priesthood Committee in Salt Lake." Behind this double-talk was an admission that the group operated under centralized authority and was an officially organized arm of the church. Mecham wrote: "If the Council is going to be involved politically then they need to be forthright and honest publicly. In light of the intense scrutiny this group will inevitably receive from the press during the next two years as they intensify their political involvement and lobbying efforts, I foresee major legal and image problems for the Church in Missouri."[175]

While many Mormons accepted the explanation that the ERA was a moral issue, others like Mecham felt uncomfortable about the duplicity, which for them was the greater moral issue. For those who further disagreed over the church's assessment of the merits of the ERA, their personal judgment put them at cross-currents with the divinely inspired leaders in Salt Lake City. It was an uncomfortable position to be in, especially where local leaders and the hierarchy itself saw them as being out of harmony with the church as much as if they had taken up drinking coffee.

Illinois

As in Missouri and North Carolina, Illinois repeatedly voted against the ERA. The difference was that the state was still considered vulnerable. In 1976 the various groups supporting the ERA came together under the umbrella "ERA-Illinois" with a full-time director and staff. But the campaign in Illinois became entangled in party politics and special interests. Black legislators in Chicago were struggling with the Democratic Party over control of the house of representatives. The powerful AFL-CIO favored equal rights but opposed the increase in federal authority.[176] Whether any given legislator would vote for or against the ERA became twisted in deals struck over issues unrelated to women's issues. In most states, women who supported the ERA tended to be well educated and relatively affluent—professionals and businesswomen—but a poll conducted in 1977 of Illinois's most conservative rural counties showed a 60 percent favorable view of the ERA.[177]

Other Illinois groups were strongly opposed to the ERA. These included STOP-ERA, the National Council of Conservative Women, the John Birch Society, and a group that called itself Right to Be a Woman. All of these were self-funded and worked independently, but many of them had women in their ranks whose husbands were well-connected.[178] The strategy employed by these groups was to play on the divisions in the Democratic Party and align themselves with the Republicans—swapping support on other issues for opposition to the ERA.

In the midst of these groups appeared the Illinois Citizens for Family Life (ICFL). Created in 1979, it was divided into three regional branches: northern, central, and southern. Within each region were smaller groups that focused on local issues in addition to those of statewide or national interest. The group maintained cohesion through newsletters, chapter and regional meetings, and a telephone hotline that could mobilize members on specific issues. Prospective members were told on a recruitment flyer that their support of "ICFL will enable it to be more effective in supporting the family values you hold dear."[179] The group's leaders, the flyer said, were Mormons: LeRoy C. Shannon, president; George Berry, treasurer; and Max Gilbertville and Jackie Summer representing Iowa. ICFL literature resembled that of other Mormon citizen groups in format and arguments. It was funded largely by Illinois Mormons.

Conclusion

Each of the campaigns in states that seemed favorable for Mormon influence, where the ERA had not been ratified, was successful. The agitation quickly neutralized the effects of the pro-ERA campaigning, in some cases focused on the same uncommitted states. It began with the IWY conferences, which provided a gauge of a state's vulnerability. Interestingly, the conferences in Illinois, Nevada, and Virginia were so contentious, they dismissed without producing a slate of resolutions. This only highlighted the fact that the ERA's future was beginning to look uncertain in those states. In Arizona and North Carolina, the IWY conferences adopted all the national resolutions including the ERA, so the amendment seemed favorably positioned. However, a campaign must have been warranted there because of the results that were realized. In Florida, the men and women who attended the IWY conference defeated all the national resolutions and those proposed by the state coordinating committee, so Florida would have looked as ripe for the picking as Illinois, Nevada, and Virginia. These were the areas the LDS Church moved into to organize political action committees to successfully defeat the ERA.

11. Trouble in Virginia

> There are many women's groups, with different agendas. Some are to the right and some are to the left; some are feminist and some are Moral Majority. That is fine; let them go on. But somewhere in the middle are issues of concern for us all. Let us find areas of commonality on which we can all agree.
>
> —Beverly Campbell, Chair,
> Virginia LDS Citizens Coalition

The Virginia senate came within a single vote of support for ERA ratification, 20-18, with twenty-one votes needed for a majority of the forty-member senate. The Virginia International Women's Year meetings, held June 10-11 in Richmond, endorsed some of the national commission's resolutions but took no action on others. The state seemed to be ideal for the church's campaign against ratification—the chance still remaining that the legislature could call for another vote. In Virginia, the church had a loyal core of political savvy, intelligent men and women who took orders from Salt Lake City, a sufficient body of literature from both STOP-ERA and Salt Lake City on the "evils" of the ERA, and enough wealthy Mormons to keep the activity afloat. Stake president Clifford I. Cummings had given an anti-ERA speech at the Sterling Park ward, but there were still Mormon women in Virginia who were committed to the ERA, believed in the separation of church and state, and were stimulated by the call to arms by the national women's movement to change the world. Starting in the winter of 1978, they called themselves "Mormons for ERA" and went about trying to change the world they lived in—the Mormon world.

The LDS Church's activity in Virginia is instructive for three reasons: (1) proximity to the national capital meant more sophistication about the political process and the national actors, (2) the body of particularly detailed and complete records about the church's organized activities, and (3) the presence of Mormons for ERA under the leadership of Sonia Johnson, then a fervently active Latter-day Saint, that raised both the quality and the quantity of the debate among Mormons themselves.

A mother of four and organist in the Sterling ward, Johnson had a doctorate from Rutgers University and had taught school in several Third World countries. She described her own espousal of the ERA as a quasi-religious conversion that came in response to the church's statement against it when it was read in church and circulated to the members in November 1978.[1] She obediently read the amendment, expecting to be convinced of its evils since, she said, she had "never gone contrary to the church on anything before." But regarding the amendment, she said: "I loved it. I just loved it. That was the beginning."[2] As pressure mounted for church members to show a united front against the ERA, she took a decided step away and with a few associates organized Mormons for ERA in the winter of 1978. Her co-founders were three good friends: Hazel Davis Rigby, Maida Rust Withers, and Teddie Wood, who together incorporated as a nonprofit, tax-exempt organization on April 11, 1980. A few weeks later on May 7, the group appointed Sonia as its president and spokesperson. When she resigned the position on December 11, 1982, she remained on the board of directors. Alice Allred Pottmyer, a member from the first, became the next president.[3] According to Lee Roderick, a political reporter in the nation's capital and Utah Senator Orrin Hatch's biographer, "Sonia Johnson was Hatch's worst nightmare come true."[4]

The Fight to Extend the Deadline

As 1978 opened, the initial skirmishing over the ERA was over. Many people had chosen their positions and the focus was now on the extension of time allowed for ratification. The frequent news coverage the previous year had stirred up new divisions and polarization between traditional women and those who believed the ERA was long overdue as an important symbol of change for American women. The LDS Church narrowed its focus in 1978 to a single, immediate goal: challenging the ratification extension.

Apostle Gordon B. Hinckley told a reporter in February: "If Mormons seem to have a cohesiveness, it springs from the convictions of basic Mormon principles" rather than from "tell[ing] a person specifically how to vote." But he "admitted it is not unusual for Mormons to be of a like mind."[5] This tendency was encouraged by church leaders in both subtle and not so subtle ways, ultimately insisted on through the threat of excommunication.

On May 25 the First Presidency sent a letter to Congressman Don Edwards, a Democrat from California and chair of the Subcommittee on Civil and Constitutional Rights, opposing the extension. They expressed concern that such an act would strain civility, pervert the Constitution, and continue the divisive fight over equal rights. "In affirming our allegiance to the United States of America," they wrote, "we express confidence that this nation is sufficiently strong and fair to be able to resolve any problems of inequality and unfairness to women, or any other group in our society, without abusing the amending process for our most basic document."[6] It concluded, "Any such gross abuse of the democratic process and of the process of amending the Constitution could send a surge of cynicism through the land which might damage the Constitution itself."[7]

In the early fall, President Cummings and counselors Robert E. Bateman and Charles W. Dahlquist sent a letter to "All Families in the Oakton Virginia Stake" reminding them of the church's opposition to the ERA and any extension of time needed to ratify it.[8] They referred to the First Presidency's original 1976 statement, letter to Congress, and an August 1978 "Reaffirmation of the First Presidency's Position on ERA." "As your Stake Presidency," it read, "we wholeheartedly sustain the First Presidency's statements and enclose a copy of each of them for your information and edification. We are providing these materials to you so you may be informed, and clearly understand the position of the Church on this vitally important issue. We recommend that, as a family, you prayerfully consider each of these statements."[9]

Utah Senators Jake Garn and Orrin Hatch were inevitably enmeshed in the national aspects of the Virginia campaign because both were Republicans and active Mormons. On May 26, Garn inserted the First Presidency's letter into the Congressional record.[10] The letter confirmed the church's allegiance to the Constitution as "divinely inspired" and explained that, coupled with its "very deep and everlasting commitment to the preservation and strengthening of the family, including its individual members," the church had done "what it rarely does—spoken out against a proposed constitutional amendment."[11] In substance, the letter argued that extension of the time allowed ratification would be "unfair to the interests of women" by further polarizing them and diverting money better used to serve their more immediate interests to promoting the ERA; the amendment lacked political consensus, and enough time had passed to demonstrate that lack of support; and finally, "it would be tragic if an amendment which claims to bring constitutional equality to women ended up injuring our Constitution."[12]

A month later in June 1978, M. Dale Ensign, LDS Public Communications director for Washington D.C., handed out to stake presidents in the area the names of members of Congress who were undecided about extending the ERA deadline and urged them to have their members lobby against extension.[13] Senator Hatch may have been involved in this effort. In any case, his personal opposition to the ERA was a matter of public record despite a relatively enlightened record on specific legislation benefitting women.[14] On Pioneer Day, July 24, Hatch wrote in his diary: "I feel so strongly that women are not treated fairly in our society, especially at the work place, . . . but to lock into the Constitution that there can be no discrimination based on sex may well lead to disastrous, unchangeable Supreme Court and lower court rulings. The statutory route is better."[15]

That summer, Sonia Johnson, her husband, Rick, and twenty of their friends marched in an ERA parade down Pennsylvania Avenue a few days before the vote in the House of Representatives to extend ratification. They carried a banner that read, "Mormons for ERA."[16] On one of the hottest days of summer, the temperature matched the political climate for the LDS Church and Utah's federal office holders when Senator Bayh invited Maida Withers of Mormons for ERA to a White House reception.[17]

Bayh chaired the Senate Subcommitte on Constitutional Rights, and in that capacity he had recently invited Sonia Johnson to testify at a Senate hearing. Senator Hatch, a member of the committee, had become so visibly upset while questioning Johnson that he attracted media attention. At one point, Bayh interrupted his colleague's monologue with a rebuke: "Senator Hatch, we know what you think. We are trying to find out what these witnesses think."[18] Hatch's staffers were allegedly passing him notes urging him "to get . . . tougher." UPI reporter Cheryl Arvidson saw it like this: "He never did really get loud, but he got mean and personal. He denigrated her. It was more his tone. There was a point where I thought he was really losing control."[19]

Despite the unpleasantness, Johnson read her views into the record, perhaps best captured in a statement distributed by the Equal Rights Coalition of Utah:

> It is our belief that passage of the ERA does not threaten the family unit. What it may do, however, is to encourage more conscious personal definitions of the shared responsibilities and commitments undertaken at the time of marriage. Commitment to the family can be as strong or stronger in marriages where the man and woman are afforded legal equality as in marriages where the state gives legal advantage to either spouse at the expense of the other.[20]

Johnson noted instances of genuine inequality in the church: women were prohibited from praying in sacrament services, young women had to be older than young men before they could go on a proselyting mission, and women were asked to support their husband's education rather than complete their own. "Mormon women do not wish to be exalted in this or any real way," she astringently added.[21]

Even in Utah, some stepped forward to voice support for Johnson. Hatch had suggested that Mormons for ERA should not be taken seriously because its numbers were small. Johnson countered that the number of people who supported the ERA in Utah did not square with the number of church members in the state. The *Salt Lake Tribune* published a letter on August 19 from ten Mormon women who wrote: "Sen. Orrin Hatch is wrong in assuming that only 1/10th of 1 percent of Mormon women support ERA. The names listed below belong to a segment of Mormon women that are not afraid to sign their names in support of the Equal Rights Amendment. We urge other LDS women who share our views to step forward and do the same." An LDS study group sent Hatch a similar protest that his numbers were off. Members of the Alice Louise Reynolds Club meeting in Provo informed Hatch of their dissent.[22] The fires were still smouldering on September 9 when the *Tribune* published another letter: "Sonia Johnson's testimony . . . eloquently voiced the sentiments of thousands of Mormon women who dare not speak in favor of ERA because they have been intimidated. We sincerely feel the ERA has been distorted and misrepresented by its opponents. We do not believe it threatens the family any more than women's suffrage did in 1920. Add our names to the growing list of women who are not afraid to speak out in its favor."[23]

Johnson told a reporter that "the climate is bad everywhere in the church," but especially in Utah where "the pressure on them is incredible to conform. They get it from their families, their bishops, . . . their stake presidents. The women in Utah are afraid they will lose their jobs, be ostracized in the community, or that their families will be harassed. . . . When we get discouraged here, we think of them as a great inspiration."[24] Membership in Mormons for ERA grew to about 500 over the next couple of months.

The Church Leadership Retaliates

Hartman Rector Jr. of the First Council of the Seventy—one of the highest administrative councils of the LDS Church and third in authority behind the First Presidency and Quorum of the Twelve Apostles—wrote to Teddie Wood of Mormons for ERA on August 29:

> The very belligerent tone of Sister Johnson's remarks will do little to win the favor of the Brethren of the Lord. He who made them made both Male and Female and there is a difference. The female has the greatest influence on the children of our Heavenly Father, because she prepares their earthly body and then nurtures them during the most formative period of their life. Therefore there is no power on earth as strong as mother love and mother influence.

His explanation for the difference between men and women reflected his own sense of the relative power of the sexes.

> In order to attempt to get the male somewhere near even [with the female,] the Heavenly Father gave him the Priesthood or directing authority for the Church and home. Without this bequeath[al] the male would be so far below the female in power and influence that there would be little or no purpose for his existence[,] in fact would probably be eaten by the female as is the case with the black widow spider.

He then challenged Wood's commitment to the church:

> The Lord has spoken through his Prophet Spencer W. Kimball. If you are really serious about being a Mormon, you will sustain the Prophet. Besides, if you have a grievance against the position of the First Presidency of the Church, you should take it to them and not before a United States Senate Subcommittee. So far as I am concerned—you are not a "Mormon" and shouldn't make pretenses that you are—certainly you don't . . . represent the rank and file membership of the Church.[25]

Relief Society President Barbara B. Smith felt equally compelled to chastise Sonia Johnson, challenging her use of Mormon historical examples:

> I think it is entirely possible that those [pioneer] women would have looked upon prayers in sacrament meetings and blessings of babies as priesthood assignments knowing that they have nothing to do with male superiority. I think they would have been able to listen to the counsel of the leaders of the Church and realize that they do not ask women to sacrifice their education for their husbands. . . . It seems to me that the mighty heritage of "courage and conviction" these women left us was founded and nourished by their faith in God and His prophets. They believed that the heavens were opened and that all mankind were being blessed by continuing revelation.

Revelation aside, there was a clear, underlying message of obedience to the male priesthood: "While we have our agency to reject this great blessing, we cannot enjoy what we will not accept."[26]

Dale Ensign responded to Johnson's Senate testimony as well. He told a reporter that Mormon leaders had always "affirmed the importance and exalted role of women in our society." He warned that the ERA would result in "far more restraints and repressions than benefits," that it "could strike at the family, . . . bring ambiguity in its interpretation, and could invite litigation." He flatly denied that the church had lobbied against the ERA—only that individual members had done so. He dismissed Mormons for ERA as a "relatively small splinter group that seeks to do as they please."[27]

When the vote on the proposed extension was announced in mid-August, Hatch was so irritated that he and Garn stated their intent to lead a Senate filibuster against it. Sonia Johnson sent Hatch a telegram on 18 August: "I am announcing my intention to begin fasting on the Capitol grounds in Washington as soon as the filibuster begins—a genuine Mormon fast, without food or liquid—and to continue until you stop talking or I die."[28] A spin-off group, Utah Mormons for ERA, announced they would also respond to the proposed filibuster with meditation and daily group prayer. Becky Cornwall, president of the small group, said: "We feel that the time has come when all the children of our heavenly parents should regard one another with equal respect and reverence."[29]

In mid-August, Johnson had visited Salt Lake City and was interviewed on KSL Radio, owned by the LDS church. The even-handed program created a huge uproar, which became even more heated when rival KALL Radio newsman Ray Friess asked Charlie Gibbs, assistant director of press relations for the LDS Church, if the church would "take action about Mormon ERA supporters" in light of the church's "public opposition to the ERA?"[30] Off the record, Gibbs said he thought such people might be in danger of censure. Friess fed the story to the wire services, and when it ran on the ten o'clock evening news on KSL-TV, it carried the provocative teaser, "The LDS Church says members who actively support the ERA could lose their Church positions." Gibbs quickly phoned in a correction, saying he had been misunderstood.[31] Meanwhile, the scrappy *Utah Holiday* magazine interviewed Johnson, who said about her fellow ward members in Sterling: "[They don't agree with me,] but they love me. It's very surprising and heartening. Now things are out in the open. It's okay to be for the ERA."[32]

By contrast, the August 1978 newsletter for the Vienna, Virginia, ward included an unsigned editorial and bishop's message portending what kind of rhetoric was to come: "One of the basic concepts of the gospel is that of free agency, and the Church has always encouraged its members to vote according to their own consciences. However, the First Presidency is so strongly opposed to the Equal Rights Amendment that they have urged us to fight its ratification." The subtle warning was to not disagree with the First Presidency, that this went beyond politics to a kind of article of faith that would be incumbent on members to accept.

This and other arguments circulated through the church until they became so familiar and oft-repeated that they showed up in virtually every lobbying effort from informal gatherings in people's homes to sermons from the pulpit. Collectively, it represented conservative folk wisdom about women's roles and one's place in society and within the strict priesthood hierarchy. Over time, this achieved the status of something like an authoritative revelation. The Vienna ward newsletter concluded:

"If you would like to support the Prophet in his opposition to the ERA, call or write to Congressman Fisher or Senators Byrd and Scott."[33]

As matters turned out, there was no filibuster; but it proved to be a lively stalking horse. Senator Garn announced separately plans to oppose extension, but met resistance because the delaying tactics would jeopardize other important pieces of legislation then moving through Congress. Garn joined Phyllis Schlafly for a press conference on September 12 and bluntly discounted the criticism, saying there was plenty of time for Senate leadership to bring up other legislation when they were ready.[34] He accused "supporters of the extension" of not "playing the rules of the game."[35]

In response, various members of Mormons for ERA—Rigby, Wood, Withers, and Jeraldine Glover—attempted to speak with Garn personally about the issue.[36] When they secured an appointment, they brought with them a basketball painted red, white, and blue and inscribed: "Overtime is part of the Game." According to Withers, Garn was less than pleased. In her words, he "proceeded to filibuster us for an hour." What they did not realize was that while they talked, a vote to limit discussion on the extension came up and was passed by the Senate. "We were unaware of our historical impact," she said, "until the press contacted us the next day. Another true-life, faith-promoting incident to build the testimonies of Mormons for ERA!"[37]

In Virginia the ERA had stalled in a house committee for five long years. In early 1979 it again failed to reach the house or senate floor even though the senate was thought to have a two-vote majority in favor. The LDS Citizens Coalition was simultaneously busy, ultimately unsuccessfully, trying to place an anti-ERA referendum on the ballot. But the legislature would conclude its work the first week of March without making progress one way or the other, leaving the commonwealth in a key battleground category as a potential swing state and high on the agenda of both sides of the conflict.[38]

Meanwhile, in late 1978, Hatch placed a pamphlet he had written called *The Intelligent Woman's Guide to the Equal Rights Amendment* into the Congressional record. In it, he argued that discriminatory laws should be removed from the statutes and that the Fourteenth Amendment should be applied to women.[39]

Mormons for ERA rallied to lobby the twenty-two "wavering senators" on the issue of the national extension bill. High on the lobbying list, and reflecting the ambivalence of the Old Dominion, were the two Senators from Virginia.[40] As the Senate debate approached, scheduled for October 3, 1978, there was renewed lobbying on all sides. Various interests supported extension but not rescission or rescission without extension.

It took three days for the Senate to follow the earlier action by the House of Representatives in extending the deadline another three years and three months to mid-1982 without allowing states to rescind previous favorable votes. A week later, on October 12, the LDS First Presidency sent out yet another letter to stake presidents and bishops in the United States to voice opposition to the ERA and the extension. The statement was published in the church's magazine, the *Ensign*.

It was a moment of triumph for the pro-ERA forces. Mormons for ERA were ecstatic and would begin to invest even more energy to maintain a steady tempo of activities over the next year: rallies, demonstrations, and speeches before various women's organizations. Numerous articles would appear in national newspapers such as the *Los Angeles Times* ("Feminist Mormons Speak out for ERA"), the *Seattle Times* ("Mormon Women Come Out of the Closet"), and the *Washington Post* ("Even Institutions Reap What They Sow").[41] In July 1979 a plane towing a banner reading "Raise the Flag for ERA" flew over the LDS temple in Washington D.C. during a flag ceremony presided over by conservative apostle Ezra Taft Benson. On July 4 women would wear "Mormons for ERA" T-shirts on the Washington Mall during the Honor America Day Rally, at which Benson delivered the prayer. Also in 1979, Mormons for ERA would join the Religious Advocates for Equality in Washington as a founding organization along with women's groups associated with the National Council of Churches and others. Their goal was to make moderate religious voices heard and "to encourage leaders and members of religious groups who officially support the ERA to do something about it."[42]

The dash and verve of Mormons for ERA would have drawn little attention if the group had not supplied solid data, especially material that the church may have preferred to keep quiet, such as behind-the-scenes organizational and lobbying instructions, official statements disseminated to church members with the weight of theological pronouncements, information about the preparation and distribution of literature for outsiders, and the coordination of volunteers at the ward and stake levels.[43]

The Potomac Women's (and Men's) Coalition

Mormons constituted only 0.5 percent of the population of Virginia but were responsible, at least in the northern part of the commonwealth, for 85 percent of the anti-ERA mail received by legislators.[44] The force behind this effort was the LDS Citizens Coalition, originally called the Potomac LDS Women's Coalition—a small group, mostly comprised of male LDS leaders, that had worked in concert with other anti-ERA groups in Virginia. From the minutes of the organizational meeting of the new, expanded coalition on November 8, 1978, one can see the methods employed to get more members involved. Although there continued to be persistent denials from Salt Lake City of church involvement, the November meeting included ranking local church officers who asserted that the direction for their activities came from Elder Hinckley and the Special Affairs Committee and that the prophet himself had called them to the work. Feminism threatened to create a new and unrecognizable world that would demolish everything they valued—family, marriage, the position they held in a world they knew and understood. For most Mormon women, the risk was not worth taking.

Despite the claim to be a women's group, it was Julian Lowe, the LDS Church's regional representative, who called the meeting, originally scheduled to be held at the Oakton stake center but then moved to the home of Clifford Cummings, the Oakton stake president.[45] The three-hour meeting was attended by about sixty ward Relief Society presidents and two women who had been assigned by their bishops to attend, along with other interested members.[46] The ward newsletters for the area stated that the prophet had asked Brother Lowe to form the committee in order to battle passage of the ERA. As an example, the Vienna ward newsletter read:

> The committee's chief function is to educate itself, Church members, and the general public as to the disastrous effects ERA will have on our lives. Too many women do not understand their rights as they now stand, and see the ERA as a panacea to real and imagined slights and discrimination that can better be corrected by enforcing laws that already exist, rather than by passing an amendment that would negate any legal recognition of the differences between men and women.[47]

Church leaders had already "called" Beverly Campbell to be chair of the coalition. Campbell had been senior partner in a public relations firm in Washington D.C. and was the mother of three. She initially had favored the ERA, she said, but had independently come to a decision to oppose it. In an interview in January 1981 with Mary Lythgoe Bradford, editor of *Dialogue: A Journal of Mormon Thought,* she explained: "When it first came out, yes, it sounded like an excellent idea. I remember reading about it and thinking there were real inequities and areas of discrimination which needed to be addressed. At that time, though, there wasn't really much you could find out about the ERA." As she told it, she was being recruited as early as 1974 by "various professional organizations" to "announce an allegiance." But as she "began looking at it from a legislative standpoint, without being aware of the Church's position," she came to see that because of "the various legal ramifications and implications," it was "not something I could support."[48] She was pleased to be called by Julian Lowe four years later to head up the church's anti-ERA coalition in Virginia. Ironically, it was her professional experience in public relations, not her role as wife or mother, that made her an attractive candidate for the calling.[49]

Now in her role as the church's most visible woman in Virginia and soon the nation, she welcomed the coalition audience that had gathered in the stake president's living room, after which Julia Christensen offered the opening prayer. Elder Lowe spoke first, citing questions he and other local leaders had received from members about how to help defeat the ERA. He described how Apostle Hinckley had asked him and Don Ladd, the other regional representative from Virginia, to organize "as has been done in other states, . . . and Brother Ladd and I decided to organize in the way the church had suggested."[50] He acknowledged the nominal existence of a handful of church leaders already operating as the Potomac LDS Women's Coalition, which had changed its name to the Virginia LDS Citizens Coalition; but now as the LDS Citizen's Coalition, the group would broaden its breadth. He emphasized that it was his responsibility to find ways to fund the group's activities.[51] Elder Hinckley had called his attention to the First Presidency's letter of October 12 urging members to "actively join with other citizens who share our concerns . . . to reject this measure." Lowe and Ladd had therefore decided "that it wouldn't be inappropriate at all if we endeavored to give it (the campaign) a little bit of order and organize as has been done in other states in the West, that the services of the sisters might be appropriately focused."[52]

The authorization from Elder Hinckley was all-important because it was a crucial factor in mobilizing the energies of the church's women. When journalist Linda Sillitoe asked Lowe in February 1979: "Do the Brethren know what you've been doing?" he replied: "Oh, they know what's going on." He was sure to update them from time to time, he said.[53]

The coalition's hierarchy would be Lowe and Ladd working behind the scenes, with Beverly Campbell out front and managing the day-to-day business and coordinating the activities of volunteers. Lowe had previously worked at the CIA and was suited to the kind of camouflaged role that was being suggested for him.[54] In terms of reporting to Salt Lake City, this was done through the Special Affairs Committee rather than directly to the apostles or First Presidency. Rodney P. Foster, a secretary in the First Presidency's office, said he was not even aware of the Special Affairs Committee before about 1977, the International Women's Year, and that "the actual grassroots movement and working with regional representatives, and setting up meetings—that was all done under cloak of other authority, what they now call Special Affairs."[55] It was his opinion that Special Affairs intentionally kept the First Presidency in the dark[56] until about July 1981 when Elder Hinckley became a counselor in the church presidency. After that time, guidance would have come directly from the highest governing body of the church. It is also likely that President Kimball trusted the committee to handle the campaign without his intervention.

The way Lowe explained the organizational complexity to those gathered in President Cummings's living room made everyone laugh. Using tentative language to let them know that decisions had been made for which they needed to give approval, but not that he was dictating the direction for them, seemed ludicrous, and yet everyone understood. There would be "a kind of loose coalition committee," Lowe said, "that would serve to—not direct it—but to steer it a little bit and where everyone *could* get some counsel and guidance as how its done." With Lowe, Ladd, and Campbell, the steering committee would also include four stake Relief Society presidents; so, said Ladd, everyone else could relax. He emphasized that "NO SPECIFIC GUIDANCE HAS BEEN GIVEN AS TO HOW WE APPROACH IT, BUT I would like to mention at the outset that whatever we do we wish to do with love and kindness."

It was a tightrope walk. Lowe needed to assure the group that its authority came from headquarters and it would be supervised by local church jurisdiction, while simultaneously telling them they would be officially empowered with autonomy. He disclaimed credit for being in charge of the meeting or giving instructions. The group's intent was to oppose the ERA, "and so," he continued—sounding ever more like a clandestine operative—"I imagine what the committee should do, and I am not in charge of that, and I am not putting words in their mouths, but I guess they will take on some of that and get to know other known groups that we could ally our cause to."[57] He said they should submit and manage a budget, create literature and circulate it, and not feel "like the whole world rests with you and you have to be a flag waver and other things which are common in our time [but] in your own poised and quiet way to have impact on our society for we do indeed feel the enactment of the Civil Rights Act [sic]. Therefore," he said, "it is clear . . . it is a moral issue to have an understanding of this and be able to communicate this to those about us."[58]

Lowe's next comment was even more revealing. "Let me say one more thing," he began. "I have been given counsel in this. In other areas we have found that it is not so good for the men to be vociferous. It works against the cause, but we are indeed—and will be—supportive." Floundering through a series of sentence fragments, he sullied on: "If it looks like, in the eyes of some, that we are trying to keep the women subservient and it is far from it. This is the exact opposition of what we are trying to do, but it is always interpreted that way." He concluded with "Why don't I quit while I am ahead?"

Sonia Johnson, speaking the next year, quoted Lowe's rationale for concealing the fact that men had helped organize the coalition: "People won't understand." This, said Johnson, was "patriarchal doubletalk." She suggested that what it really meant was that "people will understand only too well."[59]

As for how this information would be disseminated to the women in the area, Lowe told the group they could distribute literature in their Relief Society meetings or leave it in meetinghouse lobbies. Moreover, he encouraged them to continue to discuss it at church meetings, saying: "We are not going to be intimidated in this [in] any way. If we don't hold full meetings [devoted to the topic], I think that will take a little sail out of their winds." He did not specify who "they" might be, but the implication was that they were pitted against a relentless and wily foe.

Campbell followed Lowe, continuing the theme of "respect and love" and identifying their anticipated opponents as members of the church; it was to them that love and respect should be extended:

> There is strength in love. And I think what has happened tonight shows us, not that we should be intimidated, not that we should be silent, indeed just the opposite, we must be very vocal because there are other people

> that are vocal and if we believe our cause is just, and right and important—and we know it is—then we must speak more loudly than we would normally speak, but we must love our sisters in the Church, and we must try to operate with love. We must still convey our message and we [must] do it with greater strength, but we must do it with a conviction of love.

Campbell introduced the campaign slogan, which was her first contribution as a public relations expert: EQUALITY YES, ERA NO. She distributed packets of literature the women could take to their legislators. Among the material was a statement from the Potomac Region LDS Women's Coalition (continuing the confusion over the shifting name of the group) prepared by Campbell and other officers to describe the church's position. Ideally, this flyer suggested, women should be "prepared to talk intelligently about the issues and the threat to the Constitution and the threat to woman's essential rights which is what this is."

Campbell encouraged the women at the stake president's house to be willing to sacrifice their time: "You have got to take this seriously as a calling. When the call comes, you march with your forces."[60] When someone objected to instructing people on how to vote on political issues, Campbell responded: "That is not what we are saying. What is being said is, women are being called because this is a moral issue. You are not being told you have to be for or against the ERA. But indeed if this is your stand, . . . if you feel that you follow the prophet, then we know where you stand. So there is no question." She emphasized that "when the prophet speaks, he speaks scripture. Right? He is the living voice of God on this earth. He has spoken."[61]

The three speakers who followed with their own anti-ERA messages advanced the rhetorical strategy that had already permeated the church. Gayle Haight, a businesswoman and mother of five, scoffed at the ERA as "an extra responsibility amendment." For her, it represented a "loss of rights for women in ways that threaten our families and harm our society." Women would be drafted, she said. Society would become sexless, hence protectionless. She finished: "I do not want to relinquish my rights, and privileges, and protections that I now have as a woman. Nor do I want to leave this legacy to my daughters and to my sons. And this is why I am working to Stop ERA. I say these things in the name of Jesus Christ. Amen."[62]

Robert Beers spoke next. Beers was the area's political action coordinator for Phyllis Schlafly's STOP-ERA and was himself a Mormon. He agreed that the ERA "would make Government sex neutral. In other words," he asserted, "you are a person under the law. You would no longer be male/female, men/women, boy/girls." Lest anyone fail to see why this would be undesirable, he warned more ominously: "We have to think of the implications of what this would mean if there were a war. We must not blind ourselves to conditions of this moment." He was the first speaker to give the women specific assignments. They were to contact public officials "as an individual citizen," remembering that their legislators were "misguided and misinformed men" who thought the ERA issue was "a frivolous exchange between women," then adding somewhat confusingly that "more men support the ERA than women." What the women should say was that they were "*pro family*" rather than that they were anti-ERA. Beers offered that this, aside from being a genuine "family concern" and direction from the church, would be "a good missionary attempt" as they worked with other anti-ERA people. "I will personally help you get anything you need," he promised.[63]

The third speaker, identified in the minutes as "Sister Parsons," had been asked by the church to run workshops on political activism throughout the country. The minutes show she was adept at identifying key issues that might arouse passions and provide specific strategies. She focused on the enemy, stressing the importance of understanding those working for the ERA. "It is an enlightening experience," she began, "to research the feminist position from their own materials and their own presentations. The whole scope of the Feminist movement is no secret. They see the ERA as an avenue on which to build their case, a plateau on which to rebuild the world to their own specifications." Her rhetoric conjured up images of social chaos and personal danger. "Their labor has been rewarded. . . . The feminists are effective because they sacrifice time and energy and money without reservation. Unless we duplicate their effort, they may win."

Parsons then described what she called "the feminist agenda," laid out by NOW in its publication *Revolution Is Now,* including abortion on demand, sex education in the schools, women in the military, and legalization of homosexuality.[64] She quoted Betty Friedan's declaration of religious skepticism or non-belief,[65] a sure bet to alienate Mormons. She cited an inflammatory statement by Gloria Steinem denouncing marriage as "a legally sanctioned method of controlling women" and read from Steinem: "The end of the institution of marriage is a necessary condition for the liberation of women. Therefore, it is important for us to encourage women to leave their husbands." Parsons thus made the crucial link between feminism and the nuclear family. She concluded by saying she thought "it is plain to see that the ERA and the pursuit of its ratification by these radical feminists is more than a struggle for equal pay for equal work, or equal credit. It is rather a war against the basic values and principles we believe in."

Campbell gave voice to what most women in the room were probably thinking when she said, "That was certainly disquieting wasn't it? To say the least. But that is what we are fighting. It is going to take sacrifices. . . . Here we have to do in seven weeks what it has taken someone else seven years to do."[66]

Beers took the floor again, laying out the legislative history of attempts to ratify the ERA in Virginia. Beginning in 1973, the amendment had been introduced or considered in each legislative session. Forty senators were up for reelection in 1979—twenty for and twenty against the ERA—and the fate of the amendment depended on who was reelected. Beers recommended that if legislators could not be persuaded, the group should come up with new candidates altogether, although cautioning them as follows: "We need to know his background, where he went to school, how old he is, religious affiliation, what organizations he belongs to, what he does for a living, who his friends are, where he goes to the country club, and everything else. The more you know about him the more effective you are going to be. That is the biggest mistake that people who come to Richmond make. . . . They don't know who they are talking to."[67]

Predicting that some women might stumble in their efforts because of their naiveté and enthusiasm, Beers continued to urge the necessity of researching their legislators: "You have got to find out what will move him. Is he a veteran? Is he interested in that aspect of it, perhaps. Does he have children and does he have daughters that are at draftable age? What is his perspective and who is he?"[68] In his mind, if they elected "twenty-five out of forty Senators in Virginia who are against the equal rights amendment, you won't even need to keep mobilizing every year. . . . We can beat this in the next year," he concluded. "So, let's give that extra special measure and do the very best we can. I am optimistic. We have everything going our way. Ask that legislator, 'Do you support our rights to have our views expressed.' See what they say." Later Beers told *Utah Holiday* he was pleased with the women's lobbying. In his opinion, "because they are trained by the church to organize, speak in public, and assume leadership" roles, they performed better than women from other right-wing or religious groups.[69]

Teddie Wood arose at this point and introduced herself as a Mormon for ERA, saying she had been an active supporter of equality for the past decade. "I feel it is important to introduce myself since we will be meeting in Richmond and other places on opposing sides of this issue." She emphasized the church doctrine of free choice, saying that each member "should exercise their own free agency in coming to a decision on this issue. . . . Mr. Don LeFevre from the Public Relations Department of the Church in Salt Lake City has made it clear that there will be no action taken against members of the Church who support ERA." She asserted that, for her, "it is a matter of individual conscience."[70] Campbell responded, "Well, I think you came a little late. We have already discussed the approach we are taking to this issue. We have decided we are doing it with great love." Wood protested that each member should decide for herself. Campbell became more firm: "That was before the letter from the

First Presidency. When the prophet speaks, it is scripture."[71] The decision was made that in the future, proponents of the ERA would not be allowed to attend coalition meetings.[72]

At a second meeting held on December 14, this time in the ward chapel, members of the stake presidency sat on the stand with Beverly Campbell and Bob Beers. The bishop opened and closed the meeting and instructed the congregation to refrain from tape recording the speeches. In the foyer a woman who had been asked to be the "key coordinator" for that ward had stacks of brochures—*Equality Yes, ERA No*—and maps of nearby neighborhoods outlined in red. Women wearing buttons with the same slogan were later reported seen visiting the offices of the state legislators. Charles Dahlquist, a counselor in the Oakton stake presidency, reinforced Campbell's theme of obedience:

> I turn now to my topic which can be summed up in just four words. Those four words: The prophet has spoken. . . . Now, it is important to understand that today, as in past years, the Lord is revealing his will and his word through his living Prophet to all, and particularly to the members of the church. . . . What the First Presidency say as a presidency is what the Lord would say if he were here in person. This is the rock foundation of Mormonism. . . . As a stake presidency, we encourage you to listen carefully tonight and to sustain the First Presidency and the stake presidency in actively opposing the ratification of the Equal Rights Amendment. Let us not proceed blindly. But as President Tanner once said, "Given a choice, I would rather proceed blindly following the Prophet than proceed on my own with little knowledge. . . . It is my personal experience that whatever we do, we must stand behind the Prophet.[73]

The committee's first task, according to the Oakton stake newsletter, was to warn voters about "the disastrous effects ERA will have on our lives." The newsletter asserted that "too many women do not understand their rights as they now stand, and see the ERA as a panacea to real and imagined slights and discriminations that can better be corrected by enforcing laws that already exist, rather than by passing an amendment that would negate any legal recognition of the differences between men and women."[74] The next month, the newsletter carried a coalition message about following the prophet: "At many meetings during the past two weeks I have heard leaders of the Church, including two General Authorities, state that the First Presidency is more concerned about this issue than they have ever been about any issue. Elder [David] Haight said 'We have only seen the tip of the iceberg of what could happen if this Amendment should pass.' The feeling is that this is no longer a political, but a moral issue." The unsigned message attempted to reconcile individual responsibility with conformity. "Education," it said, "is the key to establishing your personal stand on the ERA. The Prophet does not expect *blind* obedience, but educated, responsible, dedicated obedience."[75]

Following the coalition's organizational meeting, Elder Lowe asked local bishops to solicit donations to support the coalition's work.[76] Members of the group also placed petitions in ward lobbies and used the signatures garnered there to demonstrate widespread support. In the Vienna ward, petitions were circulated down the pews during sacrament meeting.[77] A sample petition read that the "undersigned" (registered voters), were opposed to ratification and to extension of the ratification period.[78] The most effective way the coalition rallied the troops was by adopting the church's pyramidal structure with Beverly Campbell at the top and Relief Society sisters filling out the platform at the bottom, eventually involving between 2,500 and 3,000 individuals.[79]

In response to the prophet's instruction to ally with others fighting the ERA, the coalition established an official connection with Virginia STOP ERA. This was an easy task since Bob Beers was a personal friend of Schlafly and had organized its Virginia branch. Politically savvy, Beers advised the women to influence legislators before they became supporters of the amendment "because once they are locked in and committed they would then have to go against their word. I feel uncomfortable when I do that, [but] I do it anyway. I hate to make liars out of them but I do it for a good cause. Sometimes we have to bend ethics."[80] Beers said he had spoken at several workshops to hundreds of Mormon women about becoming politically involved.

The link forged between the two groups soon resulted in a jointly produced booklet, *Equality Yes/ERA No,* printed in time to influence legislators before they convened in January 1979. By the time the legislative session began, the coalition had distributed about 80,000 of a print run of 150,000.[81] Another joint publication was *Impact,* which answered the question "Why should I get involved?"[82] Another, with a slight alteration in punctuation, *Equality Yes! ERA No!* was formatted as an open letter to "friends" warning of the "showdown" over the ERA as the mid-1982 deadline approached. The coalition printed the names of candidates who opposed the ERA and produced a group of "Concern Sheets" on a variety of topics: "The Effect of the Equal Rights Amendment on Federal-State Responsibilities," "The Effect of the Equal Rights Amendment on Private Relationships," and "The Equal Rights Amendment and Suspect Classification," among others.[83]

After procuring a small office space in Richmond, about thirty coalition women gathered every morning from mid-November 1978 through January 1979 to coordinate their efforts before fanning out through the statehouse, literature in hand, to speak with legislators. Motivated by what they considered to be a "priesthood calling" to protect their families, they energetically distributed concern sheets and other literature, along with bumper stickers and buttons with the coalition's slogan. They tirelessly expressed their concerns and desires wherever they could get a hearing.[84] On January 23, coalition men and women carried "Equality Yes, ERA No" banners at a Richmond rally.[85] Six days later, Mormons for ERA marched in a counter-parade in Richmond to encourage the legislature to allow the ERA out of committee.

That same January, Campbell told Mary Bradford she encouraged other Mormon women to bring their own talents to the fray and "accept the cause as a 'priesthood calling.'"[86] With such language applied to the work of the coalition, some women wondered why they were not formally "set apart" as they would be for an ecclesiastical calling. But Campbell had an answer for them: "Without being set apart, I will do what is appropriate to do because the prophet has asked me to do it. I don't need any of the rest of that."[87]

When Bradford asked Campbell about the appropriateness of a church leader directing political actions, Campbell replied that if the prophet gave members advice and they prayed about it, they would find a way to follow his words. For herself, "I would respond as my heart told me." For those whose hearts delivered a different message, "Your membership in the Church is not in jeopardy because you have responded the way you have," she said. She held out the possibility of a compromise between the feuding camps: "There are many women's groups with different agendas. Some are to the right and some are to the left; some are feminist and some are Moral Majority. That is fine; let them go on. But somewhere in the middle are issues of concern for us all. Let us find areas of commonality on which we can all agree."[88]

Moreover, Campbell believed the work for women's equity would need to continue after the ERA debate was finished and that talented women would be needed. It was a responsibility that came with God-given gifts:

> We cannot afford the luxury of feeling safe and comfortable and thinking that we don't have to deal with our sisters' problems. We've got to deal with them, if we are to follow the mandate of the Relief Society "to care for all our sisters who may fall under our care and supervision irrespective of religion, color or condition."[89]

Despite the strong overlay of priesthood authority for this crusade, some wards began hearing rumblings of discontent. Some members continued to suspect a misuse of ecclesiastical authority and a blurring of church and state.

The Vienna ward newsletter repeated the almost belligerently confident position published in the stake newsletter to follow the prophet, whose desire was for "educated, responsible, dedicated obedience." The article continued with the familiar argument about how the ERA would take away many of the privileges enjoyed by women without adding anything in return.[90]

In Salt Lake City, Barbara Smith steadfastly held to the position that she was for women's equality but against the ERA. In her autobiography, she related the experience of a "very attractive" fashion model who had converted to Mormonism and favored the ERA because "she did not have a clear understanding of [its] implications." During a Relief Society homemaking lesson, the model realized she was failing to maintain a "clean, neat, orderly" home. The bishop's wife came to the rescue by compiling a list of daily activities the woman could perform to achieve this goal. When the model "couldn't stay with the list," she went back to the bishop's wife in despair. This time the bishop's wife counseled her to "pray that He will change your heart" and, giving her a shorter list, suggested that her husband's approval would be helpful. "Incrementally," the woman was "given additional chores until the family learned to work together and accomplish the goal of a clean, neat, orderly home." The model told Sister Smith this experience "had made her realize that the ERA was not an amendment that she or other women needed. For women to feel equal to men, they but needed to plant good seed—a clear gospel perspective—and realize who they are and the power and potential they possess."[91]

Lobbying the Virginia Legislature

The legislative session in Virginia opened on January 10. Prior to this, the women who had found themselves in a minority in the LDS Church because of their pro-ERA stance had founded Mormons for ERA (MERA) and begun gathering support from other Mormon women around the country. The four founders lived in the Washington D.C. area—Johnson, Withers, Wood, and Rigby—and were all active LDS women with families. In January 1979, MERA allied itself with, and received some financial support from, the National Organization of Women. Because only three more states were needed to ratify the ERA, the contribution from MERA was welcomed by other women's groups. MERA women presented lectures, participated in demonstrations, lobbied legislators, and produced literature of their own. They especially proved themselves to be effective at mobilizing the media beginning in August 1978 when Sonia

Johnson stepped into the Senate committee room and the media spotlight by facing off with Senator Hatch.[92]

The group was a safe place for women who found themselves frightened by the church's reaction to their support of the ERA. Johnson told a reporter in August 1979: "It means real ostracism for them in their congregations. You know Mormons. . . . We're a very close bunch of people. It's a very serious matter if you're ostracized from your church group." For a Mormon woman, taking this type of public stance could exact a huge personal cost. "And it's not just you. Your family, your mother, your brothers, your sisters, your friends become suspect. And there's always the possibility someone might be excommunicated from the church for this position, although this has not happened as far as we know."[93] Later recalling these grueling months, Johnson said she tried to comfort women who contacted her with their personal crises: "From my library," Johnson said, "[I] stanched bleeding wounds, slapped on bandages, and called upon all the understanding and love that were in me to help ease the misery. [People] were crying, 'I don't know what to do. I love the church; at least I did love it. And I want to love it. I don't what to lose what I had there. But I don't know how to hold onto it. It hurts so much to go to church nowadays that I can barely force myself.'"[94] She was, of course, articulating her own pain as well.

Teddie Wood, one of the original organizers, was irritated when women came to church wearing LDS Citizens Coalition buttons: "Equality Yes/ERA No." She countered by wearing a neck scarf with "ERA" painted elaborately on it and parking her car in a conspicuous spot in the church parking lot with a huge "Mormons for ERA" sign in the back window.[95] Although their numbers were few, the "pros," as they called themselves, were determined and articulate women who, on the surface, seemed able to hold their own.

Funding the Campaign

On March 1, 1979, the *Reston Times* was the first to expose Mormon lobbying irregularities: "A well funded church-organized campaign against ERA ratification during the General Assembly session may have violated state lobbying laws by failing to register with the Secretary of the Commonwealth, who has begun an investigation."[96] Why the coalition neglected to register is unknown. Beverly Campbell told *Utah Holiday* the coalition had spent thousands of dollars but not more than the $100 limit per legislator; therefore, she said, "we decided we did not qualify." Early on, the coalition had hired Robert Barker of Wilkinson, Cragun and Barker to represent and advise them. Barker was an LDS regional representative and had gained some notoriety for defending Maurice Stans during the Watergate hearings. A few days after the *Reston Times* article appeared, Barker conceded that the group needed to register, although he added defensively that "the Secretary agrees with us that probably we technically don't qualify."[97]

When reporters called Public Communications in Salt Lake City, Jerry Cahill, director of press relations, declined to comment except to say that Regional Representatives Lowe and Ladd had been authorized—by whom he did not say—to organize in Virginia. In a typical statement that sounded more like personal speculation than anything authoritative, Cahill acknowledged to *Utah Holiday* he was certain the regional representatives did this "with the knowledge of the leadership of the church and its full blessing."[98]

In fact, the financial activities of the Virginia coalition were murky. Where had the funds come from and where had they gone? Elder Hinckley was unapologetic in instructing PAC leaders about raising funds. But the church's chief financial officer, Alan Blodgett, would later tell historian D. Michael Quinn in a candid interview that no church funds had gone to the church's PACs.[99] Questioned in April 1980, Lowe confirmed the same, that no money had come from the church's central coffers.[100] Individual Mormons had donated relatively modest amounts to Families Are Concerned Today (FACT) and the cumulative total of these donations was significant. But it was not the money as much as the time and commitment of the armies of women who served as foot soldiers in the skirmish that would decide the outcome.[101]

Even so, the money trail was not inconsequential. Campbell told the

Washington Post the coalition spent $3,500. She said the concern sheets for legislators cost only $88.50 and the remainder paid for "educational" items such as bumper stickers ($3,000) and buttons ($500). Virginia law required lobbyists to report all expenses incurred after November 15, 1978, regardless of expense unless it was for travel, lodging, and personal expenses, which meant that the coalition was out of compliance.[102]

When *Utah Holiday's* Linda Sillitoe questioned Don Ladd in April 1979, he maintained that "since checks for the Coalition were not made out to the Church," they should not pose a legal problem. Local bishops had solicited the funds, but contributors had made their checks out to FACT, which Ladd said was a "ubiquitous" organization that "has no activities of its own, but is an entity set up through legal means . . . that has received funds."[103]

Ron Thomas, Lowe's friend and a certified public accountant in Maryland, was the secretary of the mysterious FACT, of which Lowe and Campbell were "officers." Robert Barker incorporated FACT as a nonprofit organization in Washington D.C., describing its purpose as having to do with a concern for public issues "that have an effect on the family." Barker denied any connection between FACT and the church, but Thomas told *Utah Holiday* that funds gathered in other states had been funneled through FACT for use in Virginia.[104] FACT was equally involved in Florida. Ladd told Sillitoe, "You'll see it spring up wherever there is [a] problem," but said he did not know why such a "mechanism" existed at all—why checks were not made out to the coalition.[105]

When Sillitoe then asked Richard Lindsay, executive secretary of the Special Affairs Committee, what FACT was, he stated: "FACT is not a church network for handling finances." He said he could guess it had been formed in response to President Kimball's direction to fight the ERA in different ways. But Ladd and Cahill both confirmed that FACT funds had been used in Florida, Nevada, and North Carolina, while Cahill simultaneously denied coordination from church headquarters.[106]

Mormons for ERA wrote to Frederick T. Gray Jr., secretary of the Commonwealth of Virginia, about what they saw as hazy relationships and undocumented expenditures by the coalitions.[107] They specifically clarified for him the confusing and sometimes shifting names for the various interlocking groups that comprised the Mormon activism.[108] Gray told the *Reston Times* he believed the "in-kind contributions" received by the LDS Citizens Coalition violated the lobbying statutes[109] but would not seek a penalty if the coalition registered and disclosed its finances.[110] He wrote to Beverly Campbell on March 7 to inform her that "valuable material assistance" would need to be reported as an expense.[111] With 16,000 members, the coalition had become a force to be reckoned with and was large enough that it was now attracting unwanted official attention.[112]

The original deadline for ratifying the ERA was March 22, and it was a day of mourning for proponents and one of increased determination on the part of opponents. In early April the LDS faithful convened for general conference in Salt Lake City and were startled to see an airplane circling Temple Square trailing a banner that read "Mormons for ERA Are Everywhere!" MERA issued a press release accusing the LDS Church of stifling open discussion and "preventing any real understanding among most members." Its conclusion: "We hope that will change. We think it will change. But in the meantime, we want our leaders to know that Mormons for ERA are everywhere and that we take exception to their fierce anti-female stance."[113]

On April 27, Sonia Johnson wrote to Elder Hinckley asking for help in setting up a meeting with church president Spencer W. Kimball. In her letter, she said she had asked her bishop if she could meet with the prophet and was told her request would be forwarded through "channels," meaning first to the stake president, who would then present it to the next level. Whatever became of that process, Johnson was now writing directly to Apostle Hinckley because a friend in Salt Lake City, Marilee Latta, had told her Apostle David Haight was aware of her desire for an audience with the president.[114] In any case, Johnson's request was denied without any reason given.[115]

In frustration, Johnson wrote to President Kimball on April 30. She expressed her faith that as the Lord's servant, he "must care very much about individual lives." Her concern, she said, was for "women who are being driven out of the Church by the insensitivity and ignorance of their male leaders." She tried to show the institutional consequences: "When a woman drops from activity, often several children and a husband follow. This is currently happening on a scale which, if the extent and increasing frequency were properly understood, would cause women's problems in the Church to become top priority." Johnson argued that Phyllis Schlafly was not an appropriate source of information about Latter-day Saint women. Johnson, by contrast, was an insider who cared deeply about the church and its women.[116]

On June 19, an Associated Press reporter interviewed President Kimball about Mormon ERA activists. The church president commented that members who support the ERA should be "very, very careful" because the church is led by "strong men and able men. . . . We feel we are in a position to lead them properly." Kimball's tone and language impressed the reporter as demonstrating impatience with dissenters.[117]

On August 2 when President Kimball was planning a visit to Virginia for an East Coast conference, Johnson wrote again, asking for a meeting. He again turned her down without giving a specific reason. In an undated response, she answered: "I am sorry you will not agree to meet with me and to acknowledge and understand the heartbreak that is contained in the letters I wished to show you. It has always been my impression that leaders of any organization would be wise to gather information from as many sources as possible, since only in this way can they make sound—and credible decisions." She added, "I am reminded of Brigham Young's admonition to the early Saints not to follow their leader blindly because if they did, who, he asked, would then counsel the prophet?"[118] Johnson may have thought she was being persuasive, but her offer was certainly interpreted as presumptuous.

On September 1, Johnson delivered a speech to the American Psychological Association's annual meeting in New York City. In her media-attracting "Patriarchal Panic: Sexual Politics in the Mormon Church," she voiced anger through feminist critical theory, denouncing the church for its "recent profound disenfranchisement of Mormon women" and characterizing Mormon anti-ERA activism as "covert activity, not openly done in the name of the church." She elaborated:

> Members are cautioned not to reveal that they are Mormons or organized by the church when they lobby, write letters, donate money, and pass out anti-ERA brochures door to door through whole states. Instead, they are directed to say that they are concerned citizens following the dictates of their individual consciences. Since they are, in fact, following the very direct dictates of the Prophet's conscience and would revise their own overnight if he were to revise his, nothing could be further from the truth.[119]

Some of Johnson's comments would be quoted back to her only three months later at her excommunication.

When the area conference convened the first week of September with 17,000 Mormons in attendance, Mormons for ERA picketed the gathering and again arranged for an airplane to circle overhead, this time trailing a banner that read: "Mother in Heaven Loves Mormons for ERA."[120] Johnson described how the banner was received:

> A reporter phoned the public relations office of the church to ask how the Brethren were taking this little prank, and was told that they found it "amusing." Then the PR man suggested that the reporter put a cartoon in the next day's paper showing . . . the Angel Moroni atop the temple [taking aim at the MERA airplane and] . . . brandishing a machine gun! One does not need to be a psychoanalyst to understand how "amusing" the Brethren found our little prank.[121]

Two weeks later, Sonia Johnson appeared with Barbara Smith and host Carl Isvog on KUTV's weekly *Extra* program in Salt Lake City. Isvog introduced Johnson as a fifth-generation Mormon woman and homemaker with a doctorate. Barbara Smith attempted to gently but categorically repudiate Johnson's claim to be a faithful Mormon. When Isvog commented that church leaders seemed to find Johnson atypical, Smith said:

> Well, that's obvious because Sonia Johnson is openly questioning Church

> authorities. And in the Mormon Church that simply isn't done. The Church maintains that women are given full equality and say there's never been a more fulfilling time to be a Mormon woman. To help prove that point, fifteen Mormon men, including President Spencer Kimball, N. Eldon Tanner, Ezra Taft Benson and others have written a book called *Woman,* which shows just how great it is to be a Mormon woman. Sonia Johnson says it is that type of male arrogance that typifies the Mormon Church and infuriates women.[122]

Isvog reminded Smith that the Relief Society supported equality under the law for women—"sort of." Her response was that "women sometimes need preferential treatment." When he asked about the church president's right to be involved in politics, Smith responded: "It isn't personal opinion when it comes that way. It is the word of the Lord."[123] There was clearly no margin in which one could find some common ground.

The next month at a Utah Women's Conference in Salt Lake City, Johnson delivered a speech titled "Off Our Pedestals" in a session that included Marilyn Warenski and Jill Mulvay Derr. In her speech, she reinterpreted this traditional symbol of honoring women as a sign of "women's immobilization and isolation." She acknowledged that leaving the pedestal was "painful as well as frightening; the muscles of our deepest instincts, of our consciences, our intellect, our spirits, have been cramped for a very long time. We ache a little as we stretch."[124]

Johnson quoted from letters women had sent her expressing their fear and exhilaration at what the women's liberation movement had done for them. One woman catalogued the ways she had seen women in her ward manipulated and immobilized by fear. "I almost wonder," the woman wrote, "what it was that made me so fearful about it at first. But I do understand that it was only partly fear of the IMAGINABLE consequences. The greater fear was the irrational fear, . . . fear of the Unknown, fear of the Terrible Things that would happen to me. What terrible things? I don't know, but TERRIBLE THINGS!"[125] Another wrote: "I feel a need and desire for incentive and motivation to be an influence for good, rather than being brainwashed with guilt and fear. This is what puts me in a fighting mood—our best desires and efforts are ridiculed by the men, even in public meetings. But we aren't supposed to do that to the men anytime, anywhere. It is being disrespectful. What is it when they do it to US?"[126] "Before I got involved," a third woman confided, "I was full of conflict and anxiety. And these are making me hostile toward people and circumstances in my life [who] weren't really at fault. I can't tell you how much better I feel now. I feel like I am finally in control of my own life. And that is a tremendous feeling. I just can't put into words how good that feels."[127]

The Johnson Excommunication

Time ran out for Sonia Johnson on November 14, 1979, when she received the letter she had expected and feared, instructing her to attend a bishop's court.[128] The night before the court, the bishopric came to her house and demanded that she surrender her temple recommend, leaving her feeling "like I'd already been found guilty."[129] At the court itself on November 17, she defended herself for five hours in front of the bishopric and male secretary against allegations that she had "spoken evil of the Lord's anointed," that she had worked against the missionary program of the church, and that her general attitude and "expression" were contrary to the purposes of the church. A decision was made to recess the trial until December. However, ten days later Bishop Jeffrey Willis informed Johnson by letter that she could no longer teach in the Relief Society.[130]

Representatives of a number of women's organizations—the National Women's Political Caucus, the National Organization for Women, the National Association of Social Workers, ERA America, and Women's Equality Action League—signed a statement opposing the church's action:

> We strongly support women being protected equally under the Constitution of the United States and thereby support the Equal Rights Amendment. We also respect the separation of Church and State. Therefore we are very disturbed by what appears to be an attempt by certain members of the hierarchy of the Mormon Church to have the church supersede the state and in fact confuse issues of faith with issues of politics.

Whatever the outcome of the trial, the fact that in 1979 Sonia Johnson is facing a trial by her church that emerges from her beliefs and assertions that women belong in the Constitution of the United States is an outrage. We stand in support of Sonia Johnson and Mormons for ERA.[131]

In a second press release, dated November 30, the National Women's Political Caucus stated stingingly: "The ERA simply guarantees women equal protection under the Constitution of the United States. That this should cause such fear and hatred that they are willing to put Sonia Johnson through this ordeal is an outrage."[132]

On December 1, the court reconvened as more than one hundred supporters stood outside in the cold, some holding candles, some singing. The court rolled on through a one-and-one-half-hour session. Supporters standing outside included the Mormon White House consumer affairs advisor Esther Peterson, Congresswoman Pat Schroeder (D-Colorado), and the Reverend William Callahan, who had been disciplined by his own church for challenging the Roman Catholic position on the ordination of women. Five witnesses testified on Johnson's behalf. Hazel Rigby talked about Johnson as "a responsive, loving, and caring woman" in her personal life and "the political struggle over passage of the Equal Rights Amendment":

> I have traveled with Sonia. I have heard her speak. I have discussed her philosophies, her ideas, and her presentations with her. I am in full agreement with what she has said and done regarding the political involvement of the Church in this issue. I have watched as she has been overwhelmed with requests for interviews, for copies of her speeches, and I have heard active and inactive Mormons thank her for her "courageous" testimony.[133]

Ralph Payne, a Mormon psychology professor at Shippensburg State College, was the second witness. He had heard Johnson speak at a symposium on "Some Reflections on Women, Religion, and Mental Health" and felt the church was overreacting: "Those outside the Church either did not care about it or saw it as a positive sign that the Church could accept and tolerate, without repression, a contrary opinion from within. But now the repression is coming. It seems we cannot tolerate public differences on an issue that most people see as purely political. . . . Damage has been done to the Church's reputation, but it certainly has not been done by Sonia Johnson; it has been done by the convening of this trial."[134]

Nadine Hansen, a California attorney, was the third witness. She described how impressed she had been by Johnson's loyalty to the church and its leaders and emphasized that the church's good image had not been damaged by Johnson's activities but instead by "the organized campaign against the ERA, and even more, the near-hysteria with which some members who oppose the ERA approach the issue." She concluded: "If Church leaders do not wish to have the kind of image which inevitably results from the political involvement with this issue, then the best way to not have that image is to not be politically involved. . . . Sonia did not create the image, she simply called attention to it."[135]

The fourth witness was Reba Keele, a professor at Brigham Young University, former Relief Society president, and one of the organizers of Utah's IWY conference. She warned that the court's ill-advised action "had the power to start a witch hunt in the Church for women who deviated in any way." She asked them what she should say to the young women who came to her asking for help in understanding this event.[136]

Kathryn MacKay, another of the IWY organizers and a niece of Julian Lowe, was the last witness. She said her uncle had assured her the LDS Citizens Coalition had been organized under Elder Hinckley's direction.[137] Even so, she had found that Johnson inspired "hope that I can work through issues within the structure of the LDS Church, because she has managed to do that so effectively herself."[138]

Johnson was next to testify. Despite the fact that her husband, Rick, was with her—something that wasn't allowed during the court's first hearing—she seemed "exhausted, frantic and not in control," according to McKay, who said she was worried about her.[139] The men read the list of accusations, asked her about the APA paper, and questioned her about the term "savage misogyny."[140] After twenty minutes, she emerged to join the other witnesses and wait.

Offering only a terse comment during the trial in her own behalf,

Johnson drew from language she had found in the stake and ward newsletters about informed rather than blind discipleship. She said: "Should the Church demand that its four and a half million members blindly abandon their God-given First Amendment freedom of speech, or their right to peacefully assemble and petition the Government? I think not, and I believe that the Prophet will sustain me in that belief."[141]

Possibly in an effort to let the publicity subside, Willis waited four days until December 5 before notifying Johnson of her excommunication. In his letter to her, which was hand-delivered, he asserted that Johnson had not been charged with supporting the ERA but rather with opposing the church leadership. "As you know," he wrote,

> I have at no time tried to dissuade you from seeking ratification of [the ERA] amendment. I have counseled with you relative to your support of church leaders and doctrine. . . . You testified that you believe and have taught that missionaries should not be invited into people's homes. You testified that you believe and have publicly stated that our society, specifically including church leaders, has a savage misogyny; when, in fact, it is exaltation [which] can be gained only through the love that results in the eternal bonding of men and woman. You have publicly taught that the church is dedicated to imposing the prophet's moral directives upon All Americans; when it is the doctrine of the church that all people are free to choose for themselves those moral directives dictated by their own conscience. Your testimony and public speeches evidence, in spirit, that you are not in harmony with church doctrine concerning the nature of God, and the manner in which He directs His church on earth. Therefore, the decision of this court is that you are excommunicated.[142]

Previously, as he had emerged from the trial, Willis had told the press on December 1 "that there would be no decision immediately announced, the ERA had not been an issue, nor had any issue of immorality been raised or considered by the court." He stuck to that position during the next week.[143] For her part, Johnson told reporters that she was not bitter, although she felt "betrayed" and was experiencing "a great sense of loss."[144]

Campbell refrained from public comment on the excommunication for six months, when finally she expressed her satisfaction with it. "At first I didn't think it would help, but there has been so much more dialogue since then," she said. "Now people are much better informed about the ERA."[145] Don LeFevre, speaking for the church, commented in mid-December: "Perhaps this current publicity has been a bit negative, but once people sit back and see things in calm perspective, everything will be just fine."[146]

Sonia's husband wrote to their bishop a week after the excommunication affirming his support for his wife and requesting "immediate excommunication." He accused the bishop of taking "a few of Sonia's statements quoted out of context and incorrectly" interpreted and giving the press a dishonest account of the church's reason for trying his wife.[147] Sonia appealed the decision to the stake president on what she considered to be procedural and substantive errors. President Earl Roueche responded on March 24 that he could find no persuasive reason to grant an appeal. Furthermore, "your conduct has been observed to ascertain if there [has been] an attitudinal change concerning the Church leadership, its position on moral issues[,] or if there were expressions of repentance. I regret that I have not found any such change," he informed her.[148]

Johnson then appealed directly to the First Presidency, but was told the record of the trial—to which she was refused access—had not yet arrived in Salt Lake City. A month later, the First Presidency declined to re-hear her case.[149] "I am now irrevocably out," she told the *Washington Post*. "It makes me heartsick. It is so dishonorable. They want me to repent. But what must I repent?"[150]

At the same time Rick Johnson wrote his angry letter to the bishop, he moved out of the house and instituted divorce proceedings. Their oldest son, a teenager, moved in with Sonia's parents in Logan, Utah. The younger children remained with their mother. Over the next few years, Sonia's life became a cautionary tale for Mormons as she threw herself with even more determination into the doomed cause of the ERA, wrote a book about her feminist awakening that became a brief best seller, made a failed attempt to become president of NOW, repudiated heterosexuality, and retreated to a lesbian commune in a secluded area of New Mexico where she still lives. For some, the unraveling of her former life touched chords of sympathy, but for others, it was the fulfillment of authoritative warnings about feminism and the predictions about what befell the enemies of the church.

For Mormons on either side of the issue, what was clear was that Sonia Johnson's excommunication was an event of enormous symbolic importance. For one thing, no matter what Bishop Willis said, no one really believed the issue had not been about the ERA. As she was publicly punished for her politics, her willingness to accept martyrdom inspired a few women but frightened many more. "I, like so many of my sisters, hit the deck," Kathleen Flake wrote ten years later. "I just faded away into law school and benign inactivity in the Church."[151] Something else that was clear was that after slowly withdrawing for most of the twentieth century from overt involvement in partisan issues, the church had rediscovered its political muscle and the will to use it.

12. Death Throes of the ERA, 1980–82

> Do you feel you are the only Mormon in your neighborhood who believes the Equal Rights Amendment should be ratified? We have found there are "bunches" of us and we have organized as an affiliate of Mormons for ERA.
>
> —Utah Mormons for ERA, 1978

Thousands of Mormon women fought against the ERA on the advice of their church. They added rescission to their list of objectives as momentum swung to their side. All the while, proponents of the ERA expanded their boycotts, challenged the Constitutionality of rescission, and launched "missionaries" to canvass areas deemed ripe for conversion. Each tactic was reactionary and opposed a specific strategy of the other side. Rather than centering the endeavor on a strong philosophical position, this was a battle of point/counterpoint, each side responding in kind.

The excommunication of Sonia Johnson brought Mormons under close public scrutiny and further politicized the church's stand on the ERA. Johnson's bishop, Jeffrey Willis, wanted the trial shielded from the public eye as something "sacred and personal," but this was not possible as Johnson quickly became a martyr, especially for members of Mormons for ERA.[1] The trial drew national press coverage and was followed for months by *Utah Holiday* reporters Paul Swenson and Linda Sillitoe, who became intimately involved in its denouement. Mormons themselves and members of the community that was ripped apart by it, Swenson and Sillitoe reflected a year later on the trial's impact: "The battle lines have been drawn in the press, in chapels and church lobbies and in the hearts of 'pros' and 'antis.'" Even as LDS press spokesman Jerry Cahill continued to deny church involvement with the political action committees ("These are individuals, acting on their conscience," he said; "The leaders are community leaders who just happen to be leaders in their church as well."), the reporters disclosed that

> Mormons for ERA have infiltrated meetings of the "antis" and have reported their activities. Both sides, then, have used tactics they found to be politically advantageous at the time. Because of their full and sincere commitment on opposite sides of the ERA cause, they all could justify their actions. There is no doubt that in those states where the ERA is still a legislatible issue, the debate will get more political before it gets less.[2]

On the anti-ERA side, the church could more or less rely on the unflinching loyalty of the Relief Society women. However, the other side was equally earnest, and there were now more than a few Mormons who secretly or openly disagreed with their church's position.

The Case of Judge Callister

By May 1979, under the influence of anti-ERA lobbying, some states wanted to rethink their ratifications. Legislators from the Western states of Arizona, Idaho, and Washington jointly filed *Idaho v. Freeman* in federal court in Boise challenging the Constitutionality of the extension and seeking to validate a state's power to rescind. Ironically, it was Judge Marion J. Callister, a devout Mormon and lay clergyman, who received the case. Concerned about the potential conflict of interest, the Justice Department, on August 25, 1979, asked Judge Callister to recuse himself.

Representative Don Edwards (D-California) compared the judge's position as a former LDS stake president and a current regional representative to that of a cardinal in the Catholic church.[3] Callister found an unlikely defendant in the American Jewish Congress, which supported the ERA but was worried, "as a matter of principle," that "a judge's membership or even leadership in a particular religious group" should "by itself" render him "incapable of deciding any case in accordance with the law and facts."[4] They thought that to disqualify him solely because of religious activity would violate Callister's own Constitutional access to religion without government interference. On October 4, Callister denied the motion to disqualify himself and subsequently ruled on the major issues in the case.[5]

During the summer of 1979, NOW petitioned to join the suit as an "intervenor and codefendant." Callister refused the petition. NOW appealed, and on August 15, 1980, the circuit court of appeals overturned Callister's decision.[6]

Earlier, on December 7, 1979—a week after Sonia Johnson's excommunication—Patricia Schroeder (D-Colorado) met with President Jimmy Carter and Attorney General Benjamin Civiletti to raise questions about the Callister situation. Schroeder spoke for the group: "We find it hard to believe that a judge who is active in the leadership of a church which sees the passage of the ERA as undermining church doctrine is representative of the type of impartiality which our judicial system stands for."[7]

Carter took no action. In response, NOW demonstrated outside the White House. Newspapers editorialized that Callister should recuse himself, but he responded on December 27, hoping to mollify critics, that he had long since been released from his church position. This struck observers as odd since the *Church News* had not carried the customary announcement of retirement from such a post. When the 1981 *Church Almanac* gave his release date as October 15, 1979, rumors flew that it had been back-dated.

NOW filed a separate motion in Ninth District Court to disqualify

Callister[8] and documented, as part of its September 1980 case, the LDS regional representatives' involvement in fighting the ERA in Florida, Nevada, and Virginia.[9] A few NOW chapters during this period picketed Mormon chapels in Howard County, Maryland; near the University of Charleston in West Virginia; and in Ann Arbor, Michigan, at the Chrysler Arena as Mormons gathered there for a regional event.[10]

On January 23, 1981, a wire service article in the *Idaho Statesman* found yet another Mormon link that cast doubt on Callister's objectivity: his three law clerks, Greg Kerr, Cory Maxwell, and David Thomas, were recent graduates of the J. Reuben Clark Law School at Brigham Young University. The Maxwell appointment was particularly significant because his father, Neal A. Maxwell, was an LDS apostle and member of the church's Special Affairs Committee.[11] When Callister refused for the second time to disqualify himself, NOW petitioned the Ninth Circuit Court of Appeals with a writ of mandamus in March 1981 to reverse this decision.[12]

Callister issued a ruling on the merits of the case on December 23, affirming that a state legislature could rescind its prior ratification of the ERA and the U.S. Congress could not extend the deadline for passage. This was the first time in U.S. history that a federal court judge had declared an Act of Congress unconstitutional. NOW immediately appealed the ruling to the U.S. Supreme Court and requested an expedited hearing since the deadline was due to expire the next summer.

Acting promptly, just seventeen days later, the Supreme Court vindicated NOW's position with a unanimous stay prohibiting enforcement of Callister's decision and agreeing to hear the merits of NOW's appeal at a later date. The Court thereby negated the effect of Callister's decision and removed him from the debate.[13]

Utah Mormons for ERA

For sociologist O. Kendall White, publication of *Exponent II* in Boston represented a step toward radical feminism within the Mormon church.[14] Whether or not this is strictly true, the tabloid-style quarterly at least introduced readers to issues of interest to Mormon women and began an important dialogue about women's lives, which it assumed were profoundly different from those of men. A locus of intellectual inquiry, *Exponent II* was an outlet for creative energies and ideas. It rarely challenged specific religious doctrines or the political activities of Mormon leaders, but it created a network among women and an accepting venue for communicating their feelings about issues such as the ERA. It succeeded because it avoided polarizing readers over this most divisive of women's issues.

Mormons for ERA was the more radical in spirit and staked out its position in a way that all but precluded an objective examination of issues. It attracted women in the wake of the spectacular publicity surrounding Sonia Johnson's excommunication who wanted to express their support or have similar viewpoints heard. Organizationally, the group functioned as a federation of statewide chapters in California, Utah, Virginia, Washington, and elsewhere. Approved by the national group before they began local activities, the state groups experienced considerable autonomy while they retained the common central objective of promoting the ERA, in addition to local issues.

Ever since Utah's IWY conference and its rejection of the ERA, Utah feminists had been anxious to show their support for the amendment. Jan Tyler remembered conversations among a network of friends about organizing a Utah branch of Mormons for ERA. Despite strongly held feminist convictions, nobody was particularly eager to lead such a group. She later recalled:

> The first person to head it up was Becky Cornwall but she felt some conflict and reservations and then Jeanine Elnes and Dodie Williams emerged and that worked for a while and then Tina Martin got involved and then the non-Mormons felt we should do it ourselves. . . . I, from the beginning, was not interested in being the leader, and Sonia knew and understood that, but I was interested in training leadership and finding new, not the usual, groups of people to involve.[15]

When Becky Cornwall was in charge, the group issued an announcement on August 18 that Mormon women who cared about the amendment should pause for prayer each day at noon until the amendment was ratified. "We have the assurance that initially 20,000 Mormon women will be involved in Utah and our neighboring states of Nevada, Wyoming, Arizona, California, Idaho, Washington, and Oregon," said Cornwall. "We wish it to also be known that vigorous freedom of thought and speech exist within Mormonism and that the principles of our faith rule out leadership by fear and bullying."[16]

Venturing a step further into the spotlight, Utah's chapter of Mormons for ERA (MERA) hosted a rally at the state capitol in support of extending the ratification deadline. Other combinations of women who had played roles in Utah's IWY conference or other women's organizations throughout the state occasionally joined together for rallies, speeches, or vigils.[17] MERA held a Utah vigil at the state capitol on the morning of Sonia Johnson's church court that drew over a hundred people. The women stood in the cold, crisp air to hear speakers talk about Sonia's situation, the women's movement in general, and why it mattered that they exhibit their support.[18]

Despite her bruising experience with the IWY, Tyler found herself surprisingly energized by the coalescence of Utah Mormons with feminist leanings. "I've loved the opportunity of working with the couple hundred women and men who have been involved, working at a steady pace on things, without a lot of to-do and fanfare, just getting done what had to be done."[19]

On February 9, 1980, two months after Johnson's excommunication, a group of women gathered in Tyler's living room, some of them meeting for the first time and others already acquainted from the IWY or other events.[20] They wondered aloud who else might be interested enough to join them. They expressed mixed feelings of exhilaration, resolve, and danger. Not being newcomers to the women's movement, they understood the risk of stepping forward. But they tried to reduce that risk by agreeing to especially look for active church members with pro-ERA views.

Kathryn MacKay remembered that what united them was their commitment to ratification and their sense of urgency about its stalled progress and the legal challenges to the deadline extension. They drafted articles of incorporation and identified public education on the "merits of the Equal Rights Amendment" as their objective. To this end, Mormons for ERA proposed to "promote, sponsor and develop publications"; "promote, sponsor and organize a network of individuals"; and "conduct and carry on activities" to advance ratification.[21] They selected a governing board of eight women: Marilee C. Latta, historian Kathryn MacKay, June Fulmer, Kathleen Flake, Kathleen Bennion Barrett, Denise Posse Lindberg, Sarah Jence, and Dolores Ritchie.

The next meeting was held two weeks later on February 23 in the home of psychologist Moyne Oviatt. A large group of Mormons attended this gathering, some of whom had been involved with an organization called Mormons and Friends for ERA, founded in 1977. They had produced the pamphlet *Another Mormon View of the ERA* and participated in "Support for Sonia" fundraising; they had also published a newsletter on women's issues and networked with other local women's groups. Some of those in attendance remembered each other from the IWY activities.[22] In any case, the attendance was a tribute to the recruiting skills of the few who had met in Tyler's living room and seemed to indicate ongoing interest the women believed was stirring just beneath the surface in Utah.

At the next meeting, held in early March at Mary Ann Payne's house, four of the twenty-one women in attendance—Linda Sillitoe, Maureen Ursenbach Beecher, Kathleen Flake, and Elouise Bell—volunteered to form a writing committee to produce pro-ERA literature in response to the anti-ERA literature in circulation.[23] According to MacKay, who chaired the meeting, the women were "identifiably Mormon" but the type who simultaneously "supported by word and deed the Equal Rights Amendment." It was decided the group should meet weekly and that members would attend the Utah Conference on Families scheduled for later that month.[24]

In the first few weeks, some of the women demonstrated a high level of involvement and a "process of self selection" came into play as the governing board becoming redefined to include twelve members, Fulmer, Latta, MacKay, and Payne comprising an executive committee.[25]

In April, Jan Tyler reported that the writing committee had completed a six-part outline for an ERA brochure with an introduction, vignettes, questions and answers, theology, legality, and a bibliography.[26] The group felt committed to getting ahead of the anti-ERA forces and becoming proactive rather than simply reacting to events in Utah and elsewhere.[27] However, Kathryn MacKay reported on plans by the national Mormons for ERA, which had signed a contract for a third banner-tow—this time to fly over Temple Square during the LDS general conference in April with a banner reading "More Mormons for ERA are Everywhere." At this news, the Utah group showed the first of a widening schism over how to best, and appropriately, respond to the Mormon Church. For the time being, they decided to remain neutral, without either jumping on the bandwagon or publicly expressing reservations about the banner-tow.[28]

Even so, the group was formulating its own plans for attracting more attention to issues—larger projects that would require some funding, where previously the members had simply dipped into their own pockets to stage demonstrations and organize letter-writing campaigns. Lola Van Wagoner Redford was recruited to help develop ways to fund the expanding activities.[29] In addition, Mary Ann Payne stepped forward and said she would not mind taking a larger role as director of the group, knowing that whoever assumed the position would have to devote a considerable amount of time to coordinating events. Her appointment was heartily approved.[30]

Despite such good intentions on the part of some of the members, serious ideological conflicts simmered below the surface and were about to be exposed. The women had already experienced personality clashes, different organizational styles, and different priorities, which were making it increasingly difficult to work together harmoniously. Unlike the long-term and intimate friendships that underlay Mormons for ERA in Virginia, the women in Utah had come together out of deep concern but not as close, personal friends. It was the crisis of Sonia Johnson's excommunication and the declining support for the ERA that had brought them together—a dual motive that colored their association from the start and perhaps sealed their doom. Although they were all Mormons by heritage, they exhibited different degrees of activity and commitment to the church. And in important ways, this would be the line that divided them.

The rift became visible at the March 29 meeting when some board members expressed dissatisfaction with Payne and the direction the group was taking. Nevertheless, Marjorie McEntyre proposed a vote of confidence, although it was postponed as the women continued to disagree over such issues as whether men could join the group ("Many," the minutes read, "felt it was inappropriate"[31]) and whether there should be a liaison with the national organization—a position Jan Tyler had assumed even though it was not mentioned in the articles of incorporation. The meeting closed without a decision on these issues or the greater question of who should be leading the charge. Like child-rearing or moving in a marriage, these critical issues challenged the ability of the women in the group to work together. Good, powerful women who shared a commitment to equal rights, they were nevertheless different enough in their ideas about how far they could go to accomplish their goals that they were momentarily paralyzed. Meanwhile, the writing committee had finished a draft of the proposed pamphlet, but Dolores Ritchie raised concerns about its "content, tone, and format." Still, the group approved sending the draft to Elouise Bell, a BYU English professor, for final editing and polishing.[32]

Behind the scenes, there were tensions and a flurry of activity over next ten days. On April 9, Mary Ann Payne wrote to the board to express how upset she had been by the fervor with which they had discussed the group's future. Could the group exist and should it? she wondered. She found three sources of irreconcilable conflict with the board: her "difficulty working with other people," the board's lack of confidence in her, and "apparent difficulties in philosophy and values" over issues such as whether to include men. Upon reflection, she did not want to spend time working out these differences, and therefore, as the "unrecognized leader of our group," she was canceling the meeting scheduled for April 12 and disbanding the group. It would be replaced with a similar organization, also called Mormons for ERA, that would include a director, board, task forces, and networking opportunities. The national group had given its blessing, she added, in favor of a new group that would be unswervingly committed to ratification, while also respecting the "individual commitment" of LDS members, commitment to Sonia Johnson, and commitment to assisting other Mormons for ERA groups.[33]

Kathryn MacKay had not been present to see the contentious discussion in the previous meeting and immediately called Payne, who assured her that the new organization was a done deal. Payne was the new executive director, and her board, she told MacKay, consisted of Marjorie McEntyre, Moyne Oviatt, Jan Tyler, and two men, John Sillito and Paul Swenson, which was curious in light of the fact that Payne had previously opposed the inclusion of men. That same day, MacKay preempted Payne's plans by quickly registering the name of Utah Mormons for the Equal Rights Amendment as a nonprofit organization.[34]

The original board ignored Payne's cancellation and met on April 12. Interestingly, Payne was also present at this meeting. MacKay sent her a note afterwards: "Thank you for attending the UMERA meeting . . . and for remaining as long as you did. It was a difficult session for all of us, and Wednesday's meeting may be even more so. I look forward to seeing you then."[35] MacKay confessed that her initial response to Payne's letter had been a feeling of "defeat and resignation." However, these had given way to a sense of annoyance and the feeling that Payne considered her colleague an "insignificant" person and treated her like an "untrustworthy child." To MacKay, "the cause of ratification of the ERA [was] more important than my ego, than my being any director on any board of Utah Mormons for the ERA." She would support whatever group worked for that end, she said, but could no longer support Payne as a member of the executive board.[36]

MacKay proceeded as if Payne had not formed a rival group, seeing it only as a cheap strategy on Payne's part to maintain control—a way to remove Fulmer, Latta, and MacKay from office. Her argument was strong. She told Payne she felt the group was composed of influential women, each possessing organizational skills, "years of experience, the clear minds, the feeling hearts and the important connections in the community to organize a network, print a pro-ERA brochure, raise funds and provide capable speakers. We need each other if the fight for women's rights is to be won."[37]

The minutes of the April 12 meeting show agreement that "the way should be kept open to those who wished to rejoin Utah Mormons for ERA." But they took decisive action against Payne for having acted "without regard for the other members of the executive board and without the support of the governing board." Payne was voted off the committee. Next, the group affirmed the governing board as it had been originally created on February 23.[38]

Four days later, on April 16, seven members of the governing board met at Louise Meader's home to discuss goals and policies. Seven members of UMERA came, but Payne, Tyler, and McEntyre did not, feeling that the significant philosophical differences would prevent a harmonious solution. MacKay took the lead in urging that they work toward a compromise, but those with whom they needed to work out such a compromise were not present. As a first step toward keeping the support of moderates, they voted to disband the writing committee.[39]

The next day, Payne took her own preemptive action by issuing a press release announcing the formation of Utah Mormons for ERA as a local affiliate of Mormons for ERA, herself as director.[40] Dismayed by the splintering, MacKay wrote to Tyler on April 18, asking what she thought had happened to push them apart. "Have we all become defensive and insular?" she wondered. "Have we forgotten the commitment ties, let alone the friendship ties?" She enclosed the compromise proposed at the last meeting, but events had already moved beyond compromise.[41] On April 20, BYU professor Maureen Ursenbach Beecher, perhaps unaware of a decision to disband the writing committee, convened it to begin the process of designing, printing, and copyrighting the brochure as soon as funding was available.[42]

Payne responded to MacKay: "You must understand my hesitancy in writing any more letters. I did not foresee the anger and hurt that would follow my letter of April 9." She, McEntyre, and Tyler had hoped they could work together with either "individuals or the group," but now saw "little hope of working out differences."[43] Payne said the nature of the publications, organizational styles, and other concerns were why she and others had not come to the meeting on the 16th, and she had withdrawn from the original group because of "philosophical" differences and their lack of "confidence" and "support."

Payne also allowed a flash of anger to show through as she continued: "What were you thinking at Saturday's meeting as we labored for two and one half hours . . . . Did you feel it was a serious omission that two motions for a vote of confidence in which no confidence was given were not included in the minutes? Did it surprise you that unanimous votes reported in the minutes did not in fact take place? What information do you have of Marilee's contacts with [the] national [organization] and with me? Has she related her conversations with Sonia, Hazel Rigby, and me?"[44]

Frustrated by the stalemate, MacKay, Fulmer, and Latta wrote a summary memorandum on May 2 of the group's brief history and their hopes for reversing the present course. They suggested the following to the governing board:

> We feel that it is still possible for Utah Mormons for ERA to regroup and to go on with its efforts to minimize the impact of the LDS Church's anti-ERA position and actions. The tasks Utah Mormons for ERA has set for itself demand the skills, connections and support of all of us if they are to be accomplished. And there will be other groups and other activities which will bring some of us together and which should not be handicapped by the effects of the split in Utah Mormons for ERA.
>
> We all need to put aside the angers, frustrations and fears. We need to cease the criticizing and drawing up of sides. It will take maturity and self-confidence to commit to work together again. However, we think these worthwhile efforts.

> We feel that the split in Utah Mormons for ERA is based on differences in style being mistaken for differences in philosophy and personality. The cause of women's rights has brought together many kinds of people who may not work together for other causes. We in Utah Mormons for ERA all came together to work as Mormons for the Equal Rights Amendment; we need to come together again for that purpose.

The three announced a board meeting five days hence at MacKay's house to discuss the group's future, by-laws and incorporation, membership, and future activities, including the brochure. They asked that those who had left the group identify the specific issues they had found problematic so all could work toward reconciliation.

Although the correspondence has not survived, MacKay was in communication with Sonia Johnson, who believed the two women had both been misunderstood. In a realistic but gentle way, she told MacKay: "Although I wish you and Mary Ann, both of whom I love and trust entirely, could bring your groups together, Mary Ann is the person the Board backed—not AGAINST anyone else but because of her personal merits. Not even because of the composition of her board. We can only ratify the Executive Director in each state because usually that's the only person we know well enough in each state. . . . We can only choose our leader and hope for the best."[45] This must have been difficult for MacKay. Both she and Payne were equally committed to ratification and believed the group could have an impact, but neither was able to create a workable consensus.

In just three months of existence, Utah Mormons for ERA had already logged a volatile, tortuous record to illustrate how emotion-laden the various conflicting visions of what should be done were and the personal struggle such decisions implied. All the members were remarkable, powerful women, and each had a view of what the organization should do or be. Their views clashed. Instead of focusing their energies on the campaign, they struggled with each other. Inevitably, the group self-destructed.

The nature of such groups illustrates the more general dynamics of this period of LDS women's history. It was true in Utah, as other states, that Mormons for ERA was an internal social movement that sought change within the church itself. Rather than making the more radical move of separating from the church, these women opted to attempt to bring about change from within. Their tactics reflected that orientation: to incorporate the movement into the church, to diffuse the threat, or to end it altogether.

Although some of the women who had been in either faction of the splintered UMERA would come together for demonstrations during the next two years, both groups essentially disbanded, disappointed at their inability to effectively organize—another casualty of the ERA conflict.

Developments in 1980

As 1980 opened, the clock was ticking. Could the ERA be ratified before the extended deadline expired in June 1982? It seemed likely since only three states were needed. In Virginia, although Mormon women who had mobilized as the LDS Citizens Coalition in late 1978 had successfully blocked passage in early 1979, another season of lobbying faced them in Richmond.

On January 14, 1980, a month after her excommunication, Sonia Johnson joined more than six thousand other representatives of civil rights, labor, and women's groups from twenty states to march on the Richmond capitol as part of the year's first major rally in support of the ERA. Johnson was among the headliners on the podium along with NOW President Eleanor Smeal; Joseph Lowery, president of the Southern Christian Leadership Conference; and representatives of the United Steel Workers, the United Mine Workers, the Virginia Education Association, the Virginia state AFL-CIO, and other unions.[46]

In a snafu of classic proportions on January 16, Phil Donahue hosted Sonia Johnson on his national news program and announced that Beverly Campbell had refused to appear, which happened not to be true. For her part, Campbell claimed that Johnson had refused to appear with her, which was also untrue.[47] Donahue apologized for what he described as an "error."

While Donahue was bantering with Johnson about her excommunication, Campbell appeared on KTVX, a Salt Lake City-based television station, with broadcaster Roy Gibson. He asked Campbell if Johnson had been excommunicated for supporting the ERA. Campbell said no, reading from Johnson's bishop: "You have publicly taught that the Church is dedicated to imposing the Prophet's moral directives upon all Americans, when it is the doctrine of the Church that all people are free to choose for themselves those moral directives dictated by their own consciences."[48] Thus, as Campbell put it, the church "did not excommunicate her," she "had excommunicated herself." Described by Gibson as the "most articulate spokesman" for LDS women, Campbell continued by saying that the question "every thinking person then must ask themselves is whether there is any reason at any time for there to be any law that would make any distinction between men and women. If such is the case, then the ERA is an inappropriate means of achieving equality for women. This is one of the major concerns that I have."[49]

Donahue scheduled another show that featured Relief Society President Barbara B. Smith and Beverly Campbell together, which President Smith accepted after consulting Elders Ezra Taft Benson, Thomas S. Monson, and Boyd K. Packer. Orrin Hatch and local media people were also alerted to the broadcast. Smith later talked about the interview and said she found it stressful, perhaps because she was upset about her pregnant daughter who was toxemic and in pain from having slipped on some ice. In any case, Smith was "nervous," dry-mouthed from fasting, and dissatisfied with her performance. "I could not talk fast enough. . . . I tried to tell the audience about five things they should know about us and our belief, but time went too quickly and I didn't get all five points explained. However, I must admit that if I'd had my way the program would not have been as effective. . . . Donahue had asked questions that were on the minds of many people. Those people would not have been nearly as receptive if I had only told them what I thought they should know."[50]

On January 26, the *Church News* published another strongly worded editorial: "Is ERA a Moral Issue?" Although the question was rhetorical, the editorial conveyed the clear message that church members were not expected to sit out the controversy: "Church membership is not for spectators. The cause of righteousness ever calls for action," the editorial read.[51]

The next month, the Virginia senate once again defeated the ERA because a wavering moderate Republican, Senator John Chichester, abstained from voting because of what he claimed was a conflict of interest. With a vote of 20-19 in favor, his abstention, as he admitted, kept the resolution from passing. If he had voted against the measure, it would have gone to Lieutenant Governor Charles S. Robb, a supporter of the ERA, for a tie-breaking vote. As it was, it stood defeated.

On the other side of the country, the LDS Church scheduled a youth conference at the University of Houston on March 1, and NOW and other ERA proponents demonstrated there against the "all-male hierarchy of the Mormon Church, the nationwide campaign by the church to prevent ratification of the ERA, and the excommunication of Sonia Johnson."[52]

Later in the month, the Eighth Circuit Court of Appeals upheld NOW's right to encourage members to boycott non-ratifying states. This judgment came in reaction to a suit filed by the state of Missouri and its attorney general, John Ashcroft, affirming the 1979 ruling of Judge Elmo Hunter that NOW's activities were a valid political demonstration and protected by the First Amendment.[53] Missouri had filed the suit in 1978, claiming NOW was in violation of the Sherman Antitrust Act. In October the United States Supreme Court refused to hear the appeal.[54] A similar case had pitted NOW against the state of Nevada, but the charges were dismissed in the spring.[55]

Another development in March for LDS Church members was that, when they opened their *Ensign* magazine in the month traditionally reserved for women's issues because of the Relief Society's founding in March in 1842, they found, bound into the center, a gray-covered pamphlet the same size as the magazine entitled *The Church and the Proposed*

Equal Rights Amendment (see chap. 4). It was distributed widely to the media and to members of legislatures in unratified states as well.

That same month, the First Presidency published its annual reminder encouraging members to be concerned and active citizens. The statement was normally issued in October. Nevertheless, it included the caveat that it was "contrary to our counsel and advice that ward, branch or stake premises, chapels or other Church facilities be used in any way for political campaign purposes, whether it be for speech-making, distribution of literature, or class discussion."[56] Yet, church members continued to talk about the ERA at church. Announcements were being made from the pulpit about car pooling from the church parking lot to demonstrations. LDS members continued to circulate petitions, distribute information about the positions and voting records of candidates, and write letters—in some cases signing letters that were written by someone else.

On April 7, 1980, Apostle Gordon B. Hinckley made a rare public appearance—in fact, his first during the ERA campaign—with perhaps the nation's best-known Mormon businessman, J. Willard Marriott Jr., president of the Marriott Corporation headquartered near Washington D.C. On NBC's *Today Show,* they explained why the church opposed the ERA.

In late April or early May 1980, Hazel Rigby of Mormons for ERA wrote to Elder Hugh Pinnock of the LDS First Quorum of the Seventy with oversight for Virginia. Rigby had two purposes in writing. First, she told him what she had observed about the organization and activities of the LDS Citizens Coalition; second, she raised questions about how Sonia Johnson's bishop had handled the excommunication. She said the LDS Citizens Coalition was an "underground" group whose tactics ran counter to the spirit of the U.S. Constitution. Pinnock answered tactfully, indicating areas where he believed there were misunderstandings worth addressing, clearly wanting Rigby to know he was well informed on both situations. Although the ERA was a moral issue, those who disagreed with the church's position could do so without fear of retribution, he emphasized. He repeated the mantra that Johnson had been excommunicated not because of her support of the ERA but other reasons:

> The Church has attempted to explain that its involvement in the proceedings surrounding the proposed ERA is because it is a moral issue. Sister Rigby, this, like a number of other concepts, principles, or statements in the Church reflect the feelings and inspiration of our prophet, seer and revelator, President Spencer W. Kimball. There are a number of others besides yourself that feel he is wrong. I certainly hope that you understand that your membership is secure, as is everyone else who are opposed to his counsel. . . .
>
> In your last paragraph, you mentioned that you will continue to speak out against injustice, dishonesty and unfairness wherever you find it. . . . I would like to join with you in the crusade. My heart is full of love and concern, and I pray that if I can be of help with some of you relating to the dilemma you are having, I would be more than happy to do so."[57]

It was an unexpectedly warm response. Rigby did not leave an immediate reaction, and given her well-informed perspective about the church's political activities, she likely could not accept Elder Pinnock's assurance of the church's concerns at face value.

In May 1980, Beverly Campbell was featured at length in the *Christian Science Monitor* identifying her objections to the ERA. She made her usual arguments. First, the amendment was unnecessary. "As a philosophical statement, the language of the ERA is nice," she maintained. "There are not many people who object to the idea. But we have to look at the ERA as it will be interpreted." It simply goes too far, she said: "It's so harsh and arbitrary. There can be no exceptions under the ERA. And there are times when exceptions are needed." The Fourteenth Amendment "gives women equal protection except where the government can show reasonable cause not to." In light of this, she scoffed at the idea that existing laws needed ERA backing to retain their effectiveness: "The teeth can't be taken out of such laws, short of repealing the law, unless it can be shown that there is compelling reason for a distinction."[58]

Second, she stressed that the ERA threatened the family: "You don't abandon someone when they are in trouble. You give them more support. When I look at the interpretation of the law in states with equal-rights amendments, I don't think it will help the family. . . . Our concern is that families will suffer." The reporter asked her about a case publicized by Phyllis Schlafly's STOP ERA. In Pennsylvania a court ruled in *Albert Einstein Medical Center v. Nathans* (1977) that creditors no longer had the right to sue a husband for payment of his wife's "necessaries" because the law was "repugnant" to the state's equal rights amendment; either the law must be repealed or creditors given the right to sue wives as well. Campbell agreed that "if a woman wants to work and support her family, she can do it. We don't need a new law for that"; but "if women bear children, there should be a presumption of support, so women who want to can safely leave their work career."

Third, the amendment would give too much power to the federal government, blurring the division of powers. She warned that any law affecting men and women—whether dealing with education, inheritance, penal laws, or social services—would be under federal scrutiny. "They would be adjudicated by justices who only read and interpret the law and who can't listen to the majority of the people," she said. "At the state level, people can vote for a change of lawmakers, or have a referendum election. But you can't change anything at the federal level." For instance, most women favored laws that led to equity in the workplace, but "it is presently against the law *not* to give equal pay for equal work. The laws already exist. The ERA will not make any new laws, but it will be the constitutional amendment under which the laws will be written."[59]

The same article quoted Rosemary Thompson, mother of two sons and Illinois director of the Eagle Forum, who worked as a self-described, full-time, professional writer. Speaking for the Eagle Forum, she echoed Campbell's concern about federal intrusiveness: "Our biggest objection to the Equal Rights Amendment is that we would find ourselves with more federal regulations on our personal and domestic life." She feared "the federal government would come and tell states that all of the laws must comply with what they [the federal government] think. Illinois has a fine equal protection law that allows equal opportunity, but also a reasonable distinction between men and women."

Thompson then recited a litany of possible consequences of the ERA that cast supporters as conspirators who "want to draft women and put them in combat duty. Men and women are not absolutely equal physiologically." She accused ERA supporters of threatening Christianity and promoting amorality—also abortion. "The proponents of abortion say it has nothing to do with the ERA. There must be some tie-in or they wouldn't be calling for it," she said.[60]

The dean of BYU's law school, Rex Lee, was quoted in the article in agreement with the parade of horribles: women in combat, unisex toilets, dismantling of laws protecting women at home, and removing preferential consideration for mothers in child support. "No one can say how the ERA will be interpreted. The real question is, since there is a risk of these things happening, is there enough of a need for a new light to search out discriminatory practices? My answer is a resounding 'no.'" He concluded that "in 1970 we needed a grand leap, but we are no longer at that point. We don't need a grand leap, but fine tuning. Very simply, the Constitution is not a fine-tuning instrument, but a piece of concrete."[61] Rhetorically, the article positioned the Latter-day Saints with fundamentalist groups that feared for their security in the modern world and mistrusted the federal government. Big government seemed to be as large a foe as the amendment—an amendment all conservative Christian groups could fight together.

In June 1980 the ERA was a hot topic for the ninth year in a row in the Illinois legislature when two formerly pro-ERA Republicans voted against it, bringing the total in favor to 105, just two short of the required three-fifths.[62] About this time, Ronald Reagan, Republican front-runner for the U.S. presidency, hinted that he would push to have the ERA removed from the Republican platform before the national convention in July. His rationale was that it was no longer a national issue because the matter was in the hands of state legislatures to ratify or reject. While he refused to call for outright revocation of the plank, first adopted by Republicans in 1940, he tried to sidestep the conflicts it generated by arguing that it had become "a divisive symbol with people who probably are all together with regard to equal rights but who can be turned off or on by that as a symbol."[63] Reagan told Republican governors in June: "I would support a plank that stresses our determination to oppose discrimination of any kind, for any reason, anywhere in the land." More than 12,000 men and women, including NOW demonstrators, picketed the national convention carrying placards that read, "Keep ERA in GOP Platform." Eleanor Smeal lamented that they were "going backwards."[64] The final outcome was that the Republican platform took no position on ERA.

The Democrats reaffirmed their support, and in fact, the Democratic platform pledged to withhold campaign funds from presidential candidates who did not support the ERA. However, Utah's Democratic convention in July followed the national Republican trend. Acting quickly with a quorum but less than a third of the eligible delegates on hand, the convention removed the ERA plank from its platform. Four years earlier, the same ploy was attempted, but on that occasion the plank was reintroduced and subsequently adopted.[65]

The next month, an outraged Betty Ford warned that Reagan's shift "threatened to carry the party toward the sort of election disaster that Barry Goldwater suffered as the GOP nominee in 1964. We're treading on dangerous ground."[66] After he accepted his party's nomination, Governor Reagan sent supporters a letter reaffirming his commitment to women's rights, but not to the ERA: "In the platform, we make the strongest and most outstanding commitment to women's rights of any Republican platform in history. The only controversy which has arisen does not concern whether women's rights should be protected, for we all agree that they should. It is a difference of opinion regarding the manner in which that protection should be secured." Moreover, he promised to establish a liaison with the country's governors, encouraging them to eliminate discriminatory legislation and add statutes to state laws if necessary.[67] This was a position the Mormon Church was comfortable with, and during November's election, 71 percent of Utah voters supported Reagan versus 20 percent for Jimmy Carter.

During LDS general conference in October 1980, approximately twenty Mormons for ERA, mostly women and children, picketed Temple Square chanting "Two, four, six, eight / Ratify in every state." BYU's student newspaper reported that the picketers' signs read: "The Three Nephites Were Women," "The apple stuck in Adam's throat is about to be burped up," and "X Mormon for ERA." The article quoted a security officer shaking his head with disbelief and muttering, "The day will come when you'll have to get a pass to get on Temple Square." One distraught woman rushed at the picketers "yelling 'No! You don't know what you're doing!' She then broke into sobs. 'I've read statements by several top law schools throughout the nation.' She said, 'Any woman who reads what the law schools have to say about ERA would know it is not what women want. I just don't know what they're doing.'" She had tears streaming down her cheeks, according to the article.[68]

During the Saturday afternoon session when the vote to sustain the church's general authorities was called for, Elder Marion G. Romney gave the ritual call, "All opposed by the same sign." Three women shouted in unison: "No! ERA policy—no!" Since voting was indicated by raising one's hand, the outcry was disruptive in itself. The women, Cheryl L. Dalton, Marty LaBrosse, and Sarah Campbell, chose to launch their protest during the sustaining of the prophet, Spencer W. Kimball. Elder Bruce R. McConkie had been alerted before the meeting that this might happen and asked the women to meet with Elder Hinckley after the session.

"We realize we have made a drastic move," Dalton told a reporter. "We know we may be putting our church membership on the line, but the church leaders must be made aware of how much we resent the use of their ecclesiastical influence to defeat the ERA." For these three women, the ERA was strictly a political issue. They asked to meet with President Kimball but were denied a hearing. "We have seized our one opportunity to voice our conscience to the First Presidency . . . in order to demonstrate our deep indignation over the church's anti-ERA policy," LaBrosse said, adding that "Elder Hinckley said that we were entitled to our opinion and that he will not condemn us for our stand on the ERA."[69] Hinckley reportedly told the women that Rex Lee had been encouraged by the church to write *A Lawyer Looks at ERA*.[70]

About three weeks later, Norma Matheson, wife of Utah's Democratic governor, Scott M. Matheson, debated Republican gubernatorial candidate Robert Wright at Utah State University. In his opening statement, Wright told the audience that the Mathesons supported abortion and the ERA and that Norma was a member of NOW. Norma denied that her husband was pro-abortion and pointed out that, as governor, he "upheld federal laws requiring funding for abortions until the Supreme Court ruled otherwise." She added, "He opposes abortion on demand unless a mother's life is in danger or if she is a rape victim."[71] During her comments, some BYU students in the auditorium who had traveled to Logan for the event heckled her, repeatedly interrupting and shouting her down. Other students told them to "shut up," but the meeting ended badly. Shaken but retaining her dignity, Matheson concluded her statement: "I expected this to be a positive dialogue; I'm sorry it's deteriorated." The next day the Matheson campaign office issued a stinging rebuke: "It's unfortunate that something like this could ever happen to the First Lady of the State of Utah. She was very hurt and upset. It's too bad that the campaign has been permitted to reach such a low level." BYU student body president Jeffrey Duke and vice-president Thomas Peterson wrote a letter of apology to Matheson, saying they were appalled by what had happened.[72]

The LDS Seattle temple was dedicated in November 1980. Despite its official name indicating a relationship with Seattle, it is actually in the nearby community of Bellevue. In any case, the state chapter of Mormons for ERA, organized by Marty LaBrosse on October 28, 1979, was ready. LaBrosse and Mary Whitemore sent a packet of information to the California chapter, headed by Nadine Hansen, Bill Washburn, and Audrey McIlwrath, and the Utah chapter. Enclosed were invitations and information on a series of ERA events surrounding the dedication ceremony. First was a press conference and protest march in front of the temple on October 6 to coincide with the church's "VIP Day" open house. On November 16, Mormons for ERA would hold a rally while the First Presidency was received at the University Towers Hotel in Bellevue. Finally, during the four-day dedication itself, women would hand out leaflets at the gates. Whitemore and LaBrosse emphasized the importance of sending representatives from the California and Utah groups. This was not, they reiterated, a regional issue, but one of importance for the entire country.[73]

In a letter to Sonia Johnson, LaBrosse described how, during the demonstration, she was "knocked down, and kicked by an agent of my Mormon church—one of my good Priesthood brothers. This was an attempt by my church to intimidate and silence me."[74] In April 1981, she filed a civil suit for assault against Arthur Kay, the temple president; Brent Nash, president of Bellevue stake; and the church. She continued her letter to Johnson: "I have been injured in the expression of my religious views. The male hierarchy has organized an anti-Equal Rights Amendment illegal lobbying [and] fund raising campaign and have violated the doctrine of separation of church and state. Yet by my supporting the ERA and calling attention to the law-breaking activities of my church men, I am called names, yelled at, thrown stones at, given the finger, narrowly missed by cars and assaulted by good Mormons." The hearing was scheduled for September 29, but she decided to back away from it. The church had filed its own suit for trespassing but had dropped its charges in January.

The events surrounding the temple dedication were a prelude to what occurred on November 17 when a group of twenty-one women, modeling themselves on the radical British suffragists of the nineteenth century, chained themselves to the temple gates to protest the "Mormons' holding all American women in chains." A church spokesmen told the press that day there were two forces at work in the world: "God's and Satan's. Because the Mormons are doing God's work," those working against the church, he charged, "must be in cahoots with Satan."[75]

Meanwhile in Virginia, the LDS Citizens Coalition was gearing up for its third legislative season of lobbying. A letter of December 12 went to Virginia wards with instructions on how to organize lobbyists for the general assembly in January. Using primarily the same literature and the same basic rhetoric as previously, the group anticipated the same success from its grassroots campaign tactics.

The Final Year, 1981

NOW opened what it called its ERA Countdown Campaign offices in key cities in Florida, Illinois, Missouri, North Carolina, and Oklahoma. Learning from the opposition, they initiated massive grassroots campaigns in these locations including "phone banks, message brigades," and door-to-door "missionary" canvassing projects.[76] One Gallup poll indicated that 63 percent of Americans "who have heard or read about the ERA" supported it versus 32 percent who opposed it. It was a record high. The ERA had never before exceeded 58 percent support nationally.[77] In January, the LDS Citizens Coalition distributed Rex Lee's *A Lawyer Looks at ERA* to legislators.[78]

On February 5, designated Women's Rights Day in Congress, Mormons for ERA joined actress Mary Tyler Moore, *Ms. Magazine* editor Gloria Steinem, Speaker of the House Tip O'Neill, Doctor Benjamin Spock, and representatives from national labor, religious, civil rights, educational, and other organizations to visit with state representatives in the nation's capitol. There were 3,000 women in all, representing their professional or civic groups to send a clear message that the women's movement was alive and well.[79] Part of the lobbying that day was to oppose the so-called Human Life Amendment which would grant fetuses full legal and civil rights and allow women who had abortions to be tried for murder. Smeal, who was on hand representing NOW, described women as "the fastest growing poverty group in America. . . . There are women out there right this moment choosing between food and heating oil, and some will die from those choices."[80]

As the NOW missionaries distributed pro-ERA material across the country, their selection of pamphlets in the San Diego area included MERA's *The ERA Is a Moral Issue,* a response to the churchwide distribution of *ERA: A Moral issue.* The MERA pamphlet was distributed in front of several Mormon chapels.[81]

On April 12, Phyllis Schlafly testified before the U.S. Labor and Human Resources Committee chaired by Orrin Hatch and denied the need for guidelines against sexual discrimination. She called the employer an "innocent bystander," victimized by legislation, and claimed that a "virtuous woman" need fear sexual harassment only in the "rarest of cases" because, "when a woman walks across the room, she speaks with a universal body language that most men intuitively understand. Men hardly ever ask sexual favors of women from whom the certain answer is 'No.'" She further claimed that "the most cruel and damaging sexual harassment taking place today is the harassment by feminists and their federal government allies against the role of motherhood and the role of the dependent wife."[82]

In a witty move, but with deadly serious aim, NOW announced in May its intention to send "missionaries" to Salt Lake City, Ogden, and Provo on behalf of the ERA.[83] President Smeal stated: "We are carrying our fight for equal justice for women to the heart of the opposition, the Mormons. . . . We know there is grassroots support for the Equal Rights Amendment in Utah and in the Mormon Church. We intend to uncover and organize that support."[84]

Kathryn MacKay considered the NOW missionaries a "wonderful strategy. It was whimsical and clever." Some of the missionaries stayed at her apartment. "They were from all over the country," she explained. "It was important in the process that the missionaries not be from Utah" and that locals offer them "a network of support." Those providing housing were regaled at night by stories of how the missionaries had been received during the day.[85]

The Utah Women's Political Caucus, a group from both political parties with an interest in recruiting more women for involvement, joined with the Salt Lake chapter of NOW on July 1 to sponsor a prayer vigil in a Salt Lake City park. Speakers included Reba Keele, Karen Shepherd, and Irene Fisher.[86] The script referenced the contribution of Mormon women to the women's rights movement, placed contemporary efforts into that context, and voiced once again the issues these women had found most important. Preceding what was called a commitment ceremony, the women walked in silence with lighted candles, sang, and prayed—one of them invoking God's help to "burn into our hearts the memory of our foremothers who struggled in this . . . desert, . . . [of] our proud but hidden history." In reaffirming their dedication to the cause of women's rights, a reader pronounced: "Sisters and brothers, our silence and solidarity have given birth to new determination among us, smoldering anger has been transformed into new energy. We can move forward confidently with strength and courage. No obstacle is too great to be overcome. We have heard the call to justice and equality and we will never back down."[87]

Their specific goals had been articulated by several generations of women's rights activists: full citizenship; help for the poor; equal pay; acknowledgment of the value of the hard work and good lives of widows, divorced women, and the elderly; educational and other opportunities for young women; equality before the law; and passage of the Equal Rights Amendment.[88]

In Washington D.C. the ERA dominated a two-hour hearing before the Senate Judiciary Committee on the confirmation of forty-six-year-old Rex E. Lee for the office of U.S. Solicitor General. Representatives from NOW, Mormons for ERA, and other women's organizations testified. Teddie Wood charged that Lee "represents both the Mormon Church and the Reagan administration" and is "an extension of my church's feverish crusade against women's rights, the same crusade that resulted in the excommunication of Sonia Johnson." Judith Lichtman of the Women's Legal Defense Fund condemned Lee for his publication, *A Lawyer Looks at ERA*, saying it gave evidence of "an unacceptable bias and insensitivity" toward women. This was seconded by Iris Mitgang of the National Women's Political Caucus.[89]

Lee responded that he was committed to equality through legislation and administrative action and that if any cases came before his court involving either the Mormon Church or the ERA, he would "step aside."[90]

However, he confirmed his unwavering objection to the ERA based on his belief that Congress, instead of the courts, should resolve women's issues. He asserted that he had an "unblemished" record on women's rights issues. Senator Edward M. Kennedy asked him how many women were enrolled at BYU's law school, to which Lee responded that only 16 percent of the students and one faculty were women.[91] However, as solicitor general, he would sustain the government's policies and defend its point of view on such matters, he said.[92] When the question of his appointment came before the entire Senate on July 31, Mormons Paula Hawkins of Florida and Orrin Hatch of Utah defended him, and his nomination was confirmed with only fifteen voting against.[93]

In September the LDS Citizens Coalition was busy in Virginia placing flyers on windshields endorsing candidates who had taken a position against the ERA.[94] The next month in Utah, another prayer vigil was planned for October 2, a few days before LDS general conference. Utah state senator Frances Farley addressed the group. Karen Gibbs, a local musician, performed a short concert, followed by a series of historical vignettes depicting the lives of early Mormon women and the women's movement at Seneca Falls, New York. Those in attendance wore white, purple, or gold ribbons remembering the three colors historically associated with suffragists.[95]

The Final Moments

In the four states NOW targeted for the countdown campaign, anti-ERA forces similarly redoubled their efforts and support for the ERA waned. NOW found it significant that two-thirds of the female legislators and all black legislators in the four states voted for the ERA, meaning that the amendment was defeated due to the "gender and racial imbalance in the legislatures." NOW was unable to persuade the white male representatives, so the opposition carried the day.[96]

For the first time in eight years, the ERA appeared on the agenda in the Georgia legislature in 1982. In January, LDS regional representative Richard Winder organized the Relief Society under his jurisdiction to flood the legislature with letters. Sunday School class time was devoted to the campaign. According to the *Mormons for ERA Newsletter,* Latter-day Saints, writing as "citizens" but not identifying their religion, generated a quarter-million anti-ERA letters.[97] The Georgia house of representatives rejected the amendment, 116-57.

On January 9, a group of nine ERA supporters calling themselves the Congressional Union chained themselves to the gates of the Washington D.C. temple, hoping LDS leaders would speak with them. Although not among the nine, Sonia Johnson acted as their spokesperson. "No one will get in [the temple] until the president, . . . Wendell Eames, comes out to listen to us," she asserted. She led protest songs and carried a sign reading, "Bigots Make Bad Missionaries." Twelve other women carried hand-sewn banners in suffragist purple and gold outside the visitors center. The police arrived, but after Eames came out to talk to the women, they dispersed peaceably without arrests. The father of a bride posing for pictures on the temple grounds stated somewhat incoherently: "Don't you think it's illegal that these women are keeping us kidnaped in here? If these women knew anything about the Mormon religion they wouldn't be here. Mormon women have more freedom than any others, because they're married to their husbands for eternity. That's all they need."[98]

The day after the Virginia legislative session of January 13, Johnson spoke to the Northern Virginia Women's Political Caucus about her recent autobiography, *From Housewife to Heretic*. She voiced optimism about the ERA. "We must organize the members of the legislature to organize for us," she said, predicting dire consequences if the ERA failed because there would still be "sixteen thousand discriminatory laws" on the books throughout the country. She told reporters the patriarchs who excommunicated her "made me a feminist and a political activist. I've never been in better spiritual shape, but I'm not a Mormon anymore."[99] Perhaps enthused by the warm welcome she typically received from such groups, she said she would rather look forward than live in the past.

The pro-ERA forces in Virginia formed a coalition called "We Will Ratify in 1982" and mounted a strenuous effort with the General Assembly. "It's looking pretty good," Davey Anderson said from the coalition headquarters—"the big push from Richmond," as he called it.[100] But despite such enthusiasm, the ERA once again failed in Virginia.

Nearby in Maryland a nineteen-year-old Mormon, Melissa Mowen, who was attending college in Hagerstown, wrote several pro-ERA letters to the editor of the local newspaper, one of them protesting Judge Marion Callister's refusal to recuse himself in Idaho. Mowen, her mother, five friends, and two Mormons for ERA from Virginia carried protest signs outside Melissa's stake conference in Hagerstown, to which Melissa's bishop, Albert Taylor, responded by scheduling a church court for March 2. Fifty ERA supporters came to the chapel along with reporters from the *Baltimore Sun*, AP, UPI, Cable News, and other media outlets.[101] Taylor decided to postpone the trial "because of the intense media scrutiny" and evicted the supporters and news people from the church foyer. Unrepressed, the pro-ERA women held a rally outside the chapel.[102] The bishop never rescheduled the trial.

The Countdown Campaign in North Carolina included TV ads, door-to-door canvassing, phone banking, and speaking tours, culminating in a massive demonstration in Raleigh.[103] Polls showed that over 60 percent of North Carolinians were in favor of the ERA. Members of the senate who were anti-ERA retreated to the legislature's chapel and took a "solemn pledge" to table the amendment before it came to a vote. The next day, the senate voted 27 to 23 (ten anti-ERA Republicans being joined by seventeen Democrats) to table the issue.[104]

It was the same in Florida where thousands of ERA supporters rallied in Tallahassee after the house voted 60-58 in favor of ratification. The senate killed the measure 22 to 16. Angry demonstrators chanted outside the state house "We'll remember in November!"[105]

Sonia Johnson and some others fasted for thirty-seven days during the summer of 1982, hoping to pressure the Illinois legislature.[106] The house voted 103 to 72 in favor, four votes short of the required three-fifths majority. This was the day after the ERA was defeated in Florida. Prior to this, NOW had tried to have the three-fifths rule changed but had been unsuccessful.[107]

On June 30, 1982, the dreaded deadline for ratification passed and the ERA died a silent death. There had been a four-year lull since the last state had ratified it. Women on both sides were exhausted. Some gradually emerged to try to understand what had happened and, in that sense, revisit the issues.

Mormons for ERA proved up to this challenge by sending out a survey with their newsletter to try to determine what kind of woman had joined their campaign. One hundred and seventy women in twenty-seven different states sent in answers. Most of the respondents were from California (24.7 percent), Utah (22.4 percent), and the Washington D.C. area (10 percent).[108] They ranged in age from twenty-one to seventy-nine, with an average age of 45.7. Eighty-eight percent were women. They were exceptionally well educated: 40 percent had a graduate (master's or Ph.D.) degree. Many were employed: 68.2 percent, while the others were homemakers (15.4 percent), students (8.2 percent), retired people (8.2 percent).

Perhaps the most intriguing figure was 47.6 percent first-born children in a range of single-child families all the way to those with twelve siblings—a birth position highly correlated with independence. Thirty-one percent described themselves as active members of the LDS Church; 19.5 percent had been excommunicated or had voluntarily removed themselves from the church rolls. The correlation between feminism and disenchantment with Mormonism was high: 47.6 percent no longer attended church. In two fill-in responses, the confusion and rage that typified women's attitudes toward the ERA controversy were evident. One question, "In what way has the church's stand on the ERA influenced your religious activity or beliefs?" was answered variously:

> My activity is unchanged, but my beliefs are profoundly affected. I no longer believe unquestioningly in the church as the "only true church."

> I have been annoyed and perplexed, but have kept being active. One seldom believes in everything his/her organization does.

> I have lost a great deal of enthusiasm and would no longer consider fel-

lowshipping people. I have lost respect for the leaders because of the ERA policies.

It was the last straw. I noticed no Mormons in civil rights marches for blacks. It made me notice the church's racism, and then I saw its sexism.

It has made me examine my positions more carefully than I otherwise might; and, subsequently, I'm more sure of where I stand.

I seethe with rage, and I shall never enter the church as long as it misrepresents the ERA or subsequent efforts for equality. [This respondent was seventy-nine years old.]

The church's stand on ERA is entirely consistent with their theology which is patriarchal.

Another open-ended question asked: "Do you think that women should have equal rights within the church?" A whopping 92.4 percent of the respondents said yes, then added:

Church policies concerning priesthood and motherhood are unjustly balanced. Priesthood is for every worthy male, but motherhood is not for every worthy female, no matter how much she may desire it.

People should have equal options and equal respect. The sex of the individual should not be a factor.

I'm not concerned about holding the priesthood, but the priesthood (men) could give us more say in decision making.

Spirituality has nothing to do with the sex of the individual.

Women tend to be more faithful, diligent, and conscientious in responsibilities. So if they do the work, why shouldn't they have the authority and credit?

I do not believe Mormon theology and "equal rights" could mesh.

Interestingly, most of the women had known little about feminism or the ERA before Sonia Johnson's excommunication. As the story circulated widely in the media, it alerted them to problems they had not noticed before. "I am grateful to the church," one woman wrote, "for excommunicating Sonia because my feminist education would have been delayed many years."[109]

Conclusion

In sociologist Kendall White's opinion, pro-ERA Mormons made tactical errors that created disharmony within their own ranks and weakened their effectiveness. The decision by MERA to go ahead with the banner tow over general conference caused a crisis of conscience for members of the Utah branch, yet these same Utah members marched in the Pioneer Day parade carrying balloons reading "ERA YES."[110] What made one event acceptable and the other not? White astutely observed: "As the resource mobilization model predicts, those tactics which brought the most attention to their cause, and to which they owe much of their success, are precisely the ones causing internal divisions due to their lack of legitimacy in the broader society."[111] Non-Mormons enjoyed the modestly dressed wives and mothers who dared speak out in public; more traditional appeals through letters, speeches, debates, talk shows, and interviews in the media were less controversial than the message banners flying over Temple Square, public fasts, and women chaining themselves to the temple gates, which generated feelings of approval and outrage outside and inside the organization.

The church's activities played out in the public arena and in the private, or at least semi-public, forums within ward meetinghouses. The opening salvo in the *Church News* reached a mostly LDS audience but was effective. Byron Fisher and Beth Jarman, the original sponsors of the bill for ratification in the Utah legislature, were dismayed to see how suddenly support for the amendment evaporated after this relatively quiet appeal to readers of the church newspaper. A few would eventually criticize the First Presidency after its 1976 statement and subsequent speeches for breaching its own hands-off policy toward politics, but the cumulative impact on local politics was persuasive.

Mormon women across the nation, especially in the contested states where they were organized to work against ratification, gave of themselves unstintingly. Few besides Beverly Campbell and Barbara Smith were known outside the boundaries of their own stakes or spoke to more than local media, but the grassroots women faithfully represented the intent of their church and learned to couch their message in terms shared widely by other traditional women. It was their belief in the prophet's foresight that fueled their truly heroic efforts; yet ironically, they were most effective when they were not known as Mormons.

The public campaign, as the church's resources were used to mobilize volunteers and distribute literature, generated a debate over the use of ecclesiastical power in the political arena. The church was heavily involved in Arizona, Florida, Missouri, Nevada, North Carolina, and Utah, but only in Virginia was a counter-movement of Mormons formed. Four committed women, dedicated to the cause of women's rights, constituted the critical mass. Responding in part to the officially authorized and funded LDS Citizens Coalition, the group's immediate objective was "revealing—disclosing—the role of the Mormon church in the anti-ERA campaign, thus establishing an important niche in the feminist movement."[112] The earliest tangible result was public scrutiny of the lobby's finances, forcing the covert organizational structure to comply with state lobbying registration laws.[113] In the process, Mormons for ERA learned how to position themselves effectively with national and local media.

According to White, social dissidents eventually withdraw from the main body when they realize that their needs are not being met. "The formal expulsion of a group like Mormons for ERA may produce some internal conflict, but it is not likely to be sufficient to challenge the church.... A more probable scenario is a growing disenchantment among Mormons who are strongly committed to the ERA that culminates in voluntary forms of dissociation and withdrawal."[114] To the degree the church is able to maintain general discipline and present a united front, such defections actually ease the tension within the church in the short run because, for all practical purposes, it ends the dialogue. But negative publicity and the high emotional costs of expelling formerly loyal members can have long-range effects that cause internal questions by policy makers and a search for less drastic measures.

As soon as Mormons for ERA organized, they formalized an association with the National Woman's Party as a special committee. Sonia Johnson was welcomed by Elizabeth Chittick. It was Johnson's belief that their shared commitment to ratification had brought them together and created enough common ground that "perhaps a small group called Mormons for ERA," connected to the NWP's "solid political base, access to nearly seventy years' experience with ERA, [its] financial assistance, and lots of encouragement, could play a role in neutralizing the effects of the church's Schlaflyesque performance in the United States."[115] But Mormons for ERA proved to be too independent to maintain this relationship for long and soon moved to a more comfortable affiliation with NOW. A frequent speaker at NOW meetings, Johnson liked the strategies of this group, which made an alliance easy to establish and maintain. Perhaps the most colorful example was NOW's plan to send out missionaries modeled after the Mormon missionary program.

In response to Mormons for ERA, local LDS leaders occasionally moved to discredit its members and neutralize or overwhelm them by more widespread activities and cooperation with other anti-ERA groups, according to White. The church also moved to appropriate LDS women's history, frequently mentioning the historical contributions of LDS women and specifically the early contributions to the women's rights movement. By embracing feminist history within the church itself, it went a long way toward neutralizing the claim that pro-ERA forces were the real women's rights activists. The church positioned itself as the true advocates for women, casting Mormons for ERA members as misguided malcontents.

Another tactic on the part of the LDS Church that undermined the effectiveness of Mormons for ERA was a repeated emphasis on MERA's opposition to the First Presidency. The church stressed the importance of seeking divine answers to political questions as something each person must do in exercising individual free agency. *The Church and the Proposed*

Equal Rights Amendment reminded women that they should not blindly follow but should seek "confirmation" of which path to take: "But what if an individual feels his 'confirmation' does not support the First Presidency's statement? When the Apostle Paul was approached by members espousing their own interpretations, he resolved their dilemma by asking: 'Every one of you saith I am of Paul; and I of Apollos; and I of Cephas; and I of Christ. Is Christ divided?'"[116]

The implication was that one could disagree, but disagreement demonstrated a serious flaw in one's spiritual health. The publication suggested that true Saints do not question or "demean" their leaders or openly encourage "others to interfere with [the church's] mission."[117] The profile of the misguided critic made Johnson a believable candidate for excommunication. According to White, "If the subsequent excommunication of Ms. Johnson reminded Mormons of the consequences of challenging church authorities, it also provided the vehicle by which Mormons for ERA could effectively use the media to present its message, build its support, and confront church leaders." In White's view, "The media became the most important environmental actor for the mobilization of economic, political, and social resources."[118]

That may be something of an overstatement—one that reduces the complex forces at work to a simple shoving contest. According to historian Mary Frances Berry, the ERA failed because of the following set of obstacles:

> State by state the failure to gain ratification, although including peculiar local circumstances (such as the Illinois requirement that three-fifths of each House is necessary instead of a simple majority), proceeded from the same problems. There was a basic liberal-conservative political split, a regional split, a divergence of attitudes toward women, and differences of ideology. The proponents needed much more in the way of resources and organization because they were in the defensive position of trying to subvert the opponents, led by Schlafly, because they did not pay careful attention to the necessity for a state-by-state consensus. They then had to play catch-up. They did not understand that issues of the role of women, abor-

> tion, the draft, and the family would find so much opposition that they had to be debated and combated affirmatively.[119]

Berry's emphasis on the nature of the debate itself, the style and substance of argumentation, speaks to the power of words. Language rich in imagery was able to conjure up the darkest fears of conservative women, and this is what ultimately won the battle. The anti-ERA campaign was waged in the images placed in the minds of men and women before it ever played out in the state legislatures.

The International Women's Year also played a powerful role in the unfolding ERA drama. These conferences paraded women in front of television cameras, across stages, and onto convention floors, demonstrating to the public the widespread support for the amendment. There could not have been a louder warning cry to the new right, inviting opponents to leap onto the bandwagon and combat not only the ERA but everything feminists seemed to embrace.

In the minds of conservatives, the fact that the feminist agenda linked the ERA with other hot-button issues diffused the movement's ability to engender support. Instead of giving conservatives the opportunity to choose equity ostensibly unencumbered by other social causes, it left nothing to chance. It seemed to be an all-or-nothing proposition.

The pacing of the push for the ERA was also significant in its demise. Enthused by early successes—twenty-two states ratified in the first year—activists did not think to spend enough time to work individually with legislators in other states. Perhaps over-confident about success, feminists became complacent. Across the board, ERA proponents were insufficiently organized for ratification on a local level. As Berry points out, the conflict that emerged when conservatives entered the scene worked against ratification:

> When there is no conflict over an issue and some perceived advantages to supporting it, legislators—whatever their personal views—will often vote for it, as they did in the early ratifying states. But when conflict arises, they often try to avoid conflict by doing nothing. In this case classic legislative behavior meant not ratifying and, if they really were philosophically op-

> posed to begin with, voting in the negative. Ideology, inter-party rivalry, and partisan politics, then, may all come into play. Then only if minds can be changed, as legislators perceive they will lose office by opposition, will they vote positively. Given the deep divisions among women in the non-ratifying states, legislators did not need to fear retribution for voting against ERA, and not many minds were changed.[120]

Given the initial general inertia on the part of pro-ERA women, when a highly organized, hierarchical organization such as the Mormon Church decided to act, it was a formidable opponent. Within days of the call to arms, Mormons mobilized, gathered contributions, and willingly spent time defending cherished beliefs. Almost overnight, apathetic legislators began hearing repeatedly and forcefully from people within their districts that the ERA was a bad idea.

By the time NOW realized what was happening, it was too late. In 1977, NOW called for an economic boycott of unratified states. The following year, 202 groups intentionally convened their meetings in states that had ratified. Political scientist Slava Lubudomorova remembers planning to attend a conference of the American Sociological Science Association, originally scheduled for Nevada. Instead, planners staged the conference in a hotel straddling the border with California, thereby refusing to support an unratified state. Cities like Atlanta, Chicago, Kansas City, Las Vegas, Miami, and New Orleans lost more than $100 million in convention funds. While the boycott was a powerful weapon, it was ultimately ineffective because it did not convert individual women to the cause or further mobilize them, it hurt states, angered opponents, and confused the issue.[121]

On the other hand, some of the legislative changes ERA opponents had said would benefit women were, in fact, passed. In 1981 Congress allowed state courts to divide military pensions equally among divorced couples. In 1984 Congress passed legislation facilitating child support payments and pension payments for women.

Even if the ERA had passed, it would not have solved the myriad problems facing women. However, it would have committed the government to a particular course of action and helped create legal uniformity in women's status. More importantly, it would *not* have coerced women into particular lifestyle choices. Its influence would have been felt more by federal and state governments than by private citizens. It would not have changed public opinion or traditional attitudes or views toward women.

Why did the ERA fail? Surely one important reason was that supporters failed to credit the millions of housewives and traditional families who felt threatened by unpredictable changes that might result from the ERA. The woman's liberation movement asked America to recognize the power of women, millions of whom did not fit conveniently into feminist categories and felt threatened in what they valued most, with no guarantee of a better alternative.

Time constraints, necessity, regional diversity in ways of gaining consensus, the positive influence of Supreme Court decisions, and disinformation spread by the opponents all proved to be crucial in the defeat of the ERA.[122] Yet, despite the amendment's failure, the long-term results have been immense. Janet Boles observes:

> The debate over the ERA served as the impetus for changing the course of public policy on the status of women in court decisions, federal and state laws, and bureaucratic procedures. It was accompanied by a virtual revolution in public opinion on the proper role and rights of women in society. Furthermore, the conflict mobilized women on both sides of the issue; it brought them together in coalitions and into politics.[123]

The rhetorical strategies of each side reflected divergent understandings of the nature of women and their role in society. An examination of persuasive tactics used in the conflict contributes to an understanding of the ERA's failure. Personal attacks, character assassination, and negative accusations sought to discredit the other side; but the rhetoric of conservatives was by far the most effective.

First, scare tactics worked. Questions about what would happen if the ERA were ratified conjured up unforgettable images of social chaos and deprivation. Second, an appeal to tradition, employing a biblical model of hierarchical relationships and traditional gender roles, drew on a familiar form of reasoning that began with religious assumptions and seemed to imply religious validation. Third, patriarchal authority shifted the grounds of the argument from equity to an issue of faith, which for Mormons included support of the prophet.

Defending the status quo capitalized on the subjective experience of the women themselves. They saw what worked and what did not, and they sought to protect what they had. Experience, personal judgment, and common sense, rather than empirical research and logic, seemed to dictate the shape of this type of argument.

13. A case study

> We have got to stop living on borrowed light. Or in the shadow of husbands and church authorities. Borrowed light is a church expression. You have to live on your own light within you, make your own decisions.
>
> —Jan Tyler

Documenting the daily life of women from the past is difficult. Her daily grind might have been filled with diapers, laundry; worries about children, husbands, or friends; singing in the church choir; gardening; rounds of sewing; cooking; packing away ages of clothing outgrown by children; and pressing the tracings of lives into scrapbooks. Such daily activities serve to draft more recognizable outlines of a woman's life than changes of law which, for many, seem no more than a faint line on the horizon. In short, tracking how shifts in the women's movement impacted real lives of individual women is tricky at best. Those who cared passionately about the outcome wrote letters to the editors of their local papers. Among Mormon women, those empowered by positions in their ward Relief Societies or legislative districts and who received authoritative instructions from trusted male leaders to become involved, to form opinions, to fight on a side designated as righteous—and to do this by attending conferences and caucuses and hearings—sprang quickly into action. However, most did not. The overwhelming majority did not get involved, read about the issues, listen to media debates, form discussion groups with friends, raise questions in Relief Society classes, or telephone their legislators. Their worlds were shaped by their ideas about religion, tradition, and their historical roles in families, neighborhoods, and wards. They were more likely to act out their inclinations for political or civic involvement in PTA meetings than at women's conferences.

It was the church itself that thrust so many of these women into their state IWY conferences or into state contests against the ERA's ratification or for its rescission. For some of the women, the glimpse of how democratic politics worked was energizing and they continued their involvement even after the ERA was a dead letter. But in most cases, after the season of crisis was over, women thankfully returned to their former lives.

Those who had been drafted into their roles as conservative activists outnumbered the women who stepped forward on their own. On the other side, it was volunteers who stepped forward on their own who filled the ranks of the small organizations such as Mormons for ERA. Ironically, the MERA women had been spurred into action by the same church that was energizing the conservative women, and it was the church that had given the liberal volunteers experience in organizational and speaking skills needed to succeed in their campaign. It was at church that these women had learned how to persuasively articulate their most deeply held values and to persevere in the face of discouragement.

Both groups of women—those who supported and those who opposed the Equal Rights Amendment—sensed the power they had in numbers and believed they might use their influence to sway public opinion and shape political outcomes. They came together, like hundreds of other groups of American women around the country, for support, for advice on how others were grappling with extraordinarily challenging issues, for sharing some of their private pain and cherished hopes about what the future would be like for their daughters. They came together with the best of intentions. Many wanted to remain faithful to their church, to be supportive of their husbands and bishops, but were plagued by a gnawing certitude that something was wrong. It would be oversimplifying to say that for the liberals, it was the status quo that was wrong, while for the conservatives, it was change that was wrong. This was true at both extremes, but somewhat muddled in the middle. Many of the devout Mormons wanted better answers about the attitude of their church toward women and, perhaps more importantly, where they fit into the scheme of things in a day when women lived forty years beyond child-bearing and often finished a college degree before marriage. The pioneer model did not fit anymore, but what did?

The Alice Louise Reynolds Forum

A glimpse into one of the groups that was organized as women were struggling to make sense of this new world, the Alice Louise Reynolds Women's Forum, is possible thanks to the excellent records kept by its members during this critical period.[1] The group formed on September 24, 1977, three months after the catastrophic Utah IWY conference. Friends of Jan Tyler, the state IWY conference chair, wanted to show their support for her. Not only had she been verbally harassed during the conference, she was followed to her car by women who had hoped to prevent her from returning to the conference. Hostess for the initial gathering of the Alice Louise Reynolds Forum in Orem, Utah, was Anna Taylor. Although their intent was to support Tyler, they found they had deeper commonalities. A feeling lingered afterward that the gathering had been good.

Two months later at the national IWY meeting in Houston, Utah's women were stigmatized by association with the Ku Klux Klan and the John Birch Society (see chaps. 8-9), which the women who had met together in Orem felt to be an additional insult, but one they thought was elicited by the extremism of Utah's delegation. Several women had heard talks by the elected delegates, talks that had stressed the shock, fear, sense of siege, and polarized thinking that had characterized the state IWY conference. Troubled by the reverberations of this ongoing turmoil, Jan Tyler, Rachel Heninger, Helen Candland Stark, and Wanda Scott called another meeting on January 21, 1978. Sitting around a long table at the BYU cafeteria, winter sunlight filtering through the two-story windows, they focused on how each saw her feminist views intersecting with church doctrine. Each woman, in highlighting a particular issue, revealed much about who she was—her jobs and talents, her particular sensitivities, and a unique vantage point.

Stark noted her reaction in a summary of the meeting: "We felt almost subversive to be meeting as feminists, a dirty word. I had thought the group might just 'fold,' and maybe that would be best, but there seemed to be a felt need for it and it took off with renewed vigor."[2]

The group met monthly between January 1978 and April 1981. They gave themselves a name, a schedule, and an agenda. Fern Smoot Taylor, Anna Taylor's sister-in-law, described the format that emerged:

> For the first four or five meetings, when our group was small (15 or 20), we formed our chairs in a circle where we could discuss our problems informally, with Anna Taylor or Fern Taylor as moderator. After the public was invited (this included men) and the attendance increased (30 to 100 or more), we used a conventional seating arrangement, with officers and speakers seated on the front row. For the first year, the meetings were chaired by either Anna Taylor or Fern Taylor. At later meetings, turns at conducting were extended to Loneta Murphy and occasionally to Jan Tyler.[3]

Algie Ballif recalled that the group was "always informal" and "very loosely organized. . . . We never elected a president, we had no membership except [that we] phoned members we wanted to notify about meetings. We had no dues. It just seemed to spontaneously grow; the need was there for women to get together and discuss their problems and, of course, men too if they so desired."[4] Men did meet with them from time to time, expressing an awareness that feminist issues impacted both women and men. In a dramatic departure from most gatherings of this type, it seldom served refreshments. Within the first year, the group opened meetings to the public and even advertised in the *Provo Daily Herald.*

It might seem at first glance that highly conservative Orem or Provo would be an unlikely spot for such a gathering, but it was not. A century earlier when Utah women were fighting for the vote, women like Zina Presendia Young Williams, Brigham Young Academy's first matron, and her half-sister, Susa Young Gates, had launched ambitious, authorized programs of education for the church's young women.[5] Since that time, generations of influential, smart, faithful, and talented women in Utah County had played prominent roles in politics, education, and social life.[6]

This new group of feminists called themselves the Alice Louise Reynolds Forum after a historic ladies' literary and cultural club of the same name, honoring the revered BYU educator who had taught and mentored some of them. Reynolds (1873-1938) was the daughter of George and Mary Ann Tuddenham Reynolds and graduated from BYA at age seventeen to continue her studies at Columbia, Cornell, the University of Michigan, Berkeley, the University of Chicago, and schools in London and Paris. She was the second female professor in Utah and the first at BYU, where she taught English literature for more than four decades. Never married, she was renowned for her mix of highly demanding standards and, simultaneously, acts of kindness toward her students. She energetically worked for women's suffrage, was active in politics, served on the LDS Relief Society general board, edited the *Relief Society Magazine* for seven years, wrote curricula for the Relief Society, Sunday School, and Young Women's Mutual Improvement Association, and worked determinedly on BYU's library committee to build its collection by more than 7,000 volumes during her thirty-four years of service.[7]

Two spunky septuagenarian sisters among the membership of the Reynolds Forum, Algie Eggertsen Ballif and Thelma Eggertsen Weight, had been students of Reynolds. When they belonged to the predecessor Reynolds Club, it had had a constitution and bylaws, took attendance, and had a rule that anyone who missed more than a certain number of meetings would be dismissed from the group. In addition to other chapters located along the Wasatch Front, the organization had chapters as far away as St. George and Hurricane, Utah, and even in New York City. They kept dues, restricted the number of members, and invited guests to speak on topics of interests.

In its reincarnation, the decision on what to name the club paid tribute not just to a beloved teacher but also to the ideal of the many smart, strong women who had flourished within the early Mormon society, who had made professional and ecclesiastical as well as domestic contributions. In the same way, the women of the forum represented the combination of strength and allegiance to a church they regrettably saw as working against the women's movement.

The Reynolds Forum was like many groups nationally. As the women's movement picked up speed, consciousness-raising groups offered new opportunities for reexamining relationships between men and women and the role women played in society more broadly. "Click" and "getting it" entered the national vocabulary as expressions of when a woman first glimpsed the systemic privileging of men, no matter how healthy and happy her own relationships with men might have been. Opponents produced such nicknames as "women's libber" and "bra-burner," portraying the world of fear that opened up if a woman asked unsettling questions at home, in the workplace, in classrooms, and from the speakers' stands. Bookstores were busy adding shelves and sections to accommodate the new genre called "women's studies," as a flood of opportunities presented themselves for self-improvement, assertiveness training for energetic involvement in mainstream society, and a variety of narratives directing women through the distinctive female "passages" of their lives.

Some of the Forum's Women

In many ways, the Reynolds Forum took its tone from Algie Ballif, Thelma Weight, and Helen Stark. If there were an elite within this circle, it was typified by these three Mormon matriarchs.[8] Friends for decades, their lives had nevertheless run parallel courses; they were among the best the Mormon world had to offer—the product of church programs, Mormon culture and ideals, and shaped by almost Victorian training about the proper role of women, the relationships between men and women, and priesthood and motherhood. They were liberated by Mormonism's theology of free agency, the gospel of works, the parable of the talents, and their keen awareness of the historically autonomous role of

LDS women's organizations. Old enough to remember the suffrage movement of the 1920s, to them the ERA was simply "unfinished business."[9] Loyal to their bones, with a lifetime of committed service to church and community behind them, they had the poise to measure the efficacy of the ERA against their sense of what was right and fair rather than against the politicized discussions the church had entered.

Helen Candland Stark descended from Mormon pioneers, and her husband, Henry Stark, was a research chemist in Delaware, where they raised their adopted three children. Described by Lavina Fielding Anderson as a "teacher, actress, wife, mother, writer, environmentalist, and a feminist, all interpreted in her own distinctive style," Stark was well known as an essayist and sometime activist who was in her sixties when she and her husband moved to Utah Valley from the East Coast.[10] She had long been interested in women's issues and particularly in what she called the importance for women of developing "wholeness" in their lives. Given the BYU Emeritus Club Award in 1980, she twice won first prize in the *Relief Society Magazine*'s poetry contest (1940, 1957), served on the board of BYU Women's Archives and the Utah Women's History Association, wrote thoughtful essays on the dilemmas of modernity for Mormon women in *Exponent II*, and ultimately would be honored by having that magazine's annual essay contest named in her honor.[11] Among her many activities was expressing concern over censorship in local school districts and improving ecological awareness.

Algie Ballif was best known as a dance and physical education teacher. Helen Stark cleverly captured Ballif's essence when she said, "She has belonged actively to the human race, ministering to the educational, civic, and social needs of town and state, and through her work in the United Nations helping on a world level."[12] Ballif served for twenty-five years on the Provo City School Board, in the Utah legislature where she chaired the education committee, and was asked by President Kennedy to serve on the Commission on the Status of Women. Locally, she was active in her ward Relief Society. "For me, when Algie played Hecuba in *Trojan Women* on the stage in College Hall," commented Stark, "she was type-cast."[13]

Although Thelma Eggertsen Weight, Ballif's sister, was born in Provo at the end of the nineteenth century, she was very much a modern woman. Educated in the Provo public schools, she had graduated from Brigham Young University and then gone on to study out of state and become a social case worker in Denver. After returning to Utah, she became the Utah County welfare director under the Federal Emergency Relief Administration and chair of the women's division of the Civilian Workers Administration in Utah.[14] The two sisters were more than siblings—soul mates, best friends, and comrades in all good things. Thelma said at a September 1980 forum meeting:

> I'm proud to be Algie's sister. . . . As a family we were always ready to ask questions of our parents, and they answered us. . . . I took classes at the University of Chicago . . . [and] as we studied . . . religious experience, . . . I just couldn't leave it alone. Those things helped me to appreciate the type of searching that we are into now. . . . I do feel for the many women who have been oppressed, and whose lives, I think, have been fearful because of priestcraft; they have felt they couldn't do anything unless their husband said "that's okay," instead of being unafraid to use their own minds and their own free agency.[15]

These two compatible sisters were nearly always a team. Algie may have enjoyed the arts more, while Thelma found her greatest pleasure in politics; but they never missed an opening, a lecture, a demonstration, or a speech involving either. They were known to be forceful in their opinions, expressed with unfailing graciousness and enviable eloquence. Part of a generation that honored both depth and breadth in education and admired elocution, these two combined their Danish heritage of exemplary homemaking skills and hard work with unswerving devotion to their church, political independence, and civic responsibility.[16] They mentored younger women, setting an example of style, dignity, and intelligence that taught another generation how to be a woman of strength, faith, and warmth.

Wanda Scott brought with her extensive experience as an aide to U.S. Congressman Gunn McKay, having operated his Utah County office. She told how she was dismissed from her calling as a Relief Society teacher in 1979 because she publicly expressed support for the ERA. She shared her story in September 1980, saying: "I found a great deal of inequality between men and women in that last office I worked in. . . . Then, I was fired from my Relief Society job because they called and wanted to know how I felt about the lessons, and I thought they truly wanted to know." Candidly, she told her church leaders she was opposed to Beverly Campbell's Utah tour and was protesting by withholding her tithing for a month. "I had never ever spoken up before. I had questioned just a little, but I don't think I was really vocal. Nevertheless, those bad things happened to me because I expressed some questions or a little opposition."[17] She was born in the little alpine town of Charleston, Utah, in 1929 and received a bachelor's degree from BYU in 1951 in business education and accounting. She taught generations of young people over a twenty-three-year period at Provo High School, also serving during this time on the Provo City Power Board and as a county and state delegate to successive Democratic conventions. Because of her valuable political experience, she became a candidate for the Utah state legislature in 1980. Before working for Congressman McKay, she had served with U.S. Congressman Wayne Owens in Washington D.C. for two years.

Among the younger members of the Reynolds Forum was Nancy Kadar, who grew up in a blue-collar family where politics were debated across the dinner table each night. Like her family, she was a Democrat "because we thought it was the party of the working people."[18] In the Republican-dominated stronghold of Utah County, her political affiliation had drawn expressions of intolerance and sensitized her to the need for greater respect for diversity. She dreamed about the difference the ERA could make to divorced or single mothers, individuals with different beliefs. She was the mother of four young children and worked as an ICU nurse at Utah Valley Hospital. She was also a member of the State Nursing Board and secretary of the Governor's Commission on the Status of Women. Her husband, Omar, grew up in Provo as a Palestinian Muslim—an education in itself in minority relations—and was a BYU professor of international relations. Recognizing the unfairness of life where, for instance, the circumstances under which Omar's mother had grown up prevented her from learning how to read, Omar had become an ardent feminist. Nancy remembered the occasion when Algie called her up in 1989 to say, "Nancy, dear, did you know that so-and-so is attempting to pass this particular legislation? Why don't you take a minute to call his office and voice your concern—and get five other women to do the same?" She felt she could not turn down the request and afterward felt empowered enough to launch such initiatives on her own.[19]

Nancy was one of the first of the Reynolds Forum to take a public stand for the ERA. In August 1978, just a year after the IWY conference—a few days after Sonia Johnson's Senate testimony in defiance of Senator Hatch's filibuster threat—Kadar told a reporter: "Women for ERA have had a hard time speaking out. There are social pressures, and it can be job-threatening." She accurately read the political climate: "I believe right-wing groups have gone all-out to defeat it," she said, "and have used excessive funds to accomplish this—groups like Phyllis Schlafly, the Conservative Caucus and John Birch Society."[20] Mainstream women were frightened of being black-listed. Nancy responded sympathetically to that fear but not to the intemperate rhetoric that had created the threatening environment.

Another young member was Margaret Woodworth, a first-year law student in 1978. Her husband, Warner Woodworth, was a BYU professor of organizational behavior. As she contemplated the challenges that awaited her in balancing the demands of a legal career and motherhood, she staked out a moderate position. Interviewed during the summer of 1978, she expressed her belief that much of the contention among women originated in a general lack of respect for diversity. "There needs to be more mutual respect between them on their individual choices," she urged. "Women should not make judgments against each other. In many respects we need to be more sisterly toward each other."[21]

Woodworth considered the state's IWY conference a "great tragedy" that left "an unfortunate image of ourselves as women." She regretted that, while "we have so much to offer women in the nation," Utahns had "promoted a negative image rather than a positive one. We need to decide what we are for, rather than what we are against. We keep saying we are pro-family. But I have to ask, What families?" She said she felt shame that Utah's IWY voted down day care and aid for single mothers. She wanted Utah to be "a model" of how to "promote the family" without saying "a woman is bad because she is a divorcee; we can offer her and her children help. This would be in keeping with the pro-family image."[22]

With their similarities in interests and outlook, the women of the Reynolds Forum constituted a special interest group, but they were unlike other groups composed of young mothers, female professors, Republican or Democratic women, or those who liked discussing novels. Eventually numbering as many as a hundred, the women ranged in age from twenty to eighty. Homemakers tugged by the care of large families rubbed shoulders with younger people enthusiastically expressing ideals about, in the case of Woodworth, making the law more responsive to gender issues. Stay-at-home mothers and single mothers with full-time jobs shared their ideas with college professors who told of waging a daily war in trying to awaken young minds to powerful ideas about honoring women and defending justice. Grandmothers sympathized, comforted, and distilled their wisdom into these free-ranging discussions. Women with happy temple marriages, divorced women, never-married women all received the same respectful hearing and the same open response.

The Business of the Forum

In addition to their friendship and concern for Tyler, the women were drawn together by a more general interest in contemporary issues. On some level, they must have been conscious that they were living through a historic period and even participating in history-making; at least, their care in preserving their papers, minutes, and records seems to attest to as much.

However, their agenda was simply to host lively discussions paralleling the period of the most heated debate over the ERA. Their free-wheeling discussions served as a sort of sounding board to sift and refine their sense of what mattered and what did not. They provided personal support, safe opportunities for discussion, and the intellectual rigor that led to refined argument. Some in the group quickly adopted the description of "feminist" for themselves, and the group welcomed this self-discovery, including the inevitable anger that accompanied awareness of injustices. Others were tentative when issues seemed to challenge the traditional party line, but the group tried to accept anxiety while maintaining a common ground for feminism and faith, guarding each woman's right to speak her mind in her own voice.

Loneta Murphy joined the League of Women Voters in the late 1970s and said she found it difficult to speak with state legislators. "It was a great surprise to me to find that Utah was dragging its heels, or dragging her heels, or really his heels" on the ERA, she told the Reynolds Forum in September 1980. "This . . . has put me into some very awkward positions in the church. . . . My temple recommend was voided because of my ERA position. . . . Going against the current church policy during the decade of the seventies has cost a terrific price in my health and on my community image. But I think in the long run, in the total picture, I will be considered one of many who made things happen. So for that, I am grateful."[23]

With such vitally important issues to work through, and at such a timely period, the forum found that almost no one dropped out of the group during its first years. It was not until women's issues began to fade in the light of some more immediate social forces, particularly the economic downturn of the 1980s, and natural life events such as relocations to other states and the illness and death of two of the group's most energetic members, Thelma Weight and Algie Ballif, that interest began to wane.

When these women sat in a circle at their first meeting, it was largely a group of strangers, although everyone knew at least one other person and some had worked with each other on different church or civic projects. But most had never shared what was in their hearts in the same way or with the same objective before. Their attendance was an act of great hope and faith in what other women could contribute to a quest for meaning. Some of them had attended the sweaty, anger-charged IWY conference in June 1977. In the months that unrolled, they followed the debates, sent money to Mormons for ERA, read and reread—then carefully analyzed—the statements by Barbara Smith, Elder Packer, and President Kimball that appeared in the press. They plunged into Mormon history and theology to find empowering precedents. They found provocative explanations and predictions in sociological and feminist theory. They wept when Sonia Johnson went on trial for her membership in Virginia in December 1979.

As they fell into a routine, the group settled on the second Saturday of each month from 2:00 to 4:00 p.m. in the Harold B. Lee Library on the BYU campus in the aptly named Alice Louise Reynolds Room, for which some members of the group had helped raise funds and decorated with comfortable furniture and art. Sometimes discussions spilled over beyond the two-hour allotment and were continued at Ballif's Victorian home near campus. Procedures had more in common with the informality of a therapy group than with Roberts's rules of order. About half the meetings consisted of in-group sharing, processing, and discussing in a multi-voiced dialogue that was sometimes exhausting but more frequently energizing. Guest speakers sometimes made formal presentations. Panels were sometimes organized to give voice to a range of opinions. The topics ranged widely and were about issues that most directly shaped the lives of Mormon women—ERA, polygamy, gender roles, discrimination, Planned Parenthood, rape, poverty, the environment, and the U.S. Constitution. Key women involved in national political campaigns spoke on several occasions, thus allowing the women to establish significant connections to other women's groups in different parts of the country.

Sonia Johnson spoke at the forum on two occasions. One of her presentations carried the catchy title, "Obedience to Authority: Or the Miss Jane Pittmans of the Church Are Marching Steadily toward the Fountain Marked 'Men Only,'" a reflection on how the small choices women make pull them toward social change. On another occasion, only two weeks after her testimony before the Senate subcommittee, she gave a vivid account of that experience. According to Loneta Murphy's minutes, the group agreed with her interpretation of the event "with only a few exceptions."[24] The forum supported Johnson when, because of her excommunication, she was seen by many as an object lesson in what happens when someone goes "too far." Such support, according to historian Amy Bentley, made the group seem "radical and dangerous" to the conservatives in Utah County.[25]

Congressman Gunn McKay attended the meeting on March 29, 1978, to discuss the political threat he saw posed by the far right. He described a church meeting in his home village of Huntsville, Utah, at which Cleon Skousen, former police chief of Salt Lake City, popular lecturer on the dangers of Communism, and founding president of the conservative Freemen Institute, distributed right-wing literature and claimed that church president David O. McKay had called him into politics. The Congressman mentioned a flyer that was being distributed in Moab that smeared him as a pro-abortion Communist, and that this was convincing enough to some people that, as Helen Stark's summary read, McKay was "running scared."

That the group had little sympathy for Skousen did not mean they let McKay off the hook on women's issues. "Reba Keele asked why we should support him when he had no women in any key position (his male first aide was also present, David Lee, and had managed to project a chauvinist image that had raised the hackles of many)." McKay "became quite defensive" as the women questioned him about "his anti-ERA vote, his anti-consumer legislation bill, etc." His attempts "to defend himself" failed to convince the women. "The discussion became quite heated, and the meeting broke up on a discordant note." Some of the women felt that a few of the members had been unnecessarily harsh and that McKay had "responded with reason. Others thought that he waffled." In any case, "he certainly knew he had been confronted."[26]

After further consideration, the group wrote McKay a conciliatory letter. Signed by the "Committee for BYU Meetings," it read:

> After your meeting with us at BYU, we were oppressed by the feeling that it

> had not gone well. Somehow we had slipped into an adversary relationship which was the last thing we intended.
>
> However, our concerns are real and deep, and our frustration level has unfortunately been building for some time, which may account for our sounding shrill. Nevertheless, as educated, thoughtful, creative women, we think that we do represent a wave of the future. Therefore, we increasingly resent being swept under the rug. We consider we have gifts to offer of time, energy, money, and especially new insights. These are gifts which none of Utah's Congressional delegates seems to want. We had hoped that you would.

Anxious to be understood, to be heard, they couched their argument in the familiar language of family negotiation rather than political confrontation: "Apparently we worry and alarm you. For this we are truly sorry. We may be prickly and thorny, but we had hoped that, taken under your fatherly wing, our detractors might discover that the ugly ducklings were indeed swans." They expressed their respect for McKay, however disappointed they had been by his positions: "We empathize with you in your precarious and embattled position. Life seems not to deal to either of us in certainties. We consider you a man of sincerity and integrity (albeit perhaps somewhat rigid). You likely consider us rabid feminists (which we think we aren't). Nevertheless, we want to cheer you on your way to success in the upcoming battle. With all of our hearts we wish you well."[27] There is no record of a response from McKay.

This interaction is interesting in that it shows how the women worked within a patriarchal framework, stating their opinions forcefully but with due respect and hope for cooperation. They deferred to the existing order while remaining just a step outside of it.

Minutes of other meetings mention energetic discussions. About half the women were not employed outside the home, so sex discrimination was more-or-less unfamiliar to many of them. However, they vigorously discussed the realities of female depression, dependency, ability to bond with other women, and the hot-button topics of Planned Parenthood and contraception. To gain a better perspective of the latter two issues, they invited guests for a panel discussion. The participants were a high school counselor, a registered nurse, the local director of Planned Parenthood, and a mother of teenage daughters. As was the norm for the group, many in attendance were pregnant or had brought their infants with them.

Mary Lythgoe Bradford attended the meeting on September 30, 1980, and announced that, as editor of *Dialogue: A Journal of Mormon Thought,* she would be shepherding an issue of the journal devoted to women, that it would be published on the anniversary of the famous "pink" issue which had appeared in 1971 and was guest-edited by influential Mormon women from the Boston area—Claudia Bushman, Laurel Thatcher Ulrich, and others—who went on to found *Exponent II*. Bradford's effort, published in the winter of 1981, came to be known as the "red" issue due to the designer's color choice. Bradford sometimes contributed articles to *Exponent II*. In one of these articles, she wrote about her visit to the Reynolds Forum, which she described as a "happening" organization where "a sense of bonding and trust generated deep sharing." She commented that "so much pain surfaced that almost everyone present was deeply moved." It was "a crisis year for women," she said, explaining that "as a result of an ecclesiastic directive, the LDS sisterhood appeared to be split into two hostile camps—those snugly within the framework, and those who felt confused, angry, and outside."[28]

Snapshot at Seventeen Months

When the group had been meeting together regularly for about a year and a half, a *Los Angeles Times* reporter visited the forum, leaving a colorful and insightful interpretation: "The twenty women, young and elderly, are sitting in a circle in the living room of a comfortable home here in the Salt Lake area, the long-chosen headquarters city for those of the Church of Jesus Christ of Latter-day Saints. At first glance, it would seem they have met for a sisterhood social, or perhaps an afternoon of sewing. But the talk is far too heavy to be hindered by needles and threads."[29] This article was important. At the time, some Mormon women were shocked by their post-Houston national image as ultra-conservatives who buddied up to the John Birch Society and Ku Klux Klan. In contrast, the members of the Reynolds Forum felt the pull of the women's movement but simultaneously felt satisfaction as wives or mothers and with their still deep-held faith. They found meaning in the joyful service they rendered to their church. The portrait that emerged from this article was one of full-toned lives, vivid political views, passionate opinions, and bold life-choices. Professionally, they included teachers, retired teachers, students, professional women, and housewives.

Their main concern, according to the *Times,* was the erosion of the boundary between church and state in the LDS Church. As one member of the group said, "It was not like that when I was growing up here. The church did not tell you what to do. It was not political. The church stressed your right to choose. Now, it has made a stand on the ERA, saying it will do the thinking for all of us. That is a right-wing approach." The women objected to the characterization of the ERA as a moral issue. "That's when the whole thing turned around," said a young woman in the group, a student. "That's when everyone started saying if you agree with ERA, you oppose the prophet. A lot of people presume that when the prophet speaks, it is the word of God. They are saying God is against the ERA. That is not true, it is the church politicking, not God."[30]

Some found the space they needed for their personal position on the ERA in the foundational Mormon doctrine of free agency. Among them was Jan Tyler. "We have got to stop living on borrowed light," she said. "Or in the shadow of husbands and church authorities. Borrowed light is a church expression," she explained in an aside to the reporter. "You have to live on your own light within you, make your own decisions. Unfortunately, when you say things like that, the church authorities often misinterpret it as abandoning the family or your responsibilities. That is just not true." She assumed that others would feel the same and was surprised when more traditional women disagreed.

This dynamic of doubt versus faith and agency versus obedience was a complicated one that produced intense anxiety and fear for many people. "You must realize," a retired teacher told the reporter, "how hard it is for us to speak out. Some terrible things have been going on here. When we first started this group, about a year and a half ago, one woman came to me and said, almost whispered, 'This is the first time I haven't trusted implicitly. But I think President Kimball . . . is wrong on this. Women should be able to make up their own minds about themselves. We should have the right to choose."

An elderly matron spoke in agreement: "You understand that for Mormon women to say these things is almost heresy. Our traditions are deep-seated. We come from pioneer stock and have been good Mormons all our lives. We believe in the teachings, the doctrines of the church. But they are not discussing the issue. The issue is, 'Are you going to think for yourself?' not 'Are you going to follow the prophet?'" For her, a particularly troubling part of the problem was that the policy decisions rested with male leaders and were not distributed fairly and widely: "The whole idea is to keep the decision-making in the patriarchy. I can still believe in the prophet and support the ERA. But they don't understand that. They think if they give women too much power, we will want too much."

Teddie Wood, one of the "founding mothers" of Mormons for ERA, was visiting from Virginia and told the reporter she had been on "a quiet pilgrimage for a few days to talk with LDS women who support the Equal Rights Amendment—both publicly and from behind closed doors." She explained why some of the women would not allow their names to be used in the profile of their group. "They are afraid," she said. "And that is understandable. They would like to work within the framework of the church and change things, as we would. But there is the fear. Pure fear that speaking out would cause reprisals, or that they would not be able to function within the community. Or worse, that they may be excommunicated."

Loneta Murphy added her description of how individuals are marginalized: "You are talking about traumatic experiences of being shoved to the perimeter of the church because of your belief in the Equal Rights Amendment." Against this reality was her Mormon heritage, which she respected, honored, and felt was important to continue. "When we got statehood [in 1896]," she remembered, "we were for equal rights. Utah was one of the first three states in the women's suffrage movement in the 1890s, along with Colorado and Wyoming. And the church supported the women and equal rights. That's why we are so unhappy with the position the church is taking now. It is a 180-degree turnaround."

When the reporter asked the church's Public Communications spokesman, Jerry Cahill, about how the church treated such women, Cahill denied that the church was searching out dissenters and threatening them with ecclesiastical discipline. "Any threats or coercion is not the policy of the church," he said, but admitted there may be a few over-zealous bishops or stake presidents who had taken action against women who made their views public. He recalled President Ezra Taft Benson's statement that "the church was naturally concerned" about pro-ERA Mormons in the church, but that it was "their right to study the issues. The church will not coerce them into changing their minds."[31] Cahill no doubt represented the church as he saw it; but in the tension that followed Sonia Johnson's excommunication, even the friendliest meeting with a church officer carried, for women, the inevitable reminder of male power that could be wielded at will.

A few women calculated the cost to their own careers or to their husbands' careers at Brigham Young University or in the church hierarchy and quietly drifted away from the Reynolds group; but for most of the members, the mere fact that women were otherwise afraid to discuss the intersection of their faith with the world around them was a blaring klaxon that warned them of something dreadfully wrong. The occasional withdrawal from the group by a member who felt intimidated by the threat to her family by those who would punish feminists only stiffened the resolve of those who remained.

The Forum and the ERA

The Equal Rights Amendment was the featured topic at four meetings the first year of the forum's existence and four meetings over the next two years. At the first, Loneta Murphy gave a historical overview of equality issues in Utah, which set the stage for future discussions. Dixie Snow Huefner of Salt Lake City, who published an article in *Dialogue* about the International Women's Year convention in Houston, talked about production of the pamphlet, *Another Mormon View of ERA*. Jan Tyler paid tribute to Alice Paul, tireless proponent of the ERA who had kept the issue alive between 1923 and the 1970s. Sonia Johnson, author Linda Sillitoe, and historian Kathryn MacKay all spoke about Johnson's excommunication in 1978.

In an effort to understand the church's position, the group turned to the past, finding in their foremothers' fight for women's suffrage evidence that, at one point, the church had embraced the idea of equal rights and had now lurched off on a different course. They struggled to find appropriate ways to recall the church to what they saw as its better self, its more ennobling history, and its highest ideals. Tyler was one who pointed to the lessons of history: "Critics said the family would fall apart [back] then, . . . that women would become men and so forth. It sounds just like the same thing we are going through now. . . . The problem comes when people focus on the fringe groups, ignoring . . . groups in the middle who are seriously, intensely seeking the golden mean."[32]

Absolutely convinced of the validity of their course, representatives of the group took their grievances to President Kimball in a series of letters. Reading them reveals the increasing tension as the church's response became less and less satisfactory. There is no evidence that members of the forum sought a personal meeting with the church president despite long-standing family and civic ties to various members of the church hierarchy. Perhaps, hearing the frustrating efforts of Tyler, Johnson, and others to meet with the First Presidency, they saw their chances as slim to none. It may be, because many of the women were writers, they preferred a medium that allowed them to ponder and shape their message carefully rather than risk a misstep in person. Nevertheless, their correspondence was probably interpreted by church functionaries as confrontational, and the misunderstandings multiplied. While the forum probably represented an atypical sampling of Mormons, the women's voices were nevertheless clear and sincere. By contrast, the responses from church secretaries were perfunctory and, the women thought, dismissive and mildly threatening.

The correspondence began during the spring of 1979 when Mormon women in Virginia were vigorously, but covertly, lobbying their state legislators, when Idaho had rescinded its early ratification, and when Barbara Smith, Orrin Hatch, and Boyd Packer were speaking widely against the amendment. The first letter, dated March 10, 1979, and addressed to Spencer W. Kimball, reads:

> We speak for a sizeable minority of LDS women whose pain is so acute that they must try to be heard. Does the First Presidency really know of our plight? We cannot believe that anyone deliberately seeks to destroy us; nevertheless that is the signal we are receiving. We feel that we are the victims of a deliberate and punishing ultra-conservative squeeze to force us out of fellowship. In a classic example of guilt by association, Mormon feminists are being linked to the destruction of the family, homosexual marriages, and abortion. We are accused of rejecting family responsibility and of abandoning moral values. Women who work are publicly labeled as selfish and worldly. Suddenly many devoted Mormon women are being treated like apostates.[33]

Drafted by Helen Candland Stark, the letter revealed how these women interpreted what was happening in their Mormon world. It hinted at their ideal of a better world—one in which diversity would be a valued resource rather than a danger. Words like "plight," "victims," "deliberate," and "ultra-conservative squeeze" could be considered fighting words, but they also acknowledged the reality of the significant gap emerging between traditionalists and feminists who felt themselves being forced outside the church.

The letter continued with descriptions of specific cases of women who were threatened with disciplinary action for voicing their feminist views. It concluded with an emotional plea for a response: "We desperately need to know whether, after serious consideration, soul-searching, and prayer, you indeed and in fact find us unworthy, a minority open to attack, and ultimately expendable. If not, can the word get out that Mormon feminists are not to be subjected to intimidations, rejection for Church assignments, loss of employment, and psychological excommunication. Every difference of opinion or sincere question should not be answered with a threatening indictment of one's testimony."[34]

The women urgently affirmed their love for Mormonism and their desire to remain attached to the church: "We are women who love the Lord, the Gospel, and the Church; we have served, tithed, and raised righteous children in Zion. We plead for the opportunity to continue to do so in an atmosphere of respect and justice. For decades we have been part of the solution, whatever the need has been; we are saddened to be now considered part of the problem."

The answer on March 28 was not from President Kimball but from Francis M. Gibbons, his secretary, who curtly requested permission to pass the letter on for comment to the women's stake presidents.[35] He concluded that "the brethren also asked me to extend their best wishes to you." The brief note failed to acknowledge or respond to any of the issues raised in the letter.

This response did not sit well with the women. Helen Stark wrote back on April 14, speaking for the group and resolutely bypassing Gibbons by again addressing her letter directly to President Kimball:

> We see no advantage in zeroing in on our particular stake presidents. We are not radical feminists. But we have a real fear that in today's climate our credibility and present contributions could be jeopardized by a confrontation with our beloved and respected stake presidents. We realize that you have many demands on your time and judgment. We assure you of our devotion to you personally as well as to your great calling, which must weigh heavily. We appreciate your concern for all of us, and we are sorry to add to your burdens.

Like the women's letter to Gunn McKay, Stark utilized the familiar language of church etiquette and inter-family communication, but clearly felt strongly obligated to plead the case of women who were being pushed to the periphery. "Nevertheless," Stark continued, "our letter came to you privately out of [the] pain of some sincere daughters of Zion. We do not wish to involve other authority figures. If you do not consider [that] our plight merits further action on your part, at least we have spoken what we feel to be our truth and you have heard."[36]

There is, in fact, no indication in the correspondence or otherwise, of which I am aware, that the church president ever saw the letter. Again, Gibbons, rather than Kimball, responded with the same formulaic greeting: "President Kimball again asked me to extend his best wishes to you." Gibbons repeated the suggestion that, if the women would agree, he would forward this second letter to their stake presidents, carrying the unwritten promise of pastoral counseling to put them on the proper path and the subtle threat of punishment if a church court were deemed necessary for holding heretical views.[37]

The women may have been meditating on how to reply, but instead, they received an indirect, unexpected, but very clear response. The forum's next meeting was scheduled for May 12, 1979—an update on the ERA and a description of the National Women's Party commemoration to be held in Washington D.C. Before the meeting, Algie Ballif received a telephone call from Marilyn Arnold, professor of English at BYU and President Dallin Oaks's administrative assistant. She informed Ballif the group could no longer use the Alice Louise Reynolds Room. Ballif was "taken aback and almost shocked" by the message, although she had praise for the messenger: "She was most gracious, and I had a feeling that it was most difficult for her to tell me this. I told her of our predicament. . . . It was the beginning of a problem we had felt could never happen—but it did. We notified the women who were in charge of the meeting, and they were most kind and helpful and sympathetic and they went to work finding another place for the meeting."[38]

Ballif gathered from Arnold that the content of "various" ERA-related discussions, as reported in the *Provo Herald*, had made it difficult for the university to remain associated with the forum. It did not matter that the forum held open discussions, allowing and even welcoming divergent views. The ERA had been presented "with dignity, with respect," Ballif wrote in a history, and some had spoken in favor and others against the amendment. "In our society, which is a democracy," she noted in a style reminiscent of Pericles or Jefferson, "our decisions should be openly arrived at."[39] It was a painful irony that a democratic group was being shut down by a church that revered the U.S. Constitution. Having a woman deliver the men's message underscored the irony.

To many of the women, this was seen as a crushing punishment. Almost all the women had been educated at BYU. It was the site of a significant portion of their intellectual maturation. The room not only honored their spiritual mentor but also their own intellectual heritage. Holding their important discussions there had legitimated their efforts, steadied and reassured them. The injustice cut deeply.

Once again, in an act of both protest and faith, Stark drafted a carefully worded third letter to President Kimball on May 18:

> Our decision to write to you stems, in part, from advice often put forth in Relief Society lessons: In the event of great anxiety, seek counsel from wise and understanding authority figures. This sharing eventually, with God's guidance, leads to a positive resolution. At this time we need to have faith in the validity of our own feelings, or to be shown empathetically why we are in error. As we now fall back on our own resources for solutions, these words come to mind: "Sometimes I feel like a motherless child."[40]

For the third time, the reply came from the secretary. Gibbons repeated the mantra of "best wishes" from the president and again pressed for permission to forward the letter to the stake presidents of the "sisters" Stark represented.[41] None of the women indicated in the minutes whether they had met with their stake presidents to talk about their positions on these issues. Nor did they answer this letter.

After a hiatus of five months, Stark wrote her last letter. It was November 30, 1979. Sonia Johnson had faced her first bishop's court, and Stark's tone had become less warm, more confrontative:

> One of the criticisms leveled against Sonia Johnson is that she erred in going public with her concerns. She should have taken her complaints directly to the Church Authorities. As one of the group of women who tried to do just that, I report with pain that this does not work. We now possess a six-letter file of correspondence, the official response of which is to belittle our plight and to suggest we be dealt with by our various Stake Presidents,

> some of whom we now consider to be harsh and rigid men. So, humiliated and frustrated, we have been tempted to go public ourselves with our little sheaf of correspondence. In fact, we went so far as to share it anonymously for the article in the Sept. 1979 issue of Utah Holiday.[42] We think the tone of these letters points up the heavy-handed hierarchical attitude which is alienating many Mormon women. . . . Communication is cut off. We are presumed to have nothing of merit to say.

She signed it, "Guardedly, Helen C. Stark." This time, there was no *pro forma* response, at least not in the letters saved by the forum.

It was easy for these women to believe that President Kimball himself never saw any of this correspondence and that Gibbons intercepted and answered the letters himself as part of his official duties. It was a comforting assumption since it allowed them to believe that, despite evidence of hostility and barriers of communication on the part of those close to the president, it did not represent the prophet's personal beliefs. They could cherish the hope that, if there were only a way to reach him, they might be heard and that change was possible. There is no evidence in the papers either to support or counter the hypothesis that Gibbons diverted Kimball's correspondence.

Although the forum maintained its independence by never joining forces officially with Mormons for ERA, its members expressed their sympathy, interest, and support of much of MERA's agenda. A week after Stark's last letter, many of the forum members held a candlelight vigil while Sonia Johnson was being excommunicated. The open discussions on the ERA and the forum's hosting of pro-ERA speakers, including Johnson, provided evidence of guilt by association that was needed in some quarters. None of the forum members were excommunicated or became public personalities on a national or local level; however, they were keenly aware that they were no longer in the mainstream of Mormon life with their Relief Society sisters.

Under these circumstances, their personal associations with women at the forum became even more important. In that circle of sisterhood, they freely expressed their love for each other, the importance of the group, their allegiance to their common heritage as Mormon women, the strength they derived from their Mormonness, their disillusionment with the church's political path, and the suffering they experienced whenever their path diverged from the official road. A particularly emotional theme was the gap in understanding among many men—or even more so the failure of other women to speak for themselves. One woman expressed it in this way:

> When we are told that the reason Relief Society isn't succeeding is because we're failing as individuals, that is called by psychologists "blaming the victim." It's a common event, and we're doing it all the time to women, to singles, to questioners. When millions are spent on Reader's Digest ads that say that Mormon women are cherished and armored and (trapped) on a pedestal, . . . I wonder about my tithing.[43]

This woman recalled her "awful IWY experience" when "a woman with garment lines under her blouse" told her "the state would be better if people like me left it. I was hurt, disillusioned, and heartsick."[44]

Conclusion

In January 1984, the Alice Louise Reynolds group renamed itself the Algie Ballif Forum in honor of one of its most beloved founding matriarchs. The women met regularly in the Provo City Municipal Building until the 1990s.

Any history of Mormon feminism during this time period could probably reproduce endless stories of women who struggled with the same issues as the Reynolds Forum. Others during the same period turned more resolutely for companionship and sisterhood to their Relief Societies. For those who found service opportunities, sociability, and emotional security in formal ward organizations, the distress and discontent of women who seemed compelled to ask endless questions and point out the troubling anomalies in the church's view of women must have made such women appear to be willful rebels. Although the church does not make attendance statistics available, anecdotal evidence would point to dozens, and perhaps hundreds, of women who felt marginalized and isolated with their questions, who must have quietly slipped away into inactivity.

Groups like the Reynolds Forum served a dual function. For women who felt alienated and disenchanted with the institutional church, such groups served as a transitional zone, allowing women to voice their concerns and explore them in a supportive atmosphere even as they continued their trajectory out of church activity. For others, such groups were a way of maintaining their commitment to the institutional church and of anchoring their loyalty to the gospel principles of justice and equality. The existence of such groups helped mediate political and spiritual realities in a shared context with other Mormon women.

In a 1979 letter, Jan Tyler asked "Who is my sister?" Her rhetorical query touched on a yearning many women had to be understood and connected to other women. She wrote about how women tend to stretch away from each other and fail to recognize what they share in common. They become categorized: "Either we are for men, or we are against men, we are for families and building them, or against families and are destroying them, we know our places (as women) and stay there, or we don't know our place and move about, and the lists of comparisons go on, . . . when in fact, any position on a continuum is a part of the whole." She saw herself connected to "every woman who has preceded me . . . and those who are yet to come."

Perhaps worn down and discouraged by the painful debate that had ripped Mormon women apart from each other, Tyler still found a way to believe it could be different. She commended

> patience with those who believe there is only one way; those who need scapegoats; those just becoming aware of the problems; those who believe it all has begun with them; those who only see their anger; those who don't recognize [that] anger is rooted in pain; those who cannot deal with the anger and other emotions because they have not yet confronted their own anger and emotions; those who are ignorant, who easily become fearful; those who never become adults; those who do not see the problems.[45]

The women of the Reynolds Forum understood this and believed that the world would be better for what they shared. These final excerpts extracted from the September 1980 meeting of the forum capture the warm spirit and energy of these good-hearted, intelligent, and gentle women who believed in each other and remained passionate about women's rights.

Belle Van Wagenen:
In the fifty years that I've lived in Provo, I have never enjoyed anything as much as the Alice Louise Reynolds Forum. Algie and Thelma were my neighbors for many years, and they invited me to hear Sonia Johnson when she came the first time. And I went with some misgiving, because I felt that perhaps I was on the wrong side of this thing. Still, I really felt surprised and frustrated by the church's stand. As I told my husband when I got home, I saw all the women there whom I have admired for their intellect for all these years at this meeting, now meet to question and to find answers and to at least be unafraid to examine the problem. This meant a lot to me.

Shirley Paxman:
I, like some of you, feel no personal frustrations about a woman's role. But I am concerned about some of the things that are happening. I'm a conservative and Anna is a liberal. But Anna and I feel very much the same about a great many things. . . . I feel that we are really losing a great many wonderful things that women have by tradition in our church, and this is distressing to me. I would like to preserve and conserve those.

Algie Ballif:
I feel that this is one of the most precious hours—it may be two hours—that I will spend in my eighty-fourth—nearly eighty-fifth—year. . . . I feel a diversity of ideas that I think is remarkable. . . . I feel that many of the expressions here tonight indicate that sooner or later there will be great changes for you and me in our church. . . . I feel that we have to remember how different we all are. In each one of us, you know, there is a heritage that is different. . . . You have suffered deeply because of some of the situations that have existed. And I have suffered. And . . . I still have miles to go before I sleep. My faith and my religion have changed much over the years from the time I was here at the BYU in school. . . .We did have great free-

dom of thought . . . Our father and mother opened up our home for Sunday discussions. . . . We heard things, and we listened, and we asked questions. That has never left us. I am still asking questions. I wish I knew what my concept of a Mother God is. I know there is one, an essence of compassion, a great overriding something that I have to have in my consciousness in order to be happy. . . . In this beautiful diversity of opinion that we have had here tonight, we find the essence, I think, of great womanhood.[46]

EPILOGUE

When the extended deadline for ratifying the ERA expired in mid-1982, women on both sides, who had given too much of themselves to simply shrug it off, continued to work for its passage or defeat. People had marched and petitioned, lobbied and rallied. They had gone on hunger strikes and engaged in acts of civil disobedience. In all likelihood, few of them were aware of the historical path along a continuum in the struggle for equality in America they had traveled.

Consider the oft-quoted letter from Abigail Adams to her husband, John, in 1776: "In the new code of laws which I suppose it will be necessary for you to make, I desire you would remember the ladies and be more generous and favorable to them than your ancestors. Do not put such unlimited power into the hands of their husbands."[1] The response from her husband was playful yet dismissive, referring jocularly to "the despotism of the petticoat" against which he said he hoped "General Washington and all our brave heroes would fight." On the other hand, he added, "you are so saucy, I won't blot it out."[2]

From such privately held concerns of individual women, there gradually emerged a struggle first to be taken seriously and then to achieve fairness before the law and equal opportunity. After two centuries of development or progress, depending on one's view, the concept of equal rights gained enough respect that thirty-eight states ratified the ERA. In 1982, only three more states were needed to see the amendment added to the

U.S. Constitution, the very document Abigail Adams had hoped would include mention of women.

Having already reviewed some of the complex turns the women's movement took over the past two hundred years to arrive at the ERA's defeat, it would be instructive to review the events that have occurred since then and consider prospects for future developments.

Only a month after its demise in June 1982, the ERA was reintroduced into the U.S. House of Representatives on July 14. It failed by a margin of twelve votes shy of the 290 required (278 in favor, 147 against). The next year, in January 1983, Sonia Johnson resigned as president of Mormons for ERA and was succeeded by Alice Pottmyer of Arlington, Virginia, whom the *Washington Post* described as an active LDS member in charge of a viable organization of 1,200 members and about 20,000 sympathizers.[3] Representatives of Mormons for ERA continued to speak at women's clubs and fireside discussions in people's homes.

Within the first few days of 1983, the Democratic Congressional leadership reintroduced the ERA as House Joint Resolution 1 with 232 Congressional sponsors, although these included representatives from four nonvoting areas: the District of Columbia, Guam, Puerto Rico, and the Virgin Islands. It was a gallant gesture, but the 290-vote requirement remained insurmountable.[4]

On May 26, Senator Orrin Hatch, who had recently published his 103-page anti-ERA book, *The Equal Rights Amendment: Myths and Realities,* opened hearings on the ERA in the capacity of chair of the Senate Judiciary Subcommittee on the Constitution.[5] He achieved what he had intended by seeing that the amendment stalled in committee, as it would do every subsequent year as supporters reintroduced the ERA into Congress.

In 1993 the National Organization of Women began studying local views about the ERA in conjunction with its state chapters and researching the impact of equal rights legislation passed by the states rather than by the federal government. In 1995, NOW convened an ERA Strategy Summit, where the decision was made to rewrite the ERA. However, rather than temper the amendment to accommodate more conservative goals, the new proposal broadened the ERA's message to include reproductive and homosexual rights. Although certain to infuriate conservatives, the determination was to move forward rather than backward and once and for all "end women's historic subordination to men and guarantee full constitutional rights."[6]

An alternative strategy developed from the precedent of the "Madison Amendment," the Twenty-Seventh Amendment to the U.S. Constitution which limits legislators' ability to determine their own pay. The amendment was passed by Congress in 1789 but not ratified for 203 years when it finally succeeded in gaining support from enough states to become law in 1992. According to this precedent, the ERA, through Congressional action or legal challenge, might pass whenever three more states endorsed it, regardless of far into the future. This was the opinion of legal scholars writing in 1997 for the *William and Mary Journal of Women and the Law.*[7] Their argument was that Congress could adjust or repeal the existing time constraint. Two years later, Representative Robert Andrews (D-New Jersey) proposed a bill to do just that, House Resolution 37, which has subsequently been resubmitted.[8]

In the two decades that followed the ERA countdown, the status of American women has improved markedly by some standards.[9] Still, Roberta W. Francis, chair of NOW's ERA Task Force, believes the amendment is still necessary. She chafes against the realization that "women have had to fight long and hard political battles to win rights that men possessed automatically because they were male." The only right "the Constitution specifically affirms equally for women and men is the right to vote."[10] More importantly, the need "can be expressed simply as a warning. Unless we put into the Constitution the bedrock principle that equality of rights cannot be denied or abridged on account of sex, the political and judicial victories women have achieved with their blood, sweat, and tears for the past two centuries are vulnerable to erosion or reversal at any time, now or in the future."[11]

During the 107th Congress in 2001-02, Senators Edward Kennedy (D-Massachusetts) and Stephen Horn (R-California), and Representative

Carolyn Maloney (D-New York) introduced the Equal Rights Amendment as Senate Joint Resolution 10 and House Joint Resolution 40. Absent from these bills was a deadline for ratification. Laura W. Murphy, director of the ACLU's national office in Washington D.C., said: "We believe that it is finally time for Congress to give the Equal Rights Amendment another chance. Passage of the Equal Rights Amendment would give women of this country the constitutional affirmation of their rights for which they have long struggled."[12]

As it now stands, the ERA has primarily played a symbolic role, but the symbol carries enormous potential. It has inspired important legislative and administrative changes in social programs and employment opportunities. As views of women have gradually changed and as these have become internalized—mostly due to the actual day-to-day realities and necessities of a twenty-first-century world—people have come to accept the fact that women are present in all areas of society and that this is a good thing. Even those who still hold to an ideal of appropriate womanhood rarely themselves conform to this model. A significant gap in actual achievement on the part of women still exists, in part due to remaining legal and social barriers, but it seems that many who toiled for the ERA have become complacent or discouraged—even fearful, based on past experience—to reexamine why women have not fully arrived. Many are content to see the issue in terms of having lost a battle in order to win a war.

Even within Mormonism, feminism has continued to broaden since the mid-1980s into a larger continuum of methods and approaches, even in the face of enduring resistance on the part of those who stand vigil over the flame of orthodoxy. Despite excommunications, female theologians Janice Allred and Margaret Toscano have explored the nature of the Mother in Heaven concept as taught by an earlier generation of female leaders such as Eliza R. Snow and Zina Diantha Young.[13] Although an important anthology, *Women and Authority: Re-emerging Mormon Feminism* resulted in the excommunications of its feminist editor, Maxine Hanks, and a contributor, historian D. Michael Quinn. Still, it introduced a diverse range of women's thinking, speaking, and writing to a large audience. These modern-day Saints have helped remind Mormon women of their heritage as women of power.

Much historical and sociological research continues to be written by such women as Marie Cornwall, Carol Cornwall Madsen, and Jill Mulvay Derr. The fact that post-modern feminist criticism was applied to an examination of the Mormon experience was one reason Cecilia K. Farr, Gail Houston, and other professors at Brigham Young University were fired or forced out in the early 1990s. Yet, feminism continues to be discussed in sessions of the independent Sunstone Theological Symposium and *Sunstone* magazine, and *Exponent II* continues to chart a course that manages to avoid public controversy while supplying a warmly supportive environment for sisterly sharing. Equally valuable among the independent LDS organizations is the Mormon Women's Forum, which offers another public space for feminist studies to proceed unfettered by ecclesiastical alarm.

The Relief Society has mostly retired from politics to its former preoccupation with religion and homemaking and its *raison d'etre* by name—emergency relief, by which the sisters have quickly responded with hundreds of quilts for earthquake victims, stuffed animals for traumatized children, pints of donated blood, and hundreds of school kits for children in developing nations, all done with overwhelming goodness. Another favorite activity is the annual Relief Society women's conference at Brigham Young University. Women flock to it by the thousands to hear church leaders praise their devotion and urge them to greater efforts.

But it is also true that hundreds of Relief Society women responded with the same alacrity in 2001 as they had before when, in this case, the renamed Public Affairs Committee called on women in California to campaign for Proposition 22, a measure intended to reinforce already existing state law banning same-sex marriage. Gay marriage had become the new political obsession of the Public Affairs Committee. When the California measure passed, it was for some women a bitter replaying of the corrosive fight over the Equal Rights Amendment. Yet, as Salt Lake City TV journalist and political analyst Rod Decker has pointed out, "At times in the ERA fight, Mormon leaders seemed scarcely to know their own strength. At only a word from them, crowds of women turned out in passionate support of the church position, and it seemed the church could, if it wanted, use that power to become an important force on other national issues. Yet the church has never repeated the ERA campaign."[14]

On a personal note, I should mention that there were times when it was impossible for me to research this book due to the force of the story, the aborted dreams and pain, which seemed to slap me in the face and knock me to my knees. It was simply too much. So many women's lives were shaped for better or for worse, too often for the worse, by the dimensions of this campaign. Well intentioned people—good women with years of mature experience and wisdom—were discouraged for having expressed honest, considered opinions. Those who cast the first stone, who most loudly accused the other side of villainy, were the ones most often guilty of the very dirty tricks and concealed agendas they accused the opposition of. Things spiraled out of control and revealed an uncivil side to otherwise good people. Yet despite the ugliness, I believe this story is one we must teach and talk about and struggle to understand. We should care about it deeply and believe that it matters. It is a journey which is in each person, that brings us to this point.

As I listened to hours of taped interviews for this study, one moved me profoundly and summed it all up for me. It was an interview by Anne Looser, a brave and powerful Honors student and Service Learning Scholar at the University of Utah. She interviewed Irene Fisher, former president of the Utah Coalition for ERA and recently retired director of the university's Bennion Center, which provides humanitarian service opportunities for students. I listened to it while driving to Utah County one evening, tears falling onto my shirt as I realized that what I was hearing was a sort of changing of the guard. Anne asked Irene how a person can do community work without getting angry, or at least without letting anger take over. Irene advised her to make her passion her power and to see it as a light that would keep her going when it gets difficult. It was tender, careful advice, which Anne received enthusiastically, perhaps intuitively understanding what Irene had meant. I was privileged to see the way our stories connect us through the generations, how the insights we share with each other about how to be women in this world create bonds that are sacred, powerful, and demanding of respect and care. This book is not my story but the stories of many women who found themselves suddenly caught in the headlights of oncoming traffic.

In her book *Sex Roles,* Rose Weitz observed that society creates gender roles and definitions anew for each generation, cogently adding: "The cultural products of any given society at any given time reverberate with the themes of that society and that era."[15] This is particularly true for the ERA contest. Like private investigators, contemporary feminists are studying cultural texts—acts, discourses, and narratives—which each generation has produced. They believe that meaning is mediated, that by examining the process of production and the texts themselves, one can discover the reverse as well, the processes that have kept some texts from being created.[16] In other words, what the texts do not say is also significant. The prohibitions placed upon women by a given culture define its ability to stretch its boundaries.

These cultural artifacts of whatever form are distinguished by two properties: they have naturalistic or "found" qualities because they were not intentionally created to be studied. They are noninteractive in the sense that they do not require asking questions and observing behavior to be understood. Cultural artifacts are produced by individuals or social organizations. They are written texts or oral narratives, visual and material artifacts, and also evidence of behavioral norms.

Likewise, this type of work provides the added advantage of creating new vantage points from which to better understand the past:

> People who do content analyses study a set of objects (i.e., cultural artifacts) or events systematically by counting them or interpreting the themes contained in them. Sociologists, historians, literary analysts, anthropologists, and archaeologists—whether feminist or not—are interested in cultural artifacts as something produced by people. These products stem from every aspect of human life including relatively private worlds, "high" cultural, popular culture, and organizational life.[17]

The fight against the ERA was centered in two opposing styles of discourse, each one based on different cognitive schema, constructed to help women understand their positions in the world. Whenever women share common ways of understanding the relationship they have with men, with their community, and with each other, they depend on conceptual structures to organize their experiences within cognitive systems that make sense to them. They are based on a combination of experience and interpretation. Conceptual structures or cognitive schema are basic to social organization and help individuals find common ground and develop shared interpretations of the meanings of their experiences.

This is true of the way women in this story chose to see feminism, with a shifting definition with personal, cultural, and generational significance influenced by the forces at play at any given time. The cost of claiming ownership of feminist views was high for some, less so for others. For Marilyn Arnold, feminism was about the sisterhood women created with each other when they worked toward a common goal. She commented:

> To go to Houston gave me a huge lift. What is it when you get together with a group of women? It's easier to talk with them for some reason, or somehow there's a flavor, there's a sisterhood. And men probably feel that on athletic teams and other places, but women haven't had that so much. It's not quite the same as if you're working together at a cause.[18]

Other women pondered the same question thoughtfully:

> **Ramona Adams:**
> Well, I'd define a feminist as a person who believes that men and women should have equal rights, that there should be equality among them, and they should have the right to choose their roles in life. They shouldn't be designed and told what they should be. And that's really what the women's movement is about. It's not about burning bras and getting women ahead. That's not what it's about. It's about equality and having the right to choose, and I am 100 percent a feminist when you define it in that regard.[19]

Cheryll Lynn May:

Feminism to me has many dimensions, and it begins on a spiritual plane, I guess. I believe that women in the eternal perspective are equal in every respect, not just in their separate sphere, but in every respect to their brothers, and that this is the only system that could be projected by a just God. On a political/economic plane, [it] means that I also believe in this total equality in every area of life. It's an equality that needs to be fought for, that has many, many dimensions and bridgeheads. It will take a constant struggle because discrimination goes back so far and is so widely practiced and just goes into the very fabric of our culture.[20]

Aileen H. Clyde:

I happily call myself a feminist, but that's because I'm interested in equal rights; and the issues I was most concerned about as I thought about this before these political implications came along were equal pay for equal work and equal opportunities in terms of education.[21]

In this sense, in the views of these LDS women who have embraced the term feminism, one can see among the cultural artifacts of the decade of the 1970s a genuine rhetoric of women's rights born out of experience, found in the tactics of mass-supported, grassroots politics, reactionary redirection of energies, and a bitterness that still lingers. Created by women who were largely inexperienced in either public life or politics but who nevertheless engaged in the campaign with all the energy and passion of social crusaders of any generation, these cultural artifacts reflect the fears, aspirations, and disappointments of women who came of age after World War II when other women simultaneously grew up in distrust of the foreign, the exotic, the deviant.

If it is true that changes in statute laws have made the ERA redundant, why is it still resisted in some quarters and, even more importantly, is it still necessary? In my opinion, particularly after studying this particular story, the answer to the latter question is an absolute yes. It is particularly necessary if you believe in the power of language to evoke shared memories on a national level, including the acknowledgment of central defining myths that tell us who we are as a group of people. As Americans, we are taught from the time we first sit in public school that the Constitution is a body of ideas and laws that distinguishes us from all other nations. We believe the Constitution establishes freedom as our central concern. Whether this is true matters less than the amazing power the idea has held for the American people. The Constitution is a structure of ideas about laws created with language that has the power to set people free, to defend against injustice, and to ensure for all of us the good life.

It is because of the power of the idea of the Constitution that it requires the inclusion of women who stand on equal footing with men rather than invisibly behind the scenes or with the possibility, as the Supreme Court ruled in 1894, that women are in fact not legally "persons" (see chap. 3). This idea must be enshrined in our most sacred national language—the rhetorical argument of the Constitution. It must celebrate who we are as American women. Is this legacy one of protecting women and their children or one of curbing and denying their potential? That is a question other historians will answer in the future.

Cynthia Boshard tells the story of her five-year-old son, Dillon, asking a friend what his mother did. The "kid kind of looked perplexed, and Dillon could tell that he didn't know exactly what he meant, so Dillon rephrased the question and said, 'You know, what does she do to help the world?'" Boshard's eyes misted as she recounted this to her interviewer, Leslie Bates, in 1991, remembering her son's idea that she was someone who was "helping the world. That was wonderful."[22] A careful examination of the ways women have worked for or against equality, particularly their activity for and against the Equal Rights Amendment, suggests that those on both sides thought they were doing what was right for the world and were engaged in what would really matter in the long run, that they were on the right side of a good fight. They believed their choices would be the best for succeeding generations. It remains for us to decide if their vision of the future was well advised.

Barbara Smith, General President of the LDS Relief Society from 1974 to 1984. *Courtesy Utah State Historical Society*

Jan Tyler, chair, Utah IWY Coordinating Committee. *Courtesy Utah State Historical Society*

A mass meeting in Provo in preparation for Utah's IWY Conference.
Courtesy Sharon Keigher Collection, Marriott Library, University of Utah

Poster for "The Voice of Womankind" conference at the Salt Palace. *Courtesy Sharon Keigher Collection*

Belle Spafford, General President of the LDS Relief Society from 1945 to 1974. Plenary Speaker at Utah's IWY conference. *Courtesy Utah State Historical Society*

Kathleen Flake, Utah IWY Coordinating Committee, mass meeting chair. *Courtesy Utah State Historical Society*

Dignitaries at the Houston IWY convention (l-r from podium): Rosalyn Carter, Bella Abzug, Betty Ford, Lady Bird Johnson. *Courtesy Utah State Historical Society*

The Utah Delegation in Houston. *Courtesy Utah State Historical Society*

At the Houston Convention (l-r): Belle Spafford, Ruth Hardy Funk.
Courtesy Utah State Historical Society

Mormons for ERA (back, l-r): Teddie Wood, Maida Withers, (front, l-r) Sonia Johnson, Hazel Rigby. *Courtesy Sonia Johnson Collection, Marriott Library*

Cynthia Boshard, Utah IWY Coordinating Committee. *Courtesy Utah State Historical Society*

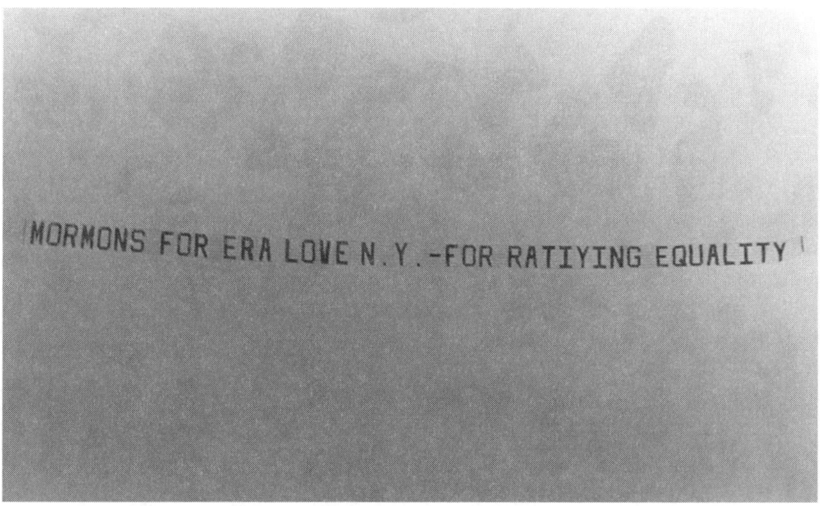

Mormons for ERA banner, 1978.
Courtesy Sonia Johnson Collection, Marriott Library

Appendix 1

CHRONOLOGY, 1842–1983

1842 Founder and president of the Mormon Church, Joseph Smith, organizes the Female Relief Society to "provoke the brethren to good works in looking to the wants of the poor, searching after objects of charity, and in administering to their wants to assist; by correcting the morals and strengthening the virtues of the (female) community, and save the Elders the trouble of rebuking; that they may give their time to other duties & C. in their public teaching."

1848 Elizabeth Cady Stanton and Lucretia Mott organize a convention in Seneca Falls, New York, to consider: "The social, civil and religious condition and rights of women. One hundred men and women sign a Declaration of Sentiments calling for women to secure the "sacred right to the elective franchise."

1866 Women gather in the American Equal Rights Association after staging annual conventions dedicated to human rights and passage of the Fourteenth Amendment, which provides that "No State shall abridge the privileges of citizens."

1868 The *New York Times* reports that Congress is considering legislation to enfranchise women of the western territories. "Female suffrage might perhaps be tried with novel effect in the territory of Utah the State of Deseret. There the 'better half' of humanity is such a strong numerical majority that even if all the other half should vote the other way, they would carry the election. Perhaps it would result in casting out polygamy and Mormonism in general. . . . Here would be a capital field of women suffrage to make a start, and we presume nobody would object to the experiment."

1869 Two national organizations are formed: the National Woman Suffrage Association (NWSA), founded by Elizabeth Cady Stanton and Susan B. Anthony, and the American Woman Suffrage Association (AWSA), organized by Lucy Stone and others. The NWSA advocates a Constitutional amendment granting female suffrage, along with other reforms. The more moderate AWSA includes men in its membership and values respectability. Mormon women are embraced by the NWSA.

The Godbeites, led by William Godbe and other Mormon dissidents, form what they call the "New Movement," including the Ladies Improvement Society, led by Fanny Stenhouse, which sends a delegation to NWSA.

December: The Wyoming Territorial Legislature is the first to establish female suffrage and to give women the right to hold office.

1870 January: At the "great indignation" meeting held at the Salt Lake Tabernacle, more than 6,000 Mormon women oppose the Cullom Anti-Polygamy Bill, shifting the focus from polygamy to the legal rights of women.

February: The Utah Territorial Legislature enfranchises women but does not give them the right to hold public office, stating "that every woman of the age of twenty-one years who has resided in this territory six months next preceding a general election, born or naturalized in the united States, . . . shall be entitled to vote at any election in this territory."

LDS Relief Society leader Sarah M. Kimball initiates a civil education program to discuss government, the court system, and parliamentary law. Twenty-five Mormon women vote.

July: The Liberal Party is formed to oppose candidates nominated by the Mormon Church. In response, the church forms the People's Party. Women join both parties and attend their conventions and rallies.

August: More than two thousand Utah women vote, entering through separate entrances to polling places.

1871 Anthony and Stanton visit Utah on their national tour to campaign for suffrage. They meet with both Mormon and New Movement women, seeing women's rights as more important than religion's differences.

1872 Utah's fourth bid for statehood is unsuccessful. In mass meetings, women participate in selecting delegates to attend a constitutional convention. Some women, such as Cornelia Paddock and Sarah Ann Cooke, believe statehood will strengthen the LDS hold on power and therefore initiate a petition drive opposing statehood. Two of the first female attorneys in the territory, Georgiana Snow and non-native Phoebe W. Couzins, join the Utah Bar. Couzins will oppose female suffrage, saying women are not necessarily better at resolving society's ills, even though she herself is an unmarried career woman; she encourages women to follow their "natural" destinies and become good "homekeepers" and wives.

April: The Wheeler bill moves through Congress, disfranchising Utah women.

June: The first issue of the *Woman's Exponent* is published with the intent of supporting women's rights and disputing attacks made against Mormonism, particularly against polygamy with Louisa Greene Richards as first editor.

1877 Emmeline B. Woodward Wells becomes the second editor and publisher of the *Woman's Exponent* until 1914. She, rather than Charlotte Cobb Godbe, represents the territory's women and is the first "leading sister" the NWSA recognizes.

The new state of Colorado fails to pass woman suffrage. In 1893 a referendum in Colorado granting women the vote passes there.

1878 Sarah Ann Sutton Cooke, founding president of the Ladies Literary Club, organizes the Ladies Anti-Polygamy Society, whose publication, the *Anti-Polygamy Standard,* maintains that suffrage is a tool of the LDS Church to overwhelm the "gentiles" in the territory, and holds an anti-polygamy meeting in Salt Lake City. The society associates with the Women's Christian Temperance Union among other "social purity" movements.

A federal suffrage amendment is introduced in Congress. It is reintroduced each year until 1887.

1879 Delegates from the LDS Relief Society (Zina Young Williams and Emmeline B. Woodword Wells) represent Utah women at the NWSA convention.

Federal anti-polygamy legislation, upheld by the U.S. Supreme Court, is protested at a rally of Mormon Women

1882 Congress passes the Edmunds Act, disfranchising all polygamous men and women and sending many underground into hiding.

1886 Mormon women again hold mass meetings, penning a resolution entitled "Appeal for Freedom, Justice and Equal Rights": "Resolved, . . . that the suffrage originally conferred upon us as a political privilege, has become a vested right by possession and usage for sixteen years and that we protest against being deprived of that right without process of law, and for no other reason than that we do not vote to suit our political opponents."

1887 The Edmunds-Tucker bill disfranchises all women in Utah Territory, among other drastic measures designed to destroy the LDS Church's political and religious power in the territory. Simultaneously, women in Washington Territory lose, by court decision, the franchise in place since 1883.

1888 Emily S. Richards proposes the formation of a Utah suffrage association to LDS Church officials and NWSA. Anti-polygamist leader Jennie Froiseth challenges Richards. She asserts that suffrage is not good for Utah. As a result, Richards helps create the Utah Woman Suffrage Association (UWSA). Eventually there are nineteen associations in twenty-seven counties by 1894.

1890 LDS President Wilford Woodruff issues a manifesto that leads the Mormons to end the official practice of polygamy. This slows new plural marriages in the United States but not in Canada and Mexico, where they continue to be performed despite being illegal there.

In Washington D.C., the NWSA joins the AWSA and becomes the National American Woman Suffrage Association (NAWSA).

Wyoming enters the union as a suffrage state.

1891 June: The LDS Church dissolves the People's Party and encourages its members to affiliate with the national political parties. In 1892, the Liberal Party also disbands.

July: After five earlier attempts, Congress passes the Enabling Act for Utah statehood.

September: At both the Utah Republican and Democratic Party conventions, platforms supporting woman suffrage are passed.

1895 March: At Utah's constitutional convention in Salt Lake City, UWSA presents memorials summarizing why Utah women should have political equality, the most hotly contested issue of the convention. Critics maintain that Congress will not accept a constitution that allows suffrage, predicting that female suffrage will throw politics out of balance and that the vote will change women into men.

April: Delegates agree to an article borrowed from the Wyoming constitution: "The rights of citizens of the State of Utah to vote and hold office shall not be denied or abridged on account of sex. Both male and female citizens of this State shall equally enjoy all civil, political, and religious rights and privileges."

May: Joining the celebration of Utah suffrage, Susan B. Anthony and the Rev. Anna Howard Shaw visit Utah. They hold a NAWSA meeting for the Utah chapters.

August: Sarah E. Nelson Anderson of Ogden tries to vote. The territorial court rules that the Enabling Act has not yet enfranchised women, so those who had been nominated for offices (Emma McVicker, Lillie Pardee, and Emmeline B. Wells) withdraw.

November: The state constitution is endorsed by more than four-fifths of the voters.

1896 January: Utah is admitted as a state with the act signed by President Cleveland.

March: Utah's first piece of protective legislation prohibits women and children from working in mines.

November: Ogden property owner Sarah Nelson Anderson and prominent Salt Lake City matron Eurithe K. LaBarthe become members of the Utah House of Representatives. Dr. Martha Hughes Cannon, a Salt Lake City physician, is elected to the senate—the first female state senator in the nation. In Idaho, voters approve a constitutional amendment extending suffrage to women.

Utah's first settlement house, called the Neighborhood House, opens.

1898 Utah state legislator Alice Merrill Horne pushes through the bill creating the first state arts council.

1899 NAWSA leader Carrie Chapman Catt comes to Utah to form a council to support suffrage in other states. The Utah Council of Women elects Emily S. Richards president.

1901 The Socialist Party is organized, both nationally and by Kate S. Hilliard in Utah. Hilliard had been active in UWSA. Until 1912, when the Progressive and Prohibition Parties endorse suffrage, Socialists will be the only national party categorically supporting full voting rights for women; they will run female candidates throughout the 1910s.

1911 The National Association Opposed to Woman Suffrage (NAOWS) is organized with members from several state and local groups. They publish the *Woman's Protest* that opposes woman suffrage, particularly in the West.

1914 Women's rights activists introduce a federal woman suffrage amendment to Congress.

1915 At hearings at the U.S. Senate Committee on Woman Suffrage, Alice George, one of the leaders of the NAOWS, testifies. She asserts that the Western states are inordinately influenced by the

LDS Church, which it believes uses women's votes to augment its political power.

Carrie Chapman Catt becomes president of the NAWSA. In Utah her "Winning Plan" is endorsed and a campaign to get the suffrage amendment passed.

1916 The key organizer of the National Woman's Party, Alice Paul, advocates employing more radical tactics for women's rights. Hundreds of NWP women are arrested for picketing the White House, hunger strikes, and other extreme measures.

1917 Utah state senator Elizabeth A. Pugsley Hayward is the sponsor of a memorial to Congress that supports passage of a suffrage amendment to the constitution.

1919 Finally, the U.S. Senate passes a woman suffrage amendment. In suffrage states, organizer Carrie Chapman Catt creates new associations, now called the League of Women Voters.

1920 February: Susa Young Gates represents Utah in the newly organized National League of Women Voters.

August: Tennessee approves the Nineteenth Amendment, the thirty-sixth and final state needed for ratification. The amendment states that "the right of citizens of the United States to vote shall not be denied or abridged by the United States or by any State on account of sex."

1923 Alice Paul and the NWP introduce the Equal Rights Amendment to Congress. It reads: "Men and women shall have equal rights throughout the United States and every place subject to its jurisdiction. Congress shall have power to enforce this article by appropriate legislation."

1924 The Senate Judiciary Committee begins hearings on the Equal Rights Amendment.[1]

1936 The Women's Charter is drafted to counter the ERA. It reads: "Women shall [have] full political and civil rights: full opportunity for education, full opportunity for work according to their individual abilities, with safeguards against physically harmful conditions of employment and economic exploitation. They shall be assured security of livelihood, including the safeguarding of motherhood. The provisions necessary for the establishment of these standards shall be guaranteed by government, which shall ensure also the right of united action towards the attainment of these aims. Where special exploitation of living standards attain, unhealthful working conditions or long hours of work which result in physical exhaustion and denial of the right to leisure, such conditions shall be corrected through social and labor legislation, which the world's experience shows to be necessary."

1938 The ERA is sent from committee to the U.S. Senate floor, where it fails to pass.

1943 Senator Harley Kilgore (D-West Virginia) drafts an alternative equal rights amendment: "Equality of rights under the law shall not be denied or abridged by the United States or by any State on account of sex. Congress and the several States shall have power, within their respective jurisdictions, to enforce this article by appropriate legislation. This amendment shall not require uniformity of legislation among the several States, the District of Columbia, the Territories, and possessions of the United States."

1950 The ERA, with a rider added by Senator Carl Hayden (D-Arizona), is passed by the U.S. Senate. It reads: "Equality of rights under the law shall not be denied or abridged by the United States or by any State on account of sex. The provisions of this article shall not be construed to impair any rights, benefits, or exemptions now or hereafter conferred by law upon persons of the female sex. The Congress and the several States shall have power, within their respective jurisdictions, to enforce this article by appropriate legislation. This article shall be inoperative unless it shall have been ratified as an amendment to the Constitution by the legislatures of three-fourths of the several States within seven years from the date of its submission to the States by the Congress; and if so ratified, shall take effect upon the expiration of one year after the date of such ratification."

1952 Simone de Beauvoir publishes her book, *The Second Sex,* in the United States.

1963 Powerful icon of American womanhood and social activist Eleanor Roosevelt dies.

Perhaps the single most influential book in the women's movement, Betty Friedan's *The Feminist Mystique,* voices the angst of millions of American women.

The Equal Pay Act is passed by Congress, the first of a series of measures directed at decreasing sexual discrimination.

1966 The National Organization of Women is organized by Betty Friedan and others in the wake of the conference of state Commissions on the Status of Women, where concerns were raised about whether Title VII sex discrimination procedures would be effectively enforced.

1968 LDS Relief Society President Belle Smith Spafford serves as president of the National Council of Women to 1970.

1970 Kate Millet's book, *Sexual Politics,* presents an important analysis of women in relation to political and power.

1971 March: Hearings on the Equal Rights Amendment convene in a Judiciary subcommittee of the U.S. House of Representatives.

September The Senate puts the ERA on its calendar, but postpones action until the next year.

October: The House strips the bill of riders and passes Alice Paul's version of the ERA, 354-24.

1972 March: The ERA is overwhelmingly approved by Congress and submitted to the states for ratification. The amendment reflects Alice Paul's wording but with a seven-year limit to ratification and enforcement by federal, rather than both federal and state, government. It reads: "Section 1. Equality of rights under the law shall not be denied or abridged by the United States or by any State on account of sex. Section 2. The Congress shall have the power to enforce, by appropriate legislation, the provisions of this article. Section 3. This amendment shall take effect two years after the date of ratification."

Congress passes an Equal Employment Opportunity Act, extending coverage and giving the Equal Employment Opportunity Commission (EEOC, created in 1964) enforcement authority. The commission issues improved sex discrimination guidelines.

June: Congress passes the Title IX Amendment to the Higher Education Act of 1965, prohibiting discrimination on account of sex in most federally assisted educational programs. The Civil Rights Commission is given jurisdiction over sex discrimination.

July/August: The Democratic and Republican Parties endorse the ERA and strict enforcement of anti-discrimination laws. After the National Women's Political Caucus encourages women to become delegates to party conventions, 40 percent at the Democratic convention and 30 percent at the Republican convention are women.

November: The number of women elected to state legislatures is 28.3 percent higher than the preceding year. In the U.S. House of Representatives, the number of Congresswomen increases to 16;

but with the retirement of Margaret Chase Smith in the Senate, that body once again becomes all-male.

Members of the National Council of Jewish Women conduct a study of day-care facilities in 176 areas and discover that facilities are either non-existent or of poor quality—underfunded, and understaffed—in most areas of the country.

1973 January: The Supreme Court holds that during the first trimester of pregnancy, the decision to have an abortion must be left solely to a woman and her physician. The only restriction a state may impose is the requirement that the abortion be performed by a physician licensed by the state. In the second and third trimesters, the states may impose increasingly stringent requirements (*Doe v. Bolton*, *Roe v. Wade*, 93 S. Ct. 739, 755).

August: AT& T signs an agreement with the EEOC and Labor department providing goals and timetables for increasing utilization of women and minorities. About $15 million in back pay is distributed to some 15,000 employees.

September: Billie Jean King beats Bobby Riggs in straight sets in their "Battle of the Sexes" tennis match.

November: The National Black Feminists Organization is formed with Eleanor Holmes Norton, an attorney and head of the New York City Human Rights Commission, as one of its leaders.

1974 The coalition of Labor Union Women is organized in Chicago with over 3,000 women in attendance.

More than 1.5 domestic service workers are brought under the coverage of the Fair Labor Standards Act by Public Law 93-259.

A study by Dr. Constance Uri, a Native American physician, reveals widespread sterilization of women in Indian health care facilities. This leads to an investigation of health care for poor and minority women and the 1977 revisions of guidelines by the Department of Health, Education, and Welfare.

The Housing and Community Development Act, Public Law 93-383, prohibits sex discrimination in carrying out community development programs and making federally related mortgage loans. The Civil Rights Act of 1968 is amended to prohibit sex discrimination in financing, sale or rental of housing, or brokerage services.

The Equal Credit Opportunity Act becomes Public Law 93-495 after Congresswomen Bella Abzug, Margaret Heckler, and Leonor Sullivan nurse it through Congress. It prohibits credit discrimination on the basis of sex or marital status. Abzug later leads a delegation of Congresswomen to meet with Federal Reserve Board chairman Arthur Burns to protest unsatisfactory implementation, and the board revises its policies.

Following a "Win with Women" campaign by the National Women's Political Caucus, eighteen women are elected to the 94th U.S. Congress. A nineteenth member is added in a special election early the next year. The state legislatures see a 29.5 percent increase in the number of women, from 465 to 604. The first woman elected governor is Ella Grasso of Connecticut. Mary Anne Krupsak is elected Lieutenant Governor of New York.

1975 January: The National Commission on the Observance of International Women's Year (IWY) is appointed by President Ford with Jill Ruckelshaus as presiding officer. Elizabeth Athanasakos will become the presiding officer in 1976. Members of the commission represent the United States at the United Nationals International Women's Year Conference in Mexico City in June.

An editorial opposing the ERA is published in the LDS *Church News*: "The Prophet placed the Church in the forefront of those who have taught the dignified and exalted place of women. . . . Legislative hearings . . . will not change the fact that men and women are different, made so by a Divine Creator. Each has his or her role."

The *Salt Lake Tribune* reports that a member of the Utah legislature who had committed himself to the ERA defected, saying: "It is my Church, and as a bishop, I'm not going to vote against its wishes."

February: The ERA is overwhelmingly defeated in the Utah legislature.

December: Barbara Smith, president of the LDS Relief Society, kicks off the church's high-profile anti-ERA campaign, speaking to the student body of the LDS Institute of Religion near the University of Utah. Two weeks earlier, survey data had shown that most Utahns favored the ERA.

A bill introduced by Congresswoman Bella Abzug directs the IWY commission to organize and convene a National Women's Conference, preceded by state meetings. The bill is passed by both houses of Congress and signed by President Gerald Ford to become Public Law 94-167.

Ms. Magazine publishes a petition for sexual freedom signed by 100 prominent women. They pledge to work for repeal of all laws and regulations that discriminate against homosexuals and lesbians.

1976 May: James I. Gibson organizes the "Citizens Quest for Quality Government" in Nevada. The Nevada senate majority leader, Gibson is an LDS regional representative and uses the church structure to mobilize a campaign. He asks bishops to appoint two people from each LDS ward to be a Quest member and fight the ERA.

July/August: The number of women at the Republican convention rises slightly to 31.4 percent and drops to 34 percent at the Democratic convention. A women's caucus at the Democratic convention in New York meets with presidential nominee Jimmy Carter and obtains a pledge to support the ERA and other women's issues.

October: The LDS First Presidency issues its first formal anti-ERA statement: "We recognize men and women as equally important before the Lord, but with differences biologically, emotionally, and in other ways. . . . ERA, we believe, does not recognize these differences."

November: The major parties nominate more women to the House of Representatives, but the net effect is the loss of one seat. The number of women in state legislatures increases to nine percent of the total.

1977 President Jimmy Carter names a new National Commission on the Observance of IWY and appoints Bella Abzug presiding officer. He names two women, Patricia Harris and Juanita Kreps, to his cabinet. Of the 526 top positions in the Carter administration, only 11 percent go to women.

January: Apostle Boyd K. Packer speaks in Pocatello, Idaho, to promote rescission of the ERA. On the podium is Allen Larsen, who is a Mormon stake president and Speaker of the Idaho House of Representatives. Afterward, the two hold a joint press conference. A few days later, the ERA is rescinded by a simple majority, whereas it originally passed with a two-thirds majority.

Relief Society President Barbara Smith gives anti-ERA speech in Coeur D'Alene, Idaho, urging the audience to defend the ERA rescission.

Indiana becomes the thirty-fifth and final state to ratify the ERA, three short of passage.

February: Utah Senator Jake Garn inserts the anti-ERA speech of Apostle Boyd K. Packer into the Congressional Record (s. 1980-

1982). Elder Packer repeats his speech for a South Carolina audience.

March: Mormons begin organizing in Florida and lobby the state legislature to reject the ERA.

April: At an LDS Church function in Sterling Park, Virginia, stake president Clifford Cummings gives an anti-ERA speech, initiating the local campaign against the ERA.

June: On the same platform with Phyllis Schlafly, LDS Relief Society President Barbara Smith gives an anti-ERA speech in Newport Beach, California, and praises Schlafly.

Approximately 14,000 Mormon women and men crowd into the IWY conference at the Salt Palace in Salt Lake City. They vote down all proposals including the ERA and world peace.

July: In the state of Washington, Mormons attempt to take over the IWY conference. Mormon men with walkie-talkies instruct women on which meetings to attend and how to vote. Mormons comprise 2 percent of the state's population.

Anti-ERA Mormons take over the IWY conference in Honolulu and elect an anti-ERA slate to the national convention in Houston. Hawaii was the first state to ratify the ERA and has its own state ERA law.

November: The National Women's Conference (IWY) convenes in Houston, Texas, to adopt a National Plan of Action.[2]

1978 May: Sen. Orrin Hatch inserts the official Mormon position against the ERA into the Congressional Record (s. 844-8442).

June: Based on research conducted by the LDS Church, the Washington D.C. area public communications director, Dale Ensign, gives Beltway church leaders the names of Senators and Congressmen thought to be on the fence about extending the deadline for the ERA and encourages them to contact these legislators to lobby against extension.

August: Sonia Johnson testifies before the Senate Subcommittee on Constitutional Rights, upsetting Senator Orrin Hatch (R-Utah). This attracts wide media attention. Membership in Mormons for ERA quickly grows to about 500.

The LDS First Presidency reiterates its position on the ERA in the *Church News*: "We believe ERA is a moral issue. . . . We express confidence that this nation is sufficiently strong and fair to be able to resolve problems of inequality . . . without undermining our most basic institution, the family."

October: Effective local campaigning prevents ERA supporters from gaining office in several state legislatures. Seventeen days before the election in Florida, Mormons raise $26,000 for four anti-ERA candidates; fifty-three percent of the money comes from California Mormons.

A brochure entitled *Why Mormon Women Oppose ERA* is printed with LDS Church funds and distributed to Relief Society women throughout the United States. It reads: "We take this opportunity again to bring to your attention our position on this important question. . . . Because of their unique capacities and responsibilities as wives and mothers, women should be the beneficiaries of such special laws as will safeguard . . . the interests of children and families. . . . We are convinced that . . . the matter is basically a moral rather than a political issue." "Because of our serious concern," it continues, "we urge our people to join actively . . . in working to reject this measure."

The First Presidency opposes the proposed extension of ERA ratification. Its statement is sent to all male church leaders in the United States and published in the church magazine, the *Ensign*.

November: The *Oakton Stake Newsletter* publishes an article, "Prophet Calls for Positive Action against ERA." It reads: "President Kimball recently asked President Julian Lowe, Regional Representative to the Council of the Twelve, to call a committee of Mormon women to work together against the passage of the Equal Rights Amendment."

BYU professor Stan Taylor gives an anti-ERA speech at the Oakton stake center in Virginia.

Effectively mobilizing ward members, Mormons in Nevada spend their Monday family home evening distributing anti-ERA literature and asking people to vote against the ERA referendum the next day. An estimated 90 percent of Mormons registered to vote in Nevada turn out to the polls to defeat the referendum.

The LDS Citizens Coalition is organized in Virginia at the home of stake president Clifford I. Cummings under the direction of Regional Representative Julian Lowe, who states that he was requested to organize the political action group by Apostle Gordon B. Hinckley, head of the LDS Church's Special Affairs Committee.

December: Spreading the word about the local campaign, anti-ERA petitions are distributed in Mormon wards in Virginia. In Orrin Hatch's ward in Vienna, petitions are sent down the pews during the sacrament service. They are later presented to members of the Virginia assembly in Richmond.

1979 January: Members of the Virginia LDS Citizens Coalition lobby the commonwealth's general assembly, although without having registered as a lobbying organization. Mormons will generate 85 percent of the anti-ERA mail sent to Virginia legislators. On the twenty-third, Mormon men and women will carry "Equality Yes, ERA No" banners at a Richmond rally.

George Romney, former governor of Michigan and an LDS regional representative, reiterates his anti-ERA stand in a letter to the Salt Lake City *Deseret News*.

United Press International reports in the Boise *Idaho Statesman* that the three law clerks of Judge Marion Callister—Cory Maxwell, David Thomas, and Greg Kerr—are recent BYU law school graduates. Maxwell is the son of Neal A. Maxwell, a Mormon general authority and member of the Special Affairs Committee, which is orchestrating the church's anti-ERA campaign.

March: After newspaper articles and an investigation by the Virginia Secretary of the Commonwealth, the LDS Citizens Coalition registers as a lobbyist.

June: The LDS First Presidency "encourage[s] all members as citizens of the nation to be actively involved in the political process," adding that "only the First Presidency and Twelve can declare a particular issue to be a moral issue worthy of full institutional involvement."

October: Over 125 Mormons attend a Kansas City council meeting to oppose a suggested endorsement of the ERA to the Missouri legislature. The group claims to represent 9,000 citizens but neglects to mention that they are LDS.

November: Relief Society President Barbara Smith gives her "How ERA Will Affect the Family" speech in a chapel in Frontenac, Missouri, sponsored by the LDS Missouri Citizens Council.

Sonia Johnson receives a letter telling her to appear before a church tribunal in three days. When she arrives on the seventeenth, she is confronted by five inquisitors who keep her five hours in what is called a "pre-trial hearing."

December: Sonia Johnson's church court is shifted to 8:00 p.m. at the Oakton, Virginia, stake center. Three hundred supporters stand outside in the cold (25 degrees) on the first evening in December to offer support. Four days later, Johnson receives word that she has been excommunicated.

George Romney tells the *Detroit News* that the equal rights movement has attracted "moral perverts" who want to undermine the family.

Judge Callister announces he is no longer an LDS regional representative and has not been for months, which is a surprise to church members. The 1981 *Church Almanac* will give his release date as October 15. Major newspapers around the country editorialize that Callister should recuse himself.

1980 January: The LDS *Church News* publishes an editorial titled: "Is ERA a Moral Issue?" It concludes that "Church membership is not for spectators. The cause of righteousness ever calls for action."

February: A staff member and former staff member in the office of Senator Jake Garn (R-Utah) write anti-ERA letters to the *Washington Post,* posing as private citizens.

Mormons for ERA member Arlene B. Wood requests excommunication after learning the church released Judge Callister as a regional representative retroactively rather than give up the chance to have an LDS judge rule on an ERA case.

March: The LDS Church publishes *The Church and the Proposed Equal Rights Amendment: A Moral Issue,* first as an insert in the *Ensign* magazine, and asserts that "the ERA is a serious moral issue. . . . For those . . . who choose to remain in the home, . . . passage of the ERA may make their choice more difficult. . . . Great pressures could be brought to bear on a woman not to marry or have children. . . . The First Presidency has spoken out against the amendment. In addition, many local Church leaders on stake and ward levels have encouraged their membership to keep informed and perform their civic duties. . . . Because of this counsel, many Church members have joined with other similarly minded citizens in their efforts to defeat the ERA."

April: LDS Apostle Gordon B. Hinckley and Marriott Corporation President J. Willard Marriott Jr. attempt to explain to NBC television host Tom Brokaw of the *Today Show* why the church opposes the ERA.

May: The *Salt Lake Tribune* publishes survey results showing that most Mormons favor the ERA in concept if its wording is read to them, but not in name.

August: Senator Orrin Hatch tells the *Deseret News* that "no member of Congress will have a greater ability to defeat the ERA than I."

October: Apostle Hinckley tells Cheryl Dalton, Marty LaBrosse, and Sarah Campbell that Rex E. Lee, dean of Brigham Young University's law school, was encouraged through church channels to write his book *A Lawyer Looks at the Equal Rights Amendment*, published by BYU Press and favorably reviewed in the *Church News*.

November: The *Deseret News* praises Rex Lee's book. A news article by Gordon Eliot White reports that Lee is being recommended to the new Reagan Administration by the Utah Congressional delegation.

December: The "LDS Coalition to Stop ERA" hands out a letter in Virginia wards with instructions on how to get organized to influence the January general assembly session.

1981 January: Lobbyists with the LDS Citizens Coalition distribute Rex Lee's *A Lawyer Looks at the Equal Rights Amendment* to Virginia legislators.

July: Mormon Senators Paula Hawkins (R-Florida) and Orrin Hatch (R-Utah) defend Rex Lee's nomination as U.S. Solicitor General. Fifteen Senators vote against his appointment.

September: LDS volunteers in northern Virginia place flyers on car windshields promoting anti-ERA candidates in the primary election.

December: On Joseph Smith's birthday, Judge Callister rules that Congress may not extend the time limit for ERA ratification but that, rather inconsistently, state legislatures may rescind their ratification at any time.

1982 January: LDS Regional Representative Richard Winder organizes Relief Society women to write letters to Georgia legislators. Time is also set aside in Sunday school for letter writing, with instructions not to identify oneself as a Mormon. Approximately 14,000 Mormons in Georgia produce about 250,000 letters.

March: The LDS Church cancels disciplinary action against a nineteen-year-old Maryland student, Melissa Mowen, for her support of the ERA after the national media has drawn attention to her plight.

June: The extended deadline for ratifying the ERA passes, three states short of the thirty-eight needed for ratification.

Appendix 2

UTAH IWY CONFERENCE SCHEDULE

The Voice of Womankind[1]

FRIDAY, JUNE 24, 1977

7:00 a.m.-7:00 p.m.
Registration, Salt Palace foyer

8:30-11:15 a.m.
Plenary session, exhibit hall

Presiding
Esther Landa

Invocation
Alice Kasai, member, Coordinating Committee

Presentation of colors
Girl Scouts of America, led by Dorothea Livingston, member, Coordinating Committee, in American Indian dress

Song
"America the Beautiful,"
conducted by Helen Knox; accompanist, Kathryn F. Kirk

Introduction of
Jan Tyler, chair, Coordinating Committee
Kathryn Putnam, recording secretary
Adelyn Logan, parliamentarian
Coordinating Committee and staff
Workshop leaders and Coordinating Council chairs

Credentials Committee report
Doris Wilson, chair

Adoption of State Meeting rules
Adelyn Logan, parliamentarian

State Meeting program
Sharon Keigher, vice-chair, Coordinating Committee

Voting instructions
Janet Darley, chair, Elections Committee

Nominating Committee report
Kathleen Flake, vice-chair

9:45-10:15 a.m.
Nominations from the floor

10:15 a.m.-7:30 p.m.
Film festival, room 220

10:15-11:45 a.m.
General session, exhibit hall

Presiding
Jan Tyler

Film
"Decade of Our Destiny"

Speech
"Today the Prelude for Tomorrow"
Belle Spafford, member of Executive Committee of
the National Council of Women of the United States

Introduction of speaker
Brenda Hancock, member, Coordinating Committee

Comments
Mary Anne Krupsak, Lieutenant Governor, State of New York, and member, National Commission for the Observance of International Women's Year

Meet the delegate nominees
Assembly hall

11:45 a.m.-7:30 p.m.
Voting on national recommendations
2nd level, top of escalators

11:45 a.m.-1:00 p.m.
Luncheon on your own

1:00-3:00 p.m.
Workshop groups
Aging
Child abuse
Employment
Enforcement of laws
Legal status of homemakers
Lifestyles
Mental health
Polarity
Power: Elective, appointive, personal
Women as students
Women offenders
(Film festival)

3:30-5:30 p.m.
Workshop groups
Arts and humanities
Basic needs

Child development
Equal Rights Amendment
Media
Men
Minority women
Reproductive health
Teen-age pregnancy
Women in Utah history
(Film festival)

5:30-6:30 p.m.
General session, exhibit hall

Presiding
Shauna Adix, member, Coordinating Committee

Open mike
Opportunity for anyone to express her/his ideas on issues of concern to women

5:30-6:00 p.m.
Meet the delegate nominees
Northern corner of exhibit hall

6:30-7:30 p.m.
Dinner on your own

7:30-10:00 p.m.
Plenary session, exhibit hall

Presiding
Esther Landa

Credentials Committee report
Doris Wilson, chair, Recommendations from Workshop Groups

SATURDAY, JUNE 25, 1977

7:00 a.m.-2:00 p.m.
Registration, Salt Palace foyer

8:30-8:45 a.m.
Plenary session, exhibit hall

Presiding
Esther Landa

Credentials Committee Report
Doris Wilson, chair

Voting Instructions
Janet Darley, chair, Elections Committee

8:45 a.m.-2:00 p.m.
Film festival, room 220

8:45-9:45 a.m.
General session, exhibit hall

Presiding
Katie Dixon, vice-chair, Coordinating Committee

Speech
"The First Step: Getting Involved"
Lola Redford, member, Coordinating Committee

Introduction of Film
Sharon Keigher, co-vice chair, Coordinating Committee

Film
"Soul of Iron"

Conclusion

9:00 a.m.-3:00 p.m.
Balloting for Delegates
2nd level top of escalators

10:00 a.m.-12:00 noon
Workshop groups
Basic needs
Employment
Equal Rights Amendment
Health education
International interdependence
Legal status of homemakers
Lifestyles
Men
Rape
Wife abuse
Women as educators
Women in Utah history projects inc.
Young women (life-span planning)
(Film festival)

12:00 noon-1:00 p.m.
Luncheon on your own

1:00-2:00 p.m.
General session, exhibit hall

Presiding
Dolores Bennett, member, Coordinating Committee

Introduction of Speaker
Jan L. Tyler, chair, Coordinating Committee

Speech
"Women's Voice in International Affairs"
Holvi Sipila, Secretary General of the United Nations for Social Development and Humanitarian Affairs

2:00-5:45 p.m.
Plenary session, exhibit hall

Presiding
Esther Landa

Credentials Committee report
Doris Wilson, chair

Recommendations from Workshop Groups

Elections Committee
Janet Darley, chair

Recommendations from Workshop Groups

Unfinished Business

New Business

5:45 p.m.
Adjournment of State Meeting

Appendix 3

NATIONAL IWY RESOLUTIONS, 1977

The vote tallies below indicate action taken on the national recommendations at Utah's IWY conference, June 1977.

1. **Arts and Humanities**
   1. The President should take steps to require that women (1) have equal opportunities for appointment to managerial and upper level posts in Federally-funded cultural institutions, such as libraries, museums, universities, and public radio and TV; (2) are more equitably represented in the staffing of grant-awarding agencies; (3) benefit more fairly from government grants, whether as individual grant applicants or as members of cultural institutions receiving Federal or state funding.

      - Agree: 1,486
      - Disagree: 8,041
      - Don't know: 73

   2. Judging agencies and review boards should use blind judging for musicians, singers, articles, and papers being considered for publication or delivery, exhibits, and grant applications, wherever possible.

- Agree: 2,091
- Disagree: 7,199
- Don't know: 130

2. **Child Care**
   1. The federal government should assume a major role in providing universal voluntary child development programs with ability-to-pay fee schedules and with direct parental involvement in operation.
      - Agree: 623
      - Disagree: 8,894
      - Don't know: 76
   2. Employers and labor unions should be encouraged by tax policies of Federal and State governments to establish nonprofit child care programs.
      - Agree: 693
      - Disagree: 8,858
      - Don't know: 67
   3. Education or parenthood programs should be improved and expanded by local and State school boards with technical assistance and experimental programs provided by the Federal government.
      - Agree: 1,020
      - Disagree: 8,424
      - Don't know: 75

3. **Credit**
   1. The Federal Equal Credit Opportunity Act should be vigorously, efficiently, and expeditiously enforced by all the Federal agencies with enforcement responsibility.
      - Agree: 2,021

- Disagree: 7,485
- Don't know: 152

4. Education

1. The President should direct the vigorous and expeditious enforcement of all laws prohibiting discrimination in education, including sports, and oppose any amendments that would weaken the protections.

    - Agree: 905
    - Disagree: 8,732
    - Don't know: 76

2. Federal surveys of elementary and secondary schools should gather data needed to indicate compliance with Federal anti-discrimination laws, and these data should be collected by sex and race or ethnicity.

    - Agree: 657
    - Disagree: 8,910
    - Don't know: 115

3. The Civil Rights Commission should conduct a study to evaluate the enforcement of laws prohibiting sex discrimination in physical education and athletics.

    - Agree: 1,666
    - Disagree: 7,864
    - Don't know: 148

4. Bilingual vocational training and education programs should be extended and significantly expanded.

    - Agree: 1,148
    - Disagree: 8,326
    - Don't know: 177

5. Leadership programs for working women in post-secondary schools should be upgraded and expanded, and private foundations are urged to give special attention to research on women in unions.

- Agree: 1,148
- Disagree: 8,326
- Don't know: 117

5. Employment

1. The President should direct the vigorous and expeditious enforcement of all laws, executive orders, and regulations prohibiting discrimination in employment, including discrimination in apprenticeship and in construction.

- Agree: 1,197
- Disagree: 8,455
- Don't know: 85

2. The Executive Branch of the Federal government should abide by the same standards as private employers.

- Agree: 2,217
- Disagree: 7,227
- Don't know: 223

3. Protections and privileges afforded minority business owners should be extended to women business owners.

- Agree: 2,043
- Disagree: 7,473
- Don't know: 131

4. All enforcement agencies should follow the guidelines of the Equal Employment Opportunity Commission.

- Agree: 1,304
- Disagree: 8,137
- Don't know: 222

5. The Equal Employment Opportunity Commission should be expanded to cover discrimination in job evaluation systems.

    - Agree: 1,108
    - Disagree: 8,357
    - Don't know: 199

6. Unions should review the impact of women of all their practices [*sic*] and correct injustices to women.

    - Agree: 1,724
    - Disagree: 7,838
    - Don't know: 1,020

7. The President should take into account in appointments to the National Labor Relations Board and in seeking amendments to it the obstacles confronting women who seek to organize in traditionally nonunionized employment sectors.

    - Agree: 1,241
    - Disagree: 8,221
    - Don't know: 252

8. Extra attention should be given the employment needs of minority women, especially blacks, Hispanics, Asian-Americans, and Native Americans.

    - Agree: 951
    - Disagree: 8,624
    - Don't know: 144

9. Enforcement of the Fair Labor Standards Act and the Social Security Act as they apply to household workers should be improved.

    - Agree: 1,297
    - Disagree: 8,149
    - Don't know: 255

10. All statistics collected by the Federal government should be gathered and analyzed so that information concerning the impact of Federal programs on women and the participation of women in the administration of Federal programs can be assessed.

    - Agree: 1,210
    - Disagree: 8,334
    - Don't know: 158

6. Female Offenders

1. Federal and State governments should cooperate in providing more humane, sensible and economic treatment of young women who are subject to court jurisdiction because they have run away from home, have family or school problems, or commit sexual offenses ("status offenders").

    - Agree: 1,831
    - Disagree: 7,678
    - Don't know: 154

2. Disparities in the treatment of male and female juvenile offenders should be eliminated.

    - Agree: 1,591
    - Disagree: 7,910
    - Don't know: 195

3. States should review their sentencing laws and their practices re-

lating to women in penal facilities with a view to eliminating discrimination and reforming treatment.

- Agree: 1,591
- Disagree: 7,910
- Don't know: 195

7. Health

1. The President should direct a review of whether women and their mental and physical health needs are being treated equitably in the health related functions of the Federal government.

    - Agree: 1,118
    - Disagree: 8,452
    - Don't know: 135

2. Women should be represented in all aspects of health-related federal programs, including policy, administration, research design, research populations, and general service availability to women.

    - Agree: 1,729
    - Disagree: 7,825
    - Don't know: 105

8. Legal Status of Homemakers

1. Federal and State laws relating to marital property, inheritance, and domestic relations should be based on the principle that marriage is a partnership, in which the contributions of each spouse are of equal importance and value.

    - Agree: 1,281
    - Disagree: 8,202
    - Don't know: 208

2. Homemakers should be covered under Social Security.

- Agree: 1,405
- Disagree: 8,039
- Don't know: 247

3. Alimony, child support, and property arrangements at divorce should be such that minor children's needs are first to be met and spouses share the economic dislocation of divorce. As a minimum the economic provisions of the Uniform Marriage and Divorce Act should be enacted in every State.

    - Agree: 1,405
    - Disagree: 8,039
    - Don't know: 247

4. More effective methods for collection of support should be adopted.

    - Agree: 1,145
    - Disagree: 8,282
    - Don't know: 232

5. Homemakers displaced by widowhood or divorce should be helped to become self-sufficient members of society through programs providing job counseling, training, and placement; advice on financial management; and legal advice.

    - Agree: 2,091
    - Disagree: 7,442
    - Don't know: 101

9. International Interdependence

1. The President and the foreign affairs agencies of the Federal government should see to it that many more women participate in the formulation and execution of U.S. foreign policy, including greater

consultation with women in citizen voluntary organizations which are concerned with international affairs.

- Agree: 1,364
- Disagree: 8,200
- Don't know: 135

2. More women should be appointed to U.S. delegations at international conferences and to governing bodies of international organizations.

- Agree: 462
- Disagree: 8,093
- Don't know: 141

3. The U.N. Commission on the Status of Women should be continued and should meet annually.

- Agree: 1,463
- Disagree: 7,949
- Don't know: 259

10. Mass Media

1. The mass media should employ women in all job categories and especially in policy-making positions.

- Agree: 1,371
- Disagree: 8,247
- Don't know: 141

2. Affirmative efforts should be made by the media to expand the portrayal of women to include a variety of roles and to represent accurately the number of women in society.

- Agree: 1,371
- Disagree: 8,214
- Don't know: 111

3. Appropriate federal agencies, such as the Equal Employment Opportunity Commission, the Federal Communications Commission and the Department of HEW, among others, should vigorously enforce those laws which prohibit employment discrimination against women working in the media.

- Agree: 1,433
- Disagree: 8,089
- Don't know: 146

4. Federal agencies should continue studying the impact of the mass media on sex discrimination and sex-role stereotyping in the American society. Special consideration should be given to media which are publicly funded or established through acts of Congress.

- Agree: 918
- Disagree: 8,577
- Don't know: 141

11. Equal Rights Amendment

1. The Equal Rights Amendment should be ratified.

- Agree: 666
- Disagree: 8,956
- Don't know: 84

12. Older Women

1. Public and private women's organizations should work together to give publicity to the positive roles of women over 50 and to provide the services that will enable elderly women to function comfortably in their own homes instead of moving to institutions.

- Agree: 1,591
- Disagree: 7,896
- Don't know: 224

13. Rape

1. State and local governments should revise rape laws to provide for graduated degrees of the crime, to apply to assault by or upon both sexes; to include all types of sexual assault against adults; and to otherwise redefine the crime so that victims are under no greater legal handicaps than victims of other crimes.

    - Agree: 2,296
    - Disagree: 7,235
    - Don't know: 164

2. Local task forces to review and reform law and practices of police prosecutors and medical personnel should be established where they do not now exist.

    - Agree: 2,414
    - Disagree: 7,008
    - Don't know: 173

14. Teenage Pregnancy

1. The IWY Committee believes that the moral decisions relating to reproduction are rightfully the responsibility of individual women and that every woman, regardless of her economic circumstances, education, race or ethnic origin, age, rural or metropolitan residence, is entitled as a basic human right to have readily available the means of controlling reproduction. The IWY Commission: supports the series of Supreme Court decisions guaranteeing reproductive freedom to women; Urges all branches of Federal, State, and local governments to give the highest priority to complying with these Supreme Court decisions and to making available all methods of family planning to women unable to take advantage of private facilities; Condemns any interference, open or subtle, with a woman's right to control her reproduction; and Urges organizations concerned with improving the status of women to monitor how government complies with these princi-

ples. Particular attention should be paid at all levels of government to providing family planning services for teenagers, education in responsible sexuality, and reform of laws discriminating against illegitimate children and their parents.

- Agree: 627
- Disagree: 9,048
- Don't know: 66

15. Women in Elective Appointments

1. The President, Governors, political parties, women's organizations, and foundations should join in an effort to increase the number of women in elective and appointive office, including especially judgeships.

- Agree: 1,463
- Disagree: 8,057
- Don't know: 121

Appendix 4

UTAH TASK FORCE RECOMMENDATIONS

The Utah IWY task forces summarized their recommendations and how the votes went at the workshops and plenary sessions, June 24-25, 1977.

1. **Aging. Recommendations. Reform present social security guidelines as follows:**
   a. Make provision for individually maintained social security accounts without regard to marital status.
   b. Raise the earning limitations. This would permit women and all other retired persons to earn more without reducing benefits.
   c. Repeal any mandatory retirement provisions.
   d. Eliminate or shorten the six months waiting period when separated couples cannot be eligible for individual benefits under the supplemental security income programs.
   e. Permit SSI benefits to continue during periods of temporary institutionalization.

Passed in the plenary session were items b, c, and e. All three recommendations fulfill the substance of the national recommendations.

2. **Arts and Humanities. Recommendations:**
   1. The Arts and Humanities Task Force recommends that agencies

offering grants to arts and humanities related projects more publicly announce the availability of grants and educate the residents of the state on the procedure of applying for grants.

2. We further recommend that the state legislation allocate funds for a public information person attached to the Utah State Division of Fine Arts to achieve this end.
3. Special consideration is due the communities away from large, metropolitan areas.

The first recommendation passed in the plenary session, the others did not. No other discussions of these national recommendations persisted past the workshop.

3. **Employment. Recommendations:**

The governor should direct the Utah Anti-Discrimination Division to:

1. Develop training programs for employers, employees and public regarding fair employment practices,
2. Fill the UADD position of division coordinator (required by statute) and hire other staff representing the interests of women,
3. Develop a more efficient and timely investigation/conciliation process.

The Utah Legislature should:

1. Change the name of the UADD to the Utah Office of Fair Employment Practices,
2. Change the Utah Anti-Discrimination Act of 1965 as amended to conform with federal law.

The workshop also recommended that:

1. MEDCU and SBA should consider women as another economically disadvantaged group and develop outreach and technical assistance programs for women;
2. The governor should issue an executive order requiring that women be invited to bid in purchasing activities of the state and agencies contracting with the state, and should

direct development services to develop programs to attract women business owners to Utah.

The governor and local elected officials should:

1. Develop management training programs for women and awareness training programs for current administrators,
2. Make affirmative efforts to appoint qualified women to high level administrative jobs,
3. Designate funds, including present special CETA funds, to allow women job opportunities,
4. Direct detailed study of merit and civil service systems to remove barriers to women's advancement in state, city and county jobs.

The final group of recommendations included the following ideas:

1. WIN and CETA programs should redirect programs and support services to train more women in non-traditional occupations.
2. The governor should earmark a portion of existing state and federal discretionary funds to develop and test pilot programs for women entering nontraditional occupations.

The recommendations coming out of the workshop reflected the national agenda. The plenary session passed none.

4. Equal Rights Amendment. Recommendations:

1. Because the women of Utah are opposed to ERA, we propose that all proponents or opponents of ERA from this time forth finance their causes with whatever privately sponsored funding they may obtain. We oppose the use of our public monies to promote or oppose the ERA.
2. We go on record as being opposed to the Equal Rights Amendment.
3. Resolved that, we, the participants of the largest IWY meeting in our nation's history, direct the Congress of the United States to appropriate no new funds for International Women's Year.

5. **Child Abuse. Recommendations:**
   1. Increase public education and expand treatment and prevention in all existing outreach programs.
   2. Appoint more juvenile court judges to deal with the cases in a more expeditious manner.
   3. Expand the state Advisory Committee on Child Abuse to effect better coordination of existing resources and conduct a public awareness program.
   4. Establish within the Division of Family Services an effective central registry in coordination with hospitals, pediatricians, other medical personnel and related agencies.
   5. Follow through with the State Plan on Child Abuse and Neglect (June 1975) which received approval of the governor. Provide adequate funding for increasing not only the number of social workers in the Division of Family Services, Protective Service, but provide specific training programs in neglect and abuse prevention.

Recommendations 1, 2, 4, and 5 passed the plenary session.

6. **Child Development. Recommendations:**

   The total local community must make a commitment to improve, expand, and coordinate parent education classes at the junior high, high school, and post high school levels. We support the Utah State Board of Education policy in recommending training for responsible adulthood and parenthood classes for all students in the secondary schools subject to community approval as per type of material taught. This education should be provided by teachers who have proven competence in the areas of child development and family relationships.

These task force recommendations represented the national recommendations. All were rejected in the plenary session.

7. **Wife Abuse. Recommendations:**

   Establish a network of emergency safety haven shelters for physically and emotionally battered wives to be sponsored by local organizations and the Division of Family Services. Furthermore, the task force recommended that:

1. The legal system be responsive to battered wives cases,
2. Information on legal alternatives be made readily available,
3. That stronger state laws be adopted for the punishment of wife abusers and protection of wives,
4. That a husband have a legal obligation to provide financial compensation for losses suffered by a battered wife; i.e. medical expenses, child care during recovery, and compensation for missed employment;
5. That all city, county, and state law enforcement bodies be encouraged to maintain separate statistics on wife-abuse incidents,
6. That churches, volunteer groups, civic organizations, and the media be encouraged to educate the public about the existence of wife abuse and available alternatives for victims.

These recommendations capture the essence of the national recommendations. All of these recommendations were passed both in the workshop and the plenary sessions.

8. Rape. Recommendations:

1. Enact a statute which would limit introduction of evidence of the victim's past sexual conduct or general sexual reputation to specific incidences where it is clearly relevant and where the court, after a closed hearing, makes a determination as to relevancy and admissibility.
2. Eliminate all language in Utah's laws which discriminate on the basis of gender of the attacker of a victim. The method is to enact changes in the statutes which would eliminate all sexually discriminatory language from Utah's laws on rape and sexual assault.
3. Bring rape and sexual assault laws into harmony with other criminal statutes by including spouses as victims.
4. Provide counseling for victims of sexual assault by individuals

specifically trained to deal with this unique problem, and increase medical sensitivity to the needs of the sexual assault victim.

5. Insure the victim of rape freedom of choice in terminating or sustaining pregnancies resulting from rape.
6. Provide compensation to victims for property damage, loss of income, and medical and counseling expenses.

The plenary session voted down items 2, 3, 5, and 6.

9. Minority Women. Recommendations:

1. Adequate funding for child care services for low-income women.
2. Improved multi-cultural educational opportunities.
3. Bilingual and multi-cultural education in educational institutions.

All recommendations defeated at the workshop stage.

10. Health Education. Recommendations:

1. Ask that the Federal Drug Administration compile and distribute a table of bioequivalent drugs.
2. Remove taxes from eye-glasses and hearing aids.
3. Improve existing school health programs with qualified teachers.
4. Place more women in decision-making bodies at policy-making levels in health areas.
5. Abolish discriminatory acts by insurance companies.
6. Establish local boards of interested and eminent health professionals to review, research, train and educate women and the public on pertinent health issues.

The plenary session approved 1 and 2.

11. Mental Health. Recommendations:

1. Implement in the secondary school system a curriculum which includes the teaching of parenting and child development skills. Credit for these classes should be allowed toward graduation.
2. Launch an educational program by utilizing existing community organizations and agencies through which classes and support systems may be available to those citizens desiring them.

3. Provide training and services through local rather than federal funding which includes job skills development, job preparation, financial management, availability of cooperative day care and temporary welfare programs.

The plenary session modified but passed all three recommendations.

12. Legal Status of Homemakers. Recommendations:

1. The establishment of a mandatory family court system in Utah.
2. Tax reform to allow tax deductions for expenses accrued by the disability of full-time homemakers. The provisions of the Internal Revenue Code and state legislation relating to estate and gift taxes should be amended to eliminate taxation on all transfers of property between husband and wife at death and on all gifts between husband and wife during their lifetimes.
3. Social Security Act benefits presently accruing to the spouse employed outside the home should accrue equally to the homemaker and the spouse.
4. Support for the Utah Parentage Act.
5. Urge women in Utah to become aware of and to cooperate with state and county recovery services.

The plenary session passed 1, 2, 4, and 5. None of the following items in the national recommendations were addressed in the task force recommendations: divorce law reform, job counseling, training and placement after divorce or widowhood, or property.

13. International Interdependence. Recommendations:

No task force was assigned to prepare recommendations before the workshop; but in this workshop, recommendations emerged against foreign aid, international interdependence, and "any world government body which attempts to dilute our national laws and personal sovereignty." This action was not necessarily a rejection of the ideas in the national resolutions but rather a different focus.

The plenary session adopted all the resolutions except the one against foreign aid.

14. Media. Recommendations:

1. The media should support as an ultimate goal the employment of women in policy making positions, make special efforts to employ women who are knowledgeable, employ qualified women at all job levels, and support equal pay, opportunity, training and promotion of women.
2. Media content should avoid the exploitation of women and broaden subject matter to include stories about women.
3. Because the media has such a tremendous impact on public opinion, it should serve as a vehicle in educating the public, for example, dealing with rape as a crime of violence, rather than focusing on sexual aspects of rape.
4. A person's right to determine her or his own title should be respected.
5. Television and radio should withdraw all commercials concerning women's personal health products.

Rejected items 1, 2, and 4.

15. Men. Recommendations:

1. Efforts should be made to work for stringent enforcement of current anti-pornographic legislation and to seek even stronger control of the distribution of pornographic materials. This effort should recognize fully that pornography is as damaging to men as to women.
2. Alternative living accommodations should be provided for victims of family violence either as a private effort (members of churches and other organizations volunteering their homes as a refuge), or through public funding for facilities.
3. Training in parenting skills should become mandatory for all secondary high school students.

The workshop passed these three recommendations. The plenary session passed an amended version of the first.

16. Reproductive Health. Recommendations:

1. Distinction between male and female should remain in textbooks,

although they should stress equality in opportunities.

2. Sexual information in textbooks and in classrooms is not allowed, with the exception of basic anatomically natural reproduction.
3. Teaching this information should not begin until sixth grade.
4. Unnatural sex acts such as homosexuality and self-stimulation are not to be taught in public schools.

Abortion. Recommendations:

1. All state and federally funded abortions should be ruled unlawful.
2. "We, the people of Utah, propose that it be on record that we support the Right to Life Amendment."
3. Funds now used for abortion should be used for medical research to eliminate birth defects and to assist those who choose to give their children up for adoption to parents who are unable to conceive and who want these children.

Sex education. Recommendations:

1. Steps should be taken to strengthen the family unit.
2. Sex education is the sacred responsibility of all parents; thus, classes should be made available through local religious and civic organizations to teach parents how to teach their children about sex and its responsibility.

All task force recommendations were rejected at the workshop stage.

17. Women in Utah History. Recommendations:

1. Women should be included in the history of Utah as it is written in textbooks and monographs, as it is taught in the public schools and institutions of higher learning, and as it is ritualized in programs, pageants, and monuments.
2. History departments, historical societies, museums, and archives should hire more women as managers, actively collect women's materials, and conscientiously promote the inclusion of women in Utah history.

These recommendations were passed both in the workshop and in the plenary session.

18. Recommendations Affecting Young Women

1. Life Span Planning. Recommendations:
    1. Families and schools should emphasize training young women in decision-making skills centering around conscious life choices to give them the training both to be self-supporting, if and when that option arises, and to prepare time to be adequate wives and mothers, if and when that option arises.
    2. We propose the increase and improvement in sex education for parents so that sex education in families may be strengthened.
    3. We propose the improvement of sex education for the medical profession, clergy, and professional counselors so they may be better prepared to counsel adults and young people.

The plenary session rejected all three recommendations.

2. Teenage Pregnancy. Recommendations:
    1. Schools should provide vocational training for pregnant students or students who are also parents.
    2. Schools should sponsor education programs to prevent teenage pregnancy.

The workshop rejected the second item and passed the first, which also passed in the plenary session.

Appendix 5

LDS FIRST PRESIDENCY STATEMENTS ON THE ERA

October 12, 1976
First Presidency Statement Opposing Equal Rights Amendment

From its beginnings, The Church of Jesus Christ of Latter-day Saints has affirmed the exalted role of woman in our society. In 1842, when women's organizations were little known, the Prophet Joseph Smith established the women's organization of the Church, the Relief Society, as a companion body of the priesthood. The Relief Society continues to function today as a vibrant, worldwide organization aimed at strengthening motherhood and broadening women's earning and involvement in religious, compassionate, cultural, educational, and community pursuits. In Utah, where our Church is headquartered, women received the right to vote in 1870, fifty years before the Nineteenth Amendment to the Constitution granted the right nationally. There have been injustices of women before the law and in society generally. These we deplore. There are additional rights to which women are entitled. However, we firmly believe that the Equal Rights Amendment is not the answer. While the motives of its supporters may be praiseworthy, ERA as a blanket attempt to help women could indeed bring them far more restraints and repressions. We fear it will even stifle many God-given feminine instincts. It would strike at the family, humankind's basic institution. ERA would bring ambiguity and possibly invite extensive litigation. Passage of ERA, some legal authorities contend, could nullify many accumulated benefits to women in present statutes. We recognize men and women as equally important before the Lord, but with differences biologically, emotionally, and in other ways. ERA, we believe, does not recognize these differences. There are better means for giving women, and men, the rights they deserve. (*Church News*, Oct. 22: *Ensign*, Dec. 1976)

May 25, 1978
Statement of the First Presidency of The Church of Jesus Christ of Latter-day Saints Opposing Extension of the Time for Ratification of Equal Rights Amendment

We feel that to extend the time for the ratification of the Equal Rights Amendment would be unwise as well as unfair.

The Church of Jesus Christ of Latter-day Saints (Mormon) has a profound veneration for the Constitution of the United States of America. We believe it was divinely inspired, and we take a serious interest in any proposed amendments to that basic document and the process itself by which the Constitution is amended. Furthermore, the Church has a very deep and everlasting commitment to the preservation and strengthening of the family, including its individual members. As a people who have in our history known the loss of our constitutional rights, we have long been concerned with the rights and interests of both men and women.

For these reasons, the Church has done what it rarely does—spoken out against a proposed constitutional amendment.

Our opposition to the Equal Rights Amendment as stated in our message of October 22, 1976 (attached) is clear and expresses genuine concern. But our concern over the Equal Rights Amendment has now been deepened by what appears to be a tampering with and an abuse of the process of amendment itself. To couple the extension of time with a restriction against reconsideration of previous ratifications would be most unwise for at least these reasons:

First, the continuation of the ERA ratification effort will increasingly divide and polarize this nation. Rather than bringing opposing sides closer together, any extension will see them grow farther apart and become more set in their opposing views.

Second, to continue the divisive struggle for the ratification of the ERA is unfair to the interests of women. The additional time, money and energy which would be employed attempting to insure its passage could be more effectively used in other ways in the interests of women. If and where specific laws or practices exist which discriminate against women, we should devote our most conscientious efforts toward changing them. Each woman should be encouraged in her honorable aspirations for fulfillment and special esteem. Because all human life begins with her, The Church of Jesus Christ of Latter-day Saints has always held her in revered light.

Third, it seems clear that support for ERA lacks the powerful consensus of that very large majority of people in the United States (two-thirds for action in the national Congress; three-fourths in the state legislatures) which is so wisely required by its framers to change the Constitution. Indeed, some states which have previously passed the amendment have now voted to rescind ratification. The formal procedures set up by the framers of the Constitution by which the Constitution is amended are part of the vitality of the Constitution. If these processes are abused, the Constitution is itself damaged and its power and influence among our people are proportionately diminished.

Fourth, we believe the Equal Rights Amendment has had its full chance to build the support that any constitutional amendment should have to secure passage. Any extension beyond seven years is unnecessary, unwise and unprecedented. The proposed amendment has enjoyed almost twice the time to seek ratification of any previous amendment which has been passed and three and one-half times longer than the average. The very careful process of amending the Constitution gives our nation time to arouse our intellects, to search our hearts, and to consult our consciences. That time has now passed.

Fifth, it would be deeply offensive to any sense of fairness to extend the deadline for ratification of the proposed Equal Rights Amendment so that some states which have refused ratification can change their mind but, at the same time, to refuse to allow other state legislatures the right to change their mind and rescind their previous acts of approval. Any such gross abuse of the democratic process and of the process of amending the Constitution could send a surge of cynicism through the land which might damage the Constitution itself. Why should there be an eccentric method of legislation applied to this one amendment?

Any extension at all is unwise, but a one-sided extension of the amending process regarding the Equal Rights Amendment would set a precedent for constitutional revision that could haunt America for years to come. Great uncertainty about the revision process would emerge if the amending process is extended over 14 years. And why not 21 years? Would the Americans of 1943 wish to have been bound by the action of state legislatures passed in 1929? Is it fair to allow a state to pass the Equal Rights Amendment in 1986 which refused to pass it in 1972, while refusing a state which passed it in 1972 the opportunity to rescind it in 1986? If the latest action of a state legislature is not valid, when is the will of the people as expressed through state legislatures not the will of the people?

Thus, changing the rules for a proposed amendment adds the possibility of great uncertainty in the amending process of the Constitution. An unduly protracted process of approval could raise doubts and encourage litigation. Once an amendment to the Constitution has been approved and is in place in that document, it would be unthinkable to let a state alter its action concerning that amendment. Prior to the formal placement of an amendment in the Constitution, states should be equally free, within a relatively short period of time, to approve or rescind their actions concerning any proposed amendment.

It would be tragic indeed if an amendment which claims to bring constitutional equality to women ended up injuring our Constitution. Our political process and institutions have, from time to time, been tainted and corrupted. However, when our nation has followed the procedure outlined in the Constitution to amend that document its integrity has been preserved. When thus amended, our Constitution has reflected a sufficiently strong will of the people that an issue is settled rather than being in doubt. This wise process permits our Constitution to remain safely above the fray and beyond the reach of corruption and manipulation, and hold the special place it enjoys in the hearts and minds of the people.

In affirming our allegiance to The United States of America, we express confidence that this nation is sufficiently strong and fair to be able to resolve any problems of inequality and unfairness to women, or any other group in our society, without abusing the amending process for our most basic document, the Constitution, and without undermining our most basic institution, the family. (Letter, addressed to the Honorable Don Edwards, Chairman, Subcommittee on Civil and Constitutional Rights, Committee on the Judiciary, Rayburn House Office Building, Washington D.C.)

NOTES

Notes to the Introduction

1. Linda Sillitoe, "Don't Use My Name," 1979, photocopy of typescript, Utah Women's Issues Collection, Special Collections, Marriott Library, University of Utah, Salt Lake City. The quotations that follow are from this typescript.

2. Ruth Murray Brown, *For a "Christian America": A History of the Religious Right* (Amherst, NY: Prometheus Books, 2002).

3. Addressing discrimination based on sexual orientation is an even thornier political issue and will probably become *the* moral/ethical/social fight of the twenty-first century.

4. bell hooks, *Feminist Theory: From Margin to Center* (Cambridge, MA: South End Press Classics, 1984), 5. Ms. hooks doesn't capitalize her name.

5. Ibid., 28, 35. For hooks, the campaign for and against the ERA would have been better served by stressing the transformative effect of "a massive political campaign to build a feminist constituency." Instead, "Where one stood depended largely on what one perceived to be the appropriate position of women in American society and what threatened to change it" (35).

6. Dan L. Thrapp, "Mormon Church Has Answer for All Needs, Its New Leader Says," *Los Angeles Times,* Oct. 5, 1974.

7. "BYU Women Oppose ERA, Survey Says, Men Prefer 'Pretty Faces,'" *Salt Lake Tribune,* Feb. 13, 1977.

8. Elaine Cannon, "What Is a Girl Good For?" *New Era,* Feb. 1968, 35.

9. "LDS Mother Speaks Out against Women's Lib," *Church News,*Dec. 18, 1976.

10. See Barbara Welter, "The Cult of True Womanhood: 1820-1860," in *The American Family in Social-Historical Perspective,* ed. Michael Gordon (New York: St. Martin's Press, 1983), 313-28. According to Welter, ideal women of this period were characterized by piety, purity, submissiveness, and domesticity.

11. My thanks to Edward L. Kimball for checking his father's diaries at my request.

Notes to Chapter 1: The Uses of History

1. See Anne Firor Scott, "Mormon Women, Other Women: Paradoxes and Challenges," *Journal of Mormon History* 13 (1986-87): 3-19; Maureen Ursenbach Beecher, "Three Women and the Life of the Mind," *Utah Historical Quarterly* 43 (Winter 1975): 26-40; Jill C. Mulvay, "Eliza R. Snow and the Woman Question," *BYU Studies* 16 (Winter 1976): 250-64; Jill C. Mulvay, "The Liberal Shall Be Blessed: Sarah M. Kimball," *Utah Historical Quarterly* 44 (Summer 1976): 205-21; Judith Rasmussen Dushku, "Feminists," and other essays in *Mormon Sisters: Women in Early Utah,* ed. Claudia L. Bushman (Salt Lake City: Olympus Publishing, 1976); Jill Mulvay Derr, "Woman's Place in Brigham Young's World," *BYU Studies* 18 (Spring 1978): 377-95; Jill Mulvay Derr and Ann Vest Lobb, "Women in Early Utah," in *Utah's History,* ed. Richard D. Poll, et al. (Provo, UT: Brigham Young University Press, 1978); relevant essays in Vicky Burgess-Olson, ed., *Sister Saints* (Provo: Brigham Young University Press, 1978); Leonard J. Arrington, "Persons for All Seasons: Women in Mormon History," *BYU Studies* 20 (Fall 1979): 39-58; Maureen Ursenbach Beecher, "Women's Work on the Mormon Frontier," and Sherilyn Cox Bennion, "Enterprising Ladies: Utah's Nineteenth-Century Women Editors," *Utah Historical Quarterly* 49 (Summer 1981): 276-90, 291-304; Carol Cornwall Madsen, "Mormon Women and the Struggle for Definition: The Nineteenth-Century Church," *Sunstone* 6 (Nov.-Dec. 1981): 7-11, rpt. in *Dialogue: A Journal of Mormon Thought* 14 (Winter 1981): 40-47; Maureen Ursenbach Beecher, "'The Leading Sisters': A Female Hierarchy in Nineteenth-Century Mormon Society," *Journal of Mormon History* 9 (1982): 25-30; Leonard J. Arrington and Susan Arrington Madsen, *Sunbonnet Sisters: The Stories of Mormon Women and Frontier Life* (Salt Lake City: Bookcraft, 1984); Linda King Newell, "Gifts of the Spirit: Women's Share," and Jill Mulvay Derr, "Strength in Our Union: The Making of Mormon Sisterhood," in *Sisters in Spirit: Mormon Women in Historical and Cultural Perspective,* ed. Maureen Ursenbach Beecher and Lavina Fielding Anderson (Urbana: University of Illinois Press, 1987), 111-50, 153-207; and Carol Cornwall Madsen,

"'Feme Covert': Journey of a Metaphor," *Journal of Mormon History* 17 (1991): 43-61.

2. Scott, "Mormon Women, Other Women," 6.

3. Carl Degler, *At Odds: Women and the Family in America from the Revolution to the Present* (Oxford: Oxford University Press, 1980), 26.

4. Alexis de Toqueville, *Democracy in America,* ed. J. P. Mayer, transl. George Lawrence (1830; New York: Perennial Classics, 2000), 23.

5. Nancy Woloch, *Woman and the American Experience* (New York: Alfred A. Knopf, 1984), 167. Woloch suggests that toward the end of the nineteenth century, "a proliferation of women's associations . . . splintered, multiplied, federated, and expanded at an energetic pace. The basic units of this outburst, the temperance society and the women's club, arose spontaneously and won adherents rapidly. Temperance gained momentum in the 1880s, and the club movement in the 1890s. Like the settlement, these associations had many functions. They enabled thousands of conventional middle-class women to learn from others [and] share female vision; they created an avenue to civic affairs, or what temperance leader Frances Willard called 'the home going forth into the world.' Not only did they give wide exposure to female 'influence,' but they invigorated their members and politicized their leaders. And they created a separate space for women in public life" (287).

6. Recent scholarship suggests a powerful feminist thrust in both the temperance and women's club movements. In her book, *The Clubwoman as Feminist: True Womanhood Redefined 1868-1914* (New York: Holmes and Meier, 1980), Karen J. Blair contends that clubs promoted autonomy while providing a covert feminist agenda. The groundswell of female associations is examined by William L. O'Neill in *Everyone Was Brave: A History of Feminism in America* (Chicago: Quadrangle Books, 1969), chap. 3. O'Neill coined the term "social feminist" to describe women who had activist desires but "generally subordinated them to broad social movements they thought more urgent." In *Womanhood in America* (New York: New Viewpoints, 1975), Mary P. Ryan uses the term "social housekeeping" to describe women's reform work. Estelle Freedman assessed the significance of separate women's institutions—colleges, associations, and reform movements—in her important article, "Separatism as Strategy: Female Institution Building and American Feminism, 1870-1930," *Feminist Studies* 5 (Fall 1979): 512-49.

7. Barbara Welter, "The Cult of True Womanhood: 1820-1860, in *The*

American Family in Social and Historical Perspective, ed. Michael Gordon (New York: St. Martin's Press, 1983), 313.

8. Ibid.

9. Ibid., 328.

10. Claudia Bushman addresses the question of whether they were more liberated than other women of their day in her preface to *Mormon Sisters:* "They probably were. The next question will be whether the pioneers were freer to carry out their ambitions than today's Mormon women. They probably were not. Looking back it appears that nineteenth-century Mormon women were remarkably free to act in the world and that they were independent of their husbands. Yet it is also clear that they practiced their traditional mothering role and assumed that it was of primary importance" (xxxi).

11. Brigham Young, *Journal of Discourses,* 26 vols. (Liverpool and London: LDS Booksellers Depot, 1854-86), 13:61. At least part of his motivation was to free men for more physically arduous tasks.

12. Articles of Incorporation, 1875, Brigham Young University Archives, qtd. in Virginia B. Poulson, *History of the College of Family Living* (Provo: College of Family Living, 1975), 13.

13. "Advice to Girls," *Young Woman's Journal* 6 (Dec. 1894): 137. Louisa "Lula" Green, founding editor of the *Woman's Exponent,* earlier advised: "Let women shine by the intelligence of their own minds and not by that reflected from man. Let woman be qualified to stand alone, if necessary, and then if she become a wife or mother, she can act with wisdom and judgment; and if her path be in smooth and quiet places, she is none the less womanly because of her innate powers. But should her lot be cast in rough and thorny paths, how great her need of strength from within and without to endure. Remember there are many lonely walks in life, and it is necessary to be well armed with courage and fortitude." "The Centennial Year of America," *Woman's Exponent* 5 (1 July 1876): 20.

14. Leonard J. Arrington, *Brigham Young: American Moses* (New York: Alfred A. Knopf, 1985), 330.

15. Heber C. Kimball, 1 Mar. 1857, *Journal of Discourses,* 4:252.

16. Orson Hyde, *Journal of Discourses,* 4:258.

17. Heber C. Kimball, 9 Nov. 1856, *Journal of Discourses,* 80.

18. Anne Firor Scott, qtd. in Bushman, introduction, *Mormon Sisters,* 1997 edition from Utah State University Press, xxi.

19. Carol Cornwall Madsen, introduction, *Battle for the Ballot: Essays on*

Woman Suffrage in Utah, 1870-1896 (Logan: Utah State University Press, 1997), 13.

20. See Carol Cornwall Madsen: "A Mormon Woman in Victorian America," Ph.D. diss., University of Utah, 1985; "Emmeline B. Wells: 'Am I Not a Woman and a Sister?'" *BYU Studies* 22 (Spring 1982): 161-78; "Emmeline B. Wells: A Voice for Mormon Women," *John Whitmer Historical Association Journal* 2 (1982): 11-22.

21. Judith Rasmussen Dushku, "Feminists," in *Mormon Sisters,* 179.

22. Qtd. in Susa Young Gates, "Brigham Young," *Woman's Exponent,* 10 (1 June 1881), 4. See also Susa Young Gates, *The Life Story of Brigham Young* (London: Jarrolds, 1930), 232.

23. Dushku, "Feminists," 181.

24. Emmeline B. Wells, untitled article, *Woman's Exponent* 11 (Sept. 15, 1883).

25. Emmeline B. Wells, "Woman against Woman," *Woman's Exponent* 7 (May 1, 1879).

26. *Woman's Exponent* 3 (Sept. 30, 1874): 67.

27. *Woman's Exponent* 1 (Jan. 31, 1873): 131; 1 (Aug. 15, 1872): 46; 6 (Feb. 1, 1878): 132.

28. Susan B. Anthony and Ida Husted Harper, eds., *The History of Woman Suffrage,* 6 vols. (Rochester: Susan B. Anthony, 1902), 4:936-37. A basic starting point for a history of female suffrage in Utah, this six-volume history was written by Anthony and Harper with Elizabeth Cady Stanton and Matilda Joslyn Gage. These women, principals in the struggle for women's suffrage generally, were conscious that they were making history and wanted to document this important struggle. It includes two sections by Mormon women: Emmeline B. Wells wrote about the early history of the movement in Utah and Susa Young Gates brought the history up to 1920.

29. Katherine Anthony, *Susan B. Anthony: Her Personal History and Her Era* (Garden City, NY: Doubleday, 1954), 262.

30. See Martha Sonntag Bradley and Mary Brown Firmage Woodward, *Four Zinas: A Story of Mothers and Daughters on the Mormon Frontier* (Salt Lake City: Signature Books, 2000), for a fuller description of the relationship between Mormon women and the national suffrage movement.

31. Alma Lutz, *Created Equal: A Biography of Elizabeth Cady Stanton* (New York: John Day, 1940), 271. The split between the two women's organizations hampered their ability to achieve their shared goal. The American group felt

the vote would be obtained only if they stuck to that narrow issue without alienating potential supporters. National, by contrast, defined women's rights broadly as including advocacy for employment opportunities, improved work conditions, and the elimination of the double standard in sexual morality.

32. Elizabeth Clark, *Religion, Rights, and Difference: The Origins of American Feminism, 1848-1860* (Madison: University of Wisconsin Institute for Legal Studies, 1987), 2.

33. Margaret Fuller, *Woman in the Nineteenth Century* (1845; Columbia: University of South Carolina Press, 1980), 27.

34. Emmeline B. Wells quoted this phrase from a William Thackeray novel, *Woman's Exponent* 7 (Dec. 1878): 102-3.

35. Eleanor Flexner, *Century of Struggle: The Women's Rights Movement in the United States* (Cambridge, MA: Harvard University Press, 1975), 163.

36. Madsen, *Battle for the Ballot,* 3.

37. Thomas G. Alexander, "An Experiment in Progressive Legislation: The Granting of Woman Suffrage in Utah in 1870," *Utah Historical Quarterly* 38 (Winter 1970): 20-30.

38. Alexander (ibid., 113) argues that the public reasons were "the real ones because they are congruent with the progressive sentiment among the Mormons at the time." He mentions the "progressive and optimistic" tone of George Q. Cannon's editorials in the *Deseret News.* "They speak of the perfectibility of man, the need for equality in the community, and the high place of women in Mormon society. Though women did not hold ecclesiastical offices, they had always voted on matters brought before the congregation, and Eliza R. Snow and her companions led the Relief Society and the Young Ladies' Department of the Co-operative Retrenchment Improvement Association. Women were encouraged by church leaders to participate in public affairs, and such leaders as Sarah M. Kimball had a high place in the public esteem."

39. Beverly Beeton, "Woman Suffrage in Territorial Utah," in *The Battle for the Ballot,* 130. See also Beverly Beeton, "Woman Suffrage in the American West, 1869-1896," Ph.D. diss., University of Utah, 1976.

40. Flexner, *Century of Struggle,* 163.

41. Blanche Beechwood [Emmeline B. Wells], "Action or Indifference," *Woman's Exponent* 5 (Sept. 1, 1876): 54. See also Carol Cornwall Madsen, "'Remember the Women of Zion': A Study of the Editorial Content of the *Woman's Exponent,*" M.A. thesis, University of Utah, 1977.

42. Beechwood, "Action or Indifference," 54.

43. "E.," "Woman's Rights and Wrongs," *Woman's Exponent* 1 (1 June 1872): N.p.

44. Jean Bickmore White, "Woman's Place Is in the Constitution," *Utah Historical Quarterly* 42 (Fall 1974): 363.

45. See the 1895 Constitutional Convention's *Official Report of the Proceedings and Debates,* 2 vols. (Salt Lake City, 1898). Jean Bickmore White described the larger context in her "Woman's Place Is in the Constitution."

46. Heber J. Grant, "Equal Suffrage Department," *Young Woman's Journal* 6 (Feb. 1895): 225; Heber J. Grant to Anthon H. Lund, 20 Sept. 1895, Heber J. Grant Letterpress Copy Book, Archives, Family and Church History Department, Church of Jesus Christ of Latter-day Saints, Salt Lake City (hereafter LDS Church Archives).

47. Joseph F. Smith, "Relief Society Conference," *Woman's Exponent* 24 (Aug. 15, 1895): 44-46.

48. Charlotte Perkins Gilman, qtd. in Nancy Woloch, *Woman and the American Experience* (New York: Alfred A. Knopf, 1984), 325.

49. See Martha Sonntag Bradley, "'Protect the Boys and Girls': The Child Welfare Movement in Utah, 1888-1920," Ph.D. diss., University of Utah, 1987.

50. Woloch, *Woman and the American Experience,* 270.

51. Ibid., 270.

52. See Patricia Albjerg Graham, "Expansion and Exclusion: A History of Women in Higher Education," *Signs* 3 (Summer 1978): 759-73.

53. Bradley, "'Protect the Boys and Girls.'"

54. Qtd. in Woloch, *Woman and the American Experience,* 297.

55. Qtd. in ibid., 299. Woloch also credits them with the 1908 Pure Food and Drug Act, the 1912 establishment of a Children's Bureau in the Labor Department, and the Women's Bureau after World War I, all of which became "permanent female outposts in the federal government." The two decades surrounding the turn of the century "represented a peak of female activism. By the early twentieth century, the vital, energetic women's movement had many bases—college, profession, settlement house, and a loose coalition of overlapping interest groups—all committed to woman's causes, social service, and civic improvement."

56. For the history of feminism, see Flexner, *Century of Struggle;* Betty Friedan, *The Feminine Mystique* (New York: W.W. Norton, 1963); O'Neill, *Everyone Was Brave;* Celestine Ware, *Woman Power: The Movement for Women's Liberation* (New York: Tower Publications, 1970); Shulamith Firestone, *The Di-*

alectic of Sex: The Case for Feminist Revolution (New York: Morrow, 1970); and June Sochen, *The New Feminism in Twentieth-Century America* (New York: Quadrangle Books, 1971).

57. Flexner, *Century of Struggle*, ix.

58. Loneta Murphy, untitled comments at a rally in support of Sonia Johnson, Dec. 1979, photocopy, Box 3, fd. 8, Sonia Johnson Collection, Special Collections, Marriott Library, University of Utah, Salt Lake City.

59. Barbara B. Smith to Sonia Johnson, Sept. 1, 1978, Box 3, fd. 11, Johnson Collection.

60. "The Church of Jesus Christ of Latter-day Saints (Mormon) and the Equal Rights Amendment," Mormons for ERA handout, n.a., n.d., Box 8, fd. 2, Sonia Johnson Collection. The statements about being "equal in heavenly things" and being "anxiously engaged" are from the Doctrine and Covenants 78:6 and 58:27.

61. Madsen, introduction, *Battle for the Ballot*, 6.

Notes to Chapter 2: A Brief History of the Equal Rights Ammendment

1. Allen F. Davis, *Spearheads for Reform: The Social Settlements and the Progressive Movement, 1890-1914* (New York: Oxford University Press, 1967); Anne Corinne Hill, "Protection of Women Workers and the Courts: A Legal History," *Feminist Studies* 5 (Summer 1979): 247-73; and William O'Neill, *Everyone Was Brave: A History of Feminism in America* (New York: Quadrangle, 1969).

2. See Robert H. Wiebe, *The Search for Order, 1877-1920* (New York: Hill and Wang, 1967); Richard Hofstadter, *The Progressive Movement, 1900-1915* (Englewood Cliffs, N.J.: Prentice Hall, 1973); and Richard Hofstadter, *The American Political Tradition* (New York: Knopf, 1973).

3. Joan Hoff-Wilson, ed., *Rights of Passage: The Past and Future of the ERA* (Bloomington: Indiana University Press, 1986), 33.

4. Nancy Woloch, *Women and the American Experience* (New York: Alfred A. Knopf, 1984), 342-43.

5. U.S. Census Bureau, 1890. See also Elizabeth Faulkner Baker, *Technology and Women's Work* (New York: Columbia University Press, 1964); Robert W. Smuts, *Women and Work in America* (New York: Columbia University Press, 1959); and Lucy Maynard Salmon, *Domestic Service* (1897; New York: N.p., 1927).

6. Grace Abbott, *The Immigrant and the Community* (New York: Century Company, 1917), 22.

7. Mary P. Ryan, *Womanhood in America: From Colonial Times to the Present* (New York: Franklin Watts, 1963), 202.

8. Woloch, *Women and the American Experience,* 302-3.

9. Ryan, *Womanhood in America,* 231.

10. *Muller v. Oregon,* 208 U.S. 412 (1908).

11. Ibid., 422.

12. See Martha Sonntag Bradley, "'Protect the Boys and Girls': Child Labor, 1880-1920," in *A World We Thought We Knew: Readings in Utah History,* eds. John S. McCormick and John Sillito (Salt Lake City: University of Utah Press, 1995), 200-14.

13. Florence Kelley, "Shall Women Be Equal before the Law?" *The Nation,* Apr. 12, 1922, 421.

14. Woloch, *Women and the American Experience,* 302.

15. Alice Hamilton, "What the American Woman Thinks," *Woman Citizen,* Mar. 8, 1924, 16.

16. U.S. Department of Labor, "The Effect of Labor Legislation on the Employment Opportunities of Women," *Women's Bureau Bulletin* 65 (1928): 50-54.

17. Grace Abbott, "Maternity and Infant Welfare: The United States," *Women in American History* (http://search.eb.com/women), downloaded Jan. 2003.

18. Woloch, *Women and the American Experience,* 85-386. See also, Children's Bureau, U.S. Department of Labor, *Reports of the Administration of the Maternity and Infancy Act* (Washington D.C.: U.S. Government Printing Office, 1923-25); George T. Palmer, *A Health Survey of Eighty-six Cities* (New York: American Child Health Association, 1925).

19. Esther Dunshee, untitled article, *Woman Citizen,* Mar. 8, 1925, 19.

20. See Sheila M. Rothman, *Woman's Proper Place: A History of Changing Ideals and Practices, 1870 to the Present* (New York: Basic Books, 1978), chaps. 1-3; Carl Degler, *At Odds: Women and the Family in America from the Revolution to the Present* (New York: Oxford University Press, 1979), chaps. 7-13; Elaine Tyler May, *Great Expectations: Marriage and Divorce in Post-Victorian America* (Chicago: University of Chicago Press, 1980); and William L. O'Neill, *Divorce in the Progressive Era* (New Haven: Yale University Press, 1967).

21. Qtd. in Lady Willie Forbus, "The Lucretia Mott Amendment," *Equal Rights,* Apr. 26, 1924; qtd. in Hoff-Wilson, *Rights of Passage,* 89.

22. *Congressional Record* 118 (Mar. 28, 1972), 10450-56.

23. Here it drew on *Muller v. Oregon,* which stipulated that "the difference between the sexes may justify a different rule respecting hours of labor in the case of women than in the case of men" (*Adkins v. Children's Hospital* [261 U.S. 525, 43 S.Ct. 394], 552-53).

24. *Adkins v. Children's Hospital* challenged Section 8 of the Act, which authorized the board: "(1) To investigate and ascertain the wages of women and minors in the different occupations in which they are employed in the District of Columbia; (2) to examine, through any member or authorized representative, any book, payroll or other record of any employer of women or minors that in any way appertains to or has a bearing upon the question of wages of any such women or minors; and (3) to require from such employer full and true statements of the wages paid to all women and minors in his employment" (ibid., 539).

25. Kathryn Kish Sklar, "Why Were Most Politically Active Women Opposed to the ERA in the 1920s?" in Hoff-Wilson, *Rights of Passage,* 32.

26. J. Stanley Lemons, "Feminists against Feminists," in *The Woman Citizen: Social Feminism in the 1920s* (Urbana: University of Illinois Press, 1973), 181-208.

27. Amelia R. Fry, "Alice Paul and the ERA," in Hoff-Wilson, *Rights of Passage,* 11.

28. Woloch, *Women and the American Experience,* 351.

29. Ibid.

30. Qtd. in ibid., 351.

31. Qtd. in Mary Frances Berry, *Why ERA Failed: Politics, Women's Rights, and the Amending Process of the Constitution* (Bloomington: Indiana University Press, 1986), 17.

32. Entry for July 9, 1977, "Feminist Chronicles," *Feminist Majority Foundation Online* (www.feminist.org), downloaded Jan. 2003.

33. Bradley, "Protect the Children," 200-14.

34. Kathryn K. Sklar, *Florence Kelley and the Nation's Work* (New Haven: Yale University Press, 1998).

35. Ibid.

36. See Allen F. Davis, *Spearheads for Reform: The Social Settlements and the Progressive Movement, 1890-1914* (New York: Oxford University Press, 1967).

37. Ryan, *Womanhood in America,* 234.

38. Ibid., 235. She explains: "The tradition of the mother of civilization

could be a source of strength to social reformers. . . . an incentive to social activism, nourishing their humanistic impulses and leaving them reserves of talent and time for social benevolence. In fact, mothers of small families were more prone to join the ranks of social reformers and suffragists than were childless wives, single women or more prolific mothers."

39. Mirra Komarovsky, *The Unemployed Man and His Family* (1940; New York: Arno Press, 1971), 49.

40. Berry, *Why ERA Failed,* 57.

41. Susan Ware, *Holding Their Own: American Women in the 1930s* (Boston: Twayne, 1982), 89-94.

42. Berry, *Why ERA Failed,* 19.

43. "Equal Rights," *Woman's Home Companion,* Apr. 1939, 2.

44. Woloch, *Women and the American Experience,* 440.

45. Joan Ellen Trey, "Women in the War Economy," *Review of Radical Political Economies,* July 1972, 40-57.

46. Berry, *Why ERA Failed,* 58.

47. Ryan, *Womanhood in America,* 317.

48. William Henry Chafe, *The American Woman: Her Changing Social, Economic, and Political Roles, 1920-1970* (New York: Oxford University Press, 1972), 144-45.

49. Ibid.

50. Ryan, *Womanhood in America,* 318-19.

51. Chafe, *American Woman,* 180.

52. Amelia R. Fry, "Conversations with Alice Paul," conducted for the Regional Oral History Office, Bancroft Library, University of California, Berkeley, 1972-73, 19.

53. Ibid.

54. Fry, "Conversations with Alice Paul," 517.

55. *Congressional Record,* July 18, 1946, 9225.

56. Alma Lutz, "Only One Choice," *Independent Woman,* July 1947, 199.

57. Qtd. in Berry, *Why ERA Failed,* 61.

58. Ibid., 62.

59. Janet K. Boles, *The Politics of the Equal Rights Amendment: Conflict and the Decision Process* (New York: Longman, 1979), 37-39.

60. Karen Offen, *Toward an Historical Definition of Feminism: The Case of France* (Stanford: Center for Research on Women, Stanford University, 1991).

61. Berry, *Why ERA Failed,* 6.

Notes to Chapter 3: The Poising of Nation and Church to 1972

1. "American Woman's Dilemma," *Life,* June 16, 1947, 101-12.

2. William Henry Chafee, *The American Woman: Her Changing Social, Economic, and Political Roles, 1920-1970* (New York: Oxford University Press, 1972), 199.

3. "Blueprint for a Wife," *Newsweek,* Oct. 4, 1954, 81.

4. National Manpower Council, *Work in the Lives of Married Women* (New York: Columbia University Press, 1958), 199; F. Ivan Nye and Lois Wladis Hoffman, eds., *The Employed Mother in America* (Westport, CT: Greenwood Press, 1976), 7-9.

5. Robert Blood, "The Measurement and Bases of Family Power: A Rejoinder," *Journal of Marriage and the Family* 25 (Nov. 1963): 475; Robert O. Blood and Donald M. Wolfe, *Husbands and Wives: The Dynamics of Married Living* (Glencoe, IL: Free Press, 1960).

6. *Harper's,* Oct. 1962, 115-19, claimed that although modern women shunned the slogans of their predecessors, they tended to retain the same concerns. A modern phenomenon, which *Harper's* called "crypto-feminism," produced women with "uncommitted hours" during the day while their children were in school and, because meaningful work was reduced by the increasingly mechanized home, an accumulation of blank years.

7. George Gallup and Evan Hill, "The American Woman," *Saturday Evening Post,* Dec. 22, 1962, 127.

8. Betty Friedan, *The Feminine Mystique* (New York: Simon and Schuster, 1963), 28-61, 95-141, 197-223.

9. Mary P. Ryan, *Womanhood in America: From Colonial Times to the Present* (New York: Harper and Row, 1975).

10. "The National Organization for Women, Statement of Purpose," in *Perspectives on American Civilization,* eds. Robert A. Goldberg and L. Ray Gunn, 3rd ed. (New York: Simon & Schuster Custom Publishers, 1990), 335.

11. Kate Millet, *Sexual Politics* (New York: Doubleday, 1970), 26, 62.

12. Peter James Caulfield, "Rhetoric and the Equal Rights Amendment: Contemporary Means of Persuasion," Ph.D. diss., University of Michigan, 1984, 38.

13. U.S. Department of Labor, *Employment and Earnings,* Jan. 1976, Table 1 and unpublished data.

14. bell hooks, *Feminist Theory from Margin to Center* (Cambridge, MA.: South End Press Classics, 1984), 5.

15. Bureau of the Census, "Money Income in 1974 of Families and Persons in the United States," *Current Population Reports* (P-60/101), Jan. 1976, Table 67.

16. Women's Bureau, *Handbook on Women Workers,* 1975, chart L.

17. Ibid.

18. Mary Wollstonecraft, *A Vindication of the Rights of Woman* (1792; Farnborough, Eng.: Gregg, 1970); Alice S. Rossi, ed., *The Feminist Papers* (New York: Bantam, 1973); William L. O'Neill, "Feminism as a Radical Ideology," in *Dissent: Explorations in the History of American Radicalism,* ed. Alfred F. Young (Dekalb: Northern Illinois University Press, 1968); Zillah Eisenstein, *The Radical Future of Liberal Feminism* (New York: Longman, 1981).

19. Margaret Fuller, *Woman in the Nineteenth Century* (1845; New York: Norton, 1971); Charlotte Perkins Gilman, *Women and Economics* (1898; New York: Harper, 1966); Eliza Burt Gamble, *The Evolution of Woman: An Inquiry into the Dogma of Her Inferiority to Man* (New York: G. P. Putnam's, 1893); Charlotte Perkins Gilman, *Herland* (1915; New York: Harper, 1979).

20. Karl Marx and Frederick Engels, *Manifesto of the Communist Party* (1848; New York: International, 1948); David McLellan, ed., *Karl Marx: Selected Writings* (Oxford, Eng.: Oxford University Press, 1977); David McLellan, *The Thought of Karl Marx: An Introduction* (New York: Harper, 1971); Angela Davis, "Reflections on the Black Woman's Role in the Community of Slaves," *Black Scholar* 3 (Dec. 1971): 7; Zillah Eisenstein, "Developing a Theory of Capitalist Patriarchy and Socialist Feminism," in *Capitalist Patriarchy and the Case for Socialist Feminism,* ed. Zillah Eisenstein (New York: Monthly Review, 1979), 11; and Max Horkheimer, *Critical Theory* (1936; New York: Herder & Herder, 1972), esp. "Authority and the Family."

21. Rosemarie Putnam Tong, *Feminist Thought* (Boulder, CO: Westview Press, 1998).

22. Maxine Hanks, introduction, *Women and Authority: Re-emerging Mormon Feminism,* ed. Maxine Hanks (Salt Lake City: Signature Books, 1992), xvii.

23. President Richard M. Nixon's 1969 task force also summarized progress and outlined the job ahead. See *A Matter of Simple Justice: The Report of the President's Task Force on Women's Rights and Responsibilities* (Washington DC: U.S. Government Printing Office, 1970).

24. National Commission on the Observance of International Women's Year, *"To Form a More Perfect Union": Justice for American Women* (Washington DC: U.S. Government Printing Office, 1976), 8.

25. *In re Lockwood,* 154 US 116 (1894).

26. *Reed v. Reed,* 404 U.S. 71 (1971).

27. Bernice R. Sandler, "Too Strong for a Woman," *About Women on Campus* 2 (Spring 1997): 6.

28. N. P. Stromquist, "Sex-Equity Legislation in Education: The State as Promoter of Women's Rights," *Review of Educational Research* 63 (Winter 1993): 379-407.

29. Significant progress was reported by the U.S. Department of Education, *Title IX: Twenty-five Years of Progress* (Washington DC: Office of Educational Research and Improvement, 1997). In 1995 women made up 37 percent of collegiate athletes compared to 15 percent in 1972; in 1996 girls composed 39 percent of high school athletes compared to 7.5 percent in 1971. Women won 10 Olympic medals in the 1996 summer Olympic Games, more than ever before. Furthermore, the status of women in education improved generally. In 1994, 63 percent of female high school graduates attended college, compared to 43 percent in 1973; in 1994, 27 percent of women earned bachelor's degrees compared to 18 percent in 1971; in 1994, women received 38 percent of the medical degrees compared to 9 percent in 1972.

30. Janet K. Boles, *The Politics of the Equal Rights Amendment: Conflict and the Decision Process* (New York: Longman, 1979), 37-39.

31. *Congressional Record* 117: H9392.

32. Ibid.; Boles, *Politics of the Equal Rights Amendment*, 37-39.

33. *Congressional Record,* 117:35815. See also "Mormons Who Have Served in United States Government (as of October 1982)," in the *Deseret News Church Almanac* (Salt Lake City: Deseret News, 1983), 284.

34. *Congressional Record* 118: S4247-72; S4372-4430; S4531-4615; Boles, *Politics of the Equal Rights Amendment,* 39-49.

35. Ibid.

36. *Congressional Record,* 117:35815. See also "Mormons Who Have Served in United States Government," 284.

37. Mary Frances Berry, *Why ERA Failed: Politics, Women's Rights, and the Amending Process of the Constitution* (Bloomington: Indiana University Press, 1986), 65.

38. Lester Orfield, *The Amending of the Federal Constitution* (Chicago: Callaghan & Company, 1942), 74-75; *Guide to Current American Government* (Washington DC: Congressional Quarterly, Inc., 1983), 3-4; Boles, *Politics of the Equal Rights Amendment,* 61.

39. The biographical information on Schlafly comes from Ruth Conniff, "Left-Right Romance," *The Progressive* 64 (May 2000): 12-15; Carol Felsenthal, *The Sweetheart of the Silent Majority: The Biography of Phyllis Schlafly* (Garden City, NY: Doubleday, 1981); Judy Klemesrud, "Opponent of the ERA Confident of Its Defeat," *New York Times,* Dec. 15, 1975, 1; Sean Price, "Housewives 1, Feminists 0," *New York Times,* Mar. 11, 2002, 26-28; Phyllis Schlafly, 1978 entry in *Current Biography,* online at *H. W. Wilson* (www.hwwilson.com; downloaded 2003).

40. Sally Quinn, *Washington Post,* July 11, 1974. See also: *New York Daily News,* Nov. 22, 1977, 39; *New York Times,* Dec. 15, 1975, 44; *National NOW Times,* Dec. 1977, 8; *Newsweek,* July 25, 1977, 35.

41. Thomas F. O'Dea, *The Mormons* (Chicago: University of Chicago, 1957), 263.

42. Thomas G. Alexander, "From War to Depression" and "Integration into the National Economy, 1896-1920," in *Utah's History,* ed. Richard D. Poll, et al. (Provo: Brigham Young University Press, 1978), 463-80; Alexander, *Mormonism in Transition: A History of the Latter-day Saints, 1890-1930* (Urbana: University of Illinois Press, 1986); Alexander, "Reed Smoot, the LDS Church, and Progressive Legislation, 1903-1933" *Dialogue: A Journal of Mormon Thought* 7 (Spring 1972): 447-56.

43. Wayne H. Hinton, "The New Deal Years in Utah: A Political History of Utah, 1932-40," M.A. thesis, Utah State University, 1963; Leonard J. Arrington and Hinton, "Origin of the Welfare Plan of the Church of Jesus Christ of Latter-day Saints," *BYU Studies* 5 (Winter 1964): 67-85; Alexander, "From War to Depression"; Hinton, "Some Historical Perspectives on Mormon Responses to the Great Depression," *Journal of the West* 24 (Oct. 1985): 19-26.

44. E. Cecil McGavin and Albert L. Zobell Jr., "Grain Storage among the Latter-day Saints," *Improvement Era,* Mar. 1941, 142-45; Jessie L. Embry, "The Relief Society Grain Storage Program, 1876-1940," M.A. thesis, Brigham Young University, 1974; Embry, "Grain Storage: The Balance of Power between Priesthood Authority and Relief Society Autonomy," *Dialogue: A Journal of Mormon Thought* 15 (Winter 1982), 59-66; Carol L. Clark, "The Effect of Secular Education upon Mormon Relief Society Curriculum, 1914-1940," Ph.D. diss., University of Utah, 1979; Lori L. Hefner, "This Decade was Different: Relief Society's Social Services Department, 1919-1929," *Dialogue: A Journal of Mormon Thought* 15 (Fall 1982): 64-73; G. M. Chandler, "Belle S. Spafford: Leader of Women," M.A. thesis, Brigham Young University, 1983.

45. See "Amy Brown Lyman," in Andrew Jenson, *Latter-day Saint Biographical Encyclopedia,* 4 vols. (Salt Lake City: Andrew Jenson History Company, 1901); Amy Brown Lyman, *In Retrospect: Autobiography of Amy Brown Lyman* (Salt Lake City: General Board of the Relief Society, 1945); Lori L. Hefner, "Amy Brown Lyman: Raising the Quality of Life for All," in *Sister Saints,* ed. Vickie Burgess-Olson (Provo: BYU Press, 1978); Jill Mulvay Derr and Susan Staker Oman, "These Three Women: They Presided over Relief Society in the Twentieth Century" *Ensign,* Feb. 1978, 66-70; Hefner, "This Decade Was Different"; David R. Hall, "Amy Brown Lyman and Social Service Work in the Relief Society," M.A. thesis, Brigham Young University, 1992; Ann Engar, "Lyman, Amy Brown," *Encyclopedia of Mormonism,* 4 vols. (New York: Macmillan Publishing Company, 1992).

46. Jill Mulvay Derr, Janath Russell Cannon, and Maureen Ursenbach Beecher, *Women of Covenant: The Story of the Relief Society* (Salt Lake City: Deseret Book, 1992), 326.

47. Relief Society General Board Minutes, Feb. 3, 10, 1916, qtd. in ibid., 184.

48. Ibid., 183.

49. Relief Society General Board Minutes, Oct. 4, 1911, qtd. in ibid.

50. Kathryn L. Mackay and Maureen Ursenbach Beecher, "Women in Twentieth-Century Utah," in *Utah's History,* 576.

51. Ibid., 577.

52. Martha Sonntag Bradley, "'Protect the Boys and Girls': Child Labor, 1880-1920," in *A World We Thought We Knew: Readings in Utah History,* ed. John S. McCormick and John Sillito (Salt Lake City: University of Utah Press, 1995), 200-14.

53. Beecher and MacKay, "Women in Twentieth-Century Utah," 575. Alice Paul's version of the Equal Rights Amendment surfaced repeatedly after 1923.

54. J. Reuben Clark, Office Diary, Jan. 25, 1959, qtd. in D. Michael Quinn, *J. Reuben Clark: The Church Years* (Provo: Brigham Young University Press, 1983). See also Martin B. Hickman, "J. Reuben Clark, Jr.: The Constitution and the Great Fundamentals," *BYU Studies* 13 (Spring 1973): 255-72. Clark may have felt differently about the 1971 version which did not contain the exemption clause, but he died before the shortened ERA became a divisive national issue.

55. Joseph Fielding Smith, "Message from the First Presidency," *Ensign,* Jan. 1971, 1.

56. Thomas S. Monson, "The Women's Movement: Liberation or Deception?" *Ensign,* Jan. 1971, 17, 19.

57. H. Burke Peterson, "Mother, Catch the Vision of Your Call," *Ensign,* May 1974, 31-33.

58. Lois Gogarty, "LDS Women Unaffected by Women's Lib," *Ensign,* Aug. 1973, 73.

59. N. Eldon Tanner, "No Greater Calling: The Woman's Role," *Ensign,* Jan. 1974, 7.

60. Ezra Taft Benson, "The Honored Place of Woman," *Ensign,* Nov. 1981, 104-7.

61. Ibid., 106.

62. Hanks, *Women and Authority,* xviii, identifies the prominent Mormon feminists of this era as Algie Ballif, Cheryl Dalton, Christine Meaders Durham, Sonia Johnson, Reba Keele, Beatrice Marchant, Carol Lynn Pearson, Grethe Ballif Peterson, Alice Pottmeyer, Linda Sillitoe, Helen Candland Stark, Joanne Thomas, Jan Tyler. Feminist history appeared from Lavina Fielding Anderson, Leonard J. Arrington, Maureen Ursenbach Beecher, Vicki Burgess-Olsen, Claudia Lauper Bushman, Jill Mulvay Derr, Judith Rasmussen Dushku, Audrey Godfrey, Carol Cornwall Madsen, Cheryll Lynn May, Linda King Newell, Susan Staker, Laurel Thatcher Ulrich, and Linda P. Wilcox.

63. Claudia Bushman, "Introduction," *Dialogue: A Journal of Mormon Thought* 6 (Summer 1971): 7-8.

64. Ibid.

65. Ibid., 7.

66. Lavina Fielding, "Problems, Solutions: Being an LDS Woman Today," *Ensign,* Mar. 1976, 16-22.

67. James B. Allen and Glen M. Leonard, *The Story of the Latter-day Saints* (Salt Lake City: Deseret Book Company, 1976), 593.

68. Barbara Brown, Thomas Emerson, et al., "The Equal Rights Amendment: A Constitutional Basis for Equal Rights for Women," *Yale Law Journal* 80 (1971): 871-985, 884; *Congressional Record* 118:S4247-4272.

69. Brown, Emerson, et al., "Equal Rights Amendment," 884.

70. Lester Orfield, *The Amending of the Federal Constitution* (Chicago: Callaghan & Co., 1942), 74-75; *Guide to Current American Government,* 3-4. Some feminist leaders recognized the mistake in accepting the deadline. See, e.g.,

Gloria Steinem, *Outrageous Acts and Everyday Rebellions* (New York: Holt, Rinehart & Winston, 1983), 348; Boles, *Politics of the Equal Rights Amendment*, 61. In *Dillon v. Gloss* (1921), the Supreme Court had decided Congress could prescribe a reasonable time if it so chose. In the case of the Eighteenth Amendment, the first with a prescribed deadline, the court found seven years reasonable.

71. See Kate Gardner, "What the ERA Will Mean to You," *Exponent II* 1 (July 1974): 2.

72. Qtd. in "Gem Legislature Ratifies Amendment to Ensure Women's Equal Rights," *Idaho Statesman*, Mar. 25, 1972; "Idaho Ratifies Equal Rights," *Idaho Post Register*, Mar. 25, 1972.

73. Louis Harris, "Public Support for ERA Soars as Ratification Deadline Nears," *Harris Survey*, May 6, 1982, 1.

74. Berry, *Why ERA Failed*, 64.

75. Ibid., 65.

Notes to Chapter 4: The Arguments and the Allies

1. "The National Organization for Women, Statement of Purpose," 1966, in *Perspectives on American Civilization*, eds. Robert A. Goldberg and L. Ray Gunn (New York: Simon and Schuster, 1990), 335.

2. Ibid., 336.

3. Joan Hoff-Wilson, *Rights of Passage: The Past and Future of the ERA* (Bloomington: Indiana University Press, 1986), 39. See also Gilbert Y. Steiner, *Constitutional Inequality: The Political Fortunes of the Equal Rights Amendment* (Washington DC: Brookings Institution, 1985).

4. For these and other definitions, see Val Norman Edwards, "A Rhetorical Analysis of Three Policy Statements of the Church of Jesus Christ of Latter-day Saints," M.A. thesis, University of Utah, 1987, 7.

5. Vella Evans, "Woman's Image in Authoritative Mormon Discourse: A Rhetorical Analysis," Ph.D. dissertation, University of Utah, 1985, 245.

6. Thomas S. Monson, "The Women's Movement: Liberation or Deception?" *Ensign*, Jan. 1971, 17.

7. Peter James Caulfield, "Rhetoric and the Equal Rights Amendment: Contemporary Means of Persuasion," Ph.D. diss., University of Michigan, 1984, 13.

8. Ibid., 14.

9. Ibid., 21.

10. Hugh B. Brown, *Improvement Era,* Feb. 1970, 70.

11. LDS First Presidency, "Official Statement," *Church News,* Oct. 7, 1978.

12. David B. Magleby, "Contemporary American Politics," online at *All about Mormons* (www.lightplanet.com/mormons; downloaded Jan. 2003).

13. Stephen L Richards, "Awake, Ye Defenders of Zion," *Improvement Era,* Dec. 1951, 877-80.

14. Ibid., 3.

15. Copy in my possession.

16. LDS First Presidency, letter, qtd. in *The Church and the Proposed Equal Rights Amendment: A Moral Issue,* 22; insert in the *Ensign,* Mar. 1980.

17. First Presidency, *Church and the Proposed Equal Rights Amendment,* 20.

18. It is perhaps ironic that their worst fears have been fully realized despite the failure of the ERA.

19. Caulfield, "Rhetoric and the Equal Rights Amendment," 18.

20. The best summary of these positions is in the First Presidency's *Church and the Proposed Equal Rights Amendment.*

21. Gary and Gordon Shepherd, *A Kingdom Transformed: Themes in the Development of Mormonism* (Salt Lake City: University of Utah Press, 1984), 8.

22. Ibid., 39.

23. Gordon and Gary Shepherd, "Mormonism in Secular Society: Changing Patterns in Official Ecclesiastical Rhetoric," *Review of Religious Research* 26 (Sept. 1984): 28-42. See also their *Kingdom Transformed.*

24. Ibid., 36.

25. Max Weber, *The Sociology of Religion,* transl. Ephraim Fischoff (Boston: Beacon Press, 1963).

26. Bryan Wilson, *The Social Dimensions of Sectarianism: Sects and New Social Movements* (Oxford, Eng.: Clarendon Press, 1990), 21.

27. Laura L. Vance, *Seventh-day Adventism in Crisis* (Urbana: University of Illinois Press, 1999), esp. the introduction, "Religious Identity and Gender" (1-12) and chap. 5, "Definition of Sectarian Identity and Delineation of Gender in the Adventist Review" (101-30).

28. "Equal Rights Amendment Is Opposed by R.S. President," *Church News,* Dec. 21, 1974, 7.

29. Edwards, "A Rhetorical Analysis," 39.

30. Jane Cartwright, "Relief Society President Assails ERA: Proposal Tabbed 'Step Backward,'" *Salt Lake Tribune,* Dec. 14, 1974, B1.

31. "A Conversation with Sister Barbara B. Smith, Relief Society General President," *Ensign,* Mar. 1976, 7-12.

32. John Unger Zussman and Shauna M. Adix, "Content and Conjecture in the Equal Rights Amendment Controversy in Utah," *Women's Studies International Forum* 5 (1982): 476.

33. Hal Knight, "Most Favor Full Rights for Women," *Deseret News,* Nov. 15, 1974, 1, 7.

34. "Equal Rights Amendment," *Church News,* Jan. 12, 1975, 4.

35. Ibid.

36. "Rally, Vigil Show Support for ERA," *Deseret News,* Feb. 18, 1975, B1.

37. "Utah ERA Coalition Charges Unfairness," *Deseret News,* Jan. 22, 1975, B1.

38. Peter Gillins, "Church Stand Apparently Dooms ERA Amendment," *Herald Journal* (Logan, UT), Jan. 19, 1975, 1.

39. Ibid.

40. Charles Seldin, "Equal Rights Amendment Suffers Defeat amid Emotional Voting," *Salt Lake Tribune,* Feb. 19, 1975, 1.

41. First Presidency Statement, *Church News,* Oct. 30, 1976, 2.

42. "First Presidency Issues Statement Opposing Equal Rights Amendment," *Ensign,* Dec. 1976, 79.

43. "ERA Opposition Voiced in Idaho," *Church News,* Jan. 15, 1977, 11.

44. Boyd K. Packer, "The Equal Rights Amendment," *Ensign,* Mar. 1977, 7.

45. Title IX reads: "No person in the United States shall, on the basis of sex, be excluded from participation in, be denied the benefits of, or be subjected to discrimination under any education program or activity receiving federal assistance."

46. Packer, "Equal Rights Amendment," 7.

47. Ibid., 9.

48. Ibid.

49. "LDS Oppose Additional Time for ERA Approval," press release, Church of Jesus Christ of Latter-day Saints, 25 May 1978, published as "Reaffirmation of the First Presidency's Position on ERA," *Church News,* Aug. 26, 1978, 2, and *Ensign,* Aug. 1978, 80.

50. "Statement of the First Presidency of the Church of Jesus Christ of Latter-day Saints Opposing Extension of Time for Ratification of Equal Rights Amendment," submitted to the Honorable Don Edwards, chair, Subcommittee on Civil and Constitutional Rights, Committee on the Judiciary, May 24, 1979,

Box 6, fd. 1, Sonia Johnson Collection, Special Collections, Marriott Library, University of Utah, Salt Lake City.

51. Randall V. Douglass, "Mormons Defeat ERA," *Royalton Guard,* 28 Nov. 1979, Johnson Collection.

52. Although there had been a steady and even voluminous trickle of biographies and autobiographies of Mormon women since Edward Tullidge's *The Women of Mormondom* (New York: Tullidge, 1877) and August Joyce Crocheron's *Representative Women of Deseret* (Salt Lake City: J. C. Graham & Co., 1884), it was future LDS Church Historian Leonard J. Arrington who inaugurated women's historical studies in 1971 with the publication of "Blessed Damozels: Women in Mormon History," *Dialogue: A Journal of Mormon Thought* 6 (Summer 1971): 22-31. The 1970s saw an increase in "recovered" history, particularly the accounts of individual Mormon women; but scholarly and critical treatments were comparatively rare until the 1990s. Two exceptions were John R. Sillito, ed., *From College to Market: The Professionalization of Women's Sphere* (Salt Lake City: Utah Women's History Association, 1983), the proceedings of a conference with limited circulation; and Maureen Ursenbach Beecher and Lavina Fielding Anderson, eds., *Sisters in Spirit: Mormon Women in Historical and Cultural Perspective* (Urbana: University of Illinois Press, 1987).

53. The chief author was Rex E. Lee, dean of BYU's law school, with assistance from the *Ensign*'s production editor.

54. At least one observer in the aftermath of Utah's IWY conference noted the irony of traditional Mormon women asserting their "free agency" in battling their feminist opponents. Barbara C. Terry of Murray, Utah, wrote in "Say Enough," a letter to the *Salt Lake Tribune,* 9 July 1977, B4: "I suspect the actions of the Mormon women at the Salt Palace are quite in character with their political positions. In opposing an amendment that would affirm the right of all citizens to make free choices and to have all laws applied equally, the LDS women are denying the principles of democratic government which they purport to hold so dear. They are unwilling to pay the price of living in a democracy. That price is that we must allow other people to make personal choices that we would not choose for them. Perhaps this is the greatest price the church must pay for its victory—the denial of democracy. The Mormon women attended the meetings to destroy and disrupt, not to participate. I am sickened at what has become of my once strong and courageous people. It is time for thinking LDS women to say enough, enough."

55. At the time, Gordon B. Hinckley was a spokesman for the church and a

member of its Quorum of the Twelve Apostles, the ecclesiastical and administrative council next in line in authority to the First Presidency. At age seventy, Hinckley also served on the Church Education Executive Committee (as chair), Church Board of Education, BYU Board of Trustees, and the General Welfare Services Committee. After 1974 he was the leader of the Special Affairs Committee, which organized the nationwide opposition to the ERA.

56. Prior to June 1978, African-descended men were prohibited from ordination to the Mormon priesthood. The announcement of a revelation terminating this prohibition did not apply to women, who are still not allowed ordination.

57. Norman Sclarewitz, "Interview with Gordon B. Hinckley," *PSA Magazine,* June 1980, 115-28.

58. Thomas G. Alexander, *Utah: The Right Place* (Salt Lake City: Gibbs Smith Publisher, 1995), 419.

59. Ezra Taft Benson, "The Honored Place of Woman," *Ensign,* Nov. 1981, 104-7.

60. Robert Gottlieb and Peter Wiley, *American Saints: The Rise of Mormon Power* (New York: G. P. Putnam's Sons, 1984), 195.

61. See Lynn M. Anderson, "Issues in Contemporary Mormon Feminism," in *Mormon Identities in Transition,* ed. David J. Davies (New York: Cassells, 1996), 159-65; Marie Cornwall, "The Institutional Role of Mormon Women," in *Contemporary Mormonism,* eds. Marie Cornwall, Tim B. Heaton and Lawrence A. Young (Urbana: University of Illinois Press, 1994), 239-64.

62. Harold B. Lee, *Conference Report,* Oct. 1964, 81; also on *Gospelink 2001,* CD-ROM (Salt Lake City: Deseret Book, 2001).

63. In 1897 the *Improvement Era* replaced *The Contributor,* which had been in circulation since 1879 as voice of the Young Men's Mutual Improvement Associations. In 1929 the *Improvement Era* merged with the *Young Women's Journal,* which had been published since 1889 for the YWMIA. By the 1940s, and increasingly from that point on, the *Improvement Era* became a general-interest magazine for adults, adding a pull-out section for teens in the 1960s. Richard D. McClellan, "Periodicals," *Encyclopedia of Latter-day Saint History,* eds. Arnold K. Garr, Donald Q. Cannon, and Richard O. Cowan (Salt Lake City: Deseret Book, 2000), 908.

64. Qtd. in Gottlieb and Wiley, *American Saints,* 195.

65. Spencer W. Kimball, "The Family Influence," *Ensign,* July 1973, 17.

66. Mirabelle Morgan, *The Total Woman* (Old Tappan, NJ: F. H. Revill,

1973); Helen Andelin, *Fascinating Womanhood* (San Luis Obispo, CA: Pacific Press, 1966).

67. David W. Brady and Kent L. Tedin, "Ladies in Pink: Religion and Political Ideology in the Anti-ERA Movement," *Social Science Quarterly* 56 (Mar. 1976): 564-75. Brady and Tedin were both raised Mormon.

68. Ibid., 574.

69. Ira Rohter, "Social and Psychological Determinants of Radical Rightism," in *The American Right Wing,* ed. Robert A. Schoenberger (New York: Holt, Rinehart, and Winston, 1969), 196.

70. Barbara S. Stone, "The John Birch Society: A Profile," *Journal of Politics* 36 (Feb. 1974): 184-97.

71. Seymour Martin Lipset and Earl Raab, *The Politics of Unreason* (New York: Harper and Row, 1970), 248-64.

72. Dan Smoot, "The Dan Smoot Report—Reject or Rescind the E.R.A.," *Review of the News,* Mar. 13, 1974, 31-38.

73. Lisa Cronin Wohl, "A Mormon Connection? The Defeat of the ERA in Nevada," *Ms. Magazine,* July 1977, 70.

74. Thomas J. McIntyre, with John C. Obert, *The Fear Brokers* (Philadelphia: Pilgrim Press, 1979), 13.

75. Ibid., 10-11.

76. John Cooper, *The Turn Right* (Philadelphia: Westminster Press, 1970), 69.

77. Irving Louis Horowitz, *Ideology and Utopia in the United States* (Oxford, Eng.: Oxford University Press, 1977), 191.

78. Cheryl Arvidson, *Las Vegas Sun,* Sept. 8, 1977.

79. N.a., "The New Right Political Apparatus: A Well Greased Machine for God, Family, and True-Blue Americanism," N.p., 1978, Box 35, fd. 2, Johnson Collection.

80. Cy Ryan, "Anti-Church Prejudice Grows," *Valley Times,* Sept. 24, 1975.

81. "The Blank Check Called ERA," *Eagle Forum Newsletter,* Jan. 1980, 1, Utah Women's Issues Collection, Marriott Library, University of Utah.

82. This judge was Marion Callister. As a regional representative, he was the liaison between local church officers and the Quorum of the Twelve Apostles.

83. "Blank Check Called ERA," 1.

84. Carol Mueller and Thomas Dimieri, "The Structure of Belief Systems among Contending ERA Activists," *Social Forces* 60 (1982): 657-75.

Notes to Chapter 5: Goals of the International Women's Year, 1975

1. "Feminist Chronicles," Oct. 24, 1973, *The Feminist Majority Foundation Online* (www.feminist.org; downloaded Jan. 2003).

2. Bureau of Labor Statistics, *Employment and Earnings,* Jan. 1976, Table 1 and unpublished data (Washington DC: Government Publications Office, 1976).

3. Bureau of the Census, "Money Income in 1974 of Families and Persons in the United States," *Current Population Reports,* Series P-60, No. 101, Jan. 1976, Table 67 (Washington DC: Government Publications Office, 1976).

4. Women's Bureau, *Handbook on Women Workers,* 1975, Chart L (Washington DC: Government Publications Office, 1975).

5. Ibid., 3, 20, 25, 26.

6. Ibid., 76, 78.

7. Bureau of the Census, "Population Profile of the United States: 1975," *Current Population Reports,* Series P-20, No. 292, Mar. 1976, 1, 3, 9 (Washington DC: U.S. Government Publications Office, 1975).

8. *Handbook on Women Workers,* 1975, 5.

9. *Chronicle of Higher Education,* 9 Feb. 1976, 5.

10. The twenty-two states were Alaska, California, Colorado, Delaware, Hawaii, Idaho, Iowa, Kansas, Kentucky, Maryland, Massachusetts, Michigan, Nebraska, New Hampshire, New Jersey, New York, Pennsylvania, Rhode Island, Tennessee, Texas, West Virginia, and Wisconsin.

11. In Maryland the vote was 2-1 in favor; in Hawaii, 6-1; New Mexico, 2-1; Colorado, 3-1; and Texas, 4-1. In Washington the ERA was 10,000 votes behind before absentee ballots tipped the balance, passing with a margin of 3,000. "Feminist Chronicles," Nov. 7, 1972.

12. "Feminist Chronicles," under Lifestyles, Media, 1972.

13. Ibid., Dec. 7, 1975.

14. Ibid., Mar. 1, 1973.

15. In *The Spirit of Houston: The First National Women's Conference, An Official Report to the President, the Congress, and the People of the United States* (Washington DC: National Commission on the Observance of International Women's Year, March 1978), 9.

16. In July 1975, JoAnn Freed interviewed twenty-nine of the forty-one Utah participants: Sally Hess Barlow, Elouise Bell, Cynthia Boshard, Kelly Brailsford, Maxine Chabries, Joan Draper, Kathleen Flake, Pat Freston, Anita Gardner, Teri Holleran, Margaret Hoopes, Ann Hunter, Pat Jarvis, Kitsy

Keetch, Jinnah Kelson, Leslie Kelson, Lorraine Killpack, Sharon Kreigher, Mary and Rex Lowe, Anna Jo Martin, Tina Martin, Anne Nicoll, Carol Lynn Pearson, Kelly Pennington, Barbara Pulsipher, Marie Scott, Jan Tyler, and Margaret Wilde. Transcripts of these interviews are available in the JoAnn Freed Collection of Oral Histories, 1975-1977, Utah State Historical Society, Salt Lake City.

17. Marie Scott, interviewed by JoAnn Freed, Freed Collection, 3.

18. Office of Media Services, "United Nations Conference of the International Women's Year," *Department of State Bulletin,* N.d., copy in the Valora P. Treshow Papers, IWY Project, in author's possession (see introduction).

19. Ibid.

20. *Spirit of Houston,* 10.

21. JoAnn Robinson Freed, "Summary of Findings on the United Nations International Women's Year Tribune [Conference], Mexico City, 19 June-2 July 1975," 2-3, Utah State Historical Society.

22. *Report of the World Conference of the International Women's Year* (New York: United Nations, 1976), 58. See also Sen. Charles H. Percy, Committee on Government Operations, *World Conference of the International Women's Year* (Washington DC: Government Printing Office, 1976).

23. *Spirit of Houston,* 10.

24. Elouise Bell, interviewed by JoAnn Freed, Sept. 23, 1977, Freed Collection, 54.

25. Margaret Wilde, interviewed by JoAnn Freed, Sept. 8, 1977, 13, Freed Collection.

26. Teri Holleran, interviewed by JoAnn Freed, Sept. 21, 1977, 15, Freed Collection.

27. Bell, interviewed by Freed, Sept. 23, 1977, 27, 31-32.

28. *Spirit of Houston,* 10.

29. "Bella Abzug, 1920-1998," *Biography Today,* Apr. 20, 1998, 7.

30. "Hats Off," *People Weekly,* Apr. 13, 1998, 64.

31. Christine Cowern, "Gloria Steinem Remembers Bella Abzug: A Tribute," *WE International* 44 (Spring/Summer 1998): 18-24.

32. Dough Ireland, "Ciao Bella," *New York Magazine,* Apr. 13, 1998, 14; Laura Mansnerus, "Bella Abzug, 77, Congresswoman and a Founding Feminist Is Dead," *New York Times,* Apr. 1, 1998, A1.

33. *Spirit of Houston,* 10.

34. Caroline Bird, *What Women Want* (New York: Simon and Schuster, 1977), 1-27.

35. Ibid., 7.

36. National Commission on the Observance of International Women's Year, *Manual for State and Territorial IWY Coordinating Committees for Planning and Conducting the Meetings for Women* (Washington DC: National Commission, Nov. 1976), 1, copy in the Ruth Hardy Funk Papers, IWY Project.

37. See Appendix 3 for a summary of the national resolutions.

38. *Manual for State and Territorial IWY*, 7.

39. *Spirit of Houston*, 114-15.

40. *Manual for State and Territorial IWY*, 51.

41. *Salt Lake Tribune*, Jan. 25, 1973, cited in John Unger Zussman and Shauna M. Adix, "Content and Conjecture in the Equal Rights Amendment Controversy in Utah," *Women's Studies International Forum* 5 (1982), 476.

42. "Proposition No. 1 Controversial," *Deseret News*, Oct. 26, 1972, A12; and "Most Utah Solons Like 'No-Fault' Insurance Idea," *Deseret News*, Oct. 31, 1972, B9.

43. "HOTDOGS Want Rights," *Salt Lake Tribune*, Jan. 5, 1973, B2.

44. Zussman and Adix, "Content and Conjecture," 476.

45. Marilyn Warenski, *Patriarchs and Politics: The Plight of the Mormon Woman* (New York: McGraw-Hill, 1978), 194-96.

46. See Janet K. Boles, *The Politics of the Equal Rights Amendment: Conflict and the Decision Process* (New York: Longman, 1979); and Margaret I. Miller and Helene Linker, "Equal Rights Amendment Campaigns in California and Utah," *Society* 11 (1974).

47. The Equal Rights Coalition Records, ca. 1970-79, are located at the Utah State Historical Society, MSS B-501.

48. *Salt Lake Tribune*, Dec. 14, 1974, B2; Warenski, *Patriarchs and Politics*, 200, 204.

49. Irene Fisher, interviewed by Anne Looser, June 21, 2003, Salt Lake City, IWY Project.

50. Irene Fisher, "Application for Nominee as Utah Delegate to National Women's Conference," Treshow Papers.

51. Ibid.

52. [Utah Order of Women Legislators], *The Equal Rights Amendment: Pertinent Issues Affecting Women* 1 (Sept. 1974), 2 (Oct. 1976); Delilia M. Abbott and Beverly J. White, *Women Legislators of Utah, 1896-1993* (Salt Lake City:

N.p., 1993); LDS censuses, 1914-60, Family History Library, Church of Jesus Christ of Latter-day Saints, Salt Lake City.

53. Rose Mary Pederson, "Woman Power Has Become a Mighty Force in Politics," *Deseret News*, Jan. 4, 1975, W8.

54. Ibid.

55. Hal Knight, "Most Favor Full Rights for Women," *Deseret News*, 15 Nov. 1974, A1.

56. In 1983 under managing director and future general authority Richard P. Lindsay, this department became Public Communications/Special Affairs. Since 1991, it has been the Public Affairs Department. Keith Atkinson and LeAnne Hull, "Public Affairs," *Encyclopedia of Latter-day Saint History*, eds. Arnold K. Garr, Donald Q. Cannon, and Richard O. Cowan (Salt Lake City: Deseret Book, 2000), 963-64.

57. James B. Allen and Glen M. Leonard, *Story of the Latter-day Saints* (Salt Lake City: Deseret Book/LDS Church History Division, 1976), 659. The relationship between Special Affairs and the current Strengthening Church Members Committee is not known. Neither have had a public presence, and the latter only became known in 1992 when it was mentioned during a question-answer period at the Salt Lake Sunstone Symposium. According to Vern Anderson's Associated Press story, "LDS Official Acknowledges Church Monitors Critics," *Salt Lake Tribune*, Aug. 8, 1992, D1, D-2, church spokesman Don LeFevre acknowledged that this committee "provides local church leadership with information designed to help them counsel with members who may hinder the progress of the church through public criticism." In a pre-release version of the story dated August 7, 1992, LeFevre confirmed that the committee consisted of "three General Authorities."

58. Barbara B. Smith, oral interview by Jessie L. Embry, July 8, 1977, 65, in the James H. Moyle Collection, Archives of the Family and Church History Department, Church of Jesus Christ of Latter-day Saints, Salt Lake City (hereafter LDS Church Archives).

59. Ibid.

60. *Phyllis Schlafly Report*, Sept. 1986, 2.

61. Ibid., 2.

62. Rex E. Lee, "Thoughts Concerning the Equal Rights Amendment," unpublished paper, ca. 1974-75, photocopy in the Funk Papers.

63. Smith, interviewed by Embry, 1.

64. Ibid. See also "LDS Leaders Oppose ERA," *Deseret News*, Oct. 22,

1976, B1; Robert Gottlieb and Peter Wiley, *America's Saints: The Rise of Mormon Power* (New York: G. P. Putnam's Sons, 1984), 204, 269. The authors cite Smith's correspondence with Doris M. Harker of the law firm of Romney, Nelson, and Cassity as their source for this discussion.

65. Smith, interviewed by Embry, 66.

66. Ibid.

67. Gottlieb and Wiley, *America's Saints*, 204, 269.

68. Smith, interviewed by Embry, 66. Alice Colton Smith, an educator in Logan, Utah, was a member of President Smith's general board. They were not related, although their husbands were distant cousins.

69. "Equal Rights Amendment Is Opposed by Relief Society President," *Church News*, Dec. 21, 1974, 7; see also "Relief Society Head Sees Peril in ERA," *Salt Lake Tribune*, Dec. 14, 1974, B1.

70. Smith, interviewed by Embry, 66.

71. Ibid.

72. Ibid., 67.

73. Ibid.

74. Ibid.

75. Qtd. in Molly Ivins, "Many Mormon Women Feel Torn between Equal Rights Proposal and Church," *New York Times*, Nov. 26, 1979, B9.

76. *San Jose Mercury News*, Jan. 5, 1975.

77. "Boycott over ERA," *Church News*, Jan. 11, 1975, 16.

78. Warenski, *Patriarchs and Politics*, 208.

79. Peter Gillins, "Church Stand Apparently Dooms ERA Amendment," *Herald Journal* (Logan, Utah), Jan. 19, 1975, 13.

80. "ERA Effort Fails to Take Hold," *Salt Lake Tribune*, Jan. 22, 1975, A4.

81. Qtd. in Linda Sillitoe and Paul Swenson, "A Moral Issue," *Utah Holiday* 9 (Jan. 1980): 32.

82. "The Right to Oppose ERA," *Deseret News*, Jan. 22, 1975, B8.

83. Zussman and Adix, "Content and Conjecture," 475-81. They cite polls reported in the *Deseret News*, Nov. 15, 1974, A1; Feb. 5, 1975, A1, A8. These differences on the basis of religion continued through April (*Salt Lake Tribune*, May 8, 1977, A1).

84. "Utah ERA Coalition Charges Unfairness," *Deseret News*, Jan. 22, 1975, B1. See also Equal Rights Coalition of Utah, Minutes and By-laws, May 6, 1975, Equal Rights Coalition Records.

85. Charles Seldin, "Equal Rights Amendment Suffers Defeat amid Emo-

tional Voting," *Salt Lake Tribune,* Feb. 19, 1975, A1; DeAnn Evans, "Utah House Rejects ERA by 54-21 Vote," *Deseret News,* Feb. 19, 1975, A-1.

86. "Rally, Vigil Show Support for ERA," *Deseret News,* Feb. 18, 1975, B1.

87. Fisher, interviewed by Looser.

88. Warenski, *Patriarchs and Politics,* 213-14.

89. Robbie B. Snow, "Committee Vows Discrimination Fight," *Salt Lake Tribune,* Sept. 29, 1976, A12; Judy Magid, "Package of Eighteen Bills Aims at Halt to Discrimination," *Salt Lake Tribune,* Sept. 29, 1976, A16.

90. "LDS Leaders Oppose ERA," *Deseret News,* Oct. 22, 1976, B1; "First Presidency Opposes ERA," *Church News,* Oct. 30, 1976, 2.

91. O. Kendall White, "Overt and Covert Politics: The Mormon Church's Anti-ERA Campaign in Virginia," *Virginia Social Science Journal* 19 (Winter 1984): 14.

92. Ezra Taft Benson to All Stake and Mission Presidents in the United States, Dec. 29, 1976, qtd. in D. Michael Quinn, "The LDS Church's Campaign against the Equal Rights Amendment," *Journal of Mormon History* 20 (Fall 1994): 108.

93. "ERA Opposition Voiced in Idaho," *Church News,* Jan. 15, 1977, 11.

94. Boyd K. Packer, "The Equal Rights Amendment," *Ensign,* Mar. 1977, 9.

95. Smith, interviewed by Embry, 68.

96. *Idaho v. Freeman* 529 F. Supp. 1107, 1125-26.

97. Smith, interviewed by Embry, 68; "Chronology: The Mormon Anti-ERA Campaign," Mormons for ERA Collection, MSS 225, Special Collections and Archives, Merrill Library, Utah State University, Logan. Utah Senator Jake Garn (R) had this speech inserted into the Congressional Record on May 26, 1978 (s. 8441).

98. "Chronology," Mormons for ERA Collection.

99. Ibid.

100. "A Conversation with Sister Barbara B. Smith, Relief Society General President," *Ensign,* Mar. 1976, 7.

101. Barbara B. Smith, A *Fruitful Season* (Salt Lake City: Bookcraft, 1988).

Notes to Chapter 6: Planning Utah's IWY Conference

1. Jan Tyler, interviewed by Marci Goodman, Feb. 21, 1992, International Women's Year Records, Manuscripts Division, Marriott Library, University of Utah (hereafter IWY Records).

2. Jan Tyler, qtd. in Linda Sillitoe, "A Foot in Both Camps," *Sunstone* 3 (Feb. 1978): 11.

3. "Utah State Coordinating Committee International Women's Year," Ruth Hardy Funk Papers, IWY Project, in author's possession (see introduction).

4. Katie L. Dixon, "Application for Nominee as Utah Delegate to National Women's Conference," Valora Treshow Papers, IWY Project.

5. Sharon Keigher, "Application for Nominee as Utah Delegate to National Women's Conference," Treshow Papers.

6. Ibid.

7. Margaret L. Wilde, "Application for Nominee as Utah Delegate to National Women's Conference," Treshow Papers.

8. Tyler, interviewed by Goodman.

9. The coordinating committee worked for six months on the IWY conference, meeting at least weekly through this period. Although some members missed meetings, each had a separate assignment and responsibility they performed before the event. There were twenty-six general members of the committee.

10. Lynne Van Dam, "Application for Nominee as Utah Delegate to National Women's Conference," Treshow Papers.

11. Valora P. Treshow, "Application for Nominee as Utah Delegate to National Women's Conference," Treshow Papers.

12. Alberta Archuleta Almada, "Application for Nominee as Utah Delegate to National Women's Conference," Treshow Papers.

13. Barbara Bradshaw Smith, interviewed by Jessie L. Embry, July 8, 1977, James H. Moyle Collection, Archives of the Family and Church History Department, Church of Jesus Christ of Latter-day Saints, Salt Lake City (hereafter LDS Church Archives).

14. Tyler, interviewed by Goodman.

15. Smith, interviewed by Embry.

16. Barbara Bradshaw Smith, interviewed by Leah Koldweyn, Oct. 14, 1992, IWY Project. Barbara Hales, one of the board members, recalled that about fifteen women were involved (Hales, interviewed by Leah Koldweyn, Feb. 8, 1993, Salt Lake City, IWY Project).

17. "Response to *Deseret News* Questionnaire," and "Questions by Relief Society Presidency to International Women's Year Officials Concerning the IWY Utah State Meeting," both in the Funk Papers.

18. Norma Matheson, interviewed by Ann Boyle, Aug. 12, 1991, IWY Project.

19. Valora Treshow, interviewed by Catherine Jorgensen, Aug. 14, 1991, IWY Project.

20. Utah State International Women's Year Coordinating Committee, Minutes, June 9, 1977, IWY Project (hereafter cited as Coordinating Committee, Minutes, by date). A copy of the minutes also appears in the Funk Papers.

21. Tyler, interviewed by Goodman.

22. Press release, "Esther R. Landa Tapped as Presiding Officer for International Women's Year Meeting," June 13, 1977, Treshow Papers.

23. Coordinating Committee, Minutes, Feb. 14, 1977.

24. Ibid. The task forces were composed as follows: minority concerns, Maria Elena Perez, Dorothy Livingston, Alberta Archuleta Almada, and Bertha Graham; international issues, Belle Spafford and Kathleen Flake; state history, Alice Kasai and Maureen Ursenbach Beecher; basic needs, Bonnie Hartley; the environment, Lola Redford; work and income, Brenda Hancock and Zelma Brundage; relationships, Shauna Adix and Janet Darley; politics and civil rights, Lynne Van Dam; education and awareness, Afton Forsgren; outreach (to adults), Georgia Thompson and Bonnie Rodgers; outreach (to youth), Kalleen Butters; and the Utah State Plan of Action, Beth Jarman.

25. "Utah Coordinating Committee for the Statewide Meeting of the Observance of the Decade of the Woman," news release, Mar. 24, 1977, Box 2, fd. 4, Sharon Keigher Papers, Special Collections, Marriott Library, University of Utah.

26. Ibid.

27. Ibid.

28. Coordinating Committee, Minutes, Mar. 24, 1977.

29. National resolutions absent from this list were enforcement of the Federal Equal Credit Opportunity Act, strategies for change, reproductive freedom ("family planning services for teenagers, education in responsible sexuality, and reform of laws discriminating against illegitimate children and their parents"), and women in elective and appointive office. See Appendix 1.

30. IWY Task Force Chairs, Minutes, Apr. 18, 1977, Treshow Papers.

31. Coordinating Committee, Minutes, Mar. 8, 1977, Box 1, fd. 8, Keigher Papers.

32. Sharon Keigher to All IWY Task Force Chairs, Apr. 18, 1977, Box 1, fd. 19, Keigher Papers.

33. Resolutions Subcommittee, untitled document presented at April 14, 1977, meeting of the Coordinating Committee, Funk Papers.

34. Ibid.

35. "Staff Development and Training Grant Proposal," Coordinating Committee, Minutes, May 23, 1977, Box 1, fd. 26, Keigher Papers.

36. Sharon Keigher to Tony Mitchell, May 11, 1977, Box 1, fd. 32, Keigher Papers.

37. "Feminist Chronicles," Feb 11, 1977, *The Feminist Majority Foundation Online* (www.feminist.org; downloaded Jan. 2003).

38. Ibid., Feb. 26, 1977.

39. Ibid., Mar. 1977.

40. Ibid., Mar. 5, 1977.

41. Mary L. Bradford, "The Odyssey of Sonia Johnson," *Dialogue: A Journal of Mormon Thought* 14 (Summer 1981): 20; "Northern Virginia LDS Citizens Coalition," Box 17, fd. 2, Allice Allred Pottmyer Papers, Special Collections, Merrill Library, Utah State University.

42. "Feminist Chronicles," Apr. 13, 1977.

43. Qtd. in John M. Crewdson, "Mormon Turnout Overwhelms Women's Conference in Utah," *New York Times,* July 25, 1977, 26.

44. Barbara B. Smith, *A Fruitful Season* (Salt Lake City: Bookcraft, 1988), 106-7.

45. "IWY-Parley Involvement Urged," *Deseret News,* June 1977, clipping file, Jayne Ann Morgan Payne Papers, IWY Project.

46. Smith, interviewed by Koldweyn.

47. Ibid.

48. Smith, interviewed by Embry.

49. "Utah Women Plan for the First Statewide Meeting," *Deseret News,* June 15, 1977.

50. The high schools and chairs were (May 12): Orem, Naomi Udall; (May 13): Provo, Loneta Murphy; (May 16): Bonneville, Kathy Cartwright; Dugway, Kitsy Keetch; Morgan, Cindy Randall; Tintic, Lorna Hannifan; and Weber, Diane Leatham and Diane Pallet; (May 17): Ben Lomond, Linda Ogden; Box Elder, Sarah Yates; Brighton, Sherry Auer; Cedar, Jeanne Pensis; Cottonwood, Emily Hall and Jane Markosian; Cypress, Joyce Petersen; East, Lynne Van Dam; Granger, Jessica Hill; Granite, Virginia Husband; Highland, Nancy Melling; Hillcrest, Jan Johnson; Jordan, Rita Acker; Kearns, Zelma Brundage; Logan, Chris Leidich; Murray, Gwen Rowley; Ogden, Sally Bradshaw; Roy,

Norma Fawcett and Barbara Fawcett; Skyline, Katie Dixon; Skyview, Janet Skabelund, JoAnn Barnes, Leslie Jones, and Stephanie Sperry; South, Martha Olson; and West, Adrianna Sampson and Ellen Hurst; (May 18): Kamas, DeAnne Van Tassel; Park City, Anne Prince; Richfield, Judy Busk; and Spanish Fork, Lucille Tayler; (May 19): Clearfield, Lynn Smith; Olympus, Irene Fisher; Panguitch, Diane Houston; Tooele, Carole Jean Copley and Kay Gollahar; Viewmont, Jane Ann Lamph, Jean Kelly, and Eleanor Willhard; and Wendover, Terri Linaris; and (May 20): Juab, Eileen Tolboe; and Parowan, Joan Mortenson.

51. Despite the committee's effort to contact as many organizations as possible, not everyone felt that they had had the opportunity to contribute. "A Minority Report," sent to Valora Treshow from "Right to Life of Utah against International Women's Year," asserted they had not been informed of the mass meetings nor asked to participate or contribute. In addition, at the conference itself, this group felt it was prevented from voicing its opinions.

52. Georgia Beth Thompson, "Participate in: GRASS ROOTS DEMOCRACY!" N.d. Box 1, fd. 2, Keigher Papers.

53. "Suggested Agenda for Mass Meetings," ca. April 1977, Box 1, fd. 1, Keigher Papers.

54. Ibid.

55. "Top Twenty Issues by Number of Times Ranked as a Priority," Box 1, fd. 1, Keigher Papers. Mary Boltz, Susan Greene, and Martha Olson analyzed and prioritized these reports for use in the conference workshops (Coordinating Committee, Minutes, June 9, 1977, Box 1, fd. 2, Keigher Papers).

56. Valora Treshow, interviewed by Catherine Jorgenson, August 14, 1991, IWY Project. Other members of this committee were Kalleen Butters, Beverly Dalley, and Peggy Kearney.

57. Flake, "Draft of an Article for the NCW Bulletin," Box 1, fd. 2, Keigher Papers.

58. Women's Council of Provo, Minutes, April 30, 1977, Box 1, fd. 1, Keigher Papers.

59. Norma Cheney and Barbara Reynolds, report to President Barbara B. Smith, May 23, 1977, Box 1, fd. 32, Keigher Papers.

60. Norma Cheney to Barbara B. Smith, May 23, 1977, Box 1, fd. 32, Keigher Papers; copy in Jayanne Payne Papers, IWY Collection, Special Collections, Harold B. Lee Library, Brigham Young University. The women discovered it was not necessary for the opinion to be publicly aired to be included in

the report, so they took additional time to write it and did not present it on the floor.

61. Ashton, interviewed by Esplin.

62. Ezra Taft Benson to All Regional Representatives in Utah, June 3, 1977, Equal Rights Coalition of Utah, Utah State Historical Society, Salt Lake City; Sheri L. Dew, *Ezra Taft Benson: A Biography* (Salt Lake City: Deseret Book, 1987), 453-54. According to Jill Mulvay Derr, Janath Russell Cannon, and Maureen Ursenbach Beecher, *Women of Covenant: The Story of Relief Society* (Salt Lake City: Deseret Book, 1992), 371, "First came a 'priesthood telephone call' to the Utah regional representatives; then a follow-up letter was sent from Relief Society to the regional representatives and also to stake Relief Society presidents."

63. Qtd. in Smith, *Fruitful Season,* 106-7.

64. Tyler, interviewed by Goodman.

65. Kathleen Flake to the First Presidency, June 13, 1977, photocopy in my possession.

66. Ibid.

67. Ibid.

68. Ruth Hardy Funk to John Madsen, June 6, 1977, Funk Papers.

69. Peterson, interviewed by Goodman.

70. Ibid.

71. Ibid.

72. Florence Smith Jacobsen, interviewed by Catherine Jorgenson, August 9, 1991, Salt Lake City, IWY Project.

73. Jan Tyler to Coordinating Committee, June 8, 1977, Treshow Papers.

74. Tyler, interviewed by Goodman.

75. Ibid.

76. Ibid.

77. "State Women's Year Leader Urges Unity, *Salt Lake Tribune,* June 20, 1977.

78. "Mormon Turnout Overwhelms Women's Conference in Utah," 26; "IWY Issues Missing as State Meetings Take Sides on Abortion, ERA," *Salt Lake Tribune,* July 11, 1977, A2.

79. Angelyn Nelson, "Women's Meeting Nears amid Rumors of 'Meddling,'" *Salt Lake Tribune,* June 23, 1977, B4.

80. "Let's Govern Ourselves," n.d., copy in my possession.

81. Georgia Peterson, oral interview by Marci Goodman, Jan. 19, 1992, Salt Lake City, IWY Project.

82. Dennis Ker, interviewed by Linda Sillitoe, July 2, 1977, Salt Lake City, transcript, Box 6, fd. 10, Utah Women's Issues Collection, Special Collections, Marriott Library.

83. Tyler, interviewed by Goodman.

84. Ibid.

85. Erma J. Christensen, "Equality and the IWY," *Utah Independent,* June 23, 1977, 1, 4, 11.

86. Erma Christensen, "Stop ERA on June 24-25," *Utah Independent,* June 23, 1977, 11.

87. Ker, interviewed by Sillitoe, 1.

88. Ibid. The women he mentioned were Ruth Gulbranson of Bountiful and Arlene Headon, Jayne Ann Payne, and Gloria Firmage of Provo.

89. Ker, interviewed by Sillitoe, 3.

90. "Caucus Leader Claims LDS Aware of Plan," *Salt Lake Tribune,* June 25, 1977, B4. Ker clarified that Barbara Smith had "neither supported nor opposed his plans" because "that's not her place."

91. Ibid.

92. "One Thousand Cautioned on Electing Women Delegates," *Salt Lake Tribune,* June 24, 1977, B1.

93. Ker, interviewed by Sillitoe, 2.

94. Ibid., 4.

95. Peterson, interviewed by Goodman.

96. Smith interviewed by Koldweyn.

97. "Mormon Turnout Overwhelms Women's Conference in Utah," 26.

98. Norma Udall, interviewed by Catherine Jorgensen, Aug. 8, 1991, Orem, Utah, IWY Project.

99. Ashton, interviewed by Esplin.

100. Zelda B. McAllister, "Application for Nominee as Utah Delegate to National Women's Conference," Treshow Papers.

101. Dixie Snow Heufner, "Church and Politics at the Utah IWY Conference," *Dialogue: A Journal of Mormon Thought* 11 (Winter 1977): 59. Heufner reported that one of her neighbors was contacted by her Relief Society "recruiter" to be a ward representative at the conference, to vote against the ERA and other resolutions, and to attend an informational caucus at a local high school (i.e., the Conservative Caucus meeting organized by Ker).

102. Peterson, interviewed by Goodman.

103. Ker, interviewed by Sillitoe, 5.

104. Smith, interviewed by Embry.

105. Ibid.

106. "One Thousand Cautioned," B1.

107. "Caucus Leader Claims LDS Aware of Plan," B4.

108. Smith, interviewed by Embry.

109. Ibid., 14.

Notes to Chapter 7: Turmoil, June 1977

1. Charlotte England, interviewed by Leah Koldwyn, Jan. 29, 1993, Provo, Utah, IWY Project, in author's possession (see introduction).

2. Daphne Dalley, interviewed by Martha Dickey Esplin, Aug. 16, 1991, Cedar City, Utah, IWY Project.

3. Belva Ashton, interviewed by Martha Dickey Esplin, August 30, 1991, Salt Lake City, IWY Project.

4. Mary Blundell, "Application for Nominee as Utah Delegate to National Women's Conference," Valora Treshow Papers, IWY Project.

5. Suzanna Mae Grua, secretary, Coordinating Committee, Minutes, June 23, 1977, Treshow Papers.

6. Esther Landa, interviewed by Sara Knudson, June 8, 1991, Salt Lake City, IWY Project.

7. Ibid. Much of Esther Landa's public service was focused on women's issues. From 1964 to 1969, she directed women's programs in the Division of Continuing Education at the University of Utah, including a statewide women's conference. She chaired a faculty-community committee which surveyed equal opportunity at the university, resulting in the creation of the Women's Resource Center. She also served as the representative of the National Council of Jewish Women to the Equal Rights Amendment Coalition.

8. "Schedule for Utah Women's Meeting, June 24-25," Box 1, fd. 7, Utah Women's Issues Collection, Special Collections, Marriott Library, University of Utah (see Appendix 2).

9. Spafford's remarks are reported in Angelyn Nelson, "Anti-ERA Stance Cheered at Meet," *Salt Lake Tribune,* June 25, 1977, A1; "Affirm Time-Tested Values," *Church News,* July 2, 1977.

10. "Anti ERA Stance Cheered," A1.

11. Angelyn Nelson, "Women's Convention Hostility Mounts," *Salt Lake Tribune*, June 26, 1977, A1.

12. Coordinating Committee, Minutes, June 9, 1977, Treshow Papers.

13. Janet Darley's final report noted several violations of the no-campaigning rule. Campaign literature was scattered throughout the Salt Palace. Many of the women who had attended informational meetings the week before came with a slate of candidates in hand. Many left their lists in the voting booth or on the floor. Darley also noted that she heard women say they had come only to vote and that they weren't interested in the conference itself (Darley, "Election Chair Report," June 30, 1977, Treshow Papers).

14. "Women's Convention Hostility Mounts."

15. Ibid.

16. Barbara Walker, Motion, Utah IWY Meeting; "The Voice of Womankind" program, June 25, 1977, Treshow Papers.

17. Registration records, IWY Collection, Utah State Historical Society, Salt Lake City. Two excellent articles detailing the IWY conference are Linda Sillitoe, "Women Scorned: Inside Utah's IWY Conference," *Utah Holiday,* Aug. 1977, 12-63; and Dixie Snow Huefner, "Church and Politics at the Utah IWY Conference," *Dialogue: A Journal of Mormon Thought* 11 (Spring 1978): 62-75.

18. Marilyn Arnold, interviewed by Leah Koldwyn, Nov. 23, 1992, Provo, Utah, IWY Project.

19. Betty Kingsford, interviewed by Martha Dickey Esplin, August 16, 1991, IWY Project.

20. Cheryll Lynn May, interviewed by Leslie Bates, Aug. 13, 1991, Salt Lake City, IWY Project.

21. Christine Meaders Durham, interviewed by Leslie Bates, Aug. 16, 1991, 4, Salt Lake City, IWY Project.

22. Ramona Adams, interviewed by Martha Dickey Esplin, September 21, 1991, IWY Project.

23. Aileen Clyde, interviewed by Anne Looser, June 21, 2002, Springville, Utah, IWY Project.

24. "Anti-ERA Stance Cheered at Meet," A1, 2.

25. Ibid.

26. Durham, interviewed by Bates.

27. Shauna Adix, "Task Force Report on Lifestyles Workshop," IWY Collection, Utah State Historical Society.

28. Dalley, interviewed by Esplin.

29. Lisa Bolin Hawkins, "Application for Nominee as Utah Delegate to National Women's Conference," Treshow Papers.

30. Garments are underclothing worn by LDS members who have participated in temple ceremonies. Because access to the temple depends on passing worthiness interviews with one's bishop and stake president, temple-going Mormons are usually considered to be among the most faithful.

31. Reba Keele, interviewed by Marcie Goodman, Feb. 28, 1992, 7, Salt Lake City, IWY Project.

32. Lisa Bolin Hawkins, interviewed by Catherine Jorgensen, Aug. 7, 1991, Provo, Utah, IWY Project.

33. Cynthia Boshard, interviewed by Leslie Bates, July 9, 1991, Salt Lake City, IWY Project.

34. Patricia Brim, "The IWY Conference in Utah," 2, unpublished paper, Sonia Johnson Papers, Special Collections, Marriott Library.

35. Boshard, interviewed by Bates.

36. Keele, interviewed by Goodman, 6.

37. Ibid.

38. Georgia Peterson, interviewed by Marcie Goodman, Jan. 19, 1992, Salt Lake City, IWY Project.

39. Landa, interviewed by Knudson.

40. Gloria Firmage, interviewed by Anne Looser, August 8, 2002, Salt Lake City, IWY Project.

41. Boshard, interviewed by Bates.

42. "Seventy Pickets Protest IWY Meeting," *Salt Lake Tribune,* June 26, 1977, A1. Some of the groups involved were the American Civil Liberties Union, Equal Rights Legal Fund, Parents for Good Day Care, Phoenix Center, Utah Welfare Rights Organization, Women Aware, Women Entrepreneurs, Women's International League for Peace and Freedom, and Young Women's Christian Association.

43. Brim, "IWY Conference in Utah," 1.

44. "Seventy Pickets Protest IWY Meeting."

45. "Women's Convention Hostility Mounts."

46. Dalley, interviewed by Esplin.

47. This "Pro-Life—Anti-ERA Slate" was supported by Utah Right to Life, Eagle Forum, and Let's Govern Ourselves; photocopy in my possession.

48. Landa, interviewed by Knudson.

49. Keele, interviewed by Goodman.

50. England, interviewed by Koldweyn.

51. Dorothy Littrell, "Memoirs of IWY," July 1977, photocopy of typescript in my possession.

52. Ballot tabulation, IWY Collection, Utah State Historical Society.

53. Barbara B. Smith, interviewed by Jessie L. Embry, July 8, 1977, Salt Lake City, Moyle Oral History project, LDS Church Archives.

54. Barbara B. Smith, interviewed by Leah Koldwyn, October 14, 1992, Salt Lake City, IWY Project.

55. She wrote: "The situation was complicated because many women, unfamiliar with parliamentary law, saw it as a way to suppress their comments rather than a tool to allow all viewpoints equal opportunity. Some believed it to be intentionally placed as a stumbling block by ERA supporters" (Dorothy L. Behling, "Thoughts on the IWY Conference," n.d., typescript, Ruth Hardy Funk Papers, IWY Project).

56. Ibid.

57. Barbara Hales, interviewed by Leah Koldwyn, Feb. 8, 1993, Salt Lake City, IWY Project. In the film *Stepford Wives,* a community of uniformly contented, attractive, sexually complaisant women turn out to be artificially manufactured to meet masculine dreams.

58. Patricia Hill, "Minority Report," July 7, 1977, Treshow Papers.

59. Dalley, interviewed by Esplin.

60. "Future of IWY 'Hangs in Balance,'" *Salt Lake Tribune,* July 22, 1977.

61. Linda Schrenk, "Minority Report," n.d, Treshow Papers. Schrenk made the common mistake of assuming the U.S. Constitution, which assures freedom of worship and forbids the establishment of a state church, specifically requires separation of church and state.

62. Marilee Latta, interviewed by Sara Knudson, Sept. 8, 1991, Salt Lake City, IWY Project.

63. Broshard, interviewed by Bates.

64. Jan Tyler, qtd. in Linda Sillitoe, "A Foot in Both Camps," *Sunstone* 3 (Feb. 1978): 11.

65. Jan Tyler, interviewed by Marci Goodman, Feb. 21, 1992, Salt Lake City, IWY Project.

66. Durham, interviewed by Bates.

67. Dan Marriott to Utah Delegates, July 6, 1977, photocopy in Treshow Papers.

68. "IWY Aim Topic of Women, Governor," *Salt Lake Tribune,* July 20, 1977. The meeting was held on July 19.

69. Ibid.

70. *Salt Lake Tribune,* June 27, 1977.

71. Qtd. in John Crewdson, "Mormon Turnout Overwhelms Women's Conference in Utah," *New York Times,* July 25, 1977.

72. Erma J. Christensen, "IWY Conference Resolutions Go Down the Drain," *Utah Independent,* July 7, 1977, 1.

73. Ibid. The pre-conference issue of the *Independent* reported that $5 million had been spent on the national IWY observance and that "President Carter has appointed only pro-ERA women" to the national commission—specifically Bella Abzug, Gloria Steinem, and Eleanor Smeal, but not Phyllis Schlafly ("Stop ERA Now," *Utah Independent,* June 23, 1977, 1).

74. Aileen H. Clyde, "Further Reflection on Meaning of Conference," *Provo Herald,* June 30, 1977, 35.

75. "No Corner on Truth," *Salt Lake Tribune,* Dec. 2, 1977, A22.

76. Allen Rasmussen, *Salt Lake Tribune,* Dec. 2, 1977, A22.

77. Robert G. Vernon, "Height of Intolerance," June 29, 1977.

78. Letters to editors, June 29, 1977.

79. Kathleen Christison, "Ashamed of Some," *Salt Lake Tribune,* June 30, 1977.

80. Dorothy Littrell, "Devil Won Out," *Salt Lake Tribune,* July 20, 1977.

81. Davis and Wadsworth to the editor, *Salt Lake Tribune,* June 20, 1977.

82. Tyler, interviewed by Goodman.

83. Editorial, *Deseret News,* June 27, 1977.

84. Jan Tyler to Kathryn MacKay, Apr. 13, 1980, Utah Women's Issues Collection, Special Collections, Marriott Library.

85. Ibid.

86. Qtd. in "IWY Conference Told Women's Views," *Deseret News,* July 4, 1977.

87. "LDS Women Seen Through Years," *Church News,* July 2, 1977.

Chapter 8: The National Convention

1. *The Spirit of Houston: An Official Report to the President, the Congress and the People of the United States* (Washington D.C.: National Commission on the Observance of International Women's Year, 1978), 9; the national commission will hereafter be abbreviated NCIWY.

2. Jill Ruckelshaus, "Women's Voices: Quotations by Women," ed. Jone Johnson Lewis, *Women's History* (online at http://womenshistory.about.com; downloaded 2003).

3. Qtd. in *To Form a More Perfect Union: Justice for American Women* (Washington D.C.: NCIWY, 1976); *Spirit of Houston,* 9.

4. *To Form a More Perfect Union*, 102. Another development was President Ford's Interdepartmental Task Force to oversee a self-study of government programs and policies affecting women (see chap. 5).

5. *Spirit of Houston,* 10.

6. Ibid.

7. Ibid., 9.

8. Ibid., 106.

9. "Women's Meetings Turn into ERA Battlegrounds," *Deseret News,* July 11, 1977.

10. Ibid., 100.

11. Ibid., 114.

12. NCIWY, "Update on the State Meetings & the National IWY Conference," July 25, 1977, 1, Valora Treshow Papers, IWY Project, in author's possession (see introduction).

13. Ibid.

14. Mark Sableman, "Twelve D.C. Women to Attend Conference," *Washington Post,* June 23, 1977, DC2.

15. *Spirit of Houston,* 104.

16. Ibid., 104.

17. Ibid., 114.

18. Ibid., 108-9.

19. Ibid., 113.

20. Patricia McCormack, "Women Getting Ready for National Conclave," *Rocky Mountain News,* Aug. 16, 1977, 32.

21. Ibid.; *Spirit of Houston,* 109.

22. "Twelve D.C. Women to Attend Conference." The other delegates were Mary Jo Binder, Charlotte Ann Bunch, Theresa Clar, Alexa Freeman, Helen H. Helfer, Etta M. Horn, Juanita Morgan, Mary Spottswood Pou, Barbara Lett Simmons, Ruth Anita Sykes, and Paquita Vito.

23. Ibid.

24. *Spirit of Houston,* 110.

25. John M. Crewdson, "Mormon Turnout Overwhelms Women's Conference in Utah," *New York Times,* July 25, 1977.

26. "Women's Meetings Turn into ERA Battlegrounds."

27. "Montana IWY Meeting Raked by Controversy," *Salt Lake Tribune,* n.d., clipping file, Box 7, fd. 18, Sonia Johnson Collection, Special Collections, Marriott Library, University of Utah, Salt Lake City.

28. Ibid.

29. "Women's Meetings Turn into ERA Battlegrounds."

30. *Spirit of Houston,* 110.

31. Nan Robertson, "New York Delegation to Women's Conference," *New York Times,* July 25, 1977, 34.

32. Elaine Bissell, "Eight Thousand Converge on Albany; Local Woman Creates Fracas," *Daily Times* [Maruaroneck, New York], July 10, 1977.

33. Stake Relief Society Presidency to All Sisters of the Relief Society in New York, New York Stake," n.d., Box 7, fd. 26, Sonia Johnson Collection.

34. Ibid.

35. Ibid., fd. 2.

36. D. Michael Quinn, "The LDS Church's Campaign against the Equal Rights Amendment," *Journal of Mormon History* 20 (Fall 1994): 118.

37. See mention of walkie-talkies in "Mormon Turnout Overwhelms Women's Conference," 26; "IWY Issues Missing as State Meets," *Salt Lake Tribune,* July 11, 1977.

38. "New York Delegation to Women's Conference," 34.

39. *Honolulu Star-Bulletin,* July 8, 1977, see also "Conservative Block Exceeds Liberals," *Honolulu Star-Bulletin,* July 9, 1977; clippings in Conservative Women Opposed to Equal Rights Amendment Collection, MSS SC 1827, L. Tom Perry Special Collections, Harold B. Lee Library, Brigham Young University, Provo, Utah.

40. Bosgra and Atkinson to NCIWY, July 15, 1977, Conservative Women Opposed to the Equal Rights Amendment Collection, Box 2, fd. 1.

41. Helen Triester to whom it may concern, July 11, 1977, Jayne Ann Payne Papers, IWY Project. The letter was sent to the National IWY Commission, President Jimmy Carter, Hawaii's Congressional delegation (Senators Daniel Inouye and Spark Matsunaga and Representatives Daniel Akaka and Cecil Heftel), Winona Rubin, Elizabeth Atharasakos, Governor George Ariyoshi, Mayor Frank Fasi, state senator Patricia Saiki, and the *Honolulu Star Bulletin.*

42. On the other hand, if the accounts can be believed, the dancers clearly

crossed the line of good taste. The word from a conservative newsletter in Kennewick, Washington, reporting on the Hawaii conference, was that "a workshop listed on the program as 'Coming Together' turned out to be a lesbian dance performance that exhibited suggestive movements, self-examination of private parts of the body, and two lesbians making love in a pay toilet. Filthy speech narrations accompanied this 'entertainment'" (*Citizens for Youth Newsletter* 2 [1977]: 2, copy in the Payne Papers).

43. Ray Yuen, "Women Meet, Disagree—Again," *Logan Herald Journal,* July 11, 1977.

44. Ibid.

45. Ibid. Nevertheless, it is unclear whether the women holding the sign were conservative or liberal.

46. "LDS Women Defend Stand," *Church News,* July 16, 1977, 7.

47. *Spirit of Houston,* 130. The poll by the National Women's Political Caucus, Women's Action Alliance, and ERAmerica turned out to be remarkably accurate. About 300 delegates opposed the ERA.

48. Ibid., 130.

49. *Spirit of Houston,* 119.

50. Ibid.

51. "Women's Voices" editorial, *Washington Post,* Nov. 18, 1977, A18.

52. "Update on the National Women's Conference, November 18-21, Houston, Texas," NCIWY, Nov. 1977, 5, Payne Papers.

53. Ibid., 5.

54. "For Immediate Release," NCIWY and the Office of Public Information, U.S. Department of State, Washington D.C., Payne Papers.

55. Ibid.

56. "Diverse Delegations to Attend National Women's Conference," NCIWY and the Office of Public Information, Oct. 3, 1977, Payne Papers.

57. "For Immediate Release," Payne Papers.

58. Angelyn Nelson, "Utah Delegation Arrives for IWY Conference," *Salt Lake Tribune,* Nov. 18, 1977, A7. The articles in the press briefing book were from the *Daily Journal American* (Washington State), *Equal Rights Monitor, Honolulu Advertiser, New York Times,* and *Ripon Forum.*

59. Ibid.

60. Megan Rosenfeld and Bill Curry, "Women's Conference Votes Abortion, Gay Rights Measures: Unburned Brassiers and Other Vignettes," *Washington Post,* Nov. 21, 1977, A6.

61. Ibid.

62. Anna Quindlen, "Anticipating a Historic Occasion, Women Stream to Conference," *New York Times,* Nov. 18, 1977, II-4.

63. "Houston Votes Aim at Assessing Progress, Charting Goals," *Washington Post,* Nov. 20, 1997, A28.

64. Megan Rosenfeld, "Reflections on an All-Female World," *Washington Post,* Dec. 2, 1977, A17.

65. Anna Quindlen, "Women's Parley Brings Action over a Rights Agenda for Nation," *New York Times,* Nov. 20, 1977, A1; Judy Klemesrud, "At Houston Meeting a Kaleidoscope of American Womanhood," *New York Times,* Nov. 19, 1977, 22.

66. Elizabeth Ford, *Current Biography,* 1975 entry, online at *H. W. Wilson* (www.hwwilson.com; downloaded 2003).

67. Rosalynn Carter, *Current Biography,* 1978 entry, online at *H. W. Wilson* (www.hwwilson.com; downloaded 2003); see also *Family Circle,* Oct. 1976, 4; *Good Housekeeping,* Aug. 1977, 102; *New York Times,* Sept. 15, 1976, 45; *New York Times Magazine,* Mar. 20, 1977, 19.

68. Edward Walsh, "Post's Report of Bottle Tax Plan," *Washington Post,* Mar. 29, 1977, A2.

69. Mary L. Morse, "Steinem Says Delegates on the Edge of History," *Daily Breakthrough: Where Women Are News,* Nov. 19, 1977, 22, Payne Papers.

70. Roger Piantadosi, *Washington Post,* Oct. 1, 1977, D3 (*LexisNexis* keyword search: National Women's Conference).

71. *Spirit of Houston,* 129.

72. Marilyn Arnold, interviewed by Leah Koldwyn, Nov. 23, 1992, Provo, Utah, IWY Project.

73. Megan Rosenfeld, "Women's Conference Opens with a Display of Political Muscle," *Washington Post,* Nov. 19, 1977, A1.

74. Ibid.

75. Ibid.

76. *Spirit of Houston,* 124.

77. Judy Klemesrud, *New York Times,* Nov. 20, 1977, 32 (downloaded from *LexisNexis*).

78. "Home from Houston," C6.

79. Klemesrud, 32 (*LexisNexis*).

80. Bill Curry, "Throng Rejects 'Antifamily Goal' of ERA: Support for Historic Sex Roles," *Washington Post,* Nov. 20, 1977, A1.

81. Ibid.

82. Ibid.

83. "Klan vs. Feminists," *Washington Post,* Sept. 2, 1977, A4.

84. Pamela Horowitz, "Personalities," *Washington Post,* Nov. 21, 1977, C3.

85. Ruth Hardy Funk, interviewed by Catherine Jorgenson, August 29, 1991, Salt Lake City, IWY Project.

86. Qtd. in Mary Gaber, "Houston Wasn't Camelot—But There Was a Shining Moment," *Utah Holiday* 7 (Jan. 1978), 6.

87. Ibid.

88. *Spirit of Houston,* 138-39.

89. Ibid., 141.

90. Ruckelshaus, "Women's Voices."

91. *Spirit of Houston,*13-97. The resolutions that survived fell under the headings of arts and humanities, battered women, business, child abuse, child care, credit, disabled women, education, elective and appointive office, employment, the Equal Rights Amendment, health, homemakers, insurance, international affairs, media, minority women, offenders, older women, rape, reproductive freedom, rural women, sexual preference, statistics, and welfare and poverty.

92. Becky Cassier, "National IWY Gets Utah's Plan," *Deseret News,* Aug. 1, 1977, B24.

93. *Spirit of Houston,* 15.

94. Ibid., 83.

95. Megan Rosenfeld, "Women's Conference Delegates Pass Abortion, ERA Measures," *Washington Post,* Nov. 21, 1977, A1.

96. Ibid.

97. Ibid., 49.

98. Ibid.

99. Ibid.

100. *Bradwell v. State,* 83 US 916, Wall. 130 (1872).

101. *Goesart v. Cleary,* 335 US 464 (1948) and *Hoyt v. Florida,* 368 US 57 (1961).

102. *Spirit of Houston,* 49-50.

103. Ibid., 51.

104. Ibid., 52. The list included the American Baptist Women, American Home Economics Association, American Jewish Congress, American Veterans Committee, B'nai B'rith Women, Child Welfare League of America, Coalition

of Labor Union Women, Common Cause, Disciples of Christ, General Federation of Women's Clubs, League of Women Voters, National Catholic Coalition of American Nuns, National Council of Churches, National Council of Jewish Women, National Council of Negro Women, National Federation of Business and Professional Women's Clubs, National Organization for Women, National Secretaries Association, National Woman's Party, National Women's Political Caucus, United Auto Workers, United Methodist Church, United Presbyterian Church, Young Women's Christian Association, and others.

105. Cheryl Knott and Janet Sanders, "Pro-Plan Progress," *Daily Breakthrough,* Nov. 20, 1977, 2, Treshow Papers.

106. *Spirit of Houston,* 148.

107. Reba Keele, interviewed by Marcie Goodman, February 28, 1992, Salt Lake City, IWY Project.

108. *Spirit of Houston,* 149.

109. Ibid. Section 2 reads: "The Congress shall have the power to enforce, by appropriate legislation, the provisions of this article."

110. Ibid., 149.

111. *Spirit of Houston,* 152.

112. Anna Quindlen, "Women's Conference Approves Planks on Abortion and Rights for Homosexuals," *New York Times,* Nov. 21, 1977, 44; Quindlen, "Women End Parley with Plan for Rights," *New York Times,* Nov. 22, 1977, A1.

113. "Home from Houston," *Washington Post,* Nov. 27, 1977, C6.

114. Bill Curry and Megan Rosenfeld, "Conference Over, the Mission Begins," *Washington Post,* Nov. 22, 1977, A1.

115. "Home from Houston" editorial, *Washington Post,* Nov, 27, 1977, C6.

116. Qtd. in Curry and Rosenfeld, "Conference Over, the Mission begins," A1.

117. Qtd. in ibid.

118. Sue Kaufman, "Strong for ERA," *Daily Breakthrough,* Nov. 19, 1977, 6, Payne Papers.

119. *Spirit of Houston,* 11.

120. Ibid.

121. David S. Broder, "Woman: The Aftermath," *Washington Post,* Nov. 22, 1977, A1.

122. Donna Wayment, qtd. in Georgia Peterson, "For Immediate Release," Nov. 21, 1977, in author's possession.

Chapter 9: Utah's Delegation

1. Jan Tyler to Delegates and Alternates, July 5, 1977, Jayne Ann Payne Papers, IWY Project, in author's possession (see introduction). See also Judy B. Rollins, "IWY State Meeting Runs by the Rules," *Salt Lake Tribune,* June 17, 1977.

2. Utah IWY Coordinating Committee, Minutes, June 29, 1977, Ruth Hardy Funk Papers, IWY Project.

3. Valora Treshow to the National Commission on the Observance of International Women's Year, July 6, 1977, Valora Treshow Papers, IWY Project.

4. Kathleen Flake, "Report of the Utah State IWY Nominating Committee," June 29, 1977, Treshow Papers.

5. Angelyn Nelson, "Group Files Formal Challenge to National Commission," *Salt Lake Tribune,* Aug. 13, 1977.

6. Angelyn Nelson, "IWY Commission Rejects All Challenges," *Salt Lake Tribune,* Aug. 13, 1977.

7. Georgia Peterson, interviewed by Marci Goodman, Jan. 30, 1977, Salt Lake City, IWY Project.

8. "Hatch Says IWY Leaders Trying to Load Utah Group," *Salt Lake Tribune,* 1977, undated clipping, Payne Papers.

9. "At Large IWY Delegates 'Not Appointed to Counter,'" *Salt Lake Tribune,* 1977, undated clipping, Payne Papers.

10. Ibid.

11. "Future of IWY Hangs in Balance," *Salt Lake Tribune,* July 22, 1977, D5.

12. Utah Delegation, Minutes, July 5, 1977, Payne Papers.

13. "Open Letter to the National IWY Commission," n.d., Funk Papers.

14. Tyler to Delegates and Alternates, July 5, 1977.

15. *Utah Women Speak* (Salt Lake City: Utah IWY delegation, July 1977), 1; Ruth Hardy Funk Notebook, Funk Papers.

16. Qtd. in Georgie Ann Geyer, "Utah Women Typify Divisions in IWY," *Salt Lake Tribune,* Nov. 15, 1977.

17. Angelyn Nelson, "IWY Delegates Take More Moderate Abortion Stand," *Salt Lake Tribune,* Oct. 28, 1977.

18. Utah IWY Delegation, Minutes, Aug. 5, 1977, Payne Papers.

19. "Workshops for IWY Delegates," n.d., Payne Papers.

20. Angelyn Nelson, "Women Seek Public Comment," *Salt Lake Tribune,* Oct. 13, 1977.

21. Utah IWY Delegation, Minutes of Workshop, Sept. 23, 1977, Funk Papers.

22. Ibid., Sept. 24, Funk Papers.

23. Angelyn Nelson, "IWY Delegates Open Meet to Public; Six Comment," *Salt Lake Tribune,* Oct. 16, 1977.

24. Utah IWY Delegation, Minutes of Workshop, Oct. 15, 1977, Funk Papers.

25. Jayne Ann Payne, "The Equal Rights Amendment or the Equivocal Rights Amendment," n.d., Payne Papers.

26. Sally Ehlinger, "The League of Women Voters of Utah," Oct. 25, 1977, Funk Papers.

27. Bella Abzug to Delegates and Alternates, Oct. 2, 1977, Payne Papers.

28. Utah IWY Delegation, Minutes, Oct. 27, 1977.

29. Angelyn Nelson, "Utah Delegates Request IWY Audit, List Gripes," *Salt Lake Tribune,* Nov. 11, 1977.

30. Angelyn Nelson, "Group Alleges 'Secret IWY Fund,'" *Salt Lake Tribune,* Oct. 29, 1977.

31. Qtd. in Angelyn Nelson, "Utahn Asks End to Dispute on IWY Funds," *Salt Lake Tribune,* Nov. 13, 1977.

32. Angelyn Nelson, "Equal Rights Group Tells Fund Source," *Salt Lake Tribune,* Nov. 15, 1977.

33. Georgia Peterson, "Utah Delegation Falsely Accused," press release, Payne Papers.

34. Angelyn Nelson, "Utahn Shares Spotlight at IWY Meet," *Salt Lake Tribune,* Nov. 20, 1977.

35. Karen Malnory, "Women on the Move," *Daily Breakthrough: Where Women Are News,* Nov. 19, 1977, Payne Papers.

36. Angelyn Nelson, "One Hundred and Fifty Utahns Fly to Houston to Join Protest against Conference," *Salt Lake Tribune,* Nov. 20, 1977.

37. "Schedule of Special Events," Houston Women's Conference, Payne Papers. In the "Seneca Falls South" room, conference attendees could "relax, listen and learn." On Saturday the diverse offerings included, "Seneca Falls: Where It All Began," "Self Defense," "Folk Singing," "Seneca Soapbox," and a "Black Ensemble." The same varied mix continued on Sunday and Monday. A third group of "Success Stories and Skill Clinics" included eight "how-to success stories and fifteen skills clinics" focused on such issues as "Separation and Divorce," "Volunteer Skills and Experiences," and "Service to Rape Victims."

38. "Press Kit Contents," Women's Conference Network, n.d., Treshow Papers. Other items in the press kit were an IWY brochure, a tentative schedule of events, historical background on the conference and a copy of Public Law 94-167, the national Plan of Action, delegates-at-large (first announcement of these appointments), biographical sketches of the conference spokespeople, myths about the national conference, facts about women, a fact sheet on discrimination against women, demographics and analysis of the elected delegates, a press release titled "Diverse Delegations to Attend National Women's Conference," radio-spot scripts (30- and 60-second sound bites), "Surely, Phyllis, Even YOU Can See That" from the *Washington Star* (a story on homemaker rights), "Showcase in Houston" from the *Christian Science Monitor*, reports on some of the state meetings, and the legal status of homemakers.

39. Angelyn Nelson, "Utah Senators and Church Ask Apologies," *Salt Lake Tribune*, Nov. 22, 1977.

40. Angelyn Nelson, "Utah's IWY Delegates Outnumbered, But They Will Push Cause," *Salt Lake Tribune*, Nov. 14, 1977.

41. "Utah Delegation Challenges the IWY, Resents Smear Tactics," undated press release, Payne Papers; Angelyn Nelson, "Utah's Delegates to IWY Will Protest 'Radical' Label," *Salt Lake Tribune*, Nov. 21, 1977.

42. "Utah Delegation Challenges the IWY."

43. Angelyn Nelson, "Solon Clarifies LDS View," *Salt Lake Tribune*, Nov. 24, 1977.

44. Kay Mills, "Those Aren't Prayer Meetings They Hold on Sunday. Those are Precinct Meetings," *Daily Breakthrough*, Nov. 19, 1977, 3, Payne Papers.

45. Jack Anderson, "Bella Harms Cause by Attack on Mormons," *Deseret News*, Dec. 28, 1977, A3.

46. Robert W. Lee, "Perversion of Reality," *Salt Lake Tribune*, Dec. 2, 1977, A22.

47. Georgia Peterson, "After Houston, What?" *Exponent II* 4 (Winter 1978): 9.

48. Ibid., 9.

49. Ibid., 17.

50. Florence Jacobsen, interviewed by Catherine Jorgenson, Aug. 9, 1991, Salt Lake City, IWY Project.

51. Naomi Udall, interviewed by Catherine Jorgenson, Aug. 8, 1991, Orem, Utah, IWY Project.

52. Open Letter to the National IWY Commission, n.d., Funk Papers.

53. Esther Landa, interviewed by Sara Knudson, June 8, 1991, Salt Lake City, IWY Project.

54. Georgia Peterson, "For Immediate Release," Nov. 21, 1977, copy in my possession.

55. Angelyn Nelson, "Most Americans Support Positions Approved at Women's Conference," *Salt Lake Tribune,* Dec. 4, 1977.

56. Angelyn Nelson, "Capitol Rally Supports IWY Delegates," *Salt Lake Tribune,* Nov. 20, 1977.

57. National Commission on the Observance of International Women's Year to All Delegates, Dec. 5, 1977, Payne Papers.

58. "Four Utah Women Named to Panel," *Salt Lake Tribune,* Mar. 21, 1978.

59. "Carter to Speed Women's Rights," *Salt Lake Tribune,* Mar. 23, 1978.

60. "What Next for U.S. Women," *Time,* Dec. 5, 1977.

61. Angelyn Nelson, "Momentum for Women Advancement," *Salt Lake Tribune,* Dec. 5, 1977.

Chapter 10: Anti-ERA Activism in Key States

1. Georgia Peterson, interviewed by Marci Goodman, Jan. 19, 1992, Salt Lake City, IWY Project, in author's possession (see introduction).

2. "Feminist Chronicles," Jan. 30, 1976, *The Feminist Majority Foundation Online* (www.feminist.org; downloaded Jan. 2003).

3. Ibid., Jan. 3, 1976.

4. Ibid.

5. Ibid., Jan. 18, 1977.

6. Ibid., Mar. 1977.

7. Ibid., Jan. 16, 1978.

8. Ibid., Feb. 7, 1978.

9. Ibid.

10. Ibid., Mar. 30, 1978.

11. Ibid., July 9, 1978.

12. At a joint press conference with Phyllis Schlafly at the end of a day-long meeting called "Coalition for Fair Play" comprising several hundred women from Catholic, Mormon, and Southern Baptist congregations, Utah Senator Jake Garn announced he was planning a filibuster against the extension of the ERA ratification period. He said, "I do not intend to misuse the Senate rules, and therefore am puzzled when asked if this is appropriate. The arrogance of

power and its steam-roller effect can only be offset by filibuster as a tool of the minority." See Virginia Robicheaux, "ERA Filibuster Won't Snag Bills," *Salt Lake Tribune*, Sept. 13, 1978. Garn later backed away from this decision.

13. "Transcript of a Meeting of Latter-day Saint Women's Coalition," Vienna, Virginia, Dec. 4, 1978, Bx. 7, fd. 22, Sonia Johnson Collection, Manuscripts Division, Marriott Library, University of Utah, Salt Lake City.

14. *Oakton Stake Newsletter*, Nov. 1978, Oakton, Virginia, Bx. 7, fd. 22, Johnson Collection.

15. See Karen Mecham, Memorandum, Oct. 5, 1979, Bx. 7, fd. 26, Johnson Collection.

16. Ezra Taft Benson to All Stake and Mission Presidents in the United States, Dec. 29, 1976.

17. D. Michael Quinn, "The LDS Church's Campaign against the Equal Rights Amendment," *Dialogue: A Journal of Mormon Thought* 20 (Fall 1994): 123.

18. "Church Leaders Reaffirm ERA Stand," *Church News*, Aug. 26, 1978, 2; "First Presidency Re-affirms Opposition to ERA," *Ensign* 8 (Oct. 1978): 63.

19. Spencer W. Kimball, Marion G. Romney, and Nathan Eldon Tanner to General Authorities, Regional Representatives, Stake Presidencies, Mission Presidents, Bishops, and Branch Presidents in the United States, Oct. 12, 1978, Johnson Collection; hereafter "First Presidency to Church Brethren."

20. In Linda Sillitoe, "Women Scorned: Inside the IWY Conference," *Utah Holiday*, Aug. 1977, 26-28; Linda Sillitoe, "Fear and Anger in Virginia: The New Mormon Activists," *Utah Holiday*, Apr. 1979, 9-12; and Dixie Heufner, "Church Politics and the Utah IWY Conference," *Dialogue: A Journal of Mormon Thought* 11 (Spring 1978): 58-75.

21. *The Alexandrin*, Oct. 1978, Alexandria, Virginia, Bx. 7, fd. 22, Johnson Collection.

22. *Vienna Vision*, Aug. 1978; *Oakton Stake Newsletter*, Nov. 1978.

23. Petition distributed in Oakton ward meetinghouse lobby, Bx. 7, fd. 22, Johnson Collection.

24. O. Kendall White, "Overt and Covert Politics: The Mormon Church's Anti-ERA Campaign in Virginia," *Virginia Social Science Journal* 19 (Winter 1984): 11-16.

25. See Ruth Ann Alexander, "South Dakota Women Stake a Claim: A Feminist Memoir, 1964-1989," *South Dakota History* 19 (Winter 1989): 552; *Church Almanac, 1993-94*, (Salt Lake City: Deseret News, 1994), 162.

26. See James T. Richardson, "The 'Old Right' in Action: Mormon and Catholic Involvement in an Equal Rights Amendment Referendum," in David Bromley and Anson Shupe, eds., *New Christian Politics* (Macon, GA: Mercer University Press, 1984), 223; [Lori Winder Stromberg],"Chronology: The Mormon Anti-ERA Campaign," *Mormons for ERA Newsletter,* 5 (Feb. 1983): [5], Johnson Collection.

27. O. Kendall White Jr., "Mormonism and the Equal Rights Amendment," *Journal of Church and State* 31 (Spring 1989): 249-67.

28. *The Fairfax Star,* Mar. 1978, Fairfax, Virginia, Bx. 7, fd. 22, Johnson Collection.

29. White, "Overt and Covert Politics," 15.

30. James T. Richardson and S. W. Fox, "Religious Affiliation as a Predictor of Voting Behavior on Abortion Reform Legislation," *Journal for the Scientific Study of Religion* 11 (June 1972): 347-59.

31. Ibid. Using telephone trees, virtually entire wards were mobilized within a few hours. The response was impressive. During the 1978 election, about 9,000 Mormons distributed flyers to the doorsteps of almost every home in Las Vegas.

32. See Richardson, "'Old Right in Action"; Anson Shupe and John Heinerman, "Mormonism and the New Christian Right: An Emerging Coalition?" *Review of Religious Research* 27 (Dec. 1985): 146-57. On March 26, 1978, the Senate held a hearing to help clarify the key issues on both sides. At the beginning of the hearing, and in the absence of Orrin Hatch, "historic official statements of the Church of Jesus Christ of Latter Day Saints opposing the extension of time for ERA ratification" were added to the record.

33. See, e.g., Orrin G. Hatch, *The Equal Rights Amendment: Myths and Realities* (N.p.: Conservative Press, 1983); Mills, "Groups Split over ERA."

34. Dallin H. Oaks to faculty and staff, qtd. in "President Oaks Attacks ERA Groups in Letter," *Daily Universe,* May 2, 1978.

35. Ibid.; "Boycotts Part of U.S. History: ERA No Different," *Daily Universe,* May 4, 1978; Dallin H. Oaks to Sybel Alger, May 5, 1978, qtd. in Quinn, "LDS Church's Campaign against the Equal Rights Amendment," 135n147.

36. Lenata Murphy to the editor, and Dennis and Robyn Savage Jensen to the editor, *Daily Universe,* May 11, 1978.

37. See the BYU president's weekly minutes of meetings, Jan. 23, 1980, 4, qtd. in Gary James Bergera and Ronald Priddis, *Brigham Young University: A House of Faith* (Salt Lake City: Signature Books, 1985), 223.

38. Heber G. Wolsey to Public Communications Directors, Dec. 14, 1979, Bx. 7, fd. 23, Johnson Collection.

39. "Gem Legislature Ratifies Amendment to Ensure Women's Equal Rights," *Idaho Statesman,* Mar. 25, 1972, 14; "Idaho Ratifies Equal Rights," *Idaho Falls Post-Register,* Mar. 25, 1972, A-11.

40. "The Equal Rights Amendment Has Been Ratified in Idaho," Mormon flyer, copy in the Johnson Collection.

41. Stromberg, "Chronology."

42. Ken Driggs to the editor, *Dialogue: A Journal of Mormon Thought* 11 (Autumn 1978): 6.

43. See "State Official Probes Mormon Lobbying," *Reston Times,* Mar. 1, 1979; "Mormon Lobby on ERA Probed," *Alexandria Gazette,* Mar. 1, 1979; "Mormon Anti-ERA Group to Register as a Lobby," *Arlington-Alexandria Star,* Mar. 15, 1979 ; "Mormon Money Worked against Florida Anti-ERA Drive, Report Details," *Salt Lake Tribune,* Apr. 21, 1980; Linda Cicero, "State to Probe Mormon Contributions," *Miami Herald,* Apr. 22, 1980, II-1.

44. Linda Sillitoe, Notes of Interview with Julian Lowe, LDS Regional Representative in Virginia, Feb. 14, 1979, Box 5, fd. 10, Utah Women's Issues Collection, Manuscripts Division, Marriott Library.

45. John Herbers, "Equal Rights Amendment Is Mired in Confused and Emotional Debate," *New York Times,* May 28, 1978, 1.

46. Mormons voted in significantly elevated numbers. Estimates suggest that 90-95 percent of all eligible Mormon voters cast votes. A useful comparison might be the 76.8 percent of registered voters in Utah who voted in 1980 or the national average of 53.2 percent. See Richardson, "'Old Right' in Action," 223; Stromberg, "Chronology," 5.

47. Lisa Cronin Wohl, "A Mormon Connection: The Defeat of the ERA in Nevada," *Ms. Magazine,* July 1977, 69.

48. Ibid.

49. Sheila Caudle, "Religion, ERA Issue Tied," *Las Vegas Review Journal,* Sept. 7, 1976.

50. Ibid.

51. Ibid.

52. For a full report on this investigation, see Myram Borders, "Mormon Group's ERA Stand Probed," *Las Vegas Review Sun,* Sept. 28, 1976.

53. bid.

54. Renee Rampton to Charles Waterman, chairman, Fair Campaign Practices Committee, Feb. 8, 1977, Bx. 7, fd. 7, Johnson Collection.

55. "Mormon Group's ERA Stand Probed."

56. Rampton to Waterman.

57. Wohl, "A Mormon Connection," 69.

58. Ibid.

59. Rampton to Waterman.

60. Ibid.

61. Ibid.

62. Ibid.

63. Ibid.

64. Wohl, "A Mormon Connection," 69.

65. Rampton to Waterman.

66. Ibid.

67. Charles Waterman to Renee Rampton, Oct. 15, 1976, Bx. 7, fd. 7, Johnson Collection.

68. James K. Seastrand to Charles Waterman, Mar. 8, 1977, Johnson Collection.

69. Ibid.

70. Ibid.

71. Dean Schank to Charles Waterman, Mar. 9, 1977, Johnson Collection.

72. Wohl, "A Mormon Connection," 69.

73. P. Butler, "Mormon Church against the ERA: 'Full Institutional Involvement' in Politics," included in NOW missionary packets, Mar. 30, 1981, Johnson Collection.

74. Wohl, "Mormon Connection," 68.

75. Renee M. Rampton, "The Role of the Mormon Church in the 1978 Nevada Election," Jan. 19, 1979, unpublished typescript, Bx. 7, fd. 7, Johnson Collection.

76. Qtd. in Wohl, "A Mormon Connection," 69.

77. Ibid., 71.

78. Ibid.

79. Ibid., 68.

80. Lou Cannon, "Obstacle of Tradition Faces the Proponents of ERA Initiative on Ballot," *Washington Post,* Oct. 12, 1978.

81. Linda Cooper, "Vegas Mormons Dare to Support the ERA," *The Valley Times,* Jan. 29, 1978, A1.

82. Ibid, 32.

83. Ibid.

84. Wohl, "A Mormon Connection," 68.

85. Qtd. in ibid.

86. Richardson, "'Old Right' in Action," 218.

87. Ibid.

88. George Franklin, *Las Vegas Sun,* Apr. 4, 1978.

89. Transcript of untitled talk by Assemblywoman Karen Hayes, Las Vegas Second and Eighth Wards, Feb. 15, 1978, 4-6, 13, Bx. 7, fd. 7, Johnson Collection.

90. Ibid.

91. Wohl, "A Mormon Connection," 80.

92. Ibid.

93. "Mormon Group's ERA Stand Probed."

94. Renee Rampton, "Mormons Conduct Illegal Political Campaign," Oct. 28, 1978, Bx. 7, fd. 7, Johnson Collection.

95. Qtd. in Wohl, "Mormon Connection," 70.

96. Transcript of untitled talk by Noreen Ray, Las Vegas Second and Eighth Wards, Feb. 15, 1978, Johnson Collection.

97. Ibid.

98. First Presidency to Church Brethren, Oct. 1978.

99. Rampton to Waterman, Feb. 8.

100. Rampton, "Mormons Conduct Illegal Political Campaign."

101. Wohl, "A Mormon Connection," 68.

102. Transcripts of talks by Hayes and Ray, Feb. 15, 1978.

103. Sheldon Rampton, "Church Newspaper Used to Endorse Candidates," 1978, Bx. 7, fd. 8, Johnson Collection.

104. "Mormons Raked for Politicking," *Salt Lake Tribune,* Sept. 7, 1978.

105. First Presidency to Church Brethren, Oct. 1978.

106. Kent White to Whom It May Concern, 1978, Johnson Collection.

107. "Mormons Wage Letter-Writing Blitz against ERA in Virginia General Assembly," *Washington Star,* Jan. 10, 1979.

108. Stromberg, "Chronology," 5.

109. Sheldon M. Rampton, Statement, Apr. 11, 1979, Bx. 7, fd. 7, Johnson Collection.

110. Ibid.

111. "Equal Rights—Yes! ERA—No!" Bx. 7, fd. 8, Johnson Collection.

112. "LDS Officials Deny Involvement in Nevada's Political Campaigns," *Deseret News*, Sept. 7, 1978.

113. Diane Divoky, "Mormon Muscle: Members' Funds Fought ERA," *Sacramento Bee*, April 19, 1980, A1.

114. Ibid.

115. Nadine Hansen, "California-Florida Cover-Up," *Mormons for ERA Newsletter*, Fall 1979, Bx. 10, fd. 7, Johnson Collection.

116. Ibid.

117. Ibid.

118. Ibid.

119. Peterson interviewed by Goodman.

120. Hansen, "California-Florida Cover-Up."

121. "Mormon Muscle: Members' Funds Fought ERA."

122. Ibid.

123. Ibid.

124. Qtd. in Hansen, "California-Florida Cover-Up."

125. Linda Cicero, "Mormon Money Worked against Florida's ERA," *Miami Herald*, Apr. 20, 1980, A1.

126. Ibid.

127. See statement by Doris Enderle of Huntington Beach in Ann Terry, Marilyn Slaght-Griffin, and Elizabeth Terry, *Mormons and Women* (Santa Barbara: Butterfly, 1980), 101. A Mormon mother-daughter team, the Terrys joined with non-Mormon Slaght-Griffin to produce a positive treatment of LDS women, including interviews with key figures in the ERA battle: Sonia Johnson, Marilee Latta, and Nadine Hansen on one side and several anti-ERA women on the other.

128. Hansen, "California-Florida Cover-Up." Carmack was later called as a mission president and then to the First Quorum of Seventy (*Church Almanac, 2001-2002* [Salt Lake City: Deseret News, 2000], 32).

129. Joan S. Carver, "The Equal Rights Amendment and the Florida Legislature," *Florida Historical Quarterly* 60 (Apr. 1981): 475n62.

130. "Feminist Mormons Speak Out for ERA," *Los Angeles Times*, May 6, 1979.

131. "Mormon Money Worked against Florida's ERA," A1. See also "Church Orchestrated Florida Anti-ERA Drive," D1; "State to Probe Mormon Contributions"; Carver, "Equal Rights Amendment and the Florida Legislature," 475.

132. Ken Driggs to the editor.

133. Wohl, "A Mormon Connection," 70.

134. Ibid.

135. Ibid.

136. Sonia Johnson, "The Mormon Church and the ERA," 1, typescript, Bx. 8, fd. 4, Johnson Collection.

137. Ibid.

138. Johnson, "Mormon Church and the ERA," 2.

139. "Mormon Money Worked against Florida's ERA."

140. Ibid.

141. Ibid.

142. Ibid.

143. "Church Orchestrated Florida Anti-ERA Drive."

144. "State to Probe Mormon Contributions," *Miami Herald,* Apr. 22, 1980.

145. Ibid.

146. "Mormon Anti-ERA Money," *Washington Post,* Apr. 22, 1980.

147. "How the Mormons Helped Scuttle ERA," *Miami Herald,* Apr. 20, 1980, A33; "Church Orchestrated Florida Anti-ERA Drive"; "Florida ERA Campaign," *Sunstone* 5 (May-June 1980): 6.

148. "How the Mormons Helped Scuttle ERA"; "Church Orchestrated Florida Anti-ERA."

149. "How the Mormons Helped Scuttle ERA."

150. Qtd. in "Mormon Money Worked against Florida's ERA." Chapple's pronouns were probably meant to imply universality, as in "one" or "you all," and the changes here (within brackets) are for ease of understanding. What Chapple told the reporter was, "I cannot divest myself from seeing you as my spiritual leader."

151. Linda Sillitoe, interview with Bill Evans, n.d., notes, Bx. 5, fd. 10, Utah Women's Issues Collection.

152. "Mormon Money Worked against Florida's ERA"; see also "Mormon Muscle: Members' Funds Fought ERA."

153. Maxine Hanks was a full-time missionary in the Florida Tampa Mission; she is quoted in Quinn, "LDS Church's Campaign against the Equal Rights Amendment," 125-6. See also President Lyle M. Ward to Dear Missionaries, Dec. 8, 1979, Bx. 7, fd. 27, Johnson Collection: "I have been authorized to put a copy of the attached statement of the Church position on the ERA in the hands of each missionary to assist you in answering questions you may be

getting. I know you will handle this matter prayerfully." Ward was president of the Washington D.C. mission.

154. "ERA Appears Dead this Year," *Phoenix Gazette*, Feb. 10, 1978, A8; "Without Women's Lib," editorial, *Arizona Republic*, Mar. 15, 1974.

155. Lou Ann Stoker Dickson to Sonia Johnson, n.d., accompanying Arizona anti-ERA packet, Bx. 7, fd. 1, Johnson Collection.

156. Bishopric to ward members, Tempe Eighth Ward, in Arizona anti-ERA packet.

157. Ibid.

158. Arizona anti-ERA Packet.

159. Ibid.

160. Ibid.

161. Ibid.

162. "ERA Appears Dead This Year."

163. Mecham Memorandum.

164. Benson to All Stake and Mission Presidents, Dec. 29, 1976. This was the official position of the First Presidency since the 1960s; see "Statement of the First Presidency," *Deseret News*, Aug. 12, 1962, A1.

165. Butler, "Mormon Church against the ERA," 9.

166. Andrew Hacker, "ERA-RIP," *Harper's*, Sept. 1980, 14.

167. Charles R. Davis, qtd. in Quinn, "LDS Church's Campaign against the ERA," 133.

168. Donald G. Mathews and Jane Sherron DeHart, *Sex, Gender, and the Politics of ERA* (New York: Oxford University Press, 1990), 67; memoranda concerning NCAERA and Save Our Families Today (SOFT), Bx. 7, fd. 26, Johnson Collection.

169. Mathews and DeHart, *Sex, Gender, and the Politics of ERA*, 67.

170. Ibid.

171. Linda Sillitoe and Paul Swenson, *Utah Holiday*, Jan. 1980.

172. Missouri Citizen's Council, "Equality Yes—ERA No," Nov. 1980, Johnson Collection.

173. Ibid.

174. Robert Mecham to Neal A. Maxwell, Dec. 5, 1979, photocopy, Bx. 7, fd. 5, Johnson Collection.

175. Ibid.

176. Janet K. Boles, *The Politics of the Equal Rights Amendment* (New York: Longman, 1979), 176-78.

177. Ibid., 176.

178. Mary Frances Berry, *Why ERA Failed: Politics, Women's Rights, and the Amending Process of the Constitution* (Bloomington: Indiana University Press, 1986), 68.

179. "Illinois Citizens for Family Life," 1979, Bx. 7, fd. 26, Johnson Collection.

Chapter 11. Trouble in Virginia

1. First Presidency to General Authorities, Regional Representatives, Stake Presidents, Mission Presidents, Bishops, and Branch Presidents in the United States, Oct. 12, 1978. This statement reiterated the position which had appeared in the *Church News* on August 26, 1978.

2. Register, Mormons for ERA Collection, Mss 225, Special Collections and Archives, Utah State University Libraries, Utah State University, Logan, Utah. The collection includes correspondence, newsletters, pamphlets, minutes, testimonies, speeches, press kits, news clippings, photos, books, financial records, legal records, and memorabilia donated by Alice Allred Pottmyer, Hazel Davis Rigby, and Maida Rust Withers.

3. The original board of directors included Sonia Johnson, president; John Bailey, secretary; and Hazel Davis Rigby, Maida Withers, and Teddie Wood, who resigned on January 27, 1981. In 1985 the board consisted of Alice Pottmyer, president; John Bailey, secretary; and Margot Cheney, Marjory Hart, Sonia Johnson, Hazel Davis Rigby, Ronald K. Rigby, and Maida Withers.

4. Lee Roderick, *Leading the Charge: Orrin Hatch and Twenty Years of America* (Carson City, NV: Gold Leaf Press, 1994), 106.

5. Qtd. in "Mormon Politicians Not Told How to Vote: No Church Conspiracy," *Las Vegas Review-Journal,* Feb. 25, 1978.

6. First Presidency to Don Edwards, May 25, 1978, Sonia Johnson Collection, Manuscripts Division, Marriott Library, University of Utah. The content of the letter appeared in the *Church News,* Aug. 26, 1978, 2; it quoted the church's official statement of October 1976, explaining and defending it.

7. Ibid.

8. President Clifford I. Cummings, Robert E. Bateman, and Charles W. Dahlquist to All Families in the Oakton Virginia Stake, Sept. 8, 1978, Bx. 7, fd. 2, Johnson Collection.

9. Ibid.

10. Senate Hearing on the Equal Rights Amendment, May 26, 1978, *Congressional Record* 124 (s. 8441, 8442).

11. First Presidency statement opposing a ratification extension, Aug. 26, 1978, in ibid.

12. Ibid.

13. "Chronology: The Mormon Anti-ERA Campaign," *Mormons for ERA Newsletter,* Winter 1982, Bx. 10, fd. 7, Johnson Collection.

14. For a summary of Hatch's legislation to benefit women, see Roderick, *Leading the Charge,* 231-35.

15. Ibid., 105.

16. Paul Swenson and Alice A. Pottmyer, "The Church, the Press, and the ERA," *Utah Holiday,* Sept. 1978, 12; Sonia Johnson, "Mormons for the ERA have been active," typescript narrative history, 1978, Bx. 10, fd. 11, Johnson Collection.

17. Swenson and Pottmyer, "Church, the Press, and the ERA," 12.

18. Sonia Johnson Testimony before the U.S. Senate Constitutional Rights Subcommittee, August 4, 1978, beginning with her prepared statement, followed by questions and answers, transcript, Bx. 9, fd. 1, Johnson Collection.

19. Ibid.

20. Ibid.

21. Ibid.

22. *Salt Lake Tribune,* Aug. 19, 1978.

23. *Salt Lake Tribune,* Sept. 9, 1978.

24. Lynn Simross, "Feminist Mormons Speak Out on ERA," *Los Angeles Times,* May 6, 1979.

25. Hartman Rector Jr. to Teddie Wood, Aug. 29, 1978, Bx. 3, fd. 11, Johnson Collection.

26. Barbara B. Smith to Sonia Johnson, Sept. 1, 1978, Bx. 3, fd. 11, Johnson Collection.

27. Judy Mann, "A Mormon for ERA Fearful of Ostracism," *Washington Post,* Aug. 10, 1979.

28. Quoted in ibid., 102.

29. Swenson and Pottmyer, "Church, the Press, and the ERA."

30. Ibid.

31. Ibid., 9.

32. Ibid.

33. "The Church and ERA," *Vienna Ward Newsletter,* Aug. 1978, Bx. 7, fd. 21, Johnson Collection.

34. Virginia Robicheaux, "ERA Filibuster Won't Snag Bills," *Salt Lake Tribune,* Sept. 13, 1978.

35. Ibid.

36. Glover was a member of Mormons for ERA from Virginia.

37. Hazel Rigby, "It Really Happened," *Mormons for ERA Newsletter,* Sept. 1979, Bx. 10, fd. 7, Johnson Collection.

38. Linda Sillitoe, "Fear and Anger in Virginia: The New Mormon Activists," *Utah Holiday,* April 1979, 9.

39. Ibid. The first printing of the pamphlet was titled *An Intelligent Guide to the Equal Rights Amendment* (Johnson Collection).

40. "Chronology: The Mormon Anti-ERA Campaign," Winter 1980, 1.

41. See "Statement of the First Presidency," *Rexburg Standard Journal,* June 19, 1979; Linda Sillitoe, "The New Mormon Activists: Fighting the ERA in Virginia," *Utah Holiday,* Mar. 1979, 12-14; Sillitoe, "Fear and Anger in Virginia," 9-12; Linda Sillitoe. "Sometimes I Feel like a Motherless Child," *Utah Holiday,* Sept. 1979, 12-14.

42. Linda Sillitoe and Paul Swenson, "A Moral Issue," *Utah Holiday,* Jan. 1980, 18-34; see also "Chronology: The Mormon Anti-ERA Campaign," Winter 1980, 1.

43. Press packets included statements from the LDS Church and Mormons for ERA; a transcript of the LDS Citizens Coalition meeting, Nov. 8, 1978; ward and stake newsletters and petitions ("The Hour Is Here," Oakton Stake petition, 1978); news and feature articles from *Dialogue* ("ERA Again," Autumn 1978), the *Los Angeles Times* ("Mormons for ERA Are Everywhere," Apr. 1, 1979), *Ms. Magazine* ("A Mormon Connection?" July 1977); *Reston Times, Rexburg Standard Journal, Utah Holiday* magazine, and wire services ("Mormons Raked for Politicking," UPI, Las Vegas, Sept. 1978); Johnson's Senate testimony and speeches to the American Psychological Association, Utah Women's Conference, and other venues; and the *Congressional Record,* 26 May 1979 (S8441); see Bx. 3, fd. 9, Johnson Collection.

44. "Chronology: The Mormon Anti-ERA Campaign," Winter 1982, 1.

45. "Minutes of a Meeting of 'Latter-day Saint Women's Coalition,'" Nov. 8, 1978, typescript, Bx. 3, fd. 13, Utah Women's Issues Collection, Manuscripts Division, Marriott Library, University of Utah, Salt Lake City. A version of

these minutes (Latter-day Saint Women's Coalition, Minutes, Nov. 8, 1978), is found in Bx. 7, fd. 21, Johnson Collection.

46. Lowe received calls from members complaining about using the chapel for a political meeting and changed the location at the last minute. He explained: "I thought it best that we have a policy, all the way, that we do not use our chapels, for any of these meetings, although we have a perfect right to, it is certainly proper to take up in the church, but we do not want to have hard feelings among our own people. We would almost take any end to keep this from happening. This doesn't mean we want to lose our position of strength; I think we will gain strength by taking such a view. We do not want confrontations where there will be bitter animosities. I was told this afternoon they're out for blood." Lowe did not explain who "they" were. See ibid, punctuated slightly for clarity; also Sillitoe, "Fear and Anger in Virginia," 9.

47. *Vienna Ward Newsletter,* Nov. 1978.

48. Mary Bradford, "A Conversation with Beverly Campbell," *Dialogue: A Journal of Mormon Thought* 14 (Spring 1981): 45.

49. Campbell rejected the criticism that she was not a "typical" Mormon. "We seem to describe the 'typical Mormon woman' in terms of tasks: she stays home, has a large family, bakes bread and cans fruit. When you ask about a typical Mormon man you talk in terms of values; he does well at his work, he holds many church positions, he cherishes his family. Why can't we describe women in value terms?"(ibid., 56).

50. Ibid., 164.

51. Ladd acknowledged the "line between the Coalition and [the] Church [was] fine, but [he was] not concerned because of Pres. K[imball's] commitment to defeating ERA." Linda Sillitoe, notes of an interview with Regional Representative W. Don Ladd, Feb. 15, 1979, Bx. 5, fd. 10, Utah Women's Issues Collection; see "Regional Representatives," *Church Almanac* (Salt Lake City: Deseret News, 1983).

52. "Minutes of a Meeting of 'Latter-day Saint Women's Coalition,'" 1.

53. Sillitoe, "New Mormon Activists," 14.

54. Ibid.

55. D. Michael Quinn, "The LDS Church's Campaign against the Equal Rights Amendment," *Journal of Mormon History* 20 (Fall 1994): 148.

56. Rodney P. Foster, interviewed by D. Michael Quinn, Sept. 5-6, 1992, in ibid.

57. Latter-day Saint Women's Coalition, Minutes, Nov. 8, 1978, 10, Bx. 7, fd. 21, Johnson Collection.

58. Ibid., 2.

59. Sonia Johnson, "Patriarchal Panic: Sexual Politics in the Mormon Church," paper presented at the American Psychological Association meetings, New York City, Sept. 1, 1979, 2, Bx. 24, fd. 2, Johnson Collection.

60. Latter-day Saint Women's Coalition, Minutes, 17.

61. Ibid.

62. Ibid., 4-5.

63. Ibid, 9.

64. The complete list included education about the ecology of overpopulation, the removal of expectations of masculine and feminine behavior in children, legal proscriptions against churches that discriminate on the basis of gender—specifically the Catholic Church, although it required little imagination to envision the challenge to the LDS Church—and other hot-button topics.

65. Latter-day Saint Women's Coalition, Minutes, 10.

66. Ibid., 11.

67. Ibid., 12.

68. Ibid.

69. Sillitoe, "Fear and Anger in Virginia," 11.

70. Latter-day Saint Women's Coalition, Minutes, 36.

71. Ibid.

72. Ibid. When Sonia Johnson tried to attend the meeting the next week, Campbell asked her to leave. Johnson said, "Why is the church holding secret meetings?" to which Campbell responded, "This isn't secret, it's just private."

73. Sonia Johnson, *From Housewife to Heretic* (Garden City, NY: Doubleday, 1981), 179. See Charles Dahlquist, address delivered at the Sterling Park Ward chapel, Oakton Stake, Virginia, December 14, 1978, transcript, 1, Bx. 3, fd. 21, Utah Women's Issues Collections.

74. "Prophet Calls for Positive Action against ERA," *Oakton Stake Newsletter,* Nov. 1978, 1, Bx. 3, fd. 21, Johnson Collection.

75. "Prophet Sends Message of Urgency," *Oakton Stake Newsletter,* Dec. 1978, 1.

76. Sillitoe, "New Mormon Activists," 12.

77. "Chronology: The Mormon Anti-ERA Campaign," Winter 1982, 2.

78. "We consider the Equal Rights Amendment a nonpartisan issue," the petition read, "and will, in the 1979 elections, vote only for those candidates

who oppose ratification of the Equal Rights Amendment," Bx. 7, fd. 18, Utah Women's Issues Collection.

79. Sillitoe, "Fear and Anger in Virginia," 9.

80. Qtd. in Sillitoe, "Fear and Anger in Virginia," 9.

81. Sillitoe, "New Mormon Activists," 12.

82. *Impact,* Sept. 1, 1979, a publication of the LDS Citizens Coalition and FACT, Bx. 7, fd. 22, Johnson Collection.

83. Other Concern sheets included: *ERA and Abortion, Equal Rights Amendment or Legislative Remedies? ERA—How Broad Its Scope? ERA—An Amendment Whose Time Has Gone, The Equal Rights Amendment and Legislative History Projects Inc., ERA and the Draft, ERA and Title IX,* and *ERA and Women in the Workforce,* Bx. 7, fd. 22, Johnson Collection.

84. Sillitoe, "New Mormon Activists," 14.

85. "Chronology: The Mormon Anti-ERA Campaign," Winter 1981.

86. Sillitoe, "New Mormon Activists," 14.

87. Bradford, "A Conversation with Beverly Campbell," 46.

88. Ibid., 50.

89. Ibid., 52.

90. "Prophet Sends Message of Urgency," *Vienna Ward Newsletter,* Dec. 1978, 1.

91. Barbara B. Smith, *A Fruitful Season* (Salt Lake City: Bookcraft, 1988), 154-55.

92. Register, Mormons for ERA Collection.

93. Mann, "Mormon for ERA Fearful of Ostracism."

94. Johnson, *Housewife to Heretic,* 152.

95. Sillitoe, "Fear and Anger in Virginia," 12.

96. Karen Rypka, "State Official Probes Mormon Lobbying," *Reston Times,* Mar. 1, 1979.

97. Sillitoe, "Fear and Anger in Virginia," 10.

98. Ibid., 12.

99. Alan Blodgett, interviewed by D. Michael Quinn, August 29-30, 1992, qtd. in Quinn, "LDS Church's Campaign against the Equal Rights Amendment," 149.

100. Diane Divoky, "Mormon Members' Funds Fought ERA," *Sacramento Bee,* Apr. 19, 1980; Linda Cicero, "Mormon Money Worked against Florida's ERA," *Miami Herald,* Apr. 20, 1980.

101. Donald G. Mathews and Jane Sherron DeHart, "The Cultural Politics

of the ERA's Defeat," in Joan Hoff-Wilson, ed., *Rights of Passage: The Past and Future of the ERA* (Bloomington: Indiana University Press, 1986), 45-46.

102. Sillitoe, "Fear and Anger in Virginia," 9.

103. Ibid.

104. Ibid.

105. Ibid., 10.

106. Ibid.

107. Sonia Johnson to Frederick T. Gray Jr., Secretary of the Commonwealth of Virginia, n.d., copy in Bx. 7, fd. 21, Johnson Collection. The date on one of the attached articles was March 1, 1979.

108. They sent the secretary a transcript of the coalition's organizational meeting; *Reston Times* articles quoting Campbell saying the coalition had circulated 80,000 pamphlets and held 600 workshops; anti-ERA material distributed to legislators; pamphlets sent to between 50,000 and 80,000 homes; four pages on instructions on how to write lobbying letters; copies of petitions circulated in Mormon chapels; a *Washington Post* article quoting Campbell's plans for a Richmond office; and a Knight-Ridder article by Vera Glasser on Mormon lobbying in Virginia.

109. Karen Rypka, "Mormon Group to Register with State," *Reston Times,* Mar. 15, 1979.

110. Ibid.

111. Ibid.

112. Ibid.

113. "Mormon Women Fly Pro-ERA Banner over Mormon Temple," press release, Mar. 26, 1979, Bx. 10, fd. 5, Johnson Collection.

114. Sonia Johnson to Gordon B. Hinckley, Apr. 27, 1979, Bx. 3, fd. 2, Johnson Collection.

115. Sonia Johnson to Spencer W. Kimball, April 30, 1979, Bx. 3, fd. 2, Johnson Collection.

116. Ibid.

117. William C. Wertz, "LDS President Opposes ERA, Encourages Women to be Wives," *Rexburg Standard,* June 19, 1979.

118. Johnson, "Patriarchal Panic."

119. Johnson, "Patriarchal Panic," 2. Mary Bradford ("The Odyssey of Sonia Johnson," *Dialogue: A Journal of Mormon Thought* 14 [Summer 1981]) suggested that by using the word *patriarchy,* which "in the minds of most Mormons is a benign term," Johnson was "treading on dangerous ground. . . . Though

Sonia always claimed that she didn't mean 'priesthood,' and that she meant 'patriarchy' in a strictly political sense to refer to man's inhumanity to women, words deemed sacred to Mormons—'patriarchal order,' 'stake patriarch'—seemed suddenly tainted. Many Mormons thought her use of these terms spelled apostasy" (24).

120. "Supporters of ERA Picket Mormons," *Washington Post,* Sept. 14, 1979.

121. Johnson, *Housewife to Heretic,* 157.

122. Ibid., 199-200.

123. Ibid.

124. Sonia Johnson, "Off Our Pedestals, Or the Chronicles of the Uppity Sisters," an address delivered to the Utah Women's Conference, Oct. 1979, Bx. 24, fd. 3, Johnson Collection.

125. Qtd. in ibid., 1.

126. Ibid.

127. Ibid.

128. Jeffrey H. Willis to Sonia Johnson, Nov.14, 1979, Bx. 3, fd. 3, Johnson Collection.

129. Marjorie Hyer, "ERA Advocate Facing Mormon Trial Finds Her Family Life in Disarray," *Washington Post,* Nov. 27, 1979.

130. Jeffrey Willis to Sonia Johnson, Nov. 28, 1979, Bx. 3, fd. 3, Johnson Collection.

131. "Statement of Support for Sonia Johnson by Major National Organizations," Nov. 30, 1979, Bx. 4, fd. 17, Johnson Collection.

132. "NWPC Supports Mormon Woman Facing Excommunication for ERA Stand," Nov. 30, 1979, Bx. 4, fd. 17, Johnson Collection.

133. Hazel Rigby, "Testimony Prepared in Behalf of Sonia Johnson for a Bishop's Court, December 1, 1979," Bx. 3, fd. 7, copy in the Johnson Collection.

134. Ralph Payne, prepared statement for Sonia Johnson's excommunication trial, Bx. 3, fd. 8, Johnson Collection.

135. Nadine Hansen, prepared statement for Sonia Johnson's excommunication trial, Bx. 3, fd. 8, Johnson Collection.

136. Reba Keele, prepared statement for Sonia Johnson's excommunication trial, Bx. 3, fd. 8, Johnson Collection.

137. Johnson, *Housewife to Heretic,* 331.

138. Qtd. in Sillitoe and Swenson, "Moral Issue," 27.

139. Kathryn MacKay, notes on the trial, Bx. 2, fd. 10, Johnson Collection.

140. Sonia Johnson, comments at excommunication trial, Bx. 3, fd. 7, Johnson Collection.

141. Ibid.

142. Jeffrey Willis to Sonia Johnson, Dec. 5, 1979, Bx. 3, fd. 3, Johnson Collection.

143. Qtd. in Sillitoe and Swenson, "Moral Issue," 28.

144. Marjorie Hyer, "Mormon Bishop Excommunicates Woman Who is Supporting ERA," *Washington Post,* Dec. 6, 1979. Excommunication meant that Johnson would not be able to speak in church, partake of the eucharist, teach Sunday school, play the pipe organ, or otherwise participate in any way other than by simply attending services.

145. Qtd. in Victoria Irwin, "The Equal Rights Amendment: The Case Against," *Christian Science Monitor,* May 6, 1980.

146. Qtd. in Sillitoe and Swenson, "Moral Issue," 31.

147. Richard Johnson to Jeffrey Willis, Dec. 11, 1979, Bx. 3, fd. 3, Johnson Collection.

148. Earl J. Roueche to Sonia Johnson, Mar. 24, 1980, Bx. 3, fd. 3, Johnson Collection.

149. Francis Gibbons to Sonia Johnson, Apr. 25, June 6, 1980, Bx. 3, fd. 3, Johnson Collection.

150. "Rebuff to ERA Supporter," *Washington Post,* June 30, 1980.

151. Kathleen Flake, "Bearing the Weight," *Sunstone* 13 (Oct. 1989): 34.

Chapter 12. Death Throes of the ERA, 1980-82

1. Linda Sillitoe, "A Moral Issue," *Utah Holiday,* Jan. 1980, 28.

2. Linda Sillitoe and Paul Swenson, "The Press, Politics and Sonia Johnson," *Utah Holiday,* Jan. 1980, 28.

3. Qtd. in "Mormon Judge and ERA," *Washington Post,* Aug. 25, 1979.

4. Ibid.

5. *Idaho v. Freeman,* 478 F. Supp. 33 [1979], 507 F. Supp 706 [1981]. See "Marion J. Callister Papers: The File on *Idaho v. Freeman,*" MS 1512, L. Tom Perry Special Collections, Harold B. Lee Library, Brigham Young University, Provo, Utah; chronology of Callister's role in the Equal Rights Amendment, Bx. 2, fd. 15, Utah Women's Issues Collection, Special Collections, Merrill Library, Utah State University, Logan, Utah; "Judge's Removal Sought in Suit against ERA," *New York Times,* Aug. 26, 1979, 25; "NOW Renews Effort to Remove LDS Judge," *Deseret News,* Dec. 3, 1979, A1; "Eight in House Seek Mor-

mon Judge's Ouster in Rights Amendment Case," *New York Times,* Dec. 7, 1979, A23; "Idahoans Say Religion Won't Sway Judge on ERA," *New York Times,* Jan. 29, 1980, 18; "Judge Refuses to Drop Case on Rights Amendment," *New York Times,* Aug. 19, 1980, 8; "Mormon Judge Challenged on Rights Amendment Suit," *New York Times,* Sept. 24, 1980, A7; "Laws of the Land: Callister's Decision," *Sunstone* 7 (Mar./Apr. 1982): 60-63; Mary Frances Berry, *Why ERA Failed: Politics, Women's Rights, and the Amending Process of the Constitution* (Bloomington: Indiana University Press, 1986), 79.

6. "Idahoans Say Religion Won't Sway Judge," 18; "Judge Refuses to Drop Case," 8; "Mormon Judge Challenged," A7; "Laws of the Land," 60-63; Berry, *Why ERA Failed,* 79; "Feminist Chronicles," Aug. 15, 1980, *The Feminist Majority Foundation Online* (www.feminist.org; downloaded Jan. 2003); "Judge's Removal Sought," 25; "NOW Renews Effort," A1; "Eight in House Seek Mormon Judge's Ouster," A23.

7. Qtd. in Marjorie Hyer, "Mormon Ouster of ERA Backer Adds to Pressure on U.S. Judge," *Washington Post,* Dec. 7, 1979.

8. "Judge Refuses to Drop Case," A7.

9. Ibid.

10. Lorie Winder Stromberg, "Chronology: The Mormon Anti-ERA Campaign," *Mormons for ERA Newsletter,* Winter 1982, 3, Bx. 10, fd. 7, Sonia Johnson Collection, Special Collections, Marriott Library, University of Utah, Salt Lake City.

11. United Press International, "LDS Official's Son Works for Idaho Judge," *Salt Lake Tribune,* Jan. 21, 1980, C6.

12. "Feminist Chronicles," Mar. 6, 1981.

13. *National Organization for Women, Inc., et al. v. Idaho et al.,* 459 U.S. 809 [Jan. 1982]. See also Robert E. Riggs, "Legal and Judicial History of the Church," in Daniel H. Ludlow, ed., *The Encyclopedia of Mormonism* (New York: Macmillan Publishing, 1992), 2:823-27.

14. O. Kendall White, "A Feminist Challenge: Mormons for ERA as an Internal Social Movement," *Journal of Ethnic Studies* 13 (Spring 1985): 32.

15. Jan Tyler to Kathryn MacKay, Apr. 13, 1980, Bx. 4, fd. 7, Utah Women's Issues Collection, Special Collections, Marriott Library (hereafter UWIC).

16. United Press International, "Pro-ERA Group to Pray," *Salt Lake Tribune,* Aug. 18, 1978.

17. Jan Tyler to Kathryn MacKay, Apr. 18, 1980, Bx. 4, fd. 7, UWIC.

18. Sillitoe, "A Moral Issue," 26.

19. Ibid.

20. A list of individuals affiliated with Mormons for ERA in Utah is found in Bx. 4, fd. 1, UWIC. It includes Ramona Adams, Marlena Ahanin, Algie E. Ballif, Linda Christiansen, Louise Davis, LeJetta Fenton, Kathleen Flake, Afton Forsgren, Suzanna Mae Grua, Margaret Hayes, Virginia Husband, H. W. Kelson, Virginia Kelson, Marilee Latta, Lucy Beth Rampton, Kay Senzee, Sharon Lee Swenson, Eldon Tolman, Thelma E. Weight, and E. R. West.

21. "Articles of Incorporation of Utah Mormons for the Equal Rights Amendment," Bx. 4, fd. 2, UWIC.

22. Kathryn MacKay to Mary Ann Payne, Apr. 14, 1980, Bx. 4, fd. 7, UWIC.

23. MERA Utah, Minutes, Mar. 8, 1980, Box 4, fd. 10, UWIC. Others in attendance were Kathleen Barrett, Gladys Carling, Camille DeLong, June Fulmer, Reba Keele, Marilee Latta, Denise Posse Lindberg, Kathryn MacKay, Judi McConkie, Marjorie McEntyre, Louise Meaders, Maria Ortiz, Moyne Oviatt, Mary Ann Payne, Dolores Ritchie, Jan Tyler, and Linda Wilcox.

24. Ibid.

25. MERA Utah, Minutes, Apr. 12, 1980, Bx. 4, fd. 10, UWIC; see also Memorandum from Executive Board to Governing Board of Utah Mormons for ERA, May 2, 1980, Bx. 4, fd. 16.

26. Ibid.

27. Ibid.

28. Ibid.

29. MERA Utah, Minutes, Mar. 16, 1980, Bx. 4, fd. 10, UWIC.

30. Memorandum, May 2, 1980.

31. MERA Utah, Minutes, Mar. 29, 1980, Box 4, fd. 10, UWIC.

32. Ibid.

33. Mary Ann Payne to Kathryn MacKay, Apr. 9, 1980, Bx. 4, fd. 7, UWIC.

34. Memorandum, May 2, 1980.

35. MacKay to Payne, Apr. 14, 1980.

36. Ibid.

37. Ibid.

38. MERA Utah, Minutes, Apr. 12, 1980.

39. Kathryn MacKay to Jan Tyler, Apr. 18, 1980, Bx. 4, fd. 7, UWIC.

40. Memorandum, May 2, 1980.

41. MacKay to Tyler, Apr. 18, 1980.

42. Memorandum, May 2, 1980.

43. Mary Ann Payne to Kathryn MacKay, Apr. 21, 1980, Bx. 4, fd. 7, UWIC.

44. Ibid.

45. Sonia Johnson to Kathryn MacKay, May 8, 1980, Bx. 4, fd. 7, UWIC.

46. *New York Times,* Jan. 14, 1980.

47. According to Barbara B. Smith's autobiography, *A Fruitful Season* (Salt Lake City: Bookcraft, 1988), 163, Phil Donahue's program manager had invited Smith to appear with Johnson. Smith had refused, explaining that "Johnson was already, although inaccurately, considered a martyr for women's rights and that if we appeared together on his program, what I had to say would not get proper attention. I suggested that Phil Donahue give Sonia Johnson the full program time, and then later give me a full hour." The program director would not consider it, so Smith suggested Campbell, who was at the beauty parlor having her hair done for the show when the program director reached her to cancel the appearance because "Johnson had refused to appear with her."

48. KTVX Channel 4, Salt Lake City, Interview with Beverly Campbell, Roy Gibson host, transcript, Jan. 16, 1980, Bx. 7, fd. 23, Johnson Collection.

49. Ibid.

50. Smith, *Fruitful Season,* 163. She does not mention Campbell's presentation.

51. Stromberg, "Chronology"; "Feminist Chronicles," Feb. 12, 1980.

52. "Feminist Chronicles," Mar. 1, 1980.

53. Ibid., Mar. 28, 1980.

54. Ibid., Oct. 6, 1980.

55. Ibid., Mar. 6, 1981.

56. "Political Involvement Urged," *Church News,* Mar. 8, 1980, 3; "Keep Partisan Political Actions Out of Church, Urge LDS," *Salt Lake Tribune,* Mar. 6, 1980, A17.

57. Hugh W. Pinnock to Hazel R. Rigby, May 5, 1980, Bx. 1, fd. 4, UWIC.

58. Qtd. in Victoria Irwin, "The Equal Rights Amendment: The Case Against," *Christian Science Monitor,* May 6, 1980.

59. Ibid.

60. Ibid.

61. Ibid.

62. "The Feminist Chronicles," June 18, 1980.

63. Howell Raines, "Reagan Cool to Equal-Rights Plank," *Seattle Post-Intelligencer,* June 21, 1980.

64. Ibid.

65. Peter Gillins, "Utah Demos Reject ERA," *Logan Herald Journal,* July 13, 1980.

66. Donald M. Rothberg, "Betty Ford Criticizes ERA Plank," *Oakland Tribune,* July 18, 1980.

67. Ronald Reagan to Dear Friends, from the Reagan & Bush Committee, ca. Aug. 1980, UWIC.

68. Qtd. in Jerry Painter, "ERA Supporters Protest LDS Church Stand," *Daily Universe,* Oct. 6, 1980.

69. Qtd. in Deana Lloyd and Bob Sallander, "Three ERA Supporters Refuse to Accept Church Prophet as 'Political Leader,'" *Daily Universe,* Oct. 6, 1980.

70. Stromberg, "Chronology," 3.

71. Donna Anderson, "BYU Hecklers Taunt First Lady of Utah," *Salt Lake Tribune,* Oct. 23, 1980, B3.

72. Ibid.

73. Mary Whitemore and Marty LaBrosse to MERA, California and Utah chapters, Sept. 3, 1980, Bx. 4, fd. 8, UWIC.

74. Marty LaBrosse to Sonia Johnson, Apr. 21, 1981, Bx. 4, fd. 10, UWIC.

75. Sonia Johnson, *From Housewife to Heretic* (New York: Doubleday, 1981), 253.

76. "The Feminist Chronicles," Aug. 1981.

77. Ibid.

78. Stromberg, "Chronology."

79. Leslie Bennetts, "A Day of Lobbying for Women's Rights Issues," *New York Times,* Feb. 6, 1981.

80. Ibid.

81. "Feminist Chronicles," Apr. 5, 1981.

82. Qtd. in Lee Roderick, *Leading the Charge: Orrin Hatch and Twenty Years of America* (Carson City, NV: Gold Leaf Press, 1994), 166.

83. D. Michael Quinn, "The LDS Church's Campaign against the Equal Rights Amendment," *Dialogue: A Journal of Mormon Thought* 20 (Fall 1994): 143; "NOW Will Take Case to Mormons," *Los Angeles Times,* May 7, 1981, V-22; *ERA Yes* (Salt Lake City: ERA Missionary Project, 1981); qtd. in *An Appeal to Members of the LDS Church* (Salt Lake City: National Organization for Women, 1981), Bx. 1, fd. 15, UWIC.

84. Qtd. in Randy Shipp, "Women's Group to Push ERA in Mormon Country," *Washington Post,* May 8, 1981.

85. Kathryn MacKay, interviewed by Anne Looser, Aug. 12, 2002, Bountiful, Utah, IWY Project, in author's possession (see introduction).

86. Each of these women would go on to make significant contributions to the quality of public life in Utah: Reba Keele as dean of undergraduate studies at the University of Utah, Irene Fisher as director of the Lowell Bennion Community Service Center at the University of Utah, and Karen Shepherd as a U.S. Congresswoman.

87. Memorandum, headlined, "Please announce in Relief Society meetings and Sunday School classes only," Bx. 4, fd. 8, UWIC.

88. Script for Prayer Vigil, typescript, Bx. 7, fd. 30, UWIC.

89. "ERA Backers Lash Out at Rex Lee Nomination," *Deseret News,* June 20, 1981, A5.

90. Ibid.

91. Ibid.

92. "ERA Critic for Women's Rights," *Seattle Times,* June 20, 1981.

93. Stromberg, "Chronology," 3.

94. Ibid.

95. Script for Prayer Vigil, typescript.

96. "Chronology of the Equal Rights Amendment, 1923-1996," June 1982, online at *National Organization for Women* (www.now.org/issues; downloaded Jan. 2003).

97. Stromberg, "Chronology."

98. Qtd. in Michael McQueen, "ERA Supporters Protest outside Mormon Temple," *Washington Post,* Jan. 10, 1982.

99. Margo Kline, "Virginia Weekly," *Washington Post,* Jan. 14, 1982.

100. Ibid.

101. Frank Somerville, *Baltimore Sun,* Mar. 2, 1982.

102. Alice Pottmyer, "Church Cancels Trial of ERA Advocate Melissa Mowen," *Mormons for ERA Newsletter,* Apr. 1980, Johnson Collection.

103. "Feminist Chronicles," Mar. 1982.

104. Ibid., May 19, 1982.

105. Ibid., June 21, 1982. In the wake of this final failure of the ERA in Florida, a record eighty-one women filed to run in legislative races, nineteen of whom survived the primaries and went on to win their elections—four in the senate and fourteen in the house (see "1982 General Election Official Results,"

Florida Department of State, Division of Elections [http://election.dos.state.fl.us/elections/resultsarchive]; downloaded May 2005).

106. Stromberg, "Chronology," 3.

107. "Feminist Chronicles," June 22, 1982.

108. Phyllis Rueckert, "A Profile of 170 Mormons for ERA," *Mormons for ERA Newsletter,* May 1983, 3-5, Bx. 10, Fd. 7, Johnson Collection. The survey was restricted to Mormons in the United States, with one foreign response. Eleven percent of the respondents said they had been registered by friends or did not know how they had ended up on the MERA mailing list, but the others declared that they had intentionally signed up. Some of the respondents were in their twenties (9.6 percent) and some in their seventies (6.6 percent). Those with a bachelor's degree or higher constituted 72.4 percent of the sample.

109. Ibid.

110. Stromberg, "Chronology," 3.

111. White, "Feminist Challenge," 33.

112. Ibid., 35-36.

113. "State Official Probes Mormon Lobbying," *Reston Times,* Mar. 15, 1979; "Mormon Group to Register with State," *Reston Times,* Mar. 15, 1979.

114. White, "Feminist Challenge," 38.

115. Sonia Johnson, quoted in ibid., 40.

116. *The Church and the Proposed Equal Rights Amendment* (Salt Lake City: Church of Jesus Christ of Latter-day Saints, 1980), 19.

117. Ibid.

118. White, "Feminist Challenge," 45.

119. Berry, *Why ERA Failed,* 68.

120. Ibid.

121. Slava Lubudomorova, conversation with Martha Bradley, Sept. 17, 1998.

122. Ibid., 56.

123. Janet K. Boles, *The Politics of Equal Rights Amendment: Conflict and the Decision Process* (New York: Longman, 1979), 4-5.

Chapter 13: A Case Study

1. This chapter is greatly strengthened by Amy L. Bentley's award-winning article, "Comforting the Motherless Children: The Alice Louise Reynolds Women's Forum," *Dialogue: A Journal of Mormon Thought* 23 (Fall 1990): 39-61; and from the forum's papers (letters, minutes of meetings, biographical

sketches, newspaper articles) in the Algie Ballif Collection, Special Collections, Marriott Library, University of Utah.

2. Helen Candland Stark, Summary of 1978 meetings, typescript, Ballif Collection.

3. Fern Taylor, "Format of Meetings," n.d., Ballif Collection.

4. Algie Ballif, "A Report on the Alice Louise Reynolds Women's Forum," n.d., Ballif Collection.

5. See Martha Sonntag Bradley and Mary Firmage Woodward, *The Four Zinas: Mothers and Daughters on the Mormon Frontier* (Salt Lake City: Signature Books, 2001).

6. For a helpful context, see Karen J. Blair, *The Clubwoman as Feminist: True Womanhood Redefined, 1868-1914* (New York: Holmes and Meier Publishers, 1980), who documents how women's clubs created a means for women to become engaged in public life. Progressive and concerned with women's rights, these groups provided their members with the organizational experience necessary to push through suffrage and other social policies. See also Theodora Penny Martin, *The Sound of Our Own Voices: Women's Study Clubs, 1860-1910* (Boston: Beacon Press, 1987).

7. Julie Hunsaker, "Alice Louise Reynolds," in Arnold K. Garr, Donald Q. Cannon, and Richard O. Cowan, eds., *Encyclopedia of Latter-day Saint History* (Salt Lake City: Deseret Book, 2000), 1015.

8. Lavina Fielding Anderson, "A Strenuous Business: The Achievement of Helen Candland Stark," and Helen Candland Stark, "The Good Woman Syndrome," *Dialogue: A Journal of Mormon Thought* 23 (Fall 1990): 12-33, 34-38.

9. Bentley, "Comforting the Motherless Children," 45.

10. Anderson, "Strenuous Business," 12.

11. "Helen Stark Fosters Balanced Life, Environment," *Provo Herald,* Jan. 28, 1979.

12. Helen Candland Stark, biographical sketch of Algie Ballif, Bx. 1, fd. 4, Ballif Collection.

13. Ibid.

14. Helen Candland Stark, biographical sketch of Thelma E. Weight, Bx. 1, fd. 4, Ballif Collection.

15. Thelma Eggertson Weight, qtd. in Maxine Hanks, *Women and Authority: Re-emerging Mormon Feminism* (Salt Lake City: Signature Books, 1992), 107-8.

16. Bentley, "Comforting the Motherless Children."

17. Qtd. in Hanks, *Women and Authority,* 109-10.

18. "Activist Nancy Kadar Expands Her Heritage," *Provo Herald,* Aug. 13, 1978.

19. Qtd. in Bentley, "Comforting the Motherless Children," 44.

20. "Activist Nancy Kadar Expands Her Heritage."

21. "Margaret Woodworth Addresses Herself to Social Issues," *Provo Herald,* June 11, 1978.

22. Qtd. in Lynn Simross, "Feminist Mormons Speak Out for ERA," *Los Angeles Times,* May 6, 1979, viii-1.

23. Qtd. in Hanks, *Women and Authority,* 110.

24. Alice Louise Reynolds Women's Forum, Minutes, Aug. 12, 1978, Ballif Collection.

25. Bentley, "Comforting the Motherless Children," 49.

26. Stark, summary of the March 29, 1978, meeting, Ballif Collection.

27. Committee for BYU Meeting to Congressman Gunn McKay, n.d, Ballif Collection.

28. Mary Lythgoe Bradford, "Focus," *Exponent II* 14/4 (1989): 7. The minutes of this particular meeting were considered so intimate, they were closed to researchers until after 1986.

29. Simross, "Feminist Mormons Speak Out."

30. Ibid.

31. Ibid.

32. Ibid.

33. Helen Stark to Spencer W. Kimball, Mar. 10, 1979, Ballif Collection.

34. Ibid.

35. Francis M. Gibbons to the Sisters, Mar. 28, 1979, Ballif Collection.

36. Helen Candland Stark to Spencer W. Kimball, Apr. 14, 1979, Ballif Collection.

37. Francis M. Gibbons to the Sisters, Apr. 25, 1979, Ballif Collection.

38. Algie Ballif, "A Report on the Alice Louise Reynolds Women's Forum," n.d., Ballif Collection. The forum met in various locations in Provo, including the city hall, library, and high school auditorium or cafeteria, where they drew even larger crowds than on BYU campus.

39. Ibid.

40. Helen Candland Stark to President Spencer W. Kimball, May 18, 1979, Ballif Collection.

41. Francis M. Gibbons to the Sisters, May 23, 1979, Ballif Collection.

42. Linda Sillitoe, "Sometimes I Feel Like a Motherless Child," *Utah Holiday,* Sept. 1979, 13.

43. Alice Louise Reynolds Women's Forum, transcript of meeting, Sept. 30, 1980, Ballif Collection.

44. Ibid.

45. Qtd. in Hanks, *Women and Authority,* 104-7.

46. Ibid., 111-13.

Epilogue

1. Abigail Adams to John Adams, March 31, 1776, in Alice S. Rossi, ed., *The Feminist Papers: From Adams to de Beauvoir* (New York: Columbia University Press, 1973), 10-11.

2. John Adams to Abigail Adams, April 14, 1776, ibid.

3. Jack Eisen, "Mormon ERA Group," *Washington Post,* Jan. 11, 1983.

4. "Feminist Chronicles," Jan. 3, 1983, online at *The Feminist Majority Foundation Online* (www.feminist.org; downloaded Jan. 2003).

5. Orrin Hatch, *The Equal Rights Amendment: Myths and Realities* (N.p.: Savant Press, 1983).

6. "Chronology of the Equal Rights Amendment, 1923-1996," January and July 1995, online at *National Organization for Women* (www.now.org/issues; downloaded Jan. 2003).

7. Allison Held, Sheryl Herndon, and Danielle Stager, *William and Mary Journal of Women and the Law* 3 (Spring 1997): 113-36.

8. In 1996 a Congressional legislative analyst agreed that the Madison Amendment paved the way for Congress to declare ERA ratification complete if ratified by three more states. In 2002 backers resubmitted the ERA for consideration by five state legislatures in Illinois, Mississippi, Missouri, Oklahoma, and Virginia. See David C. Huckabee, Congressional Research Service, Library of Congress, "Equal Rights Amendment: Ratification Issues," Memorandum, March 18, 1996, cited by Roberta W. Francis, "The History behind the Equal Rights Amendment," online at *The Equal Rights Amendment* (www.equalrights amendment.org; downloaded May 2005).

9. See Mary Frances Berry, *Why ERA Failed: Politics, Women's Rights, and the Amending Process of the Constitution* (Indianapolis: Indiana University Press, 1986); Janet K. Boles, *The Politics of the Equal Rights Amendment: Conflict and the Decision Process* (New York: Longman, 1979); Renee Feinberg, comp., *The*

Equal Rights Amendment: An Annotated Bibliography of the Issues, 1976-1985 (Westport, CT: Greenwood Press, 1986); Cynthia Harrison, *On Account of Sex: The Politics of Women's Issues, 1945-1968* (Berkeley: University of California Press, 1988); Sylvia Ann Hewlett, *A Lesser Life: The Myth of Women's Liberation in America* (New York: William Morrow, 1986); Joan Hoff-Wilson, ed., *Rights of Passage: The Past and Future of the ERA* (Bloomington: Indiana University Press, 1986); Jane J. Mansbridge, *Why We Lost the ERA* (Chicago: University of Chicago Press, 1986); Leila J. Rupp and Verta Taylor, *American Women's Rights Movement, 1945 to the 1960s* (New York: Oxford University Press, 1987); Gilbert Y. Steiner, *Constitutional Inequality: The Political Fortunes of the Equal Rights Amendment* (Washington D.C.: Brookings Institution, 1985).

10. Roberta W. Francis, "Why We Need the Equal Rights Amendment," online at *The Equal Rights Amendment* (www.equalrightsamendment.org; downloaded May 2005).

11. Ibid.

12. "Equal Rights Amendment Re-introduced in Congress; ACLU Says Measure Necessary to Protect Women," press release, March 22, 2001, online at *ACLU: Women's Rights News* (www.aclu.org; downloaded Jan. 2003). The ERA has been resubmitted to Congress each year since 1983.

13. See Janice Merrill Allred, *God the Mother and Other Theological Essays* (Salt Lake City: Signature Books, 1996); "'Do You Preach the Orthodox Religion?'" *Sunstone* 15 (June 1991) 23-33; and "Toward a Mormon Theology of God the Mother," *Dialogue: A Journal of Mormon Thought* 27 (Summer 1994): 15-40. Margaret Merrill Toscano is the author of "Making Love with God: Sex and Identity in the Late-Medieval Women Mystics Mechthild of Magdeburg and Margery Kempe," Ph.D. diss., University of Utah, 2002; "Peripheral Visions of the Mormon Mother God: Making Invisible the Visible," *Mormon Women's Forum Newsletter* 8 (Fall/Winter 1997): 3-9; "If I Hate My Mother, Can I Love the Heavenly Mother? Personal Identity, Parental Relationships and Perceptions of God," *Dialogue: A Journal of Mormon Thought* 31 (Winter 1998): 3-52; and with her husband, Paul James Toscano, *Strangers in Paradox: Explorations in Mormon Theology* (Salt Lake City: Signature Books, 1990).

14. Rod Decker, "The Mormon Church and Utah Politics: A Journalist's Appraisal," in Jeffery E. Sells, ed., *God and Country: Politics in Utah* (Salt Lake City: Signature Books, 2005).

15. Rose Weitz, *Sex Roles* (New York: Oxford University Press, 1977), 194.

16. Shulamit Reinharz, *Feminist Methods in Social Research* (New York: Oxford University Press, 1992).

17. Ibid., 146.

18. Marilyn Arnold, interviewed by Leah Koldewyn, Nov. 23, 1992, Provo, Utah, IWY Project, in author's possession (see introduction).

19. Ramona Adams, interviewed by Martha Dickey Esplin, Aug. 9, 1991, Salt Lake City, Utah, IWY Project.

20. Cheryll Lynn May, interviewed by Leslie Bates, Aug. 13, 1991, Salt Lake City, Utah, IWY Project.

21. Aileen H. Clyde, interviewed by Anne Looser, June 21, 2002, Springville, Utah, IWY Project.

22. Cynthia Boshard, interviewed by Leslie Bates, July 9, 1991, Salt Lake City, Utah, IWY Project.

Appendix 1: Chronology, 1842-1983

1. See a complete history of the Senate and House committee hearings in: Joan Hoff-Wilson, ed. *Rights of Passage: The Past and Future of the ERA* (Bloomington: Indiana University Press, 1986), 13-16.

2. See *The Spirit of Houston: An Official Report to the President, the Congress and the People of the United States* (Washington D.C.: National Commission on the Observance of International Women's Year, 1978) also William Chafe, *The American Woman: Her Changing Social, Economic and Political Roles, 1920-1970* (New York: Oxford University Press, 1972); Linda Grant DePauw, *Fortunes of War: New Jersey Women and the American Revolution* (Trenton: New Jersey Historical Commission, 1975); Eleanor Flexner, *Century of Struggle* (New York: Atheneum, 1975); Jo Freeman, *Women: A Feminist Perspective* (Palo Alto, CA: Mayfield, 1975); Judith Hole and Ellen Levine, *Rebirth of Feminism* (New York: Quadrangle, 1971); Gerda Lerner, "The Lady and the Mill Girl: Changes in the Status of Women in the Age of Jackson," *American Studies Journal* (Spring 1969); Gerda Lerner, *Black Women in White America* (New York: Vintage, 1972); William O'Neill, *Everyone was Brave* (Chicago: Quadrangle, 1969); Judith Papachristou, *Women Together: A History in Documents of the Women's Movement in the United States* (New York: Knopf, 1976); Barbara Wertheimer, *We Were There: The Story of Working Women in America* (New York: Pantheon, 1977). Carol Cornwall Madsen, *Battle for the Ballot: Essays on Woman Suffrage in Utah, 1870-1896* (Logan: Utah State University Press, 1997).

Appendix 2: Utah IWY Conference Schedule

1. "Schedule for Utah Women's Meeting, June 24-25," Bx. 1, Fd. 7, Utah Women's Issues Collection, Manuscripts Division, Marriott Library, University of Utah, Salt Lake City.

INDEX

Martha Sonntag Bradley is a professor in the College of Architecture and Planning and director of the Honors Program at the University of Utah, where she has received the Distinguished Teaching Award, the Student Choice Award for Excellence in Teaching, the Bennion Center Service Learning Professorship, and the honorary title of "University Professor, 1999-2000." She taught previously in the history department at Brigham Young University, where she received a Teaching Excellence Award. She has served as president of the Mormon History Association and co-editor of *Dialogue: A Journal of Mormon Thought*. Her many books include *Kidnapped from that Land: The Government Raids on the Short Creek Polygamists; Four Zinas: A Story of Mothers and Daughters on the Mormon Frontier;* and *A History of Kane County.*